CLINICAL AND
COUNSELING
PSYCHOLOGY

CLINICAL AND COUNSELING PSYCHOLOGY

BY John M. Hadley

millard, 1915-

PURDUE UNIVERSITY

Alfred A. Knopf NEW YORK

✯ ✯ 1961

L.C. catalog card number: 58–5048

THIS IS A BORZOI BOOK
PUBLISHED BY ALFRED A. KNOPF, INC.

Published 1958; reprinted 1960, 1961

Preface

CLINICAL AND COUNSELING PSYCHOLOGY IS A DYNAMIC AND BUR-
geoning field. Although the number of its practitioners is growing
rapidly, the demand for trained personnel is far outrunning the
supply. This book has been designed as a tool for training the needed
men and women. Intended as a preview of the profession, it is a textbook
for the introductory course in clinical and/or counseling psychology.

I have also been mindful that students and professional workers in
such fields as medicine, psychiatry, social work, nursing, education,
speech pathology, and religion may want to investigate clinical and counseling psychology in search of ideas that can be applied in their own
work. Lecturing to the general public has shown me that many laymen
are eager to learn what a psychologist is, what he does, and how he can
serve them. I have tried to present the material in such a way that it will
be found comprehensible, stimulating, and informative also by readers
who are not specialists in psychology.

Necessarily in a survey of so vast a field, the analysis of some topics
will not include the amount of detail that a reader may want. This problem has been met by listing, in a bibliography at the end of each chapter, specific books and articles that deal more comprehensively with
each topic, so that the reader can pursue his individual interests in a
more intensive and exhaustive fashion. Since the references are cued into
the text itself so as to make an annotated guidebook to the vast body of
literature in the field, the volume should be helpful in more advanced
study. The extensive Glossary should also be useful to many readers.

My approach to the subject matter has been greatly influenced by
my own experience. I was trained in the field of psychology generally, not
primarily as a specialist in one area. I have worked not only as a teacher
but also as an experimental psychophysiologist, a speech pathologist, a
school psychologist, a communications specialist, an aviation psychologist, a classification specialist; in human engineering, in educational counseling; and as an administrator of a university training program in clinical, counseling, and school clinical psychology. This background has led
me to emphasize in the following pages the broad base of psychology and
the similarity in function of clinical, counseling, and school psychology.

It has also led me to emphasize that the subject matter of psychology is human behavior. The ultimate purpose of all clinical and counseling procedures is the alteration of a person's behavior into more constructive channels. Techniques of testing and assessment are ways of

getting the information that will enable us to better understand an individual's current behavior and thus to plan for its modification. These views have prompted me to change the order of topics followed in many similar textbooks; I have discussed therapeutic and counseling procedures before describing the methods for evaluation of a client. I hope this will help to reduce the tendency to regard the psychologist as mainly a tester or a diagnostician.

The problems presented to the practical clinician are the problems of specific individuals. They are not problems simply to be studied; they are problems to be solved or mitigated. All methods that may be useful in that task should be available to the clinician, and the problems of the client should determine which techniques will be used. My approach in this book is consistently client-oriented. At the same time the importance of the research attitude—of being constantly alert, in all our practical efforts, to the discovery of better theories and techniques—is recognized throughout.

This book approaches its subjects from the perspective of modified field theory, which regards human behavior as determined by the vectors or forces operating in any given situation. While environmental or extrapersonal forces are emphasized, this does not imply neglect of the qualities and tendencies of the specific client. Attention has been focused on the interaction of the person with his environment.

For the ideas that he propagates, every teacher and writer owes to others far more than he can recognize, and it is with humility that I acknowledge my debt to my own teachers. Dr. George A. Kelly, my first teacher and long-time friend, has influenced my professional life more than anyone else. Another benefactor, whose direct assistance was tragically brief because of his untimely death, was Dr. F. B. Knight. To all of my colleagues at Purdue University whose ideas have contributed so much to this book, I am deeply grateful. My greatest debt is to my students: Beatrice Barrett Ribback contributed substantially to Chapter 4; she, Erwin J. Stegman, and Thomas A. Wickes to Chapters 5–8; Stephen H. Pratt to Chapter 18; and Elsie Sjostedt Fosdick to Chapter 19. Ruth Baker Hines read and criticized a number of chapters, and many others will see their ideas in almost every chapter.

I have quoted extensively from my predecessors and contemporaries. The longer quotations are acknowledged in footnotes, and I would like here to express gratitude to the publishers and authors who have granted me permission to use many briefer quotations and to adapt their materials. Perhaps sometimes I have unconsciously quoted or adapted ideas that are not specifically credited, and I trust that these involuntary contributors will realize that my appreciation, if not overt, is nonetheless warm.

Mrs. Ruth Carter Bundy, my secretary and assistant, has expended untold effort in editing, typing, and preparing the manuscript. Miss Zita de Schauensee of the College Department of Alfred A. Knopf, Inc., has given excellent editorial assistance, and Ray Ginger, also of Alfred A. Knopf, Inc., has given invaluable advice and assistance. My wife Doris typed a considerable part of the manuscript, and in my writing, as in much else, provided the real impetus to my work. To her and to my children Joan and John, who have had only a part-time father for several years, this book is dedicated.

J. M. H.

PURDUE UNIVERSITY

September, 1957

Contents

1. INTRODUCTION   3
   What This Book Is About   3
   The Field of Clinical and Counseling Psychology   6
   The Knowledge and Skills of the Clinical and Counseling
       Psychologist   7
   Who Does the Clinical or Counseling Psychologist
       Work with and What Does He Do?   8
   How the Present Concept of Clinical and Counseling
       Psychology Has Evolved   9
   Recent Factors Contributing to the Development of the
       Field   11
   How Methods for Individual Evaluation Have
       Developed   12
   How the Research Function Has Evolved   14
   Background in the Therapeutic Area of Application   15
   Other Important Events   16
   Professional Psychology, a Science or an Art?   17
   How a Clinical or Counseling Psychologist Can
       Achieve Objectivity   18
   Summary   20

PART I. APPLICATION OF PSYCHOLOGICAL THEORY

2. ORIENTATION TO PSYCHOLOGICAL COUNSELING   25
   The Elements of Psychological Counseling   28
   The Course of Psychological Counseling   37
   Summary   39

3. THEORETICAL FRAMEWORK   41
   How Theory Can Help Us in Planning Counseling or
       Therapy   43
   What Is Meant by Planning Counseling or Therapy   54
   Summary   59

4. THE ROLE OF INSIGHT   62
   Insight in Gestalt Psychology   65
   Classical Psychoanalytical Approaches to Insight   68

Insight in the Neo-Analytical Schools of Thought 78
The Function of Insight in Client-Centered Counseling 95
Insight in Counseling Procedures Developed from
    Learning Theory 102
Summary 116

5. EMOTIONAL RELEASE AND TENSION REDUCTION 121
Emotional Release as a Function of Formal
    Psychological Counseling 122
The Theoretical Implications of Emotional Release 127
Techniques to Encourage Emotional Release 136
The Encouragement of Release Outside the Formal
    Counseling Situation 138
The Control or Reduction of Overexpression of
    Emotions 140
Summary 141

6. SUPPORTIVE RELATIONSHIPS AND ACTIVITIES 144
The Emphasis upon the Relationship Aspects of
    Psychological Counseling 146
Supportive Procedures and Psychoanalysis 150
Environmental Manipulation as a Supportive Device 151
The Supportive Aspects of Reassurance 152
Suggestion and Advice as Supportive Techniques 156
Support Through Pressure and Coercion 157
Muscular Relaxation, Rest, and Diversional Therapy as
    Supportive Procedures 158
Summary 160

7. RELEARNING 162
Some Postulates About Behavior 163
Reinforcement Theory 165
Cognitive Theory 168
Combined Theory of Reinforcement and Expectancy 170
Goals and Procedures of Re-education 174
Re-education Through Manipulation of the
    Environment 175
Can These Theories Be Brought Together? 177
Summary 181

8. SOCIALIZATION 183
Social Orientation and Psychopathology 183
Learning Theory and Socialization 186

The Directive Counseling Approach and Socialization　190
Nondirective Counseling and Socialization　193
Socialization as an Aim in Educational Guidance and
　Counseling　194
Socialization in the Hospital Situation　195
Some Philosophical Thoughts on Socialization　197
Summary　199

PART II. PRACTICAL PROCEDURES
AND TECHNIQUES

9.　ENVIRONMENTAL TREATMENT　203
Environmental Treatment Defined　203
Examples of Environmental Treatment　206
Environmental and Personal Therapy with Children　207
The Purpose of Institutional Treatment with Children　210
Environmental Treatment with Little Change in the
　Environment　211
Environmental Treatment with Adults　214
The Psychologist's Responsibility in Environmental
　Modification or Manipulation　216
Environmental Treatment in an Institution　218
The Psychiatric Social Case Worker and Environmental
　Therapy　222
Summary　224

10.　GROUP COUNSELING AND THERAPY　227
The History of Group Counseling and Therapeutic
　Activities　230
The Lecture-Discussion Technique　234
Activity Group Procedures　236
Client-Centered Group Counseling　237
Analytically Oriented Group Procedures　239
Psychodrama　240
Group Work with Children　241
Evaluation of Group Counseling　244
Summary　245

11.　VOCATIONAL GUIDANCE AND COUNSELING　249
The Significance of Vocational Counseling　250
What Is Vocational Counseling?　253
Factors to Be Considered in Vocational Counseling　256
Occupational Information　258

The Use of Tests in Vocational Counseling   259
Some Examples of Vocational Counseling Problems   264
Summary   268

12. SPECIAL COUNSELING TECHNIQUES   270
Counseling with the Physically Handicapped and
   Disabled   273
Special Problems with the Speech-Defective Client 276
Counseling and Reading   282
Study-Habit Counseling   285
Summary   290

PART III. EVALUATION AND ASSESSMENT

13. THE PHILOSOPHY OF CLINICAL EVALUATION   295
What the Psychologist Evaluates   296
Is the Psychologist Concerned only with the Person? 299
The Assessment Tools of the Psychologist   300
The Contributions of Psychological Tests   302
Structure in a Test   306
Summary   306

14. THE ANAMNESIS   308
How to Use the Case History   308
Sources of Information   313
Completeness and Form of the Case-History Record 314
The Registration   318
Educational History   325
Family History   333
Developmental History   339
Sociological History   346
Occupational History   346
Summary   347

15. THE DIAGNOSTIC INTERVIEW   349
Structuring the Interview   350
Principles of Interviewing   354
Pattern of the Diagnostic Personal Interview   360
Content of the Diagnostic Interview   361
The Clinician's Observations   377
An Example of the Use of an Interview   378

16. THE EVALUATION OF INTELLIGENCE   385
Definitions of Intelligence   386

The Constancy of Intelligence 390
Cautions Concerning the Use of Intelligence Tests 392
Classification of Tests of Intelligence or Capacity 395
The Stanford-Binet 396
The Wechsler Intelligence Scale for Children 401
Performance Scales 406
Scales for Infants and Preschool Children 412
The Wechsler-Bellevue 416
Group Intelligence Tests 426
How to Select a Test 429
Summary 430

17. THE EVALUATION OF INTELLECTUAL EFFICIENCY 436
Evaluation of Deficit from Intelligence Tests 438
Tests of Intellectual Deficit 443
Evaluation of the Thinking Process in Brain Injury 445
Relationship Between Intellectual Processes and
    Personality 455
The Evaluation of Language and Symbolic Activity 460
Summary 462

18. STRUCTURED PERSONALITY TESTS 469
What Personality Tests Measure 470
The History and Development of Structured Personality
    Tests 473
Validity 474
The Minnesota Multiphasic Personality Inventory 478
Other Structured Tests 482
General Evaluation of Structured Personality Tests 486
Summary 489

19. PARTIALLY STRUCTURED PERSONALITY TESTS 495
The Thematic Apperception Test 497
The Children's Apperception Test 511
The Michigan Picture Test 512
The Blacky Test 513
The Make-a-Picture Story Test 514
The World Test 515
Structured Doll Play 516
Drawing and Painting Techniques 518
The Szondi Test 521
Sentence-Completion Techniques 524

The Purdue Multiple Choice Sentence Completion
Test 525
Word-Association Tests 527
Other Partially Structured Procedures 528
Summary 528

20. UNSTRUCTURED PERSONALITY TESTS 534
The Rorschach Test 536
The Mosaic Test 553
Summary 554

PART IV. PROFESSIONAL ISSUES

21. QUALIFICATIONS OF THE CLINICIAN 559
The Training of a Psychological Clinician 560
Personal Attributes of the Psychological Clinician 565
Summary 574

22. THE SCOPE OF PROFESSIONAL PSYCHOLOGY 577
The Psychologist in the Medical Setting 580
The Psychologist in the Educational Setting 587
Psychologists and Correctional Services 592
The Psychologist in Schools or Homes for the Mentally
Retarded 595
The Clinical and Counseling Psychologist and Industry 596
Do and Should Psychologists Enter Private Practice? 599
Rules Governing the Practice of the Clinician 601
Summary 603

23. PROFESSIONAL RELATIONS AND THE PUBLIC INTEREST 609
Psychology and Psychiatry 611
Clinical Psychology and Psychiatric Social Work 617
Clinical Psychology and Counseling Psychology 620
Clinical Psychology and Vocational and Educational
Guidance 623
Clinical Psychology and Education 625
Clinical and Counseling Psychology and Industrial
Psychology 626
Clinical Psychology and the Law 627
Clinical and Counseling Psychology and Religion 628
Psychology and Legislation 629
A Final Thought 635
Summary 635

24. RESEARCH AND SERVICE   639

     Future Developments in the Area of Research in
       Clinical and Counseling Psychology   642
     Future Trends in Clinical Evaluation   645
     The Future of Counseling and Therapy   646
     Summary   649

GLOSSARY   651

INDEX OF NAMES
INDEX OF SUBJECTS   follow page 682

CLINICAL AND
COUNSELING
PSYCHOLOGY

✵

CHAPTER

I

Introduction

WHAT THIS BOOK IS ABOUT

A HANDSOME YOUNG MAN FOURTEEN YEARS OF AGE IS IN THE SEVenth grade. He repeated the first grade, the second grade, and the third grade. After his second year in the third grade he was advanced to the fourth grade, and he has been advanced every year since then. He is not doing seventh grade work—in fact, he has never done adequate school work for any year level at which he has been placed. Because he was advanced to grade levels that were beyond his educational capacity, he fell further and further behind each year, and he is now confused, frustrated, and exceedingly unhappy. His father and mother are college graduates, his brothers and sisters are good students, and he gives every appearance of being a healthy, normal boy. He is a competent worker on his father's farm. He understands stock and has won a number of blue ribbons by showing animals at county fairs. He drives a tractor, does minor repairs on equipment, and, in general, is very apt in mechanical activities. Why does he have such marked school difficulties?

A youngster of twelve is living in a dream world. He sits for hours simply looking out of a window. He occasionally makes peculiar noises and has been observed to run and flap his arms like a bird. He has been this way since he was four. Until that time he was regarded as a perfectly normal child. He has never been to school. He seldom talks except when he has some physical need, such as when he is hungry or thirsty, or when it is necessary for him to go to the toilet. On some of these occasions his vocabulary and manner of expression have been as mature as that of a much older person. How can we understand this unusual behavior?

A veteran of World War II is continually plagued by a distinctive, irritating, unpleasant voice which he hears in dreams, in crowds, and even on radio or television. Occasionally he is disturbed by characteristics in the speech of his friends which remind him of this voice. Loss of sleep and anxiety about having something wrong with him combine to interfere with his work, and he is impatient with his family and his working associates. He does not feel that he can endure this any longer and is pleading for help.

A college girl has developed a facial grimace that results in a constant display of her unusually perfect teeth. Although not unattractive, she is rather stout and plain in appearance. She is exceptionally intelligent but does not apply herself to her academic studies and, as a consequence, makes very mediocre grades. She has a beautiful twin sister and two brothers who are atomic physicists, and she has high aspirations for graduate and professional study. She does much independent reading but seldom prepares her regular assignments. She has presented herself at a university clinic, asking for help in study habits.

A former business-machine statistician, following an automobile accident, finds that he is partially paralyzed and that he cannot perform even the simplest statistical operations. He can perform arithmetical and computational operations, but such less concrete tasks as programing a machine for a complex problem are entirely impossible. He can concentrate only for brief periods of time, finds himself irritable, and is able to carry out only a very small part of his previous activities. At thirty years of age he is faced with the prospect of preparing for some new area of work. The very thought of this is depressing, and for the most part he sits and broods over his poor fortune. Who can help him to think constructively about his future?

A brilliant field engineer has made an outstanding record for himself as a practical trouble shooter on a large number of projects. He has worked mostly by himself and has had no experience with the supervision of personnel or with administrative detail in general. Because of his reputation, he has been appointed to a high-level executive position in a consulting firm. After having worked for ten years to achieve a position of this kind, he finds that he is ineffectual as an administrator. People do not seem to like to work for him, and he is frequently tactless in his approach to important clients. His colleagues are convinced that he should be valuable in the firm but wonder how he can be used. Can he do anything to help himself?

These are actual problems that were presented to a professional clinical and counseling psychologist in one working day. Later in the book we will see the methods and procedures he used in planning his approach to them and to other problems. In the hospital or in the clinic the psychologist is faced with equally varied and perhaps more bizarre examples of inefficient behavior and unhappy people. The broad field of clinical and counseling psychology attempts to provide solutions to difficulties such as these. This book will focus attention on those applications of psychology that are concerned with the intra- and interpersonal aspects of the behavior of individuals. We hope to describe a general area of study and work in which are included such specialized applications as clinical psychology, school psychology, and counseling psychology. Whatever the emphasis, whether it is on work with children or adults, industrial workers or hospital patients, we will discuss the professional applications of psychology which direct attention to the study of the individual case. Regardless of the descriptive label used from this point, whether it is "clinical" or "counseling" psychology, the reader must be aware that these terms are used interchangeably. To the extent that we discuss sub-specializations in the more general area, they are to be interpreted as differences in application rather than as differences in basic knowledge or fundamental procedures.

The purpose of this book is to provide an overview of the theory, the methods, and the application of the individual-study approach in psychology. We hope to answer some of the questions that are frequently asked concerning this rapidly developing professional field. Our philosophy, which will be stressed many times, is that the end product of the efforts of the clinical, the counseling, or the school psychologist should be changes in the attitudes and the behavior of the individuals who are presented as clients. These efforts should not be haphazard. They are more than "common sense," although a lot of this enters into the work of the professional psychologist. There is a considerable body of research and theoretical thinking which can be applied to the practical problems clamoring for solution. This material is not always well organized, nor are all theories in agreement. Many are only partially supported by scientific investigation. In any case, the person who is beginning a career in any of the specializations within our general area of study must be introduced to these theories. In the last analysis he must select or construct a theory for himself. To this end we will suggest a possible frame of reference which may allow the reader to entertain and possibly to integrate this burgeoning mass of facts and theory. Then we will present the application of these ideas and this factual knowledge to the promotion of behavioral change. We will survey methods for the evaluation of the individual; it is by the use of such methods that we can gain the information necessary to implement the changes suggested by the various theories and to achieve the objectives of psychological counseling and therapy. Finally, we will look at the present status of the profession and speculate about the future.

THE FIELD OF CLINICAL AND COUNSELING PSYCHOLOGY

As suggested above, our field of study may be defined as the specialized application of the principles of general psychology to the study of the individual. Whereas psychology may be defined as the study of behavior in general, the clinical application is regarded as the study of the behavior of individuals as they function in their total life situation. The professional clinical or counseling psychologist must consider each individual as a unique problem. The clinical method must achieve objectivity by intensive study of the individual. Kurt Lewin (25) has described the problem of the clinician quite nicely in his statement that behavior is a function of the interaction between the person and his environment. According to this point of view (which will be frequently reiterated in this text), the person is functioning in an environment in which there are many forces acting upon him. Added to these environmental influences, there are numerous forces operating within the individual. At any given moment the environmental and personal tendencies combine in many ways to modify each other. Thus behavior is seen as the resultant of this complex of interacting forces. Clinical and counseling psychologists utilize all the general and specialized tools of psychology to identify and evaluate as many as possible of the forces acting upon or within the individual. The psychologist's evaluations of the individual will be adequate only to the extent that he has observed or anticipated most of the major factors affecting the individual's behavior.

Traditionally, the general study of psychology is concerned with understanding, predicting, and controlling behavior. In the clinical and counseling applications we endeavor to evaluate and/or to understand the individual's behavior so that we can contribute to its modification or control. We are constantly searching for new information and new ways of organizing old information so that we will be better able to anticipate forces not directly observable, and improve the accuracy of our predictions. This leads us to define our field as *that discipline which utilizes the principles and knowledge of general psychology to evaluate and understand individual behavior; to make recommendations for, or to engage in activities designed to contribute to, the modification of behavior; and to conduct research into the regularity and predictability of individual behavior.* We believe that this definition applies to all the specialized applications of psychology which are concerned with the behavior of individuals and their interaction with their complex environments.

Our subject matter is *behavior*, but we must not divorce behavior from the subjects who present it. We are interested in the behavior of people—living, feeling, thinking, knowing people. This seemingly obvious statement should be studied carefully. Our unit of study is not personality, or emotion, or intelligence, or any of the various attributes that may be regarded as aspects of behavior—our concern is with the attitudes, motives, ideas, responses, and needs of the person. The clinical or counseling psychologist respects his subjects; he recognizes their right to feel and act as they do. He does not think of them as behavior problems, speech problems, or schizophrenics, but as persons presenting certain varieties of behavior. The philosophy of respect for the worth of the individual client—of client-centeredness—is the distinguishing characteristic of the modern-day clinician.

THE KNOWLEDGE AND SKILLS OF THE CLINICAL AND COUNSELING PSYCHOLOGIST

One writer (30) has suggested that the clinical psychologist resembles the clergyman or the physician more than he resembles the general psychologist. It is to be hoped that his belief is not shared by many psychologists, for it cannot be too strongly emphasized that the clinical psychologist should also be a general psychologist. Furthermore, if the clinical psychologist is to apply the principles of general psychology effectively, he must be well grounded in all the specialized aspects of psychology. For example, he must be a child psychologist: all of his subjects are or have been children, and most if not all of the behavior problems of adults have their roots in childhood. The clinical psychologist must also be a social psychologist: since his subjects function in a social structure, few problems can be understood without reference to social relationships and pressures. Because his subjects do not function as disembodied spirits, the clinical psychologist must be a physiological psychologist. Since many adults spend approximately one third of their lives at their work, the professional clinician must know about vocations, occupations, the preparation required for different kinds of work, and the abilities and aptitudes required for specific vocational careers. In addition he needs techniques for furthering his knowledge and improving his contributions to the field; so he must be well grounded in experimental and statistical techniques. Finally, he must understand the process of learning, the dynamics of motivation, and the complications of the emotions.

It is this knowledge that characterizes the professional worker in clinical and counseling psychology. These are the attributes that differentiate his work from that of the clergyman or the medical man and that of many other disciplines as well. It is granted that there is similarity in that these persons or professions minister to individuals, but it is submitted that the resemblance ends with this concept of individual counseling. The procedures employed by the psychologist and the knowledge behind them are uniquely those of psychology. If all these disciplines did not bring different points of view to bear on the problems of mental health, there could be no team effort and little justification for separate specialty areas.

WHO DOES THE CLINICAL OR COUNSELING PSYCHOLOGIST WORK WITH AND WHAT DOES HE DO?

The reader should note that our definition is not restricted to any particular subjects or groups of subjects. To the extent that the methods employed are essentially psychological in nature, they may be employed with any individual. They may be applied to the "normal" as well as to the "abnormal," and they may be directed toward prevention or hygiene as well as toward remedial procedures. Furthermore, we must not limit the definition of psychology to observation, measurement, and analysis merely for purposes of diagnosis or prognosis. Just as we have described the aims of general psychology as the understanding, prediction, and control of behavior, we may describe the aims of clinical and counseling psychology as the understanding, prediction, and control of the behavior of individuals. If we are to understand and predict, we must conduct research into the dynamics of behavior, both "normal" and "abnormal." The control of behavior may involve the changing of patterns of response, the learning of new responses, and the direction or channeling of behavior. In a general sense these activities have been described as therapeutic, and such activities are regarded as the ultimate aim of clinical and counseling psychology.

Such considerations as these have resulted in the description of the clinical psychologist's functions as including diagnosis, research, and therapy. The point of view of this text is that even these terms are too formalistic and restrictive. The term "diagnosis" connotes the study of the patient or client. As the next chapters will indicate, the psychologist does apply his skills and knowledge to the problem of diagnosing or evaluating the behavior of persons presenting behavior disorders. However, in addition, his work may take him into a variety of settings where, instead of diagnosing in the usual sense of the word, he may evaluate or assess or, better yet, simply try to understand why a given person— whether he is a school child, factory worker, business executive, or officer—behaves as he does. The purpose of the evaluation may be to judge a person's fitness for educational, business, or military promotion. It may be to interpret the individual's behavior to the teacher, the foreman, the business associate, or to any one of many other persons. The psychologist may assist in planning an educational program or an industrial training program. Many, if not all, of these activities involve behavioral changes but they go beyond the traditional concept of therapy. The professional psychologist does not (or should not) evaluate or recommend on the basis of hunches or simple guesses. He should utilize all of the content of psychology applicable to his individual problem. He should be constantly developing new principles and acquiring new information as well as testing the applications of old knowledge. In other words, the functions of clinical and counseling psychology are broad indeed and must not be conceived of as being restricted to diagnosis, research, and therapy—and certainly not as dealing only with a narrow segment of the population.

HOW THE PRESENT CONCEPT OF CLINICAL AND COUNSELING PSYCHOLOGY HAS EVOLVED

First, let us examine specific definitions of clinical psychology that have been suggested by earlier writers.[1] A definition is supposed to include all that belongs to the object defined and to exclude all that does not. It should become apparent, as we discuss the definitions, that these early psychologists, having received their training in several fields, including physiology, medicine, education, and religion, as well as psychology, described the field in terms of their own experience and training. Their definitions are not indicative of the extent or the limits of the field as it is today; they are, however, of historical interest and give a shorthand picture of the changing ideas about the meaning of clinical psychology.

One of the early attempts at definition identified the practice of clinical psychology with the practice of medicine. Louis E. Bisch (7, p. xiii) stated, "Clinical psychology . . . is psychology based on clinical experience. No person should consider himself a qualified clinical psychologist who has not had some medical training nor should a physician qualify as such who lacks training in psychology." Although the statement was made several years ago, this concept is by no means uncommon even today. It is based on the assumption that psychologists deal with persons who are ill in the medical sense. This is not consistent with the present interpretations of the subject matter of professional psychology. The issue is confused by the derivation of the word "clinical," which can be traced to the Greek word "*klinikos*," meaning "of a bed." It has been suggested (43) that the use of the word "clinical" is unfortunate, but, as C. M. Louttit (27) has pointed out, this objection to the use of the term seems to have little validity since its general connotations are not necessarily limited to medicine. Unfortunately, however,

[1] Louttit (26) reported that he had collected about forty different definitions.

for several periods in the history of clinical psychology we do seem to have patterned our field after the discipline of medicine, and, in fact, have sometimes identified ourselves with medicine. This tendency seems to have disappeared in favor of the concept of professional psychology as a discipline in its own right and as one with unique contributions to make. Consequently, it does not seem logical to restrict the practice of clinical psychology to persons with medical training. Aside from their historical significance, definitions of clinical psychology in terms of medical practice do not seem to warrant our further consideration.

Another way in which clinical psychology has been defined is to equate it with the study of abnormal or subnormal individuals. For example, Henry H. Goddard (16, p. 85) suggested, "Clinical psychology should mean personal examination of someone who is mentally abnormal or subnormal." This description of the field is consistent with the activities of the early clinical psychologists who worked with subnormal or feeble-minded subjects. Most modern psychologists would find this definition rather restrictive. Examination of abnormal subjects comprises a rather small proportion of present-day clinical practice. Still other concepts have stressed the function of psychometrics and have defined the field in terms of the evaluation of abilities, aptitudes, and achievements (19). Some early definitions of the field of counseling psychology identified counseling with vocational guidance, and school psychologists have equated the field with remedial education. Here again, to present-day psychologists these definitions are too restrictive and refer only to a limited aspect of their work.

A somewhat more acceptable definition was formulated by a committee of the Clinical Section of the American Psychological Association (1, p. 5):

> Clinical psychology is a form of applied psychology which aims to define the behavior capacities and behavior characteristics of an individual through methods of measurement, analysis, and observation; and which, on the basis of an integration of these findings with data secured from the physical examinations and social histories, gives suggestions and recommendations for the proper adjustment of that individual.

Although an improvement on earlier definitions, this definition is still not wholly acceptable to most psychologists today. It places the emphasis on the definition and description of behavior and gives little thought to the understanding of how behavior patterns may develop. Furthermore, modern clinical practice frequently provides the psychologist with an opportunity to implement some of his recommendations.

However this definition, formulated as far back as 1935, does approximate our definition in one significant respect. It emphasizes the study of the individual by means of measurement, analysis, and observation. These are the methods of general psychology. The clinical psychologist has been described as one who uses clinical methods. Since clinical methods are nothing more than psychological methods, we might better say that the clinical psychologist uses those psychological methods that are particularly well adapted to the study of the individual.

RECENT FACTORS CONTRIBUTING TO THE DEVELOPMENT OF THE FIELD

Frederick C. Thorne (38) has discussed the effect of the first and second World Wars on the rapid growth of the profession of clinical and counseling psychology. The influence of World War I was principally in the development of psychometrics. It gave impetus to the development of group tests and to the first mass application of these devices. This same period saw the development and standardization of individual intelligence tests.

World War II set up conditions that contributed to the maturation of psychology as a profession. During the war military services assigned to psychologists responsibilities that went beyond those which had previously been thought to be within the scope of psychology. These psychologists for the most part had been trained in general psychology rather than as specialists in clinical psychology. Their responsibilities ranged from personnel testing to counseling and therapeutic activities. Psychologists participated in research projects ranging from those of human engineering to problems related to the causes of aviation accidents. They were even assigned duties in connection with ward administration in neuropsychiatric and other hospitals. The competence with which they carried on these many activities demonstrated the value of psychological training and opened up new vistas for the application of psychology.

Since the war, emphasis has been on the development and training of clinical and counseling psychologists. This emphasis has resulted in improvement of training facilities. The Veterans Administration envisaged the use of psychologists on a large scale, but immediately recognized that there were not enough persons trained in the individual applications of psychology to staff its many hospitals and clinics. It subsequently conceived training programs that would be conducted in cooperation with universities qualified to train professional psychologists. The United States Public Health Service inaugurated a training program to prepare clinical psychologists for work in the field of mental health. The Army developed a plan for training professional psychologists to work in Army medical and research centers. Concern about the quality of psychology training programs prompted the American Psychological

Association to appoint a Committee on Training in Clinical Psychology. This committee developed procedures for evaluating and accrediting training universities. It has now been expanded to the Education and Training Board, which is concerned with training in these specialty areas. The result has been a general improvement and a degree of desirable standardization in the training of clinical and counseling psychologists.

HOW METHODS FOR INDIVIDUAL EVALUATION HAVE DEVELOPED

To fully understand the development of psychology as a profession, we must go further back than the recent wars. The functions of diagnosis (or evaluation), research, and therapy (or behavior modification) have had somewhat separate but, to an extent, overlapping histories. The function of diagnosis has been traced historically by Saul Rosenzweig (33). He suggests that diagnosis in psychology derives from two chief sources—the psychometric and the psychodynamic.

The psychometric origins of diagnosis stem from the work of many men, of whom two, Sir Francis Galton and Alfred Binet, stand out and must be given special credit. Earliest in point of time was Galton, who, because of his pioneer work in this area, is frequently called the "father of individual differences." Galton's investigations were exceedingly varied. He studied such diverse problems as the measurement of sense perception, the experimental induction of paranoia, the heredity of genius, the geographical distribution of female beauty, and the measurement of mentality. The first recorded study of the associative process was authored by Galton (14).

1. INTELLIGENCE TESTS.   Although James McKeen Cattell (9) is generally credited with using the term "mental testing" for the first time in 1890, the name most frequently associated with the development of intelligence tests is that of Binet. Binet, in collaboration with Theodore Simon, an elderly physician, constructed a test to measure specific psychological functions such as attention, imagination, reasoning, judgment, and memory. His first test, of thirty carefully selected questions arranged in order of difficulty, was published in 1905 (5). He revised the test in 1908 (6) and again in 1911 (3). In these revisions he arranged the questions or tasks in age groups and originated the concept of mental age. If a child of ten could not pass the tests for an age higher than age eight, Binet considered him to have a mental age of eight. William Stern (34) then conceived the idea of dividing the mental age by the chronological age and getting a quotient. Lewis M. Terman (35) later called this the "intelligence quotient" or I.Q.

Most credit for the development of mental tests is given to Binet, although several earlier workers had been interested in the general problem. We have mentioned Galton's contributions, as well as those of Cattell (10), who administered tests of reaction time and free and controlled association to students at Columbia University. Joseph Jastrow (20) published a group of mental tests in 1892; Hermann Ebbinghaus (11) published a sentence-completion test, which was a form of intelligence test, in 1897; and Edwin A. Kirkpatrick (22) and Robert L. Kelly (21) compared children on the basis of mental tests in 1900 and 1903. However most of these tests measured simple sensorimotor functions rather than such processes as reasoning, imagination, or judgment. Binet's tests were accepted in the United States almost as soon as they were reported. Goddard made the first English translations and published his revision of the 1908 scale in 1911 (15). In 1916 Terman (35) published the Stanford revision, and Frederick Kuhlman (23, 24) revised the Binet tests three times—in 1912, 1922, and 1939. John P. Herring (17) also revised the Binet test, as did Robert M. Yerkes (46, 47), who published two different revisions of it. One of the major contributions of the Yerkes scales was their influence upon experimentation and development of group tests in respect to scaling of items and point scoring. Terman, assisted by Maude A. Merrill (36), revised the Stanford-Binet in 1937, and this revision is still one of the most widely used of the individual intelligence tests for children. While the functions of the clinical psychologist have developed well beyond the measurement of intelligence, the emphasis here should serve to underline the historical significance of the work of Binet and other workers in the area. The history of testing can be brought up to date only by mentioning the name of David Wechsler (40, 41), whose work will be discussed later. However, his tests for children, adolescents, and adults are recent historical landmarks.

2. PROJECTIVE TESTS.   The psychodynamic origins of psychological evaluation are closely related to the contributions of the nineteenth-century French psychopathologists and to the work of Sigmund Freud and his associates. One of the most important developments in the history of clinical psychology in recent years has been the increasing use of projective techniques. The first explicit formulation of the projective hypothesis was made by Lawrence K. Frank (12) in 1939, but the concepts resulting in the widespread use of projective techniques date back into the nineteenth century. Leopold Bellak (2) has traced the historical development of the concept of projection. The term itself was introduced by Freud (13) in 1894 in his paper on the anxiety neurosis. It seems apparent that the projective methods of diagnosis have evolved largely from the psychodynamic thinking of Freud and his fellow psychoanalysts.

The earliest of the present commonly used projective devices is the Rorschach technique. Hermann Rorschach (32) published his work in 1921 after ten years of experimenting with ink blots as stimuli for personality diagnosis. It is rather amazing that the major elements of administration, scoring, and interpretation developed by Rorschach are still used in much the same manner as he originally proposed. The Rorschach technique is undoubtedly the most important single historical landmark, but other projective devices have followed and have been widely used by clinical psychologists. Mention should also be made of the historical importance of the work of Christiana D. Morgan and Henry A. Murray (29) on the Thematic Apperception Test and of the contributions made by Margaret Lowenfeld (28). All these tests will be discussed in detail in Part III.

The use of projective methods has made it possible for psychologists to play a much more important role in diagnosis and evaluation than that of simple psychometrics; they have become explorers of the personalities of their subjects. Such techniques allow the diagnostician to bridge the gap between the phenotypical description of the person and the study of the underlying or genotypical dynamics of behavior. The important contributions that the psychologist can now make to the understanding of the person and the planning of his treatment have done much to raise psychology from the status of a technique to that of a profession.

HOW THE RESEARCH FUNCTION HAS EVOLVED

The history of the research function of clinical and counseling psychology is tied in closely with the history of research and laboratory study in experimental psychology.[2] Problems in mental testing, as well as those in learning or sensory discrimination, have been studied by the methods of psychophysics developed in the early research in Leipzig in 1879. The development of statistics was a direct outgrowth of the testing movement. Galton and one of his students, Karl Pearson, were among the pioneers in the development of this research tool. Despite the early relationship between the invention of research methods and the origins of clinical psychology, the research function of clinical psychology has lagged far behind the development of its other functions. Research techniques have been widely applied to problems of measurement and testing, but well-controlled experimental research on psychodynamics has been chiefly conspicuous by its absence. The leadership in research on psychopathology and the etiology of behavior disorders has been taken by psychiatry, and the published material is more anecdotal and biographical than experimental. Although it seems possible that significant

[2] See Boring (8) for a detailed history of experimental psychology.

historical events in the research applications of clinical psychology are yet to be recorded, there have been many changes in research methodology brought about by the import of clinical and counseling orientation and ideas.

Until very recently the experimental psychologists have not concerned themselves extensively with behavior disorders. This has been due to the difficulty and near impossibility of the application of experimental controls. Clinical psychologists in particular have been primarily concerned with the problems of individual diagnosis and therapy and have not interested themselves in carefully controlled experimental studies. Within the past few years a number of events have contributed to an increased interest in such topics as anxiety, motivation, and perception. This interest has led almost automatically to a consideration of psychodynamics. The experimental psychologist has become interested in problems of behavior pathology. The clinician or the counselor has developed a scientific attitude and has begun to question some of his assumptions. As a consequence we now see the rapid development of research in the clinical setting. Most encouraging is the evolution of what we shall describe later as a scientist-practitioner, who is developing new research tools to fit his unique research problems. Most prominent among these tools is the adaptation of statistical procedures by which the research worker, while allowing many factors to vary, is able to assess the relative influence and the interaction between these uncontrolled but recognized and measured factors. The scope for research in the field of clinical and counseling psychology is wide indeed, and it is perhaps in this function that the psychologist can make his most distinctive contributions of the problems of behavior pathology.

BACKGROUND IN THE THERAPEUTIC AREA OF APPLICATION

Discussion of the therapeutic function of psychology will appear in Parts I and II. It is sufficient to say here that psychology has yet to make its real, significant, unique contributions in the area of therapy. Some may feel that the contributions of Freud are being slighted by this statement. Certainly, Freud considered himself more a psychologist than a physician, and obviously psychology claims Freud in its history—just as does psychiatry. However, in spite of this, psychoanalysis can be thought of as stemming more properly from the medical than from the psychological traditions. The work of Carl R. Rogers (31) is essentially a psychological contribution to the field of therapy, and the influence of his philosophy has had drastic effects on the psychology of interpersonal relationships. Although Rogers is a psychologist, careful study and exam-

ination of the concepts and techniques of client-centered therapy which
he developed will reveal their rather direct descent from psychoanalytically oriented forms of therapy. The development most nearly psychological in its origin is the recent interest in the applications of learning theory to behavior modification. Within this framework we can structure
counseling and therapy in such a way as to take advantage of the knowledge of psychology. In general, though, just as in the case of research, it
seems safe to conclude that history is yet to be made insofar as psychology's contributions to therapy are concerned.

OTHER IMPORTANT EVENTS

The most important single date in the history of clinical psychology is
1896. In that year Lightner Witmer (44, 45) presented a series of pro-
posals concerning the use of the laboratory study techniques in practical
investigation of the problems of school children. Witmer anticipated
many of the principles and procedures of present-day clinical psychology
and earned the right to be called the "father of clinical psychology." The
methods and techniques of Witmer and his students could be used to
good advantage in many clinics today. It is he who first suggested the application of the principles of general psychology to the individual case. It
seems likely that he was the first to recognize the value of co-operation
between the psychologist, the psychiatrist or physician, and the social
worker. In these respects, as well as others, clinical psychology has spent
fifty years in catching up with Witmer.

Still other events [3] have made both direct and indirect contributions
to the development or "coming of age" of professional psychology. Mo-
mentous in its history was the establishment of the laboratory for the
study of feeble-mindedness at the Vineland Training School in 1906. The
contributions of its first director, Goddard, and its subsequent directors,
Stanley D. Porteus and Edgar A. Doll, were of the utmost importance to
the maturation of clinical psychology. The establishment by William
Healy in 1909 of the behavior clinic in connection with the Cook County
Juvenile Court in Chicago was another significant event in the history of
professional psychology. (This clinic has remained in continuous operation and is now known as the Illinois Institute for Juvenile Research.) In
the same year Clifford W. Beers founded the National Committee for
Mental Hygiene. This committee must be given special credit for its pio-
neering efforts in the modern child guidance movement.

Paralleling the development of clinical methods in the field of psychology, there have been many developments in remedial education and
in vocational and educational guidance which have been incorporated

[3] For further discussion of historical factors, see Watson (39).

into the field of professional psychology. These contributions must be recognized, but they have so blended into the general development of clinical methods and procedures as to be practically indistinguishable from them. Certainly the prewar professional psychologist expected to be called upon for vocational and educational counseling, for remedial education and industrial counseling. Perhaps we have digressed slightly in the immediate postwar years, but the present-day clinician can trace his history in part to events in the profession of education as well as to those already discussed in this chapter.

The student of clinical and counseling psychology should remember that the history of this profession is really very short as compared with that of other disciplines, such as medicine or psychiatry, which have common interests. We are scarcely more than adolescent, and many of our problems may be related to this extreme youth. Professional psychology does have a rich heritage.

PROFESSIONAL PSYCHOLOGY, A SCIENCE OR AN ART?

A science is defined as an exact and systematic statement or classification of knowledge as to facts, laws, and approximate causes, gained and verified by exact observation and logical thinking. An art may be thought of as the practical application of knowledge, natural ability, skill, dexterity, facility, or power. A considerable amount of discussion —much of it heated—has centered around whether the application of psychology is a science, an art, or an undetermined and indeterminable mixture of both. Although this can be viewed as an academic or even philosophical question of little practical importance, the attention given to it prompts some discussion.

Historically, psychology has been regarded as a science, and it has earned that regard by attempting to provide, through accurate observation, measurement, and experiment, the knowledge with which to understand how and why living organisms behave as they do. So long as psychology remained almost totally in the laboratory, few questions were raised as to its scientific nature. Many argued, however, that the skill required in practical application of the knowledge of psychology might more properly be regarded as an art. There seems to be no doubt that the profession is striving to become more scientific and to insure that its practices are indeed sound and based on facts and on laws that have been established by exact and objective observations.

Edward M. Westburgh (42) has contended that clinical psychology is an art. Louttit (26) appears to agree with him, although he describes a "practical art" as the application of basic sciences and implies that psychology falls into this category. William A. Hunt (18) has posed the question as to whether clinical psychology is a science or a superstition. A superstition is defined as a fixed, irrational idea or a notion maintained in spite of evidence to the contrary. In his excellent and humorous discussion of this question Hunt concludes that psychology is a science but that it is tinged—he calls it "fringed"—with superstition. Many of the arguments involve a certain amount of quibbling or hairsplitting. The major question would seem to be whether clinical methods can be scientific. We must agree that a large ingredient of skill (or art) enters into the work of the professional psychologist; however, he must also be objective in his observations and procedures.

HOW A CLINICAL OR COUNSELING PSYCHOLOGIST CAN ACHIEVE OBJECTIVITY

The science of psychology arrives at its principles and generalizations about behavior either by the study of large groups of persons and the use of statistical controls or by studies in the laboratory in which the behavior of subjects is carefully controlled so that the only factor allowed to vary is the one under study. The clinical or counseling psychologist does not study large groups of individuals, at least not all at the same time. As a matter of fact the size of the sample for his experiment is usually one. The clinical or counseling psychologist can seldom delimit the behavior of an individual with any degree of preciseness. In dealing with our subjects, we cannot be sure what it is in the functioning of the organism that makes a difference in behavior. We cannot see what the subject's behavior was when he was behaving normally, so we cannot be sure of what seems to be a disorder of behavior. As already discussed, it is difficult and in many instances ethically impossible to experiment on people in the professional setting. We cannot expose subjects to influences that might be permanently damaging to them, nor can we withhold treatment that would be beneficial. Actually, the individual must be observed as he lives in a very complicated, uncontrolled environment. How then can the professional psychologist expect to be scientific? Since the clinical psychologist cannot control the behavior of his subjects, *the clinical method must achieve scientific status by insuring objectivity in the observations made of individual behavior.*

Objective or scientific observation may be accomplished in several ways. One method involves the elimination of biases in the observer. The clinical situation is a social situation. Clinical observations are made by human observers. The psychologist functions as a participant observer. He must be constantly alert to the possibility that his observations may be biased by predetermined ideas which he may have developed concerning what he expects to discover. Perhaps the most subtle and yet the most important source of bias is the personal frame of reference or theoretical beliefs of the participant observer. Unfortunately, psychologists seem to have difficulty in remaining objective insofar as theories of personality or behavior are concerned. Various theoretical points of view have been advanced to explain behavior. These theories can probably be best regarded as tentative maps of unknown territory. All undoubtedly have some degree of correctness. However, many of them are drawn from the inside looking out, and others only after observation of certain aspects of behavior but without observation of other aspects. Some theories tend to resemble the New Englander's map of the United States, in which Boston is as large as Texas and Texas as small as Rhode Island. Certain portions are stressed entirely out of proportion because of the map artist's preoccupation with the segment he knows best. If we could always regard our theories as theories and not as absolute truths, we could remain more objective. Often a personal theory or belief seems so logical and we become so enamored of it that either we cannot entertain any observations that do not fit into the theory or we distort the observations to make them fit. In clinical observation we should be aware of our personal biases and attempt to avoid this type of distortion in our observation and reporting. Maps are sometimes drawn as one thinks a territory ought to be, rather than as it really is; and just as all maps may be partially correct, they are all probably partially fallacious. Consequently, the job of research workers in clinical psychology is to superimpose the theories—the maps—and reconcile some of the areas of agreement and disagreement. There is much exploration to do as well, since it is very likely that there is territory not described with accuracy by any of the theories.

The clinician searches out all the available information concerning his subject, just as does the researcher. This procedure or group of techniques has been called the case-study method. The case study is the core of the clinical method and will be discussed in detail in Chapter 14 but at this time let us glance at some of its elements. The case study begins with a clarification of the present problem and a definition of factors leading up to the current situation. It must include a family history, since it is important to estimate pertinent environmental factors as well as possible hereditary limits. Also important is the developmental history, which involves a survey of contributing factors influencing the behavior of the individual from conception to the present. The educational history, the vocational history, the collection of sociological data, and the personality interview round out the case-study or case-history data. The case study should be so thorough that no significant information is neglected. Such thoroughness will tend to operate against any tendency to form conclusions that are prompted only by personal biases on the part of the clinician. The case study also gives the clinician an opportunity to check on the accuracy of information collected. Information obtained from one source should be compared with that obtained from other sources. This procedure of cross-validation is the essence of scientific observation. Although information that cannot be validated should not be disregarded, it should be regarded as of tentative validity.

On the basis of this body of collected information, the clinician proceeds to the next step in the scientific method. He now begins to put the information together and to formulate tentative hypotheses that will explain the behavior of the subject. These hypotheses can be partially evaluated by the use of psychological tests. Such tests will be discussed in Part III, but at this time we wish to emphasize that tests do not, in, of, and by themselves, provide basic information. They must be regarded as supplementary to other observational techniques. They have their greatest value as techniques by which the validity of other observations can be checked in order to make preliminary tests of hypotheses. The final test of any hypothesis is of course the accuracy by which the behavior of a subject can be predicted by the use of the hypothesis.

To summarize, clinical and counseling psychology is scientific to the extent that unbiased attitudes can be maintained, that thorough observations can be made, that observations can be cross-validated; on the basis of these observations hypotheses are formulated and subjected to preliminary tests before they are subjected to final tests. Despite the fact that observations are limited to one subject and that the factors affecting this subject cannot be regulated, the clinical method can be scientific if the observations are scientifically controlled. The problem of making the clinical method scientific reduces itself in part to the problem of training observers to be objective and scientific.

SUMMARY

This introductory chapter has attempted to offer a very general definition of the applications of psychology to the individual. We have defined clinical and counseling psychology as a specialized application of the principles of general psychology to the study of the individual. We have discussed the functions or aims of clinical and counseling psychology as those of evaluation, research, and behavior modification. We have mentioned some of the very important historical events that have occurred in the first half century in the life of our profession and have discussed its genealogy or family history. We have attempted to indicate how clinical methods can be scientific in spite of the absence of the statistical and/or experimental controls ordinarily used in general psychology. Controlled observation has been suggested as a necessary characteristic of a scientific psychological approach.

BIBLIOGRAPHY

1. American Psychological Association, Clinical Section, "The definition of clinical psychology and standards of training for clinical psychologists." *Psychol. Clin.*, 1935, 23, 2–8.
2. Bellak, L., "On the problems of the concept of projection." In Abt, L. E., and Bellak, L. *Protective psychology*. New York: Alfred A. Knopf, 1950.
3. Binet, A., *"Nouvelles recherches sur la mesure du niveau intellectuel chez les enfants d'école."* L'Année psychologique, 1911, 17, 145–201.
4. Binet, A., and Henri, V., *"La psychologie individuelle."* L'Année psychologique, 1895, 2, 411–65.
5. Binet, A., and Simon, Th., *"Methodes nouvelles pour le diagnostic du niveau intellectuel des anormaux."* L'Année psychologique, 1905, 11, 191–336.
6. Binet, A., and Simon, Th., *"Le developpement de l'intelligence chez les enfants."* L'Année psychologique, 1908, 14, 1–94.
7. Bisch, L. E., *Clinical psychology*. Baltimore: Williams & Wilkins, 1925.
8. Boring, E. G., *History of experimental psychology*. New York: D. Appleton, 1929.
9. Cattell, J. McK., "Mental tests and measurements." *Mind*, 1890, 15, 373–81.
10. Cattell, J. McK., and Farrand, L., "Physical and mental measurements of students of Columbia University." *Psychol. Rev.*, 1896, 3, 618–48.
11. Ebbinghaus, H., *"Ueber eine neue Methode in Prüfung geistiger Fähigkeit und ihre Anwendung bei Schulkindern."* Zeitschrift für Psychologie und Physiologie der Sinnesorgane. 1897, 13, 401–57.
12. Frank, L. K., "Projective methods for the study of personality." *J. Psychol.*, 1939, 3, 389–413.
13. Freud, S., "The anxiety neurosis." In *Collected Papers*, Vol. I. London: Hogarth, 1940.
14. Galton, F., "Psychometric experiments." *Brain*, 1879, 2, 149–62.
15. Goddard, H. H., "A revision of the Binet Scale." *The Training School Bulletin*, 1911, 8, 56–62.
16. Goddard, H. H., Gesell, A., and Wallin, J. E. W., "Fields of clinical psychology as an applied science." *J. Appl. Psychol.*, 1919, 3, 81–95.
17. Herring, J. P., *Herring Revision of the Binet-Simon Tests*. Columbia University: Teachers College, 1924.
18. Hunt, W. A., "Clinical psychology—science or superstition." *Amer. Psychologist*, 1951, 6, 683–7.
19. Institute for Juvenile Research. *Child guidance procedures*. New York: Appleton-Century, 1937.
20. Jastrow, J., "Some anthropological and psychologic tests on college students." *Amer. J. Psychol.*, 1892, 4, 420–7.
21. Kelly, R. L., "Psychological tests of normal and abnormal children." *Psychol. Rev.*, 1903, 10, 345–72.
22. Kirkpatrick, E. A., "Individual tests of school children." *Psychol. Rev.*, 1900, 7, 274–80.

23. Kuhlmann, F., *A handbook of mental tests*. Baltimore: Warwick & York, 1922.
24. Kuhlmann, F., *Tests of mental development: a complete scale for individual examination*. Minneapolis: Educational Test Bureau, 1939.
25. Lewin, K., *A dynamic theory of personality*. New York: McGraw-Hill, 1935.
26. Louttit, C. M., "The nature of clinical psychology." *Psychol. Bull.*, 1939, 36, 361–89.
27. Louttit, C. M., *Clinical psychology*. New York: Harper, 1947.
28. Lowenfeld, M., "The world pictures of children." *Brit. J. Med. Psychol.*, 1939, 18, 65–101.
29. Morgan, C. D., and Murray, H. A., "A method for investigating fantasies: the Thematic Apperception Test." *Arch. Neurol. Psychiat.*, 1935, 34, 289–306.
30. Richards, T. W., *Modern clinical psychology*. New York: McGraw-Hill, 1946.
31. Rogers, C. R., *Client-centered therapy*. Boston: Houghton Mifflin, 1951.
32. Rorschach, H., *Psychodiagnostik*. New York: Grune & Stratton, 1942.
33. Rosenzweig, S., *Psychodiagnosis*. New York: Grune & Stratton, 1949.
34. Stern, W., *The psychological methods of testing intelligence*. Baltimore: Warwick & York, 1914.
35. Terman, L. M., *The measurement of intelligence*. Boston: Houghton Mifflin, 1916.
36. Terman, L. M., and Merrill, M. A., *Measuring intelligence*. Boston: Houghton Mifflin, 1937.
37. Thorne, F. C., "A critique of nondirective methods of psychotherapy." *J. Abnorm. Soc. Psychol.*, 1944, 39, 459–70.
38. Thorne, F. C., "The field of clinical psychology: past, present, and future. A critical survey in 1945." *J. Clin. Psychol.*, 1945, 1, 1–20.
39. Watson, Robert I., "A brief history of clinical psychology." *Psychol. Bull.*, 1953, 5, 321–46.
40. Wechsler, D., *The measurement of adult intelligence*. Baltimore: Williams & Wilkins, 1944.
41. Wechsler, D., *Wechsler intelligence scale for children*. Psychol. Corp., 1949.
42. Westburgh, E. M., *Introduction to clinical psychology*. Philadelphia: Blakiston, 1937.
43. White House Conference on Child Health and Protection, Sect. I. C., Sub-committee on Psychology and Psychiatry, *Psychology and psychiatry in pediatrics: the problem*. New York: Appleton, 1932.
44. Witmer, L., "Practical work in psychology." *Pediatrics*, 1896, 1, 462–71.
45. Witmer, L., "The organization of practical work in psychology." *Psychol. Rev.*, 1897, 4, 116–17.
46. Yerkes, R. M., Bridges, J. W., and Hardwick, R. S., *A point scale for measuring mental ability*. Baltimore: Warwick & York, 1915.
47. Yerkes, R. M., and Foster, J. C. *A point scale for measuring mental ability*. Baltimore: Warwick & York, 1923.

Part One

✻ ✻

APPLICATION OF PSYCHOLOGICAL THEORY

Orientation to Psychological Counseling

IT WILL BE REPEATEDLY EMPHASIZED THROUGHOUT THIS TEXT THAT the purpose of psychological evaluation is to plan for the future of the client. In truth, the entire purpose of clinical or counseling psychology is to promote the efficiency and the happiness of the individuals who present themselves to the psychologist. This section of the book, Parts I and II, will be devoted to a discussion of counseling and therapeutic procedures as they are conducted by psychologists. The range of such procedures is tremendous. We will attempt to indicate something of the variety of activities involved, but again we want to stress that the justification for the existence of clinical and counseling psychologists is their contribution toward the adjustment of their clients. All the evaluative procedures that will be discussed in later portions of this text are regarded as significant only insofar as they may lead up to or allow us to plan for this final objective. If we are to plan, we must know what we are planning. Traditionally, in clinical and counseling psychology much emphasis has been placed on diagnosis and evaluation. This is as it should be, and it seems likely that psychological procedures of evaluation yield invaluable information. The question frequently arises as to the purpose of psychological examinations—evaluation for what? Consequently, we will discuss first the theory behind procedures that are designed to contribute to behavior change; then some of the more specific procedures; and finally, interviewing, observation, and testing procedures, with special emphasis on the integration of these procedures with the theory and practice of psychological counseling and therapy.

Psychological evaluation may aid in the planning of all kinds of therapy, from medical treatment to psychological and psychiatric procedures.

Many psychologists work in situations in which their primary objective is to make recommendations as to treatment procedures. Others may have the responsibility for instituting and carrying out the recommendations. We shall attempt to survey and to discuss the various kinds of procedures which may be involved. Although we may subdivide the problem for convenience of discussion, it is hoped that the reader will constantly bear in mind that it is the client who is important and that the procedures or concepts may apply to any client if the evaluation of the individual so indicates.

We shall not engage in a detailed discussion regarding the differences between counseling and therapy, as such a differentiation would be meaningless for purposes of this text. There is a considerable amount of confusion about these terms, and they appear to be used interchangeably. Many psychologists who deal with people's problems in an intensive and comprehensive fashion refer to their work as therapy; others who are engaged in remedial education and/or vocational counseling call this therapy. In a very general sense procedures that stem from the discipline of medicine or psychiatry and involve personality reorganization as the goal might be regarded as therapeutic procedures. These procedures might be roughly placed at the opposite end of the continuum from those stemming from the disciplines of psychology and education, which are oriented toward behavioral changes. The latter might more properly be regarded as counseling techniques. Since our point of view will be to emphasize the latter, we shall ordinarily use the term "counseling." This choice of terms is quite arbitrary, but the above discussion may provide a rationale for it.

The procedures which we are to call counseling procedures are also closely related to educative and rehabilitative activities. When applied to children or adolescents, they might be referred to as guidance activities, and they are certainly included in the goals of education—promoting the development of happy and efficiently functioning human beings. When our procedures are applied to adults, we might accurately describe them under the heading of rehabilitation. In dealing with the poorly adjusted adult, we hope to aid him in his attempts to rid himself of symptoms and to discover and deal with the underlying causes of these symptoms. To this extent, our aims overlap with those of psychiatric therapy. However, it is exceedingly important for the reader to realize that the purposes of psychological counseling do not end with the identification of causes or symptoms, or even with the elimination of symptoms. The most essential goal is to aid the individual in his efforts to achieve an effective relationship with his environment. This includes his relationship with his family, with members of his community, and with his associates at work—his adjustment to his particular living situation. This, then, is the final goal of counseling, rehabilitation, guidance, re-education, or therapy, regardless of the name by which it is called. It is with this total adjustment that psychology is primarily concerned.

To repeat, we are concerned with activities which result in changes of attitudes or changes in behavior and which effect a happier adjustment to the environment on the part of individuals or groups of individuals. Psychological counseling is concerned with behavioral adjustments to the environment, and may involve environmental manipulation, as well as personal counseling. When we speak of psychological counseling, we are *not* referring to activities that have personality reorganization as the basic or only purpose. Personality changes and reorganization may occur, but such changes are associated with the specific aims of psychological counseling and are not the basic or ultimate goals. As the term is used here, psychological counseling is not synonymous with psychiatric therapy or psychoanalytical therapy. Psychiatry and psychology are closely related disciplines, and there are many similarities between them. Much of their history is intertwined, and much of their knowledge is so overlapping that we may find it difficult to distinguish them. For example, both disciplines have at one time or another claimed Freud, and a substantial portion of their vocabularies is derived from his teachings. However, there are differences as well, of which the most important is that the psychologist should not take any responsibility for treating the individual in a medical sense. Other differences are not so obvious and may depend largely on the theoretical orientation of specific psychologists and psychiatrists. Psychological counseling is not necessarily a long-time process, nor is it ordinarily deep therapy in the sense of exploring early memories and experiences. On the other hand, many psychiatrists and present-day psychoanalysts advocate brief methods of therapy and concentrate on current adjustment rather than on past experiences. Thus we see that the differences are tenuous and not clearly defined. It should not be necessary to differentiate the disciplines of psychology and psychiatry in any explicit fashion. Certainly both disciplines can contribute to the public welfare. Suffice it to say that we firmly believe that psychology has unique contributions to make to the field of psychopathology, which develop primarily from the subject matter, theory, and doctrines of psychology and only secondarily from medicine and psychiatry. Hence psychological counseling is regarded as a discipline in its own right and with its own individual contributions to make. Perhaps the most important contribution is the emphasis on the total behavior of the person and on the long-range implications of his adjustment to his particular environment.

One marked characteristic of the psychological counselor is his concept of the client and the client's role in the counseling or therapeutic process. Any changes that take place in the behavior of the client are accomplished by the client. The psychologist does not *do* anything *to* the client. Rather, he works with him, guides him, and assists him in the process of effecting behavioral changes. The psychologist does not, or should not, assume that he cures anyone. He may help to a considerable degree, but he does not effect a cure. If a cure is effected, it is accomplished by the client. The psychologist may provide an opportunity for problem solving, he may provide essential information, he may offer support, he may guide the client's efforts in constructive directions, and he may even suggest helpful environmental changes, but ordinarily, in the final analysis, the client must accomplish his own emotional and behavioral alterations. The client who cannot effect the necessary changes without someone doing something *to* him may require very special education, or the services of a medically trained therapist, or it may be necessary to give careful consideration to the realism of the specific objectives to be established. It is of course understood that the professional psychologist should proceed in co-operation with medically trained personnel, and it is mandatory that psychological diagnosis include a thorough medical examination.

Actually, the term "cure" is confusing and somewhat meaningless. It is usually used to describe the removal of symptoms of a disease and the prevention of the recurrence of these symptoms. This medical usage can hardly be applied to psychopathological conditions. It is doubtful whether we have much knowledge concerning the cure of so-called "mental diseases." The term "cure" is sometimes used to describe what is thought to be a relatively complete personality reorganization or overhaul. Psychology is not striving primarily for cures; in fact the term is not used by most psychologists. Even when cures, in the limited sense of reduction and control of symptoms, are effected, the job of the psychologist has only begun.

THE ELEMENTS OF PSYCHOLOGICAL COUNSELING

In general, psychological counseling aims to improve the functioning of the individual in his environmental field. To achieve this, psychological counseling must be concerned with the total situation. This includes the person himself, amid the various environmental forces surrounding him. If the person's functioning in the environmental field is to be altered, changes must take place in the environment, in the person, and in the interaction between them. Consequently, the psychologist deals with the environment as well as with the person and, most important, he is concerned with the interaction between the two.

As applied to the person, psychological counseling consists of techniques and activities that promote insight, provide for emotional release and tension reduction, give support, encourage relearning, and contribute to socialization. No order of importance should be implied from this order of presentation. All these aims will be discussed in detail in Chapters 4, 5, 6, 7, and 8 of this Part. In this chapter we will introduce each aim, since it is believed that these aims are basic to all behavioral change. In the actual counseling situation with a particular client one objective may be emphasized more than another, but some aspect of each should be considered in planning for most clients. In the next chapter we will discuss the planning of the counseling process for a given client. Such planning will of course involve aims more specific than these primary aims, as, for example, the need for special remedial procedures or vocational planning. The reader should understand that much of our discussion is purposely kept at a general level. We are not restricting ourselves to any age group or problem group. Specific training with different groups will be necessary before an individual can qualify as a counselor—this discussion serves only as an orientation to the total field.

1. ENVIRONMENTAL THERAPY.   Environmental therapy may extend to the treatment of other persons within the client's environment. It may involve minor or temporary changes in the environment, and it may go to the extreme of changes in job, living conditions, or even institutionalization. Environmental therapy is often the primary treatment for some problems of childhood adjustment and, in this and other instances, it may be the only possible treatment. Environmental manipulation or treatment is usually accompanied by personal counseling or therapy. Sometimes personal counseling takes place with no attempt to deal directly with the environment. This course is seldom desirable, since its probable results will fall far short of our goal of efficient, happy adjustment of the client to the environment.

2. INSIGHT.   This aim of psychological counseling is concerned primarily with helping the client to gain insight into the current situation. For our purposes insight is almost, although not entirely, synonymous with the definition and clarification of the client's problem or problems. The psychological counselor is most concerned with promoting the client's objective understanding of the current and present situation. He does not probe into the past except as the past has direct bearing on the present situation; he does not explore unless some definite connection is to be established. At the risk of appearing facetious, we are inclined to agree with Stanley G. Law (9, pp. 6–7) who commented on unnecessarily probing indiscriminately into the client's unconscious life as follows:

> In the realm of medical diagnosis, one does not resort to vivisection. In the realm of psychiatry, the orthodox history is a comparable procedure—just as brutal, yes, just as sadistic,

and just as unnecessary. How ridiculous to extract each juicy morsel of the details of a sensitive man's sex life, when the problem to be dealt with is that his mother-in-law insists on living under the same roof with him! [1]

This is not to deny that deep exploration may be indicated for some clients, since they may profit only from such an analysis. On the other hand, it is not believed to be necessary for all, and many clients may profit extensively without such an examination of the unconscious antecedents of their behavior.

In discussing the constructive-synthetic approach of analytical psychology, Gerhard Adler (1, p. 4) suggests that the value of childhood recollections must become relative and limited. Adler says:

> Both analyst and patient spend laborious hours painstakingly angling in the dark waters of childhood recollections; they are very proud when they have hooked a particularly large or handsome fish, and nevertheless, at the end of it, things may be no better than they were. *The mistake is that what is prior in time is also regarded as prior in value.*[2] From the point of view of analytical psychology, however, the present situation is regarded as more important both because of its irreducible immediate significance and because of its significance for the future.[3]

The point of view of psychological counseling as described in this text is practically identical on this point with the view expressed by Adler.

Another viewpoint that coincides with our concept of psychological counseling is that expressed by Franz Alexander (2, p. 20). He points out that the belief is still held by many psychoanalysts that the recovery of memories is, in itself, one of the most important therapeutic factors. He feels that this belief—that the filling in of memory gaps is the therapeutic goal of psychoanalysis—has hampered both the understanding of why patients remember repressed events and the correct evaluation of their therapeutic significance. Alexander believes that he has demonstrated that the recovery of memories is ". . . not the cause of therapeutic progress but its *result.*"

J. S. A. Bois (4, p. 308), too, has suggested that effective psychological counseling does not necessarily mean a complete overhauling of the personality structure. He points out that the client, when in the throes of psychosomatic trouble, may not have the time, the money, the breadth of

---

[1] By permission from *Therapy Through Interview*, by Stanley G. Law. Copyright 1948 by McGraw-Hill Book Company, Inc.

[2] Italics ours.

[3] By permission from *Studies in Analytical Psychology*, by Gerhard Adler. Copyright 1948 by W. W. Norton & Company, Inc.

vision, or the endurance to undergo personality reorganization or painful emotional retraining. He suggests, "It may even be dangerous to pull apart the coarse and imperfect texture of his past life. In the end of the process you may have in your hands a pile of shreds which cannot be woven again into solid warp and woof."

In a similar vein Peter Blos (3), differentiating between psychological counseling and psychoanalysis, suggests that psychological counseling does not attempt to resolve infantile conflicts but deals with the derivatives of these conflicts into ego reactions. In the present discussion we do not wish to be quite so restrictive. It is not believed that psychological counseling is limited to the ego. On the contrary, psychological counseling is applicable to problems in which the involvement is more extensive than the ego. Blos believes that psychological counseling should be limited to those individuals who have not yet established a rigid, repetitive, neurotic pattern, but who are acutely overwhelmed by inner or outer pressures and have resorted to protective reactions. The bulk of the psychologist's clients fall into this category, and psychological counseling may be most effective with these clients. Still, the psychological counselor must be prepared to deal, when necessary, with the clients who have developed such overlaid reactions as are characterized as neurotic.

Interpretative and cathartic procedures should be a part of the therapeutic resources of the psychologist, but the psychologist's main objective is not to analyze or interpret so-called "deeper layers of the personality." By virtue of the support given and the opportunities for free expression provided by the counselor, the client may recognize and clarify deeper feelings, but this is an indirect not a direct result of the therapist's behavior. Ordinarily the psychologist does not regard insight as equated with deep therapy, and in most instances he does not assume the responsibility for deep analytical procedures.

In dealing with a client's problems and in trying to help him gain insight or understanding of them, we start with the present. A discussion of present attitudes and behavior will inevitably lead to a consideration of early life experiences and conflictual experiences that have been repressed or are not in his immediate awareness. In such instances the past cannot be ignored, because it is essential to a definition and clarification of the present. As far as possible the counselor will leave to the client the responsibility for this search into the unconscious, but he will not avoid such material simply because it would be "deep therapy" and not counseling. Rather it is regarded as necessary that any pertinent material be clarified. The psychological counselor has no preconceived ideas about what is pertinent but follows the lead of each client in making judgment. In psychological counseling the promotion of insight or understanding consists, therefore, in structuring the situation, defining the problem, and identifying only such antecedent factors as seem pertinent to the current problems of the client. Much of the insight derived from psychological counseling will be incidental to other areas of therapy such as release, tension reduction, and support.

Although many problems are complicated by the repressions of certain materials, some problems are rendered insolvable because of the client's lack of necessary information about himself and the world around him. If valid information that would be useful or helpful to the client is available, we feel that the counselor must supply it. The criterion of legitimate practice in this regard is based on whether the information presented by the clinician can be regarded as fact or fancy, whether it is scientific knowledge or merely the personal opinion of the clinician. Finally, in the defining of the problem the psychological counselor should utilize the diagnostic tools of psychology to the fullest possible extent. The definition of the problem is frequently synonymous with the treatment. That is, when the client understands the problem, he may be able to deal with it.

3. EMOTIONAL RELEASE AND TENSION REDUCTION.   Another aim of psychological counseling is that of *emotional release*. Many clients need a satisfactory outlet for their emotional energy. Although it is impossible to describe any typical client or categories of clients, there are, roughly, two extremes. At one extreme is the individual who has had or is experiencing severe trauma. Ordinarily this individual will be able to adjust normally if he is given the opportunity for appropriate emotional release in a permissive, warm, friendly, uncritical atmosphere. A tragically large portion of our population have no friends, relatives, or confidants who can provide such an atmosphere. At the other extreme are those clients who have repressed or bottled-up their feelings for so long that their importance has become entirely exaggerated. This large fraction of the population is ordinarily too inhibited or too proud to allow itself appropriate emotional release even when the opportunity is provided. Persons in this group may even have emotional reactions that are out of all proportion to the stimuli evoking them. However, opportunity for release, especially socially acceptable release, is nearly always palliative, and it may be definitely therapeutic in the sense of encouraging permanent changes in attitudes or behavior. It is obvious that the aims of insight and release, as well as other aims that will be discussed later, go hand in hand and thus, for the most part, are inseparable. In the process of talking, reliving experiences, or otherwise expressing emotion, the client often arrives at certain insights. In some instances insights may have been obscured by some emotional cloud. In still other instances the person's cognitive resources or ability to think clearly may have been lessened by the degree of emotional or subcortical excitation.

Individuals often zealously guard embarrassing experiences or supposedly shameful memories for years, only to discover that they are not nearly so embarrassing or so shameful once they are expressed. For example, when a group of persons are "letting their hair down," you may tell about your "most embarrassing experience" and even laugh about it, without experiencing any of the emotional feeling originally associated with it. Popular speech has several expressions that reflect this phenomenon. "The dirty clothes are not nearly so gray when they are brought out of the dark closet" is sometimes used in this connection. A young man referred himself to our psychological clinic because he said he had a "horrible" thing which he had to tell someone. He appeared extremely anxious and distracted. With much blocking, emotional confusion, and some weeping, he proceeded to describe an experience about which he had never before told anyone. When he had finished, he turned to the clinician and asked, "Doesn't that seem pretty bad to you?" The clinician, a little puzzled as to how to respond, decided to be frank and answered with a blunt, "No, it doesn't!" Whereupon the client said, "It's a funny thing, but it doesn't seem bad to me any more either." He left the clinic and was not seen again, except that he returned to thank the clinician for the "wonderful help" he had received.

Closely related to emotional release is the problem of *tension reduction*. Tension is a concomitant of any unresolved situation, and it is perhaps the most evident characteristic of frustration and anxiety. A certain degree of tension is constructive, since it provides the motivation necessary for problem-solving behavior. On the other hand, too much tension hampers and complicates the individual's attempt to adjust. Extreme tension often makes rational, intelligent behavior difficult, and at times, impossible. Many unhealthy behavior patterns are the consequence of an individual's need to find some way, perhaps even a bizarre, atypical, or disorganized way, of reducing tension. Tension reduction is an important by-product of several other aims of counseling. Emotional release is almost always accompanied by reduced tension. To a lesser degree, support, and perhaps insight, may bring about a lessening of tension. Conversely, some of the techniques employed in reducing tension often result in insight, emotional release, and other positive effects.

One of the most effective means of reducing tension is talking about the situation. Talking is also essential to other aims. An important mental-hygiene principle states that every individual needs someone to talk with. Healthy adjustment is encouraged by the possession of a confidant. This confidant is ideally not a psychologist or psychiatrist, but a friend, parent, teacher, or mate. The psychologist will discover that many clients are relieved by verbalizing about their problems. Other forms of tension reduction, such as exercise, are frequently recommended by the psychologist. An old saying suggests that it is much healthier after a bad day at the office to hit a golf ball rather than the wife or children. Many frustrated persons probably maintain their balance by physical exertion such as taking long walks, engaging in recreational and avocational activities that "work off steam." The frustrated housewife may rearrange the furniture several times a day; this may be a bit confusing, but it is healthy if it serves to relieve tension. In addition to the above examples, psychological counselors may also employ techniques of relaxation such as those described by Edmund Jacobson (8) or by us (6).

4. SUPPORT.   Support is a necessary aspect of most counseling and therapy. In certain instances the psychologist will not endeavor to offer any other assistance. This is particularly true when the individual is incapable of dealing with his problem or in those cases in which it appears that an examination of the problem would be traumatic. In other instances, too much support may encourage overdependence and discourage the client from an active attack on his problems. Thus the use of supportive techniques, as is true for all counseling techniques, depends entirely upon the individual and his peculiar problems.

Supportive counseling is self-definitive. Support in the individual counseling situation is encouraged by the warm, friendly, permissive atmosphere of the relationship. In the counseling situation the clinician gives the client something to fall back on. To this extent, it may seem to be quite similar to the dependence characterizing the transference situation in psychoanalytic therapy. However there exists a real, though perhaps subtle, difference between support and dependence. In support the client is encouraged to make definite attacks upon his problems, with the clinician providing a place for the client to turn when things get rough. The therapeutic relationship becomes a port in the storm, a haven in which the client can reorganize his resources. It may be the margin of safety that makes the difference between helplessness and adequate adjustment. The presence of such a relationship may provide the person with sufficient security to make for healthy functioning. The aviator wearing a parachute may feel less anxiety than if he were without one. He may never need to use it, but its presence offers a degree of support. This role of support is not limited to the counseling situation. As a matter of fact, we contend that supportive relationships are essential to good mental hygiene. To illustrate, the desirable parental relationship is one in which the parents or other members of the family are always at hand to pick up, soothe, and dust off the fallen child, then guide him back to his attempts to deal with a complicated environment. This healthy relationship must be contrasted with that in which all problems are solved for the child by an overprotective parent, who actually leads the child through childhood rather than guiding and supporting him, or the therapeutic situation in which the client is led back through childhood and has his feelings interpreted to or for him. The parental supportive relationship should function until gradually the support is provided by friends, by sweethearts, and finally by husbands or wives.

In describing the functions of the psychiatric therapist, one writer (9, pp. 9–10) describes the role of support as follows:

> Since the effort to recover must be expended by the patient and must be consciously directed—in this respect the process differs from that of recovering from an organic illness—the patient must never be allowed to expect too much from his physician. He must be kept constantly aware of the fact that it is his life and his suffering and that it is his own efforts that will produce a cure. *You stand ready and willing to give all the moral support he needs to help him understand himself, to accept in him those traits of character and the guilt he cannot accept himself,*[4] but, beyond this, you are powerless. Your acceptance of him and the rights to function and feel as he will can be a very potent therapeutic tool, at times dramatically effective.[5]

The dynamic basis for many adjustment problems arises out of the loss of, or sudden change in, supportive relationships. Such a case was that of a male client whose female analyst married and moved to a different section of the country within two months after his mother's death. Each spring the Purdue University Psychological Clinic receives many requests for counseling from graduating seniors who require support when faced with leaving the University after four years, looking for jobs, and perhaps getting married. Most persons need supportive relationships when meeting new or different situations, and many have no source for such support. Sometimes they are either too proud or too confused to accept existing possibilities. At times problems become so complex that just a little extra support is needed. With many clients the counselor must look for substitute supportive relationships. Most well-adjusted persons normally find a degree of support and security from many groups, such as the family, community, church, clubs, work situations, and recreational activities. Thus one function of psychological counseling is to provide support, when indicated, and to aid the individual in accepting or discovering permanent supportive relationships. This function of counseling will be mentioned frequently in the following pages. Alexander (2) has discussed it as one of the more important therapeutic aims.

5. Socialization.   Most psychologists would agree that there are social implications in all adjustment. We live—unless we become re-

---

[4] Italics ours.
[5] By permission from *Therapy Through Interview*, by Stanley G. Law. Copyright 1948 by McGraw-Hill Book Company, Inc.

cluses—in a world of people. We have active and passive relationships with many groups. Consequently, if counseling is to result in healthy, happy, efficient behavior, socialization is an important part of any remedial or developmental counseling process. The counselor must consider the need of the individual to learn social skills, to experiment with social situations, and to gain experience in social activities. In many clients, young and old, this is a developmental process; that is, the individual must learn to interact with people. In other instances it might be a remedial process because the client has developed ineffectual or undesirable attitudes and habits of responding toward others.

The concept of socialization is broad. It has vocational implications, at least insofar as persons have social contacts in their work; it involves family relationships and relationships within the church, the school, and the community. Psychological counseling cannot prepare the client for all eventualities, but ideally it provides him with the motivation, the necessary basic attitudes, and opportunities for learning. The individual counseling situation itself is, in the simplest sense, a social situation. Out of this situation the client may be encouraged to experiment with other situations with which he comes into contact. The first step may be merely saying "hello" to people on the street. The counselor may encourage and support the client in other attempts to gain social skills. He may suggest all kinds of activities from dancing and sports to clubs and recreation or service groups. Group therapy and role playing may be engaged in. We shall elaborate more fully later on various aspects of socialization as an aim of counseling.

6. RELEARNING.   The sixth and perhaps ultimate aim of psychological counseling is relearning. We have suggested above that therapeutic techniques may be defined as those techniques that contribute to changes in behavior and attitudes, resulting in a more efficient and happy adjustment of the client. In the end, counseling can hardly be said to have been successful unless some behavioral patterns have been changed. Some behavioral changes may result from activities directed toward the other therapeutic aims, but distinctly abnormal behavior is likely to persist until the client has learned new patterns of behavior. Psychological counseling involves all the relevant techniques of re-education, reconditioning, and retraining.

Although the sponsors of most therapeutic approaches would undoubtedly concur on the necessity for re-education, in actual practice this important phase of therapy is frequently neglected. Therapists at times become so engrossed in tracing a hysteriform disorder back to the Oedipus situation or an obsessional disorder back to the pregenital stage that they overlook the ultimate readjustment of the individual. They stress the importance of insight into conflicts at these levels, the clarification of intervening material, and lose sight of the present behavior of the client. Although the hysteriform symptoms may show improvement after the recall of the Oedipus, we should not attach too much importance to the magic of insight. Although, as previously mentioned, many clients may effect changes in behavior if they understand its source, others may require guidance if they are to change well-established habits of thinking and acting. Such retraining or re-education ranges from the extinction of conditioned reactions of a complicated nature, the altering of nonadjustive compensatory reactions, or the development of previously inhibited behavior, to the more direct therapeutic methods of remedial training in special subjects, motor training, or speech correction.

Alexander (2, p. 18) reports the evolution of Freud's psychoanalytic techniques through five periods, culminating in a "procedure aimed at achieving permanent changes in the ego's functional capacity by a slowly progressing emotional training—more an educational process than a therapy in the original sense." He notes that this transformation from therapy in the original psychological sense to an educational process is seldom complete and may be a strong point for the use of re-educative techniques. Alexander Herzberg (7) has presented a strong case for the use of organized or directed experiences in the daily life of the patient to augment the work being accomplished in the analytic sessions.

Rogers (11) considers that re-education is an observable factor in the closing phases of the process of counseling. However, he points out that in client-centered therapy the therapist does not manipulate the client's environment or suggest action to him to bring about a series of experiences. Rogers contends that if therapy is progressing successfully, the evolving insights will enable the client to recognize and meet and handle situations arising in his daily living, and this will demonstrate to him his own progress and strengthen his confidence in himself. In contrast to this it is our contention that the psychological counselor, following upon a complete diagnosis, may frequently encourage very direct activities for re-educational purposes.

John Dollard and Neal E. Miller (5), O. Hobart Mowrer (10), Franklin J. Shaw (12, 13), and Edward Joseph Shoben (14) have all discussed the role of learning in therapy. Their suggestions, as well as therapeutic techniques of others which are directed toward learning and relearning, will be discussed thoroughly in Chapter 7.

THE COURSE OF PSYCHOLOGICAL COUNSELING

Lest the general course of counseling be lost in a consideration of the elements or specific aims of counseling, we must look at the total process.

Counseling begins with the referral or the earliest meeting between client and clinician. A division between evaluation and counseling can be made only for convenience of description and discussion. The clinician should orient his thinking toward the ultimate goal of efficient, happy behavior; from the time of the first professional contact, his efforts should be guided by the need to make recommendations and plan activities that might be expected to contribute to a more satisfactory life situation for the client. When we conduct an intake interview with a patient in the hospital or clinic, we should be collecting information that might have relevance to his ultimate vocational, social, and economic readjustment. We should contrast this attitude of long-range planning for total rehabilitation with the unfortunately short-sighted attitude of some clinicians who think only of the immediate therapeutic process and the likelihood of the client's being eventually discharged from the hospital or clinic. Counseling with a physically handicapped person must ordinarily be concerned with his psychological acceptance of the disability. However it should not end with a change in the attitude of the client toward himself but should eventuate in the training, employment, and the absorption of the client into society as an integral part of his family and community. Academic and vocational counseling with the high school or college student should not be basically directed toward the choosing of a course of study which the student could enjoy and complete successfully. Rather, the long-range perspective should include the fitting of the person for a happy, constructive life.

The examples that have been cited may aid the reader to understand the meaning of the statement that will be repeated so many times in this book—that the entire aim of diagnostic or evaluative procedures is to plan treatment. In practice, the first phase is evaluation of the individual in an attempt to understand his current situation and factors leading up to it. Then we plan activities and experiences that might be expected to result in a more satisfactory adjustment of our client. After carefully considering and examining our plans, we enter the next phase, which consists of the implementation of these plans. This must be a careful experimental procedure in which we constantly re-evaluate our progress as we go along. In many, if not most, instances plans must be revised or changed as the process of counseling progresses. We hope to reach the point at which the client, his family, his teacher—whoever is regarded as responsible—can proceed without the counselor's immediate assistance. Eventually the process should carry itself along without the participation of the psychological counselor.

It is hoped that the reader can understand and accept our philosophy that psychological counseling and therapy is related to the total process of a client's maturation or rehabilitation. The specific aims and techniques to be described in the following chapters are not ends in themselves but are to be viewed as integral parts of a developmental process. By the same philosophy we are not endeavoring to describe counseling as a simple face-to-face relationship between clinician and client but rather to suggest that the client's entire life situation must be regarded as a therapeutic experience. Counseling is not planned in terms of one hour a day or week but in terms of twenty-four hours a day. The psychological counselor is not the only and probably not even the most important therapeutic influence. All the persons coming into contact with the client must be regarded as contributing to his behavioral adjustment. For example, the child's family, his teacher, and even his friends are a part of his therapeutic milieu. In the hospital all personnel who have any relationship with the patient are therapists. Ideally, the psychologist strives to mobilize and co-ordinate all these influences. This may be impossible, but we do deal with as large a segment of the total life situation as is possible.

All this discussion does not rule out the importance of individual and group psychotherapy in which the psychologist may be the prime therapist. Many clients require or profit from such formal counseling or therapeutic experiences, and planning must include such experiences to the extent that they are indicated and are feasible. In general, however, psychological counseling as herein presented is more akin to teaching than to therapy, to education than to treatment, and to rehabilitation than to personality reorganization. The counselor may co-ordinate, expedite, and facilitate, but need not influence the client more directly.

SUMMARY

In this introductory chapter we have attempted to emphasize that a discipline of psychological counseling or therapy exists. We have attempted to introduce briefly the aims of psychological counseling: environmental therapy, insight, emotional release, support, socialization, and relearning. Subsequent chapters will deal with each of these concepts in detail. It has been emphasized that these concepts would not necessarily all be used with a specific client. Neither is it likely that the counseling process with most clients would be limited to the promotion of any one or two of the objectives only. The over-all process has been broken down for purposes of discussion and understanding. In any over-all approach to counseling by a trained counselor most, if not all, of the objectives are stressed. That they are stressed, however, may not be explicitly recognized, and some may be neglected unless attention is directed toward them. After so dissecting the counseling process, we returned to the larger picture, emphasizing that psychological counseling is related to the total process—development, maturation, and rehabilitation.

BIBLIOGRAPHY

1. Adler, G., *Studies in analytical psychology*. New York: Norton, 1948.
2. Alexander, F., and French, T. M. *Psychoanalytic therapy*. New York: Ronald, 1946.
3. Blos, P., "Psychological counseling of college students." *Amer. J. Orthopsychiat.*, 1946, 15, 571–80.
4. Bois, J. S. A., "The field of the psychological therapist." *J. Clin. Psychol.*, 1945, 1, 304–8.
5. Dollard, J., and Miller, N. E., *Personality and psychotherapy*. New York: McGraw-Hill, 1950.
6. Hadley, J. M., "Various roles of relaxation in psychotherapeutics." *J. Gen. Psychol.*, 1938, 19, 191–203.
7. Herzberg, A., *Active psychotherapy*. New York: Grune & Stratton, 1946.
8. Jacobson, E., *Progressive relaxation*. Chicago: University of Chicago Press, 1938.
9. Law, S. J., *Therapy through interview*. New York: McGraw-Hill, 1948.
10. Mowrer, O. H., *Psychotherapy: theory and research*. New York: Ronald, 1953.
11. Rogers, C. R., *Client-centered therapy*. Boston: Houghton Mifflin, 1951.
12. Shaw, F. J., "A stimulus-response analysis of repression and insight in psychotherapy." *Psychol. Rev.*, 1946, 53, 36–42.
13. Shaw, F. J., "Some postulates concerning psychotherapy." *J. Consult. Psychol.*, 1949, 12, 426–31.
14. Shoben, E. J., Jr., "Psychotherapy as a problem in learning theory." *Psychol. Bull.*, 1949, 46, 366–92.

☼

CHAPTER

3

Theoretical Framework

THREE POINTS ARE BASIC TO THE THEORETICAL APPROACH TO COUN-
seling as it is discussed in the chapters that follow. First, we shall
concern ourselves with changes of behavior and attitudes. Attitudes are regarded as aspects of behavior. Attitudinal adjustments may
be far more intrinsic than physical reactions but the difference is regarded as relative. In the functioning individual, both intrinsic and extrinsic behavior is involved in his reactions to a complex environment.
Since we wish to promote behavioral and attitudinal adjustments, we are
not concerned with personality theories in a limited sense; we are basically interested in theories of behavior. Such theories of behavior must include consideration of intrinsic personality factors, but it is the total behavioral field upon which we will focus our primary attention.

Second, each individual must be regarded as a unique problem. We
will attempt to understand the specific factors contributing to the behavior of each client. We will attempt to formulate plans for changes in this
behavior, and, finally, we will try out these plans. In other words, the
general approach consists of definition of the problem, formulation of
hypotheses, and testing of these hypotheses. It is obvious, therefore, that
theories of personality, which place emphasis upon intrinsic behavior or
personality factors, must give way to behavioral theories, which consider the total life adjustment of a person.

Third, our emphasis will be on planned counseling. This is not to
imply that the psychologist does all the planning but rather that the counselor and client (if he is capable of so doing) together work out a tentative general set of goals as well as the strategy for attaining these goals.
These plans may require change, but it is strongly believed that planned
effort is always more efficient than unplanned, undirected activity. The
psychologist will use all available tools to accumulate the data necessary

to provide a basis for sound planning. In keeping with our earlier statement that the main purpose of psychological evaluation is to plan for treatment, the psychologist must utilize the results of the evaluative procedures in order to plan the general strategy of the counseling process. Franz Alexander and Thomas M. French (1) have also stressed the need for planned therapy, stating that consciously directed effort reaches the goal more easily and rapidly than does random effort. Persistent effort and good intentions may partially make up for haphazard direction, but a plan of action based on a full understanding of the problem makes success surer, quicker, and easier. In order to avoid the untenable psychological dilemma of the headless horseman who jumped on his horse and rode off in all directions at the same time, it is hoped that this and the following chapters will describe a general strategy that can guide the psychological counselor.

It is not the purpose of this presentation to outline any special techniques that will be useful to *all* psychologists with *all* their clients. Nor do we plan to suggest any specific formulations that will automatically correspond to the needs of any given client. We believe, however, that it is of value to present an outline of psychological procedures and a general method of approaching clients that will provide a framework within which to operate. There are few feelings more helpless than those of a young psychologist facing his first counseling interview without any particular strategy or general plan to follow. There can, of course, be no "handbook" giving specific instructions to follow, but we hope we can present a broad orientation that will give psychological counselors a margin of security, and that will serve as a flexible yet systematic set of guiding principles for the neophyte psychological counselor. As a person matures as a counselor, he develops his own specialized techniques and over-all procedures.

Many of the procedures to be described are concerned primarily with the client who is responsible for his own actions and who is relatively independent of family and other external controls. However, it is not intended that we neglect the dependent client, the child, the retarded or the handicapped person. Some changes can be effected in their behavior through the facilitation of re-education and other aims. Furthermore, those responsible for the behavior of others—for example, parents and teachers—may require advice or counseling so that they can effect behavioral and attitudinal readjustments in themselves as well as in their charges.

The reader should not assume that this chapter attempts to present a theory of behavior. As the title indicates, its purpose is to suggest a framework within which the scientific psychological counselor can operate. Many theoretical points of view have been advanced by psychologists and others to explain behavior and personality. In Chapter 1 these theories were viewed as tentative maps of unknown territory, and it was suggested that it is the job of the research worker and theoretical thinker to superimpose on the data that is assembled in daily practice some of the theories—the maps—and reconcile some of the areas of agreement and disagreement among them. It should be emphasized that we do not propose simply to take a little of this theory and a little of that and then throw them together. Rather, these maps need to be integrated and a "true" map constructed. The psychological counselor, however, is faced with the practical situation of dealing with the problems of a client as they are presented to him. He can hardly wait until the ultimate map is drawn before attempting to offer some assistance or guidance to his client. Consequently, it appears appropriate at this point to examine some of the theoretical considerations regarding behavior and attempt to develop a rationale for our planned approach to counseling and psychological therapy. Specifically, we shall consider some of the elements of psychoanalytical theory, learning theory, and field theory and attempt to indicate the applications of these theories to the functions of the psychological counselor.

HOW THEORY CAN HELP US IN PLANNING COUNSELING OR THERAPY

1. REQUIREMENTS OF AN ADEQUATE BEHAVIOR THEORY. O. Hobart Mowrer and Clyde Kluckhohn (10, p. 69) list four assumptions basic to a dynamic theory of personality. These assumptions are as follows:

(a) The behavior of all living organisms is functional.
(b) Behavior always involves conflict, or ambivalence.
(c) Behavior can be understood only in relation to the field, or context, in which it occurs.
(d) All living organisms tend to preserve a state of maximal integration, or internal consistency.[1]

In the larger sense we are going to accept these assumptions in the present discussion. In connection with the first concept, that of functionalism, a further assumption is to be made. This assumption—many will feel that it is more than an assumption—is that the functional aspects of behavior can best be explained and understood in terms of learning. That is to say, a person's behavioral reactions can best be seen as learned ways of easing tension.

[1] By permission from "Dynamic Theory of Personality," by O. Hobart Mowrer and Clyde Kluckhohn in *Personality and the Behavior Disorders*, edited by J. McV. Hunt. Copyright 1944 by The Ronald Press Company.

Mowrer and Kluckhohn elaborate on their second assumption to point out that the proposition that behavior always involves conflict is indigenous to psychoanalysis. It is equally inherent in field theory and learning theory. Problem-solving activity characteristically arises out of conflict situations. Conflict is so characteristic of life that it almost seems to be a case of belaboring the obvious to hypothesize that behavior always involves conflict.

In discussing their third assumption, Mowrer and Kluckhohn state that Gestalt psychologists have stressed particularly the importance of field in the determination of behavior. They contend that psychoanalysis, anthropology, and learning theory all take the importance of context for granted. We must agree completely with the contention that they adhere to it in principle, but we question whether they carry it into practice. Although in theory most of the analytical workers will admit to the importance of field or environmental factors, in actual practice these factors are all too frequently overlooked in favor of consideration of intrinsic motives. This discussion will elaborate the importance of field or context.

The final assumption of Mowrer and Kluckhohn, that "all living organisms tend to preserve a state of maximal integration or internal consistency," must also be recognized as basic to any theoretical discussion of behavior. As these authors have observed, the proposition is implied by the other three. However, the distinction between integration, adjustment, and growth must be recognized. Some theories of psychotherapy equate the principle of integration with the principle of growth. We must recognize that organisms may select certain unhealthy modes of adjustment such as repression, regression, dissociation, and escape into fantasy in order to preserve their integration. Consequently, any adequate theory of behavior must account for apparently disintegrative mechanisms of behavior as well as positive growth tendencies.

It is undoubtedly possible to conduct successful counseling or therapy within any one of the several theoretical frameworks, provided that both the counselor and the client accept the framework. It may be possible to counsel without any theory of behavior. However, it is ordinarily advantageous if the counselor operates within some kind of theoretical framework. The client must have something to believe in, and, even more important, the clinician must have something to believe in.

2. FIELD THEORY. Many authorities are of the opinion that we are going to make little progress beyond our present level of achievement in counseling and psychotherapy until we discard our "class" or "essence" theories of personality (behavior determined by the type or kind of personality) and begin to apply field or interaction theory to the understanding of behavior. Wendell Johnson (5, p. 7) points out that

"insofar as we are not scientific, we are essentially Aristotelian in our outlook, in our fundamental attitude, or set, or orientation to life." In this statement Johnson is not discussing the development of theories of personality but he does describe clearly the process by which unscientific "either-or" laws concerning human behavior have been developed. The reader should refer to the first few chapters of Johnson's book in order to see how Aristotelian thinking affects our "common-sense" beliefs. Alfred Korzybski (7) and his followers, particularly Anatol Rapaport (11), have stressed the inadequacy of Aristotelian logic as a system of inquiry. In a non-Aristotelian system knowledge is sought in the regularities with which events occur, rather than through the "nature of things." Consequently, it is the reality of behavior in general, not the nature of the individual or of individuals which we must consider if we are to develop a satisfactory scientific behavior theory.

Lewin (8, p. 28) has differentiated between the modern and Aristotelian points of view as follows:

> . . . the kind and direction of the physical vectors in Aristotelian dynamics are completely determined in advance by the nature of the object concerned. In modern physics, on the contrary, the existence of a physical vector always depends upon the mutual relations of several physical facts, especially upon the relation of the object to its environment.[2]

Lewin makes it very clear that this applies also to internal causes, which involve the mutual relation of the facts of a physical system. The most important concept so far advanced as a framework within which the clinician might work is expressed by the formula:

$$B = f \ (PE)$$

This represents the simple, obvious, but frequently overlooked fact that behavior or variations of behavior (B) can best be explained in terms of the interaction between the person (P) and the environmental forces acting upon him (E). This concept is basic to the theoretical framework of this text.

Lewin has also discussed the way in which present-day child psychology and affect psychology exemplify the Aristotelian habit of considering the abstractly defined classes as the essential nature of the particular object, and hence as an explanation of its behavior. In discussing the concept of drives Lewin (pp. 15–16) points out that the hunger drive or the maternal instinct, for example,

---

[2] This and following quotation from *Dynamic Theory of Personality*, by Kurt Lewin, are printed by permission of the McGraw-Hill Book Company, Inc. Copyright 1935 by McGraw-Hill Book Company, Inc.

. . . is nothing more than the abstract selection of the features common to a group of acts that are of relatively frequent occurrence. This abstraction is set up as the essential reality of the behavior and is then in turn used to explain the frequent occurrence of the instinctive behavior, for example, of the care of infant progeny. Most of the explanations of expression, of character, and of temperament are in a similar state. Here, as in a great many other fundamental concepts, such as that of ability, talent and similar concepts employed by the intelligence testers, present-day psychology is really reduced to explanation in terms of Aristotelian essences, a sort of explanation which has long been attacked as faculty psychology and as circular explanation but for which no other way of thinking has been substituted.

Many personality theorists are essentially Aristotelian in their approach to understanding and explaining behavior. Such concepts as "anima," "persona," and "racial-unconscious" are excellent examples of abstractions that are set up as realities and then used in turn to explain behavior. Other concepts often regarded as realities are our familiar concepts of the id, ego, and superego, or the Freudian tripartite division of the personality into conscious, foreconscious, and unconscious.

3. FIELD CONCEPTS VS. ANALYTIC CONCEPTS.   Although many would insist that such concepts as id, ego, or superego are only constructs and are not regarded as essential realities, the actual use of these terms would seem to belie this. Frequently these concepts are used *as if* they were realities, not only in writing, but even more in staff conferences and therapy planning. It is one thing to observe the existence of consciousness or to observe that certain aspects of behavior are conscious, while others are not; it is another thing, however, to ascribe certain dynamic characteristics to consciousness or unconsciousness and then to use these hypothetical characteristics to explain the frequent occurrence of specific bits of behavior. This is not to deny the existence of consciousness or unconsciousness; our criticism is directed toward the use of these concepts to explain themselves.

J. F. Brown (2) has set up a distinction between class-theoretical versus field-theoretical concepts. The simplest and earliest types of science are characterized as "class-theoretical," and the most complex and systematized sciences as "field-theoretical." Although there are many points in psychoanalytical theory which need clarification, Brown feels that Freudian psychoanalytical theory is a type of field theory. Some concepts such as regression and libidinal progression are said to be dynamic and field theoretical in nature, while the concepts of basic urges, the division of the personality into conscious, foreconscious, and uncon-conscious, and the concepts of ego, superego, and id are somewhat more difficult to fit into field theory. Brown believes that these conceptual and methodological difficulties of Freudian theory stem from the transition from class-theoretical psychology to a field-theoretical psychology which was going on during Freud's lifetime. It would be good if we could be sure that the transition is as complete as Brown insists. He suggests that the other varieties of analytic theory (Adlerian and Jungian) are less adequate, less dynamic, and certainly less consistent with field-theoretical concepts than is Freudian psychoanalysis. Although individual psychol-ogy seems to give more recognition to the importance of sociological factors in human adjustment, this recognition is very superficial. Jung's theory is regarded as much less systematic than Freudian theory. Fur-thermore, as is also emphasized by Brown, the theories of the racial un-conscious and the prophetic nature of dreams are entirely unscientific and, in the light of other scientific psychological evidence, approach the ridiculous. Many of the concepts of psychoanalysis must be studied as forces or vectors bearing on behavior, but we can hardly accept them without further experimentation and modification.

To carry this discussion one step further, it is maintained that even personality is an abstraction, and that the same is true of intelligence. However, personality and intelligence can best be regarded as *qualities* or *characteristics* of behavior and not as realities. As mentioned above, "class" or "essence" concepts, even though they may be described in a very complicated fashion, are oversimplifications. It is much easier to explain behavior in terms of an instinct, a frustrated id impulse, a type or aspect of personality, the unconscious, or by some other abstraction than it is to search for all the dynamic forces that may be affecting the behavior of a particular individual. We have always tended to develop abstractions—frequently even superstitious abstractions, and usually misconceptions—to explain hard-to-understand but frequently observed phenomena. It is much simpler to develop a theory and then explain a given phenomenon in terms of the theory than to search out the real reasons for it. And each time we can explain an occurrence within the framework of our theory, we take this as added proof of the validity of our theoretical construct. Because the theory works, it is uncritically accepted.

Unfortunately, this type of illogical and unscientific process charac-terizes personality theory as it has developed from therapeutic activities. The most common supportive evidence for a theory of personality is its workability in counseling or therapy. Somewhere in the process of think-ing we fail to realize that there may be many reasons why a treatment procedure is successful other than the accuracy of the theoretical con-structs upon which it is based or of those which have been derived from the therapeutic procedures. Some of the many reasons why a therapy might work, in a few or in many instances, are as follows: Support is a characteristic of almost all successful forms of counseling. Verbalization by the client is basic to practically every school or approach to counseling and psychotherapy. While being counseled, the client is receiving personal attention as well as attention to his problems. A warm permissive relationship is characteristic of most therapies. Opportunity for emotional release and tension reduction is either basic to, or a byproduct of, all therapeutic processes. Furthermore, practically all clients seeking help are looking for explanations. Lack of understanding is anxiety-producing. Events and experiences that are the unexplained, not understood, and unfamiliar are perhaps among the more fearful. The psychoanalyst offers a system of explanation. This is very comforting. This need for knowledge about, or for an explanation of, the unknown is largely responsible for the virtual universality of theism throughout the history of mankind.

Laurance F. Shaffer (13, p. 461) points out still another reason why theories of personality and theories of therapy have endured without experimental verification. He says,

> . . . these theories have a personal value to the therapist that holds them. They give him a sense of security and protect him from conflicts of his own that might arise in the often uncomfortable interpersonal relationships of the therapeutic interview. Perhaps this last factor explains the warm emotional, almost religious, attachment that each therapist has for his particular mode of explanation. The practicing therapist sees his theory not as an objective system of description, but as a code of values and a way of life.[3]

Shaffer further states that an explanation that satisfies one purpose is often unsuited for other purposes. It is possible that many theories of psychotherapy have more value for the counselor than for the client. Shaffer, as well as R. Nevitt Sanford (12) and Shoben (14), has stressed that one of the greatest contributions which can be made by psychologists is in the area of research. According to Sanford (12, p. 66), "It would be hard to name an area in which research is more needed than it is in therapy, or an area in which what is being done lags further behind what might be done." It is Shaffer's belief that theories of psychotherapy have up to the present time made relatively few contributions to research.

[3] From "The Problem of Psychotherapy," by Laurance F. Shaffer, *American Psychologist*, 1947, 2, 459–67. By permission of the American Psychological Association.

It is certainly not the aim of this discussion to disprove the accuracy of any personality theory. It is offered simply to support the thesis that no theory is proven by virtue of its workability in the counseling or therapeutic situation. We should never be disrespectful to any theory that has helped many people. At the same time we should regard such theory as a therapeutic approach, not as a system of laws which can be used to explain human behavior. All schools of psychotherapy can and do claim successes—if therapeutic success is proof of a theory, then all theories have been proven. However, none purports to be successful in all instances.

4. A FIELD-THEORETICAL APPROACH TO PSYCHOLOGICAL COUNSELING.   George A. Kelly (6) has made certain observations in a search for dynamic and accessible factors in intellectual development. Although his observations are primarily oriented toward intellectual development, it is possible to adapt them to development in general and, more specifically, to the problem of counseling. He has actually taken a rather broad view of intellectual development, and consequently his theoretical framework lends itself nicely to the problem of behavioral readjustment. He writes as follows (p. 5):

. . . it is possible to view intellectual development as the resultant of a number of vectors. These vectors vary in strength and direction. They vary from time to time. They vary from person to person. It may not be necessary for all of us to envisage them in the same way. They could be considered, in turn, as themselves partial resultants in the force system.

According to this view it ought to be possible to facilitate intellectual development in three ways:

(1) Increase all of the vectors which have projections upon the line of intellectual development.

(2) Modify the system so that the resultant becomes a maximum for a given vectorial total, or

(3) Increase a selected vector which does not have too great an angular separation from the line of intellectual development.

The first method would increase the internal strain upon the system, but would have the advantage of not requiring any preliminary analysis of the system. The second method would decrease the internal strain but if improperly applied, would retard intellectual development. The third method would increase the internal strain to some extent, depending on the vector selected, but would require a clinical diagnosis of each case in order to find a vector which was both related to intellectual development and susceptible to stimulation.[4]

Although Kelly would probably neither recognize nor claim his hypotheses with the changes about to be proposed, they do provide a take-off point for our theoretical position. In considering the above statements by Kelly, let us first strike out the word "intellectual" each time it occurs so that we are talking about development in general. Second, insofar as we can adapt these methods to the problems of counseling, it is believed that we must have a clear knowledge of the system before we disturb it in any way. Consequently, all methods should require a preliminary analysis of the situation. Third, we must emphasize that many of the vectors in the system are within the person as well as surrounding him. Many of these vectors may be opposed by vectors either in the environment or within the organism. According to one viewpoint one might really conceive of a force system within a force system. However, this point of view overlooks the fact that the two systems are dynamically related. For this reason, Lewin's formula, in which behavior is viewed as a function of interaction between forces both in the person and in the environment, is a more useful basic postulate.

An application of the first method insofar as intellectual development is concerned would be a general stepping up of intellectually stimulating conditions for a child. Examples, as applied to the more general problems of counseling, are mobilization of the environment in "total-push" [5] therapy, motivation therapy, and the very directive techniques of persuasion, suggestion, exhortation, and advice. As Kelly pointed out, such techniques increase the internal strain upon the system and consequently, at least as counseling techniques, should require a careful preliminary analysis of the system.

The second method would require the reduction of unfavorable tensions and perhaps the reduction of certain aspects of external stimulation so that the favorable internal trends might manifest themselves. Some forms of environmental manipulatory therapy, changes in the attitudes of those who surround the client, supportive therapy, tension reduction, and release therapy are all examples of the application of the second method. As in the case of the first method, there are dangers if the method is not properly applied. In discussing the actual manipulation of the vectorial matrix, Kelly refers to a project of ours (4) in which several case and group studies were conducted on the role of relaxation

---

[4] From "Observations Made in a Search for Dynamic and Accessible Factors in Intellectual Development," by George A. Kelly, *Fort Hays Kansas State College, Studies in Clinical Psychology*, 1940, 1, 5–10. By permission of the President, Fort Hays Kansas State College.

[5] *See* pp. 218–19.

in rational psychotherapeutics. In some cases relaxation appeared to remove tensions and to directly foster better adjustment, while in others it formed a protective frame that permitted freer expression and the formulation of the personality problems; in yet another, relaxation played all these roles but at different stages in the counseling process.

Obvious examples of the third method are the remedial and reeducative techniques. Others are the uncovering and insight therapies, which result in the formulation of a course of action by the client; this may occur through the removal of repressions or inhibitions, thus allowing the client to direct his behavior along a definite vector or toward a specific goal.

It should be clear that we regard behavior as the resultant of a force system. As Lewin (8) has pointed out, this is a *dynamic* force system, and for this reason it is constantly in a state of change or flux. The job of the psychological counselor is to isolate as many of the forces in this system possible. If enough of the forces are defined, the direction and character of behavior can be predicted with some degree of accuracy— but only to a degree, for it is impossible to define all the forces affecting the behavior of a complex human being. Complete accuracy can never be attained because the force system is dynamic, and any diagnostic technique, whether an interview or a projective test, is relatively static. All the tools of the clinician should be brought to bear on the dynamic evaluation. It is believed that the psychologist is better equipped to analyze and describe this force system than is anyone else. Predictions should be formulated concerning the direction of the resultant of the vectors and further tests or observations should check the accuracy of these predictions. Even though the prediction of behavior will never be 100 per cent accurate, recommendations can usually be made regarding the control of this behavior.

The clinical psychologist is in every sense an experimentalist. Although the N (number of cases) of his experiment at any given time is only one, he is a researcher in his treatment of this individual. His task is to become so familiar with the force system for any single case that its behavior can be predicted and controlled. Counseling or therapy should be an experimental procedure. It should consist of varying certain factors, holding others constant, and carefully observing the results. As an experimentalist, the psychologist is willing to discard a hypothesis if it does not work, and try another. This concept of therapy coincides with the doctrines of planned and flexible therapy as described by Alexander (1). Therapy must be planned but, even more important, it must be flexible. Therapists whose procedures are structured within the framework of an Aristotelian "class" or "essence" theory of personality will find it difficult to vary their procedures to the optimum advantage.

5. THE CONCEPT OF LEARNING AS APPLIED TO COUNSELING.
One characteristic in the behavior of biological organisms which may
not seem to be completely explained by field theory is the phenomenon
of learning. Certain patterns of behavior tend to be repeated even though
all the original dynamic forces that resulted in the behavior are not present in the force field. If we were interested in maintaining the semantic
framework of field theory, we would say that the force field has changed
and that certain secondary acquired devices are now factors in the force
field. In any case, whether we attempt to incorporate learned responses
into our field theory or whether we simply utilize field theory to explain
the perpetuation of such responses, we need to examine how responses
are learned and how they can be unlearned.

Shoben (14, p. 379) has examined and discussed contemporary
theories of learning with a view to presenting psychotherapy as a problem
in learning theory. He points out that reinforcement theory seems to
"account rather adequately for the acquisition of striped muscle acts;
but at least in the conditioned defense situation—most germane to the
clinical problems here under scrutiny—its adequacy is dependent on the
operation of secondary motivational states, for the acquisition of which
it is hard put to explain." Consequently Shoben looks to two-factor
rather than monistic theories to explain the learning of complex behavioral adjustments. One of the two-factor theories he discusses is that
of Mowrer (9). This basic theory would appear to be satisfactory to explain the learning of both "skeletal" and "emotional" learning. Furthermore, the theory seems to explain satisfactorily the processes of unlearning, relearning, and re-education which characterize the behavioral
changes accompanying counseling activities. The intent here is not to
endorse this approach but rather to use it as an example. Learning and
psychotherapy will be discussed at greater length in Chapter 7.

6. DIRECTIVE CLIENT-CENTERED COUNSELING.   At this point the
reader may be thinking that counseling based on such hypotheses must
be quite directive, quite prescriptive, and with little responsibility given
to the client. This is not necessarily true. To the degree that the client is competent, he should be an integral part of the planning process.
Furthermore, the psychologist should not make any prior decisions about
the competence of the client. The diagnostic resources of the clinician
should be fully utilized to evaluate the resources, the motivation, and the
control of the client. The counseling program will be more or less directive, depending upon the client's ability to take responsibility for his own
behavior. It is client-centered at all times. This is an important concept
and should be carefully noted. To be client-centered, counseling need
not be nondirective. We propose the concept of directive client-centered
counseling. If the counselor is concerned with the single case of his ex-

periment, every activity will necessarily be centered about the client's problems. On the other hand, if the counselor projects himself or his theories into the experiment, client-centeredness is lost. We maintained that the counselor cannot actually be client-centered if he is guided by a personality theory (as contrasted with a field-behavior theory). Client-centered counseling can exist only if he is interested in behavior.

7. Research Needs in Psychological Counseling. Research in counseling should not be directed toward the essential characteristics of the person or his personality; it should be concerned with the process of adjustment, with the learning process, and with the characteristics of certain counseling activities. According to our post-Galelian field theories of behavior, no laws can be derived concerning the characteristics of the person without taking into consideration the force system of which he is a part. Our research should be directed toward understanding the effect of certain influences upon this force system. To illustrate, what is the effect of verbalization? In what way is the force system changed by talking about the problem?

Recent trends in dynamic psychology have been very healthy, especially to the extent that they have broken away from the "either-or" concept of normal and pathological. Another notable effect of the dynamic theories has been to stress the importance of the individual. Even with these healthy trends, however, personality theory is at a level of development comparable to that of physics in ancient times. It would not be just to imply that the Greek physicists did not give careful consideration to many natural phenomena, but until the beginning of the sixteenth century, so far as we know, there were no programs of planned experimental study and research. The Greeks displayed remarkable creative genius in mathematics, metaphysics, literature, and art, but they achieved very little in natural science. They lacked the incentive to conduct experimental tests, but nevertheless some of their ideas seem to have been close to the truth. *They delighted in speculative philosophy.* So it is today with personality theories that speculate about the essence of the personality and with theories that attempt to determine the direction of behavior in advance by the nature of the object concerned. In spite of the extensive acceptance of the theories of Sigmund Freud, Alfred Adler, Carl Jung, and their disciples, few, if any, experimental tests have been made of their concepts.

Many of our readers may be disturbed by the mechanistic way in which behavior is being treated. One of our students once objected to the "reduction" of human behavior to a physical science and reproached us for being unemotional and impersonal. Exception is taken to the notion that any actual "reduction" is involved, but the following quotation from the Foreword to an article in which a physicist, Willard Gardner

(3), discusses the scientist's concept of the physical world may answer the charge of unemotionality:

> To those who are aesthetic, there is perhaps nothing more inspiring than a beautiful sunset, with brilliant colors above the horizon and with banks of dark clouds above, set in the deep blue of the heavens or the brilliant hues of the rainbow forming a halo about the majestic mountain with its coat of green, purple, brown, or gray. By these things are the emotions stirred.
>
> The physicist too is emotional but he is also at times realistic. He becomes sentimental but he also seeks to explain the behavior of nature. By means of devices and instruments his perceptual world is expanded. He tries to translate it all into numbers and equations. He seeks for invariance in a world which constantly changes. By the power of his intellect he achieves a measure of success; he discovers harmony in chaos, and he lays a foundation upon which the engineer and the artisan may build.[6]

The physical world is relentless and without emotion. It is but a part of a vast universe that transcends it. The psychological investigator may feel that there is some intelligence that transcends the person and his physical environment. Let us remind ourselves that we cannot plot or predict the strength and direction of such supernatural vectors. Consequently, let us do the best we can with the forces that we can isolate. If we can look objectively, experimentally, and nonspeculatively at the realism of behavior, we will make progress in the formulation of behavioral theory.

WHAT IS MEANT BY PLANNING COUNSELING OR THERAPY

Planning is the phase most important to psychological counseling. We have stressed again and again that the entire purpose of diagnostic methods and clinical psychology in general is to plan treatment or at least to furnish information and make recommendations that will be useful in planning for the future of the client. The diagnostic phase must of course progress to doing something about the client's problems. It must be emphasized that this does not necessarily mean doing anything *to* the individual; it does mean, however, that eventually some systematic plans must be made concerning the general strategy of the counseling process.

The philosophy of counseling to be discussed in this text is quite

[6] From *The Scientist's Concept of the Physical World*, by Willard Gardner, 1942. By permission of Dr. Gardner and the Faculty Association, Utah State Agricultural College.

eclectic. We are not dedicated to any one school of thought and will simply attempt to fit several schools of thought into a scientific psychological framework. If we are really scientific psychologists, we should be able to use scientific procedures in deciding which of the many available procedures are best adapted to the needs of a particular client. In the area of counseling it is not very scientific to assume that there is any one procedure that will suit the needs of all clients. As we begin the counseling process, we shall continue to be experimentalists. Once we decide upon a course of action, we are in effect trying out a given hypothesis; if this course does not prove to be a satisfactory solution to the needs of the client, we must look for an alternate hypothesis.

1. ENVIRONMENTAL AND/OR PERSONAL COUNSELING.   Planning for the client involves making a series of critical and crucial decisions. These decisions are not necessarily final. They may in some instances be reversed or revised as we progress with the counseling process, but they are nonetheless crucial and should not be made on a trial-and-error basis. The first decision to be made is whether environmental manipulation or personal counseling (or therapy) is indicated. In reality neither this nor any of the other decisions to be made is merely an "or" decision; it is rather an "and/or" decision. In other words, we must decide whether we are to deal with the environment *and/or* the person. Usually both will be indicated but occasionally *only* environmental manipulation or *only* personal counseling may be possible. It is recommended that the psychological counselor carefully survey the possibilities for some beneficial environmental manipulation with every client, as psychological counseling with important figures in the environment is consistent with our philosophy of situational and behavioral treatment, as contrasted with *personality* therapy.

The difference between this concept of psychological counseling and other therapeutic approaches may be largely semantic. Total personality therapies, such as the various analytical systems, certainly recognize the function of environmental forces in determining personality. However, we feel that it is more advantageous to orient counseling toward behavior which is considered a function of the person and the environment than to orient it toward personality. No matter how broad our conception of personality may be, the latter orientation tends to encourage the counselor to concentrate on personality reorganization and to lose sight of the total situation in which the individual must function. Behavioral adjustments will be effected most easily when both environmental and personal adjustments are made. Personality therapy sometimes fails because the individual is attempting to function amid environmental stresses that are too severe for him (or perhaps any individual) to cope with. By the same token we often find situations in which the environment *can-*

not be altered and to which the client must learn to adjust. When it is impossible or impractical to consider environmental manipulation, efforts must be directed toward effecting an efficient adjustment of the individual to the reality situation.

The psychological counselor will consider carefully whether any form of environmental manipulation is possible or practical. The distinction between environmental and other forms of therapy is of course always relative. Some of the aspects of counseling which are primarily environmental will overlap with ameliorative, supportive, and even insight approaches. Environmental manipulation may range from complete change of environment, to minor changes in the attitudes of those associated with the client or to the mobilization of environmental forces to the aid of the client.

2. INSIGHT AND PROBLEM-SOLVING VS. AMELIORATIVE AND SUP-PORTIVE PROCEDURES.   Let us now assume that some form of personal counseling is indicated, whether or not accompanied by environmental manipulation. The next decision concerns the necessity or practicability of procedures directed toward insight and problem-solving behavior as against the use of ameliorative, supportive, and nondirective techniques. As in the case of the decision between environmental and personal counseling, we are not making a decision to use one approach to the exclusion of the other. Many of the supportive, ameliorative, and so-called "superficial" procedures must accompany insight-oriented counseling. With certain clients insight may be impossible, dangerous, or otherwise not indicated, in which case superficial procedures will comprise the principal remedial activities. Here again, though, the distinction is entirely relative, for a degree of insight will come with emotional release, tension reduction, and other ameliorative procedures. Insight may be possible only if support is offered or perhaps when some opportunity for overdependence has been removed. A degree of insight certainly accompanies the use of nondirective procedures, and many of the directive techniques of reassurance, persuasion, and explanation promote insight.

The term "superficial" is used in the preceding paragraph to designate techniques other than "deep" therapy. Unfortunately, the term "superficial" carries a certain undesirable connotation, as of second-best or less effective. The reader should bear in mind that it is not used in this sense; the so-called "superficial" techniques are no less real than those discussed under insight. Superficial procedures are nearly always necessary, and they are often the only ones used. The counselor should always be alert to the advisability of using techniques oriented toward ameliorating symptoms. Thorne (15) discusses various conditions under which the use of these techniques is indicated: (a) when crises in adjustment arise in which emotional stability or other distressing symptoms require immediate action to tide the client over his troubles; (b) during periods of maladjustment or instability due to environmental stresses, when the client is basically healthy and normal; (c) in situations impossible of satisfactory solutions; and (d) for the treatment and relief of distressing symptoms that must be attended to before more basic therapy can be effectively attempted. Palliative or ameliorative procedures are indicated as basic under certain conditions, particularly (b) and (c) above. Under (a) and (d), ameliorative procedures may be complimentary to other procedures. When such is the case, care must be taken not to "overdo" the amelioration and thus hinder behavior change. A client might become too comfortable and one necessary condition for successful problem solving and learning is a degree of tension. Ameliorative techniques include such procedures as reassurance, catharsis or ventilation (expression of feeling), symptomatic treatment, and relaxation. These techniques and other ameliorative devices will be discussed in Chapters 5 and 6.

Closely related to the ameliorative procedures are the supportive procedures. Supportive counseling is certainly ameliorative in nature, and it is indicated in many conditions of acute stress. Support consists primarily of acceptance of the client by the clinician or by others, and the main purpose of supportive techniques is to give the individual a margin of security. As Alexander (1) points out, supportive therapy might even be grouped under the environmental therapies because of its frequent dependence upon the environment. The counselor is, of course, one element in the environment, but the client may also look to family, friends, working associates, lodge, and church for support. Support may take the form of activity therapy, since a great deal of security can frequently be gained by skill in some activity.

Psychotherapy is, to a large degree, identified in most persons' thoughts with insight or uncovering therapy. The point of view of psychological counseling as herein discussed has stressed the applicability of forms of counseling which are not directed toward insight or, as the analytic therapist would say, limited to the level of the ego. Some psychologists and psychiatrists feel that *real* therapy exists only when the sources of the conflict are uncovered and the ego is given a chance to adjust to the conflict in the therapeutic relationship. We believe that other approaches may be just as real, but we do not deny that insight, problem solving, and uncovering activities are indicated when the client is deemed capable of gaining insight and of handling conflict. Several philosophies of counseling which are designed to promote insight and emotional understanding will be discussed in Chapter 4.

3. Directive or Nondirective Procedures. The decision as to whether nondirective or directive procedures are to be followed is one

that will to a large extent make itself, particularly if the clinician can be sufficiently nondirective to ascertain whether the client can carry the responsibility himself. The point of view of this text is that the nondirective philosophy should prevail as long as the individual is productive and as long as the procedure is efficiently profitable. Nondirective procedures are indicated when essentially supportive nonthreatening counseling is the plan. However, such procedures may also be indicated for the productive client when insight is the goal. In this second instance the efficiency of the nondirective procedures must be carefully evaluated, since clients may gain so much support from the nondirective procedures that their insight may remain protectively superficial. Still other clients may gain satisfaction from preoccupation with some aspect of their problem and concentrate on this aspect to the exclusion of the larger view; in such cases, the clinician must either become somewhat directive or offer some interpretation instead of the nondirective technique of reflection.

When the diagnostic picture indicates, the counselor may become quite directive. Directive counseling is better described as a number of directive techniques, than as a procedure by itself. Directive techniques are used on occasion by almost all counselors, but we must give credit to Thorne (15) for organizing and synthesizing thought about directive procedures. Although some of the directive techniques, such as suggestion, persuasion, advice, and coercion, have been in ill repute, we feel that they are valuable and safe when used with full awareness of their limitations and with reasonable skill. After all, every person is daily subjected to gratuitous advice and suggestions from a multitude of people. The psychological scientist possesses the most valid source of knowledge concerning mental hygiene problems and certainly the best tools for studying the individual. Admitting that this source may be fallible and incomplete, it is still the best available. This is true, of course, only if the psychologist utilizes the objective measures at his command. Objective advice based upon these measures and other sources of evidence is sometimes indicated.

4. Individual and/or Group Counseling. The psychological counselor must make still another decision. He must evaluate the relative merits of individual and/or group methods for each client; that is, individual and group counseling may be conducted at the same time or separately as the needs of the client indicate. Group activities have certain practical advantages. With the large numbers of patients in hospitals and clinics, and the shortage of trained personnel, adequate individual counseling for all needing it is practically impossible. We must endeavor to provide beneficial experience for as many clients as possible with the personnel available. However, group counseling must not be thought of as a makeshift or an improvisation. Actually, participation in a group

offers certain experiences that are not available in the individual counseling situation. Many of these extras, as well as different techniques of conducting group counseling, will be discussed in Chapter 10 on group procedures.

5. SPECIALIZED PROCEDURES. Finally, there are many specific problems with which the psychological counselor must be prepared to cope. Many clients will come to the psychologist for education and vocational counseling, for consultation on matters of work efficiency, or for remedial teaching in such areas as speech and reading. The well-trained psychological counselor must meet these problems. In some of these instances the need for counseling may appear to be superficial or symptomatic; however, the scientifically oriented worker should not make this assumption. Treatment oriented toward guidance or remedial education may be merely a part of a total counseling program. On the other hand, the need for vocational counsel may be a real problem with no relation to the emotional life of the client, or poor reading habits may need consideration in and of themselves. Knowledge of techniques for dealing with such specific problems is needed, and this must be recognized in the training of the psychological counselor.

SUMMARY

Three concepts have been described as basic to the theoretical approach to counseling that we are presenting. First, we are concerned with changes in attitudes and behavior. Second, each individual is regarded as a unique problem. Third, counseling should be a planned process. The requirements of an adequate behavioral theory were discussed, and with these requirements in mind the reader was encouraged to examine field-theory, psychoanalytical-theory, and learning-theory approaches to counseling. Although most theories strive to be dynamic and field theoretical at the level of concepts and constructs, it was suggested that in actual practice many of the dynamic constructs are treated as if they were static, essence, or class-theoretical constructs.

A tentative field-theoretical model for psychological counseling was suggested; this model views behavior as the resultant of interacting force systems. Psychological counseling can be thought of as the process of modifying this force system in order to alter the resultant behavior in hoped-for directions. This modification is ordinarily not drastic in the sense of disrupting the over-all integration of the force system; it consists rather of increasing and decreasing certain vectors so that interactive relationships are changed. Although resultant behavior could certainly be altered by innumerable modifications of the complicated force systems in which individuals function, three examples were given:

(a) We can increase the probability that a given course of behavior will result by increasing the strength of all the vectors which project upon that line of behavior. The relearning and socialization objectives would generally contribute to such an effect. Unless this is carefully planned and unless these objectives are accompanied by other objectives, the tension or strain upon the system would be increased.

(b) Such objectives as environmental modification, emotional release, and support may contribute to the reduction of certain forces so that other forces may have an opportunity to affect the resultant behavior.

(c) Special remedial techniques, insight, and the removal of repressions may strengthen or release certain vectors and reduce the strength of others so that the chances of occurrence of certain behavior may be increased.

The process of planning was presented as a series of crucial decisions, and the psychological counselor was urged to check off certain possible areas of activity. (a) Can the client profit from change in the environment or from more extensive use of environmental resources? (b) What ameliorative, palliative, and/or supportive measures are indicated? (c) To what extent can the client profit from a nondirective approach? (d) Should the counselor offer any suggestions or advice—assume a directive role? (e) What decision will be made concerning insight or uncovering activities? This will involve the choice of a particular technique for promoting insight, as well as the indications for using it. (f) Should group procedures be used in addition to, or in lieu of, individual procedures? (g) Are any special remedial procedures indicated? If the clinician has considered all these alternatives, he can feel that he has really been a psychologist and a scientist.

BIBLIOGRAPHY

1. Alexander, F., and French, T. M., *Psychoanalytic therapy*. New York: Ronald, 1946.
2. Brown, J. F., *Psychodynamics of abnormal behavior*. New York: McGraw-Hill, 1940.
3. Gardner, W., *The scientist's concept of the physical world*. Logan, Utah: The Faculty Ass., Utah State Agricultural College, 1942.
4. Hadley, J. M., "Various roles of relaxation in psychotherapeutics." *J. Gen. Psychol.*, 1938, 19, 191–203.
5. Johnson, W., *People in quandaries*. New York: Harper, 1946.
6. Kelly, G. A., "Observations made in a search for dynamic and accessible factors in intellectual development." *Fort Hays Kansas State College, Stud. Clin. Psychol.*, 1940, 1, 5–10.
7. Korzybski, A., *Science and sanity: an introduction to non-Aristotelian systems and general semantics* (2nd ed.), Lancaster: Science Press, 1941.

8. Lewin, K., *Dynamic theory of personality*. New York: McGraw-Hill, 1935.

9. Mowrer, O. H., "On the dual nature of learning—a reinterpretation of 'conditioning' and 'problem solving.'" *Harvard Ed. Rev.*, 1947, 17, 102–48.

10. Mowrer, O. H., and Kluckhohn, C., "Dynamic theory of personality." In Hunt, J. McV., *Personality and the behavior disorders*, Vol. I. New York: Ronald, 1944.

11. Rapaport, A., *Science and the goals of man*. New York: Harper, 1950.

12. Sanford, R. N., "Psychotherapy and counseling: introduction." *J. Consult. Psychol.*, 1948, 12, 65–7.

13. Shaffer, L. F., "The problem of psychotherapy." *Amer. Psychologist*, 1947, 2, 459–67.

14. Shoben, E., "Psychotherapy as a problem in learning theory." *Psychol. Bull.*, 1949, 46, 366–92.

15. Thorne, F. C., *Principles of personality counseling*. Brandon, Vt.: J. Clin. Psychol., 1950.

The Role of Insight

THE TERM "INSIGHT" IS USED IN VARIOUS WAYS AND WITH DIFFER-
ent meanings by writers and workers in the field of psychological
counseling. But although there is relatively little agreement regarding the use of the term, there is considerable agreement that the phenomenon represented by it is one of the fundamental aims of psychological
treatment. Insight was listed in Chapter 2 as one of several basic aims of
psychological counseling; although the term was not specifically defined,
the point was made that uncovering or promoting the realization of repressed memories should not be the only goal of the psychologist. Uncovering repressed memories is merely one aspect of the promotion of
insight. The psychological counselor is most often concerned with definition and clarification of the current situation, and his direct efforts appear
to be most effective when they are concerned with the conscious, intellectual aspects of understanding the development of current problems. However, we must never forget that if deeper exploration is indicated for a
given client, counseling procedures should be oriented toward that objective.

We mentioned earlier the man who was disturbed by characteristics
of certain voices. For the most part the voices appeared to be real, not
imaginary voices or hallucinations, but nonetheless he was often irritated by the sound of voices he heard on the radio or in a crowd, and
even by the voices of his friends. These voices evoked several reactions
in him. They were frightening, and when he heard them in his dreams,
he would wake up screaming with fright. Sometimes he was angered by
them, and not infrequently he would have an impulse to destroy the
voices or even the persons who possessed them. He also wanted to run
away from them and had developed what amounted to a phobia of
crowds—when surrounded by strange people, he was almost certain to
hear some fragment of speech that would disturb him.

He was certain that these voices were associated with something that had been extremely traumatic to him, but, search as he might, he could not find an explanation that satisfied him. As is to be expected, the voices were not his only problem or symptom. He also had a vague feeling of guilt, represented mainly by a desire to atone or make up for something. Driven by this feeling, he was active in church work, was a leader in various community and social service projects, and, in general, took advantage of opportunities to help other people. In his memories of his war experiences there was one rather long blank period. It extended from a week before he was seriously wounded until a month after he was injured. In reality, even though his tank had exploded and he had suffered extreme concussion effects all over his body, there did not appear to be a very good explanation for the amnesia after the injury. He was unconscious for a few hours but, according to medical records, recovered rather quickly, and his main symptom was amnesia for events preceding and following the tank explosion.

By careful and laborious effort, utilizing his dreams, free association and controlled association, it was eventually possible to piece together the events repressed during this period. It was felt that he was getting very close to the root of the trouble when he recalled an experience that occurred several days before he was wounded. His group had been "mopping up" in a small village, and in the process of going through every building looking for remnants of the enemy forces, he had entered a small church. In the front of the church, partly obscured by the pews, he had seen a German soldier. Automatically and almost involuntarily he had shot and killed him. His instantaneous reaction before he shot had been that he himself, outlined by the doorway, was an excellent target, and that he must shoot first. However, when he approached the enemy that he had killed, it was obvious that the German had been kneeling in prayer. The young soldier had not entered the church to hide but to worship.

Prior to this incident our client had been an efficient, methodical, and cold-blooded fighting machine. He had been proud of his skill as a soldier and enjoyed his activities; he had not experienced fear, but had been stimulated and exhilarated by the war. After the incident he lost his zest for fighting. He was disturbed by guilt feelings, thinking he had committed an unpardonable sin. Furthermore, he came to feel very unsure of himself and believed that the loss of his tank and the death of the crew was due to his error of judgment. The insight gained at this point was more disturbing than comforting. Our client was bothered by anxiety as to why he had been such a cold-blooded fighter. He felt that if he had not been so quick to act and so vicious, he would not have killed the soldier. In other words, he now began to despise himself for his love of fighting, and his anxiety increased.

The counseling was now oriented toward prewar and early life experiences. Later on we will go into these in more detail, but at the moment let us merely add that as his childhood history was explored, it became clear that he had built up a tremendous amount of aggression. When he entered combat, the expression of aggression was sanctioned, even rewarded by commendations and decorations. Although this realization (insight) was not pleasant or easy to accept, it did allow him to understand and accept his war behavior, and his over-all anxiety diminished. Throughout this period of treatment the voices continued to plague him. At some point he had recalled that he had some personal effects which he had taken from the body of the soldier killed in the church. These effects were locked in a trunk in the attic of his home. The fact that he possessed them had been either forgotten or repressed. He was encouraged to bring them to show to his counselor. While he was showing them, he began to perspire and then reported that he knew "where the voice came from." He remembered an elderly German lady who had attempted to keep him from entering the church. She had screamed at him, cursed him, and hung onto him to prevent his entrance. Her efforts had angered him and he had pushed her roughly aside to enter the church. After this realization he no longer heard the voice.

This case illustrates the varying roles that insight can play in clinical practice. Indeed, it illustrates several "kinds" of insight. In the instance of this client, insight was an indispensable aim of the counseling process. In other cases, such as that of the girl with the compulsion to exhibit her teeth, insight was not as effective. No particular traumatic experiences could be discovered in her early life history. What was revealed was a series of experiences in which she was unable to compete socially with her beautiful sister and in which the academic and scientific achievements of her brothers were continually before her. Her understanding of the total picture appeared quite complete. She had an intelligent understanding of the facial grimace and her inability to apply herself. Still, the behavior seemed to be so firmly established and the lack of direct gratifications was so lacking that her habits could not change. Insight appeared to make her happier with her pattern of behavior, and the efficiency of her behavior did not improve. In truth, she fully accepted her behavior after seeing how it had developed, and, no longer feeling guilt, she became less anxious to change. For her a program of relearning was necessary.

In this chapter we will discuss the concept of insight as it is viewed by various theoretical systems of psychological and psychiatric counseling or therapy. We will examine the meaning of insight within these various theoretical approaches so that we can utilize the different conceptualizations of insight as they may be pertinent to the needs of any particular client. At the same time we will have an opportunity to compare and evaluate the different theoretical positions. Although this comparison and evaluation of theories could be included in any of the several chapters in this section, it seemed most appropriate to include it here because of the importance of insight to a wide variety of theories. As a result, this chapter reviews both the different applications of insight as a counseling goal and a number of relevant theories.

The psychologist who is planning counseling experiences for a client will, of necessity, employ ideas from different theoretical systems if he plans with the needs of the client in mind. This is a practice that we believe to be more effective than using the same concept with all clients. Some years ago there was a beloved old physician who was regarded as one of the best tonsillectomists in western Kansas. He had an excellent reputation, and people came to him from miles around. He was exceedingly skillful and eminently successful, the only difficulty being that the tonsillectomy was almost his sole treatment procedure. Regardless of symptoms, if a patient he was treating was still in possession of his tonsils, he took them out. Unfortunately, the practice of some counselors is almost as ridiculous as this. Since the term "insight" probably has a different meaning for every clinician, it is hoped that the psychological counselor will not assume that insight will aid all clients, without considering the meaning he gives the term. There are some instances in which we should encourage, and others in which we should discourage, the attainment of any given aspect of insight. At times one aspect of insight will be suppressed and another promoted: as for example when the psychologist assists a client in defining a current problem but avoids the uncovering of certain earlier traumatic events; or when it is indicated that the client should be distracted from the current problem by placing emphasis upon unraveling and analyzing events that led up to the current situation. It may seem desirable with one client to promote an objective and unemotional consideration of previous experiences, and with another the expression of appropriate emotions may actually be desirable. Considering in this way the needs of each individual, we plan selectively and choose from a variety of concepts, attempting to use the one or several concepts that will be most helpful for a particular client. With the above discussion serving as a rationale, we will now examine insight from a number of theoretical viewpoints.

INSIGHT IN GESTALT PSYCHOLOGY

The concept of insight is commonly associated with, and probably originated with, Gestalt learning theory, particularly with the comparative psychology of Wolfgang Kohler. In his studies of the thought processes of apes Kohler described what he regarded as reorganization of the perceptual field and an integration of a system of cues which are responded to simultaneously. One of the most characteristic aspects of the Gestalt concept of insight is its spontaneous and sudden nature. Kohler believed that his apes, when presented with a novel problem situation, related the various elements of the situation to each other and then perceived the "whole" (Gestalt), thus being able to perform the correct solution. Kohler's use of this concept led to a great deal of experimentation revolving around the validity of insight in the Gestalt orientation as well as the fundamental properties of insight in both animals and men.

The chief opponent of the concept expounded by Kohler was Edward L. Thorndike, whose major efforts had previously been directed toward animal learning, which he explained on the basis of trial-and-error behavior. Although experimentation along this line may at first glance seem somewhat removed from counseling, closer scrutiny indicates its relevance. The emphasis on insight in counseling and on counseling as a learning process makes experimental investigation of insightful learning particularly important.

After a review of the literature John A. McGeoch (23, p. 47) concluded in 1942 that

> . . . the abrupt changes which occur are functions of transfer from prior training, of the subject's experience with the particular problem he is trying to solve, of passage from one level to another in a hierarchy of response, and of many other conditions which are continuous with such concepts as trial and error and association. The subject's trials and errors need not be overt to be trials and errors but may take place symbolically or in some other fashion beyond the direct observation of the experimenter. Actually, many of the descriptions of insight behavior contain rich descriptions of pre-solution trials and error.[1]

Several workers (6, 36) have found that chimpanzees either did not solve Kohler's problems at all or solved them only after much previous experience with the tools of solution. Harry F. Harlow (17) obtained data on the formation of learning sets or tendencies to respond in a particular manner by training monkeys on a large number of discrimination problems. At first it took the monkeys a long time to master a problem, but after they had learned several problems, a new one was easier for them, and eventually they could solve a new problem almost immediately. The importance of Harlow's data lies in showing that monkeys can learn to solve problems with insight—with apparent suddenness and

[1] By permission from *The Psychology of Human Learning*, by John A. McGeoch. Copyright 1942 by Longmans, Green & Company, Inc.

with few trials and errors—after they have had much experience with similar types of problems. Harlow does not feel that there is any evidence that primates solve problems suddenly, but that with experience gained from many problems, they may master new problems with few or no errors. This improvement in performance is seen by Harlow as a result of the experiences.

Although there appear to be many gradations between intelligent insight and trial and error, the research on this topic as a problem in learning theory has given us a few leads that can be used in counseling. For example, Harlow's research might suggest that, in discussing a variety of problems with the client, we can provide him with a background of experiences so that he may suddenly perceive a solution to other problems that have not even been discussed. If we assume that the client can achieve a suddent intelligent solution, we must be sure that he is aware of all the elements in the situation. To this end, such sudden solutions should be expedited by thoroughly discussing the problem situation, making sure that the problem is completely defined and described. Discussion, description, and definition of the problem are valuable aids to problem solving, even if one leans to McGeoch's belief that there is much covert trial and error preceding sudden insight.

Another concept emerging from research on problem solving in human subjects is the importance of direction. The direction or set given to the subject determines to a large extent how rapidly and how successfully he will solve a problem. The psychological counselor, then, should give the client some idea of the direction in which he might work. This can be done by suggestion, by instruction, or by hypotheses offered by the counselor, as well as by transfer of training whereby the client applies what he has previously learned to solution of the problem at hand. If the application is correct, positive transfer will result, but if the application is incorrect, negative transfer will result. In the case of incorrect application the counselor can be most helpful not only by pointing out the direction, but also by guiding the client as he relates his experiences to solution of a problem.

The above paragraphs describe in general the concept of the role of insight in psychological counseling which is favored by the theoretical orientation and philosophy of this text. Although the concept had its origin in Gestalt psychology and is also consistent with field theory, it is likely that research on problem solving and learning has contributed to its development. The reader should be able to see many applications of this approach if he views the counselor as one who encourages problem-solving behavior. The role of "cues," "signs," "associations," and many other similar constructs can be used by the ingenious and alert counselor.

The preceding discussion assumes that the tools and elements necessary to problem solving are available to the client. It further assumes that the client has had appropriate experiences that can be applied to solving current problems and that these experiences can readily be recalled. In many instances these assumptions are valid, and problem solving can be approached quite directly. On the other hand, it will be necessary for many clients to gain experiences and learn new tools. This aspect of counseling will be discussed under re-education or retraining in Chapter 7.

CLASSICAL PSYCHOANALYTICAL APPROACHES TO INSIGHT

1. SIGMUND FREUD.   Personal problems are not always available for direct attack because a person is often unable to recall or remember all the factors contributing to his current difficulty. The explanation of this involves the concept of repression and leads us to a consideration of the psychoanalytic interpretation of the meaning of insight. Freud (11, p. 939) once stated, "The theory of repression is the pillar upon which the edifice of psychoanalysis rests." Freud attributed motivation to unconscious sexual and aggressive instincts that are unacceptable to the larger social world within which man exists. He believed that these primal impulses are banished from consciousness and held in check in the unconscious; repression serves as the device by which the conscious intellectual aspect of the personality (the ego) maintains its integrity. Since these impulses are continually striving to break through to awareness, the process of repression must be continuous and unrelenting. If the ego becomes incapable of co-ordinating these conflicting forces, if it fails in its attempts to mediate between the basic biological urges (id impulses) and the excessive demands of the conscience (superego), the repressed impulses find substitute expression in the form of symptoms.

Psychoanalysis aims at improving the ego's capacity to deal with its own conflicts. By uncovering repressed forces and re-exposing the ego to the impulses it had earlier repressed, psychoanalysis attempts to free it of its neurotic defenses and thus enable it to control, through conscious intelligent judgment, the impulses that had previously been unavailable for co-ordination and integration. In this way Freud conceived the task of psychoanalysis as the undoing of repression. Analysis is a process of tracing the neurotic symptoms back to their source in childhood, of bringing to the client's knowledge his unconscious repressed impulses and wishes, and of uncovering the resistances that prevent his fuller knowledge of himself. Freud believed that every symptom has a meaning in terms of unconscious instinctual motives and satisfactions, and that if these motives could be discovered and accepted by the client, he would be in a position to deal with them rationally. Freud seemed to imply that *conscious awareness of the dynamics of one's disturbance constitutes the goal of analysis.*

Freud's principal tool for exploring the unconscious was free association. The client reclined on a couch and endeavored to verbalize his thoughts in an uninhibited fashion. The analyst maintained a relatively passive role and was guided only by the client's associations, which he interpreted at intervals so that the client might become more aware of their meaning. Dreams were regarded as "symptoms" and interpreted in terms of sexual symbolism. This procedure was designed to allow maximum opportunity for the recovery of unconscious material. The client was relieved of the necessity of logical thought and presumably could allow his impulses to be expressed freely and reveal his basic conflicts. Nevertheless, Freud discovered that the ego was sometimes unwilling to dredge the unconscious of painful wishes of the past, and "resistance" was inferred from the client's inability to recall or from his mounting anxiety when inner conflicts were being approached or discussed. Resistance, for Freud, represented a protective barrier to be penetrated before insight could be obtained. The entire analytical process is focused on uncovering these resistances, bringing them to the client's attention by interpretation, and enabling him to relinquish them.

In view of the highly verbal nature of communication in psychoanalysis and the relative ease with which a client may accept interpretations at the verbal level, it might seem that the insight to be achieved is of a logical, intellectual type. While some critics maintain that Freud's method was directed toward rational understanding, he was firmly convinced that insight into the relationship between a previously repressed urge and a present symptom is possible only when the emotions appropriate to the early wish are re-experienced or re-enacted in the therapeutic situation. He pointed out that clients who consciously remember nothing proceed to express the forgotten material in action; thus the repressed content is reproduced not in awareness but in unconscious behavior. Freud's interpretation of this phenomenon of "acting out" was in terms of the concept of the "repetition compulsion." Since most neurotic conflicts were assumed to be generated from the "Oedipus complex" [2]—undue attachment of a child to the parent of the opposite sex and corresponding antagonism toward the parent of the same sex—it seemed to follow that, in reliving his conflicts from early childhood onward, the client re-experiences these urges, identifying the analyst with the original object of his desires. This unconscious "acting out" in the "transference neurosis" was seen by Freud as a blessing in disguise, which he considered to be the most powerful tool of the analyst. He saw it as the vehicle by which the deepest forgotten emotions become mani-

---

[2] The Oedipus complex takes its name from a character in Greek tragedy who married his mother after killing his father.

fest and accessible to the analyst for interpretation and to the client for integration into his active conscious life. The analyst's interpretations of repressed conflicts in the transference situation are timed in such a way that the ego is able to assimilate them and thus become strengthened in its new control over previously unsolvable problems. Thus, Freud's concept of insight is more than the pure intellectual acceptance of an interpretation. It involves reliving and "working through" of the deepest and most strongly repressed affective reactions, which can then be integrated into the conscious life of the client.

Concerning the question of re-education or the recombination of the instinctual elements that are isolated and examined during analysis, Freud (10) contended that this is unnecessary because psychosynthesis is achieved *automatically* during analysis without any intervention by the analyst. The way for it is opened by reducing symptoms to their instinctual elements and by overcoming resistances. Freud attributed to the mind an instinctual energy impelling it toward cure—an innate tendency to reorient and redirect itself once it is in control of all its elements. Such control is achieved through insight into the nature of the instinctual motives of one's symptoms. While this might take place only at the intellectual level, its full impact and penetrating benefits could be derived only from emotional reliving of the incidents in which repression first occurred (frequently referred to as abreaction) and acceptance of the instincts at work, both of which are acted out in the formation and final resolution of the transference situation.

Earlier in the chapter we passed briefly over the uncovering of repressed childhood aggressions, in the example of counseling with the veteran who had gloried in the experience of expressing aggression in combat. This aspect of his long-range adjustment was not clarified easily. He was able to recall many early life experiences in which he was frightened and punished by his father, but each of these recollections came with difficulty and with strong emotional reactions. Although his father had been very unkind to his mother, who had died when the client was quite young, it was difficult for him to accept and express his feelings toward his father. This resistance may have been related to his strong religious background and the associated feeling that he should not have such attitudes toward his father. Certainly his early life attitudes toward religion had something to do with the intensity of his reaction to the church incident. In any case, the reconstruction of his childhood history was more than intellectual and was accompanied by physical sickness, anger, grief, and acute fear. The counselor was the focus of a considerable amount of negative feeling during this period, and on at least two occasions he was destroyed in the client's dreams. After the mass of complicated feeling was expressed and worked through, the client was able to view himself with much more objectivity and to accept some of his subsequent behavior as the result of the unconscious expression of these repressed aggressions.

2. CARL GUSTAV JUNG. Although Jung differed from Freud on many basic formulations, he, too, conceptualized that man possesses an innate tendency toward adjustment. He conceived that man is propelled by an inborn spiritual or religious need for "wholeness" or "completeness." He believed this process of "individuation" to be a force that (1, p. 168) "struggles to make man fulfill his individual task to approximate more closely his real self." According to Jung, the "wholeness" or state of integration is latent and predetermined within every individual. A person not only experiences his individual totality but also discovers his relatedness to the "collective unconscious." Clarification of the content of the collective unconscious—containing the archaic memories of all mankind—and recognition of its influence on present life is, for Jung, equivalent to what Freud called insight. Counseling or therapy, as the Jungian would describe it, aims essentially at the achievement of this insight—recognition of one's relatedness not only to one's inner mental life, but also to the outer world and the universe.

Although Jung postulated two layers of the unconscious, the personal and the collective unconscious, he showed relatively little concern for the former, whose forgotten or repressed infantile contents he regarded as peculiar to the individual. However since every problem belonging to the layer of the personal unconscious blocks the experiencing of images in the collective unconscious, he considered uncovering and understanding of the personal unconscious, with resolution of personal conflicts, to be necessary, not as an end in itself, but rather because this would enable the individual to grasp the superpersonal, collective foundations of life. Jung's greatest emphasis was on man as a social being (rather than as the more isolated individual with whom Freud was concerned) who shares certain mental functions with all men. These are the "inherited potentialities of human imagination," the archaic residues of the evolution of the species, which are represented in the collective unconscious by primordial object-images. Jung called these images archetypes or "universal categories of intuition and apprehension." It is through recognition and understanding of these primordial trends of thought and emotion that the individual advances in his progress toward individuation or self-realization (31, pp. 145–8).

Jung's concept of the unconscious differs vastly from that of Freud. Although infantile sexuality, repression, and the Oedipus complex were not rejected by Jung, they receded in importance with his de-emphasis of infantile sexual trauma in the production of later neurotic conflicts. This change in emphasis seems due to Jung's broadened concept of libido. Jung accepted a multiplicity of instincts, one of which was sexual and all of which arose from a "primal" libido, an outgrowth of the evolution of the species. He saw the libido as a continuous source of undifferentiated energy related to all desires, preserving not only the individual but all mankind. Thus Jung's libido is composed of constructive as well as destructive features. It follows, then, that Jung's unconscious also differs in character from that of Freud, its contents being not merely primarily evil, primitive, infantile id strivings.

Since Jungian analysis was designed to release the individual's creative potentialities, to construct a "psychic totality" by rendering accessible the wisdom of the collective unconscious, it may be characterized as a "prospective" method, rather than a retrospective one that seeks cure in revelation of past causes. Jung's is a therapy oriented toward the future of each client, toward his formulation of a philosophy of life to help him actualize his ambitions. The *present* positive aspects of each client form the raw material of therapy. The achievement of insight or "self-knowledge" becomes a forward rather than a backward movement within the individual's life span.

The course of analytical work follows two steps, (a) anamnestic analysis and (b) synthesis of conscious with unconscious. The first step consists of a reconstruction of the client's biography, which is rearranged and interpreted in order to gain a picture of the conscious situation and to establish personal contact between the client and the analyst. The personal unconscious is revealed by free association and analyzed only after conscious material is exhausted, and the analysis aims to establish a causal relationship between a symptom and a definite experience in the past. Jung believed that this method was particularly valuable in calling to the client's attention the unconscious psychological history of his behavior problem, enabling him to discover related external facts that might help him lose his feelings of insufficiency and guilt, thus releasing psychic energy previously invested in his inadequate behavior. While this method bears resemblance to that of Freud, Jung believed that, for the necessary discovery of "inner facts," conflicts must be interpreted as existing not in the past but in the present, as the result of problems demanding greater output of "psychic energy" than the client could muster. The task of analysis is to uncover problems or conflicts that the client is trying to evade and to find constructive expression for the newly gained energy. This departure from Freudian theory brought with it the addition of the synthetic method, which is the core of Jungian therapy. Essentially it is a process by which the fantasy life of the client is interpreted in terms of archetypes, thereby establishing a relationship between the individual and the racial heritage that he shares with all men through the ages.

Primordial images are approached by Jung's principal therapeutic tool, dream analysis. In contrast with Freud, Jung regarded dreams as natural, normal functions indicating an attempt of the mind to free the dreamer of his complexes. Rather than achieving "sterile" wish fulfillment, dreams represent the individual's unacknowledged potentialities, which are symbolic manifestations of the collective unconscious. They are interpreted with reference to the actual situation of the dreamer rather than his infantile sexuality. Such interpretations are supplemented by a re-educative process of "amplification" designed to facilitate further development and individuation by opening to the client the mystical pre-established realm of "inner truth and reality." Amplification is an enrichment of the original material by analogous images from mythology and folklore. It is here that the analyst contributes his own associations, which then determine the direction of future associations by the client. The symbolic material necessary for understanding the actual situation of the client is explained to him and enhanced (rather than reduced) by positive contributions of the analyst (1).

Jung's psychotherapy is a dialectical process, a dialogue between two persons in which the therapist participates to the same degree as the client. Gerhard Adler (1) describes it as a mutual psychological process between the client and the analyst. Jung's method is designed to confront the contents of the conscious with that of the unconscious, thereby calling forth a reaction between them that is a synthesis or solution of the relationship between inner and outer reality. What corresponds to Freud's insight is the realization of the relation between "conscious" and "collective unconscious."

Since the ultimate to be attained is of such a nebulous, mystical nature, it eludes precise definition. To find the meaning of oneself and of the universe seems to imply a continuous search, and apparently Jungian therapy, because of its goal, is often a process terminated only by the death of the patient or analyst. After all, some patients may never be *sure* of self-realization, hence they may feel the need for ever new and more broadening "insights" far beyond the bounds of Freud's conception of the therapeutic goal. Thus it appears that both Jung and Freud considered consciousness of cause-effect relationships as essential, but what constituted "cause" and "effect" to the two men was vastly different.

3. ALFRED ADLER. In place of Freud's libidinal instincts and Jung's principle of individuation Alfred Adler substituted an innate ego motive, propelling the individual toward a goal of security and adaptation to life. Adler's basic instinct was self-assertion, an inherent tendency in the organism to achieve superiority. This tendency was deemed necessary to compensate for an original "organ inferiority" present from birth. Adler later modified his idea of innate constitutional inferiority (organ inferiority) to stress feelings of social inadequacy resulting from

hereditary or environmental deficiencies. The basic driving force of the "will to power" underlies both motivational constructs. The process of living was regarded as a struggle toward a positive adaptation to the demands of society, particularly in the spheres of interpersonal relations, vocational life, and love. Thus, in contrast with Freud, Adler emphasized the relation of the individual to his environment rather than to levels in the individual's consciousness.

According to Adler, the manner in which the individual strives for security and adaptation constitutes his character or his "life style." This orientation toward life is unique with every individual, for it is determined by the individual's opinion of his own capacities, which, in turn, reflects his image of the sentiments of the community. Because of the superiority accorded the male in our Western culture, men have become a symbol of power and dominance, and the subordinate position of women carries with it feelings of inferiority against which is raised the "masculine protest." The neuroses and psychoses, like normal behavior, arise from inferiority feelings, the difference being in the failure to compensate adequately within the limitations of social reality. Because they lack confidence, the mentally ill are unable to develop social feelings for their fellow men, hence their life styles are inappropriate and poorly modified in accordance with their life goals.

Adlerian psychotherapy has the ultimate aim of channelizing the will to power into a more realistic scheme for attainment of the client's goal. Although Adler recognized an unconscious containing "biological memories" derived from the personal experiences of the individual, the unconscious was of minor therapeutic significance in his orientation. His therapeutic approach was focused not on the resurrection of childhood repressions but on the individual's forward-moving, positive adaptation to society. The past life of the client was important only as it enabled the therapist to understand the direction of the client's expressed ideas and to identify the real cause of inferiority feelings. In this connection Adler did stress the importance of early childhood problems, but only as the source of psychological insecurity.

Free associations and dreams were interpreted by Adler in terms of life goals and present problems rather than as the expression of unconscious desires. Insight consisted of recognition by the client of the reasons for his feelings of inferiority and the ways in which these feelings have caused his life style to diverge from the reality of his life goal. Although the therapist might facilitate this process by playing the role of a parent, Adler, unlike Freud, saw no practical utility in elaborating the transference. Bertrand S. and Evelyn P. Frohman (12) point out that Adler's approach attacked the basic etiology. His therapy was obviously not designed to probe the unconscious, nor did he dwell on repression or resistance. Adler was more interested in re-educating the client to realistic ways of integrating his capacities with the demands of his social milieu. Behavioral changes and redirection of ideas were the desired ends to be reached. He assumed emotional life to be subject to conscious desire and control, hence therapeutic rearrangement dealt with ideas and attitudes rather than with emotions and instinctual strivings. In his orientation intervention by the therapist often took the form of persuasion and encouragement to convince the client of the need for readjusting his methods in order to attain his goal of power or psychological adequacy.

Adler posited no deep and visionary concept of racial heritage with which one must become related for self-knowledge. He denied the importance of unconscious sexual motivation. He dealt with the individual's inferiority feelings only as they impeded practical application of his real capacities in striving for adequacy within himself and with his fellow men. While insight into the cause and effect relationship of inferiority feelings and life style was a necessary aspect of this therapy, the constituents of causality lay much closer to the surface in his theory than in that of Freud; they were explained in less esoteric terms of the relation of man to environment. This kind of insight is far different from that of Freud and occupies a much less important and central place in the treatment process.

4. OTTO RANK. Although Rank remained a disciple of Freud much longer than did either Jung or Adler, Otto Rank's break with traditional Freudian theory concerned a point so crucial as to revolutionize his entire concept of psychotherapy. The resulting innovations, far more drastic than those of Adler and Jung, emanated originally from Rank's theory of motivation, and ultimately from his basic concept of the integrity of the individual. To Rank, the average man was a relatively unstimulating person; the neurotic, on the other hand, was actively searching for himself and attempting to accept what he found. He, unlike Freud's neurotic, did not passively succumb to the overwhelming conflict between instinctual impulses and social pressures, but was active, creative, and instrumental in his own self-determination. However, although his creativity elevated him above the average man, he was still ignorant of himself. It was the task of psychotherapy to assist him in discovering this valuable creative aspect of his own being, in accepting and finding confidence in himself, and thus eventually in enabling him to establish his own philosophy of life.

These were Rank's later ideas but his original departure from Freud was the "birth trauma." Rank conceived the core of neurosis to be the trauma of birth, the painful separation of the infant from intra-uterine bliss, which produces immediate "primal anxiety," subsequently motivating man's entire life toward the search to obtain adequate substitutes for this pleasant state. It was his contention that the period of childhood is particularly important as a time during which this primal anxiety is gradually discharged through repeated experiences of emotional expression. In the neurotic, insufficient childhood abreaction leaves residual anxiety which motivates him to by-pass the substitutes found satisfactory by the average person, in an effort to achieve *complete* fulfillment of the primal wish to return to the mother.

Rank diverged further from Freud as he developed the trauma of birth, from a biological phenomenon into a concept of the birth of creativity or individuality in response to the loss of "wholeness" at birth. The latter he further extended into a basic life principle by which biological dependence on the mother is broken by independent self-development. To follow this principle, the individual, through identification and through introjection of the outer world, achieves a "drive" or "initiating power" that guides and integrates the self in creative assimilation of the outer world. This force, which Rank called the "will," constitutes man's inner protection against the external factors with which he must contend in order to live. Composed of both approved and disapproved contents, the "will" impulse does not serve the id as does Freud libido; rather it is an ego impulse that not only initiates but also controls human activity.

Just as Freud's therapy is concerned with the recovery of repressed libidinal wishes relating to his central concept of Oedipal strivings, so Rank's therapy revolves around development of the ego's capacity to "will," which, itself, is closely associated with *his* core concept, the birth trauma. In view of the disparity in their fundamental concepts of human motivation, it is not surprising that Rank's therapeutic technique and rationale bears little similarity to that of Freud. Independence, individuality, creativity, in short the capacity to "will" and hence to gain the psychological totality lost in the process of birth is the ultimate goal of Rank's therapy. Rank (32, p. 149) wrote, "Real psychotherapy is not concerned primarily with adaptation to any kind of reality, but with adjustment of the patient to himself, that is, with his acceptance of his own individuality or that part of his personality which he has formerly denied."

Since, presumably, the neurotic has not been permitted the full beneficial catharsis of childhood which discharges primal anxiety, and hence has been blocked in effectively separating himself from his mother, it follows (if we accept Rank's premises) that a rebirth should take place in the therapeutic situation. The client is permitted to release the primal anxiety associated with his fear of separating from his mother, and his guilt-laden avoidance of "willing" which is also associated with this fear. It is assumed that until the person is truly "separated" from the mother he will not feel free to have an individuality or a "will" of his own. Rank's therapy provides a setting in which the patient learns to "will" without guilt. It is an experience of rebirth, a release making possible future emotional development, a process of reliving the birth trauma. Just as the child's emotional ties with his mother are paramount in his real infancy, so his emotional relationship with the therapist is the nucleus of the therapeutic process. What Freud referred to as transference is here analogous to the child's relationship with his mother. Rank considered the task of analysis to be twofold: first, the bonds with the mother must be severed, then the newly released energy must be utilized for the formation of a new ego ideal through individuation and progressive development of the will.

Rank went further than any of Freud's original collaborators in his emphasis on the present, most particularly the immediate relationship between client and therapist. In a sense Rank's clients were making a new start from scratch, and since Rank was not interested in events prior to "birth," there was no past to explore, but rather a future individuality toward which to develop. The content of associations, and biological and historical material, were abandoned as unimportant in themselves, and therapy was devoted to utilization of the present relationship. Material produced during analysis was to be understood not by reference to the past but only as it related to the artificially created rebirth relationship between patient and analyst.

While transference and interpretation were regarded by Freud as instruments by which to explore the unconscious, Rank elevated the patient-analyst relationship to this position. What occurred in this relationship was important in and of itself, not simply as a means toward some other end. He did not dwell on the technique of interpretation but wrote of "understanding." He believed that simple verbalization by the client, rather than an explanation or interpretation by the analyst, was the principal therapeutic agent. The client in therapy was striving for an *immediate* understanding of experience, at the level of *consciousness,* in the very act of *experiencing.* This seemed to apply equally to both client and analyst.

Since this new conception of therapy involves a basic respect for the client and his capacity to "will," and since its course is directed by the conscious intellectual conflicts of the moment (not the repressed impulses of the past), it follows that there should be no definite preformulated prescribed sequence of techniques, no predetermined patterns of expectations as guides to interpretations. Although the trauma of birth is the fundamental concept in Rank's theory of neurosis, it has little direct bearing on the actual events in therapy. Rank did not believe in the preconceived hypotheses underlying the more intellectualized procedures of Freud and others. Rank's therapy remained almost entirely on the emotional level where feeling experiences were central and where spontaneous expression of unique individuality was accorded full value as a sign of growing will and as a means of acquaintance with oneself. He wrote (32, p. 149), "My technique is essentially in having no technique but in utilizing as much as possible experience and understanding that are constantly converted into skill but never crystallized into technical rules."

In a therapeutic approach designed to foster expressiveness and emotional growth without recourse to past history and unconscious material, one would hardly expect to find emphasized the type of insight conceived of by analysts employing "deeper" therapy. Although Rank capitalized on the growth experiences in the present patient-analyst relationship with interpretations in terms of this relationship *only,* he did mention that, in order to prevent fixation and reproduction of the birth trauma when leaving the analyst, the client's mother attachment, as expressed in the transference relation, should be revealed. He did not explain clearly just how this interpretation was to be given and how its acceptance or rejection by the client was to be handled. Rank maintained that the client's reactions were seen as arising, not from infantile patterns, but from the immediate therapeutic experience. He saw no necessity for intellectual genetic understanding of symptom etiology. The client, through "understanding" or feeling his immediate emotional reactions toward the analyst, discovers his individuality, his initiative, and, in general, the positive aspects of himself. Presumably the experiences of the therapeutic situation equip him with the power to "will," which is assumed to have been latent in him from birth. This positive force, when set in action by the release of primal anxiety, is then utilized in constructive, creative expression that obviates the necessity of retaining former symptoms. Whatever insight is attained is at the conscious level and focuses on an *occurring* expression. The resistance that Freud would wish to overcome is valued and developed as the power to will and to deal with the problems outside the therapy situation with assurance and self-confidence that is uniquely one's own and not a product of continued dependence on maternal protection. The "understanding" and "self-knowledge" that Rank wrote of as one of the goals of therapy may be conceived of as the result of a series of "insights" regarding the *immediate* cause and effects of emotional experiences with the analyst. Only the "here and now" is relevant to the future emotional maturity of the client.

INSIGHT IN THE NEO–ANALYTIC SCHOOLS OF THOUGHT

While most of the more recent developments in theories of personality dynamics and therapy of mental and emotional disorders can be traced to the concepts and practices of Freud, Jung, Adler, and Rank, there have been other advances whose impact on the field of psychotherapy must not be overlooked. The data of sociologists and anthropologists, in particular the cross-cultural studies of the last score of years, have shed new light on factors associated with behavior disorders. They have invalidated such concepts of universal causality as the Oedipus complex, and they have demonstrated and clarified the highly significant role of culture in producing behavior disorders.

In this country Karen Horney was one of the earliest psychoanalysts to incorporate these findings into her own theory of neurosis and her concepts of therapy. In time, a group composed of Horney, Erich Fromm, Harry Stack Sullivan, Frieda Fromm-Reichmann, Ernest E. Hadley, and others became known as the Washington School of Psychiatry under the leadership of William Alanson White. While each of these "neo-analysts" instituted some unique modifications of "classical" analytic theory, they share a common awareness of man's interaction with his cultural milieu as a formative influence upon his personality development. In general, they discarded Freud's mechanistic, biological instinctual interpretations in favor of a more realistic and practical consideration of individual conflicts in terms of actual relationships within the existing superstructure of cultural pressures and demands.

In the previous discussions we have attempted to trace the deterministic relationship between theoretical conceptualizations of mental illness and the associated goals and techniques of therapy. With the shift of emphasis in the neo-analytic theories of motivation, we can justifiably anticipate corresponding modifications in therapeutic concepts and procedures. What becomes of the role of insight as a result of these changes?

1. Karen Horney.   Perhaps the most conspicuous and most basic deviation in Horney's theoretical stand is her rejection of Freud's unsubstantiated libido or instinctual theory of human behavior and her substitution of safety and satisfaction as guiding principles. In place of Freud's instinctual drives, Horney introduced the term "neurotic trends" to designate strivings powered by a search for safety. While Freud viewed personality disorders in terms of sexuality, Horney believed them to be the ultimate outcome of disturbances in actual human relationships, and although she recognized that sexual problems may be (but are not necessarily) associated with neurosis, she considered them merely as symptoms of this deeper conflict (21).

Horney did not believe the Oedipus complex to be biologically based but due instead to concrete describable conditions in the patient's family situation. Furthermore, character is molded not by relations with one's mother alone, but by the totality of one's early experiences. Although Horney conceded that childhood does leave imprints that can be directly traced, what is more significant is that a character structure evolves from the sum-total of childhood experiences which is the frame of reference guiding individual behavior and attitudes. Later experiences are not repetitions of infantile experiences, but emanate from the character structure laid down in childhood in the process of dealing with one's environment (21). Thus, while Freud viewed man as motivated by instincts inherent in his biological make-up, Horney's formulation is broader and more environmentally oriented.

Anthropological studies have shown that the biological make-up of man remains fairly constant, while social conditions show extreme variations. Horney contended that, since man's biological equipment is never observed in isolation, notions of opposition between the person and his environment should be discarded in favor of a view toward interaction between the person and his environment as the fundamental determinant of human personality. While Freud relegated the environment to a peripheral position in his system, endowing it with negative suppressive features, Horney placed it in a central position in her theory. She stressed its importance in the etiology of mental disorders by describing a "situational neurosis" in which the personality remains intact but an external situation full of conflict produces a neurotic reaction (31). Thus, some forms of anxiety may be entirely accounted for by conflict-laden objective or external situations. While Freud postulated a universal basic conflict between life and death instincts, Horney did not believe that a basic neurotic conflict would arise under the proper environmental conditions—under those that furnish maximum safety and security without arousing "basic anxiety" generated by repressed hostility.

Horney also recognized a "character neurosis" involving alterations in character structure which begin in early childhood and which take precedence over the external life situation. In such cases the anxiety must be understood in terms of the individual's past history, especially his hostility toward parental control. However, while infantile anxiety is a necessary condition for later development of neurosis, its influence may be counteracted by favorable environmental changes which may bring affection, approval, and security to the child. Without such intervention, the child reacts to his "destructive" environment with anxiety that he projects onto the outer world, with (20, p. 92) "a feeling of being small, insignificant, helpless, endangered, in a world that is out to abuse, cheat, attack, humiliate, betray, envy." While neurotic trends and the neurotic character structure may be rooted in infantile anxiety (a product of social conditions), Horney (22, p. 233) stated that knowledge of their genesis does not explain their perpetuation in present real life relationships. "No conflict is merely a relic of the past but is determined by stringent necessities in the existing character structure." As one might expect, it is in connection with this point that Freud and Horney differ in their therapeutic procedures.

According to Horney, neurotic trends function as a means of coping with life with a minimum of anxiety. Because they are ways of avoiding potential danger, of obtaining satisfaction, and of expressing resentment toward the world, the neurotic follows them compulsively. Adherence to this pattern provides a rigid individual who is not only personally inefficient and unhappy because his productivity and real spontaneity become stifled, but who is also impaired in his relationships with people due to increased dependency on them, which in turn generates hostile feelings.

With this conception of the neuroses Horney debunked any approach that (a) attacked symptoms without first grasping the character structure or (b) attempted, as did Freud's, to relate actual problems to childhood experiences and to establish a causal relationship between the two. Freud's primary objectives in therapy were (a) to recognize the existence of neurotic trends and (b) to relate them to their sources in frustrated infantile sexual and aggressive impulses. These are, then, the constituents of the insight that Freud thought to be the goal of therapy. He assumed that recognition by the client of the infantile nature of his behavior would automatically insure not only recognition of its incongruity with adult patterns but also subsequent mastery over it (21). Horney (21, p. 146) pointed out that, since one's real picture of childhood is so muddled and vague, any attempt, such as Freud's, to "penetrate through the fog represents an endeavor to explain one unknown—the existing peculiarities—by something still less known—childhood. It seems more profitable to drop such efforts and to focus on the forces which *actually* drive and inhibit a person; there is reasonable chance of gradually understanding these, even without much knowledge of childhood." [3] Hence, in therapy, Horney went along with Freud only to the extent that the presence of neurotic trends should be recognized by the client. Her next step is concerned not with the genetic understanding of these trends but with the *present functions* they serve, the reasons why these trends are maintained in the existing character structure, and the consequences they have for the client's adequacy in interpersonal relationships. Her emphasis is, then, on the analysis of the actual character structure. She contended that, in the process of working through the consequences of neurotic trends, the client's anxiety is so diminished that he no longer finds these trends necessary. Horney did not neglect the data from childhood completely, for she found (21, p. 146) that "in the process of obtaining a better grasp of actual goals, actual forces, actual needs, actual pretenses, the fog hovering over the past begins to lift. One does not regard the past, however, as the treasure long sought, but considers it simply as a welcome help in understanding the patient's development."

[3] This and following quotations from *New Ways in Psychoanalysis*, by Karen Horney, are printed by permission of the W. W. Norton & Company, Inc. Copyright 1939 by W. W. Norton & Company, Inc.

Because Horney did not subscribe to Freud's mechanistic, biological, instinctual theory, she naturally found fault with the static concept of repetition-compulsion. Her own concept of transference does not include the reactivation of infantile experiences. She believed that interpretations of the client-analyst relationship in terms of a transfer of infantile feelings onto the analyst merely increases the client's dependence on the analyst because it leaves untouched the real underlying anxiety. By neglecting to analyze actual existing needs, Horney felt that Freud's approach runs the risk of insufficient understanding of the actual personality, and, furthermore, it often allows the analysis to become stagnant and unproductive. Insofar as transference involves observation and understanding of the client's emotional reactions in the analytic situation as a means of understanding his character structure and his present problems, Horney agreed (21, p. 34) that it is an indispensable tool of analytic therapy—"The essence of all human psychology resides in understanding the processes operating in human relationships." For her, the transference relationship was simply a special form of human relationship which is peculiarly accessible to penetrating analysis designed to allay anxieties activated in other similar relationships outside therapy.

Horney's analytical techniques are essentially those that Freud used. free association and interpretation. In contrast to the passivity on the part of the analyst recommended by Freud, Horney believed that the analyst should "deliberately conduct" the analysis, often directing the client's associations into more fruitful channels, even making suggestions as to possible solutions to current problems.

On the question of moral problems Horney was consistent in handling the therapeutic relationship as realistically as possible. She advocated development of a "constructive friendliness" in which deficiencies and potentialities, genuine qualities and pretenses can be recognized and examined without detracting from the rapport between client and analyst. It is important that the analyst make known his attitudes toward the client's moral conflicts in order to allay possible fears of condemnation and to allow the patient to recognize feelings he may have projected onto the analyst.

Horney's concept of insight is concerned with motivating the client's "psychic forces" to help him abandon his neurotic trends. Actually this concept seems to play a vitally important role in Horney's brand of psychoanalysis, which is oriented toward making the client aware of his motivations and their connection with present needs, and assisting him in deciding for himself the efficacy of his behavior trends in dealing with everyday life. Horney considered intellectual insight, when integrated into the client's actual life situation, as a "powerful motor" strong enough to activate all available energies toward a will to change. If this integration is to develop, the client's insight must include knowledge of situations that provoke undesirable behavior and realization of the consequences in terms of his anxiety, inhibitions, guilt feelings, and relationships with others.

The scope of this insight includes also the recognition of moral problems and pretenses and their function for the client. With these, as with sexual problems, Horney aims to enable the client to decide and evaluate for himself, but this is possible only after he achieves insight into their function. Insight is, then, as important in Horney's scheme as in Freud's, but cause and effect are interpreted by Horney from a more realistic frame of reference oriented toward present functions and consequences of the individual's everyday life attitudes, particularly his relationships with others. It is not produced by recall of the past nor does it revolve around Oedipal strivings alone; it is insight into *present* patterns of interaction that gives added meaning to the past.

2. HARRY STACK SULLIVAN. Harry Stack Sullivan (42, pp. 207–11) stated that "one achieves mental health to the extent that one becomes aware of one's interpersonal relations. . . . The processes of psychiatric cure include the maturation of personality; that is, the evolution of capacity for adult interpersonal relations. . . . The long term goal . . . must be the dissolving of the patient's barrier to full intimacy" [4] with other persons. The similarity between this concept of psychotherapy and that of Horney is immediately evident in the emphasis of both on the interacting individual and on the significance of self-awareness for adequacy in interpersonal relationships.

The interrelation of man and his fellow men was for Sullivan—as for Horney—the nuclear fact of human existence (42, p. 10): "A personality can never be isolated from the complex of interpersonal relations in which the person lives and has his being." Sullivan emphasized this viewpoint even more forcefully by stating repeatedly that (p. 10) "the field of psychiatry is the field of interpersonal relations, under any and all circumstances in which these relations exist." Within this interacting milieu man's behavior is goal-oriented around two "end states" (this too is much like Horney's concept of motivation): (a) the satisfaction of biological needs and (b) the attainment and maintenance of security, a response to man's cultural equipment or the man-made components of his environment. Underlying the manifestation of man's biological needs is a "power motive" encouraging extended interaction with the environment and improved ability to achieve both satisfaction and

[4] This and following quotations from *Conceptions of Modern Psychiatry*, by Harry Stack Sullivan with a critical appraisal by Patrick Mullahy, are printed by permission of the William Alanson White Psychiatric Foundation and of the publishers, W. W. Norton & Company, Inc. Copyright 1940, 1945, 1947, and 1953 by the William Alanson White Psychiatric Foundation.

security. This power drive is elicited out of the frustrations occurring in early infancy and compensates for successive thwarting which determines later personality development. The infant feels either powerful or powerless depending on the approval or disapproval of his parents (especially his mother), whose attitudes are conveyed by the (p. 17) "peculiar emotional linkage," or "emotional contagion or communion," called "empathy." Parental disapproval of the child's modes of gaining satisfaction is empathized by the infant who learns that certain of his needs threaten his security, make him feel uncomfortable and anxious. Thus anxiety develops from the conflict between the satisfaction of biological needs and the desire for security.

Sullivan believed that out of these culturally imposed restraints upon the child grows the "self" or "self dynamism," which is formed in the process of discovering how to obtain power or success in interpersonal relations. It is (42, p. 184) "a growing integration useful in dealing with others, for obtaining satisfactions and avoiding insecurity." Anxiety tends to mold the self by directing it away from disapprobation and frustration toward approval, satisfaction, and security. Thus the self, as it develops, focuses attention only on those aspects of personal interaction that elicit approval or disapproval. Contrariwise, anxiety also restricts the growth of the self by excluding from its awareness much data that would otherwise expand its capacity to handle future problem situations.

The self, then, is a product of acculturation, and the deficiencies or inconsistencies of acculturation produce impoverishment of the entire personality, which includes the self. In this and other ways the self dynamism may bear some resemblance to Horney's "character structure," but Sullivan has elaborated and refined his concept far beyond that of Horney. Being made up of reflected appraisals, the self dynamism may be hostile and disparaging toward others and toward itself or it may be loving, accepting, and appreciative, depending on whether it developed from derogation and deprivation or approbation and facilitation. Further, it tends to maintain the direction given it in infancy, thus stabilizing the course of its future development. As Patrick Mullahy (30, p. 269) suggests in his critical appraisal of Sullivan's theory, "By means of anxiety [the self] selects and organizes the conditions for its future growth, both as to direction and characteristics, in order to maintain the direction and characteristics given it in infancy and childhood."

When the self dynamism ignores needs vital to security and biological satisfactions, the person becomes mentally ill. It must be remembered that the self is a configuration pattern focused on and changing in accordance with the approval or disapproval in interpersonal relationships. It follows that the persons significant for the self are indirectly instrumental in determining both the self and the nature of what is dissociated, for the self not only generates but also restricts the quality of "me-you patterns" (30, p. 270). When the client manifests different attitudes or "me-you patterns" in the same interpersonal situation, Sullivan claimed this actual situation is seen by the patient as "parataxic," that is, the patient is reacting in this situation in terms of an earlier situation.

Sullivan's concept of parataxic refers to a period in infancy when the undifferentiated wholeness or "prototaxic" experience is broken into parts without any logical connection. The prototaxic, parataxic, and autistic modes of symbol activity are (30, p. 278) "primary forms of creative thinking and spontaneous feeling [in which] one is free to ignore, for the time being, in dreams and fantasy, the demands of 'normal life,' of 'reality,' the common and shared everyday world." They do not originate for the purpose of gaining specific satisfactions and security but rather they are expressions of overflowing energy and spontaneous activity. Consensual validation by reality testing in group experiences is lacking in this early mode of symbolization manifested by the autistic, highly individualized verbalization of the child. Perpetuation of parataxic processes in adult relationships results in barriers to effective interaction of which the client is unaware. An excellent example of this can be found in the work of one of Sullivan's colleagues, E. E. Hadley (16), who explained conflicts and disagreements between businessmen as the result of their unrecognized antagonisms carried over from earlier life.

Personality is postulated by Sullivan to account for the behavior of persons in interaction with one another. It is manifested solely in interpersonal situations, and it includes not only the self dynamism but also that which has been dissociated or selectively inattended. As a (30, p. 273) "reservoir of creative activity and original thought," the marginal personality is available to the self system under certain conditions for its enrichment. In the ideal individual the self would be synonymous with personality. In the maladjusted individual the self system is (p. 273) "impoverished by toxic experience." However, dissociated tendencies still remain in the periphery of personality and are expressed only unintentionally in dreams or fantasies. But (42, p. 97) "the basic direction of the organism is forward." Personality tends toward the state of mental health despite the handicaps of acculturation.

The problem of change in the more severe mental disorders is "enormous," because it involves accepting a dissociated tendency into the self, a process that entails extensive change in personality. Sullivan viewed mental disorder in terms of interpersonal processes (30, p. 283) "either inadequate to the situation in which the persons are integrated, or excessively complex because of illusory persons also integrated in the situation." Behavior by which the person pursues his required satisfactions is ineffective. "In other words, the mentally ill are not sufficiently able to feel and sense and understand the uniqueness and differences of interpersonal situations. For them the situation is, erroneously, of course, felt to be not unique but modeled on, or paradigmatic of old situations," that is, parataxically distorted (30, p. 294).

In the freedom of the therapeutic situation and with the help of interpretations, the client, Sullivan felt, is enabled to understand the significance of his past reactions to people and their influence on his present modes of personal interaction. Insight is fundamental, particularly the *first* insight into a parataxic process involving the relationship between patient and analyst. In Sullivan's (42, p. 205) words:

> Until a patient has seen clearly and unmistakably a *concrete* example of the way in which unresolved situations from the distant past color the perception of present situations and over-complicate action in them, there can be no material reorganization of personality, no therapeutically satisfactory expansion of the self, no significant insight into the complexities of one's performances or into the unexpected and often disconcerting behavior of others concerned.

This first insight is assumed to produce changes in the self system which allow freedom for the expression of constructive impulses. The person learns that more security can be gained by abandoning his complex ineffectual process than by retaining it, and so he is able to proceed to other anxietous situations for analysis and insight.

Sullivan (42, p. 105) believed that meaningful traces of *all* past experiences are somehow "fixed" or retained as patterns of momentary interaction between organism and environment. He does not postulate an unconscious but simply "memory"—"a relatively enduring record of all momentary states of the organismic configuration." Memory presumably records the dissociated and selectively unattended impulses that must be recovered, re-evaluated, and integrated by the self system in the course of psychotherapy. Because these impulses are assumed to have been banished from awareness in order to avoid insecurity in relationships with one's fellow men, it is these processes at work in the client's present relationships that therapy must uncover. Intensive treatment re-integrates these dissociated motivational systems and dissipates the parataxic distortions of unresolved situations in the client's past.

To promote insight, Sullivan made extensive use of the interview situation in which the therapist is a "participant observer" who listens to associations, guides their course by indirect questioning, and offers interpretations that facilitate gradual evolution of awareness in the client of the people involved. The interview allows the development into awareness of communicable statements concerning past unpleasant experiences. Insight is reached through interpretations based not on abstract esoteric concepts but on a synthesis of significant concrete statements made by the client in very personal references. If the client can become aware of an impulse whose discharge would be painful, he may find means of obtaining partial or symbolic satisfactions.

There are three "collaborative efforts" that Sullivan believed may be expected of most clients: (a) awareness of changes in his body, especially increases and decreases of tension, that may bring awareness of movements produced by dissociated impulses; (b) awareness of marginal thoughts that might disturb the self by interfering with the focus of attention; (c) the prompt statement of all that comes to mind—a difficult achievement until the client obtains security following his first insight into a parataxic process. Once past this milestone, Sullivan contended that the therapeutic situation changes from a tentative, loosely integrated relationship into a firm and reliable collaboration. Permanent benefit seems to occur more often with verbalization rather than through acting out. Sullivan contended that most clients have heretofore acted out conflicts without the therapeutically necessary awareness of what they were doing. Although acting out may be appropriate when mental illness cannot be treated by more thorough techniques, verbalization is essential to more intensive therapy where insight is a prerequisite to cure.

Sullivan believed that the client, in learning to understand the pattern of his maladjustive behavior, usually begins with a simple, apparently trifling instance rather than with a deep and penetrating insight. Interpretations and questions of the therapist are likewise simple and designed to focus on the momentary situation and to check or consensually validate the motives attributed by the client to others. Alertness is gradually released until a parataxic process can be identified and its influence on present perceptions of significant persons in the client's life demonstrated. Only after recognition of such a process is its genesis probed for. Final dissolution of the conflicts in former situations permits acceptance of the dissociated impulses originally associated with them. To be able to abandon a parataxic distortion, the client must understand its origin and realize its inappropriateness in the immediate reality relationship. Presumably, intensive therapy attacks all the more important parataxes that impair the client's adequacy in dealing with people. Thus the significance of insight in Sullivan's therapy lies in the influence of past reactions on present interpersonal relationships, especially that between patient and analyst. Although he shares with Horney, Fromm, and Fromm-Reichmann an appreciation of the interaction between the individual and his environment, he seems to retain more of the classical flavor in his genetic approach which, though giving cognizance to the significance of present interaction, resorts to the past for clarification and understanding. The concept of recurring modes of behavior modeled on past experience which block discrimination of, and adaptability to, new circumstances resembles Freud's repetition-compulsion in a way emphatically denied by Horney's functional analysis of present patterns in which insight is only secondarily concerned with the past.

Sullivan worked with neurotics as well as with hospitalized psychotics, and he believed that all are amenable to treatment. He included provisions for flexibility of technique and approach for cases in which the above approach would be ill advised. In his system psychiatric cure involves maturation of personality and requires premorbid development sufficient to permit the three forms of collaboration which we have listed. Where this is impossible due to barriers that have blocked the individual's successful advancement through the preadolescent stage, the goal of amelioration rather than cure is sought. This approach applies with clients who are unable to progress beyond juvenile competition for superiority and with those of asocial development whose remoteness handicaps the treatment situation. Failure of therapies that purport to bolster the self dynamism is explained by the simple reason that it is the self that obstructs the personality's strivings toward mental health. Exceptions are admitted, however, in traumatic reactions where supportive therapy often enables the client to regain perspective at least temporarily, during which time some remedial work may be effective (42).

3. ERICH FROMM.   Erich Fromm's frame of reference is more sociological than psychiatric, and his writings deal more with the analysis of problems and conflicts of society during various historical periods than with the application of theory in clinical practice. He believes that the pressures and frustrations (particularly economic) impinging on man from his social environment are crucial in the production of neurotic patterns. In this respect Fromm shares with other neo-analysts the appreciation and recognition of the findings of sociologists and anthropologists which throw new light on the concepts and theories of psychopathology. Along with his colleagues in Washington and New York, he sees man more as a part of a larger unit characterized by "relatedness" to the world than as an isolated entity whose problems are the result of conflicting inner "instinctual" forces.

4. FRIEDA FROMM-REICHMANN.   In contrast to Fromm, Fromm-Reichmann is more directly oriented toward a therapeutic approach and technique. Her theoretical stand is apparently derived from Sullivan. In fact, her discussion of therapeutic procedures implies a general acceptance of Sullivan's complicated theory of interpersonal relations. In therapeutic interviews with severely disturbed mental patients, she has expanded and clarified in greater detail the specific applications of Sullivan's conceptual framework. Hers is a genetic approach making use of

interpretation based on direct questioning, dreams, and free association, and it is designed to bring about insight into the historical and dynamic factors that cause present disturbances. Interpretations are made in the light of these memories and principally in relation to the patient-doctor interpersonal experience (15).

Fromm-Reichmann, like Sullivan, modifies her approach in working with subjects who are too disturbed to participate in "generic and dynamic scrutiny." Her basic theoretical orientation prescribes ultimate goals that seem to remain constant and applicable for most patients; the principal point of flexibility is in varying the choice of technique with the degree of the client's disturbance. For instance, she advises against the use of free association with psychotics whose expressions are already so disorganized that more directive techniques are indicated (14).

Fromm-Reichmann seems convinced of the curative power of insight, which she defines as both an intellectual and an emotional grasp by the client of the dynamics of his conflicts while he is re-experiencing them and working them through in his interrelationship with the analyst (13). Transference is, thus, the medium through which such formerly dissociated emotions are activated and old conflicts brought to awareness. Interpretations are concerned mainly with the vicissitudes of the doctor-patient relationship and the influence of parataxic distortions rooted in historical events in the client's life. While Fromm-Reichmann believes these data from the past to be extremely important, she cautions against neglect of the subject's current interpersonal experiences, the problems he is presenting, and possible recent crisis situations.

Because Fromm-Reichmann is more interested in ego defenses or "security operations" (the motivation behind dissociations and the reactions of the patient to newly recovered repressed material) than in the contents of associations per se, she prefers an interview technique rather than free association. She feels that in free association, the subject is prone to avoid material that would clarify the defense operations, and that such dynamics are best revealed by directive questioning to elicit relevant information from the client.

Insight into the genetics and dynamics of the problem is the crux of Fromm-Reichmann's therapy. It involves, first and foremost, a complete grasp of the dynamics of the doctor-patient relationship and all changes occurring in this relationship during the course of therapy. Dissolution of parataxic distortions is, of course, paramount, and here, as in Sullivan's therapy, symptoms and distortions are interpreted in terms of their protective functions to the ego at the time of their adoption. Insight need not be extended in scope to include all conflictual material but is necessary only for the central problem. She assumes that once the client understands his major conflicts, he will be able to handle the side issues on his own.

Fromm-Reichmann points out that intellectual understanding of an interpretation is not identical with a therapeutically valid grasp of its meaning, nor is understanding of a single interpretation of, say, a parataxic distortion, sufficient. Here she seems to contradict, in part, Sullivan's contention that the first insight into a parataxic distortion is the turning point in therapy. Fromm-Reichmann believes that even a single insight should be "reconquered" and repeatedly tested in new connections and contacts. This "working through" of newly acquired understandings as they are reflected in the doctor-patient relationship is essential to insure emotional integration of new knowledge as well as intellectual understanding. The verbal exchange between doctor and patient is only half the function of this collaborative "working through" process. The accompanying discharge of affect, the nonverbal interplay, and the affective connotations of statements are an integral part of the emotional experience underlying attainment of lasting and curative insight. It is only by the process of "working through" that (15, pp. 141–2) "the intellectual and rational grasp of one interpretation of a single experience . . . will be changed . . . into the type of integrated creative understanding which deserves to be termed 'insight.' " Such insight is viewed as creative in that it is curative and promotes change in the structure of the patient's personality.

Once achieved, it is Fromm-Reichmann's opinion that the client's insight should be evaluated at intervals by reviews of material and interpretations presented up to that point. Beyond this, the patient should test his new insight in its relatedness to daily life and other relationships outside of therapy. Although Fromm-Reichmann recognizes a necessity to modify techniques for particularly disturbed patients, and while she is fully aware of other less intensive approaches which seek for "social recoveries" and symptomatic cures, she believes (15, p. x) that "there is no valid *intensive* psychotherapy other than that which is psychoanalytic or psychoanalytically oriented," that is, which promotes personality changes through insight into the genetics and dynamics of a patient's problems.

5. FRANZ ALEXANDER AND THOMAS M. FRENCH.   At the Institute for Psychoanalysis in Chicago another group of analysts has made prominent contributions to the theory and therapy of behavior disorders. Probably the most prolific of these writers are Thomas M. French and Franz Alexander, of whom the latter was a recent Director of the Institute. Although they have introduced various theoretical and methodological elaborations and modifications of the classical analytic approach, the associates of the Chicago Institute, like those of the Washington School, have generally accepted the basic principles of psychodynamics advanced by Freud, and so they, too, may be called "neo-analysts."

While, in general, it appears that the Chicago School has probably devoted more consideration to new applications of Freud's basic ideas than to theoretical innovations such as those of Sullivan or Fromm of the Washington School, nevertheless, the impact of sociological and anthropological findings is reflected also in the revisions offered by the Chicagoans. They, too, have gone beyond Freud's sharp etiological focus on childhood Oedipal impulses to recognize three broad factors: heredity, early experiences, and actual difficulties, the latter of which includes culturally determined situational pressures beyond the individual's control.

Franz Alexander states that neurosis must be defined in a relativistic manner as a relationship between a personality and its social setting, neither of which remains constant in any two cases (3). Within our highly stratified society where rapid social change, mobility, and concomitant competition demand continual readjustment, he believes that the individual ego, as the personality's instrument of integration, must be flexible enough to adapt to repeated shifts for maintenance of needed security. Neurosis results from breakdown of the adaptive, integrative functioning of the ego, a failure of the ego to co-ordinate needs harmoniously with each other and with external conditions.

The aim of psychoanalysis, according to Alexander (3, pp. 275–6), is "to effect permanent changes in the personality by increasing the ego's integrative power . . . to change the ego by exposing it to conflictful repressed material." This general statement mirrors Freud's concept of analytical therapy. However Alexander carries it further in saying (pp. 204–5) that "the aim of psychoanalysis is to increase the effectiveness of the conscious ego by replacing automatic adaptations and repressions with conscious control and flexible adjustments to the changing conditions of modern life." [5] With slightly different connotations, Alexander and French (2, p. 26) consider as the aim of psychoanalysis "to increase the patient's ability to find gratifications for his subjective needs in ways acceptable both to himself and to the world he lives in, and thus to free him to develop his capacities." [6] The latter concept implies recognition of the larger, more inclusive social context within which the individual's problems have developed and with which he must learn to deal effectively. Thus, the unit under consideration far exceeds the scope of Freud's concentration on the individual in isolation from the pressures and demands of his environment.

The influence of Sandor Ferenczi is immediately discernible in

[5] This and following quotations from *Fundamentals of Psychoanalysis*, by Franz Alexander, are printed by permission of W. W. Norton & Company, Inc. Copyright 1948 by W. W. Norton & Company, Inc.

[6] This and following quotations from *Psychoanalytic Therapy*, by Franz Alexander and Thomas A. French, are printed by permission of The Ronald Press Company. Copyright 1946 by The Ronald Press Company.

Alexander's principle of surplus energy, according to which sexuality is a quantitatively determined specific mode of discharge of any unused and undirected excitations within the organism. Hence, when impulses are not co-ordinated with or subordinated to other impulses in the service of self-preservation, these unattached surplus impulses must be discharged to maintain homeostasis. Such discharge is pleasurable in and of itself and is not subordinated to other goals. According to Ferenczi, Alexander, and French, surplus energy is the source not only of sexuality but also of man's creativity and progressive growth (3).

In the light of the surplus energy principle and the strong influence of Ferenczi, we should anticipate some emphasis on release and constructive utilization of surplus energy—on bringing such energy under control and adapting it to social and cultural demands. Such is the case in the therapeutic emphasis of the Chicago Institute on what they term the "corrective emotional experience." This concept does not appear to be essentially an original concept but simply a new label for abreaction and "working through" which re-emphasizes the significance of a type of therapeutic experience whose emphasis has undergone fluctuations during different phases of psychoanalytic development. Nevertheless, the main therapeutic conclusion of Alexander and French (2) is that alleviation of basic neurotic conflicts can be accomplished only if the client undergoes new emotional experiences that undo the traumatic influences of earlier experiences. All other therapeutic phenomena are secondary to this central principle. It involves re-experiencing the heretofore repressed feelings within the transference relationship in which the therapist, as the object of these formerly forbidden impulses, responds with permissive acceptance rather than with the punitiveness with which they were met by the original figure in the client's past. In repeatedly re-experiencing repressed material in such a permissive atmosphere, the intensity of former conflicts is reduced until the client's behavior changes, and impulses formerly repugnant become integrated by the strengthened ego. It is only by actually experiencing a new solution in the transference setting or in everyday life outside of therapy that the client is convinced that a new reaction is not only possible but more desirable. This experience enables the client to deal with previously unmanageable life experiences before termination of treatment is considered.

Alexander and French (2) have carried through the newer analytical approach in going beyond the therapeutic situation to the present everyday life problems of the client. In fact, they warn against allowing the client to become too comfortable in his transference neurosis. The corrective emotional experience includes not only the release or abreaction of repressed impulses but also their modification and their constructive utilization in dealing with real life. The client is encouraged toward outside experiences parallel with those in therapy, and he is guided toward the application of his therapeutic gains in ever broader areas of daily living. In this way an attempt is made to further increase the ego strength and to counteract future regression (2, 3).

Two basic principles govern Alexander and French's adaptation of psychoanalytic procedure: the principles of planning and flexibility. With a uniform technique for all subjects and all phases of treatment Alexander and French again depart from the orthodox procedure of passively following the subject's lead in his free associations and dreams. They recommend a plan of treatment based on a diagnostic appraisal of the client's personality and his actual life problems. Although subject to change in the course of analysis, their plan is to outline what is to be accomplished, what complications may be anticipated, how the subject's problems should be approached, and what methods seem indicated by the nature of these problems and the individual's personality. Implicit in this plan of treatment for all clients is the second principle, flexibility. The plan differs from classical Freudian analysis in that there is no "standard" procedure or rigid technique, rather various techniques are adapted in a flexible manner to each individual case. Not only is the approach varied from client to client, but seldom is the same method used consistently during the treatment of one client. Thus, even with a single case, the therapist may employ both free association and the more directive interview technique; he may vary the frequency of interviews in accordance with the level of emotional intensity desired for best results. In general, he regulates the transference relationship and his specific techniques to make maximum use of the client's real life experiences as an integral part of therapy. Alexander and French believe that therapy moves faster when there is heightened emotional participation, and that there is less chance of an encumbering transference neurosis when it not only embraces the therapeutic relationship but also deals actively with external factors in the client's environment.

In preparing an individually planned course of therapy, the choice of approach is dependent upon a host of relevant factors gleaned from family history, interviews, and other diagnostic devices. Supportive therapy is recommended for acute and situational neuroses in which the ego is only temporarily impaired and in which no permanent ego change is deemed necessary. This type of therapy, which strengthens defenses and gives needed guidance, may be beneficial also in the treatment of severe chronic cases in which the ego is beyond hope of change. In such cases no attempt is made to trace the genesis of guilt feelings or to develop and resolve a transference neurosis. Although limited insight may be achieved, it plays a subordinate role where immediate emotional support is needed.

Alexander and French believe that insight therapy is applicable in a large range of cases in which changes in ego functioning and the structure of personality are indicated. This type of therapy is conceived of as a re-educative process, the resumption of a learning process that was interrupted by the development of constricting neurotic defenses. The transference neurosis is used here to bring out the subject's reaction patterns where they may be observed and interpreted, enabling the client to understand his motives and to become aware of differences between past situations that elicited certain defensive reactions and present situations in which such reactions are now quite maladaptive. In their emphasis on actual life problems Alexander and French do not believe in repetition of the entire childhood situation with all its conflicts. They prefer to concentrate only on those phases related to the client's central conflict. While memories and unconscious repressed feelings are important in providing a background for the present behavior, their recovery is not a goal in itself but an instrument or means by which the client's misinterpretations of the present are brought into relief. Hence it seems that, while insight is facilitated by understanding the genesis of neurotic patterns, it is therapeutic only in its relevance to present problems and emotional readjustment.

Intellectual insight is only an accessory to the more significant emotional readjustment that enables the patient to give up his defenses. Essentially, the plans and goals of treatment for each client are formulated not in terms of insight alone but according to the emotional readjustment of which the client is capable. Although the standard use of insight as a device for stimulating this emotional reorientation may be applicable with patients who are able to tolerate the concomitant disturbances involved, it is often impossible to achieve insight until after preliminary readjustment, often fostered by supportive techniques that presumably provide new ego strength and thus eliminate the necessity for protective resistance (2).

In the course of therapy many different approaches and techniques may be employed. The pace and depth of therapy are geared to the individual subject in a flexible fashion and are subject to modification according to the exigencies of the therapeutic situation—this includes the subject's emotional reactions both to the therapist and to the persons in his extra-therapeutic environment. Since there is no iron-clad, step-by-step, rigidly specified procedure, the significance of insight as a factor in therapeutic progress is relative to many other contingent variables but always to the emotional readjustment that is the general goal of this more modern psychoanalytic approach.

The general trend among neo-analysts has been toward a more realistic concept of the individual as molded not alone by mechanistic biological instincts but by the dynamic social patterns of his culture and the expectancies of his social group. Although recognized as formative

of the individual's present personality, childhood experiences ?
pal wishes have receded in theoretical significance and, subsec
therapeutic relevance as increasing consideration has been gi
individual's later experiences, principally those revolving arou... .
cial relationships. With vitiation of Freud's theory of universal Oedipal
strivings, a variety of other real-life factors productive of later neurotic
and psychotic behavior have been substituted. If therapeutic procedures
are in any way determined by theoretical formulations, it would seem
natural to expect variations in approach in line with recently accepted
theories of multiple causation. This expectation is further reinforced by
the increased heterogeneity of the therapist's clientele commensurate
with the growing interest in mental hygiene and the expansion of clinical
facilities for the lower socioeconomic groups. The larger number of cases
and the diversity of problems brought to the therapist provide plentiful
raw material for new dynamic theories of personality, each of which
eventuates in modifications of therapeutic endeavors.

The role of insight in the various neo-analytic approaches has waxed
and waned in prominence contingent upon such other variables as the
relative importance of the past in understanding and alleviating present
conflicts, the place of the client-analyst relationship in therapy, the depth
and scope of the emotional experience to be achieved, and the nature of
the relationship between intellectual and emotional constituents of a truly
therapeutic experience.

THE FUNCTION OF INSIGHT IN
CLIENT–CENTERED COUNSELING

As an outgrowth of his work in the child guidance field, Carl Rogers developed a method and a theory of counseling which provide a consistent
set of hypotheses heretofore conspicuously absent in psychotherapeutic
theory. His thinking appears to be rooted in the relationship emphasis of
Rank, with a blend of the neo-analytic influence of Horney and Sullivan. Rogers' approach differs from earlier ones in both goal and technique. His aim is to assist the individual to grow. Rogers (35, p. 195)
states that the one basic tendency of every individual is toward growth,
in the sense of a drive toward "maintenance and enhancement of the
self." [7] He (33, p. 221) assumes that "the satisfactions of independence
and growth far outweigh the comfort of remaining dependent." [8] Fur-

---

[7] This and following quotations from *Client-Centered Therapy*, by Carl R.
Rogers, are printed by permission of Houghton Mifflin Company. Copyright 1951
by Carl R. Rogers.

[8] This and following quotations from *Counseling and Psychotherapy*, by
Carl R. Rogers, are printed by permission of Houghton Mifflin Company. Copyright
1942 by Carl R. Rogers.

ther, and more fundamental, is Rogers' underlying belief in the inherent worth and significance of the individual, a philosophy that regards the individual as capable of assuming responsibility for his own self-direction, his own choice of values; he is not an object to be dissected, diagnosed or manipulated. Concerning the counselor, Rogers (35, p. 21) states, "He can be only as 'non-directive' as he has achieved respect for others in his own personality organization." This attitudinal orientation regarding the possibility of self-understanding and self-direction is, for the client, actually a hypothesis to be tested and proved in the course of therapy. This is the "client-centered" hypothesis to be "implemented" by the counselor.

In Rogers' basic framework the individual exists in a private world (the phenomenal field) composed of all his conscious and unconscious experiences. Unconscious sensory and visceral sensations become conscious if associated with a need, and all such consciously perceived and experienced components of the field constitute reality *for that individual* who reacts to it, as an organized whole, to maintain homeostasis. Behavior, then, is goal-oriented around present needs and tensions in the field *as perceived now*, subject to secondary modifications from past experience. Quite naturally, such behavior can best be understood from the individual's own internal frame of reference. This frame of reference can only be transmitted by communication which, in a permissive atmosphere that minimizes need for defenses, brings more experiences into awareness and thus broadens the individual's perceptual field or reality.

Rogers theorizes that in the course of development a portion of the infant's perceptual field gradually becomes differentiated as the self,—that is, recognized as "I" or "me"—and only those objects or experiences within the control of the self are admitted as a part of it. The structure of this self, formed through interaction with people, is a fluid but consistent, organized perceptual configuration that includes awareness and evaluation only of those experiences and aspects of the self that maintain or enhance the self. Other satisfactions and values not consistent with the self are either denied awareness or distorted, as in the case of repression. The individual is able to discriminate and react according to threatening and nonthreatening stimuli even though they are not consciously recognized as such. The more inconsistent the threatening experiences that are perceived, the more rigid becomes the self-structure in order to maintain itself. Nor is perception alone dictated by the self-concept but also behavior or the means by which needs are satisfied. Needs inconsistent with the self-concept which are denied awareness may persist. In neurosis, behavior that the self accepts is employed to satisfy an unrecognized need that has been rejected (repressed) by the self to preserve its existence or equilibrium. Behavior that is inconsistent with the structure of the self is not felt to be a part of the self; that is, it has not been (35, p. 510) "organized into the gestalt of the self-structure." Maladjustment or a state of tension ensues when there is a discrepancy between the actual behavior of the individual and the individual's self-concept, which governs his behavior. Conscious control is more difficult when the individual attempts to meet needs not consciously recognized. When the individual becomes aware of the existing tension, he experiences a general "indirectedness," a feeling that he has no substantial unique core or self, that he is living only by the values he has taken over from others.

What occurs in Rogers' counseling may be inferred from the above propositions. In the complete absence of threat to the self the individual is free to perceive and examine inconsistent experiences, and the structure of the self can be revised to include these inconsistencies. Adjustment is attained when the self is able to assimilate all experiences of the organism into a consistent, organized, integrated relationship with the self. Once attained, this state assures greater understanding and acceptance of others—that is, self-acceptance—and enables the individual to enjoy more satisfying relationships with people. Self-acceptance permits spontaneous behavior, heretofore guarded because it satisfied needs unacceptable to the self. Further, as the individual grows in his ability to perceive and accept more of his experiences into his self-structure, he replaces his former rigid value system (probably largely introjected from others) with a flexible valuing process based upon what he himself experiences as satisfying. When the individual is in a state of adjustment, he is aware of all his needs, including the need for social approval, for affectional, sexual, and aggressive expression, and the need to avoid guilt. Since all persons have basically the same needs, the values that each individual espouses form the commonality of a socialized value system.

A first aspect of the task of counseling is to foster the client's feelings of complete acceptance, thereby freeing him from the need for defensive guardedness and permitting him to relax his rigid self-structure and become aware of experiences and feelings that had previously been denied awareness due to their inconsistency with his self-structure. The concept of self, having been disorganized or loosened, is then expanded to include these new facets which, when tested and assimilated, produce a reorganized, newly integrated self. Since counseling is founded on the individual's basic tendency toward enhancement of self, it assumes self-initiation of this process leading toward perception of new feelings. The client proceeds at his own pace with whatever material he brings up. He is never rushed or subjected to probing by the counselor, as this would merely tighten the existing perceptual constriction originally developed to exclude the unacceptable. Initial, immediate acceptance of the client as he is, sets in motion a process of change in the self-concept which subsequently allows recovery of denied or repressed material. Because the therapist also accepts the new perceptions, the client is able to introject this acceptance and admit these experiences into his self-concept.

In accordance with Rogers' fundamental principle of growth and belief in the worth of the individual, the role of the counselor is essentially to "implement" or to provide an atmosphere most conducive to the individual's growth and reorganization. The counselor should accept and respect his client's capacity for forward-moving change even to the extent that he will accept *any* outcome or direction the client may choose. The counselor's role is more than a simple supportive role; it is an "empathic identification" enabling him to assume as closely as possible the client's internal frame of reference, to experience with the client, and thus to see through the client's eyes. He must do this objectively, without any personal emotional involvement that might paralyze his therapeutic function. By perceiving the client as the client sees himself, the counselor is able to reflect and to clarify the client's feelings and attitudes; and in this way he is able to communicate deep understanding of and respect for these feelings.

A second aspect of the client-counselor relationship is the security from threat which it affords not through approval, but simply from consistent acceptance of the client without evaluation, interpretation, or personal reaction by the counselor. While Rogers admits that transference attitudes develop in such a relationship, this rarely occurs in the psychoanalytic sense, largely because of the absence of those aspects of analysis that create dependence. Rogers claims that the evaluation in analysis weakens self-confidence by making the client feel that the counselor knows more about him than the client knows about himself. Analytic probing activates strong and forbidden impulses, often elicited in a turmoil of emotion, which itself is often interpreted and encouraged. This, in conjunction with the free association technique, encourages the client to passively avoid responsibility and leaves him in a relationship with a technique-pursuing counselor who, in the client's eyes, acquires the attributes of a strong authority figure on whom the client must depend for direction. In contrast, the client-centered approach is designed to promote awareness of the self as the "perceiver" and "evaluator," while the therapist remains truly "nondirective." Rogers hastens to point out that the counselor's procedure is not "*laissez faire,*" for this might be experienced by the client as a rejection and it would not communicate the counselor's respect for him. In his earlier book Rogers (33) approved of occasional interpretations by the counselor, but only on the basis of material already verbalized by the client. The present practice of the client-centered counselor is to avoid interpretation which deals with material outside of awareness—and to reflect meanings and intents that already exist in the client's awareness. As Nicholas Hobbs (19) interprets it, the counselor attempts to reconstruct the client's perceptual field at the moment of expression by statements that clarify, reflect, or restate the feeling content of the expressed material.

With some idea of Rogers' theoretical orientation and the counseling procedures he recommends, let us now consider his concept of insight and its role in reintegrating the self-structure of the client. Insight involves reorganization of the perceptual field or, in the language of Donald Snygg and Arthur W. Combs (41), a differentiation of the phenomenal field. If the client has been living in a poorly defined phenomenal field with a maladaptive, unrealistic self-concept, he has been prone to overgeneralize his feelings, to disregard space and time changes, to be dominated by concepts rather than by actual facts, and generally to neglect reality-testing of his experiences. Differentiation means a change in figure-ground relationships, a bringing into focus of hitherto unrecognized perceptual elements which clarify the reality of one's experiences. It may mean a change from perceiving elements as rigid and fixed to perceiving them as flexible and changeable. Often it means exposing the falsity of previous generalizations of feeling through a more detailed examination of the experiences on which they are based (35). In his earlier book Rogers distinguished at least three categories of perception which comprise insight: (a) the perceived relationship between previously known facts (apparently possible only when, through catharsis, the client is freed from defensiveness); (b) perception of the related nature of all impulses, that is, acceptance of the self (which entails the relationship of unacceptable impulses to the present self-concept); and (c) the positive choice of more satisfying goals (possible, presumably, only after perceptual differentiation of the alternatives) which seems to involve abandoning the desire for immediate satisfaction in preference for deferred gratification as a more acceptable pattern of behavior. Achievement of insight, then, is substantiated by actions that enable the client to move toward his new goals, thus creating new self-confidence and independence (33).

It appears that the most crucial aspect of therapeutic insight is the awareness of, or differentiation of, experiences that contradict the client's present self-concept. In other words, it is the discrepancy between the self as perceived by the client and the self as it actually is in its functioning capacity—the inconsistency of behavior and desires. Since emotions play so vital a role in the process of reorganization, this type of differentiation may be conceived more concretely as the discrepancy between the feelings and attitudes the client believes he now has and those to which he has denied awareness, or which he has distorted, to avoid threat to the self. Rogers states that when these inconsistencies are perceived, the client is motivated to discover the reasons behind them, whether inaccurate description of his feelings or his behavior (35).

If, as Rogers implies, the concept of insight is considered synonymous with self-understanding, and if it encompasses the aspects of change described above, then insight is a prerequisite to therapeutic success—perhaps even the goal of counseling. This is not always the case, however, for Rogers cites examples in which no verbalized insights seemed necessary. In these the client benefited simply from the therapeutic relationship as an opportunity to experience the warmth and acceptance of a nonpunitive figure. Also, Rogers implies that the relative significance of achieved insight in the structural reorganization of the self may depend largely upon the breadth and scope of this new perceptual extension—whether it is a segmental insight of highly circumscribed nature or a more general and all-inclusive *process* of insight, in which case its importance is definitely augmented.

Attempting to isolate the constituents of insight for purposes of analysis and comparison is a difficult task, primarily because one encounters at every turn Rogers' global concept of the self, which is somewhat amorphous in its abstractness. To find concrete components of insight, to categorize them, and then generalize regarding their nature is, to say the least, somewhat futile, for two immediate reasons. First, Rogers, unlike most of the theorists discussed thus far (Freud in particular), postulates neither a universal nor even a usual etiological factor or group of factors. Neurotic behavior is assumed to satisfy needs that are not recognized. Beyond assuming that these repressed or distorted needs are threatening to the self, Rogers does not venture. He does not offer specific formulations as to why such needs are threatening. The self-structure, having been formed through interaction with the environment, particularly with other individuals, is delimited by such interaction, and thus it might be assumed that repression and distortion are ultimately brought about as a result of this same interaction. Rogers says nothing of a drive for power or of unacceptable wishes toward the mother, nor does he single out specific biological needs or the effects of cultural restraints. These are far too removed from the client's perceptual frame of reference to be useful in Rogers' system. Why, he reasons, should the counselor introduce further complications by trying to mold the client's feelings to a set of constructs preformulated by someone else? Whatever caused the client's phenomenal field or self-structure to constrict in self-defense is peculiar and unique to *that* client, so the causal end of such cause-effect relationships that might be perceived with insight is not something about which one can generalize. Since the counselor can never wholly and completely share the client's frame of reference, he is in no way qualified to accurately evaluate its adequacy in terms of the client's experience. Likewise, the theorist is not equipped to generalize on matters highly personalized for each client. We are left with only a nebulous notion of therapeutic insight, because it is a phenomenon whose exact nature neither the theorist nor the counselor can predict since at least part of it is beyond the scope of their experience.

A second problem in analysis of Rogers' system is created by variability in his definitions of insight. Basically, insight is understood to be a reorganization of the perceptual field in much the same sense that Kohler used the term. "Differentiation," as it is used in this context by Snygg, Combs, and Rogers, appears to be nothing more than articulation, and the entire phenomenon may involve either thorough change in figure-ground relationships or simply a differentiation or articulation of "new" figure-ground relationships out of sensations and perceptions that were at one time available to consciousness. At the perceptual level the process of counseling seems to consist of expanding the perceptual field and clarifying its contents. Presumably, the material dealt with in a counseling interview is all at the conscious level since it has all been verbalized by the client. Also, the orientation is focused on present problems and needs, as these are the determinants not only of one's present behavior but also of one's perception of the past. Apparently, however, the phenomena that Rogers calls insight are not always confined to material in conscious awareness (if we consider what is verbalized to include all of the conscious phenomenal field) but may include awareness of some relationships with previously experienced, and then repressed, feelings and events. From case protocols Rogers points out instances of so-called insight which often seem to be inferred from unverbalized material and which also vary from the client's simple awareness of feelings, past or present, to his deeper understanding of the effects of past or present feelings and events on his present attitudes toward himself. The content of insight may involve a small segment of behavior within a brief period of time or it may encompass a long-range pattern established in the past and maintained consistently since then. Some clients are apparently capable only of the former and never reach a deeper level of "self-understanding." In his earlier book Rogers included as insight even the positive choice of more satisfying goals—an occurrence which we believe is more accurately designated as an act from which we may infer insight, or an event made possible in part by insight. Evidently Virginia Mae Axline (5) also separates insight from behavioral modifications, for she points out that while the counseling relationship may hasten development of insight, the responsibility for instituting change remains with the client.

Nevertheless insight as a therapeutic phenomenon certainly has its place in Rogerian thought. Rogers seems much less concerned with the origin of feelings and attitudes than with bringing these feelings into awareness, a process that, he believes, in itself, changes one's perceptual field. In accordance with his fundamental growth principle (34, p. 419):

. . . the client can and will uncover all the repressed elements which it is necessary to uncover in order to build a comfortable adjustment. . . . The client can achieve for himself far truer and more sensitive and accurate insights than can possibly be given to him. . . . The client is capable of translating these insights into constructive behavior which weighs his own needs and desires realistically against the demands of society. . . . Only one condition is necessary for all these forces to be released, and that is the proper psychological atmosphere between client and therapist.[9]

In this therapeutic atmosphere the client directs himself toward insightful "self-understanding," hence a systematic analysis of insight would have relatively little practical value for the counselor. Whatever insights are achieved may be analyzed by the client himself in his growth process.

Rogers' principal therapeutic endeavor is the creation of the "proper psychological atmosphere," mentioned above. While insights are surely indicative of a desirable change and growth of the client's self-structure, they are arrived at "spontaneously" and "naturally" without special effort by the counselor. Thus it seems that the client does his own probing, his own interpretation, in short, his own theorizing. If the client needs insight, whatever its scope or depth, he will achieve it, but the decision as to its necessity for growth is to be made by the client, not by the theorist or counselor.

INSIGHT IN COUNSELING PROCEDURES DEVELOPED FROM LEARNING THEORY

1. JOHN DOLLARD AND NEAL MILLER. Among contemporary learning theorists Dollard and Miller (7) offer the most methodically developed application of learning principles to counseling. For the most part they accept the variables or concepts of psychoanalysis and organize them within a broad Hullian learning framework. They schematize the development of inefficient neurotic behavior as follows: Sex and aggression are considered among the basic drives, and fear and guilt among the secondary or learned drives. Fear, produced by cues from a goal toward which an individual is directing his behavior, motivates an avoidance response that may conflict with a goal-approaching response. Fear is reduced and the conflicting avoidance responses are reinforced when the neurotic individual halts his goal-directed behavior,

[9] From "Significant Aspects of Client-Centered Therapy," by Carl R. Rogers, *American Psychologist*, 1946, 1, 415–22. By permission of the American Psychological Association.

but this halting leaves the goal drives (sex and aggression) unreduced (in a state of "misery"), and as a result the individual is ready to make other approaching acts that again elicit fear. The strong fear or guilt of the neurotic which is elicited by response-produced cues is reduced when the responses producing these cues have ceased. Because they are reduced in this manner, these drives may motivate repression of verbal and other cue-producing responses (thoughts) that form the basis of the higher mental processes. Repression, then, renders the neurotic "stupid," unable to discriminate between situations in which he was punished and those in which he was not, and thus apt to make maladaptive generalizations that perpetuate his unrealistic fears. Unable to think clearly because of his misery, he becomes preoccupied with thoughts motivated by his unreduced drives. Fear and high drives produce symptoms that often partially reduce both the fear and the goal drives, the whole process reinforcing the neurotic symptoms. The more numerous the conflicts involved, the greater are the sources of motivation and reinforcement of symptoms.

According to this theory, while these symptoms provide partial drive reduction, their long-range effects augment the neurotic's fear and unreduced drive strength. Due to repression, he is unable to label (verbalize) the cause of his symptoms. Because these unlabeled impulses are unconscious, they are uncontrolled. Due to his inability to label them, the neurotic individual is less able to guard against the impulses that evoked his symptoms. Since the social conditions of our culture favor maintenance of repression, the neurotic is unable to free himself from its influence—to unlearn it—without help.

The therapeutic situation of Dollard and Miller is designed to foster the unlearning of repression. In the permissive, accepting, reassuring therapeutic relationship the neurotic is encouraged in free association, and to express his feelings verbally. Impulses and feelings that had heretofore brought disapproval and resulting anxiety are now accepted. The therapist's understanding and calm acceptance is also rewarding to the client. By not punishing, the counselor creates a reversal of the circumstances in which fear was learned. Since the client is not punished, his fear is extinguished (reinforcement is absent), and this extinction generalizes to weaken the motivation to repress other thoughts and feelings that had previously brought punishment or disapproval. The counselor should not reduce all fears indiscriminately, however, for in order to achieve extinction of the fear associated with verbal expression, the client must verbalize his feelings while he is still afraid so as to insure that absence of reinforcement (lack of punishment) will be associated with the anxiety-producing responses.

By weakening repression, the permissive condition of counseling allows fuller strength to the client's inhibited impulses, which generalize first toward the counselor, toward whom his avoidance reactions are greatly diminished. Since these responses have long been inhibited, the majority of them have never been labeled. The counselor labels them as they occur, thus making them available in the client's consciousness, subject to his reasoning and planning abilities. This generalization of emotional responses, which Freud called transference, along with the data from free association, provides material from which past conditions may be reconstructed, as well as evidence which indicates the neurotic's habits in everyday life. One of the first jobs of the counselor is to help the client identify these habits, which were acquired in childhood, and to recognize the similarity between his habits as a child and as an adult. By placing his habits in groups according to similarity and then naming the categories, the client is enabled to see relationships between his present feelings and those of his childhood. He is then in a position to become aware of the inconsistency of similar feelings toward dissimilar objects; for example, his mother and his wife. Verbal labels and responses clarify the difference between past responses followed by punishment and present responses where punishment is absent. In this manner verbal cues prevent generalization of anxiety from past to present. When the neurotic has become aware of various differences in cues producing his responses, he can see the maladaptiveness of his present behavior, and is challenged to try new responses better adapted to existing conditions. In this process of anxiety reduction by extinction, reassurance, and discrimination, the client becomes less restrained. When his new responses are rewarded—reduce his goal drives—they become the basis of new habits that resolve his conflicts.

The importance of labeling (verbalizing, symbolizing) in the analyses of Dollard and Miller becomes clear from their (7, p. 281) statement that "the neurotic is a person who is in need of a stock of sentences that will match the events going on within and without him." Once previously unconscious (unlabeled) feelings and thoughts are labeled (made conscious), they are subject to control by the client's higher mental processes. Labels permit more accurate discrimination and generalization of cues and responses. More specifically, labels or words are responses that can be attached to particular cues as when a person describes how he feels. When this labeling function is absent, the material is "unconscious." Labels also produce cues that can elicit specific responses, as when an individual responds to directions given by others or when he gives directions to himself. However, if he possesses labels, he does not necessarily respond to them appropriately, since he may never have learned to respond to such cues or his fear may be strong enough to block correct responses that were once learned. In the latter case, the response made is "unconscious." According to Dollard and Miller, labels aid the client in motivating himself and in becoming "logical, reasonable, and planful." A label enables him to initiate an intervening series of cue-producing responses controlled by higher mental processes. Labels help define the neurotic's problem and help suggest an appropriate, more adaptive course of action. Without labels, the client can only respond directly and unconsciously to his drive or emotion.

When new labels are given, as in interpretation, anxiety may be intensified so that further extinction trials are needed. In order to apply a correct label to other relevant situations, the client may have to relearn the label under other similar circumstances, and this is the familiar process of "working through." The greater "mental freedom" of the counselor enables him to see the connections and contradictions in the client's verbalizations, to make the necessary discriminations and generalizations, to see the underlying forces influencing the client's behavior. He has, in short, a "construction" of what has been repressed. With this "construction" in mind, the counselor helps the client to learn new labels by (a) verifying those the client discovers himself, (b) selectively repeating certain responses of the client, and (c) providing labels that are missing in the client's account. The latter method is referred to as "interpretation." The new element in this learning procedure is not necessarily the word itself but the connection between the word and the right cue (the verbal unit). The new response will be extinguished if it is useless or strengthened if it is rewarded—if it reduces fear or produces other drive-reducing responses.

In their book Dollard and Miller made few references to insight, and there is little discussion of its role in therapy. They do state that insight is the sudden generalized change mediated by a newly acquired verbal hypothesis (7). It is contrasted with the slow changes (trial and error) that occur without such verbal responses. They further state that to have insight is to have the correct sentences with which to describe one's own behavior. Throughout their discussion of the process involved in psychotherapy, Dollard and Miller reiterate the tremendous significance of these verbal responses. It is the possession of a stock of sentences for appropriate description of the events within and without the individual which distinguishes the normal from the neurotic. Their statements concerning insight are confusing. Is insight the acquisition of verbal symbols, or is it the behavioral change that follows acquisition of verbal units? Consciousness is equated with possession of verbal labels for thoughts and emotions. Is insight, then, synonymous with consciousness? Although they speak of insight as the acquisition of verbal labels, this appears to be simple association of cue and response, a *rote* type of learning as distinguished from the superior *logical* learning involving words and thoughts, that is, symbols. The latter *logical* learning entails insight or reasoning which functions to produce new responses. In view of this distinction it seems most likely that Dollard and Miller conceive of insight as the change made possible by the labeling of cue-response connections. Such connections, when labeled, are verbal units that permit new and more accurate discriminations. In this sense, then, insight would include the label plus the discrimination it facilitates, the latter being under control of the higher mental processes. This is consistent with the concept of insight as functioning to produce new responses. Despite their negligent treatment of this concept in their analysis, its components (labeling and discrimination) are indispensable prerequisites for the learning of new more adaptive responses.

Thus it seems that insight, as the product of label-learning, as the conscious awareness of relationships between responses and cues, is, in this analysis—as in many others—the core of therapy, but here its theoretical interpretation is considerably different from any other we have discussed. Apparently, labeling or insight is not the *sine qua non* of *all* therapeutic success, since Dollard and Miller point out that mere reassurance and acceptance from the therapist reduce fear, and that, in the absence of further conscious learning, such fear reduction should be applicable to the rest of the patient's life and should reduce to some degree his motivation for symptoms. They reason that although no new thoughts will be learned, anxiety reduction will enable the patient to better utilize his present repertoire of thoughts. These changes will not, however, effect complete cure, which is accomplished only by the removal of repression, by new labeling, new discrimination, and renewed control by the higher mental processes. Because verbal responses are the means through which higher mental processes operate, their acquisition is essential for more intelligent, more flexible behavior.

2. O. HOBART MOWRER.   While Dollard and Miller took Freud's theory and molded it into their preferred Hullian framework, the writings of another prominent learning theorist, O. Hobart Mowrer, reflect a perhaps equally strong but somewhat negative reaction to Freud's influence on contemporary psychotherapeutic practices. Whereas Dollard and Miller claim to accept Freud's notion of the relevant variables in psychoanalysis, which they cast in Hullian terms, Mowrer refers to Freud's theory only as a point of departure for his own, which directly refutes some of the fundamental postulates of both orthodox and modern psychoanalytic theory.

In his theory of neurosis Freud emphasized frustration of libidinal desires and wishes and their subsequent repression by the pressure of social demands introjected as the superego. The repressed impulses and desires struggle against the thwarting restrictions of the superego and produce neurotic anxiety. Neurotic anxiety is reduced by releasing the id impulses and strengthening the ego's capacity to deal with the superego. Freud's superego represents the influence of the socialization process;

it is first acquired by learning through identification with one's parents and reinforced later through the school and the church. Mowrer interprets Freud's concept of neurosis as a phenomenon of overlearning and oversocialization, the product of an oversevere superego. But overlearning, he claims, does not solve the "neurotic paradox" in which self-defeating, self-punishing behavior is not extinguished but perpetuated.

According to Mowrer (26), no monistic learning theory can account for the dynamic opposition in neurosis. Mowrer's resolution of the neurotic paradox is accomplished to his satisfaction by his two-factor theory based on the assumption that we not only learn solutions to problems but we also learn that problems exist. Problem-solving or solution learning follows the principle of reinforcement (drive reduction); it is under voluntary control of the central nervous system, and it is the means by which we acquire tendencies to action. Conditioning, or sign learning, is governed by contiguity principles; it is mediated by the autonomic nervous system and hence is involuntary. This latter aspect of learning provides the avenue through which we acquire expectations, sets, and predispositions. Since it is the mechanism by which secondary drives attach themselves to new objects, it is also instrumental in creating problems that must be dealt with by the voluntary actions of problem-solving.

With his dichotomous conception of learning, Mowrer theorizes that by utilizing his problem-solving ability, the neurotic learns how to bypass or ignore the restrictive demands of social authority vested in his parents—he avoids learning by conditioning ("emotional learning"). In this way instead of complementing each other in harmonious integration, problem-solving learning is turned against sign learning. Problem-solving learning is used defensively to protect the self against new conditioning (new fears and anxieties) and attitudinal changes that would be more rewarding in the long run. Herein lies the crux of psychopathology (29). The primary drives (sex and aggression) retain control over problem-solving processes and cause these to be directed toward blocking or inhibition of secondary drives (guilt and fear). Translated into Freud's terms, neurosis arises when the ego remains id-dominated and directs repressive action against the superego. In Mowrer's theory problem-solving serves the primary drives rather than the superego. Thus, *in contrast with Freud's concept, Mowrer conceives of neurosis as superego deficiency*—a deficit in "attitudinal" learning. In seeking pleasure the neurotic "has learned how not to learn" (24, 25, 27). Neurosis is a state of "personal immaturity," and the neurotic's fears correspond to society's disapproval of the characteristics of neurosis (25). Resistance set up by the infantile ego against various socializing forces plus the ego's later opposition to the internalized agents of these forces (superego) keep the ego in an immature, asocial, id-dominated state. Nevertheless, since the ego has instituted such an avoidance mechanism, Mowrer attributes the root cause of neurosis to the individual himself rather than to the externally imposed superego demands stressed by Freud (29).

In Freud's system the superego is all-powerful and unmerciful in its repression of the id. In Mowrer's theory it is the superego that becomes repressed (dissociated). Mowrer agrees with Freud that anxiety is the basis of neurotic symptomatology and that anxiety arises only when there has been prior repression. But Mowrer interprets clinical experience as evidence that it is the "socially derived" drives (conscience), rather than the primal biological drives (sex and aggression), that are repressed. By dissociating guilt and self-condemnation, one achieves at least temporary relief from persistent deception following transgression of authority.

This brings up another major disagreement with psychoanalytic theory. Whereas Freud stressed the thwarting of the forbidden desires and impulses for which the id seeks gratification, Mowrer (25, p. 515) takes a more concrete behavioristic view, stating that "human beings fall victim of neurosis not because of what they would do but cannot, but because of what they have done and would that they had not." Mowrer contends that it is an overt act or series of acts, rather than mere thoughts, which initiate a sequence eventuating in neurotic symptoms. A shameful experience plus fear of its consequences is followed by persistent deception and guilt, which is then dissociated (repressed). But since the influence of the superego is continually nourished and vitalized by the existing social realities it represents, it is not forever silenced by dissociation. Rather, the superego, like the id in Freud's scheme, constantly pleads for a hearing and in so doing produces neurotic anxiety that is warded off by symptoms.

According to Mowrer, the neurotic's original shameful actions are the result of inadequate learning (conditioning) from his parents due to disturbed, "defensive" identification. In this situation an ambivalent attitude toward the parents prevents complete assimilation of their authority. The influence of the superego becomes walled off in order to avoid anxieties, and the neurotic, through continual dissociation, progressively heightens the barrier between his ego and the standards and values he once repressed. His "outraged conscience" is ignored and forced to assert itself indirectly through symptoms. The neurotic is morally a partial failure because he is not yet willing to listen to, or live with, his conscience (28).

In Mowrer's framework the task of counseling with the immature, developmentally fixated neurotic is quite logical. The client must grow up, become a mature socially responsible individual. Counseling, then, attempts to resume the task left uncompleted by the parents; it helps the neurotic person to see his feelings as a consequence of his habit of dissociation and to pull together and integrate the dissociated parts of his personality, and it furthers his developing maturity to the extent that he is able to recognize and fulfill the demands of his superego. Counseling does not endeavor to strengthen the superego, but rather to re-establish communication between the ego and the superego. There is no attempt to reverse the socialization process (as Mowrer interpreted Freud's weakening of the superego), as this would only strengthen the present immaturities that have generated the existing neurosis. The client's high standards should be accepted as evidence of good character, and counseling should make these standards more understandable and helpful to him so that he can live by them rather than isolate them from the remainder of his personality.

Mowrer (29, p. 79) has stated that "once a patient is accepted for therapy, the procedure is, in principle, the same in all cases." The subject is invited to talk about whatever comes to mind. Eventually, in this chaotic mass of material, the counselor sees "connections" that the subject will not allow himself to see, and he (p. 472) "wages a campaign of association in opposition to the patient's dissociative trends." The counselor, in a very real sense, undoes the subject's dissociations, by-passes his defensive barriers, thus doing for the client what he has been unable to do for himself. The counselor offers *tentative* exploratory interpretations, which are simply his associations to the client's material. Interpretation is the major tool for bringing to consciousness the client's repressed conflicts. By means of this technique the counselor works to gain admission to consciousness for the denied superego energies, on the assumption that only when these have been brought to consciousness can the ego acquire the strength it has previously lacked. Mowrer does acknowledge the possibility of ego support merely from the counselor's acceptance of the "returning" superego, but he implies that strength so derived from the counselor is less significant and less intense than that afforded by reunion with the superego (29). The counselor helps bring back to the client's consciousness the sense of self-criticism and the capacity for vivid experiences of guilt. Beyond that, he must attempt to revive also the occasion of the original repression. Presumably the re-experiencing of guilt encourages growth. The counselor helps the client to resist dealing with his conflicts by dissociation, as he once did, and to learn new and more integrative ("mature," "characterful," "adult") solutions to his problems. The objective is, then, to replace the habit of dissociation with the habit of association, thus changing the client's method of problem-solving (29). With this procedure the counselor is able to resynthesize those elements or strata of the client's personality which he has endeavored to isolate.

The role of the counselor has been interpreted in various ways by Mowrer. In terms of his two-factor theory, the counselor must aim at effecting behavioral changes in the client which will so alter his relationships with others that reinforcement of his painful emotions will be minimal (26). Such a role is necessarily authoritarian and directive in nature. It consists of opposing the subject's present efforts to solve his problems in a disintegrative manner by deception and dissociation, and of strengthening the subject's ego so that it may eventually reintegrate the recovered superego. The counselor attempts to prevent the client from choosing the shortsighted, self-defeating "short cuts" toward an immediate goal, pointing out to him the "detours" or indirect routes toward a more distant goal. In other words, he attempts to block old habits and create circumstances in which more permanently satisfactory ones may be acquired.

The neurotic's conflict was, presumably, generated in his inadequate relationship with his parents as a child. It was his fear of their punishment and desire for their love which brought guilt and necessitated repression of indulgences which might be against their wishes. The emotional significance of parent-child relationships is strongly reflected in the transference situation which, here, as in Freud's approach, is the pivotal phenomenon of therapy. The reality of transference clearly indicates that the client reacts to the counselor as a parental and social authority. As his conflicts become externalized, his internal struggles are cast into an interpersonal frame of reference. The fact that the client endows the counselor with superego qualities suggests to Mowrer that it was this component of his personality which had been dissociated and thus avoided (29). Mowrer believes that in transference the unassimilated superego is extrojected onto the therapist and the client relives his childhood problems. This encourages a "therapeutic regression" whereby the substitution of interpersonal conflicts for internal ones creates an occasion for new learning. Counseling thus provides a "second childhood" and a second chance to grow up (25). The patient is able to go back to the "choice points" of his childhood, and he is helped to select more beneficial avenues of development.

In his discussion of counseling procedures Mowrer finds himself in a dilemma (29). He emphasizes that the responsibility for neurosis lies with the client, in the unacceptable acts he has performed and in the subsequent dissociation of his guilt. At the same time he stresses the importance of the counselor's active interference to block dissociative trends and maintains that without this opposition by the counselor the neurotic is unable to help himself. Mowrer "solves" the dilemma by calling to attention the fact that the counselor cannot acquire new habits for the client—he cannot "implant" the neural changes involved. However, he can clarify by interpreting the self-defeating character of old habits, helping the client to understand their nature and origin, and then preventing the client from reverting to these modes of problem-solution. From this, Mowrer concludes that counseling is a genuine "client-counselor collaboration" in which neither party is either "active" (directive) or "passive" (nondirective); each works on the task he has to perform.

A discussion of insight in Mowrer's psychotherapy must be based on inferences drawn from scattered general statements and from Mowrer's (25) review of insight in studies of animal learning, as unfortunately, his only attempt at analysis occurs in the context of these experimental investigations. Here again, as with Dollard and Miller, the facts are "second order"—they are not drawn from actual clinical experience. Mowrer's neglect of insight as an element in psychotherapy may reflect his earlier years of devotion to the reinforcement theory and to experimentation on animal behavior. Like most well-grounded stimulus-response theorists, Mowrer does not seem at home in discussing concepts that evolve from Gestalt theory. Although he tends to analyze the sudden insight or "Aha!" experience as tension-reducing—as a reduction of secondary drives which reinforces the immediately preceding responses—he suggests that analysis of learning processes is greatly clarified by a systematic distinction between learning, as defined by his two-factor theory, and insight. Mowrer acknowledges that these two processes commonly occur simultaneously in everyday life and that they interact in a complicated manner; for this reason they can be abstracted and thought of independently only for purposes of analysis.

Mowrer believes learning to be a slow inductive process, whereas insight is a deductive process involving reasoning or thinking in which the individual experiences immediate secondary reinforcement before the direct instrumental results of an act have occurred (25). By means of the two kinds of learning, generalizations (attitudes, habits) are developed. When the organism experiences the two kinds of sequences involved in sign learning (conditioned stimulus followed by unconditioned stimulus) and solution learning (a particular response leads to solution of the problem) regularly enough to have some confidence in their predictability, and when more than one of such "confidences" or generalizations have been established, they "run together" and generate "deductions." "When pertinent generalizations are combined, their combination may be creative, and lead to those arresting events we call 'insights,' to the having of an 'idea' " (25). Insight, in any event, involves "combining something in an immediate situation with something that is temporally remote" (presumably from the past experience of the organism). It is a "short cut" or substitute for the longer, more tedious process of learning.

Mowrer continues his speculation on insight by associating these short cuts in learning (insights) with instruction or teaching, which also helps to eliminate trial-and-error solutions. Although Mowrer is dealing in his discussion with rat behavior, he follows this somewhat anthropomorphic tangent to an interpretation of insight in the rat, which probably bears more than chance conceptual resemblance to the insight to be gained by the patient in counseling. He suggests that possibly the rat "identifies with" (acts like) the experimenter and thus learns to make a response that was made earlier by the experimenter, in order to get a food pellet (25). Although Mowrer considers this to be a very primitive form of identification, he later discusses the same process in counseling as an aspect of transference.

In counseling, the absence of countertransference enables the client to work through his anxieties and guilt without necessity for his usual defensiveness. In addition, this acceptance by the counselor changes the client's expectations and habits that had been formed following previous unpleasant parental reactions. With the dissolution of former modes of behavior in a defense-free relationship, the client is able to consider new patterns of response. Because the counselor is helpful, the client develops gratitude toward and trust in him—the client tends to identify with the counselor. This results in changed ego attitudes toward authority figures, and in this way the ego is prepared to accept the superego. Often such identification with the counselor is manifested in the client's desire to do what the counselor does, or, more important, to "see" the connections in his behavior that the counselor sees. While these "connections" may be highly specific for purposes of analysis in terms of learning theory, Mowrer would agree that they also involve broader relationships between the client's present maladjustive behavior patterns and the ultimate self-punishment they will bring. This kind of realization is essential in successful counseling because it affords motivation for learning new responses. Apparently it constitutes insight that is similar to the suggested insight of the rat. Although Mowrer notes that identification with the counselor is usually transitory, it is nevertheless preliminary to reintrojecting conscience and terminating counseling (25).

To what extent does insight in Mowrer's therapy revolve around identification with, or "acting like," the counselor (as the rat appears to have "identified with" the experimenter)? Since the client's original parental identification was incomplete, it might follow that one of the necessary tasks of counseling is to provide completion of this deficit in his development as a child. Although brief in duration, the client's identification with the superego representation or parental figure of the counselor must be more positive and thorough than his earlier identification with his parents to compensate for the inadequacies of his childhood relationship with them. Assuming that insight does involve "seeing connections" as the counselor sees them, then it apparently entails the client's learning to see himself through the eyes of the superego-counselor.

Despite Mowrer's stress on the collaborative aspects of counseling and his insistence that the counselor does not try to change the superego or impose his own values on the client (25), his description of counseling is almost wholly in terms of the counselor's role. It is the counselor who "wages a campaign" of opposition to the patient's habits of dissociation, it is the counselor who "sees connections" in the client's narrative, it is the counselor who reports his associations to the client's material, and, lastly, it is the counselor who points out to the client the alternative paths of behavior which will solve his problem by a series of detours. Apparently all the client needs to do is verbalize, rather than act out, his emotions in various disturbing events. Synthesis of isolated strata of the client's personality is stated to be the task of the counselor.

Insight, in Mowrer's therapy, seems to be much more an achievement for the counselor than for the client. The "connections" seen by the counselor in the client's material apparently concern (a) the relation between current behavior and past actions about which the client feels guilt and (b) the relation of present behavior to its punishing consequences. The counselor deduces causal relationships and interprets these to the client. If awareness of these "connections" may be considered insight, then it would seem that Mowrer, too, considers it indispensable to therapeutic progress.

Mowrer's apparent neglect of psychotherapeutic insight may be, in part, a result of his suggested dichotomizing of learning (induction) and insight (reasoning or deduction). Although he does not elaborate on the application of his two-factor theory to counseling, nevertheless, his is a learning theory, not a theory of insight. While he may analyze the rat's behavior in terms of a process of learning and a process of insight, his statement that in reality the division is arbitrary, and that the two processes occur simultaneously in everyday life, may be his way of justifying his neglect of human insight in psychotherapy. Moreover, Mowrer admits that learning theory is still far too simple to encompass all the complexities of socialization and character formation (25).

3. OTHER LEARNING THEORIES. The theories of Edward J. Shoben (40), Franklin J. Shaw (38, 39), and Laurance F. Shaffer (37) are also behavioristic in nature though differing in degree. According to Shoben, counseling consists of three interrelated processes. The first step is the lifting of repression and the development of insight, and it is presented in his theory as the acquisition of "symbolic controls" achieved by symbolic restatement of the stimuli for anxiety. This is reminiscent of Dollard and Miller in their insistence on the importance of labeling in insight. Shaw (38) also speaks of insight as a "symbolization into consciousness" that makes cues (repressed motives) available to the client for conscious control. He believes counseling should eventually enable

the client to define (verbalize) his own modes of adjustment and to recognize their punishing consequences (39). Shaffer (37, p. 465) states similarly that the purposes of psychotherapy are, first, to "induce the client to represent verbally the cues he needs for voluntary behavior," and, second, to reinforce the "appropriate" responses to these cues. Through counseling the neurotic acquires the ability to "speak" of, and to control, his behavior. Verbal representation of cues often eventuates in insight which is, for Shaffer, operationally defined as "verbalization of the person's problems and of the relationships between them."

Shoben's second and third steps involve reconditioning and reeducation. Cues once associated with movements toward a repressed activity become reconditioned to the nonanxietous reactions in the counseling situation. Before this occurs, however, the stimulus originally associated with anxiety must be discovered and made conscious so that it may be reinstated at the appropriate time. Shoben definitely believes that such insight must precede counterconditioning. After anxiety has been reduced through reconditioning, the client is helped through reeducation to formulate rational goals and to develop modes of behavior suitable to attain them.

Shaw's concept of maladjustment (38, 39) bears similarity to Mowrer's in that he characterizes it as resulting in behavior whose consequences are immediately rewarding but which bring ultimate remote punishment. His counseling, like that of Mowrer, focuses on problem-solving behavior within a Hullian framework of reinforcement theory. Assuming that reward is essential to learning, Shaw contends that "nonintegrative behavior" may be modified by making punishment more immediate and thus forcing the acquisition of new, more adaptive responses. The counselor's task is, then, to discuss with his client the consequences of his behavior. When the client discovers that he will not be punished in the counseling situation, his "conditioned avoidance reactions" (rationalization and projection to avoid perception of self) will be extinguished. The counselor also helps the client to define verbally his modes of adjustment and the functions they serve. In this way the client is assisted in acquiring insight into the punishing consequences of his behavior. As was explained above, this symbolization makes the client aware that the repressed motives which have become cues to his present behavior are also cues to later punishment. By helping the client to analyze the nature of the behavior he is trying to learn, the counselor assists him in replacing his former fearful anticipations by more constructive expectations, thus enabling him to find reward through his new behavior.

Insight (or knowledge of cues) is, in Shaw's theory, an intermediate and necessary phase in reaching the ultimate goal of behavior change. Through insight the client is able to take active steps to acquire more integrative modes of behavior. The counselor suggests new modes of response, new hypotheses or expectancies, to be tested out by the client until he finds a more adaptive pattern of response whose consequences are no longer punishing.

As a group, the learning theorists are characteristically concerned more with the acquisition of new responses than with the conditions under which maladaptive behavior developed. Since their method is to define personality disorders in terms of observable reactions, their treatments are response-oriented. Insight, however it may be defined, is just as integral a part of the learning theorists' counseling as it is of classical psychoanalytic therapy. Both Freud and the learning theorists contend that repressions must be destroyed—whether "uncovered" through analysis or "lifted" by the extinction of fear. Both theories implicitly assume the supremacy of intellectual control, requiring conscious awareness (insight) of certain relationships. Differences in the content of insights, however, vary according to the differential theoretical conceptions of causation. Thus, since in the Freudian scheme repressed libidinal wishes are at the root of neurotic conflict, psychoanalytic insight concerns the relation of these unconscious motives to present neurotic adjustment. Although the learning theorists' variable definitions of neurosis seem more descriptive than explanatory, it is nevertheless clear that they are more apt to be slanted toward seeing its cause in repressed cue-response connections acquired through maladaptive conditioning or misdirected reinforcements; accordingly, insights are concerned with overt behavioral acts. Nevertheless, both types of insight are assumed to bring about control, whether by the ego or by the "higher mental processes."

The insights in psychoanalysis and those in learning theory approaches are assumed to bring about conscious control. Beyond this point, the two schools diverge rather broadly in their concepts of counseling or therapy. To Freud, conscious awareness or insight was the end product or goal of therapy. He considered re-education unnecessary because he believed that "psychosynthesis" of therapeutic and real life experiences occurred automatically after removal of repression. Although the learning theorists generally agree that insight is a necessary part of the counseling process, they regard it not as the ultimate goal but as a preparatory step toward learning new responses. It is a necessary means by which previously repressed stimulus-response connections are made accessible to the client in a situation that reduces the fear or guilt surrounding them. Once this anxiety has been reduced, the client is helped to learn new responses, new ways of behaving, that are better adapted to his aims. This new learning is the goal of "learning" therapy.

Considering these similarities and differences, it might be concluded that since learning therapy emphasizes the acquisition of new modes of behavior, it relegates insight to a secondary role. The same might be said of all therapies that go beyond insight to a re-educative phase as, for instance, those of Jung (the synthetic phase of treatment), Adler (adaptation of life style to life goal), and even Fromm-Reichmann (evaluation of insights by review, repeated testing) whose therapy is quite emphatically insight-oriented. We believe that such discrimination is not only conducive to misleading generalizations at the theoretical level, but also that it may tend to create erroneous impressions of the actual events occurring in counseling. What is understood as the end or goal in one system is certainly no more important than the same kind of phenomenon which, in another system, is considered as a necessary means toward a new end. Indeed, it could even be argued that insight, when conceived as a "means-end" device (learning therapy), has greater significance than when conceived as a goal in itself (psychoanalysis), because its absence would halt the learning therapy sequence at an earlier phase. The distinction seems more academic than practical. A more plausible differentiation, of perhaps greater heuristic value, would be that based on the content or nature of insight rather than on the relative significance of its role in counseling.

SUMMARY

As the above discussion has shown, the theoretical conceptions of insight differ markedly within and among the different "schools" of thought. Within the psychoanalytic group there are variations in emphasis. Horney's stress on functional analysis of existing needs implies a type of therapeutic insight quite different from insightful awareness of the libidinal genesis of conflict which is so prominent in Freudian analysis. The therapies of Sullivan, Alexander and French, Adler, and Rank are also adapted to the client's present problems, particularly those emanating from his interpersonal relationships. In neo-analytic theories the emphasis on the individual plus his social and cultural setting necessitates expanding therapeutic insight to include this broader group of variables. The etiological significance accorded the unconscious also seems to bear possible deterministic relation to the "depth" and scope of insight to be achieved in therapy. At the "depth" end of this continuum Freud and Jung could be placed, and at the "superficial" end, Adler, with his educative type of therapy designed to deal with the conscious ideas and desires of the client. Alexander and French, with their flexible approach, lie somewhere between the two extremes.

Relative emphasis on the emotional acceptance or integration of changes accompanying insight also vary from Horney's belief in the necessity of intellectual insight to Fromm-Reichmann's insistence on "working through" for emotional integration beyond intellectual understanding, to Alexander and French's therapeutic formulation based on emotional adjustment.

In general, conceptions of insight among the psychoanalysts seem to be more varied than those among the learning theorists, since all learning theorists seem to regard insight as an intermediary, though necessary, phase preparatory to new learning. The conceptual distinctions both within and among these groups seem to derive largely from differences in their theoretical interpretation of insight rather than from whether or not it is important. Some form of insight occurs in all the therapies discussed here. To assess its importance in the various theoretical approaches is difficult since its role is, in many cases, masked by emphasis on other facets of therapy and by the semantic differences arising from terminological variations. Rogers' emphasis on procedures that sustain client-centered atmosphere, the learning theorists' concern for response changes, Adler's educative approach to changes in the life style, the flexible approach of Alexander and French centered on the therapeutic goal of emotional readjustment, all appear to dwell on certain components of therapeutic progress, certain goals of treatment determined by their theoretical outlooks. At first glance these variations in "central concept" might imply reduction in the psychological significance of insight. However, more careful analysis reveals that the differences are more apparent than real and that they pertain more to the counselor's theoretical interpretation than to the actual practices employed in the therapeutic interview.

The principal differences occur in the theoretical nature of insight, its scope and depth. In analysis, because of the emphasis on genetic understanding of repressed material, we think of deeper insight, whereas in the theories of Adler, Rank, and in most of the learning theories, insight remains more on the conscious level. The scope of insight appears quite restricted both in classical analysis, in which it is confined to the individual's unconscious instincts and resistances, and in the learning theories, where awareness of stimulus-response connections is important. In some of the neo-analytic approaches the concept of insight is broadened to include the individual's relation to others in his social environment, often with less emphasis on the past. Finally, in Rogers' theory the scope of insight seems limited only by the number and variety of experiences or by the life span of the individual and his ability to accommodate the experiences in his phenomenal field without threatening his self-enhancement.

Thus, insight may be regarded as a process continuous with, and augmenting growth toward, an ever-increasing understanding of one's self and one's relations with others. It is not always a static point or phase, a specific type of revelation, which automatically assures subsequent return to healthy adjustment. Nor should it be considered merely as a preparatory step to new learning. Rather, it seems to play an equally significant role in clarifying one's past feelings and motives, one's present strengths and weaknesses, and in the continuous learning and growth that accompanies more adaptive and creative living.

In counseling, the client experiences insight as self-understanding, a feeling of knowing himself better, regardless of whether he has been guided by the interpretations of a psychoanalyst or simply accepted by a permissive Rogerian—whether he has become familiar with his libido, the collective unconscious, his stimulus-response associations, his superego, or whether his phenomenal field has expanded and differentiated. It is primarily the counselor's need that is fulfilled by having theoretical assumptions to support his procedures and techniques, and it is the counselor to whom theories provide explanatory concepts that facilitate interpretations of therapeutic results. In the process of planning for him the counselor must decide whether the client can profit from any clarification, understanding, or definition of his problem or of events associated with it. If the counselor feels that some enlightenment is advantageous, he must work out its attainment utilizing the theoretical framework in which he feels most comfortable and which appears to be compatible with the client's apparent behavioral situation.

BIBLIOGRAPHY

1. Adler, G., *Studies in analytical psychology*. New York: Norton, 1948.
2. Alexander, F., and French, T. M., *Psychoanalytic therapy*. New York: Ronald, 1946.
3. Alexander, F., *Fundamentals of psychoanalysis*. New York: Norton, 1948.
4. Alexander, F., "Current views on psychotherapy." *Psychiat.*, 1953, 16, 113–22.
5. Axline, V. M., *Play therapy*. Boston: Houghton Mifflin, 1947.
6. Birch, H. G., "The relation of previous experience to insightful problem solving." *J. Compar. Psychol.*, 1945, 38, 367–83.
7. Dollard, J., and Miller, N. E., *Personality and psychotherapy*. New York: McGraw-Hill, 1950.
8. Fenichel, O., *The psychoanalytic theory of the neuroses*. London: Routledge & Kegan Paul, 1946.
9. Freud, S., *Collected papers*, Vol. I. London: Hogarth, 1950.
10. Freud, S., *Collected papers*, Vol. II. London: Hogarth, 1950.
11. Freud, S., "The history of the psychoanalytic movement." In Brill, A. A. (trans.), *The basic writings of Sigmund Freud*. New York: Random House, 1938.
12. Frohman, B. S., and Frohman, E. P., *Brief psychotherapy*. Philadelphia: Lea & Fibiger, 1948.

13. Fromm-Reichmann, F., "Recent advances in psychoanalytic therapy." *Psychiat.*, 1941, 4, 161–4.
14. Fromm-Reichmann, F., "Notes on the development of treatment of schizophrenics by psychoanalytic therapy." *Psychiat.*, 1948, 11, 263–73.
15. Fromm-Reichmann, F., *Principles of intensive psychotherapy.* Chicago: University of Chicago Press, 1950.
16. Hadley, E. E., "Unrecognized antagonisms complicating business enterprise." *Psychiat.*, 1938, 1, 13–31.
17. Harlow, H. F., "The formation of learning sets." *Psychol. Rev.*, 1949, 56, 51–65.
18. Hendrick, I., *Facts and theories of psychoanalysis.* New York: Alfred A. Knopf, 1950.
19. Hobbs, N., "Group-centered psychotherapy." In Rogers, C. R., *Client-centered therapy.* Boston: Houghton Mifflin, 1951.
20. Horney, K., *The neurotic personality of our time.* New York: Norton, 1937.
21. Horney, K., *New ways in psychoanalysis.* New York: Norton, 1939.
22. Horney, K., *Our inner conflicts.* New York: Norton, 1945.
23. McGeoch, J. A., *The psychology of human learning.* New York: Longmans, Green, 1942.
24. Mowrer, O. H., "Learning theory and the neurotic paradox." *Amer. J. Orthopsychiat.*, 1948, 18, 571–610.
25. Mowrer, O. H., *Learning theory and personality dynamics.* New York: Ronald, 1950.
26. Mowrer, O. H., "Implications of a two-factor learning theory." *Psychol. Serv. Cen. J.*, 1950, 2, 116–22.
27. Mowrer, O. H., "The therapeutic process, III. Learning theory and the neurotic fallacy." *Amer. J. Orthopsychiat.*, 1952, 22, 679–89.
28. Mowrer, O. H., "Neurosis and its treatment as learning phenomena." In Brower, D., and L. E. Abt (eds.), *Process in clinical psychology*, Vol. I. New York: Grune & Stratton, 1952.
29. Mowrer, O. H., *Psychotherapy: theory and research.* New York: Ronald, 1953.
30. Mullahy, P., "A theory of interpersonal relations and the evolution of personality." In Sullivan, H. S., *Conceptions of modern psychiatry* (2nd ed.); New York: Norton, 1953.
31. Mullahy, P., *Oedipus myth and complex.* New York: Hermitage, 1952.
32. Rank, O., *Will therapy.* New York: Alfred A. Knopf, 1936.
33. Rogers, C. R., *Counseling and psychotherapy.* Boston: Houghton Mifflin, 1942.
34. Rogers, C. R., "Significant aspects of client-centered therapy." *Amer. Psychologist*, 1946, 1, 415–22.
35. Rogers, C. R., *Client-centered therapy.* Boston: Houghton Mifflin, 1951.
36. Schiller, P. H., "Innate constituents of complex responses in primates." Reported by H. F. Harlow in Stone, C. P. (ed.), *Comparative psychology* (3rd ed.), New York: Prentice-Hall, 1951.
37. Shaffer, L. F., "The problem of psychotherapy." *Amer. Psychologist*, 1947, 2, 459–67.

38. Shaw, F. J., "A stimulus-response analysis of repression and insight in psychotherapy." *Psychol. Rev.*, 1946, 53, 36–42.
39. Shaw, F. J., "The role of reward in psychotherapy." *Amer. Psychologist*, 1949, 4, 177–9.
40. Shoben, E. J., "Psychotherapy as a problem in learning theory." *Psychol. Bull.*, 1949, 46, 366–92.
41. Snygg, D., and Combs, A. W., *Individual behavior*. New York: Harper, 1949.
42. Sullivan, H. S., *Conceptions of modern psychiatry* (2nd ed.). New York: Norton, 1953.
43. Watson, R. I., *The clinical method in psychology*. New York: Harper, 1951.

✳

CHAPTER

5

Emotional Release
and Tension Reduction

THE NOTION THAT THE EXPRESSION OF EMOTION CONTRIBUTES TO
mental health and to the related feeling of well-being is not new.
The fact that a person is usually relieved by the expression of feelings or by talking about an emotion-laden event or idea is quite widely
recognized. As Laurance Shaffer (23) noted, we have popular expressions such as "confession is good for the soul," "getting it off your chest,"
"blowing off steam," and "having a good cry" which reflect in different
ways the idea that emotional expression can be beneficial. That this idea
is not new is suggested by Aristotle's comment that Greek drama served
the purpose of mental catharsis. The concept of freeing oneself from
guilt by the expression or acting out of feelings is reflected in various religious rituals. In the ancient Hebrew tradition an instance of emotional
release was acted out annually through driving a goat, symbolically bur-
dened with the sins of the community, out into the desert to die. The
goat's death represented the death of the burden of sin which the animal carried. In the Christian tradition the sacrament of confession has
quite effectively served a similar purpose. The specific use of catharsis as
a therapeutic technique is of more recent origin, as its formal incorpora-
tion into treatment procedures dates from the nineteenth century. The
value of expressing emotion in therapy was recognized, publicized, and
promoted by Pierre Janet, Josef Breuer, and Sigmund Freud.

In this chapter emotional release and tension reduction will be
considered as closely related, and for practical purposes synonymous,
concepts. We will discuss the ventilating, undamming, erupting connotations of emotional release as well as the unwinding, relaxing connotations of tension reduction. It will be seen that the aims, emotional

release and tension reduction, can occur both within and outside the formal situation of the counseling or therapeutic interview. We will discuss emotional release from several points of view, considering the more classical therapeutic situation as well as some aspects of encouraging release and reducing emotional tension by activities outside the counseling situation. No discussion of physical and pharmaceutical means of encouraging emotional release and/or tension reduction will be included. We will see again how our aims and techniques overlap: many supportive procedures are supportive because they are tension reducing, and tension is almost always reduced when support is felt. Again, in considering emotional release, we will emphasize its importance as an adjunct to other counseling aims and as a treatment procedure in and of itself, or both, depending upon the needs of the individual client. It will be seen that emotional release can be either reconstructive or supportive or both, and that the classification of any counseling procedure as reconstructive or supportive depends on the counselor's personal frame of reference or theoretical beliefs. For example, to David M. Levy (14) emotional release and catharsis are reconstructive, while to Harrington V. Ingham and Leonore R. Love (7) they are quite supportive in nature. This kind of classification is not particularly helpful, especially if one places the needs of the individual client to the fore in planning the counseling program.

EMOTIONAL RELEASE AS A FUNCTION OF FORMAL PSYCHOLOGICAL COUNSELING

Emotional release is experienced by the client when he is able to express himself freely and openly. It is not so much an activity in itself, but a feeling tone that results when he expresses something of importance. The extent of the release may not be proportional to the reduction of "overt" signs of emotional behavior, although it usually is; and ordinarily the release is accompanied by tension reduction and a degree of relaxation. At times, however, strong emotions may be experienced or released without a great show of emotional activity. In experiencing affective, emotionally toned reactions, the client gains in several ways. His anxiety may be reduced, he is relieved of worries and preoccupations, and he finds that he can now think more objectively. In the past he may have been so bound up with emotional tension that he was not able to think intelligently or objectively about his problems; as a result he was unable to face, or consistently avoided, much of the material involved in this central problem. If he can now get it out in the open and talk about it, he will probably experience a feeling of relief; and he will no longer find it necessary to protect himself continuously against consideration of the emotionally disturbing topic and everything associated with it. Another almost automatic accompaniment of facing previously avoided material is the desensitization that occurs. Each time the client speaks of the topic, he finds it easier, and gradually the traumatizing topic holds less danger for him.

Still another advantage of experiencing or expressing feeling associated with a disturbing idea or event lies in the client's satisfaction in achieving a goal. He attains a first purpose by attacking the problems that trouble him. This is an important step since many clients avoid solvable problems simply because they have not been able to bring themselves to an initial attack upon them. Emotional release motivates the client toward therapeutic activities. This is true even when the material expressed is not closely or dynamically related to the basic problems. The removal of preoccupations with trivial daily activities frees the individual so that he can proceed to consider areas of experience which are more productive of behavior change.

The need for release may be greatest early in the counseling process, and at this time emotional expression may be more frequent and dramatic than later. However, emotional expression frequently continues until the termination of counseling. In fact, as will be suggested later in this chapter, good counseling often involves the establishment of outlets for it so that release can continue indefinitely. Most clients receive both temporary and permanent relief from emotional release. Even temporary relief is palliative, and it is important for that reason, if for no other. More important, however, is the extent to which the client can use the occasions of emotional expression and the periods of comfort accompanying them to develop insight into problem situations. Frequently, merely acting out repressed material without conscious understanding brings about improvement.

Some illustrations will help us to understand the function and value of emotional release and tension reduction in the process of counseling and therapy. The client who was upset by voices certainly gained relief through the free expression of emotions when he described both his childhood and his war experiences. He had regarded himself as a pretty tough, self-sufficient person, and he had considered the expression of feeling and emotion as a sign of weakness. As a result he had "bottled up" a rather terrifying amount of emotional material. As he expressed it, one could almost see him "unwind" and relax as he spoke of his experiences. The child mentioned in the first chapter (and referred to in others), who appeared to be an autistic or schizophrenic child, seemed to benefit more from activities that provided him with an opportunity to work off some of his emotional tensions than from any other therapeutic aims. Among other activities in the play therapy situation, he took a doll which he called "mother" and made threatening gestures and angry sounds at it for long periods of time. The business-machine operator who had been injured in a serious automobile accident seemed to quiet down and perform more efficiently after he had had an opportunity to "blow off steam" about the terrible things that had happened to him. Even though, as will be pointed out later, he had suffered severe brain damage, he was able to mobilize the resources available to him more effectively when some of his excess tension had been dissipated.

Emotional release may be most helpful for clients who exhibit extreme anxiety as a result of a suppressed or repressed traumatic event. A case in point is that of a young college instructor who complained of terrifyingly bad dreams; in these dreams he almost invariably killed his younger brother. He also had an extreme startle reaction which manifested itself whenever he was surprised by a loud noise; at such times he would throw himself on the ground or under some kind of protection. This happened once when he was riding his bicycle along a busy street abutting the campus and two cars collided near him. He threw himself from the bicycle and crawled under a steel fence for protection. Needless to say, this behavior was a source of embarrassment to him, and his anxiety and tension were increased each time it occurred. During the first counseling session the counselor suggested the need for understanding the meaning of his dreams. The client interrupted to say that he knew why he had the dreams and that he had been trying to forget the events which he felt contributed to them. It developed that he believed he simply had to suppress thoughts concerning a chain of events which had occurred in his combat experience. He had not told anyone about them; he had wanted to tell his wife but had not done so because of his conviction that talking about them would refresh them in his memory. During the day, except when startled, he could control his tension and distract himself from the anxiety-provoking thoughts. He had become very skillful at busying himself with mathematical problems—he was a mathematician—and with other preoccupations whenever he was reminded of these thoughts. With a little encouragement he proceeded to tell about his experiences during a battle in which two American groups had taken a small town in western Germany. It seems that one group had approached from one side and the other from the opposite side, but, due to confusion in communications, neither group had known that the other was in the area. In approaching the town the client's platoon had stumbled upon a small detachment of German soldiers. After a brief skirmish they had taken most of them prisoners. Only a few of the Germans had been injured, but at least one was killed. The client noticed this one in particular. He was not sure, but it seemed likely that he had shot him. He was impressed by the boy's youth and remembers thinking that his own brother was not much older. In taking the town, the two American groups had accidentally lobbed some shells into each other's ranks, and it was believed that casualties had resulted from the confusion. Patrols from the two groups had met and firing was narrowly avoided. Finally, the groups had moved into the town, and much to the client's surprise, he encountered his brother. He had not known that his brother was in Germany, much less in this particular sector. That night he dreamed for the first time that he had killed his brother. He recalls having the very frightening thought that it could have happened—he could have accidentally killed his own brother. This thought was terrifying to him. If there was any subtle basis for his extreme concern, this was not at the level of awareness.

After telling the story, the client reported much relief from tension. He was encouraged to tell his wife about the experiences. On two subsequent visits to the clinic certain details were reviewed. The important fact is that the client's anxiety cleared up immediately, and for several years he has been completely free of the terrifying dreams and the startle reactions. It would certainly seem that he gained some clarification and understanding by telling the story to someone else. The counselor's objective calm and acceptance must have been helpful, but primarily it would appear that open discussion of the memories and the client's frank expression of feeling relieved him to the point where it was no longer necessary for him to express these emotional reactions in less direct fashion.

Another sketch will illustrate the applicability of release therapy in the case of an individual who has been conditioned to anxiety by the impact of a succession of tension-provoking, guilt-laden events. This client had spent his early life in an orphanage. He had hated the orphanage and had been forever dreaming of getting out, but when prospective foster parents had come to choose children whom they might adopt, no attention had ever been paid to him. Finally, when he was fourteen, he was taken by an elderly couple who agreed to give him a home and allow him to attend high school. He discovered almost immediately that they expected him to work for his maintenance. He was expected to get up very early to do chores before school, and to come home immediately after school to do the evening work. As a result he was not able to take part in school activities after school hours. He had resented this very much and when he was sixteen he had run away from the foster home. After some wandering he arrived in a large Eastern city, where he survived for a few days by sleeping in alleys, eating garbage, and begging. He was "rescued" from this life by a young musician who took him into his apartment and gave him food, clothes, and spending money. In return he was expected to be a homosexual partner. This was physically repulsive to him, and he was also quite anxious about his role. He had had a strong religious background in the orphanage and his behavior seemed sinful. In spite of this, he lived with his benefactor for two years.

Eventually, he had felt that he could endure the situation no longer, and he talked it over with the young musician, who understood and actually helped him to obtain a position as music librarian and band boy with an orchestra. He had a "high" time during the two years he traveled with this group. He learned to drink, developed strong interests in women, mostly prostitutes, and did some experimenting in the use of drugs. After that time he began to feel that he was wasting his life, that he was sinning and, generally, he had developed guilt reactions. As a consequence he left this position and took a modest but respectable government job. He left girls alone, joined a church group, and for almost a year, led a very "clean" life. As time went on, he began to be bored and to go out more. He became interested in a girl, and began to drink excessively. His salary would not maintain his new program, so he took a part-time job selling household appliances on a door-to-door basis. He was supposed to turn in his collections to the company, and then receive a commission. However, he spent his collections, and when the time of accounting came around, he owed the company several hundred dollars, which he could not pay. He was given twenty-four hours to pay up, or be arrested. During this time, he told his story to a friend, who advised him to leave the state. This he did, and returned to the Middle West.

There he turned over a new leaf in earnest. He secured a job, joined a church, and again began to live a "clean" life. He became concerned about his foster home and visited it. He learned that the woman had died and that the old man was quite alone and destitute. He felt that he had behaved shabbily to these people who made it possible for him to leave the orphanage. To make up, he took the elderly man into his own home and began to care for him. Through the church young people's group, he met a young lady to whom he became engaged. Meanwhile he was sending back a few dollars a week to pay off the debt he had run away from. He recalled this period as the happiest of his life. All was well until he went to a New Year's Eve party in a neighboring community. His fiancee had not been able to accompany him, so he had gone alone. For the first time in more than a year he had had a few drinks. These had led to more, and, to shorten a long story, he awoke on New Year's Day sharing the bed of a young woman who had been at the party. He had been quite remorseful over the episode, but had almost forgotten it when the young woman came to tell him that she was pregnant. This had been a severe blow, but he felt he had only one course of action open to him, and he married the girl. His wife was quite intolerant of the foster father, and made life so miserable for the old gentleman that he had left their home. She could not understand why she had to save so that the client could send money away to pay on the debt. The client found her very critical in other ways as well, and he finally came to the conclusion that he could not exist in the situation.

To escape, he joined the Army, and after a brief period of training he was sent to the Pacific. Soon after he entered the combat theater, he regretted his decision. He became extremely tense and anxious, and this resulted in a long series of hospitalizations—he was usually hospitalized because of some kind of gastrointestinal complaint. Eventually he was returned to the States and given a medical discharge with the diagnosis of "anxiety reaction." He hurried home with every intention and desire to make the best of his marriage. He resumed his old position and seemed to be moderately happy until he learned that his wife was pregnant for the second time. He then began to become tense again, and this was apparent to his associates at work. As a practical joke one of them slammed a large shovel down on a concrete floor just behind him. This so startled him that he turned and kicked the man, severely injuring him. As a result he lost his job. Soon afterward he was seen at an out-patient clinic, and found to be extremely tense and anxious, with tremulous hands, perspiring continually, and reporting that he was about to "blow his top."

A considerable amount of space has been devoted to this client to develop the history of his current reactions, because we believe that emotional release and tension-reduction treatment is essential for a person who has been thus conditioned to anxiety. Other aims may also be indicated but some form of release is absolutely necessary in order for the individual to function. This is likely to be the case for most persons suffering from acute anxiety reactions. The client in the above example was given an opportunity to talk out the series of experiences. This afforded temporary relief. He was helped in securing another position and a series of interviews was arranged. These were structured to give him a place to ventilate his feelings and tensions, both those arising from the past and those in the present. Gradually, he was encouraged to develop an interest in recreational activities, and he began to do woodwork in his spare time. These activities appeared to provide an avenue for some of his energy. He has continued to function effectively, with less and less overanxiety. He is now happy with his wife, they have four children, and at the moment it appears that his adjustment will continue. He has few resources with which to withstand trauma and unforeseen circumstances may upset him, but it appears reasonable to state that he has profited from release therapy, together with support and vocational counseling, with insight only incidental.

THE THEORETICAL IMPLICATIONS OF EMOTIONAL RELEASE

1. SIGMUND FREUD.   The role that emotional release plays in counseling is dependent upon the importance a particular theory of counsel-

ing or therapy places upon emotion as an etiological factor in maladjustment. In his initial work with Josef Breuer, Freud placed great emphasis on the role of emotion in both the development and cure of hysteria. In reporting the case of Anna O., Freud traced all her symptoms to emotions experienced while nursing her father, and in this connection they became intelligible as remnants of affective situations. The treatment was called the "cathartic method" [1] because it was believed that its efficacy was based on the mental and emotional purging that the client went through during the treatment process. The cathartic method assumes that in events which are highly charged with emotion, a pathological reaction can occur when the emotion, instead of being fully released, remains "bottled-up" or "hemmed-in" and so seeks an outlet through abnormal behavioral reactions. The principle is that if the emotion is expressed freely, a catharsis and relief will result. Breuer felt that he had established the fact that there is no sign or evidence of any reduction or weakening of the symptoms when the traumatic event is described without any emotional release. Later Freud developed the idea that reliving repressed emotional situations is not the only factor operating. As a result, he emphasized the role of the transference situation and suggested that a necessary part of effective emotional release was the client's inevitable feeling toward the analyst as a part of experiencing the appropriate emotion.

2. ALFRED ADLER.   In his thinking on emotion Freud placed a great deal of emphasis on the element of force. The words "impulse" and "drive" are commonplace in his writing. These words are sometimes modified by such attributes as sexual, aggressive, or libidinal, but even then the object of the force is only loosely differentiated. Freud spoke of love, but Adler spoke of love of power. In Adler's thinking on emotion the emphasis was placed on force as a direction. His concern was primarily with order and orientation as a part of human experience. He felt that everyone, in order to make sense out of the world and his relationship to it, avails himself of "guiding fictions," schemes of understanding and orientation, frames of reference, and modes of organizing experience. He believed that the healthy person regards these guiding principles as devices for making workable distinctions, which he does not take to be fixed and infallible in the process of living. In contrast, the individual who is mentally ill chooses an unworkable and unrealistic scheme, one which is inapplicable to the world but which he nevertheless rigidly maintains. For Adler, human behavior was purposeful as well as forceful. No human being, according to Adler [see Mullahy (17)], can think, feel, will, dream, without all these activities being determined and

---

[1] For further discussion of the development of thought concerning the cathartic method, see Brill (2), Hinsie (6), and Nuttin (18).

directed toward an ever-present objective. This concept recognizes that if the individual is to achieve emotional release, not only must the force find expression, but the expression must be in a direction satisfactory to the person within his conceptual framework. Adler also pointed out that if "guiding fictions" are changed, there may be no need for emotional release of the same kind that had previously been necessary. Finally, within this concept is the notion that a change in "guiding fictions" can make possible emotional release where it could not find expression before.

3. CARL GUSTAV JUNG. Jung (9) believed that in quite a large number of cases abreaction (the reliving of emotional experiences) is not only useless but actually harmful. For Jung, the essential factor in mental illness was the dissociation of the psyche, not the existence of a highly charged affect. Thus the main therapeutic problem was not abreaction but how to integrate the dissociation. He reasoned that a traumatic complex brings about dissociation of the psyche. The complex is not under the control of the will, and for this reason it possesses the quality of psychic autonomy. Its autonomy consists in its power to manifest itself independently of the will and even in direct opposition to conscious tendencies: it forces itself tyrannically upon the conscious mind. The explosion of affect is a complete invasion of the individual. Considered from this angle, abreaction is described as an attempt to reintegrate the autonomous complex, to incorporate it gradually into the conscious mind by living the traumatic situation over again. Jung suggested that there may be other factors essential to the process. Mere rehearsal of the experience does not in itself possess a curative effect—the experience must be rehearsed in the presence of the therapist or counselor. As the client confides his experience to an understanding and sympathetic counselor, his conscious mind finds in the counselor a moral support against the unmanageable affect of his traumatic complex. In other words, when the counselor lends him moral support as he attempts to combat the uncontrolled emotions, he no longer stands alone in his struggle. In this way Jung reasoned that the integrative powers of the conscious mind are reinforced until the client is able once more to bring the rebellious affect under control. The rehearsal of the traumatic moment is able to reintegrate the neurotic dissociation only when the conscious personality of the client is so far reinforced by his relationship with the counselor that he can consciously bring the autonomous complex under the control of his will. Only under these conditions was abreaction seen by Jung to have curative value. But the curative value does not depend solely on the discharge of affective tension; it depends far more on whether or not the dissociation is successfully resolved. It stands to reason that when dealing with behavior that is traumatically determined only to a minor degree, the cathartic method of abreaction will meet with poor success.

4. OTTO RANK.   Rank (19) described personality in terms of impulse, emotion, and will. The child brings into the world a primitive impulse life. This tends immediately to motor discharge resulting in a feeling of gratification. An impulse excitation passes through two phases of tension and discharge which the person experiences as pain and pleasure. As emotion gradually develops, there are pain-tension and pleasure-discharge, but the accentuation differs. The essence of emotion consists in wanting to preserve tension in order to prolong the pleasure phase until the point is reached when it becomes unbearable and has to be discharged. In Rank's thinking the emotional life corresponded to an inhibited or dammed-up impulse life. The damming up may come from external objects or from within, because the individual soon learns to make use of impulse-inhibition for the sake of developing emotion. For Rank, verbalization constituted the only emotional expression in the therapeutic situation. He saw it not only as a symbolic substitute for action or emotion but also as actually representing a rejection (putting out) of parts of the conscious awareness (ego) of the individual. In the therapeutic process the guilt reactions are separated out and put over onto the counselor. He becomes a dumping ground on which the client deposits his old neurotic ego and, in successful cases, finally leaves it behind him. Rank assumed that the guilt reactions are suppressed and are not ordinarily expressed even though the individual has some awareness of them. These feelings must be eliminated from the ego, so that there is no longer need to deny them, if the client is to gain relief. This is only possible if the counseling experience affords the individual a potential living-out of the suppressed or denied side of his personality. Rank's theory attached importance to different aspects of the ego which he called "impulse ego" and "will ego." These parts of the ego are conceived of as being in conflict, and for efficient function it is necessary for the individual to make a choice between them. If one aspect or the other is suppressed, this choice is difficult. Through the emotional realizing of the hitherto denied ego parts, the individual is in a position to compare and, on the ground of this comparison, to choose. Although this therapeutic release of the hitherto blocked portions of the ego is a substitute for real experience, Rank believed that it has value that can be carried over into real life experiences. Insofar as guilt feelings arise from self-reproach due to the repression of one side of life, the emotional experience of this repressed or denied side in the therapeutic situation relieves it, while the opposing source of guilt feeling, prompted by the fear of release and of actual experience, is transformed into self-responsibility by the choice opened up to the individual by the process.

5. SAMUEL R. SLAVSON.   Although Slavson's (24) theory of emotional release is essentially Freudian, it is presented here because of its

application in group counseling situations. He feels that one of the aims in the treatment of maladjusted children is to release the tensions created by the conflict rather than to increase them through constant correction, faultfinding, or punishment. In Slavson's groups, restraints are completely suspended, and the child feels free to behave without fear. He returns to a state of irresponsibility and infantile patterns, but because the group sets up a primary group code, he gradually reconstructs his impulses so as to be accepted by the counselor and the other members of the group. Slavson removes social control, judgment, and censure from the child. Indeed, the counselor feels he has succeeded rather than failed when the child who has shown evidences of inner tensions caused by inhibited aggressiveness and hostility expresses his aggressive tendencies freely. This is activity catharsis, and has been reported to be successful with neurotic children. The client throws over the tyranny of his conscience, feels the release of freedom of action—release—and becomes amenable to the influences of the group, the counselor, and later also of the wider culture. Thus a new and healthier conscience (superego) is built, devoid of fear and anxiety.

Slavson believes that activity balances emotional pressures because it serves some specific corrective needs of the client. Attack upon materials and surroundings by emotionally disturbed children proves, according to Slavson, quite conclusively that children redirect their hostility upon the inanimate environment in accordance with the principle of "dispersion of emotion" and gain considerable release in this way. While it might be thought that such unimpeded activity has only release value, Slavson insists that this is not the case, for a disturbed child, through being allowed to act as he pleases, feels assured of love and acceptance by the group. Unconditional acceptance serves to attenuate the client's hostility toward what he feels to be a persecuting and rejecting world. Free play and work, therefore, have no therapeutic value if carried on in isolation. Their value in therapy springs from the fact that others witness and do not restrain or punish. Hostile and aggressive acts have therapeutic value only when they are permitted, not merely because they are committed. A destructive act alone, therefore, does not satisfy the inner cravings to be loved. It is only when the act is accepted by some adult that it releases tension and sets the stage for emotional reorientation.

6. LEARNING THEORY AND RELEASE. According to D. Ewen Cameron (3), release, or unburdening by the client, is one of the best ways of desensitizing annoyances, frustrations, anxiety, and guilt. By verbalization in a nondirective, permissive atmosphere, the client learns to communicate better, as the fear of being criticized for his communications is reduced by each communication that has not been criticized. Cameron advocates three rules to be followed by the counselor: the com-

munication must be extensive, it must be intensive, and it must be sufficiently repeated. He believes that to communicate is to re-experience, and when an action tendency is re-experienced, the probabilities that it will be modified reach their maximum. Nonleading questions by the counselor are often needed to make communication as extensive as possible. The aim is to bring about in the client as complete emotional response as possible in the telling. Repeated communications about sensitive things should be brought about with the emotional tone accompanying the communication.

Shaffer (23) explains the emotional release that accompanies verbalization, not as a purifying process during which noxious elements of thought are got out of the system, but as a form of experimental extinction. Conditioned fears are extinguished by exposing the client to fear-producing stimuli, by talking about them in reassuring and nonthreatening circumstances so that the fears are not reinforced. In addition to the experimental extinction process, as the individual tells of his difficulties, he often experiences an adequate emotional response, which has previously been inhibited. He learns that he can openly express his fears, aggressions, and motives. This emotional expression is found to be tension reducing, as are, to some degree, all responses to emotional stimuli. Shaffer believes this to be especially valuable in bringing to the fore repressed and inhibited aspects of the client's experiences. He suggests that the client tell his story again and again, adding each time any additional information that is recalled. He believes this to be necessary to extinguish the conditioned responses, since extinction is achieved only by continued repetition over a period of time. If the clinician uses this purely cathartic approach, he should remain detached from the proceedings as much as possible, since the reconditioning and insight gained from repeated expression will effect the cure.

The viewpoint of Dollard and Miller (4) is quite like the two just described. So that the client may gain emotional release, the counselor seeks to supply a permissive setting in which the client can talk freely. Because his talking is not punished, he can talk about frightening experiences until through extinction they become no longer frightening. The extinction then generalizes so that the motivation to repress other painful experiences and topics is weakened. As the fears motivating repression are reduced, the client is urged to think about his problems, and his mental life is greatly intensified. The removal of repressions restores the higher mental processes, which in turn foster further fear-reducing discriminations, reasoning, foresight, hope, and adaptive planning. In other words, when emotional tension is relieved, the client can think and plan more intelligently.

Andrew Salter (21) totally rejects the concept of emotional release, as he thinks it fails to take cognizance of the blocking or restraining of emotions. He feels that normal emotional expression has been inhibited and that the idea of counseling is to unlearn habitual, conditioned, inhibitory reflexes by practicing deliberate excitatory (expressive) emotional responses that eventually become overlearned and are then conditioned excitatory emotional reflexes.

7. THEORIES OF COUNSELING OR THERAPY BASED ON RELEASE. In Jacob L. Moreno's (16) system emotional release is evolved from his emphasis upon spontaneity of action. He feels spontaneity propels an individual to make adequate responses to new situations and new responses to old situations. Anxiety results from loss of spontaneity, so the purpose of therapy is to teach the client to become more spontaneous. When the responses reach an adequate level of spontaneity, anxiety diminishes or disappears entirely.

David Levy (15) has categorized psychotherapy into *affect therapies*, which are aimed at feelings with little use of thought processes, and *insight therapies*, which are aimed at understanding the source of a conflict. In his work with children he (13) has achieved favorable results from release therapy involving the creation of play situations that facilitate the expression of the child's anxieties. When anxieties or symptoms are thought to have arisen from excessive demands or prohibitions at an early age, the play technique is aimed at restoring the situation and remobilizing the anxieties out of which the conflict arose. This experience is repeated until the child's fears are discharged, and the child is enabled to resolve his conflicts by completing his natural reactions, which had hitherto been inhibited by fear.

Levy's methodological principle of release therapy with children is simply the acting out of emotional feelings to relieve anxieties, thus permitting expansion of the child's personality heretofore constricted by premature or excessively severe discipline. With the interpretive function of the counselor reduced to a minimum, Levy has found that very young children are often relieved of symptoms apparently without knowledge of why they were brought to therapy. Levy (14) carefully specifies the type of case he selects for release therapy; the children are not suffering from circumstances existing in the present. In other words, in selecting his cases Levy avoids the deeper problems created by long-standing family complications and the presence of secondary gains from acquired symptoms. Release therapy is not applicable for all clients, and Levy considers the latter types of case in a very different light. In these the children are suffering less from symptoms than from their exploitation of them (using them to gratify deeper needs). For these children, insight therapy is needed to help the child understand the reasons for his behavior. The material elicited in free and structured play is interpreted to the child to help him achieve insight. Levy agrees with the concept of flexibility, stating that there are no universally correct formulas and that the therapist's approach must be modified by his understanding of the child's responses. Release therapy and insight therapy may be used in combination. As a prelude to insight therapy, it may be necessary to encourage release of repressed feelings and alleviation of guilt through their acceptance by the therapist.

Resembling Levy's release therapy is Joseph C. Solomon's (25, 26) active play therapy, a similar method of relieving the child of his condemning conscience by encouraging him to re-create a traumatic situation in play, drawing, painting, or other activities. Although interpretations are given in this type of therapy, they concern only the client's hostile feelings as they are expressed toward the counselor. The child's insight here seems to be secondary to the counselor's insight, for Solomon believes that play not understood by the counselor loses its value for the child. Levy has emphasized the value of play therapy in promoting release. He does not advocate its use to the exclusion of other forms of therapy; rather he clarifies its advantages and specifies the age groups and kinds of problems which appear to profit from this form of treatment. He believes that play itself is the therapeutic agent, a direct outlet for denied impulses and desires. The relationship between child and therapist is simply a tool by which the child fulfills this primary function of play. With the more severe neurotic clients, for whom Levy prescribes interpretive methods of analysis, the relationship becomes a sustaining source of strength which helps the child to gain insight into his repressed motives and feelings. Whether play therapy or interpretative methods are used, this relatedness that develops in the process of counseling is instrumental in the attainment of a further goal whose nature varies with each client.

8. INTEGRATING THE THEORIES. Each of the theories of emotional release discussed here offers possibly a way of thinking that is of practical use in counseling. Some of them complement others and agree in many respects, while others are quite different and seem to disagree on many major points. Faced with the obvious fact that emotions do exist and that emotional release is often of value in counseling, we may well ask the question, "What are the major contributions of these theories and can these contributions be placed together in one coherent way of thinking?" The major contributions of each theory can easily be given, but combining them is not simple.

The basic contributions of Freud are that emotion is a dynamic force and that it may be operative at different levels of awareness. Adler's contribution is that this force does not operate in a vacuum, that it is directed toward a goal within the individual's conceptual field of reality. Jung recognized that with some persons emotional release is valuable, while with others it does little good and at times it is harmful. Rank combined Freud's notion of drive with Adler's notion of direction and orientation, and maintained that a will is postulated, its purpose being to control the direction and the strength of the emotion. Salter and Moreno evolved an opposing idea that at least some disorders are not the result of "bottled up" feelings but rather the result of inhibited acts or expressions. Finally, Levy, along the same vein, stresses release through play as an outlet for denied impulses and desires. With these notions in mind the following comprehensive view of emotions and emotional release is offered.

Emotion is a function implicit in behavior, and it can be observed only indirectly in the overt activity of an organism. It is not the cause of act, nor is act the cause of emotion; they are concurrent and inseparable. The construct of emotion explains an aspect of activity. "Emotion" is a descriptive term used to define the force and direction of an organism moving within a field.

Since an individual is able to perceive his activity within a field, he is also able to perceive the force and direction of his activity within that field. In other words, since the individual can experience his activity, he can also experience feelings concurrent with his acting. Yet the human faculty of attention is a simple thing, and tends to concentrate on one thought at a time. If more than one thought receives attention, the thoughts are present at different levels of awareness. Thus it is possible that a state of imbalance is attained between an individual's awareness of acting and his awareness of emotion. In this way the individual, through selective attention, may be either more conscious of the force and direction of his activity or more conscious of the acting itself. A state of imbalance in this feeling-activity continuum may easily result in nonadaptive or maladjusted behavior. Failure to adjust will then cause an increase in attention. If this attention is directed toward that side of the continuum where overattention had caused the maladjustment, a cumulative effect may take place resulting in increased nonadaptive behavior. Depending upon which side of the emotion-activity continuum is characteristically at the higher level of awareness, emotional release will have different functions. For the individual who is preoccupied with his activity within his field, release makes it possible for him to discover and examine the motives and goals of his activity. For the individual primarily concerned with emotion, release would be emphasized. Thus in the first instance, counseling would be oriented toward enabling insight, and in the latter counseling would be a teaching-to-act process through conditioning procedures similar to Salter's, through increasing spontaneous activity as advocated by Moreno, or through play as suggested by Levy.

TECHNIQUES TO ENCOURAGE EMOTIONAL RELEASE

Through clinical practice over a period of years certain techniques have been discovered which tend to foster emotional release. Freud originally used hypnosis as a means of recalling thoughts to consciousness so that the individual could relive them along with adequate expression of appropriate emotions. This technique is still used by some to secure abreaction. Samuel H. Kraines (11) still works with hypnosis in therapy, but he feels it should be used as an adjunct rather than as a primary method of treatment. Margaret Brenman and Merton M. Gill (1) have also found hypnosis of value when it is accompanied by reintegration of the newly discovered material with the current life of the client. They point out a limitation of this method in that deep hypnosis is necessary except in cases of traumatic neuroses in which the trauma is recent. They report that even when the trauma is recent, hypnosis does not always produce lasting good unless the material revealed is properly solidified by conscious working out. Abram Kardiner and Herbert Spiegel (10) report more favorably on the use of hypnosis with acute traumatic war neuroses. They found that if the client is treated in an acute phase, it can be used to abreact the emotion and to suggest a means through which the patient can gradually gain control over his symptoms. In variations of this treatment drugs have been used instead of hypnosis. The procedure is then referred to as narcoanalysis or narcosynthesis.

A second technique originated by Freud is free association, which he considered to be superior to hypnosis because with its use repressed thoughts and feelings could more easily be incorporated into consciousness. In addition, it afforded him the opportunity to study the association of ideas and feelings more easily than was possible under hypnosis. This technique led to the discovery of the value of dreams and slips of the tongue as indicators of repressed emotion. These techniques are still in use today.

Maurice Levine (12) points out the value of simple confession and ventilation. He feels that religious confession can produce psychiatric results, that absolution can resolve feelings of guilt, and that in the telling of sins the responsibility for them is shifted onto the confessor. Ventilation consists of persuading and allowing the client to talk freely. The emphasis is upon conscious material. Levine believes that in some way the therapist can "universalize the guilt" associated with certain feelings. He refers to this as "dilution therapy."

In Rogers' (20) therapy the counselor encourages the client in the free expression of feelings about the problem, partly through his friendly attitude (receptive and interested) and partly through skill gained by experience. One of his primary aims is to avoid impeding the flow of hostile feeling. In play therapy, as in therapy with adults, the counselor accepts the client's feelings by responding not to the intellectual content of what the client is saying, but rather to the feeling behind it. He often verbalizes what the client is doing without interpreting it. The counselor limits himself almost entirely to verbalizing and clarifying what the client is attempting to express. Rogers maintains that it is dangerous to go beyond what the client has already expressed, so his aim is to completely accept the feelings and to verbalize them. Positive feelings and negative feelings are accepted in exactly the same manner. No attempt is made to emphasize positive feelings. It is believed that through the expression and clarification of feelings understanding of the self occurs. Emotional expression, in play therapy, is accepted in the same manner as in other counseling situations; however certain limits are set up—aggression toward a picture or clay model of the counselor is accepted, but direct aggression toward the person of the counselor is forbidden.

Thorne (27) advocates the use of passive methods whenever possible. Passive methods are usually the methods chosen by the counselor to permit emotional release in the early stages of counseling when the client is telling his story. Passive methods are preferred until the client is no longer able to progress by the use of passive methods alone. At this point directive methods are indicated. With clients whose symptoms result from emotional pressure and frustration, free expression of the emotions may dissipate emotional tension until the emotional tension or symptoms disappear. Emotional release has little effect on basic etiologic factors. Some psychoneurotic clients can talk continuously about their problems without diminishing their symptoms. Thorne describes emotional release as one of the palliative measures which may be helpful in relieving tension when the client is so agitated that no rational approach to his problems is feasible. Frequently it is necessary to offer relief to immediate symptoms before further counseling can be pursued. Thorne emphasizes the importance of the client's understanding that under ordinary circumstances these relieving techniques are not adequate to remove the cause.

The release of feelings can be encouraged by various individual and group play activities. Lauretta Bender in her work with children stresses the importance of play situations in which feelings can be expressed without guilt (22). The child, for example, may be able to do violence without embarrassment to a doll representing the father, but in an interview situation he would never allow himself to verbalize this feeling. Activities involving the use of the plastic arts, the graphic arts, puppetry, clay modeling, dancing, music, and group play have all been used as vehicles for emotional release. Added advantages of group play over individual play have been cited by Bender. She attaches importance to the conversation accompanying group play in which the children often point out one another's faults. In group play the counselor may encourage the discussion of fears and other emotional reactions. Bender believes that this social situation provides freer, more fertile associations and better catharsis than an interview situation, as well as the opportunity of experiencing the emotions of the other members of the group and of finding that one's own experiences have social value. She believes that the mere expression of unconscious fantasies has therapeutic value even though, admittedly, some workers feel an acceptance by the child of a verbal interpretation of his expressions is necessary. The production of a drawing which expresses aggression but which is accepted and valued by the counselor (thus avoiding guilt feelings) is of therapeutic value. Levy (13) has made use of the technique of doll play in both structured and unstructured forms. The dolls are used as objects for the release of hostility. When hostility is released, a reduction of guilt feelings is believed to occur. This allows the growth of other forms of response.

THE ENCOURAGEMENT OF RELEASE OUTSIDE THE FORMAL COUNSELING SITUATION

Techniques for release outside the counseling hour may be divided into three partially discrete categories: release through activity in interpersonal situations, release by the use of indirect or substitute devices for the expression of conscious feelings, and release through activities that give expression to more typically unconscious emotions.

The first method, release through activity in interpersonal situations, would include open expression by the client of feelings of hostility, anger, envy, and resentment against people in his everyday life. Occasionally the client can find someone who will accept his tendencies to dominate or to be dependent. Perhaps all that is necessary for him to achieve release is a minimum of support or persuasion. As effective as procedures of this kind may be as vehicles for emotional release, they are seldom used because they are often productive of guilt feelings that seem to reinforce the client's neurotic needs and behavior. If such techniques are used at all, the following precautions should be taken:

1. The counselor should be aware of implications in the life of the client.

2. The counselor should be prepared to prevent or minimize feelings of guilt.

3. The client should have some insight into the rationale of the prescribed behavior as well as some degree of awareness of the expected benefits.

4. Such direct expressions of feeling are usually advisable only with normal or slightly neurotic clients.

The second method for emotional release outside the counseling hour makes use of indirect or substitute devices such as play, physical exercise, work, various forms of expressive arts and crafts, books, movies, acting, and writing. All of these can be acceptable outlets for different emotions and permit "steam" to be released without harm to the client or to others. Levine (12, p. 86) cites an incident in which a specific outlet for a specific form of aggressiveness was provided. "A patient . . . had become nearly bald because she had the compulsion to pull out her hair. A brief analysis of her problems indicated clearly that the hair-pulling was an unconscious expression of an intense hatred of her mother and of her envy of her mother's beautiful hair. The symptom was lessened by the simple expedient of having her make crayon drawings of her mother in which the hair was very ugly." This unusual example is cited as illustrative of our point. It should not be inferred that one can generalize much from it since there are probably few clients who present a similar problem, and even if there were more, the solution would probably not be as simple.

Another example of such procedures is given by John G. Watkins (28), who attempts to demonstrate the value of "poison-pen therapy." As hostility dynamics begin to emerge, it is his practice to encourage the client to verbalize them by writing a "letter" which is not to be mailed, but which is to be brought into therapy to serve as the focal point of a discussion designed to clarify feelings. Fathers, mothers, and husbands all bear the brunt of the poison-pen treatment. He says, "There appears to be something about writing in the confines of one's own room which facilitates release even better than the treatment office. The slower speed with which the material can be recorded than spoken also extends the cathartic process, giving a longer period for the reliving of each expressed feeling." To date, Watkins reports he has used this device with nine cases. In six the results were very beneficial with considerable symptomatic improvement, two were not affected, and one grew worse.

The third category for emotional release outside the therapy situation embraces the various activities through which emotions are expressed more or less unconsciously. These can be grouped in a general way under the heading of sublimation. The reality of sublimation is confirmed by many clinical observations, though once again controlled research is lacking. According to Thorne (27) the principal problems in using sublimation in therapy are concerned with securing the proper conditions so that sublimation can take place. Clients with reasonably intact personality resources can usually work out their own provisions for sublimation, even though they may feel temporarily helpless. Adequate sublimative outlets do not come without careful planning and execution, nor do they come instantly, but once the client begins to find himself, progressive momentum will be built up. The problem is more difficult with clients who are neurotically or psychotically incapacitated and not able to get started alone. Then it may require considerable environmental manipulation, suggestion, and persuasion to get the client started on newer paths of living. Many examples could be given of sublimation, but they would be of value only for the purposes of illustration since effective sublimation for a given client is a very individual and personal activity. Certainly in life we see many demonstrations of both healthy and unhealthy sublimatory activities. A very satisfactory plan was evolved by one client who was frustrated in her desire to marry and have a family and in her strong need to accumulate personal possessions, have a home, and other "creature" comforts. She had been teaching school and was deriving some satisfaction from her associations with children. However after a few years of teaching it became obvious to her that she would never have a home she could call her own, and in contemplating a lonely life, at the end of which she would have few material belongings, she became exceedingly depressed. With encouragement she began to look around for something else to do and evolved the plan of starting a turkey ranch. Keen intelligence and hitherto undiscovered business ability enabled her to prosper exceedingly well. She conceived the idea of combining the ranch with a summer camp for underprivileged children and gained added satisfaction from this association with children. This once unhappy, discouraged, frequently ill person is now optimistic, cheerful, and self-confident, and possesses one of the nicest homes in her community; much to her gratification, it is always filled with friends. Unfortunately the economic success described in this illustration cannot come to all, but the satisfaction of important needs can usually be achieved if the efforts of both client and counselor are energetically directed toward the problem.

THE CONTROL OR REDUCTION OF OVEREXPRESSION OF EMOTIONS

Although most of our discussion up to this point has been concerned with emotional release, the overexpression of emotion also has a place in this discussion. Many individuals find their problems exaggerated by uncontrolled expression of emotionality. When they exhaust the patience of one listener or physician, they search for another. In this way they go down through the years talking profusely to anyone who will listen, without achieving even symptomatic relief. In fact, if they become "talked out" of one symptom, another quickly appears to take its place.

In relating their complaints, these whining, emotionally overexpressive, neurotic patients frequently develop a melodramatic manner, obviously adopted for its psychosocial effects. Thorne (27) strongly advises that these patients not be permitted to continue these hysterical emotional outbursts, especially when they are characterized by a complete cessation of voluntary attempts at control. He advocates almost any procedure that will convince the patient of the undesirability of his behavior. Great care should be exercised that such a measure is not viewed as a punitive device.

A type of control that is used with anxious or tense clients is muscular relaxation. Muscle tension often accompanies emotional problems and contributes to the client's symptoms by providing foci for new anxieties. Muscle relaxation exercises to relieve anxiety have been used for years. Many of these are founded on the system of Annie Payson Call which combines muscle relaxation, rest, and "mind training" for purposes of control. The best-known modern exercises are those of Jacobson (8), who reports that his method is very effective with cases of nervous hypertension, chronic insomnia, and depression. Muscle relaxation is also induced by massage, cold showers, and mild heat treatments. Ordinarily we regard the use of such techniques as purely palliative, and they are usually accompanied by some form of counseling. However there are cases in which reduction of tension by itself results in extensive behavior change and readjustment.

Severe anxiety sometimes breaks out in the course of counseling. Lewis R. Wolberg (29) states that handling intense anxiety reactions requires much fortitude on the part of the counselor. By assuming a calm, reassuring manner, the therapist provides the best medium in which the client can achieve stability. The therapist must constantly convey to the client a feeling of warmth, understanding, and protectiveness, at the same time respecting the client's latent strengths, which may have been overwhelmed by the turmoil. Helping the client to arrive at an understanding of the source of his anxiety promises the quickest possibility of relief. Where anxiety is intense, it is usually impossible to work with the client on an insight level. Here supportive measures are necessary to restore habitual defenses. Sometimes a change of environment may be necessary. If anxiety continues, the frequency of sessions may be increased and the client assured that he can reach the therapist at any time in case of a real emergency.

SUMMARY

Emotional release and tension reduction have been stressed as aims in counseling. It is recommended that they be employed for any or all of the following purposes: (a) simple palliation, (b) to prepare the client for other aims such as insight and re-education, (c) as an aim in and of themselves. The counselor should consider carefully how helpful release can be encouraged within the counseling situation, and he should aid and encourage the client to make healthy use of means of release and tension reduction in the everyday life situation. Theoretical points of view have been emphasized, and the case for release therapy has been presented. Unfortunately, methods and techniques are difficult or impossible to describe. The clinician will have to use his ingenuity and experience to plan for and encourage expression of feeling in his client whenever the need for it is indicated.

BIBLIOGRAPHY

1. Brenman, M., and Gill, M. M., *Hypnotherapy*. New York: International University Press, 1947.
2. Brill, A. A., *Freud's contribution to psychiatry*. New York: Norton, 1944.
3. Cameron, D. E., *General psychotherapy, dynamics and procedures*. New York: Grune & Stratton, 1950.
4. Dollard, J., and Miller, N. E., *Personality and psychotherapy*. New York: McGraw-Hill, 1950.
5. Glass, A. J., "Psychotherapy in the combat zone." *Amer. J. Psychiat.*, 1954, 110, 725.
6. Hinsie, A. E., *Understanding psychiatry*. New York: Macmillan, 1950.
7. Ingham, H. V., and Love, L. R., *The process of psychotherapy*. New York: McGraw-Hill, 1948.
8. Jacobson, E., *Progressive relaxation*. Chicago: University of Chicago Press, 1938.
9. Jung, C. G., *The practice of psychotherapy*. New York: Pantheon, 1954.
10. Kardiner, A., and Speigel, H., *The traumatic neuroses of war*. New York: Hoeber, 1947.
11. Kraines, S. H., *The therapy of the neuroses and psychoses*. Philadelphia: Lea & Febiger, 1941.
12. Levine, M., *Psychotherapy in medical practice*. New York: Macmillan, 1949.
13. Levy, D. M., "Release therapy in young children." *Psychiat.*, 1938, 1, 387–90.
14. Levy, D. M., "Trends in therapy, III. Release therapy." *Amer. J. Orthopsychiat.*, 1939, 9, 713–36.
15. Levy, D. M., "Psychotherapy in contemporary psychiatry (A symposium): psychotherapy and childhood." *Amer. J. Orthopsychiat.*, 1940, 10, 905–910.
16. Moreno, J. L., *Who shall survive?* Beacon, N.Y.: Beacon House, 1953.
17. Mullahy, P., *Oedipus myth and complex*. New York: Hermitage, 1952.

18. Nuttin, J., *Psychoanalysis and personality*. New York: Sheed & Ward, 1953.
19. Rank, O., *Will therapy*. New York: Alfred A. Knopf, 1936.
20. Rogers, C. R., *Client-centered therapy*. Boston: Houghton Mifflin, 1951.
21. Salter, A., *Conditioned reflex therapy*. New York: Creative Age Press, 1949.
22. Schilder, P., *Psychotherapy*. New York: Norton, 1951.
23. Shaffer, L. F., *The psychology of adjustment*. Boston: Houghton Mifflin, 1936.
24. Slavson, S. R., *The practice of group therapy*. New York: International University Press, 1947.
25. Solomon, J. C., "Active play therapy." *Amer. J. Orthopsychiat.*, 1938, 8, 479–98.
26. Solomon, J. C., "Active play therapy: further experiences." *Amer. J. Orthopsychiat.*, 1940, 10, 763–81.
27. Thorne, F., *Principles of personality counseling*. Brandon, Vt.: J. Clin. Psychol., 1950.
28. Watkins, J. G., "Poison-pen therapy." *Amer. J. Psychotherapy*, 1949, 3, 410–18.
29. Wolberg, L. R., *The technique of psychotherapy*. New York: Grune & Stratton, 1954.

CHAPTER

6

Supportive Relationships
and Activities

THE CONTRIBUTION OF SUPPORTIVE RELATIONSHIPS TO THE EFFEC-
tiveness of human functioning, although not often recognized as
such, is probably as old as mankind. Man has derived support
from his relationships with his kind since the earliest use of language, if
not before. The very nature of clustered dwellings brings support, as do
different forms of government and leadership. The witch doctor of primitive cultures, through his prestige and his advice and guidance, was a
source of support for those influenced by him. The churches and their
clergy have offered moral and spiritual support to church members of all
faiths. The security that religion gives to a believer is undoubtedly the
most important source of support which has been available to human beings in the history of our civilization. Persons find further security and
support from many other groups and from participation in various activities. We gain support from our fraternities, our clubs, our lodges, and our
professional or social societies. Our self-confidence is bolstered by identifying with our schools, our political organizations, and from the feeling of
belonging in worker groups. We feel good because of all our social supports from the church and the state down to our families; the family
structure provides the most personal and intimate supports for most persons, and it is a source of security which in our society is one of the more
essential supports.

Unfortunately, many of us cannot achieve sufficient support from
the more "natural" kinds of associations and must turn elsewhere for
help. One available source is psychological counseling and therapy. In
this chapter we will emphasize that the offering of support is an important

and legitimate aim of psychological counseling. Whereas some writers (1, 10) contrast supportive techniques with "reconstructive" or deeper therapeutic techniques, we regard support as a supplement to other counseling aims and, in many instances, as an aim in its own right. Support is herein regarded as the utilization of any one or of a group of techniques that tend to give the client an uplifting or "shot in the arm," either for the moment or over a longer period of time, by altering in some fashion his adequacy or effectiveness in meeting life as he views and meets it from day to day. Therapeutic support is often used to make the client more secure and self-respecting in the counseling situation so that he can gain greater benefit from counseling through trust or participation, and/or it may be intended to generalize to the functioning of the client outside the counseling situation.

In the last analysis one of the principal goals of psychological counseling is to provide the client with a sense of security and self-reliance which will carry through all his behavioral reactions. This sense of security may come from within, or it may be a function of supportive relationships provided for, or utilized by, the client. The support that comes from within may be a direct or indirect result of counseling, but frequently a counselor must actively encourage and direct the client in the development of such inner supports. David Riesman (11), in his provocative book *The Lonely Crowd*, has elaborated upon the theme that there is cause for alarm in the fact that members of our society do not have adequate "built-in," inner value systems and are leaning too heavily upon mass media, which may influence our way of thinking and being in a detrimental fashion. The present stress in our modern culture on group thinking and group "doing," from nursery school years into adulthood, may actually serve as a deterrent to an individual value system—offering support and a form of security in one sense, but at the same time robbing the individual of "inner" support and security. Individuals have a need to feel secure: they need the acceptance of others, and they need to feel safe from being hurt by others. Programs purporting to fulfill this need will gather followers, whether they are based on rational plans or sheer suggestion. It is a part of the task of the counselor to help his client develop a rational plan for deriving healthy, socially acceptable support from his activities and his associations.

Although supportive counseling is most often seen as complimentary and supplementary to other aims of counseling, we wish to stress again that support may be the most important, and at times the only factor, that is necessary to enable clients to function efficiently and happily. Let us consider, for example, a young person whose home has been broken, who has spent half of his life with one parent and half with another, who has gone to a new or different school every year, who has never had the opportunity to develop a group of friends, and who is confused about many questions of value, morality, and ethics. Can insight into, or awareness of, the many aspects of his chaotic life be of striking value to this person? Insight into, or understanding of, the situation or of self would appear inadequate alone. If, however, he can decide upon a program of training and ultimate work which is interesting to him, and if he can begin to form associations with persons interested in some of his personal objectives, he may begin to feel a purpose and a central theme around which he can organize his behavior. He may develop a code of ethics about his work and perhaps subsequently a set of personal values. As he succeeds in his work and gains in reputation and stature with his colleagues, his self-confidence will increase and he will continue to feel more secure. Then he will make closer associations with people and probably acquire a family, a community, and a church. Thus, our hypothetical client may develop into a healthy, efficient, happy adult.

Often the healthy trends just described will occur without the intervention of a counselor. Frequently, they can be expedited by a counselor, and sometimes they may never occur without counseling or therapy. We will now turn to a discussion of the various aspects of support as an aim and as an adjunct of psychological counseling.

THE EMPHASIS UPON THE RELATIONSHIP ASPECTS OF PSYCHOLOGICAL COUNSELING

The function of support as a self-conscious aim in psychological counseling and therapy probably received its earliest formal recognition from Rank, whose concepts were discussed at length in an earlier chapter.[1] Rank placed considerable emphasis upon the client-counselor relationship as the chief therapeutic agent. Following Rank, the foremost proponents of relationship counseling or therapy were Frederick H. Allen, Jessie Taft, and John Levy. Many of their ideas and practices culminated in the development of some aspects of Carl Rogers' counseling. Although Rogers sees self-understanding and self-acceptance as the goal of his counseling process, we question whether many of these benefits, as well as additional effects, are not the result of the warmth and absence of threat which are characteristic of the relationship between a client-centered counselor and his client.

In writing about emotional release as a function in therapy, Allen (3) suggests that mere release of feeling has little therapeutic value; it is the use and direction of feelings which constitute growth. It is clear that Allen's concept of growth goes beyond simple release of feeling to what is basically a learning or re-educative phenomenon. Our present concern is with the emphasis upon the supportive relationship in counseling,

[1] *See* pp. 75-8.

which is the principal therapeutic tool utilized by Allen. We must note carefully that Allen's objective is not the mere removal of distressing symptoms. He describes his concept of counseling as applicable where change in the subject's personality is the goal. His concept of counseling is more than a specific approach geared to clients with more or less specific symptoms. It is a philosophy or theory of individual growth of sufficient generality to be useful with a larger group of clients with varied symptoms. It departs from the usual analytic concepts; with a flavor of Rankian and later Rogerian thought, Allen speaks of counseling as a growth experience established around the child's own present feelings toward himself, with a counselor whose goal is to help him make more creative use of his potentialities, to achieve a more positive acceptance of himself and a capacity to relate himself to others. It is a process of self-discovery made possible in his relationship with his counselor, who helps him to a healthier way of being himself.

Allen (4, p. 54) disapproves of genetic approaches because he feels that the use of the counseling relationship to reactivate earlier experiences and the interpretation of present phenomena in terms of past relationships may complicate the growth process by binding the child more to the very past that aids him to avoid the realities of the present. Since the neurotic client is too tightly bound to the past, it is the task of the present experience to unburden him from those destructive aspects of the past and "to help him affirm certain positive values in that past which he may have denied." Allen points out that the past has aspects of safety which protect the individual from the necessary realities of the present. While he reiterates his belief that "growth-inducing" values lie not in probing the past but in emphasizing the client's role in making more creative use of his assets, he recognizes that the client's talk about his past is almost essential and that the client will usually react to the counselor as he has reacted to others in his past. It then becomes the counselor's responsibility to maintain the reality aspects of the present, including himself, to help the client recognize the immediacy of his relationship with the counselor, and to avoid being drawn into the past to the exclusion of the here and now. When the client reactivates the past, he does it in a present relationship that changes the meaning of former feelings. The counselor must help the client to use his recollections of the past to form a more realistic evaluation of the present self.

Therapy is not just the application of a technique or the giving of insights but a living experience (4) in which the client is helped to help himself by participating in determining his own change. It begins when the client brings the counselor into a relationship out of which the client achieves a new sense of his own worth. Growth is a process of individuation of the real self which Allen tends to regard [as do Snygg and Combs (13)] as a perceptual differentiation of the self from others and the present from the past self. It is not a process of manipulation by the counselor, for such a process would violate the basic principle of growth and the belief in the individual's inherent capacities for mature acceptance of himself and relatedness to others. To encourage a process of individuation of the real self, the counselor must be constantly sensitive to what the client is doing, for it is through this positive client-counselor relationship that direction and meaning are given to the changes that the client effects in himself. What Freud called "resistance" and Rank, the "will," Allen accepts as the core of strength from which will emanate a new attitude toward the self. The phenomenon of projection is considered important as the means by which the client uses the counselor to symbolize the unacceptable parts of himself (4). Through repeated projection and reality testing of the feelings expressed, the client begins to find his assets and, with the counselor's support, to accept his limitations. The changes that the client is able to effect in himself depend on the feeling he can express in relating himself to the counselor. Allen cautions the counselor against distraction by verbal content when the real raw material of the therapeutic process is the client's feeling, in particular his positive feeling toward himself. The counselor's primary function in the client's growth is to support and clarify, and always to help the client toward a more realistic definition of and acceptance of himself.

Jessie Taft (14, pp. 75–7), who employs Allen's principles in her therapeutic case work, writes more about the technique:

> In my opinion, the basis of therapy lies in the therapist himself, in his capacity to permit the use of self which the therapeutic relationship implies, as well as his psychological insight and technical skill. . . . In the last analysis, therapy as a qualitative affair must depend upon the personal development of the therapist and his ability to use consciously for the benefit of his client the insight and self-discipline which he has achieved in his own struggle to accept self, life, and time as limited, and to be experienced fully at the cost of fear, pain, loss. I do not mean that knowledge is not necessary, that technical skill is not necessary. They are. But they are of no value therapeutically without the person.[2]

Taft's comments leave the impression that in relationship treatment the counselor takes a more active role and is freer to express his own personality than in the more theoretically bound analytic procedure.

It is difficult, for purposes of comparison, to pin down the tools and techniques of Allen's procedures. The relationship and participation features bear strong resemblance to Sullivan's technique, but Allen's ap-

[2] From "The Time Element in Therapy," by Jessie Taft, *American Journal Orthopsychiatry*, 1933, 3, 65–79. By permission of the editor.

proach is not psychoanalytically oriented. The dynamic experience of growing in a relationship, without interruption or reversal of direction necessitated by prolonged probing for infantile genesis, gives a progressing, ongoing, forward-moving quality to Allen's idea of counseling. It is an educative rather than an analytic exercise. It includes and emphasizes release of feelings as their expression is cushioned in the counseling relationship and clarified by the counselor in terms of the individual's growth to maturity. "Insight," as an awareness of cause-effect relationship, recedes in significance as unfolding of feeling and creative growth become the quintessence of successful counseling. So complete is Allen's reaction against genetic, analytic understanding that he neglects discussion of insight, preferring to think more in terms of self-awareness. Interpretation is referred to as clarification, and apparently deals more with feelings than with thought. Feelings are not emphasized in terms of their past source but because of their implication for the present relationship. The cause and effect components of what we have defined as insight might here refer either to the relationship or to the individual. Perhaps the most growth-inducing awareness concerns the reasons for, and consequences of, certain feelings arising out of the various specific or general aspects of the relationship. This type of awareness is, of course, of a limited, focal nature. The other kind of insight, to which Allen refers only parenthetically, may well concern those feelings from the past which the client spontaneously expresses. Allen does not seem interested in *why* such feelings were first elicited, but rather in what use they serve in the present and in their effect on the child's present attitudes toward himself and toward the counselor.

Although Allen prefers to think in very general terms such as "self-definition" and "self-evaluation," these phenomena would be unlikely to occur without some variety of insightful awareness. Allen, rather than specifying precisely the type of awareness which occurs, is more concerned with what the child does with awareness, the uses to which he puts his new knowledge of himself. The means used to achieve this knowledge are not labeled and are not concretized, hence to the present writer, not fully communicated. Something must mediate between catharsis (expression of feeling) and the attainment of self-understanding, and this may well be insight. Of course the fact that Allen deals principally with children has greatly influenced his thinking. It may be argued that, as Anna Freud [see Hendrick (7)] pointed out, the child whose ego is undeveloped, and whose problems are less of his own creation than are those of an adult, is incapable of experiencing the insight one might expect from an adult. She believes that the problems of the child are as amenable to resolution by educative as by analytic techniques. In her terminology, then, the process described by Allen seems designed to foster the child's ego development. To this end, it implies a predominately supportive function, which presumably furnishes the child with the most healthy and satisfying relationship he has yet experienced.

John Levy [*see* Durkin (6)], in relationship counseling with children, has used a modified technique in accordance with his more analytic approach. He believes that interpretation of the relationship is essential. The counselor points out all the unconscious attitudes that have been repressed because of the anxiety associated with them and later displaced or expressed indirectly to protect the child's ego. Levy realizes the necessity of giving reassurance or building ego strength when feelings are pointed out. When the child tries out on the counselor all the attitudes he typically experiences in his day-to-day relationships, the counselor points out to the child his real needs; and, by maintaining a constant feeling toward the child, he clarifies the inappropriate attitudes, which the child finally abandons, being then free to function more fully. In such a relationship the "distortions" to which the child reacts are not counted against him. Thus an insightful relationship is clarified between the child's expressed feelings, as elicited by his expectations derived from past experience, and the realities of the present relationship in which these feelings are unwarranted and inappropriate.

SUPPORTIVE PROCEDURES AND PSYCHOANALYSIS

In describing the historical development of supportive treatment, Thorne (15, p. 180) points out that "although psychoanalysis is the antithesis of supportive therapy, Freud recognized that methods other than depth analysis may be effective in ameliorating a disorder." [3] He further indicates that Freud recognized multiple causation as being involved in the etiology of the neuroses and that the existence of neurotic behavior depends upon the total load upon the nervous system and its capacity to maintain this load. Consequently, Freud is quoted as indicating that anything that can keep this factor below a certain threshold, or bring it back below it, is effective therapeutically. Freud apparently believed that there is a quantitative relationship between etiological factors and that these factors can replace each other in quantitative terms. Thus, if one factor is alleviated, the total effect of the etiological factors may fall below the neurotic threshold and the client may be relieved to some degree. Freud stressed that anything that attacks any of the factors causing a neurosis is good in a therapeutic sense. Although Freud undoubtedly regarded supportive treatment as superficial in comparison with the depth approach of analysis, he appears to have acknowledged that supportive procedures

[3] From *Principles of Personality Counseling* by Frederick C. Thorne. Copyright 1950 by Frederick C. Thorne. Reprinted by permission of the author.

do attack some etiological factors, and to have given a degree of credence to such procedures.

Alexander (1) indicates that supportive measures are knowingly or inadvertently used in all psychotherapy. He divides therapeutic techniques into two groups: the supportive and the reconstructive. He places the heaviest emphasis on insight (or emotional re-education) and stresses that some degree of insight is almost never absent in any beneficial psychotherapeutic approach. Even though an academic distinction is made between the supportive and reconstructive procedures, actual practice does not follow such a distinct line. Since transference is a characteristic aspect of psychoanalysis, and since regression to the dependent attitudes of one's early years is a constant aspect of transference, this regression has a supportive effect on the client. The client is apt to stay clear of adult responsibility and decision-making by simply retiring into a dependent attitude toward the analyst. This dependency on the analyst as an aspect of the transference situation may be advantageous or disadvantageous. Consequently the relationship should be carefully controlled. Alexander suggests that support reduces emotional tension and increases the client's natural integrative capacity. On the other hand, it would seem that some clients simply give in to the dependency situation and have no motivation to make active attacks on their problems. Alexander believes that primarily supportive measures are indicated when the client is under acute emotional stress. He lists five procedures that constitute the core of supportive treatment: (1) gratification of dependency needs, (2) abreaction, (3) intellectual guidance, (4) support of neurotic defenses, (5) manipulation of the environment or life situations.

Support is of course a part of psychoanalytic therapy as well as of most other approaches to counseling and therapy. It may be considered as basic to the treatment process or as a necessary adjunct. In either case, the promotion of support is an aim of planned psychological counseling, and it will be helpful to examine some of the ways in which the client may gain such support.

ENVIRONMENTAL MANIPULATION AS A SUPPORTIVE DEVICE

Environmental manipulation can be very supportive for a client, in that alterations in the environment often serve to neutralize or counteract the development of extreme behavioral reactions. If an individual is being made anxious and tense by his vocation, by members of his family, by conditions in his family situation or in his marriage situation, or even by the location of his dwelling, changes in these conditions may make life more satisfactory and livable from day to day—thus reducing his anxiety. Although we discussed environmental manipulation as a treatment aim in its own right, the supportive aspects of changing the environment in which the person functions cannot be overlooked.

In the past, social case workers and psychiatric case workers have probably accomplished the most in this type of work. Jeanette Axelrode (5) has discussed the "old-fashioned case worker" who knew nothing of personality therapy, but was nevertheless able to deal successfully with many children simply by providing realism in the form of wholesome activities such as trips to the circus and to the zoo—recreational activities in the company of the case worker, who had a real, deep, personal attachment to, and interest in, the child. Giving a child real and warm affection, trusting and respecting him and providing wholesome activities may counteract tendencies toward delinquent and maladjustive behavior. The steady devotion and interest of an adult may offer support to a child which would not be possible in interview therapy or formal counseling.

The psychological counselor need not feel that he is confined to his office; he should be willing to take advantage of practical opportunities of showing interest in his client by joining him in appropriate activities. We once spent many hours with a twelve-year-old client in a woodworking shop. Other counselors had tried and failed to establish a relationship with this boy in an office situation, but in the shop, where he felt more secure, he was able to reveal and discuss many of his personal problems. The playroom can certainly be construed as a supportive situation for many children, and much of the activity therapy in hospitals owes its success to the security feelings developed by successful participation in various activities. The counselor may also find it possible to search out supportive relationships for his client in his real life environment. He may encourage teachers to take an interest in a child, he may recommend participation in group activities such as the Boy Scouts, or he may encourage church participation. Such examples should suffice to show the relationship between environmental manipulation and supportive therapy. These aims, as do all our aims, overlap in many ways.

THE SUPPORTIVE ASPECTS OF REASSURANCE

Reassurance is one of the most frequently used techniques in supportive counseling, but it is also one of the most delicate to manipulate properly. To use reassurance beneficially, the counselor must find all conditions propitious, use it with complete honesty and sincerity, and realize fully the exact amount that will be acceptable to the client. The very nature of the client-counselor relationship can afford great reassurance, especially if the client finds security, self-respect, and a sense of well-being in the presence of the counselor. Reassurance is most often used for supportive purposes at the beginning of counseling, to strengthen the relationship or to relieve the intensity of the anxiety that the client may feel. The initial anxiety of the client is, understandably, usually severe. He may be anxious about the relationship and fearful of the new experience. In many instances the client has referred himself because his anxiety has become so intense that he feels he needs help. The counselor may be able to give his client greater confidence in himself as an individual, in his counselor, and in the counseling relationship in general by the judicious use of reassurance.

Reassurance, if it is carefully, tactfully, and appropriately used, is also a potent force in alleviating anxieties that build up suddenly during the counseling process. Verbal reassurance can consist of pointing out to the client his positive abilities, his attributes, and other positive forces with which he has to work. It may take the form of stating an honest understanding of the client's problems, at the same time pointing out that his situation is by no means unique. Gains or progress in adjustment can be pointed out. The proper structuring of the plan of the counseling process during the early sessions provides a form of reassurance. Reassurance can be supportive—by alleviating fears and notions the client may have about "going crazy," "having an inherited mental illness," "having a malignant disease," or "being stigmatized for life."

Julian B. Rotter (12) holds that the client requires several types of reassurance. He must first be reassured that his problems are genuine and that he is justified in seeking psychological help. He must be reassured of the potential value of counseling and of the wisdom of seeking help. He must be assured that some value can be had from talking about his problems; that his attitudes, fears, and concerns are related to problems; and that these concerns are sufficiently important to justify his spending time, and on occasion money, in an attempt to effect a change.

A second mode of reassurance is used in attempting to build up the client's expectation that counseling will be successful. This type of reassurance helps the client to continue counseling, and increases the potential of alternative behaviors so that he will attempt new ways of dealing with his problems. Social learning therapy (of which Rotter is an advocate) emphasizes more than do most counseling approaches the use of reassurance to provide the client with satisfying alternatives before he is willing or able to give up his defenses. As the client learns to be more trusting of the counselor, he accepts the counselor's assurances that there are more satisfying ways of dealing with his problems and he will try some of them. Assurances must be given in general terms and in terms of the possibilities and probabilities, so that the client will be prepared for setbacks in his search for a better adjustment. As new behavior is tried out and success met, reassurance is strengthened.

In a third type of reassurance the client is made to understand directly that a specific goal can be reached. Its purpose is to convince him that he need not avoid attempts to reach the goal for fear of failure. Two cautions are inserted here: the counselor should avoid conveying the impression that he views the situation as no problem at all, and he should avoid this type of reassurance when the client obviously mentions an inadequacy in order to obtain reassurance. Individuals often seek reassurance regarding potential ability as a substitute for accomplishment. It then becomes the counselor's task to point out the potential and to show the client that it is his responsibility to make attempts to reach his goals, rather than using neurosis as an excuse for not dealing with problems directly. Toward termination of counseling the client may seek reassurance about his ability to solve future problems. He may try out his success in the later stages of counseling by extending the time between appointments. Rotter (12, p. 365) summarizes his remarks on reassurance as follows:

> Reassurance, then, from the social learning point of view is actually a direct reinforcement made by the therapist, or perhaps it should be called an event, the occurrence of which increases the expectancy for future reinforcement for some specific or general pattern of behavior.[4]

Thorne (15) calls reassurance *symptomatic therapy* in which certain superficial needs of the client are satisfied so that some of the factors most disturbing to the client can be dealt with. He lists some of the most elementary types of reassurance:

1. Reassurance that the individual's case is not unusual.
2. Reassurance that the nature of the condition is known.
3. Reassurance that the symptoms are annoying but not dangerous.
4. Reassurance that something can be done.
5. Reassurance that cure is possible.
6. Reassurance that he is not going "crazy."
7. Reassurance of setbacks, when the client thinks he is getting worse.
8. Reassurance that the client is not sinful or blameworthy.

Reassurance should not be given too frequently. Thorne feels that the safest technique is to allow the client to express himself completely, and then to offer reassurance to strengthen the insights and new behavior patterns as they develop during the course of counseling. Reassurance is most effective when it is applied on behavioral as well as verbal levels— actions speak louder than words. Most clients need to be reassured that they are receiving the best available treatment; some counselors use the

---

[4] From Rotter, Julian B., *Social Learning and Clinical Psychology*. Englewood Cliffs, N.J. Copyright, 1954, by Prentice-Hall, Inc.

cost of treatment—others impressive offices and elaborate methods—to reassure the client of the prestige and success of the counselor. Specific fears and anxieties should be dealt with factually and directly. If the counselor is doubtful or evasive, it may cause the client's insecurity to mount. "Affective reassurance" is the term applied by Thorne to the reassurance emanating from the smiling, friendly, noncritical manner of the counselor. Suggestible individuals benefit greatly from reassurance. It is quite useful with children; the younger they are, the more suggestible. Reassurance is very effective with mental defectives. Clients starting out on new adjustment patterns may need constant reassurance.

The use of reassurance has been criticized on the grounds that its effects are superficial and do not reach the appropriate mechanisms. However criticism of it has more often been directed toward its unskilled use rather than toward its value. Louise D. Laing (9) describes the use of verbal and nonverbal reassurance. More skill is required for verbal reassurance and more damage may result from its inept use. Nonverbal reassurance may take the form of mere silence on the part of the counselor when the client expresses self-condemnation. Relieving the client of his feelings of peculiarity, showing respect for him, giving him responsibility for his own improvement, and reminding him of his positive feelings are all forms of verbal reassurance.

George A. Kelly (8) classifies reassurance and support under the general title of "palliative techniques." He calls reassurance an expedient to be used so that the client's ideas appear at the time to be plausible, this procedure operating as an aid until a more substantial structure can be built. Reassurance temporarily reduces anxiety, but Kelly does not feel that this is necessarily undesirable in a counseling relationship. He does feel that the counselor must know how to use reassurance. He cautions that it may backfire if the counselor attempts to allay the client's fears by assuring him that future events will progress smoothly and then later the reverse occurs. If this happens the client will probably become reluctant to put faith in the counselor's reflections of reality. To use Kelly's terminology, reassurance has value in maintaining the client's "faulty constructs" until he can develop more adequate ones. Apparently Kelly feels that having a faulty construct is better than having no construct at all.

Methods promoting reassurance in the client may be used to further the client's confidence in his counselor. This may be achieved by predicting outcomes, as for example "You will probably feel a bit depressed the next day or so, but you will begin to feel better after that." Likewise postdictions may aid—"You have been feeling upset over this, haven't you?" All new and anxiety-laden material the client reveals should be accepted with no sign of approval or disapproval. Imposition of value labels, such as "You are right" or "That is fine," should be avoided, because they commit the client to a position that he cannot change without appearing inconsistent. The counselor's acceptance of any values elicited does not necessarily mean that he concurs or agrees. Because Kelly believes that reassurance always tends to slow up the immediate progress in the counseling or therapeutic situation, he feels that it should be used only when the counselor is willing to accept this slowing up. It may be used when counseling is progressing so rapidly that the client does not have a basic structure upon which he can depend. Reassurance may be used to let the client know that his ideas "are not silly." It may be used to control anxiety between sessions, or to keep an "important chain of associations" going during the interview. It may also be used in traumatic situations. Kelly cautions that reassurance may be "habit forming" and encourages its careful use.

Kelly further differentiates between support and reassurance. He defines support in terms of the responsiveness of the counselor to the client. He advocates that the counselor build up a repertory of response patterns that will offer support to his clients. He suggests that a primary support technique is promptness in keeping appointments. This should hardly require discussion, since the client who has been "stood up" can scarcely be expected to feel very secure in his relationship with his counselor. Another relatively simple technique is to recall clinical material of previous meetings at appropriate times. The client will feel support in knowing that the counselor remembers what took place in the previous session. Support is also offered if the counselor can respond to communications in the way the client anticipates or hopes. Such responses provide the client with support for the plausibility of his way of thinking. The above examples of responsiveness to the client should suffice to illustrate how both verbal and nonverbal reassurance can be supportive to the client.

Despite the fact that reassurance as a counseling technique is held in disrepute by some counselors, its usefulness should be apparent. Actually, reassurance itself is seldom dangerous or disadvantageous. It becomes undesirable only through misuse, by overassurance or nonfactual or baseless reassurance. Honest, sincere, factual reassurance can hardly be considered undesirable. Finally, there is also the possibility that withholding reassurance may actually be damaging to the client. Reassurance may be necessary on some *occasions,* and when properly used, it is a powerful counseling tool.

SUGGESTION AND ADVICE AS SUPPORTIVE TECHNIQUES

Suggestion and the giving of direct advice are techniques similar to reassurance and should be used with the greatest caution. In nearly all counseling relationships the counselor is a figure of authority to his client. Consequently, even offhand suggestions of alternative behavior patterns or remarks not intended as suggestions may do great harm to the client if they are not carefully thought out. A client is very apt to select from the total content of what the counselor says some single point that fits his needs as he sees them, and by taking the point out of context, he sometimes alters the "suggestion" to the extreme—he interprets the counselor's remark very differently from the way the counselor intended. Often a client will take a statement and read into it broad implications that were not intended, acting upon it in accordance with his own desires. It is also possible for a counselor to voice suggestions as strict injunctions that are intended to "make" a client react in a specific, precalculated manner. If the client views the counselor as a figure of strict authority, he may take such suggestion well—occasioning the removal of some deep symptoms—due to his need to abide strictly by the word of the authority figure in the counselor. Submission to and identification with an omnipotent authority figure plays a profound part in such instances. It is clear that in such a relationship the counselor must use extreme caution and have explicit knowledge of exactly what he is doing and how his client will react. Suggestion is sometimes used in periods of immediate anxiety or depression when it seems imperative for the client's mental or physical well-being. It is probably true that suggestions of the type discussed here function best when client defenses are weak and when the drive to operate in a symptom-free manner is a potent force. Symptom removal itself can alter one's total adjustment, and symptom removal can derive from suggestion, which is supportive. But suggestion, like any other technique, must be used with the greatest care and with full awareness on the part of the counselor of his own self-interests, of the specific relationship, and of the specific client. There are occasions when the client is in definite need of expert advice, and if the counselor is qualified by experience and knowledge to offer advice, he should feel free to do so. If the psychologist's training stands for anything, he should be qualified to offer constructive advice on occasion.

SUPPORT THROUGH PRESSURE AND COERCION

Pressure and coercion are two methods—used in conjunction with extreme authority on the part of the counselor—that are employed to bring specific rewards or punishments to the client in order to motivate him toward specific behavior or action patterns. Thorne (15) emphasizes that these two techniques are most useful in dealing with clients who live in extreme dependency and can function effectively and adequately only under rather extreme authority. They are also found useful in dealing with clients who are somewhat immature and tend to act out their problems, who nearly always fail to face reality, who proceed into emergency situations endangering themselves or others, who have little control over their emotions, and who will not adopt any decisive action pattern, and in situations where other methods have not been effective. It should be remembered that at all times permissive techniques should be exhausted before coercion is tried in counseling. Relative to such pressure techniques, Wolberg (16, p. 24) states:

> Pressure may be exerted in the form of assigned tasks. Thus, Herzberg advises that tasks be assigned the patient which are directed against (1) impulses that maintain the neurosis, attempting to remove them or lower their intensity below the critical threshold, (2) obstacles toward satisfaction of impulses, (3) "essential predispositions," (4) neurotic gains and (5) "delaying factors" which operate to prevent impulse fulfillment.

It has been said that clients are apt to react to pressures and coercion in a manner resembling their reactions as children to parental authority and injunctions, for the defenses and situations in which pressure or coercion are used often find the client in similar states of hostility, aggression, and defensiveness. For example, if pressures and coercion are used, the adult client is apt to react as a child might by "running away" (leaving the situation) or by rebelling violently. For this reason, the two techniques are to be used only in extreme cases and always with moderation. We must be sure that the "ends justify the means" and that we are prepared for the consequences.

MUSCULAR RELAXATION, REST, AND DIVERSIONAL THERAPY AS SUPPORTIVE PROCEDURES

Relaxation, rest, and recreation are conceived to have similar functions although they may encompass a wide range of activities. Accompanying nearly all neurotic patterns there seems to be a definite degree of muscular tension that in turn often provokes muscle spasms, tics, spasms of the internal organs, and even severe headaches and other symptomatic conditions. These are not only discomforting, but to many individuals they are shameful and embarrassing as well. To the extent that activities can relieve this tension and reduce the discomfort and embarrassment, they are supportive.

Rest is probably the first means tried by individuals in attempting to treat their "nervous conditions." It is fairly well accepted today that long periods of rest, changes in one's job, or long vacations will in themselves do very little to alleviate neurotic conditions or anxiety states. If the source of the suffering is only muscle fatigue, the individual will probably be restored to a balanced condition by rest alone, but if there are deep neurotic tensions, such as those complicated by neurotic exhaustion states or other neurosthenic symptoms, rest will be ineffective, for it is very likely that the client will be unable to sleep when the opportunity is afforded or to relax sufficiently to restore his physical well-being. In these instances some supportive value may come from systematic relaxation or the facilitation of relaxation by diversional activities.

The proper and beneficial use of leisure time is one of the greatest problems for many people, and it presents a special problem for the maladjusted individual. For the maladjusted individual these "free" hours, when neither the mind nor the body are actively engaged, are probably the most difficult periods of the entire day. The counselor can often give untold support by suggesting and even assisting the individual to enter into beneficial leisure-time activities. Leisure-time activity is more difficult to provide for the older, especially the retired, individual. Many of the supportive techniques listed by James L. McCary (10) are almost totally diversional in nature. They include reading, dance therapy, inspirational group therapy, music therapy, all recreational activities—diversions such as handicraft and art work, athletic participation, model building, further education—all kinds of club membership, and traveling. It would appear that such supportive techniques are a necessity in nearly all effective counseling with neurotic clients, so that their minds or bodies or both are kept occupied, not preoccupied. The task of the counselor is not merely to suggest such diversional outlets; he should aid the client in finding suitable and satisfactory activities. Each individual is unique, especially when selecting a diversional pastime activity, and each client should be presented with a wide variety of activities from which he can select on the basis of his natural ability and interest. This is an area of supportive counseling that calls for follow-up work to see that the individual does seek and participate in some leisure-time activity. The increased socialization to be derived from these activities is a key aspect of all supportive counseling programs.

There are many other forms of treatment that can be termed "supportive," since any form of counseling that builds the organism in any constructive and positive manner toward better and easier daily living with its environment serves a supportive role. Any counseling activity that acts as a "crutch" for the individual has supportive aspects. Anything that builds a more healthy mind, body, and daily routine is supportive to the client. For more complete discussions of techniques such as guidance, externalization of interests, persuasion, emotional catharsis and desensitization, hydrotherapy, shock and convulsive therapy, drug or chemical therapy, brain surgery, inspirational group therapy, music therapy, improved nutrition, material security, hospitalization, habitual routine, occupational therapy, and all forms of medical treatment, the reader is referred to Axelrode (5), Thorne (15), and Wolberg (16). These authors provide comprehensive discussions of supportive counseling and the methods and techniques it uses.

SUMMARY

In this chapter we have reviewed some of the ways in which supportive relationships, both within the counseling situation and in the environmental field, can be used to give the client the extra security and energy that will enable him to deal better with his problems. We have noted the application of support in the relationship school of therapy, in the classical psychoanalytic approach of Freud, in the neo-analytic approach of Alexander, in the social learning theory of Rotter, and in the personal construct theory of Kelly, and we have made frequent references to its use by Thorne in his eclectic approach. Whatever the school or philosophy of counseling, it would appear that supportive factors are involved, whether this is recognized or not. And we should plan specifically for their effective use.

BIBLIOGRAPHY

1. Alexander, F., "Current views on psychotherapy." *Psychiat.*, 1953, 16, 113–23.
2. Allen, F. H., "Some therapeutic principles as applicable to psychiatric work with children." *Amer. J. Psychiat.*, 1937, 94, 671–80.
3. Allen, F. H., "Trends in therapy, IV. Participation therapy. *Amer. J. Psychiat.*, 1939, 9, 737–42.
4. Allen, F. H., *Psychotherapy with children.* New York: Norton, 1942.
5. Axelrode, J., "Some indications for supportive therapy." *Amer. J. Orthopsychiat.*, 1940, 10, 264–71.
6. Durkin, H. E., "Dr. John Levy's relationship therapy as applied to a play group." *Amer. J. Orthopsychiat.*, 1939, 9, 583–97.
7. Hendrick, I., *Facts and theories of psychoanalysis.* New York: Alfred A. Knopf, 1950.
8. Kelly, G. A., *The psychology of personal constructs*, Vol. II. New York: Norton, 1955.
9. Laing, L. D., "The use of reassurance in psychotherapy." *Smith Coll. Stud. Soc. Work*, 1952, 22, 75–90.
10. McCary, J. L. (ed.), *Six approaches to psychotherapy.* New York: Dryden, 1955.
11. Riesman, D., Glazer, N., and Denney, R., *The lonely crowd.* New York: Doubleday, 1955.

12. Rotter, J. B., *Social learning and clinical psychology*. New York: Prentice-Hall, 1954.
13. Snygg, D., and Combs, A. W., *Individual behavior*. New York: Harper, 1949.
14. Taft, J., "The time element in therapy." *Amer. J. Orthopsychiat.*, 1933, 3, 65–79.
15. Thorne, F., *"Principles of personality counseling."* Brandon, Vt.: J. Clin. Psychol., 1950.
16. Wolberg, L., *The technique of psychotherapy*. New York: Grune & Stratton, 1954.

☼

CHAPTER

7

Relearning

FROM A RELEARNING POINT OF VIEW THE GOAL OF PSYCHOLOGICAL counseling is to understand and alter an individual's behavior and attitudes by means of principles of learning and constructs derived from various learning theories. In this chapter we will discuss the counseling process, as it is conducted both in and beyond the interview room, from the standpoint of theories of learning. One of the ultimate purposes of psychological counseling is to encourage and promote new or altered patterns of behavior and thinking. To most psychologists this is a problem in learning. The goals of relearning and socialization are the aims of psychological counseling which come closest to our ultimate goal—promoting changes in behavior and attitude to effect a happier and more efficient adjustment of the individual to his environment.

The order in which we have discussed the various aims or goals of counseling only approximates the sequence of events in the counseling process. We have placed relearning and socialization toward the last to suggest that it is these goals toward which we are always working. Environmental change, insight, support, and emotional release are significant only as they result in changed ways of acting and thinking and more effective functioning in the social field. In some instances they may appear to more or less automatically bring about these terminal aims but often they prepare the person for the alteration of his habits. Our reason for placing relearning before socialization is almost entirely arbitrary. Much relearning must take place through social experimentation, and so one might argue for a reversed order. On the other hand, socialization is the proving ground where the individual applies and tests his new understanding, his security feelings, his relaxed attitude, and the new response habits he has built up. This entire problem of order is one that must be determined for an individual client in terms of his immediate and delayed problems, and the order of presentation is, therefore, largely academic.

The counselor, when performing his professional role, carries out an ambitious and unique function in society. He enters into a relationship with an individual who is a complex, functioning organism made up of a multitude of on-going processes, all of which have been affected in relatively unknown ways by innumerable more-or-less obscure experiences that stretch back to the day of his birth, perhaps even before. This organism (the client) functions in a world inhabited by many other organisms. Despite the infinite variety of behavior theoretically within the client's potential, he has developed a limited number of acceptable behavior patterns. To a large measure this learned behavior has been determined by the culture in which he functions, and he has learned to react to the expectations of others. His repertory of behavior has not been maximally effective—else, for the most part, he would not be in need of help—and so the counselor's problem is to aid him in altering this behavior. Not only must the counselor promote new learning; he must contribute to unlearning as well.

For this ambitious task, the psychologically oriented counselor can apply learning concepts effectively. The value of using learning concepts would seem to be in their specificity, their amenability to the formation of hypotheses, and their usefulness in avoiding the reification of tentative constructs. Further, at the molar clinical level, they offer a substantially homogeneous set of generalizations with which to work. Although there are certainly differences among the various learning theories, many of them seem reducible to differences in emphases or to biases in the personality characteristics of particular investigators.

SOME POSTULATES ABOUT BEHAVIOR

Before discussing particular learning theories, let us review a few of the basic postulates commonly used by clinicians. In some instances these assumptions are explicitly stated, and in others they are not formally stated but are implicit in the clinician's procedure. In our discussion we will lean heavily on Rotter (18) and Cameron (2) whose assumptions are explicitly stated and are substantially representative.

1. ASSUMPTION OF FIELD FORCES.   In dealing with a person, the clinician is dealing with the interaction of an individual with his environment. In this assumption the emphasis is on the interaction. This emphasis gives us a phenomenal world for the individual which is only more or less congruent with the real or objective world. The behavior of the person is a phenomenon, and since much of the meaningful environment is

social, we can speak of the behavior as a social phenomenon. Theorists, in addition to the two mentioned above, who make this assumption are Lewin (10), Snygg and Combs (22), and others (8, 24).

2. ASSUMPTION OF UNITY OF BEHAVIOR.   Nearly all schools of thought make this assumption. It is true that some talk about personality instead of behavior, but most theorists assume that new experiences are a partial function of previously acquired meanings, and that old acquired meanings or learnings are changed by new experiences. From some points of view behavior has at its core some kind of "innate" or developed organization; this core organization is usually called the "personality" of the individual. Other writers view this unity as the interdependence of self and environmental influences. Cameron emphasizes the nonunity nature of the organism; according to his thinking, the individual is not complete in himself, rather he possesses a number of functions that cannot be carried out except in interaction with others. Excellent examples of socially dependent functions are activities such as breast feeding, sexual functions, and the functions of communication. From Cameron's point of view the unity lies in the individual's normal tendency to reach out, to relate himself to others or to communicate.

3. ASSUMPTION OF GOAL-DIRECTED BEHAVIOR.   Aggressive goal-seeking is considered normal and healthy—all persons are striving toward goals. This results in a motivational principle that provides a basis for predicting behavior by evaluating a given situation in terms of the potential satisfactions and gratifications that may result from it. This aggressive, healthy goal-seeking should be carefully distinguished from aggressive behavior that is destructive of human relations and, therefore, designated as hostile. It must be noted, however, that not all aggressive behavior is necessarily hostile in nature. Examples of the assumption of goal directiveness are Freud's psychic determinism, Adler's (16) striving for superiority, Lewin's (11) vector psychology, and even William McDougall's (13) propensities. Clark L. Hull's concept of organismic need underlies his use of reinforcement (7). Cameron's (2) premise is somewhat broader in nature; he sees the organism as basically concerned with extending its control of both the internal and external environment.

4. ASSUMPTION OF THE MODIFIABILITY OF LEARNED BEHAVIOR.   Man is superior to other living organisms in his ability to modify his behavior in response to a changing situation more quickly and more extensively. Theoretically, all behavior, deviant or normal, is susceptible to modification. This has important implications for counseling or psychotherapy. We view beliefs, fantasies, and thinking as behavior, even though there is no overt evidence of activity. Beliefs and thoughts are potential patterns of activity which can be modified in thinking or fantasy.

Talking about a reaction to a situation approximates the experience of reliving it. To relive a situation in a supportive setting may modify it in the sense of freeing the reaction from whatever hostility, anxiety, guilt, or embarrassment may be associated with it. There are, of course, limits to the modifiability of behavior imposed by organic damage, age, intelligence, and the importance to the individual of the particular segment of behavior under examination.

5. Respect for the Individual.   The concept of the client as a living, feeling, thinking individual is basic to all clinical work and has already been mentioned many times. When we deal with a subject in the clinical setting, we must regard the individual with more than a laboratory interest. Many formal learning theorists have a predilection for machine models and view the complexities of the human client as artifacts or impediments. The clinician who is attempting to apply learning theory to the counseling process must always respect his client as a person, making sure that the rights of the individual are not disregarded. This is more than an assumption; it is a basic ethical rule of practice.

REINFORCEMENT THEORY

There are two main classes of learning theory today: (a) *stimulus-response (S-R) reinforcement theory* and (b) *cognitive,* or *expectancy, theory.* The main difference between the two lies in the use of the concept of reinforcement. The S-R theorist uses a *drive-reduction* theory of reinforcement, according to which learning proceeds as a result of the occurrence of events, known as reinforcements, which reduce the physiological drives activating behavior. The behavior that avoids punishment is learned because it reduces the tension set up by the punishment or its anticipation. Performance is determined by the strength of the drive and the strength of the habit, which is in itself a function of historical learning and drive reduction. Hull's principle of secondary reinforcement, whereby a goal acquires reinforcement value through its association with primary reinforcement, provides the opportunity to explain social behavior.

As contrasted with "S-R" theories, the "cognitive" theories of learning emphasize as the central concept subjectively held *hypotheses* or *expectations.* The effect of reinforcement is to create expectations or hypotheses with respect to their reoccurrence. Behavior is a function of the subject's expectations and the role of reinforcement is to change (increase or decrease) these expectations, or to verify or negate the subject's hypotheses regarding the situation.

Since counseling from the standpoint of learning theory aims to understand and alter an individual's behavior and attitudes, it follows that a sharp distinction between insight and relearning is difficult to maintain. The learning theory approaches of Dollard and Miller, Mowrer, and several others have been discussed [1] from the standpoint of their emphases on insight. Insight was in fact described in part as the unlearning of repression and the learning of the proper labels with which behavior can be described. Here, in connection with our discussion of relearning as a goal in counseling, we come again to a discussion of the philosophies of several of these learning theorists (Dollard and Miller and Mowrer, in particular). We will now review some of the concepts suggested earlier, this time emphasizing the learning of new modes of response in contrast to the unlearning of inefficient or handicapping modes of response. If the reader will compare the analysis of the stimulus-response reinforcement theories presented earlier with the review of these theories in this chapter, he will see that reinforcement theories are more concerned with the elimination of old learning than with the establishment of new learning. Cognitive or expectancy theory, on the other hand, concerns itself more specifically with the formation of new expectancies and new modes of response.

1. JOHN DOLLARD AND NEAL E. MILLER.   Dollard and Miller (5), who attempt to systematize principles of human behavior, especially as they relate to counseling, from a Hullian point of view describe four basic factors that they believe underlie all learning phenomena: drive, response, cue, and reinforcement. Drive, in conjunction with cues from other stimuli which are not strong enough in themselves to act as drives, impels responses. If the first response is not rewarded by an event reducing the drive, it will drop away and others will appear. When a succession of nonrewarded responses are extinct (because of lack of reinforcement), the result is called random behavior. If a response is followed by reward (reducing the drive), the connection between the cue and this response is strengthened; and the next time the same drive and other cues are present, this same response is more likely to occur. This strengthening of the cue-response connection is described by Dollard and Miller as the essence of learning.

Essentially, this concept of learning is based on the functioning of primary physiological drives. To explain social behavior, it is necessary to hypothesize secondary or learned drives, which are derived from primary drives. In this instance, previously neutral cues have gained the capacity to play the same functional role in the learning and performance of new responses as do primary drives. The rationale for learned reinforcements follows the same logic. Learned drives are strengthened by reinforcement and weakened by non-reinforcement, and otherwise vary

[1] *See* pp. 102–16.

with the principles and conditions of learning. The great variability of behavior springs from the fact that different conditions of learning may attach learned drives as reinforcements to different cues. On the other hand, different drives may be attached to the same cue, and these may be conflicting (as in the instance of fear and anger) or they may be complementary.

The solution of emotional problems is normally a function of the higher mental processes. As distinguished from simple automatic habits, these higher mental processes refer to a series of internal responses which mediate between cue and response. Dollard and Miller believe that neurosis has its source in intense emotional conflict, a conflict that is unconscious in the sense that it is unverbalized by the neurotic. In order to reduce the painful effects of such conflicts, the individual tends to learn and to have reinforced those behaviors that permit him to escape or avoid the situations that stimulate conflicting drives. Since he finds such avoiding behaviors rewarding, the conflict itself is never resolved by the higher mental processes because it can never be considered by them.

The general process of counseling consists first in providing a nonpunishing situation in which avoidant behaviors tend to extinguish. The extinction generalizes and weakens the motivation to repress related material. As this material is made available to the higher mental processes, normal learning of appropriate responses becomes possible, and the neurotic is ready for relearning. Dollard and Miller advocate five specific conditions of counseling: (a) free association under conditions of (b) permissiveness on the part of the therapist who rewards the client by (c) a nonjudgmental attitude and (d) by understanding and remembering the client. Finally, (e) the counselor helps the client clarify the distinctions between thinking and acting. All of these are intended to reduce the anxiety and fear motivating avoidance, and to enable the client to use his thoughts more freely and flexibly.

2. O. HOBART MOWRER. Mowrer (14) has proposed that there are, in fact, two kinds of learning: (a) conditioning, in which contiguity is a condition sufficient for the occurrence of learning, and (b) problem-solving, for which reinforcement is a necessary condition of learning. He stresses anxiety as the basis of neurosis, and maintains that it arises only from the act of repression. The individual, fearing the consequences of his behavior, develops strong negative feelings with respect to punishing consequences, instead of learning behavior that will be acceptable and therefore lead to positive reinforcement. By adopting the role of a nonpunishing parent, the counselor permits all the "bad" impulses and habits to arise in the defense-free relationship. This permits the dissolution of old habits sufficiently for the client to be able to consider alternative modes of adjustment, which can then be satisfactorily reinforced.

According to Mowrer, the fears, loyalties, and attitudes of the individual are acquired by conditioning, and constitute the superego or conscience. However, they become an effective part of personality only when the individual finds it necessary to accept them as restrictive, coercive dictates in order to resolve conflict-produced anxiety. It is important to note here that neurosis is not forced upon an individual by too severe moral training, but represents a "decision" or "choice" on his part to deal with conflicts by means of deception and dissociation, rather than by more constructive, more consistent, more integrative means. In the Nebraska Symposium (15, p. 175) Mowrer states, ". . . I have argued against the idea of 'habit' and have proposed that we replace it with the older notion of voluntary, consciously directed action."

This appears to be one of the basic attributes of Mowrer's approach to counseling. In effect, he teaches the client to take voluntary, consciously directed action, in lieu of automatic, emotional, reflexive action, when confronted by a conflict situation. The procedure may be very didactic, with the client being instructed to follow certain new courses of action until they become learned responses. Presumably, the suggested or taught responses will be learned by virtue of the reinforcement resulting when anxiety is reduced in the problem situation. Basically, according to reinforcement theories of learning, the counselor aids the client to behavior that will lead first to the extinction, or dropping out, of previously ineffective responses because of lack of reinforcement; and second, to the learning of new substitute responses, which will be reinforced because they are more effective than the old responses. In the practical counseling situation the counselor should capitalize on opportunities for applying these principles. The ingenious counselor will be able to guide the client in experimenting with his environment in such a way as to take maximum advantage of the reinforcement principle.

COGNITIVE THEORY

1. EDWARD C. TOLMAN.   The first person to formulate this concept clearly was Edward C. Tolman (23). He conceived of mental processes as dynamic aspects, or determinants, of behavior. "Expectations" are bits of knowledge concerning the nature of the goal object, its position, and modes of behavior which will lead to its attainment. Evidence for such expectations is the fact that if any of these entities (the goal, its position, or the "path" to it) are changed, and hence prove not to be as predicted, the behavior of the subject shows disruption and alteration until a new expectation is developed. The expectation itself is a cognitive event having relational or gestalt properties. When one pattern of stimulation is followed in time by another, a relation develops between them

(cognitively, centrally, or perceptually) which is the knowledge (expectation) that behaving in a certain manner to the prior stimulus-complex will eventuate in the pattern customarily following it. Tolman refers to broad orientational expectancies as "means-end-readinesses." Such *sets* may be innate or transferred from previous experience. The more specific expectations relative to "what leads to what" are called "hypotheses." These hypotheses are strengthened when confirmed, and weakened when not confirmed. Thus, the organism builds up a more and more refined and accurate "cognitive map" of the situation. Tolman's statements about the "gestalt-like" nature of "sign-significate-expectancies" follow along the same line as the model provided by Lewin.

2. KURT LEWIN.   Kurt Lewin employed both an expectancy and a reinforcement point of view (11). He emphasized the importance of the cognitive expectations and hypotheses of the subject. He also employed the principle of "valence," a premise that behavior is essentially determined by the value of various goal-objects in the field. He was not always clear as to whether the effect of goal attainment is to reduce tension (or drive) for the acquisition of the goal or simply to reduce the general tension of the organism. In any event, to the extent that tension is reduced when goals are attained we must infer that reinforcement occurs. Lewin was mostly concerned with the field conditions that result in the occurrence of a given behavior, and less so with the effect of its occurrence. The basic statements of Lewin's field theory are: (a) behavior has to be derived from a totality of coexisting facts, and (b) these coexisting facts have the character of a *dynamic field* insofar as the state of any part of this field depends on every other part of the field. According to this theory, behavior depends neither on the past nor on the future, but on the present field. Objects in the psychological environment have positive or negative "valence" according to whether they promise to meet present needs or threaten injury. To Lewin, an awakened need produced a state of tension in the person—a readiness for action. Frustration of the need by a barrier may result in random or ill-directed activity. Chronic frustration can result in the barrier acquiring a negative valence, which in turn leads to angry attack or fearful avoidance.

The re-educative process, from Lewin's point of view, affects the individual in three ways: (a) it changes his cognitive structure, (b) it modifies his valences and values, and (c) it affects motoric action, involving control over physical and social movements. He points out that first-hand experience does not automatically create correct concepts, that the possession of correct knowledge does not rectify false perception, and that changes in sentiment do not necessarily follow changes in cognitive structure. To effect such changes, he believed it necessary to induce a change in the culture *or,* from the individual's viewpoint, a new set of values. Since a new set of values will usually be met with hostility, it is important to create an atmosphere of freedom and spontaneity as part of the re-educative process. The new set of values must be accepted willingly, freely, wholeheartedly. Lewin suggests 12, p. 66): "Methods and procedures which seek to change convictions item by item are of little avail . . ." The chances for such re-education are increased whenever a strong "we-feeling" is created, and the client becomes more friendly and less hostile.

Neither Lewin nor Tolman directed much of their thinking to problems of counseling or therapy, although Lewin did become interested in the resolution of social conflicts and problems of group dynamics. We can speculate though, that they would have advocated the changing of the client's "cognitive maps" or "phenomenal fields." This would result in the changing of patterns of behavior which is the goal of counseling. Our earlier conceptualization of counseling as a process involving the manipulation of a matrix of vectors is consistent with Lewin's presentation of the re-educative process. Both Lewin and Tolman would certainly have envisaged the eventual goals of counseling to be re-education and socialization, with environmental manipulation, support, emotional release, tension reduction, and probably insight regarded as necessary to the attainment of the desired end results.

COMBINED THEORY OF REINFORCEMENT
AND EXPECTANCY

1. FRANKLIN SHAW. A number of writers, more concerned with developing tentative but usable formulations rather than formally rigorous models, have felt it necessary to incorporate aspects of both reinforcement and expectancy theories in their attempts to construct theories of counseling. Among these, Shaw and Rotter are representative. In his early theorizing Shaw (19, pp. 389–90) stated certain principles describing what he conceived to be the conditions under which changes in behavior and attitudes take place:

1. Affective states are subject to conditioning; that is, situations may come to arouse them by occurring in conjunction with other situations that already arouse them. This principle indicates that instigations to action, when occurring repeatedly in conjunction with punishment, would become conditioned to anxiety.

2. Participation is directed toward the reduction of affective states. Since the reduction of affective states is problem-solving, we can say that participation is oriented toward the solution of problems. This principle would lead us to expect that anxiety would be reduced by "getting

away from," removing, or repressing whatever arouses it. It follows from (1) and (2) that instigations to action would be repressed.

3. Problem-solving is facilitated by the presence of cues. In psychotherapy, patients arrive at new solutions by getting cues as to how they have contributed to their problems. It follows from this principle, in combination with (1) and (2), that maladjustment or inadequate solution would occur, because repression would do away with the possibility of cues being perceived as to the role that the individual's own instigations to action play in his adjustive efforts.

4. Participation which solves problems, or reduces motives, tends to be learned and retained (*i.e.,* the law of effect).[2]

In practice the counselor finds that the maladjustive responses of his client have both a positive and negative value. However, the rewarding aspects of the responses are immediate, while the punishing consequences are remote and, for the most part, unrealized. The first job of counseling, then, is to make the unfortunate consequences of behavior more available to the client, that is, more immediate. Following the inhibition or extinction of maladjustive behavior, the second essential part of counseling involves influencing the client's motivation and level of aspiration according to the principles of reward and conditioning. The client's relearning in his social milieu is aided greatly by what he learns in the therapeutic situation itself.

More recently Shaw (20) has been influenced by the current trend that encourages the client to make active efforts to solve his own problems (that is, to relearn) during the period of counseling, and by the cognitive learning theories (especially that of Tolman) which emphasize expectancy concepts. Specifically, he regards psychological counseling as a relearning experience in which the counselee exposes his expectancies to someone (the counselor) who is skilled in discerning these expectancies and in "undermining" or "upending" them in a "constructive" fashion. It is assumed that the organism orients itself in its environment by means of expectancies, the inference being that behavior disorders are based upon expectancies that in one way or another are at odds with reality. One means of undermining expectancies suggested by Shaw is the counselor's failure to answer questions as the client expects, or his failure to answer them in a neat, packaged way. Shaw illustrates another means of undermining expectancies with a client who has the idea that external forces control him, leaving him helpless in the situation. Shaw suggests that the counselor simply ask him what courses of action are open to him (the client), in this way changing his expectancy and forcing him to con-

[2] Adapted from "Clinical Psychology and Behavior Theory," by Franklin J. Shaw, *Journal of Abnormal and Social Psychology*, 1950, 45, 388–91. By permission of the American Psychological Association.

sider alternative behaviors that in turn help him to learn. The effect of this procedure seems to be the denial of the immediate positive or rewarding value of the maladjustive behavior, thus heightening the negative or punishing aspects.

We believe that any one of several general reactions may follow such undermining. One possible reaction is that the client will simply persist in his behavior until he finally flees from the field and discontinues counseling. Or the client may vary his behavior, probably with regressive reaction patterns, until the counselor is satisfied. Again, if he is not successful in solving his immediate problems, the client may withdraw from counseling. Still another possibility is that with the counselor's help the client may be able to proceed to a consideration of the punishing consequences of his behavior. This latter reaction is presumably the one that Shaw hopes for. In a sizable number of clients the desired reaction will probably result, but the counselor must be cautioned against expecting favorable results in all instances. Shaw (21) has introduced the concept of "mutuality" to describe the relationship between client and counselor in which the client is amenable to the upending or undermining of expectancies. If the client and counselor are relating to each other "fully" and "deeply," the upending of expectancies is not so apt to shock the client and destroy the counseling relationship. Shaw appears to be emphasizing the often observed fact that our counseling aims are overlapping. Relearning (whether by changes in expectancies, by reinforcement, or by any other means) is not likely to take place unless a desirable relationship exists between counselor and client. We have described this relationship as a supportive relationship—it has also been described as a condition of rapport. In any case, the customary behavior of the client is precipitately disrupted by the undermining of expectancies, with a good deal of accompanying anxiety and other generalized emotion becoming prominent in the client's overt behavior. Because of the threatening nature of this experience, it is of the utmost importance that the counselor himself behave in a nonthreatening and nonjudgmental way. Further, the undermining of expectancies must be carefully timed and planned so that the client can make a fairly rapid recovery. It is easy to imagine that abuse of these strictures could lead to the counseling itself becoming becoming severely traumatic.

2. JULIAN B. ROTTER.   We have seen how Shaw hopes to encourage more rapid and effective relearning by the active manipulation of emotionally conditioned cognitive processes, with the assumption that changes in expectancies lead to changes in behavior. We will now turn to Rotter's approach (18) which is also based on an expectancy-reinforcement principle. The behavior of a person is determined not only by the nature or importance of goals or reinforcements, but also by his antici-

pation or expectancy that these goals will occur. Such expectations are determined by previous experience. In discussing why a maladjusted person does not learn adjustive behavior automatically, Rotter accepts the explanations given by Mowrer and by Dollard and Miller. Since the person is characterized by avoidant behaviors, the nature of these avoidant behaviors deters him from situations or experiences from which he might learn more adjustive behavior. This is particularly so because the punishment is usually delayed and thus has less effect on reducing the maladjustive behaviors.

According to Rotter (18, pp. 338–44) the counselor should devote his efforts along two main lines:

1. Toward weakening inadequate responses, which includes most of the time-honored therapeutic techniques such as reflection, catharsis, insight, discussion, projection, and transference.

2. Toward strengthening adequate responses, occurring as a function of an increased expectancy for some gratification or positive reinforcement.

Rotter cites five ways in which the counselor may attempt to increase the potentiality of alternative or adjustive behaviors by increasing the expectancy of gratification (positive reinforcement):

1. The direct reinforcement of the behavior, either by the therapist or by others, in which the therapist uses the knowledge of what reinforcements are of high value for the patient.

2. Placing the patient, or helping him to find and enter, into situations where he may observe in others alternative behaviors and their consequences, or where by discussion and interpretation, he can try to understand the behavior of others retrospectively.

3. Dealing with the patient's past history of alternative behaviors and reducing his expectancies that they will now result in the same frustrations or negative reinforcements as they did in the past, and verbally increasing his expectancies that these alternative behaviors will result in gratification.

4. Discussing with the patient possible alternatives apparently for the first time, including discussions of how the behaviors are actually carried out, and creating for him an expectancy that they may lead to gratification in life situations.

5. Creating and reinforcing for the patient an expectancy that he may solve his own problems more effectively by looking for and trying out alternative solutions or behaviors.[3]

[3] From Rotter, Julian B., *Social Learning and Clinical Psychology*. Englewood Cliffs, N.J. Copyright, 1954, by Prentice-Hall, Inc.

GOALS AND PROCEDURES OF RE–EDUCATION

D. Ewen Cameron (2, p. 190) emphasizes that "what we are concerned with under the heading of re-education is (rather) the matter of an extensive reorganization of the action patterns of the individual. The kind and range of ways in which an individual can deal with events arising in a given field depends on his concepts of that field. . . . Where the individual's concepts of a field are unrealistic and limited, his ability to deal with events occurring within that field will be correspondingly ineffective. Among other things his ability to understand cause and effect relations will be circumscribed." [4] More specifically, he believes that the client exists in a society that imposes considerable stress upon the individual; that demands conformity to standards in sex behavior and hostility control, many of which are well-nigh impossible; that accords much significance to success and to winning in competition. In particular, this society uses guilt and anxiety as means of social control. It is natural, therefore, that in certain fields of individual activity (personal failure, hostility, or unusual sexual behavior) there is little or no communication between people. If this is pertinent to the case, re-education concerning how people actually do behave in these fields of individual activity is of the greatest value and is an absolute prerequisite to modification of deviations in behavior arising from misconceptions. For some people, re-education as to the possibility of other ways of dealing with problems is essential.

Cameron advances several specific re-educational methods: (a) the direct provision of information, (b) educational movies illustrating the genesis and effects of rejection, hostility feelings, and overdependence, (c) lectures on human behavior, and (d) explanation. Cameron (2, pp. 175–7) indicates three situations in which he considers explanation to be appropriate:

1. When the concepts necessary for the patient to comprehend the material that he has brought out are not available to him.

2. In the situation where the concept is familiar to the patient but the data have been incorrectly categorized, *e.g.,* a fast heartbeat during an anxiety attack is a result, not a cause.

3. When current problems are patterned after earlier ones which the patient has survived despite failure to manage them.

Thus, explanation furnishes the client with specific tools or skills for managing specific situations. Re-education is somewhat broader, bringing

---

[4] From *General Psychotherapy*, by D. Ewen Cameron, printed by permission of Dr. Cameron and Grune & Stratton, Inc. Copyright 1950 by Grune & Stratton, Inc.

about a new orientation which in turn suggests a whole series of new ways of dealing with problems. Retraining is the actual working out with the client of new skills or techniques and the practicing of these skills.

The work of Kraines (9) may be taken as representative of the working psychotherapists, mostly psychiatrists, whose formulations are less empirical and less affected by the modern trends of functionalism and operationism. To Kraines, the aim of psychotherapy is threefold: (a) to remove stress, (b) to eliminate immature traits, and (c) to substitute mature, healthful reaction patterns. In general, the eventuation of desirable changes depends on the attainment of considerable rapport between client and counselor. No laws or hypotheses of learning are appealed to for technique. Within this major condition of re-education, the attitudes and reaction patterns of the individual are changed by (p. 178):

1. Bringing to conscious attention in specific detail the unhygienic attitudes and their attendant irritating memories.

2. Removing the emotional tone attached to the memories, by intellectual understanding and by desensitizing the patient through repeated discussion.

3. Then, retraining the patient so that he will react in a hygienic, efficient, and non-symptom-forming manner to the various stresses of life.[5]

As noted, the all-important factor in effecting behavior changes is positive rapport with the clinician. These changes are accomplished: (a) through free association and dream analysis, and (b) mainly by discussion in which the client formulates very specifically what it is that he is irritated about, in this way being enabled to recognize the immaturity of his reactions. Other writers who have stressed the importance of explanation and discussion are Rudolf Dreikurs (6) and John F. Cuber (4). The latter cautions against the exaggeration of the role of intelligence and reason, and suggests that "reason-reward-punishment" must recognize the physiological limitations of the individual.

RE–EDUCATION THROUGH MANIPULATION OF THE ENVIRONMENT

Most of the techniques discussed so far have emphasized the direct manipulation of the client, with or without his consent and co-operation. However, from the field theoretical point of view, the client and his en-

[5] From *The Therapy of the Neuroses and Psychoses*, by Samuel H. Kraines, printed by permission of Dr. Kraines and Lea & Febiger, Publishers. Copyright 1948 by Lea & Febiger.

vironment are regarded as one interrelated whole or life space. If, then, we engage in specific environmental manipulation, some reorganization of the client's field may be expected. Certain examples from those favoring environmental manipulation are presented below.

Rotter (18) presents the general theory that the child's behavior is determined by the reinforcements he receives. Therefore, a change in the social environment or the people in it leads to change in the child's behavior. There is the implication that the obtaining of direct gratification from activities that do not lead to punishment is sufficient to build up behavior potentials for adjusted reactions without the counselor's having to weaken the child's earlier learned "bad" behavior. Rotter discusses the following forms of environmental treatment: (a) institutionalization, (b) adoption and foster placement, (c) the use of camps and clubs, and (d) changing parental attitudes. The first two procedures are not deemed desirable except under unusual conditions, since they tend to create more problems than they solve.

According to Gerald H. J. Pearson (17), a psychoanalytic counselor, the real aim of educational counseling is to make the child less afraid of instinctual impulses and to teach him to direct them in a culturally acceptable way. Suggestion and re-education are the appropriate methods for accomplishing this goal. The purpose of re-education is to remove guilt and fear surrounding instinctual impulses, so that the child may be able to gratify them more adequately. There are three types of re-education: (a) The patient is given retraining as to the nature of human beings through the promotion of intellectual insight into better ways of adjusting to life. To gain the therapist's love, the child gives up certain ways of acting and adopts others. (b) The child is urged to use existing facilities for the expression of instinctual drives. When he sees that such methods are possible and do not lead to punishment, he can continue to use them and so be relieved of tension. Environmental change is a special example of this type of therapy. (3) Reconditioning, which is not favored by Pearson. Environmental therapy is stressed as the method for changing or removing the influence of significant persons in the child's life.

Jacob H. Conn (3) believes that if re-education is to occur the child must be able to express his dissatisfactions, fears, and hopes in a natural fashion, so that he will begin to understand how he has contributed to the total situation, and to accept his share of responsibility for what is going on. Conn believes this is best accomplished through the medium of play, especially doll-play. During the doll-play the child is treated as a respected equal. No interpretations are made, and attention is focused on the child's complaints. The child expresses his thoughts and feelings through the dolls, as though they were responsible for the actions. In this way, the client is at the same time an impartial observer and an active participant in a discussion of his attitudes and problems. The counselor structures the session with directed questions.

Austin Riggs used environmental manipulation as an adjunct to re-educative therapy. He saw neurosis as a resultant of conflict within various levels of the individual, such as the instinctive, reflexive, intellectual, social, and ethical. He considered, for example, that in emotionally over-active or temperamental individuals, emotional stress may bring about symptoms whose meaning is not comprehended by the individual experiencing them. Intense overactivity, he thought, may hinder the functioning of the intellect and manifest itself in psychoneurotic misinterpretation. As a first step in treatment Riggs advised removal of the client from home, vocational, and social environments in which stress had developed. In the neutral environment of a sanitarium he was acquainted with the fact that he needed re-education in the principles of adjusting to life. Regimentation and scheduling of activities in such an environment served several purposes: (a) it minimized stress and regularized the patient's life, (b) it removed responsibility for decision-making from the client, (c) it helped develop habits of social co-operation, (d) it taught the client to do things because they had to be done, instead of avoiding them because of dislike or disinterest. Activities included occupational therapy, mental exercises, recreation, social events, and regular periods of rest and relaxation. This was the "regularizing" basis upon which retraining was superimposed. Retraining was accomplished through interviews with the therapist, group discussions, lectures, and assigned readings (1), and a "therapeutic re-educative" attitude prevailed on the part of the entire hospital staff.

CAN THESE THEORIES BE BROUGHT TOGETHER?

We have reviewed several applications of learning theory to the problems of counseling and psychotherapy, and we have seen that there is no one learning approach to counseling; rather, there are a number of different approaches. We have not summarized and integrated these approaches into a single cohesive counseling technique. Our discussion has illustrated ways in which counseling can be construed as a process of learning. In fact, in a general way, all the other aims of counseling could be included under the principles of learning. Our purpose has been to encourage the prospective counselor to constant awareness that old behavioral patterns may have to be unlearned or altered and new patterns learned. All that we know about the learning process must be directed toward this goal.

The complete process of behavioral change frequently requires that the counselor plan learning experiences for his client. Behavioral changes may result more or less automatically from environmental change; and, similarly, insight, emotional release, and support may prepare the person so that he will change his modes of behavior and thinking without any special habit retraining. However, since this does not always happen automatically, specific emphasis on learning is indicated. In other instances the process of change can be expedited by planned learning experiences. For these reasons the goals of the counseling process must be directed toward learning, re-education, and relearning.

Let us now examine, through examples, how these goals can be attained, and at the same time study the similarities and differences between the several theoretical approaches. Earlier we mentioned the plain twin who had the beautiful sister and the intelligent and professionally accomplished older brothers. She presented the very specific symptom of a facial grimace that exposed her beautiful teeth. Much more serious was her inability to apply her own excellent intelligence in any directed and organized fashion. Insight and self-understanding in themselves did not enable her to deal with her symptoms. Insofar as the first symptom, the grimace, was concerned, it is true that insight, or something akin to it, undoubtedly was of considerable value. Quite early in the counseling process her attention was called to the grimace, and several possible hy-potheses to explain its development were discussed with her. She claimed not to be aware that she was producing any facial distortion. The hypothesis that was most comprehensible and acceptable to her was that it was a compensatory mechanism through which she exhibited her beautiful teeth to make up for other unattractive characteristics that she felt she possessed. She recalled that her father had frequently complimented her on her teeth and lovely smile, and remembered crawling into his lap when she was of preschool age and saying, "See my teeth, Daddy!" The idea that she had used the device to gain attention was expanded by the recall of other occasions on which her teeth and smile had been favorably commented upon.

Dollard and Miller might say that she had labeled this bit of behavior. She was certainly able to look upon it objectively after she had some words to describe it. This objectivity allowed her to deal with it as a habit, and with conscious effort she was able to bring the mechanism under control until it gradually disappeared. Mowrer might say that our client learned, or was taught, to take voluntary action instead of automatic emotionally determined action. Lewin might have said that the cognitive structure had been changed, that positive valences were now attached to the absence of the grimace, and that through practice motoric action was influenced so that control was gained over the behavior. Shaw might suggest that the counselor had helped the client to become aware of the punishing consequences of her behavior. Perhaps Rotter would emphasize the client's increased expectancy that the modified response would lead to gratification. Cameron might stress the value of the explanation offered the client and the gaining of concepts necessary to understand what she had been doing. We have purposely simplified these various explanations to demonstrate the similarity among them; such differences as do appear to exist may be largely semantic.

The more disturbing symptom of inability to apply herself to required or assigned tasks seemed to be most amenable to an expectancy approach. As her childhood experiences were discussed, particularly her school experiences, it developed that she had one characteristic memory. Whenever she entered a new grade, she was always told, "Oh yes, you are the sister of Mark and David. I remember them well. I'm sure you will have no problems with school work." This thought was presumably presented to her time and again. If the thought was not actually expressed, she assumed that the teachers were thinking this. She early developed the belief that great achievement was expected of her. At the same time she gradually began to lose confidence in her abilities. This was due in a degree to some real or imagined failures, but mostly to the unrealistically high aspirations she had set for herself. Finally, she began to expect that she would fail and as a result found it impossible to attempt any assigned task upon which performance might be judged.

In the process of counseling these expectancies were attacked quite directly and objectively. She was encouraged to examine why she felt she could not accomplish certain tasks. At first she offered the defense that she could do them if she tried but that she simply had not tried. In time, she was able to accept the fact that she was really afraid to try. Then, in a gentle and cautious fashion, she was encouraged to entertain the expectancy that she would do well if she tried to apply herself, and eventually she slowly, but surely, regained her confidence or expectancy of success. As a matter of record, she reversed her grade record in college from fifty semester hours of "C" and ten hours of "B" in her first two years to fifty hours of "A" and ten hours of "B" in the second two years.

Even though we have used the simplest language of expectancy learning theory to describe the above counseling process, other concepts might have been used. Dollard and Miller could certainly call attention to the process of free associating and remembering the early school experiences in the presence of a presumably permissive, nonjudgmental counselor, who seemed to understand the client and helped her to realize that she had been confusing in her thinking what *would* happen with what *might* happen. Mowrer might emphasize the reduction of anxiety resulting when the accepting counselor was substituted for authority figures who were regarded as potentially punishing. So, too, we might use the language of still other theoretical systems. In general, we prefer to think that in the counseling process the counselor radically reorganized the force field in which the client was operating. The more analytically oriented counselor might place more emphasis upon other factors in the total counseling situation, but in the case of this client, it is not believed that behavioral changes would have resulted without consciously directed relearning experiences. The discussion of this case has been presented to underline the importance of supportive relationships. The idea of acceptance by the counselor and the warmth and permissiveness of the relationship is inherent in all the theoretical approaches that have been considered.

In Chapter 1 we mentioned an engineer who, although successful in the field, found that he was not effective as an administrator. The counseling problem with this man also seemed to be one in which relearning was a major objective. Although none of his attitudes or behavioral reactions were extreme enough to be regarded as pathological, it was discovered that this client was quite suspicious and distrustful of people. He had the feeling that people are basically undependable, and he felt that this was especially true in the business world. His whole orientation was competitive; the main goal to him was to stay a jump ahead of everybody else. His discussion of this problem was redundant with statements like, "You have to look after Number One first." This attitude was definitely affecting his relationships with people. He knew that it was wise to cover it up, but his veneer wore thin most of the time. The counseling program involved several activities, some of which were quite didactic and consisted of study and training in administrative procedures. Other activities might more appropriately be discussed under socialization in the next chapter. The counselor hoped that he would broaden his experience with people so that his perspective might be modified. Even if this did not occur, it was hoped that his social graces might improve. In addition to these approaches, the counselor attempted to attack his perceptions of people directly. Individual counseling time was devoted to analyzing experiences with people in which he had believed himself wronged or betrayed. Some progress was made in that he became less sure that he had perceived many of these situations accurately, and he expressed the belief that he was better able to trust people than he had been in the past. It was hoped that, as he was able to entertain different expectancies about people, the counselor could support him through some successful and rewarding experiences with them. Unfortunately, before the plans were much more than initiated, the counseling sessions were interrupted by an emergency that arose in his firm. He had to make a hurried trip abroad, and he has not been seen since. He may still be abroad—or he may have decided that the counseling plans would not help him. In any case, we cannot report the ultimate outcome since we have no knowledge as to whether or not he is adjusting more favorably.

Certain kinds of relearning experiences are indicated for use both with the young stockman and with the brain-injured business-machine operator. In their cases, procedures are so specific that we will discuss them under another heading. For the purposes of our discussion we will refer to the task of re-educating such handicapped persons as *retraining* rather than relearning.

Let us emphasize in closing this discussion that the solutions to counseling problems are not attained as easily as they are described. Counseling is usually a long process—more than sixty interviews were held with the college girl. Other problems may require more time, and of course, some less; but, typically, the actual implementation of plans is slow and laborious.

SUMMARY

In this chapter we have emphasized the learning aspects of behavioral change. We have discussed the application of the two main classes of learning theory, reinforcement and cognitive theory, as well as of theories that combine these two primary conceptual frameworks. Particular stress has been placed on cognitive and field theoretical approaches to the problems of counseling. In addition to the more theoretical positions, attention has been paid to the practical goals and procedures of re-education as they are applied to counseling and therapy. Finally, we have attempted to bring some of the theories and methods together by discussing them in relation to several actual examples of counseling.

BIBLIOGRAPHY

1. Appel, K. E., "Psychiatric therapy." In Hunt, J. McV. (ed.), *Personality and the behavior disorders*, Vol. II. New York: Ronald, 1944.
2. Cameron, D. E., *General psychotherapy*. New York: Grune & Stratton, 1950.
3. Conn, J. H., "The child reveals himself through play." *Ment. Hyg.*, 1939, 23, 49–69.
4. Cuber, J. F., *Marriage counseling practice.* New York: Appleton-Century-Crofts, 1948.
5. Dollard, J., and Miller, N. E., *Personality and psychotherapy*. New York: McGraw-Hill, 1950.
6. Dreikurs, R., "The immediate purpose of children's misbehavior, its recognition and correction." *Int. Zeitschrift: Indiv.-Psychol.*, 1950, 19, 70–87.
7. Hilgard, E. R., *Theories of learning*. New York: Appleton-Century-Crofts, 1948.
8. Kohler, W., *Gestalt psychology*. New York: Liveright, 1947.
9. Kraines, S. H., *The therapy of the neuroses and psychoses*. Philadelphia: Lea & Febiger, 1941.

10. Lewin, K., *A dynamic theory of personality*. New York: McGraw-Hill, 1935.
11. Lewin, K., *Principles of topological psychology*. New York: McGraw-Hill, 1936.
12. Lewin, K., *Resolving social conflicts*. New York: Harper, 1948.
13. McDougall, W., *The energies of man*. New York: Scribner, 1932.
14. Mowrer, O. H., *Learning theory and personality dynamics*. New York: Ronald, 1950.
15. Mowrer, O. H., "Motivation and neurosis." In Jones, M. R. (ed.), *Nebraska symposium on motivation*. Lincoln: University of Nebraska Press, 1954.
16. Mullahy, P., *Oedipus myth and complex*. New York: Hermitage, 1948.
17. Pearson, G. H. J., *Emotional disorder of children*. New York: Norton, 1949.
18. Rotter, J. B., *Social learning and clinical psychology*. New York: Prentice-Hall, 1954.
19. Shaw, F. J., "Clinical psychology and behavior theory." *J. Abnorm. Soc. Psychol.*, 1950, 45, 388–91.
20. Shaw, F. J., "The psychology of learning as the context of the rock 'em, sock 'em school." Presented to the MPA, Columbus, Ohio, April 30, 1954.
21. Shaw, F. J., "Mutuality and up-ending expectancies in counseling." *J. Consult. Psychol.*, 1955, 2, 241–7.
22. Snygg, D., and Combs, A. W., *Individual behavior*. New York: Harper, 1949.
23. Tolman, E. C., *Purposive behavior in animals and men*. New York: D. Appleton, 1932.
24. Wertheimer, M., "Gestalt theory." *Soc. Res.*, 1944, 11, 78–99.

✧

CHAPTER

8

Socialization

A LTHOUGH THE TERM "SOCIALIZATION" HAS DIFFERENT MEANINGS in different contexts, for the purposes of our present discussion we will consider it in two ways. In the most general sense socialization is a life-long process through which the individual learns a culture or possibly several cultures. More specifically, and from the point of view of the clinical and counseling psychologist, we can define socialization as a process whereby the individual is aided in his attempts to learn how to deal with people more effectively—vocationally, socially, and academically. In this definition we have stressed the learning of effective modes of social adjustment. In Chapter 7 we stressed the importance of socializing experiences and the dependence of changes in social behavior upon learning. In this respect the present discussion is an extension of the previous chapter. As an aim of psychological counseling, socialization is perhaps the ultimate goal. If all people were able to deal effectively with the individuals and groups with whom they come into contact, there would be little need for psychological counseling.

SOCIAL ORIENTATION AND PSYCHOPATHOLOGY

It is possible to conceptualize behavior disorders in terms of different perceptions of social reality. If we establish a hypothetical continuum ranging from extreme social orientation to extreme personal orientation, we can plot most of the common behavior disorders along this scale. At the extreme of awareness of social pressures, we might place persons with conversion reactions. These individuals are trying desperately to present themselves in a socially acceptable fashion. In an effort to ease tensions in social situations and in their attempts to find excuses that will justify their inability to adjust satisfactorily, they adopt physical symptoms of various kinds. The college girl client assumed a grimace. Another client may lose his ability to vocalize, and talk in a whisper. Sensory limitations, such as blindness and deafness, motor paralyses and associational difficulties in the nature of amnesia and fugue states, are commonly adopted without the existence of any real physical basis for these symptoms. A person may assume almost any kind of physical illness. Bodily symptoms are socially acceptable. Most of us would rather admit to a physical disability or limitation than acknowledge to ourselves and others that we are personally and socially unable to adapt to the social milieu. An elderly psychologist, who was suffering from what he regarded as a functional ailment, once said to us, "I'd thank God for one, good, honest pain."

Conversion reactions are usually suggested in some way. A fourth grader, whom we will call Danny, was referred to a psychological clinic because he became violently ill at regular intervals of about four weeks. At the time, several years ago, Kansas was a "dry" state. Each community had its bootlegger who went across the state line to bring in alcoholic beverages of various kinds. Danny worshipped his father, who was the bootlegger in a small town. His father was arrested regularly, but he was always released from jail after a week or ten days. He would then go back to his work, only to be arrested again in three or four weeks. After Danny began school in the first grade, only a few weeks elapsed before his father was arrested, and his classmates began to tease him. The chant, "Danny's father is in jail," could be heard from one end of the playground to another. Danny had to defend his father, and he fought the other children. He fought like a tiger, but, unfortunately, he took on too many children. He was rather badly beaten up, and had to be taken home; he was quite ill from the beating he had received and from the excitement attendant upon it. This happened several times, until he learned that if he were ill, he did not go to school; if he did not go to school, he was not teased; and if he was not teased, he did not need to fight. So he became ill each time his father was arrested. This extreme example shows one way in which a conversion mechanism was suggested. We must stress that this is not a conscious mechanism. The individual is not aware of what he is doing, although he appears to others either to be malingering, or to be definitely ill or handicapped. Actually he is neither. A conversion reaction is only a reasonable facsimile of the real thing, and it is unconsciously adopted.

This client responded remarkably well to a combination of environmental treatment and socialization. His father was helped to find a different occupation and Danny was taught ways of dealing with other children more effective than fighting. The counseling process was, of course, not actually this simple, but these were the main objectives, and Danny gradually became ill on fewer and fewer occasions.

At the other extreme of our hypothetical scale we have withdrawn, catatonic, schizophrenic behavior. Persons who exhibit this type of behavior have withdrawn completely into their own personal worlds. They have refused to take any responsibility for their own actions. They may be extremely compliant or extremely negativistic, but in the main they behave as if they were unaware of any interaction with social pressures. As contrasted with the conversion reactive, who seems highly extroverted, the catatonic reactive is very introverted. All his attention is turned in on himself. One man was in a stupor for eighteen months, during which time he lay rigid in his bed; he was fed by tube much of the time, and appeared oblivious to stimulation. When he finally recovered, he was asked, "Why were you this way?" He recounted a series of frustrations he had experienced in dealing with people and concluded, "I just darn well decided to do nothin'!" In treatment such an individual might be bombarded with friendly, nonthreatening, and rewarding social stimulation until he is able to react without penalty to personal attention. When his fears are diminished, he might be gently encouraged to interact with others. Small steps must be taken first, with social participation gradually increased.

Another client was so withdrawn that he walked about with his head hanging, never speaking to anyone. He was not regarded as pathologically psychotic because he was functioning as a student. He prepared his assignments, did good written work, but never participated in class discussions. When called upon, he said nothing; he simply hunched lower in his chair. He was unapproachable by the usual individual counseling activities; these require some communication since counseling is a social situation in and of itself. As a first aim this client had to be socialized. However, the initial stages had to be quite easy. As a beginning it was necessary for him to look at people. This took a lot of encouragement, but eventually he could look his counselor in the eye, and was able to smile at him, nod his head, and communicate at a simple level. In time he said, "Hello," to people he met on the street, and, finally, in a group counseling situation, he said a few words. The other members of the group were obviously so happy for him that he began to participate more and more. As is usual in counseling, other aims were also necessary before he was able to function effectively. After three years this client has been able to participate in a panel discussion in front of a class which was presented over television. His counselor had to be satisfied with extremely small gains before this most recent milestone was reached.

To return to our continuum, other behavioral reactions may be visualized between these points. Near the socially oriented end, we might place the neurasthenic behavior that will be described in the following chapter, in which the person becomes so tired because of tensions experienced in social situations that he gives up and becomes dependent on others. Further along the scale, and approaching the midpoint, are the anxiety reactions in which the person is overwhelmed by tension. Still further along, and near the beginning of the psychotic or personally oriented arm of the continuum, are the obsessive and compulsive reactions in which the person wards off anxiety by rigid and ritualistic controls over his interactions with others. Crossing over the midpoint, we might arrange the paranoid reactions, whereby the individual begins to disregard reality, and to manufacture his own world of delusions and hallucinations to explain the things that happen to him. Then we might arrange other so-called schizophrenic forms of behavior by which the person retreats from social reality or the anticipation of difficulties by returning to an earlier level of adjustment (regression), or by using equally effective forms of withdrawal. Any of these reactions may be approached, at least in part, by some emphasis on social treatment.

All these reactions differ from "normal" or adequate behavior only in degree. We do not need to go to the hospital or clinic to practice socialization. We can prevent withdrawal in individuals by helping them to enjoy healthy social experiences, or the development of neurotic mechanisms by teaching the individual more effective modes of social intercourse.

The student of the psychology of behavior disorders will note that the reactions sometimes referred to as manic and/or depressive behavior have been omitted from the above continuum. We hypothesize that these reactions are on a different continuum. They are seen as different degrees of affective lability, ranging from the extreme of excitability to the extreme of retardation and "flatness" of affect. Each of the other behavioral reactions on the above continuum could vary on this second range of mood variability. The task of adjusting the mood-reactions of a client so that they are reasonably appropriate to the situations in which he finds himself is also a problem mainly in the realm of social learning.

LEARNING THEORY AND SOCIALIZATION

1. JULIAN B. ROTTER. The significance of language as a tool for social learning has long been recognized by many workers. The statements of Rotter (22) are most explicit in this regard. Psychological counseling is to him essentially an educative and interpretative process. His procedure for promoting increased socialization for his client entails discussion of alternative modes of behavior in social situations. Rotter's method is to evaluate alternatives with his client in terms of the present and the ultimate gratifications that might result from them. Presumably, he then urges his client to engage in, or experiment with, several alternative modes of action so that the behaviors will be either reinforced or inhibited by the appropriate reward or punishment connected with them.

This is essentially the procedure suggested for use with the engineer mentioned earlier. Like Shaw (24), Rotter speaks of changing expectancies, but it would appear that his method of change is a mechanical process that results from great quantities of interpretation and conditioning. In his system the primary duty of the counselor is to foster alternative modes of behavior and point out the reward and punishment that might be associated with each alternative.

2. O. HOBART MOWRER.   Mowrer (15) does not deal specifically with the topic of socialization as a learning process. But it would appear that according to his concept, socialization takes the course of learning to conform to the restrictive aspects of a culture and assimilating the mores of that culture. Thus, to him, socialization in counseling or therapy is a process that acquaints the individual with the regulations of his culture, society, and class. Such socialization may also entail teaching the client to act in accordance with these mores to the best of his ability. This concept of socialization should be considered by the counselor in planning for the client. Many clients are not aware of some of the formal and informal rules of our society. In many instances teaching social ethics is a legitimate counseling activity, and although this interpretation of socialization is rather specific, we must not neglect its possibilities.

3. JURGEN RUESCH.   Another aspect of socialization in counseling is described by Jurgen Ruesch (23). He is in accord with the Dollard and Miller (5) viewpoint, and believes that interaction between individuals is the result of the social techniques acquired by them. The term "social technique" is used to describe all of the methods used by an individual in approaching, managing, and handling other persons. This concept of the social technique can then be separated into the four essential components of drive, cue, response, and reward. In his discussion Ruesch assumes that while drive, response, and reward are relatively fixed for each individual, the observation, nature, and management of cues is largely a social and cultural function. He believes that cultures are defined by the fact that people of a given culture observe and respond to the same cues. The presence of rewards within his culture induces the individual to learn and remember cues. Thus, the reward and punishment values that are culturally associated with the observation of cues are introjected or internalized by the individual. In this way, when a cue is perceived, it elicits in the individual a simultaneous sensation of punishment and reward. During their training, children are rewarded for the observation of cues that lead to conforming behavior and punished for the observation of cues that lead to nonconforming behavior. Thus, the observation of cues becomes a basis for individual and group behavior.

The problem of socialization in psychological counseling becomes, then, one of teaching the client new cues for new social situations, and helping him to forget old cues from prior social situations that are no longer appropriate in the present. We might speculate, as Ruesch does, that socialization is a particularly necessary part of counseling in America because our society, with its flexible social stratification, literally invites the individual to change his social status. Ruesch believes, too, that social mobility and social status have essentially a therapeutic and prognostic value. He points out that clients whose social status is declining offer poor prognoses, while social climbers tend to present more hopeful prognoses.

Ruesch (23, pp. 126–8) gives numerous examples of cultural changes that involve "adaptive behavior, a change in social techniques." Such transitions as "from childhood to adulthood, from the family circle to the wider social environment, from civilian to military life, from one social class to another one, from one American region to another, from rural to urban living, or from ethnic to American" require that attitudes be changed and that the introjected reward and punishment values be modified. Changes of this kind are encountered by the psychological counselor, and he is frequently impressed by the relative ease with which some clients make the transition, as against the difficulty experienced by others. Ruesch offers an explanation of this variation in success and illustrates his reasoning by the process of acculturation from ethnic to American. This is regarded as a difficult transition and one that is in most instances accompanied by conflict. "Areas where difficulties in acculturation are encountered usually deal with responses and cues which are characterized by strong reward and punishment values." Cues with technical value are assimilated easily, as illustrated by the ease with which the foreign worker adapts vocationally and occupationally. On the other hand, as Ruesch indicates, we find that the learning of new cues and responses is difficult in such areas as eating habits, religion, attitudes toward parents, and matters of child rearing. The old cues and responses have reward value, and the new ones frequently have punishment value since they may be counter to the teachings of the individual's old culture.

> The problem gets even more complicated in the second generation. Whenever the values of parents and environment coincide, there is no conflict. But if the new culture offers reward value, while the parent punishes for acceptance or rejection of a given cue, the result is ambivalence, confusion, and possibly total rejection or rebellion against acceptance of any values.

Ruesch suggests that cues that are predominantly culturally determined can easily be changed by pointing out to the individual that they no longer apply in the present. This suggestion is well taken except that situations are seldom this simple. Clients frequently find it difficult to reject old behavioral patterns because in so doing they feel that they are at the same time rejecting their parents. Consequently, counseling in such instances must help the client to discriminate between the cues that are associated with culture and those that are related to the parents. The counselor must be sure that he has a valid reason for suggesting social activities to an individual if these activities conflict with the individual's cultural background. It follows that the clinician should be aware of the cultural background before he suggests any course of action. We remember our embarrassment when, after we had advised a young lady to take up dancing because of her lack of grace and her awkwardness, her father came to us and berated us for suggesting dancing, which would surely send his daughter to perdition. We had neglected to attach the proper significance to the particular religious sect to which the family belonged—one in which dancing was considered a horrible sin. In spite of the need to observe certain cautions, the counselor should always be prepared to encourage the learning of new social techniques, as this is one of the important aspects of healthy behavioral change.

4. FRANKLIN J. SHAW. According to Shaw and Robert S. Ort (24, p. 311), "Learning to interact in social positions adaptively requires (1) practice or experience, (2) analysis and understanding of expectations of such interaction, and (3) the selection of modes of social interaction that are uniquely suited to one's own resources." [1] Although the discussion does not concern itself primarily with the task of the psychological counselor, this concept of learning what is called "adaptive interaction" can be applied to the promotion of socialization.

With regard to the first requirement they describe how experience in various forms of social interaction is gained in the process of development. A young child prepares for adult activities by playing games that call for him to assume the role of parent, teacher, doctor, or storekeeper. Other examples given by Shaw and Ort are the practice trials in law schools, the vicarious experience gained by medical students in observing operations, and the more general vicarious experience gained when we listen to another relate his experiences or watch another interact in a certain position.

The rationale behind all the laboratory, practicum, and internship experiences required in the training of the psychological counselor is along the same vein. These examples illustrate the principle of "learning by doing." In counseling we encourage our client to play roles of various kinds, thus giving him practice in some role he may later be called upon to assume. As we shall see, this is one aspect of group counseling, and

[1] This and following quotations from *Personal Adjustment in the American Culture,* by Franklin J. Shaw and Robert S. Ort are printed by permission of Dr. Shaw and Harper & Brothers. Copyright 1953 by Harper & Brothers.

it is also a technique that can be used in the individual setting. To carry the examples a bit further, psychological counseling can and does utilize vicarious experience and observation by encouraging the client to observe others interact in situations and to imagine himself in the same situations. In group meetings a client may relate experiences that were successful, while others listen and then in turn relate their own experiences. A form of bibliotherapy may be employed in which biographies and case histories are studied. As Shaw and Ort (p. 313) suggest, the profit gained by the individual from this type of experience or practice depends to a large extent upon what he expects of himself as he gains the experience. "If he can regard flaws in his performance as a part of the learning process . . . he will not only be more comfortable with himself, but will also be more inclined to try to gain further experience with the attitude that his mistakes are something to be profited from rather than reasons for adopting a defeatist outlook."

It follows, then, that the second and third requirements of their analysis of the learning situation must be emphasized for counseling as well as for normal development. Practice in social interaction must be accompanied by discussion of experiences by the client and the counselor. Shaw and Ort offer a rather complicated classification of social expectations into: (a) an individual's expectations of his own interaction, (b) others' expectations of his interaction, (c) his expectations of the interaction of others, and (d) others' expectations of their own interactions. Whether he follows this outline or some simpler approach, the counselor should aid the client in identifying sources of difficulty in his social relationships. Through analysis of these sources of difficulty and further practice the client is helped to understand and correct his expectations as well as his actual behavioral reactions. Finally, the client must choose social situations and modes of social interaction within these situations that are suited to his own resources. Many clients are "running in the wrong race"—or, as Shaw might say, not "leading their own lives"— and as a result are expecting to succeed in situations that provide little possibility for their personal success. Before we encourage a client to engage in any form of social experimentation, we must make certain that he has a clear idea of his own resources and limitations. In this way we can ensure that his expectations will have some basis in reality and that he chooses his situations in terms of these expectations.

THE DIRECTIVE COUNSELING APPROACH
AND SOCIALIZATION

1. FREDERICK C. THORNE (25), one of the more directive counselors, postulates that defects or disorders in learning control may be etio-

logical factors in the types of personality disorder that are characterized by desocialization under frustration or stress. Socialization is the best technique for dealing with these personality disorders. Thorne believes that all formal counseling involves putting pressure on the client to direct action toward specific goals, which are mainly social. Methods ranging from individual pressure to overt coercion are indicated when a person demonstrates inability to exert reasonable self-control. Pressure and coercion are thought to be educative and therapeutic methods, with rehabilitation rather than punishment as their objective.

Psychological counseling, according to Thorne (25, p. 192), demands that the counselor give the client information so that he can develop a more correct and up-to-date *Weltanschauung*. This type of reeducation may require more wisdom and intellectual breadth than the average counselor possesses, and as a consequence other sources or source persons may be called upon as the occasion arises.

> An individual social prescription must be made for each person. He must be introduced to a wide variety of things to discover what might interest him, and follow-up work must be done to see that he actually succeeds in getting started on his own initiative. This may mean that the counselor makes arrangements for him to join social groups, to learn new hobbies, to get started in gardening, or to learn to knit. It may include a prescription to join the young people's organization at church, or to take dancing lessons. Arrangements will have to be made for the wall-flower to meet dancing partners or for the elderly person to start going to grange meetings again.[2]

In this vein Thorne joins other counselors in his emphasis upon increased socialization as an important tool as well as a goal of counseling.

2. SAMUEL H. KRAINES. Kraines (10, p. 256), who can also be classed as directive, offers the following opinion:

> One of the best forms of constructive outlets for the pent-up energy is in *socialization*. Visiting with one's friends, going to group affairs, interesting one's self in organizational activities are excellent means for utilizing energy. Too often patients become seclusive and almost asocial when their neurotic symptoms develop; and this seclusiveness creates a vicious cycle, wherein the patient has more time to think of his own ailments which thus become exaggerated, and also, because loss of contact with others means loss of the opportunity to orient one's

---

[2] From *Principles of Personality Counseling* by Frederick C. Thorne. Copyright 1950 by Frederick C. Thorne. Reprinted by permission of the author.

self toward realities as others see them. The fact that patients state that they have no satisfaction in going out, or that the association with others merely makes them feel worse, should be overcome by the explanation given above and the patients should be urged to enter social activities, despite their reluctance to do so. It will be found in the average patient that after the first two or three visits to friends, the original antipathy disappears and the patient begins to improve. Yet, the physician must persist in urging the patient, for without the moral suasion, many patients will relapse and lose all the value they gained from their contacts.[3]

But (p. 549):

Socialization of the community is even more important than socialization of the individual. One of the fundamental and almost "inherent" aversions present in the human beast is fear and dislike of "strangers." Much of the distrust and suspicion in local communities is the result of the fact that persons are "strangers" to their neighbors. Any activity which enables members of the community to get to know each other is an aid in overcoming such distrust and in increasing community action. Toward that end, the "block" meetings which have been instituted in American cities are of great ultimate value. Such groups should eventually have national problems presented to them for analysis and for suggestions, and the sum total of such thought should be a powerful and wholesome influence on legislative bodies.

3. D. EWEN CAMERON.   D. E. Cameron (2, pp. 289–91) believes that the difficulties of a client are a manifestation of a sick society, and therefore methods of prevention should be concerned with the manipulation of social forces. This "manipulation of the forces which act upon the individual in his day-to-day living—forces derived from his home, his school, his work"—is the function of the counselor. Social manipulation is related to group counseling but it is more extensive in scope and in a way lies beyond the hospital and/or office. Its main function should be preventive, but it is often therapeutic. Although Cameron believes that socialization is indicated for the majority of clients, he states that it can best be used with the aged suffering from social dislocation, with children suffering under the stresses of a disorganized home, and with those of the mentally handicapped whose breakdowns have taken

[3] This and the following quotation from *The Therapy of the Neuroses and Psychoses*, by Samuel H. Kraines are printed by permission of Dr. Kraines and Lea & Febiger, Publishers. Copyright 1948 by Lea & Febiger.

place as a result of their inability to keep up with a demanding environment.

He outlines two principles basic to his conception of "social psychotherapy." The first of these involves the recognition and reduction of environmental stresses—the stress may be removed or the stresses may be modified if removal is not possible. The individual's response to stress may be modified. Second, he advocates the development of favorable factors in the client's environmental setting. Examples of this principle are such activities as placing the child in a favorable or a stable home, reintegration of aged individuals in group activities, and the use of such groups as AA. Cameron believes that the counselor should pay more heed to current and situational stresses and take definite steps to alleviate them. This can be done by setting up family discussion groups, in which the relatives of a client would meet under the guidance of a counselor to discuss human behavior in general. In the community area, the counselor would be called upon to manipulate existing social institutions, to create special facilities, and to manipulate the community group. Aid should be given to those suffering from anxiety states, feelings of inadequacy, feelings of rejection, the aged, and recent immigrants, by the provision of social groups and satisfying social experiences.

NONDIRECTIVE COUNSELING AND SOCIALIZATION

In turning now to less directive procedures and theories, we find that Rogers (21) views socialization as involving environmental manipulation in which group pressure in a new or changed situation seems the most efficient means of altering the individual's attitudes and behavior. This is regarded as a sound basis for treatment in many instances, although it has little application for individuals who have attained a reasonable degree of adult maturity. He believes that only in the case of the criminal, the psychotic, the defective, or the individual who is for other reasons incapable of taking responsibility for himself can we freely use socialization involving environmental manipulation with adults. Socialization may be used with the problem child in the instance where the child's problems are those of social maladjustment, or when a better group adjustment will provide satisfactions that make problem behavior less necessary in other areas. The school is in an excellent position to deal with the solitary, friendless, shy, or fearful child. It is suggested that when organized recreational groups fail, academic goals such as a class project may help in his socialization. The counselor must begin on the child's existing level of social adjustment and gradually work toward more social skills, wider circles of social activity, and more diverse types of co-operation.

Norman Cameron's (3) idea that socialization, as it is reflected in the counseling situation, is an active learning situation corresponds with Axline's (1) thoughts concerning socialization. Both conceive of the counseling situation as a miniature social community and expect habits learned in this small community to be generalized to larger social situations. Axline utilizes socialization experiences in both individual and group counseling. In the group situation she feels that children may work out by themselves problem solutions that are just as difficult as those faced by any adult or group of adults. She does warn that a child in a group should not be made to feel that he is being compared or contrasted with any other member of the group. The child's feeling of complete acceptance by the counselor is more easily established in individual counseling contacts than in group contacts because the possibility of comparison or implied criticism cannot enter into the individual situation. The group situation requires interaction between individuals, which brings about a (p. 10) "constantly changing integration within the individual" which culminates in "self-realization." Axline feels that the drive toward maturity, independence, and self-direction (Rogers' growth principle) will develop a well-balanced individual if it has "good growing ground." It is the task of the counselor to provide or find this ground.

We regard well-chosen and well-controlled socialization experiences as indispensable to child counseling. We are not quite as concerned as is Axline with the child's feeling of acceptance at all times. The child will not always experience acceptance, and he must learn to contend with nonacceptance in his broader social adjustments. Children normally learn successful social techniques through their association with children and adults in a variety of social settings. In the counseling process they should be systematically exposed to as many of these situations as possible, with care being taken that the conditions are such as to encourage the learning of effective behavior.

SOCIALIZATION AS AN AIM IN EDUCATIONAL GUIDANCE AND COUNSELING

Harold B. and Pauline N. Pepinsky (19, p. 293) have urged that it is time for a shift of emphasis in the psychological clinics of the various colleges and universities. Instead of thinking of socialization as an aspect or goal of the counseling process (as we propose in this text), they stress the importance of emphasis on socialization in addition to individual psychological counseling. They say:

> Although psychologists talk of adjustment being in terms of cultural norms, many therapists in the college counseling situation have relied on a relatively stable social environment. The

assumption is no longer tenable. This condition implies a necessity for greater breadth of training in social dynamics and a greater flexibility in the use of therapeutic techniques.

Arthur J. Jones (9) outlines many of the more useful techniques in socialization as adjuncts to counseling. He discusses such techniques as panels, forums, committee reports, individual contributions to discussion, lectures, contests, dramatics, radio, moving pictures, question boxes, case conferences, and the like. All these approaches are suggested as valuable adjuncts to counseling when dealing with students who are shy or retiring, or who do not have proper and adequate social tools at their disposal to interact with others in a satisfactory manner. Some of the aims of this type of socialization, as listed by Lester D. and Alice Crow (4), are directed at guiding the individual toward "social competence." Such aims are:

1. To develop wholesome emotional life and altruistic attitudes.
2. To develop good manners and poise.
3. To be friendly and co-operative.
4. To create and maintain congeniality in small intimate groups.
5. To become economically productive members of society.
6. To become responsible members of the community.
7. To participate in the determination of the direction to be taken by existing social forces.

These counselors, as well as David W. Lefever, *et al.* (11), illustrate the increasing recognition of the sociological aspects of adjustment. They stress the role of education in preventing, identifying, and remedying the social maladjustments of students. It is through participation in the social and civic life of the school that the student can gain personal and social adjustment, and the psychological counselor can capitalize on all such activities to further his client's social facility.

SOCIALIZATION IN THE HOSPITAL SITUATION

Socialization, in a narrower sense than the one in which we have been using the term, is applied as a formal program in many of the mental hospitals in the United States. These programs vary from hospital to hospital and no two are alike, but they all have some similarities. An example of a somewhat typical program is the one conducted by the Special Services Department of the Veterans Administration Hospital at Marion, Indiana. This department carries on, among other activities in the "total push" effort (adapted sports, music therapy, library activities, canteen activities), an activity that they call resocialization. This program consists of two parts, group resocialization and individual resocialization. In the group division the accent is on group games, dancing, popcorn mixers, smokers, and the like. These are designed to bring about maximal interaction among the patients as well as teamwork and some competition. In the individual division the focus is on activities such as reading poems, plays, essays, and editorials and recording them. Social graces, such as properly answering the telephone and introducing people, are rehearsed until the patient feels confident in the activity. This program is designed to give the individual more confidence in himself as an individual and as a part of a larger group. It is followed in the resocialization program both of the maximum security and of the open wards, with the degree of intensity geared to the ward that is being served at the time. The hospital considers that the program is a good one and, for the most part, fairly effective.

This type of program certainly offers much to the majority of patients. The limitation of many large-scale "total push" socialization efforts is that the individual patient may "get lost in the shuffle" and that his unique needs may not be met. If socialization is to be maximally successful, we must constantly think in terms of how the program can meet individual needs, and we must make adjustments and institute new variations as dictated by these individual needs. We must avoid the situation that occurred at another hospital where all patients were required to attend the hospital church service every Sunday morning. The defense of this policy was that all could profit from the social group participation in singing and in going to and from the church, and from the inspiration of the services. The only chaplain available was of a rather sectarian denomination and for this reason, if for no other, many patients rebelled at the requirement. Without further elaboration, it is difficult to comprehend how the mandatory church attendance could be of value to all patients.

In a more positive vein, we were impressed by a plan at another hospital to abolish special departments in the recreational program so that all staff members would feel free to conduct and supervise whatever activities the patients might desire at any particular time. Rather than scheduling a music hour under the leadership of the music specialist or an athletic hour to be conducted by the physical education staff member, the plan is to have recreational leaders available at all times to organize such group socialization activities as will be profitable to the patients present at the time. If a patient is to adjust outside the hospital, he must be able to take some responsibility for planning his social activity. Since this, in itself, is an aspect of socialization, individual and group planning should be encouraged in the hospital treatment program.

SOME PHILOSOPHICAL THOUGHTS
ON SOCIALIZATION

It would seem that socialization, as it is related to psychological counseling, can be approached from many points of view as well as at varying levels of complexity. In his *Civilization and Its Discontents* Freud (6) spoke of socialization as the struggle of man's original nature in opposition to his second nature (or culture). Mowrer (15), on the other hand, views neurosis not as oversocialization but undersocialization. Therapeutically, Freud would suggest the removal of restraints and inhibitions, while Mowrer would insist upon the development of more responsible controls. We have here two divergent theoretical assumptions concerning the nature of socialization, and therapeutic procedures that differ accordingly. It is interesting to note that Fromm's (7) idea of the properly socialized man contains both concepts—his autonomous man is both spontaneous and responsible. The usual methods of psychological counseling stress both flexibility and tolerance of ambiguity. This is our concept of healthy adjustment—thus our idealization of the "autonomous man," or the "integrative individual." Those who reach this stage of development, it is assumed, are truly socialized individuals. In Riesmann's (20) words, such people have good social radar, use it when they choose, but can make choices out of their own individuality.

However, there are those who suggest that our symptoms of good adjustment may be subterfuges of an unstable culture, which has little to give but ambiguity. Edith Weisskopf-Joelson (26) has pointed out that Western culture might be characterized by the absence of a strong, comprehensive, and insistent philosophy that gives the individual an interpretation of the purpose of life and a set of values by which to live. Talcott Parsons (18) in his *Patterns of Aggression in the Social Structure of the Western World* points out that in the middle classes primary (kinship) relations foster a level of socialization which makes the child anxious and forces him to repress his aggression. For this reason, he is not well fitted to make the social adjustment into his occupational system in an easy continuous manner. This discrepancy in turn produces more anxiety, and the occupational system merely reinforces the tendency to repress aggression and express it by projection to scapegoats. He characterizes our civilization as paranoid. Robert Merton (14) offers this central hypothesis: abnormal behavior may be regarded as a symptom of deviation from culturally prescribed aspirations and socially structured avenues for realizing these aspirations. The American culture emphasizes certain success goals without equivalent emphasis upon institutive means; this results in imperfect co-ordination between goals and means, which is conducive to "anomie" (normlessness). Indeed, in an "anomie" structure, the autonomous man will flourish—he has social radar, and it would seem that the end (goals) will justify the means, provided too many toes are not stepped on.

We are not implying that the ideal of counseling is to produce autonomous men; one must often settle for a functioning man. But the recognition that counselors inadvertently influence their clients to accept specific value systems suggests that the dynamics of the autonomous man be looked at more carefully. Robert J. Havighurst (8) conducted an empirical study on the adolescents of a large city, using interviews, a personality inventory, TAT, Rorschach, and Mooney Problem-Check list. He found the following characteristics in the self-directive person: he is ambitious, conscientious, and orderly; his moral beliefs are variable, and highly uncertain; he has conflicts with his parents; in his personal adjustment he is self-centered, self-doubting, somewhat anxious, concerned with moral problems, moves away from people, lacks warmth in human relationships, and gains security through achievement. It will be observed that these adolescents are deeply concerned about moral problems, yet they have variable and uncertain moral and ethical beliefs. They have good social radar, but just where do they stand in relation to their environment?

Without belittling the irrational, emotional components of man's personality, one often wonders just how much the rational capacity of man plays a role in his development. Some feel that it is of considerable importance. Joseph Nuttin (17), in his *Psychoanalysis and Personality*, observes that more than biological interaction, and even more than communion of any other kind with his fellow men, man needs a more universal sort of communication and support and integration. He needs to be able to know that he has been integrated, and to feel himself integrated, into an absolute order of existence. Rollo May (14), in his *Man's Search for Himself*, agrees in essence with Nuttin's ideas.

In the past many psychological counselors have dealt with values in a cautious way. In fact we have seen resistance on the part of counselors to take any kind of stand on problems of value. This being the case, it is no wonder that the value-system component of the socialization problem has come to be considered secondary, if it is considered at all. Yet, if socialization is the process by which man establishes a wholesome relationship with his milieu, why not a heavier and bolder emphasis on values in the counseling session and in other activities? And if a counselor adamantly denies the validity of this approach, why not have him make his values explicit—since these values have a way of inadvertently influencing the client. May not the parrying of a client's question as to what is right, by the democratic reply, "What do *you* think is right?" reinforce the idea that good is a matter of taste? It would seem that man is capable of cognitive growth—there are the emotions—but in Lewin's terms, the process of socialization is characterized by increasing differentiation of the life space. Change in the cognitive structure may result from changes within the cognitive structure itself, that is, knowledge and change may result from changes in the individual's valences, values, and hopes.

The concept of socialization is complex and far-reaching. It is a concept that has been made useful and understandable in many fields, and that overlaps with other frequently used concepts such as environmental manipulation, group therapy, and college counseling. We feel that, in the long run, it will become increasingly important in both psychology and sociology in the United States. The tensions produced by cold wars, by the geometrically increasing growth of the population, by vastly overcrowded slums, by industrial and technological advancements, all create a greater need for interpersonal harmony among people. This harmony is forthcoming only if the people who make up our culture are up to the job of adjusting well, and adjusting well is certainly a legitimate variable in socialization.

SUMMARY

Socialization has been described as a rather specialized and highly important end product of learning. The attainment of effective social interaction has been seen as an important aspect of mental health. A number of characteristics of abnormal behavior were conceptualized as differing degrees of social awareness, with the neurotic behavior reactions viewed as socially oriented, and the psychotic reactions as personally oriented. A few general suggestions were made and some examples given of the application of socialization to counseling with individuals with these behavioral reactions. The procedures and theories of Rotter, Shaw, and others were described as the applications of learning theory to the promotion of increased socialization. The more explicit re-education procedures of Thorne and Kraines, and the social manipulation approach of D. Ewen Cameron were briefly outlined. The use of socialization in the school, in the hospital, and in the community was elaborated from several theoretical and practical points of view. Finally, we indulged in some philosophizing about the functions of a healthy, efficient person in our society and culture. This speculative thought led to the suggestion that mental health may be a function of the personal adequacy of individual value systems.

BIBLIOGRAPHY

1. Axline, V. M., *Play therapy*. Boston: Houghton Mifflin, 1947.
2. Cameron, D. E., "Observations on the patterns of anxiety." *Amer. J.*

Psychiat., 1944, 101, 36–41. Also *General psychotherapy.* New York: Grune & Stratton, 1950.

3. Cameron, N., *The psychology of behavior disorders.* Boston: Houghton Mifflin, 1947.
4. Crow, L. K., and Crow, A., *An introduction to guidance.* New York: American Book, 1951.
5. Dollard, J., and Miller, N. E., *Personality and psychotherapy.* New York: McGraw-Hill, 1950.
6. Freud, S., *Civilization and its discontents.* New York: Cope & Smith, 1930.
7. Fromm, E., *Escape from freedom.* New York: Farrar & Rinehart, 1947.
8. Havighurst, R. J., and Taba, H., *Adolescent character and personality.* New York: Wiley, 1939.
9. Jones, A. J., *Principles of guidance.* New York: McGraw-Hill, 1951.
10. Kraines, S. H., *The therapy of the neuroses and psychoses.* Philadelphia: Lea & Febiger, 1948.
11. Lefever, D. W., Turrell, A. M., and Weitzel, H. I., *Principles and techniques of guidance.* New York: Ronald, 1941.
12. Lewin, K., *Resolving social conflicts.* New York: Harper, 1948.
13. May, R., *Man's search for himself.* New York: Norton, 1953.
14. Merton, R., *Social theory and social structure* (rev. ed.). Glencoe, Ill.: Free Press, 1957.
15. Mowrer, O. H., *Learning theory and personality dynamics.* New York: Ronald, 1950.
16. Newcomb, T. M., "Autistic hostility and social reality." *Human Relat.*, 1947, 1, 29–88.
17. Nuttin, J., *Psychoanalysis and personality.* New York: Sheed & Ward, 1953.
18. Parsons, T., *Essays in sociological theory.* Glencoe, Ill.: Free Press, 1954.
19. Pepinsky, H. B., and Pepinsky, P. N., "Implications of social dynamics for methods of therapy with college students." *Amer. Psychologist*, 1947, 2, 292–3.
20. Riesmann, D., Glazer, N., and Denney, R., *The lonely crowd.* New York: Doubleday, 1955.
21. Rogers, C. R., *Client-centered therapy.* Boston: Houghton Mifflin, 1951.
22. Rotter, J. B., *Social learning and clinical psychology.* New York: Prentice-Hall, 1954.
23. Ruesch, J., "Social technique, social status and social change in illness." In Kluckhohn, C., and Murray, H. A. (eds.), *Personality in nature, society and culture.* New York: Alfred A. Knopf, 1948.
24. Shaw, F. J., and Ort, R. S., *Personal adjustment in the American culture.* New York: Harper, 1953.
25. Thorne, F., *Principles of personality counseling.* Brandon, Vt.: J. Clin. Psychol., 1950.
26. Weisskopf-Joelson, E., "Some suggestions concerning Weltanschauung and psychotherapy." *J. Abnorm. Soc. Psychol.*, 1953, 48, 601–4.

Part Two

✵ ✵

PRACTICAL PROCEDURES AND TECHNIQUES

☼

CHAPTER

9

Environmental Treatment

THE USE OF ENVIRONMENTAL FACTORS IS AN IMPORTANT ASPECT OF counseling. Since, in line with the philosophy of this text, the function of counseling is to aid the individual in altering the interaction between himself and his environment, it follows that the psychologist must consider the positive benefits to be gained by manipulating the environmental situation. In actual counseling practice one cannot expect to alter the environmental forces without having an accompanying alteration in the person's reaction to the environment and thus an alteration in the total situation. For purposes of discussion, however, we must isolate a part of the total situation. Our presentation of environmental treatment will include: definition and examples, methods and techniques, its relation to and importance in various theoretical frameworks, its application in the hospital setting, and contributions to it from the field of social work.

ENVIRONMENTAL TREATMENT DEFINED

Environmental treatment may be defined as any process designed to help an individual or a group of individuals make desirable behavioral adjustments by inducing changes in the social or physical environment. The degree of alteration may vary from a change in one or several factors in the individual's normal routine, to his temporary or permanent removal from his habitual mode of life to an entirely new situation. It is probably impossible, even in permanently removing the client to a new situation, to bring about a complete change in the environment, as the individual is a part of his environment and he is not subject to complete and instantaneous alteration.

The word "designed" is used in the definition to indicate a conscious direction. A conscious direction is necessary if the process is to be regarded as therapeutic. In some situations the mere passage of time will bring about environmental changes that will have a beneficial effect. For example, after a few months of service the dejected military recruit may have become a happy, efficient soldier who can assume responsibility. However we can hardly call this the result of treatment if it was brought about simply by the passage of time. But if in a particular situation a counselor instead of taking more positive action with a client recommends waiting for events to take place, or if he consciously encourages the client to take more responsibility over a period of time, this can be designated as a counseling or therapeutic procedure. Environmental counseling and therapy can be as simple as that. The psychological counselor is urged to be constantly alert to the possibility of simple and direct solutions. As another example, neurotic tendencies in the adolescent frequently disappear as he begins to receive needed recognition. If instead of instituting a more drastic program, a counselor recommends that time be given a chance to produce situational changes, this constitutes a therapeutic goal. Even though time alone may bring about beneficial environmental changes, a counselor or therapist can often expedite the process through his conscious efforts. He must always keep environmental factors in mind as he plans for and with his client. This, then, is the aim or goal of environmental treatment.

Robert I. Watson (22) differentiates between modification of the environment and manipulation of the environment. Modification is less extreme and stresses changes in some aspects of the life setting as it exists in the present; manipulation refers to removal to a new environment. In therapy with children, for example, both procedures are designed to modify those factors in the environment which are considered either causally related or contributing to the continuance of behavior disorders. If the environment appears to be one with which the child will never learn to cope, removal is perhaps indicated; but if in the present home setting changes can be made or new experiences added that might be expected to bring about a better adjustment, they should always be attempted before more drastic measures are taken. Watson states that the history of environmental therapy shows that emphasis in the past was usually on institutional placement and that work with parents was largely confined to the authoritarian "telling-them-what-to-do" approach, the assumption being that parents should be directed to change the "outer forces" on the child. He lists the two developments that contributed most to an alteration of this directive attitude: (a) recognition that the child's personality is a composite of external as well as internal forces, and (b) wider recognition of the value and use of newer techniques such as play therapy and the interview. He notes, however, that the change from a pedagogical to a therapeutic point of view has been slow to develop. In this chapter we will consider both modification and manipulation of the environment as techniques of counseling.

No clearly defined line exists between environmental therapy and personal counseling or traditional psychotherapy. Strictly speaking, problem-solving by means of insight or the use of supportive procedures in the interview situation involves environmental therapy in that the interview itself constitutes a change in environment. Attempting to solve problems by changing the individual through personal counseling will ordinarily not lead to permanent adjustment unless the changed attitudes and behavior are applied directly in the client's daily home and social life. If a problem is situational—external to the individual—environmental manipulation may be the only means to a satisfactory solution. In instances in which the problem has become internalized, personal as well as environmental treatment will be required.

If we consider some of the persons mentioned in Chapter 1, we can see that environmental therapy is only a part of the over-all program of planned counseling. We described a man who was troubled by hearing an irritating voice. The associations that led him to attach importance to voices on the radio or to become upset when the voice of a friend reminded him of the irritating voice were within himself. He could hardly have escaped from them by changing his environment—he tried several times but the haunting voice continued to follow him. It is clear that environmental therapy would not dispose of his dreams. The girl who had developed the facial grimace (to compensate, by displaying her perfect teeth) had little control over the environmental factors that made it necessary for her to compensate. She had a beautiful, popular twin sister with whom she could not compete socially and two brothers, who were professional men, with whom she was afraid to compete intellectually. It would have been difficult to manipulate these factors. We have described how she was able to develop an objective understanding of the effects of these factors and to learn compensatory reactions that were more effective than the grimace.

On the other hand, environmental therapy played an important part in counseling with the youngster who had good practical skills with animals and farm equipment but was failing in his school work. His life situation was altered favorably when his parents and teachers were given some understanding of the reasons for his poor academic work. But even here environmental therapy (treating those within his environment) was not sufficient to enable him to make a completely effective adjustment. It was necessary to give him special education, using methods of instruction which were carefully planned to fit his abilities, and adequate vocational guidance and training to enable him to get as much satisfaction as possible from his nonverbal skills. We will have more to say about him later.

EXAMPLES OF ENVIRONMENTAL TREATMENT

Environmental treatment includes such diverse procedures as guiding the individual into satisfying activities; counseling with his family, teachers, employers, or supervisors; modifying his physical environment or removing him from a harmful environment.

Rest or vacation is a common type of environmental treatment. The rest or the change in scenery in itself may not be the therapeutic agent, as much as is removal from annoying stimuli or change of habits. The results of this type of treatment are often temporary, and in some instances rest may actually become a hindrance to adjustment as the individual may tend to become morbid and introspective because of having "time on his mind." For this reason rest is usually most effective if accompanied by well-chosen physical and mental activities.

Music and art may be conceived of as forms of environmental therapy. Such media are ordinarily used as adjuncts to other treatment or counseling activities. Music often provides an opening wedge to help the counselor or therapist gain rapport with the client—in other words, to put the client in the proper mood. The use of music in hospital wards has been found to reduce the activity of some patients and, when carefully chosen, to stimulate activity in others. The observation has been made that music often reduces the number of demands for cigarettes and the frequency of trips to the toilet. Art provides a medium for the expression of feelings and ideas. The use of music and art may also promote emotional release or tension reduction. Physical types of environmental therapy include swimming, dancing, sports, games, and physical therapy. Examples of "mental" environmental therapy are reading, writing, psychodrama, hobbies, and the intentional introduction of stress situations. Vocational counseling, job changes, and industrial or work assignments (both within and beyond the hospital setting) are procedures that may be designated as vocational environmental therapies.

Let us return to our young stock showman to illustrate one form of environmental therapy. In his case the greatest need appeared to be that of modifying the attitudes of his parents and teachers. A careful evaluation of certain test performances suggested that although he was average or above in nonverbal skills, he was extremely deficient in verbal and abstract skills. This deficiency had interfered with his learning to read. In arithmetic he could work concrete problems, but abstract ones were beyond his comprehension. The conditions of his birth gave ample reason to believe that he had suffered at least minimal brain damage. His older sister was an excellent student with high intellectual capacities. His parents were college graduates, and his father was a successful farmer. Both parents had high aspirations for the boy and were disturbed by his poor academic ability. His teachers believed him to be either lazy or stubborn. Because of the various pressures brought to bear on him, he was unhappy and frustrated because of his inability to live up to expectations. At times he became very depressed and reported fantasies of being dead. When his disabilities, along with their probable basis, were explained to his parents and teachers, they were able to see him as handicapped rather than lazy or dull. They were then able to begin to consider ways of capitalizing on his strengths, and in a general but real sense they were able to provide a vastly different psychological environment for him. He was given special remedial reading instruction, and he was taught arithmetic in concrete terms (actually, he learned to use an abacus, which reduces complex operations to the concrete counting level). And, perhaps most important, the rest of his school curriculum was tailor-made to fit his particular pattern of abilities. He was encouraged to participate more freely in 4-H work, and a dramatic psychological turning point came when he was able to "outshow" his sister in a major livestock exhibition. No direct personal counseling or therapy was attempted except to help him to understand something of the basis of his handicap. Thus, with the aid of relearning and environmental therapy, he was eventually able to achieve a highly satisfactory adjustment.

Jules H. Masserman (13) has reported some effects of environmental change on experimentally induced neuroses in cats. A kitten was made neurotic, and then removed from the experimental cage to the experimenter's home for eight weeks. Some symptoms gradually diminished: general restlessness, suspiciousness, phobia of lights and unusual sounds, and aversion to closed spaces. However the kitten continued to be a feeding problem, would not keep clean, could not be taught to use a sand box, was vicious toward a non-neurotic litter mate, and was so unpredictably destructive that she was returned to the laboratory, but she was not placed in the experimental cage. At the end of a year she was deprived of food for a day and then replaced in the experimental cage. All the former symptoms gradually returned, and her reactions were almost as intense as those after the first induction of neurosis a year before. This work speaks strongly for the influence of environmental factors in precipitating and sustaining neurotic behavior, but it does not offer much hope for behavioral change through environmental manipulation alone— at least not in cats.

ENVIRONMENTAL AND PERSONAL THERAPY WITH CHILDREN

Gordon Hamilton (6) states that the essence of child guidance lies in combining direct psychotherapy with social therapy in varying proportions. The individual cannot be expected to do all the adjusting to an unfavorable environment; the environment itself must be made more favorable. Social therapy is usually combined with psychotherapy so that one reinforces the other. This raises the question whether environmental manipulation, concurrent with direct treatment, dilutes or reinforces counseling. Hamilton feels that although active intervention with regard to the environment is not too effective with the neurotic child (whose problems are internalized), it is at times necessary even if it retards treatment. He contends that it is indispensable with very young children, that is, when the only way of treating the child is to treat the parents and alter the home situation. If a natural family is lacking, then a substitute family relationship can be effectively introduced. To be effective, this substitute family must not only like children, but must be able to like disturbed and/or deprived children in a therapeutic way. The therapeutic attitude in substitute parents does not need to be directly expressed; it is most effectively demonstrated by action and behavior. The aim of the substitute family is to achieve a better balance, channeling and distributing the child's energies so that they are available for growth.

It would appear that indirect methods of treatment such as environmental manipulation are most successful and most fully developed in therapy with children. Since the child is in a formative period, he is less rigid than an adult. It is safe to conclude that, unless circumstances are extremely poor, the true home is of greater value to the child than a foster home, and that in general the foster home is better than an institution. As Watson (22) has noted, the social worker is a specialist in the field of environmental modification and manipulation, and his services should be used whenever possible. Watson also cites what he considers to be the criteria for the use of environmental manipulation: (a) when a parent rejects a child in a way that demonstrates that the parent is inaccessible to a change in attitude; (b) when, because of their own neurotic needs, parents are personally involved in the child's problems in such a way as to prevent the progress of therapy; (c) when the child is delinquent and the behavior of the family contributes to the delinquency; (d) when the mother is absent and no adequate mother substitute is available; (e) when the care of the child places a disproportionate drain on parental resources; (f) when help from other facilities has failed; (g) when the diagnostic opinion from thorough study indicates that environmental manipulation would have greater positive value than any other approach.

In the choice between foster home placement and institutionalization of the child, the decision should be for whichever most adequately meets the basic needs of the child. In other words, will the child benefit most by an individual, personal, intense relationship, or by a group or impersonal relationship? While some institutions do emphasize personal relationships, by and large personal relationships in institutions are less intense than in foster homes. Institutional placement is indicated if the child is psychotic, a low-grade mental defective, or an advanced delinquent, or if he has symptoms that cannot be tolerated in any other setting. However the great majority of children who show mild behavior disorders and neurotic symptoms arising from need for interpersonal relationships are better placed in foster homes. On the age factor clinical opinion is practically unanimous that the younger child has a greater opportunity for therapeutic change in a foster home than in an institution; and that the adolescent who is developing a need for independence often finds the group life of the institution preferable.

Another of the children mentioned in Chapter 1 was living almost completely in a dream world. He darted about flapping his arms like a bird. He could be described as an autistic or perhaps a schizophrenic child. Although his test performance was that of an exceedingly retarded child, some of his spontaneous verbalizations and his development until he was four years of age indicated that he might have superior potential. His father and mother were persons of superior ability. They were professional people and had never given much attention or affection to their children. The boy and his sister, who was five years older than he, were raised by a succession of housekeepers, none of whom stayed with the family long enough for any personal ties with the children to develop. Until he was four, the client was a normal child with various precocious abilities. He was close to his sister, who gave him the only mothering he received. Both children received good physical care but no love except what they gave each other. They were scarcely known to their parents. When the sister was nine, she began to do superior work in school. For the first time the parents gave her some attention. They were extremely pleased with her, and as a reward for her good work took her with them on a four-week trip. Until that time they had always left both children at home and vacationed by themselves. The night they returned the client got so excited when he was awakened that he became nauseous and vomited. He was scolded for this by both his parents and sister. When the family awoke the following morning, they found him sitting in front of the window of his room staring out into space. Since that morning he has for the most part been living in his own dream world. Over the years he has talked less and less, and now at twelve years of age he never communicates in a comprehensible fashion except as required to care for his physical needs. For the past year he has been participating in play therapy and other psychotherapeutic activities. Almost no progress has been made. During the same period counseling has been done with the parents at weekly intervals. The psychologist working with them despairs that they can change their behavior or attitudes toward the children. The mother refuses to accept the idea that the boy's problems have any psychological bases and prefers to think of him as a mentally retarded child. She feels sure that some accident occurred during the vacation period, and blames the housekeeper (who was discharged) for his present condition. She finds it difficult to spend any time with the boy and punishes him frequently. When the boy recently tried to kiss his mother, she repulsed him because "It isn't nice for a grown boy to do that to his mother." Psychological counseling has failed both in personal counseling and in the modification of the attitudes and behavior of those about him. It has been concluded that the child needs institutional treatment, since no foster home can be found. Even if one could be found, it is likely that the parents would not approve of any home in which the physical environment was less adequate than in their own. It is now hoped that the impersonal, stable environment in a mental hospital, combined with personal therapy, may have positive and beneficial effects. Just a little mother love at the right times would have been most helpful, but unfortunately this was given neither consistently nor freely. In this illustration we see how little personal counseling can achieve unless significant aspects of the environmental situation can be modified along with the personal counseling and therapy.

Another child client has actually been in seven different schools in one year. Both parents are under the care of psychiatrists and both are "beside themselves" because of their son's current academic problems. The counselor strongly encouraged the parents in their desire to place the boy in a military school. It was thought that a stable environment and removal of the child from the disturbed home situation for the larger part of the year would give him a chance to develop some consistent habits of thinking and a calmer outlook. The counselor sees him as a very disturbed boy whose parents are even more disturbed than he. No variety of counseling can help him if he continues to be shifted from one school to another and is at the same time exposed to the constant conflict in the home.

Treatment institutions vary in kind. There are training schools for delinquents and mental defectives, private psychiatric hospitals, various kinds of resident schools for the treatment of emotionally disturbed children, children's wards in mental hospitals, and community living-in schools for maladjusted children. Some of these provide long-term care, others temporary treatment, and many, unfortunately, are more custodially than therapeutically oriented.

THE PURPOSE OF INSTITUTIONAL TREATMENT
WITH CHILDREN

The goal of institutional treatment has been described as the formation of a community whose purpose is the readjustment of the children committed to its care (22). The most important factor in achieving this re-adjustment is the attitude of the personnel toward the child. They should be capable of relating to the child with warmth and affection, but should avoid sentimentality. They must be fair and just, neither harsh nor punitive. They must respect the rights of the child, helping him to develop respect for the adults in the community rather than abnormally strong attachments to other children. If the staff appears to be hostile, the children will tend to unite against the institution, creating a breeding ground for further delinquency or abnormal behavior and totally defeating its purpose. This can be avoided by an accepting attitude on the part of the personnel and by a program designed to give the child an opportunity to develop personal ties with adults. One method of accomplishing this is to relieve the counselor of all administrative authority, thereby fostering better identification with him by the children. If this cannot be done, the counselor must convey the attitude of liking and accepting the child as a person even though he may not be able to like and accept the child's behavior.

Bruno Bettleheim and Emmy Sylvester (2) describe a total "therapeutic milieu" in which the objective is to facilitate the child's development of feelings of security. Training in skills and achievements and specialized programs of activities are deemed therapeutically justified only as they permit the child to develop a consistent frame of reference. This consistent frame of reference is experienced by the child as he becomes a part of a well-defined hierarchy of meaningful interpersonal relationships which is provided by the "therapeutic milieu." Through these relationships he must learn spontaneity and flexibility in dealing with people, finally attaining an internalization of controls and an integration of his behavior. This type of approach is best used with children whose interpersonal relationships have been destroyed, or those who through deprivation lack the tools for building up personal relationships. The institution provides the setting where this development can most advantageously take place.

ENVIRONMENTAL TREATMENT WITH LITTLE CHANGE IN THE ENVIRONMENT

Modification of the environment without resort to institutionalization involves treatment of unhealthy influences within the home or the social group. Treatment of the parents is, in general, oriented around their relationship with the child, and parental treatment is guided by, or limited to, the extent that his or her problems contribute to the child's problems. At least one parent is asked to accompany the child to the clinic, at which time a member of the clinic staff (frequently a social worker) attempts to orient the parents toward the problems of the child. If parental problems are inextricably interwoven with those of the child (and they usually are), the parents are included in the treatment. The role of the clinic in this case is to understand the needs of the parents, planning with them for beneficial changes. The parents, in many instances, are not emotionally disturbed themselves beyond the confines of the particular problem, and so do not need extensive personal counseling. The first step in treatment of the parents is to guide them to an emotional acceptance of the child's problems; and then to aid them in reducing their feelings of guilt or responsibility. After the parents are able to view the problem with some degree of objectivity, specific plans for the solution of the problem may be outlined, and new environmental experiences that have therapeutic value may be introduced. Clubs, social groups, and summer camps are frequently suggested to help the child develop better relations with other persons. These temporary environmental changes often reduce tension for both the parents and the child. Modification of school experiences can be achieved through consultation and mutual planning with school authorities and teachers. In schools where special services dealing with adjustment problems are provided, these can be used. When special facilities are lacking, the counselor must arrange conferences with the school authorities to discuss the problems and to outline a definite program of remedial treatment.

Alexander Herzberg (7) uses a combination of persuasion, direct influence on the person's milieu, and therapeutically oriented tasks. The client is asked to undertake some specific piece of new behavior, the primary function of which is to give him heightened self-confidence and an experience of success. He is expected to give full reports on the results of his new behavior in subsequent interviews. When he succeeds, he wins at least a temporary victory over his difficulties. Even when he does not succeed and must report that he has not been entirely successful, he has an opportunity to give free expression to his feelings about the task and the factors surrounding it, and may be able to learn better ways of handling similar tasks. Herzberg feels that it is important for the client to begin with a task on which he will not experience complete failure, because this would only lead to discouragement, and he might withdraw from counseling. The task must (a) be one in which the client is able to succeed; (b) lead toward mental health; (c) be directed against impulses that are maintaining the neurosis; and/or (d) be opposed to superficial gains that are derived from the deviant behavior. It appears that many persons cannot tolerate this type of treatment. Of 100 consecutive cases reported by Herzberg, 48 were "cured," 47 broke off treatment slightly improved or unimproved, and 5 were terminated by the therapist as not capable of significant improvement. However success was achieved fairly rapidly when it was forthcoming. The report indicates that 44 per cent required 20 interviews, 38 per cent needed 21 to 40 interviews, and 18 per cent required more than 40 interviews.

Vivian E. Fisher (4, pp. 35–8) uses the term "active therapy" for environmental manipulation and defines it as a "deliberate interference by the therapist with the implicit and overt activities outside the consultation room." The principal purposes of active therapy are fourfold. The following description of these purposes is adapted from his discussion:

(1) *To elicit or gain access to repressed material.*" When plateaus occur in the course of treatment, in order to force a move, the therapist may rule out "insofar as possible all affective outlets which the client has" and thus increase affective tension "with the usual result of additional thoughts, recollections and dreams."

(2) *To increase the client's insight.*" "Requiring the client to perform certain acts or to place himself in certain situations which he has formerly avoided because of fear or for some other reason will often give him insight" which a discussion with the therapist cannot bring about.

(3) *To reveal abilities or capacities to the client which he did not believe he possessed.*" "The most common limitation which patients come to take for granted in themselves is their inability to endure their affective neurotic tensions." As the client's "tolerance for affective tensions increases with treatment he should be helped to realize this by means of active therapy . . . He should be instructed and encouraged not to deny or ignore his affective tensions but simply to endure them. This will hasten their diversion into patterns of adjustive motivation and expression."

(4) *To encourage the client to give the matter of his treatment high priority among his everyday affairs.*" Many clients will adopt an attitude of "timelessness toward the treatment if permitted to do so." Active therapy, judiciously employed, can give treatment "its proper importance in the mind of the patient and also impress upon him that it is something to be concluded at the earliest possible moment." [1]

Although many clients would never be able to change their behavior without what Fisher has called active therapy, active therapy harbors many pitfalls and no specific rules can be given for its application.

Changes in environment are useful in the control and treatment of delinquency. It has been found in plotting the home addresses of youths in trouble with the law, that they come for the most part from the same general areas (8). Placement of recreation centers in such areas provides more normal outlets for energy, thus lowering the delinquency rate.

[1] By permission from *The Meaning and Practice of Psychotherapy*, by Vivian E. Fisher. Copyright 1950 by The Macmillan Company.

These facilities in addition to having a social hygiene value, can frequently be used by the counselor for remedial purposes.

ENVIRONMENTAL TREATMENT WITH ADULTS

Environmental therapy is a procedure that is not limited to use with children. Adults, too, can profit from environmental modification. Although occasional change is beneficial to the mental health of many people, persons with neurasthenia or fatigue symptom syndromes most often require that minor, and sometimes major, changes be made in their living or working situations. These persons may be working at jobs they do not like, with people with whom they have conflicts, or for employers or supervisors who make their workdays unhappy. Perhaps their home lives are not harmonious, or many little irritations disturb them. As many examples could be given as there are people who could be so described. Their lives are characterized by chronic emotional tensions, and they may eventually become exhausted from having to live constantly under such tension. They begin to feel too tired to go on. They develop physical ailments and hypochondriacal symptoms. Their attention may shift from the source of the tension to their health or feeling of well-being. They may be too ill or tired to go to work, or even to get out of bed in the morning. This excuses them from facing the tension-provoking situations and has secondary gain. As a consequence, the pattern of illness may be repeated and repeated.

These neurasthenic symptoms are probably a major cause of absenteeism from work, and of the instances of boredom and malaise among housewives, who find the repetitive, day-by-day disagreeable chores around the house too much to take. Factory managers have discovered that proper placement on the job, work rotation, changes of supervisors, and other alterations in the working environment may change tired, sickly, unhappy workers into efficient, productive regular workers. A husband may discover that taking his wife to dinner regularly each week, thus getting her away from the unending chore of planning meals, is a good medicine for some of her complaints. Some women find needed variety in club work or part-time jobs. The man who is unhappy with his daily routine may be able to distract himself with a hobby.

These are all forms of environmental therapy. In many instances psychological counseling will help the person to solve some of the problems he faces, and even to deal effectively with basic sources of tension, but if he has to go back to work under the same irritating conditions, the effects of personal counseling may be short-lived. There are, of course, many environmental situations that cannot be modified in any major fashion, so the individual may have to learn to tolerate irritation and frustration. Fortunately, some minor modification can be made in most situations. Even a slight change may mean the difference between endurability and breakdown.

One of many possible illustrations is that of a successful certified public accountant, who was good at his work, which was financially rewarding. In taking up accounting, he had followed in his father's footsteps; he had never really enjoyed it, and as time went on he came to hate every moment he spent at it. He developed a number of physical complaints, and gradually spent more and more time in bed. He became irritable, and when he was finally seen by a psychologist, his wife was threatening to leave him. After a short conversation it was learned that he loved music and had a small, but fine, record collection. He felt that this interest was too expensive, and he also felt guilty about the time he "wasted" listening to records, thinking that he should be working instead. It was not difficult to persuade him that it might be good for his health if he indulged his interest. With this encouragement, he began to add to his collection. He built his own recording equipment, and he recorded on tape for his own use some of the selections he could not afford, as well as many rare recordings that could not be bought. In time he developed one of the largest private record collections in his city. His work went better; he worked shorter hours, but accomplished far more when working.

In time he came to be in demand as a speaker, as he was regarded as somewhat of an authority on records. He was eventually asked by the local paper to write an article on his collection. Then he was offered the opportunity to be music critic for a daily newspaper. This led to his having a column, and he was finally able to give up accounting and earn an excellent living from what had once been a hobby. Needless to say, he is now an efficient, happy, and healthy man.

James D. Page (16) is another writer who stresses that an improvement in the client's external problems sometimes encourages recovery. He discusses changes of scenery and taking vacations as examples. In psychiatric practice removal from the immediate scene or conflict is a therapeutic procedure frequently employed. This measure undoubtedly produces marked amelioration of symptoms, but seldom complete relief. If the client is removed from the immediate scene and nothing further is done, he is apt to persist in many of his neurotic patterns. He may show evidences of all of them whenever his conflicts are reactivated by untoward circumstances in the environment, and resume his aberrant defenses on his return to the original or some related neurotigenic milieu. Moreover, sanction of "geographic escape" by the physician often leads the client to continue his futile attempts to solve problems by this means alone, rather than to co-operate in other forms of therapy more likely to produce lasting recovery. If, however, we can improve some of the environmental problems by counseling with the family or by other means while the client is absent, he may be able to cope with the improved situation when he returns.

G. Wilson Shaffer and Richard S. Lazarus (19) speak of situational therapy in which no effort is made to bring about a major change in the person; efforts are directed instead toward manipulation of the situation so that stress is relieved. With most clients this is not completely satisfactory for at least two reasons: (a) major changes in environmental situations and relationships are difficult to accomplish; (b) since a great part of the difficulty probably lies within the individual, the manipulation of the environment is likely to bring only minor relief. They maintain that for the great majority of those who come for treatment much more is necessary.

Austin Riggs was eminently successful in using methods of re-education and environmental control. He was opposed to psychoanalytic theory although he recognized the significance of early experiences in the development of psychoneuroses. He thought of conflict as existing within the individual at various levels—instinctive, reflexive, intellectual, social, and ethical. His therapy was directed toward the psychoneurotic, for whom he advised temporary environmental change. Sanitariums were considered valuable in that they provide a neutral environment away from the emotional strain of ordinary living. Here the patient was acquainted with his need for re-education, and a schedule of activities was provided to teach him the importance of regularizing his life. Regimentation was used to distract and divert the patient, and to help him to develop habits of social co-operation. The patient was taught to do things because they must be done rather than to avoid them because of dislike or disinterest. In Riggs's writings there is unusual emphasis on discipline, ideals, and the influence of reason, as well as on social goals. Although he was successful, some patients found it impossible to live up to his goals and ideals, and others suffered debilitating "conscience pangs" as a result of his teachings. Much of the success of his method may be attributed to the personality of Riggs himself.

THE PSYCHOLOGIST'S RESPONSIBILITY
IN ENVIRONMENTAL MODIFICATION
OR MANIPULATION

The degree to which the counselor participates in decisions and control of the client's life outside the therapeutic hour varies with the theoretical persuasion of the counselor. Nondirective counselors feel that treatment is most effective when the counselor does not participate at all. Limitations are set up and made clear to the client early in the treatment process. Likewise, classical psychoanalysts prefer a minimum of participation in control of the client's environment. In contrast, neo-analysts, field theorists, and learning theorists emphasize the use of the environment.

We have presented a number of different aspects of environmental manipulation and modification. Certainly, the counselor cannot use all that has been suggested with any given client, and we can hardly expect that any one approach would be successful with all clients. As discussed by Abraham H. Maslow and Bela Mittelmann (12), there is a definite relationship between a client's unusual behavior and his need for environmental change. In some instances what appears to be a very slight change in the environment may reflect itself in considerable change in a client's behavior. Environmental stresses may be alleviated simply by changing the attitudes of teachers, relatives, or associates toward the client. The counselor may be able to give these individuals an insight into the behavior of the client which they did not previously have. We recently saw a child who was described by his teacher as a troublemaker, as one who was not interested in the activities of the rest of the group, and as one who could not be kept busy. The child was apparently rebelling against the teacher's attempt to force him into conformity, and both were becoming very emotional about the situation. When the teacher was helped to recognize the fact that the child was intellectually superior (WISC I.Q. of 145), she was easily able to understand that he was bored by some of the group's activities. As a result she began to diversify his activities, and needless to say both the teacher and the child were happier. Another child was being beaten by his father and was driving his teacher to distraction because of his inability to maintain attention in school long enough to learn under usual instructional conditions. The attitudes of both father and teacher were changed when they learned that in all likelihood the child had suffered brain damage. They became more patient, and when teaching methods were adjusted to his short attention span, he was able to learn more efficiently.

Many clients are in a position to handle all their problems if minor changes alone are made in their environments. Occasionally the necessary changes are only in the attitudes of the client toward his environment. The client may have unreasonable fears concerning some element in his environment such as a person or some social situation. The persons in his environment may be reacting to these fears, and a complicated pattern of misunderstandings may have resulted. This is exemplified by a boy who came into a new school situation after he had developed many fears of meeting this new situation. He had been told by other children to "watch out" for a certain teacher. He was very uncomfortable with this teacher but did not want to show his fear, so he behaved in a way that the teacher construed as insolent. When we were able to help the boy to see that he had nothing to fear in the new situation, he became less defensive, the teacher's attitude was changed, and, in effect, the entire environment was changed.

In more acute situations the difficulties of the members of the family or associates may be so great that they cannot change without a program of counseling or personal therapy for the key persons. Assuming that the environment cannot be changed psychologically, then more radical measures are necessary, as for example, the intervention by social agencies or other agencies who can offer the client a different environment. If the situation is still more extreme, as in the instance of a "delinquent environment" that cannot be constructively changed, counseling may be impossible or limited in its effect, and the client may have to be taught to contend with the existing situation. When the attributes of the client are such that no usual environment can meet his needs, we are forced to consider the alternative of institutionalization. There are few situations, excluding physical and mental handicaps or illnesses, in which the flexible, ingenious, and alert counselor cannot find some significant modification that will be beneficial to the client.

ENVIRONMENTAL TREATMENT IN AN INSTITUTION

Environmental treatment within hospital walls has been approached in a number of different ways by persons of differing theoretical persuasions. A great deal of the work in this area has been done by psychoanalytic psychiatrists. Environmental therapy for hospital patients is not really new. For example, in the seventh century an asylum in Cairo provided storytellers, dancing, and light comedy for its patients. One of the first attempts to use a within-the-hospital approach in America was planned by Abraham Meyerson (15) and reported by Kenneth J. Tillotson (21) in 1939. They called their approach "total push." Meyerson theorized that the hospital patient lives in a motivational vacuum and as a result retreats further and further from reality. To remedy the situation and to keep the patients continually active, he proposed a four-point program: (a) medical measures including the use of physiological therapies, showers, massage, douches, rubdowns, and ultraviolet irradiation (no rationale was given for the irradiation treatment and the lack of reasons was freely admitted); (b) exercise and games; (c) vitamins and diet; (d) the psychological push. This last point involved giving the patients new and individually different clothing and using motivational techniques such as praise, blame, reward, and punishment. Tillotson reports on the application of this program to eleven chronic schizophrenic patients whose mean hospitalization time was 12.1 years. He states that none worsened under this treatment program. Results are given in the form of individual case reports. The patients showed progress in terms of better contact with reality; increased social responsiveness; increased activity, skill, and co-ordination; improved moods; and some degree of improvement in physical status.

Arpad Pauncz (17) emphasizes the intrapsychic aspects of "total push." He lists four basic ideas that are essential to its effective use: (a) that even the most psychotic patient retains some aspect of normality; (b) that many pathological manifestations are due to basic personality trends, the display of which is facilitated by psychosis; (c) that patients must be made aware of these facts and must learn responsibility for present, past, and future conditions; and (d) that self-responsibility is biologically determined and universally valid. There are those, of course, who will question the last point. However the validity of the other three does not depend upon it. Ruth Barnard (1) distinguishes between milieu therapy and "total push." She labels as "total push" any program designed to keep people as active as possible in order to prevent a lapse into vegetative existence. Milieu therapy is defined as treatment which provides activities and an emotional atmosphere that meet the needs of the individual patient. It includes individualized planning of the patient's entire day. An application of program planning in the Industrial Neurosis Unit at Belmont Hospital near London is reported by Maxwell S. Jones (9). Here, with generous support from several departments of the government, attempts were made to rehabilitate persons who had been chronically known to the various welfare agencies, courts, and jails and were generally considered untreatable and unemployable. This group was treated together in a "therapeutic community" that was oriented from the day of a patient's arrival toward his eventual role in society. The workshops, instead of attempting to be pleasant and amusing, simulated real factory conditions so that tensions associated with work roles could be worked out while the person was still in the hospital. A follow-up study on the adjustment of patients six months after leaving the hospital showed that two thirds of the group studied had made fair adjustments or better, and one third had made poor or very poor adjustments. Slightly more than half of the subjects had worked full time since leaving the hospital. Jones feels that these results could not have been achieved by hospitalization and individual psychotherapy alone.

An environmental type of therapy which took place at an Army hospital (11) illustrates an approach almost antithetical to the above. Whereas Jones's "therapeutic community" was highly structured, the army hospital situation was almost completely unstructured. The group of patients in the project consisted of neurotics and a few mild psychotics. The average population of the special unit over the twelve-month study period was fifty. New admissions averaged five a week. Restrictions in the unit were minimal. Patients were required to work out the day-to-day problems of living among themselves. Staff members were available, and once a day all patients assembled for an hour's session with the psychologist or psychiatrist. Other than this the staff gave help only when requested to do so or when asked for supplies. The patients adjusted to the situation quite readily, and it appears from this study that when patients are deliberately placed in a nonrestrictive environmental situation, many counseling goals are achieved with a minimum of counselor help. For example, the patients expressed their feelings spontaneously, both verbally and through activity, and insight and understanding developed through their having to face the fact that many of their difficulties could be traced to their own behavior. The patients developed a feeling of belonging and gained support from one another in that they all had common problems. A series of studies (18, 20) at the Chestnut Lodge Sanitarium in Maryland have focused interest on the effects of the staff on the patients. The workers at the Sanitarium conceive of a mental hospital ward as an interacting social structure or system in which the type of activity engaged in by any one person, whether he is a staff member or patient, is to some extent determined by other persons on the ward, and, reciprocally, it contributes to influencing and channelizing the activity of others. This concept is derived from the teaching of the Washington School of Psychiatry, in which mental illness is regarded as a type of participation in the social process rather than as a disease entity residing within the person. It follows from this reasoning that if one is to understand the activities of particular members of a group (even when the group is a hospital ward), one must understand the complete pattern of activities of the entire group. Examples are given in which prolonged excitement of patients was directly related to a conflict situation between two staff members in which the patient was the source of contention. When the conflict between staff members was resolved, the patients improved rapidly. The workers at the Sanitarium also hypothesized that even the most withdrawn patients, who are very restricted in their relations with others, often use obscure means for participating with the group. In one study they built quite a case showing that incontinence is a significant mode of social participation. With some patients it is likely that this is the only means they have of influencing the group or of calling attention to themselves. In any case, we can assume that the patient who feels abandoned, isolated, and neglected, or who feels that the entire situation is unconstructive, may use a variety of obscure and bizarre ways of influencing his relations with other people.

The observations at Chestnut Lodge, as well as those of a number of other hospitals, have led to the concept of organizing the hospital environment around the needs of the patients rather than planning a hospital program that sets a definite social structure to which the patient must conform whether he wants to or not. It seems quite likely that in the past many patients have learned to conform to a rigid hospital environment entirely too well. Once they have learned to conform in the hospital, they are in no condition to adjust to an environment outside the hospital. We now hear quite a bit about the "new look" in hospital management of patients. The characteristic aspect of this new look seems to be the treating of the patient as an individual, as Mrs. Smith or Mr. Jones rather than as *a psychotic*. When the patient is viewed as a real person rather than as a diseased object, we begin to be concerned about this person's personal and social needs.

Let us conclude this section with two additional descriptions of hospital care. The first, by Menninger, is highly directive in that the counselor or therapist decides what is good for the patient and then provides for his needs in the hospital framework. The second illustrates the concept of patient-government in which the responsibility for much of his behavior is given to the patient.

William C. Menninger (14) states that hospital care is desirable for many persons presenting neurotic illness and for most presenting psychotic illness. It is beneficial not only because of the availability of psychotherapy, but because of the protection afforded, the neutral environment created, and the isolation from relatives. In addition, the progress toward recovery can be greatly facilitated if the hospital program permits a more propitious outlet for expression than that which the patient has chosen in his illness. The role of the therapist is to prescribe activities that provide such an outlet. A prescription not only sets forth the therapeutic aim that is indicated to meet the unconscious conflict situation, but may also suggest specific measures in the various therapeutic departments by which the conflict may be most effectively expressed. The object of prescriptions is to furnish the patient with opportunities for expression in socially approved outlets that are psychologically kindred to his unsocial or antisocial or destructive psychopathological outlets.

To be prescribed, an outlet must meet three criteria: (a) it must give the individual gratification; (b) it must be sufficiently kindred in its expression to permit a transfer from the symptom to the activity; (c) it must be social, productive, or effective; rather than antisocial, unproductive, or ineffective. A patient's unconscious conflict must be recognized and understood before a prescription can properly be given. According to Menninger, six needs met by therapeutic aims are: an outlet for aggression, a means of atonement of guilt, a means of obtaining love, advantageous identification, acting out of fantasies, and opportunity to create. Activities such as bag punching, bowling, and wrecking meet the need for an outlet for aggression. When members of the staff play the role of understanding parents rather than of strict or overindulgent parents, this provides opportunity for advantageous identification. Atonement of guilt may be brought about through hard, menial, routine work performed under a person whose attitude is one of understanding fairness tempered with firmness and even severity. Love may be given the patient by staff members. There is some question as to whether indiscriminate showing of love, or giving of love only when it is earned, is the better procedure. Music, art, and handiwork provide outlets for the needs to act out fantasy and to create.

The major deviation from Menninger's proposal is the policy currently being widely adopted which gives the patient more voice in the planning of the program. Whereas Menninger suggested that the therapist prescribe activities, a program in which patients are given almost complete responsibility for the conduct of their wards has been described by P. Stefan Kraus (10). According to his plan patients were encouraged to take up as many of the activities of normal daily living (outside the hospital) as possible. They were given ground privileges, and the doors of various wards within a building were left unlocked. The patients were organized into groups which ate together, planned their group activities and participated in them together, planned their recreational activities, and in general assumed total responsibility for their own conduct within the hospital. The results from such programs as this strongly suggest that if we change the environment in the direction of normalcy, the behavior of patients will make a similar shift. For much too long a time we have been treating the inmates of mental hospitals as patients and not as human beings.

THE PSYCHIATRIC SOCIAL CASE WORKER AND ENVIRONMENTAL THERAPY

One group of professional workers, the social workers, consider the environment as their main concern, and have been concentrating their efforts on the environment for some time. The role of the psychiatric social case worker in environmental therapy is well described by Leona Hambrecht (5). The contributions of social treatment or case work with children have developed out of a twofold requirement: the need for study and evaluation of the social environment, and the social treatment of the environment. Psychiatric social case work with children has concentrated primarily on work with the parents and has focused attention on the child's environment. This includes his play, his schools, his friends, his interests, as well as his family life. In contrast, psychiatry has focused on uncovering and treating the child's inner and emotional life. The psychiatric social worker may help the parents to formulate their own thinking, feeling, and behavior in relation to the child. This is done, as was discussed earlier,[2] without dealing with the parents' unconscious attitudes

[2] *See* pp. 211–12.

and without treating them directly. The first aim of the worker is to give them an opportunity for emotional release, which, if handled skillfully, can lead to their gaining some insight. Secondly, the parents can learn to redirect their emotional energies toward more constructive satisfactions, in the light of their own understandings and insight. With older children the psychiatric social worker may encourage the child in the verbalization and expression of social problems, in this way aiding him toward a clear and objective understanding of these problems. After a child is discharged from the hospital or clinic, the worker may keep a sustaining contact with him in an effort to gradually ease his entrance into groups with others until such time as he no longer needs the worker's assistance.

Another function of the psychiatric social worker in a clinic or hospital setting is supportive therapy with the patient or client. Hambrecht says that this supportive therapy builds a sound therapeutic relationship and facilitates the exploration of attitudes, family experiences, and social relationships. This relationship is valuable in that it discourages the client's expectancy of an immediate or specific solution to his problem, and it substitutes instead a sense of his importance in contributing toward the mutual study of the problem. It does not commit the worker to any form of premature social treatment procedure. In psychiatric treatment of his child the parent ordinarily accepts his relationship with the worker as part of the search for the causes of the problem, and in this search he begins to examine himself. He eventually sees the members of his family in their respective relationships; knowing their life experiences, he begins to find new meaning for their behavior and better handling of himself with them.

The mental hygiene aspects of social group work, such as that done by workers in the field of recreation and leisure-time education, are discussed by Everett W. DuVall (3). He states that the mental hygienists have appeared to stress the correction of maladjustments and the developing of improved techniques of dealing with mental disorders, rather than the more positive approach of preventing their development. Since group workers have stressed the development of good habits and of relationships tending toward socialized adult behavior, the mental hygienists have not always realized their value in mental hygiene programs. The objectives of both the psychiatric and the social group work approach are the same, although their methods may be somewhat different.

A survey of a boys' and girls' organization in Los Angeles with a membership of over seven hundred indicated that nearly all the children and youth in the organization presented problems requiring individual attention. Only one in five of these problems was recognized before the survey. This points up the need for special training of group workers. According to DuVall, the group membership includes a wide range of problem behavior, some of which often go unrecognized. For example, the shy, conforming child is frequently in greater need of attention than is the more demanding, aggressive youngster. The activities of boys' and girls' club programs are similar to, or identical with, the activities utilized by the occupational therapist in the hospital setting. They include weaving, metal- and woodwork, leather craft, plastics, clay modeling, and other crafts and activities. Under the skilled worker these activities can have intrinsic value in developing expression and in channeling energy. The group work situation also provides an opportunity for the much-desired early diagnosis of instability and for resolving cultural and emotional conflicts in their early stages, and it permits a transition from individual to group life within a more protected confine.

DuVall recommends that a group program, rather than presenting formal activities in which all must participate, provide tasks and plans appropriate to the needs of the individuals involved and that the program of activities be carried out by members of the group guided by the agency staff. Individual needs must be determined by a comprehensive study of each individual participating in the program. This does not mean that the worker should discover interests, capacities, and needs and then impose a program of activities. On the contrary, the members in the recreational group should be given a wide freedom of choice, as this is essential to the development of a democratic-type group. DuVall feels that an individualized program can best meet the criterion of a mental hygiene approach to social group work.

SUMMARY

Environmental therapy has been defined as any process designed to help an individual make desirable behavioral adjustment by changing certain factors in his environment. Such changes may be brought about by counseling with persons in the environment, removing the individual to a new environment, vocational counseling, and by the use of rest, music, art, and recreational activities. Except among strict psychoanalysists and strict nondirectivists, there is fairly general agreement that environmental manipulation is a valuable adjunct to other forms of therapy and may be especially valuable in treating children. Disagreement does exist as to how far manipulation should be carried—in other words, how much is desirable or of actual value to the client. As problems become more internalized, environmental therapy becomes less effective. Environmental treatment within a hospital setting has progressed from a fevered pushing of patients into activity, just to keep them moving, to a more thoughtful approach in which an attempt is made to channel the client into activities that will meet his individual needs. There is wide divergence among hospitals in the amount of direct control exercised over the patients. Similarly, the amount of planning done varies from the forced activity of the total-push approach, with little planning, to the Menninger approach of carefully planning and tailoring activities to meet the needs of the individual. One of the most recent innovations is the concept of patient-government, whereby patients themselves take a degree of responsibility for planning their activities.

BIBLIOGRAPHY

1. Barnard, R., "Milieu therapy." *Menninger Quart.*, Spring 1954, 20–5.
2. Bettleheim, B., and Sylvester, E., "Milieu therapy: Indications and illustrations." *Psychoanal. Rev.*, 1949, 36, 54–68.
3. DuVall, E. W., *Personality and social group work*. New York: Association Press, 1943.
4. Fisher, V., *The meaning and practice of psychotherapy*. New York: Macmillan, 1950.
5. Hambrecht, L., "Psychiatric social case work with children." In Lewis, N. D. C., and Pacella, R. L., *Modern trends in child psychiatry*. New York: International Press, 1950.
6. Hamilton, G., *Psychotherapy in child guidance*. New York: Columbia Univ. Press, 1947.
7. Herzberg, A., *Active psychotherapy*. New York: Grune & Stratton, 1945.
8. Hilgard, E. R., *Introduction to psychology*. New York: Harcourt Brace, 1953.
9. Jones, M., *The therapeutic community*. New York: Basic Books, 1953.
10. Kraus, S. P., "Consideration and problems of ward care for schizophrenic patients." *Psychiat.*, 1954, 17, 283–92.
11. Malone, T. P., "Analysis of the dynamics of group psychotherapy based on a twelve-month experimental program." *J. Pers.*, 1948, 16, 245–77.
12. Maslow, A. H., and Mittelmann, B., *Principles of abnormal psychology*. New York: Harper, 1951.
13. Masserman, J. H., *Principles of dynamic psychiatry*. Philadelphia: W. B. Saunders, 1946.
14. Menninger, Wm. C., "Psychiatric hospital therapy designed to meet unconscious needs." *Amer. J. Psychiat.*, 1936, 93, 347–60.
15. Meyerson, A., "Theory and practice of the 'total push' method in the treatment of chronic schizophrenia." *Amer. J. Psychiat.*, 1939, 95, 1197–1204.
16. Page, J. D., *Abnormal psychology*. New York: McGraw-Hill, 1947.
17. Pauncz, A., "Contribution to the concept of 'total push' therapy." *Psychiat. Quart. Suppl.*, 1951, 25, 220–7.
18. Schwartz, M. W., and Stanton, A. H., "A social psychological study of incontinence." *Psychiat.*, 1950, 13, 399–416.
19. Shaffer, G. W., and Lazarus, R. S., *Fundamental concepts in clinical psychology*. New York: McGraw-Hill, 1952.

20. Stanton, A. H., and Schwartz, M. W., "The management of a type of institutional participation in mental illness." *Psychiat.*, 1949, 12, 13–26.
21. Tillotson, K. J., "The practice of the total push method in the treatment of chronic schizophrenia." *Amer. J. Psychiat.*, 1939, 95, 1205–13.
22. Watson, R. I., *The clinical method in psychology.* New York: Harper, 1951.

☼

CHAPTER

IO

Group Counseling and Therapy

TRADITIONALLY, GROUP COUNSELING HAS BEEN CONSIDERED A DIS-
tinctive approach to treatment. Group procedures have frequently
been contrasted with individual procedures, and in some instances,
viewed as substitutes for individual methods. Group counseling has also
been regarded as an adjunct to individual counseling, and it is often recommended either as a preparation for individual counseling or as a
termination activity following basic individual counseling. Our philosophy in this text differs somewhat from the above. Group counseling is
regarded here as a significant aspect of the entire rehabilitation process.
Group activities can be an important factor in environmental therapy.
Group relationships and the feeling of belonging to a group can contribute substantially to the support and security of the individual. Relearning
and socialization can often be effected in group situations and sometimes
require group participation. Group experiences are helpful in furthering
insight and emotional release. Our philosophy, then, is to conceive of
group activity and group participation as among the various media available for the accomplishment of any or all the aims of psychological counseling. In planning with and for our client, we can use group activities to
advantage in many ways. It is the task of the counselor to work out the
means most effective for utilizing group activity to accomplish the aims
or goals being emphasized for the individual client.

There is some confusion in the literature regarding the boundaries
of group counseling. Some clinicians use the term only in relation to
groups in which the director is a specially trained counselor working toward specific therapeutic aims. Others use it to include "any group
brought together for the purpose of improving interpersonal or intrapersonal relations." The latter definition describes our approach. Group
counseling and therapeutic procedures are used in education, in indus-

trial situations, in prisons, in the military, in hospitals, and in clinics. They are designed to promote educational and social goals; they are applied to problems of industrial relations; social relations are studied and improved through group activities; and individual adjustment problems are dealt with in group situations. There are many types and combinations of types of group counseling and therapy today, and their methods and purposes vary widely. In the last analysis, however, all approaches have as their basic goal improvement in the adjustment of persons both individually and collectively. To put it in a still more fundamental fashion—we are striving to help people to get along with themselves and with others.

Historically, the original factor stimulating the development of group counseling was the saving in time and money. With the large number of patients or clients in hospitals and clinics and the shortage of trained personnel, adequate individual counseling for all clients and patients was—as it still is—impossible. Group counseling was first adopted in the interest of providing therapeutic activities for as many clients as possible with the personnel available. As experience has been gained, it has become clear to workers in the field that group procedures in counseling provide many "extras." Consequently, group counseling is no longer regarded merely as a makeshift made necessary by difficult or exceptional circumstances; rather, it is agreed by all workers, as stated by Jacob W. Klapman (28, p. 83), that ". . . it may utilize a segment of the psychodynamic and therapeutic spectrum which is not quite so readily engaged by individual treatment." [1] The present attitude, that group procedures are valuable counseling methods in their own right, is well expressed by Siegmund H. Foulkes (19), who describes group counseling as an important new method for the study and improvement of human interrelations.

Let us discuss some of the extras that are offered by group counseling. Group relationships play a major role in causing emotional maladjustment, and problems developing out of group relationships can often be solved most effectively within a group situation. As Donald A. Shaskan (56) has pointed out, the ease of acceptance of group counseling by the client is striking. In many cases people find it easier to discuss their problems with a group of individuals who share the same or similar problems than to discuss them with one person. They find it easier to accept the fact that they are not alone in their particular difficulties when they are able to discuss with others, or to listen to others discuss, the same things. The group provides a miniature and controlled social situation. Clients can experiment in such a situation, trying out modes of reaction and roles before they use them in larger or personally more important

---

[1] By permission from *Group Psychotherapy: Theory and Practice*, by Jacob W. Klapman. Copyright 1946 by Grune & Stratton, Inc.

social situations. Klapman (28) has described group counseling as "experience under controlled conditions." He considers it more nearly a "living through" process in relation to social adjustments than practically any other form of counseling. Another extra is the motivation provided by the group. The cumulative effect of other clients endeavoring to change their behavior patterns has been observed to produce a far stronger incentive toward that end in the individual client than usually results from individual counseling in a comparable length of time. The group seems to have a "catalytic" effect on its members. According to Benjamin Simon, *et al.* (57), there is evidence that passive (nonarticulate) participation can be as emotionally intense and as therapeutic as active (articulate) participation in the group situation. In other words, group members may profit from the group activities and discussion even if they do not themselves engage in the activities.

Fritz Redl (49), emphasizing the value of group techniques in diagnosis or evaluation, states that teachers and group workers have for years complained that information given to them by the psychiatrist, case worker, and mental hygienist is of little help to them in handling children in groups. This difficulty is thought to arise from (p. 56) "a deep-seated difference between individual motivation and group psychology." It is pointed out that careful observation of an individual in a group situation can explain: how the client reacts to the attempt of the group to bring pressure on his actions; whose influence he accepts or rejects; how he fights outside influence; how he alibis to himself, to his friends, or (if a child) to adults; his attempts to avoid responsibility demands; how much resistance he shows toward the influence of group ethics and group prestige in his thinking or his acts.

Adaptations of group therapy have been worked out by representatives of many theoretical frameworks, several of which will be discussed in this chapter. A bibliography of group therapy containing references up to 1949 has been presented by Benjamin Kotkov (31). This bibliography alone contains 579 items, and in the period since 1949 interest in group counseling and therapeutic procedures has been accelerated. It appears safe to conclude that group procedures are widely used and that they are becoming increasingly popular. Since current practices of group counseling are of many types and combinations of types, there is no specific group-counseling approach, but there are a number of group procedures. In this presentation we will select a few approaches as illustrative of the total field of effort. There is the authoritarian approach of Abraham A. Low (35), the confessional-inspirational method of Joseph H. Pratt (48), the didactic technique of Jacob W. Klapman (26), the drama forms of Jacob L. Moreno (41), the activity groups of Samuel R. Slavson (58), the nondirective procedures of Nicholas Hobbs (24), the social-educational method of Joshua Bierer (8, 9), the round-table technique of Willis H. McCann (12, 39), the semianalytic approaches of Louis Wender (64, 65) and Siegmund H. Foulkes (18, 19), and the psychoanalytic methods of Paul Schilder (55) and Alexander Wolfe (67, 68). Alcoholics Anonymous may be considered a group therapy organization. Included among the many special techniques and devices used in group work are puppetry, music therapy, dancing, rhythm, and films. Self-perpetuating groups, requiring little help from the counselor or leader, are found in panel discussions, patient-government, and social clubs. Bibliotherapy may be conducted in groups and may take the form of educational talks by the leader, group discussion of books read by all members, or individual book reviews. Before we discuss some of the specific forms of group counseling, let us consider the history of the trend toward group work.

THE HISTORY OF GROUP COUNSELING AND THERAPEUTIC ACTIVITIES

Although socialization benefits from group activity have undoubtedly existed ever since people first gathered together for comfort and to accomplish things together, the earliest recorded recognition of group influence in the treatment of psychiatric disorders was in 1904 when Jean Camus and Phillippe Pagniez (13) noted that patients in a large ward were more cheerful than those in private rooms. The first systematic group work seems to have been done by Pratt (45, 46, 47, 48) with tuberculous patients. He organized group meetings to teach patients personal hygiene, to check their record books, and the like. He observed that the patients received a good deal of mental stimulation from these meetings. They felt encouraged, and enjoyed the society of their fellow patients. This stimulation and raising of morale was seen to benefit the organism as a whole, and Pratt extended similar treatment to other groups of chronically ill patients. Later Pratt was impressed by the writings of a French neurologist, Joseph J. Dejerine, who was one of the first to realize that psychosomatic disorders are due to emotional maladjustment and that these disorders are relieved by dealing with the emotional cause. He eventually worked out a lecture type of group therapy, the effects of which were based on the patient's faith in the physician and class teachings. This method made use of relaxation, suggestion, testimony, emotional release, and support. One aim was the objectification of problems. This type of treatment, frequently called "repressive-inspirational," was used by Pratt at the Medical Clinic of the Boston Dispensary with patients whose physical symptoms were diagnosed as evolving from functional nervous disorders.

In 1908, William R. P. Emerson (15), whom we can assume had

some contact with Pratt, began to employ a group method (or "class" method) in the treatment of undernourished children at the Boston Dispensary. The children who were under treatment met in a classroom. They were weighed before every meeting and seated according to the amount of weight gained. Thus he added an idea of competition to the gaining of weight so that it became something of a game. The children's parents were in attendance at the class meetings, and a child's failure to gain was investigated and discussed. Emerson also made good use of the reports of social workers who periodically visited the homes of the children.

The success of group techniques with medical patients soon led to the use of group techniques in the treatment of mental disorders. In 1909 L. Cody Marsh (37) began some tentative experiments on the use of group meetings with neurotic clients. Unfortunately, his experiments had relatively little effect on other early workers, as he published nothing about his work until 1931. His article in that year is one of the earliest published writings on the use of the group method on a planned basis with emotionally disturbed individuals. Because Marsh felt that the individual method was inadequate due to the lack of psychiatrists, lack of sufficient time, lack of standardized procedures, and the lengthy course of treatment, he proposed the group approach as an alternative. His method consisted of a series of therapeutic classes, in which he included lectures on various topics in mental hygiene, stunt activities, song services, and music, as well as the reading of selected books by the participants. His ideas for this type of treatment came from varied sources such as the Rotary Luncheon Club, Salvation Army revival, principles of mob psychology, principles of salesmanship, and social service methods. His purpose was to promote happiness and extroverted behavior in the participants, and he felt that the results, based on testimony of the patients and his own observation, were favorable. Through the use of this method he found that more patients received psychiatric attention, more received the beginnings of mental and emotional re-education, more obtained varying degrees of emotional release, and many were motivated toward improvement and recovery. The patients participating tended to work out social difficulties; they were made more approachable for individual treatment; and their general morale improved. Within the next few years Marsh (38) somewhat enlarged and modified his ideas concerning group counseling, noting that an additional advantage of group over individual treatment is its relatively low cost, which makes it economically available to more people. He emphasized the patients' role as that of students for whom the counseling process should be educational rather than medical. He felt that group counseling contributed to developing a helpful transference that was easily broken; enthusiasms were engendered which were not so prominent in private treatment; resistances of the patients were more easily overcome; and the impersonality of the situation made the patient more amenable to treatment.

In 1911, in Vienna, Moreno (41, 42) created a children's theater for spontaneity plays, in which children could play out their own problems. A similar theater was developed for adults in the early 'twenties. Later Moreno formulated a group treatment method based on the principles of sociometric group analysis. He brought these ideas to the United States in 1924 and used them therapeutically in institutional work. Moreno christened the group method "group psychotherapy" in 1931, and William Alanson White of St. Elizabeth's Hospital in Washington, D.C., took a leading interest in sponsoring the new method. In 1936 a theater for psychodrama was built at Beacon, New York, and four years later a theater was built at St. Elizabeth's.

In 1919, at St. Elizabeth's, Edward W. Lazell (32, 33) began to work out lecture methods and use them for the re-education of institutionalized patients. The lectures, based on psychoanalytic psychology, were constructed in simple language, Klapman (28) describes Lazell's experience in delivering a series of lectures to sixteen apparently inaccessible schizophrenic patients. Lazell noted no response to his lectures until the day when one of his patients sent for him. This patient had "snapped out" of his extreme withdrawal and wanted to "talk to the doctor." The patient attributed his sudden change to the lectures. Lazell maintained that most patients are accessible to the "correct manner of approach" provided they have intelligence enough for the subject matter of the lectures.

Louis Wender (64, 65) was one of the next to relate his experiences with group psychotherapy since 1929 at Hastings Hillside Hospital, New York. He noted that patients frequently analyzed and discussed their problems with greater candor with one another than with the physician; it was a common occurrence for a physician to learn the problems and conflicts of a patient through the patient's confidant. There was considerable difficulty in using the method of psychoanalysis because of the prohibitive cost, dearth of patients with the intellectual and cultural equipment, length of time needed, and the difficulty of establishing transference because patients compared physicians among themselves and jealousies developed—the patients could not be separated as outpatients are. In this situation group psychotherapy was purported to further social adjustment. Patients maintained the friendships that originated in the group meetings and continued to profit from the helpfulness and understanding they provided. Their drive to remain well seemed to be more dynamic, and was characterized by a competitive quality. The patients gained and maintained a capacity to discuss their problems freely, and this in turn enhanced their ability to deal successfully with new and difficult emotional material and experiences.

In the 'thirties Paul Schilder (55) set up small groups of psycho-neurotics and mild schizophrenic cases. He applied the classical analytic method, first preparing patients in individual sessions. In the same period Wender (64) was using class methods of group therapy and working out a method that combined education with the psychotherapeutic interview. The methods of Wender and Schilder were thought to be more suited to the needs of neurotics than of psychotics.

Abraham A. Low (35) is an exponent of the self-help method of psychiatric aftercare. This viewpoint is represented by the group "Recovery, Inc.," founded in 1937 by recovered mental patients who had been treated at the University of Illinois Medical School in Chicago where Low was assistant director of the Psychiatric Institute. The aim of this group is to reduce relapses in mental disorders and to combat chronicity in psychoneurotic conditions. Prevention of panic, which often brings about breakdown, is the main objective; to this end regular meetings are held during which there is panel discussion of the literature written by Low and members describe any recent disturbances that may have occurred. The psychological material and procedures are purposely kept simple so that persons of average or low intelligence can understand and follow. Important points are drilled in, and members acting as leaders are given special training. When a member panics at home, he can phone a veteran member for support. If necessary, the veteran will visit his home. The hoped-for effect of this group method is to discipline the patient and to make him share or bear the responsibility for his invalidism. He is shown the way to recovery, and can accept or reject it—it is his choice. In many ways Recovery, Inc., is similar to Alcoholics Anonymous, which originated at about the same time and is still one of the most successful ways of helping alcoholics.

World War II gave considerable impetus to group counseling. The need for treatment was much greater than the established methods could provide for. Audio-visual aids, psychodrama, puppetry, talks of the repressive-inspirational type, music, and many other techniques were tried in evacuation hospitals, front-line units, and home hospitals (11, 14, 17, 40). Some of these auxiliary techniques were found to be effective with acute, temporary disturbances resulting from immediate problems, such as those resulting from battle or when people are uprooted from their own groups. Not only did group counseling prove useful under these conditions, but its effects came to interest a large cross section of professional persons who have gone on developing it.

This completes our brief discussion of how group methods began. Let us now turn to some of the more specific and well-developed group methods and trace their development.

THE LECTURE–DISCUSSION TECHNIQUE

Although the first use of the lecture-discussion method can probably be traced to Pratt and Lazell, this didactic approach to group work is usually associated with Klapman (26, 27, 28). He has written on it rather extensively, and those interested are referred to his writings. Here we will merely describe briefly some of his ideas. Klapman writes that even though the practice of lecture-discussion methods has not been frozen into rigid techniques, no matter where these methods are introduced, and regardless of whether they are initiated by isolated units of workers or professional trained staffs, the practices and lectures employed eventually take on the same character.

Although a few workers claim success with large numbers, the common experience seems to be that six or eight patients or clients, and certainly not more than ten, form the most workable therapeutic group. The groups are usually referred to as "classes," and the subjects are told that the classes constitute a regular part of the program of treatment. As a starting point and focus for each meeting, especially in the early phase of the series, the leader gives a talk. He will discuss some topic; for example the emotions, beginning with their biological functions and physiological accompaniments. He may have something to say about defense mechanisms, starting with their familiar everyday forms. Simple diagrams or drawings on the blackboard are used whenever possible, not only to clarify what is being said but also to serve as an anchorage point for the discussion that is to follow. The talks by the leader are not to be regarded merely as a device to set the meeting in motion, as they have a genuine teaching function. An intellectual grasp of the mental mechanisms, even in simple terms, forms part of the goal of treatment. It is valuable for the subject to realize at once that emotional disorders are scientifically understandable. He learns that what he may have believed to be his own guilty secrets and contemptible weaknesses have their place in general scientific knowledge. He is reassured to find that the leader knows about them and that other patients suffer from them.

Following his preliminary remarks the counselor encourages group discussion. He invites questions and asks for illustrative experiences. At first the subjects may be reticent in talking about their own experiences, showing many varieties of resistance ranging from complete silence to argumentative attacks on the ideas presented by the leader. The group situation, however, is conducive to eventually overcoming resistance. If the leader maintains a permissive and interested attitude and avoids allowing himself to be drawn into defense of his own position, the subjects become increasingly able to speak about the things that trouble them.

Once the process is started, it goes forward fairly well. Each subject is emboldened by hearing the others talk about their problems. Each has the valuable privilege, moreover, of remaining silent if he wants to; conversation is taken over by the leader or by someone else if his own talk begins to embarrass or frighten him.

Klapman has formulated a plan whereby an entire mental institution is organized around its group therapeutic procedures. He states that there is no basis for the generally held notion that the inevitable end result of schizophrenia is severe deterioration, and he believes that carefully planned group activities designed to provide maximum stimulation in all spheres can prevent or retard deterioration almost completely, thus reclaiming many patients heretofore considered beyond help. He maintains that it is the economically feasible duty of society to make every effort to provide this stimulation for institutional patients. He outlines a series of twenty-four lectures that are the basis of his system. He often uses a mimeographed textbook in his classwork but without unduly pushing the participants to study it; nor does he otherwise make them feel responsible for their lessons. So far as possible the counselor tries to create an informal discussion group. Patient-activity, such as reading autobiographies, symposia on various subjects, debates, discussions of book reports, is utilized. Throughout the institution the patients are grouped into four forms (28, pp. 279–82):

Form D Includes "patients with (1) psychoses associated with neurological disorders, (2) psychoses associated with organic disease, (3) arteriosclerotic and senile psychoses." Group recreational and housekeeping activities are provided to the maximum abilities of the patients, and meetings of the repressive-inspirational type are held.

Form C Includes "untidy, deteriorated, destructive patients, denizens of the back wards. . . . Beginning with simple calisthenics and habit-training classes, the patient may be resocialized through such group practices as community singing, games, and other group procedures. Combined with suitable occupational and recreational therapies, it is conceivable that an appreciable percentage may be enabled to advance to higher forms." At least an improved institutional adjustment is to be expected in such a setting.

Form B Includes "the great mass of leveled-off tidy patients, who constitute the majority of the institutional patient-workers." Opportunities are provided for the members of this group to learn new trades, perform useful tasks, and advance to the next form. "Orientative" psychotherapy using the lecture system described above is provided. The class material must be held at the functioning intellectual levels of the patients.

Form A Includes "patients with most recent psychiatric onset, patients whose personalities are still organized at optimum levels, the more intelligent, the most treatable patients." Here the most intensive group and individual psychotherapy can be utilized.

Under Klapman's plan there would be a gradual gradation, and patients would be promoted from class to class and from form to form until they reached Form A, where they would get both group and individual treatment. Such a scheme provides an incentive to patients and a yardstick by which to measure progress.

ACTIVITY GROUP PROCEDURES

Samuel R. Slavson (58, 59, 60) developed his system of activity group counseling in his work for the Jewish Board of Guardians in New York City. The members of his groups engage in individual counseling with a social worker concurrently with their attendance at the weekly group sessions. The groups are composed of five or six children, and the activities consist of leather work, carpentry, clay modeling, painting, and the like. In addition to these activities the groups make trips to museums, to the zoo, to movies, go on hikes, and make similar outings. Every session is terminated with the serving of refreshments; this is intended not only as a rewarding activity but to duplicate to some extent a family situation. The purpose of these activities can best be understood from Slavson's (58, p. 139) writing:

> Frustration to an already frustrated individual is of no great value. We must rely upon successful achievements and satisfactions. The group therapist supplies the least complicated materials and situations and helps individual children when they show signs of stress or fear of failure. As tolerance to frustration is increased, the children are allowed to fail and discover their limitations.[2]

The function of the counselor is to provide a maximally permissive atmosphere in the group situation, thus aiding the children to form a new conception of what *adult* represents. The counselor's only form of disapproval is the withholding of praise. Praise is given liberally for all constructive acts except those that are performed for the group rather than for an individual, since it is the child's group and any effort put forth in the direction of its maintenance or improvement is taken for granted. Praise is withheld in the case of destructive or antisocial acts. Only when the counselor is sure that the members regard him as a "sanctioner"

[2] This and following quotation by permission from *An Introduction to Group Therapy*, by Samuel R. Slavson. New York: International Universities Press, sixth printing, 1954. Copyright 1954 by International Universities Press.

rather than a "prohibitor" does he begin to assert himself positively. There is no punishment for the prevalent fighting (which the counselor takes for granted without interfering), stealing of tools or materials, or any such antisocial or destructive behavior. After frustration tolerance is considered to have been sufficiently built up, frustrations of increasing magnitude are introduced as part of the weaning process. These frustrations include the transfer of children from one group to another, changing counselors, combining groups for one or more meetings, and other means of making the group and individuals within it less dependent upon each other and upon the counselor.

According to Slavson, the chief difficulty encountered among his clients is not weak superego but overintense superego. Since the conflict between the needs of the child and his superego results in anxiety which may be resolved by antisocial acts or by withdrawal, the aim of the activity program is to enable the child to release his tensions in a permissive atmosphere. The group gradually establishes a primary code, and the child slowly reconstructs his impulses so as to be accepted by the counselor and the other members of the group. The activity provides a cathartic outlet for the client's tensions. Of the effect of the group, Slavson (58, p. 190) says:

> The presence of others has a socializing effect through spontaneous mutual help, admiration of work done by others, cooperation of two or more in a group project, pleasurable feelings that come from constructive effort in a group, and the gradual development of an awareness of the need of others.

CLIENT–CENTERED GROUP COUNSELING

Although client-centered counseling has been associated primarily with Rogers, the work of Hobbs (24) is representative of this method as it is used in group situations. Our discussion is, therefore, closely patterned after his point of view. The nondirective or client-centered approach is based on the assumption that the individual has within himself both the ability to solve his own problems and a growth impulse that makes mature behavior more satisfying than immature behavior. For this reason the counselor is accepting and permissive, limiting his remarks to clarification of the client's feelings or ideas and to giving support. The transference relationship, interpretation, and diagnosis are avoided as much as possible. Each member of the group must find, in the counselor and other group members, a feeling of warmth and acceptance, so that there is increasingly less need for defensive behavior. This atmosphere is more difficult to achieve in a group than in an individual counseling situation, but when attained it is more effective because the person feels accepted by a social group, rather than by one person who is a professional acceptor. Another characteristic of group-centered counseling is the communality of feeling which results. Different persons have different symptoms and problems, but they usually share the same feelings, as, for example, feelings of anxiety or self-worthlessness. The expression of feelings provides the basis for group discussion, just as it forms the basis for client-centered individual counseling.

Hobbs (24, pp. 289–92) feels that group counseling has several advantages over individual counseling. These advantages are general, and not unique to the nondirective method:

1. "The group situation brings into focus interpersonal interaction, and provides an immediate opportunity for the discovery of new and more satisfying ways of relating to people."

2. "As a member of a group the person learns what it means both to give and to receive emotional support in a mature fashion. When he learns how to give and receive, the client takes on a new role which can contribute to his feelings of self-worth."

3. Some people find it easier to talk in a group. They learn from the others that it is acceptable to talk about one's problems and they learn how to go about the process of self-analysis.

4. Many issues center around the problems of values. This is more characteristic of client-centered therapy, because it is basic to this approach that the client be allowed to work out his own system of values. The therapist is neutral, but group members are not, and they can propose alternate values or perspectives without pressure being felt.[3]

In this type of counseling the optimal number of members in a group seems to be about six plus the counselor. Types of persons who do not fit well into these groups include the hostile individual, especially if he is psychologically sophisticated, and the severely disturbed person who is so far out of contact that he is insensitive to the feelings of others. The frequency and length of meetings vary with the needs of the group. In getting started, the counselor usually indicates that the group is responsible for its own pace and direction; members are told that it is their group. This is all the structure that is given. The basic unit of group interaction is the theme (a topic or point of focus in the discussion). It has a clear beginning and a clear stopping point. A few members or the whole group may participate in discussion of a theme, but frequently it centers about one person in the group who may present his problem to the group. It may be brief or last for several sessions. It may be abandoned or it may be returned to in later sessions. Movement of themes is in the direction

[3] Quoted and adapted by permission from "Group-Centered Psychotherapy," by Nicholas Hobbs in *Client-Centered Therapy*, by Carl R. Rogers. Copyright 1951 by Carl R. Rogers.

of greater detail and deeper emotional expression. The counselor plays as minor a role as possible, but he tries to understand the feelings displayed, and will reflect them to the group if other members fail to do so. The counselor also tries to reduce threat that may be directed at any group member, so as to prevent him from withdrawing from interaction. Group members tend to play the therapeutic role with greater frequency as the series of meetings progresses. Hobbs points out that it has not been established as yet that group counseling is more effective than individual counseling, because conclusive research is lacking. However, from observation he believes that for normal or near-normal persons with debilitating situational conflicts, group counseling is somewhat more effective.

ANALYTICALLY ORIENTED GROUP PROCEDURES

Paul Schilder (55) was probably the first person to apply psychoanalysis in group situations. His clients were given individual orientation in the techniques of free association and dream interpretation, and then instructed to write a detailed autobiography. Following this they were seen in groups that were conducted in a way similar to individual analysis. Either the analyst or other clients would give interpretations, and free association might be forthcoming from any member of the group. Shocking material would be interpreted by the analyst in a manner to reduce the shock. Individual therapy was carried on concurrently with the group program.

Another approach to the psychoanalysis of groups has been described by Wolfe (67, 68). His emphasis is on dream analysis, free association, analysis of resistance, transference, and countertransference. Groups are heterogeneous with regard to sex and neuroses but have a narrow age range. Wolfe feels that the family constellation produced the neurosis, so the logical agency for curing it is the surrogate family setting of the group. Excluded from his groups are: psychopaths (because they are potentially destructive), morons (who would retard group progress), alcoholics (who are treated separately), psychotics, and hypermanics. Schizoids are believed to be helpful in interpreting unrealistic material. Groups include eight to ten members. Pregroup individual therapy ranges from ten to thirty sessions for each client. Unlike the nondirective counselors, Wolfe considers diagnosis important for understanding group dynamics and for proper construction of the group.

The first four group sessions in Wolfe's approach consist chiefly of lectures concerning procedure, potential emotional stresses, and the security of the proceedings. Following these, but still during the first stages, the group members freely associate about dreams and fantasies. Dreams are taken as progress indices, and graduation from the group is on the basis of the normalcy of dreams. The next stages involve free association of the members about one another. The individual is supported as well as dissected by the group, and becomes toughened against unreality-based neurotic criticism. Resistances appear during free association, and these are analyzed and an attempt is made to break them down. Personal history is considered of value only insofar as it is relevant to the present difficulty. The largest single area of group concentration is the analysis of transference. Intragroup and group-to-leader transferences are analyzed, and the unrealistic elements are exposed. The ability of the group member to detect and resolve his own transference distortion, and to refrain from countertransfer to those who project on him, is taken as another indication of his readiness to graduate. Speculation about the leader or any absent member is encouraged at supplementary meetings, which the leader does not attend. These are started after 12 to 24 regular meetings of the group have been held. In general, the analytically oriented group leader is interested in the problem of how unconscious wishes and defenses make themselves manifest in the group, and how past and present group relationships are related to the adjustment problems of the individual. The group leader must recognize individual needs and indicate which are realistic and which appear to be unrealistic. The group provides an opportunity for working through difficulties that are associated with interpersonal relations.

PSYCHODRAMA

This type of psychotherapy was originated by Moreno in Vienna, and according to him it grew out of the observation of the play of children. Although psychodrama is based primarily upon concepts derived from the analytic approach, its primary contribution is the method of role playing. Moreno has described his procedures and unique terminology in several writings (41, 42). We will attempt to describe briefly some of the principal concepts. In general, the method consists of having an individual, or individuals, act out various roles on a stage. The objective of psychodrama therapy is a total dramatic production of the client's life. It tries to provide the participant with more reality than the struggle with life permits him to achieve spontaneously. The task of the individual is more complicated in psychodrama than in individual or other types of group therapy because he must express how he feels at present, through both words and gestures. The psychodrama may be carried out in the presence of spectators, or with only a small group of other patients who participate in the drama; these methods are known respectively as open and closed. The staff of therapeutic assistants should be as large as possible, including persons of both sexes and a variety of personality types.

The participant first starts with himself (in the director's presence) and lives through situations that are part of his daily life. Later he enacts the roles of other people who are emotionally tied to him. Presentations may relate to experiences in any period of the individual's life, and he is helped by staff members in getting started. These are the techniques of *self-representation*. Techniques of *spontaneous improvisation* are used when the participant acts out fictitious, imagined roles. He is instructed in doing this, to keep his personal character from interfering with the fictitious character. In this way his ego is presumed to be free to watch and record what goes on. The technique of *soliloquy* reflects the private reactions of players to their roles. These are spoken as asides. *Warming-up* techniques are used to induce spontaneous states. Motions, thoughts, feelings, images, and alcohol are utilized. The director may enter as a participant-actor, using his psychiatric knowledge to guide the drama.

GROUP WORK WITH CHILDREN

Although Moreno began his work in psychodrama with children, group procedures as applied to children are of comparatively recent origin. Among the first to organize groups to treat children was Ernest Papanek (43), who in 1924 organized a special group in Vienna for the "problem children" taken from the city's largest public school. His group took the form of a "club" whose schedule of activities was much like that of Slavson's activity group. Through this club Papenek sought to bring about certain personality changes in the children, changes that he felt would better fit them for group living.

Today we find writers in the field presenting many variations in group work with children. Among these writers is Virginia Mae Axline (1, p. 26), who presents a rather comprehensive description of the nature of group counseling with children. She sees group counseling as a "Non-directive therapeutic experience with the added element of contemporary evaluation of behavior plus the reaction of personalities upon one another." The group experience is seen as injecting a realistic element into counseling "because the child lives in the world with other children and must consider the reaction of others and must develop a consideration of the individual's feelings." While most writers on the subject would agree with this much of her definition, there is some disagreement as to what further constitutes group counseling. While Axline does not perceive the group as a "club," "recreational group," "education group," or above all, as a "substitute for the family," [4] Slavson (58, p. 337) emphatically states, "The chief characteristic of the therapy group is its sim-

---

[4] By permission from *Play Therapy*, by Virginia Mae Axline. Copyright 1947 by Virginia Mae Axline.

ilarity to the family." Slavson's *activity therapy* (primarily designed for children and adolescents) is also in the nature of a "recreational club." In general, however, in spite of the disagreement about the resemblance of the therapeutic group to other groups, most workers agree that the functions of group work with children are those of support, socialization, and the other aims of group procedures with adults and of counseling and therapy in general. Slavson adds one further objective, that of providing the child with genuine interests to occupy his leisure time.

In addition to Axline and Slavson, other contemporary workers who have reported their experiences in group work with children are Harry M. Little and Gisela Konopka (34), Kathleen K. Stewart and Pearl L. Axelrod (61), Fritz Redl (50, 51, 52, 53), Lauretta Bender (3), Bruno Bettelheim (6, 7), and Dorothy M. Bollinger (10). Both Redl and Bettelheim describe residential group care and group living, and for extremely disturbed children they feel that such living provides a more complete therapeutic situation. Summer camp programs have been discussed by Helen Hewitt and Margaret Gildea (23) and special problems such as the overcoming of social and cultural tensions (30) and the physically handicapped (54) have been dealt with in group situations.

Children, because they are not usually able to verbalize their problems as are adults, must depend upon nonverbal means for expressing their feelings. One of the best outlets is the "acting out" that children do so naturally and that can be used in the therapeutic situation. Louise A. Sullivan (62, p. 58), a student of Moreno, presents a study of psychodrama in a children's clinic.

> The value of play techniques in the treatment of childhood behavior disorders is well known to the psychiatric field. However, psychodrama has another advantage. Having only the child's imagination and problems as props, it is a simple matter to put his problems on a reality level, thus offering him active treatment from the time of his first clinic visit. In bringing into play this unique quality of spontaneity the patient is revealed to himself and helps remove the need for self-deception. It is a dynamic interplay of the interpersonal relationships, which the child can accept for himself as truth because it is himself in action.[5]

Sullivan found that children demonstrate certain fairly typical reaction patterns. They go through an initial period of resistance, and a second period of so-called spontaneity in which they form a transference relationship with the worker. Following this, certain standard situations are

[5] By permission from "Psychodrama in a Child Guidance Clinic," by Louise A. Sullivan, in *Group Psychotherapy*, by Jacob L. Moreno. Copyright 1949 by Jacob L. Moreno.

set up for the child in an effort to determine his difficulties. The final stage is the planned treatment period during which the actual work on the problem progresses, both in relation to the child and to his parents.

Closely related to the psychodramatic technique is the puppet drama, which involves prepared stories and/or stories written by the children. Ruth E. Hartley, Lawrence K. Frank and Robert M. Goldenson (22), Selma Horwitz (25), and Lauretta Bender (3, 5) discuss the use of puppetry, as does Axline (1). The four different procedures described by these writers all provide that the children use ready-made puppets on some occasions and that on others they make their own. Sometimes they use prepared scripts and sometimes the children write their own. Bender, however, hires special puppeteers to operate the puppets although the children may direct the action from the audience. The use of puppets in drama has the advantage that they combine reality and fantasy, but for this very reason they may prove threatening to the maintenance of contact with reality by severely disturbed children. All the writers on the subject, including Adolf G. Woltmann (69), agree that the primary value of the puppet drama lies in the follow-up after the shows, although there may be some cathartic value in the performance itself.

Musical activities, including spontaneous rhythms and dance, have been used in various group settings. Rudolf M. Wittenberg (66) used music instruction and training in a hospital ward. Bender (4) reports on various uses of music in a children's ward, including organized musical groups, rhythm bands, and group games. From the point of view of therapy and socializing activity, Bender found music most valuable with the younger children. Spontaneous bodily movement and dancing were encouraged, and a musical pageant was spontaneously evolved. Separately from this, Bender organized a group for creative dance in which certain specific emotions were expressed through the dance. Phyllis Van Fleet (63) tells of a similar project with fourteen children, five to sixteen years of age. Nine of the group were boys, and it was the boys who took the lead in the project and seemed to derive most benefit from it.

Formal studies on the results of group techniques with children are surprisingly scarce. Louise Fleming and William U. Snyder (17) report a study on 46 children living in a children's home. All the children were given the Rogers' Personality Test, a sociometric test devised by Fleming, and the "Guess Who?" test. Seven children were selected for therapy—three girls in one group and four boys in the other. After twelve weeks of therapy the entire group was retested for changes in the scores on the three tests. The conclusions of the study were as follows (p. 116):

(1) Measurable changes in adjustment do take place as a result of nondirective group play therapy. In this study, four of

the subjects showed a marked improvement, and three showed response changes on tests but no improvement on scores. (2) Improvement for the girls was greater than that for the boys. (3) Girls showed greater change in personal than in social adjustment. (4) Subjects' conflict over therapy limits has definite therapeutic advantages. (5) Water, paints and nursing bottles were the most important media for the expression of feelings. (6) The sex of the counselor may be a factor in establishing rapport with children around the age of ten. (7) It would appear that for the best therapeutic results, the children in a group should not vary too greatly in degree of intensity of maladjustment.[6]

On the basis of an N of 7, it is rather doubtful that such an impressive list of conclusions is justified. The study does point up the need, however, for some extensive research as to the efficacy of any and all of the various types of group therapy.

EVALUATION OF GROUP COUNSELING

Among the many studies and reports of group counseling and therapeutic procedures, two of the most extensive have been by Leon Gorlow, Erasmus L. Hoch, and Earl F. Telschow (20) and by Florence B. Powdermaker and Jerome D. Frank (44). Although both of these reports describe many attributes of the group process and present the results of the experience of the investigators, in general they only furnish tentative answers to broad questions and point up those aspects of group therapy which merit further intensive research. Many writers (2, 12, 21, 29, 36, 39, 40) conclude from their experience and research studies that group therapy is a profitable, successful experience but little definitive evidence is available. The difficulty is, of course, that we have no adequate criteria to use in evaluating success in any form of treatment procedures. It is, however, studies of this nature that must necessarily bring forth the necessary data from which a comprehensive group-treatment approach can evolve.

Although evaluation of group counseling, as of individual counseling, is exceedingly difficult and must be made largely on the basis of subjective judgment, results to date suggest that it is making its place as a tool of the psychologist, psychiatrist, and social worker. It seems especially efficacious in the form of activity group psychotherapy with chil-

[6] From "Social and Personal Changes Following Non-directive Group Play Therapy," by Louise Fleming and William U. Snyder, *American Journal of Orthopsychiatry*, 1947, 17, 101–16. By permission of the editor.

dren and adolescents, and as a measure to prevent deterioration among psychotic patients, with contributions, of course, on all intervening levels. The future is promising for group psychotherapy, but, more important, group psychotherapy is promising for the future of counseling and therapy.

SUMMARY

Group counseling has had broad applications. The term has been used to describe camp-meeting-like sessions with as many as 500 persons taking part, as well as group psychoanalysis sessions in which only two or three participate. The procedures have included lectures, community sings, discussions, free associations, reading of biographies, debates, manual arts activities, and mixing of these and other procedures. Though group therapy was originally "resorted to" as a matter of expedience, it has become recognized as a valuable preparation for, adjunct to, or follow-up on individual psychotherapy, and as a technique that can in itself produce some results that are uniquely attributable to the dynamics of the group situation.

Group counseling may take many forms. There are about as many specific approaches to group work as there are persons who use them. The lecture discussion technique of Klapman, the activity group methods of Slavson, client-centered counseling as outlined by Hobbs, the analytically oriented group therapy conducted by Wolfe, and the psychodramatic group activities of Moreno have been described as representative of the range of procedures that have been used or adapted in group counseling. Clinical experience has demonstrated the worth-whileness of group work, but much research is needed before we can speak authoritatively about the *how* and *why* of group counseling.

BIBLIOGRAPHY

1. Axline, V. M., *Play therapy*. Boston: Houghton Mifflin, 1947.
2. Bach, G. R., *Intensive group psychotherapy*. New York: Ronald, 1954.
3. Bender, L., "Group activities on a children's ward as methods of psychotherapy." *Amer. J. Psychiat.*, 1937, 93, 1151–73.
4. Bender, L., *Child psychiatric techniques*. Springfield, Ill.: Thomas, 1942.
5. Bender, L., and Woltman, A. G., "The use of puppet shows as a psychotherapeutic method for behavior problems in children." *Amer. J. Orthopsychiat.*, 1936, 6, 341–54.
6. Bettelheim, B., *Love is not enough*. Glencoe, Ill.: Free Press, 1950.
7. Bettelheim, B., and Sylvester, E., "Therapeutic influence of the group on the individual." *Amer. J. Orthopsychiat.*, 1947, 14, 684–92.

8. Bierer, J., "Group psychotherapy." *Brit. Med. J.*, 1942, 1, 214–17.
9. Bierer, J., "A new form of group psychotherapy." *Proc. R. Soc. Med.*, 1944, 37, 208–9.
10. Bollinger, D., "Group therapy at the Children's Center." *Nerv. Child*, 1945, 4, 221–7.
11. Braceland, F. J., "Group psychotherapy." *Sociometry*, 1945, 8, 283–7.
12. Cadman, W. H., Misbach, L., and Brown, D. J., "An assessment of round-table psychotherapy." *Psychol. Monogr.*, 1954, 68, No. 14 (Whole No. 384).
13. Camus, J., and Pagniez, P., *Isolement et psychothérapie*. Paris: Félix Alcan, 1904.
14. Cohen, R. R., "Visual aids in group psychotherapy." *Sociometry*, 1945, 8, 311–14.
15. Emerson, W. R. P., "The hygienic and dietetic treatment of delicate children by the class method." *Boston Med. Surg. J.*, 1910, 163, 326–8.
16. Fleming, L., and Snyder, W., "Social and personal changes following nondirective group play therapy." *Amer. J. Orthopsychiat.*, 1947, 17, 101–16.
17. Fontel M. C., "Psychodrama in an evacuation hospital." *Sociometry*, 1945, 8, 363–83.
18. Foulkes, S. H., "Principles and practice of group therapy." *Bull. Menn. Clin.*, 1946, 10, 85–9.
19. Foulkes, S. H., *Introduction to group-analytic psychotherapy*. New York: Grune & Stratton, 1949.
20. Gorlow, L., Hoch, E. L., and Telschow, E. F., *The nature of nondirective group psychotherapy*. New York: Teachers College, Columbia Univ., 1952.
21. Hadden, S. B., "Post military group psychotherapy with psychoneurotics." *Ment. Hyg.*, 1947, 31, 89–93.
22. Hartley, R. E., Frank, L. K., and Goldenson, R. M., *New play experiences for children*. New York: Columbia Univ. Press, 1952.
23. Hewitt, H., and Gildea, M., "An experiment in group psychotherapy." *Amer. J. Orthopsychiat.*, 1945, 15, 112–27.
24. Hobbs, N., "Group-centered psychotherapy." In Rogers, C. R., *Client-centered therapy*. Boston: Houghton Mifflin, 1951.
25. Horwitz, S., "The spontaneous drama as a technique in group therapy." *Nerv. Child*, 1945, 4, 252–73.
26. Klapman, J. W., "A didactic approach to group psychotherapy." *Ill. Psychiat. J.*, 1941, 1, 6–10.
27. Klapman, J. W., "Some impressions of group psychotherapy." *Psychoanal. Rev.*, 1944, 31, 322–8.
28. Klapman, J. W., *Group psychotherapy: theory and practice*. New York: Grune & Stratton, 1946.
29. Klopfer, W. G., "The efficacy of group therapy as indicated by group Rorschach records." *Rorschach Res. Exch.*, 1945, 9, 207–9.
30. Konopka, G., "Group therapy in overcoming racial and cultural tensions." *Amer. J. Orthopsychiat.*, 1947, 17, 693–9.

31. Kotkov, B., "A bibliography for the student of group psychotherapy." *J. Clin. Psychol.*, 1950, 6, 77–91.

32. Lazell, E. W., "The group treatment of dementia praecox." *Psychoanal. Rev.*, 1921, 8, 168–79.

33. Lazell, E. W., "Group psychic treatment of dementia praecox by lectures in mental re-education." *U. S. Veterans' Med. Bull.*, 1930, 6, 733–47.

34. Little, H. M., and Konopka, G., "Group therapy in a child guidance center." *Amer. J. Orthopsychiat.*, 1947, 17, 303–11.

35. Low, A. A., "The combined system of group psychotherapy and self-help as practiced by Recovery, Inc." *Sociometry*, 1945, 8, 332–7.

36. Luchins, A. S., "Experiences with closed ward group psychotherapy." *Amer. J. Orthopsychiat.*, 1947, 17, 511–20.

37. Marsh, L. C., "Group treatment of the psychoses by the psychological equivalent of the revival." *Ment. Hyg.*, 1931, 15, 328–49.

38. Marsh, L. C., "Group therapy and the psychiatric clinic." *J. Nerv. Ment. Dis.*, 1935, 82, 381–93.

39. McCann, W. H., Almada, A., "Round table psychotherapy: A technique in group psychotherapy." *J. Consult. Psychol.*, 1950, 14, 421–35.

40. McKay, L. A., "Music as a group therapeutic agent in the treatment of convalescents." *Sociometry*, 1945, 8, 471–5.

41. Moreno, J. L., *Psychodrama*. New York: Beacon House, 1946.

42. Moreno, J. L., "Psychodrama." In McCory, J. L. (ed.), *Six approaches to psychotherapy*. New York: Dryden, 1955.

43. Papanek, E., "Treatment by group work." *Amer. J. Orthopsychiat.*, 1945, 14, 223–9.

44. Powdermaker, F. B., and Frank, J. D., *Group psychotherapy*. Cambridge: Commonwealth Fund, 1953.

45. Pratt, J. H., "The class method of treating consumption in the homes of the poor." *J. Amer. Med. Assn.*, 1907, 49, 755–9.

46. Pratt, J. H., "The principles of class treatment and their application to various chronic diseases." *Hosp. Soc. Serv.*, 1922, 6, 401–11.

47. Pratt, J. H., "The influences of emotions in the causation and cure of psychoneuroses." *Int. Clinics*, 1934, 4, 1–16.

48. Pratt, J. H., "The group method in the treatment of psychosomatic disorders." *Sociometry*, 1945, 8, 323–31.

49. Redl, W., "Diagnostic group work." *Amer. J. Orthopsychiat.*, 1944, 15, 53–67.

50. Redl, F., "Problems of clinical group work with children." *Proc. Second Brief Psychotherapy Council*, 1944, 29–35.

51. Redl, F., "Resistance in therapy groups." *Human Relat.*, 1948, 307–13.

52. Redl, F., and Wineman, D., *Children who hate*. Glencoe, Ill.: Free Press, 1952.

53. Redl, F., and Wineman, D., *Controls from within*. Glencoe, Ill.: Free Press, 1952.

54. Rubenstein, B., "Therapeutic use of groups in an orthopedic hospital school." *Amer. J. Orthopsychiat.*, 1945, 15, 662–74.

55. Schilder, P., *Psychotherapy*. New York: W. W. Norton, 1938.

56. Shaskan, D. A., "Must individual and group psychotherapy be opposed?" *Amer. J. Orthopsychiat.*, 1947, 17, 290–2.

57. Simon, B., Holzberg, J. D., Aaron, S., Saxe, C. H., "Group therapy from the viewpoint of the patient." *J. Nerv. Ment. Dis.*, 1947, 105, 156–70.

58. Slavson, S. R., *An introduction to group therapy.* New York: International Univ. Press, sixth printing, 1954.

59. Slavson, S. R., *The practice of group therapy.* New York: International Univ. Press, 1947.

60. Slavson, S. R., *Analytic group therapy with children, adolescents, and adults.* New York: Columbia Univ. Press, 1950.

61. Stewart, K. K., and Axelrod, P. L., "Group therapy on a children's psychiatric ward." *Amer. J. Orthopsychiat.*, 1947, 17, 312–25.

62. Sullivan, L. A., "Psychodrama in a child guidance clinic." In Moreno, J., *Group Psychotherapy.* New York: Beacon House, 1945.

63. Van Fleet, P., "Rhythmic activity: A project in group therapy with children." *Amer. J. Orthopsychiat.*, 1949, 19, 79–86.

64. Wender, L., "Dynamics of group psychotherapy and its application." *J. Nerv. Ment. Dis.*, 1936, 84, 54–60.

65. Wender, L., "Current trends in group psychotherapy." *Amer. J. Psychotherapy*, 1954, 5, 381–404.

66. Wittenberg, R. M., "Psychiatric concepts in group work." *Amer. J. Orthopsychiat.*, 1944, 14, 76–83.

67. Wolfe, A., "The psychoanalysis of groups: Part I." *Amer. J. Psychotherapy*, 1949, 3, 525–58.

68. Wolfe, A., "The psychoanalysis of groups: Part II." *Amer. J. Psychotherapy*, 1949, 4, 16–50.

69. Woltmann, A. G., "The use of puppetry as a projective method in therapy." In Anderson, H., and Anderson, G., *An introduction to projective techniques.* Englewood Cliffs, N. J.: Prentice-Hall, 1951.

Vocational Guidance
and Counseling

THE SPECIAL PROBLEMS OF VOCATIONAL COUNSELING MUST BE carefully considered by the counselor because of the importance of vocational adjustment in the total adjustment of the individual. We are hesitant, however, about isolating this topic as one requiring attention aside from its place in the general discussion of counseling. In the actual counseling situation, vocational counseling *cannot* be separated from the other aims of psychological counseling. To illustrate, environmental manipulation must consider the work segment of the client's environment, which occupies approximately one third of his time. Insight or understanding of problems frequently focuses upon tensions, dissatisfactions, and the lack of satisfactions that are associated with one's occupation. Similarly, tensions can be reduced and emotions relieved through application to a job. Along the same vein, the goals of socialization and support can frequently be achieved most effectively through associations with fellow workers; through the security that comes from doing a job well; through the feeling of belonging with a group working toward the same goals; through identification with an employer, with professional groups, labor groups, and other occupational in-groups. Vocational counseling must be integrated with the entire counseling process. Let us bear in mind that counseling is a continuous process and that vocational guidance cannot be administered without consideration of educational guidance and personal counseling. As Edmund G. Williamson (28) has stated, it is often impossible to administer vocational counseling without first clearing up problems of a personal nature. We would like to add that it is just as often true that personal counseling cannot be effective unless vocational problems are solved.

THE SIGNIFICANCE OF VOCATIONAL COUNSELING

Although we agree with Milton L. Blum and Benjamin Balinsky (5) that all aspects of counseling (vocational, educational, and personal) are aspects of the total counseling process, the importance of vocational planning and work is such that a discussion of some of the special problems associated with vocational counseling seems indicated. The importance of work as a treatment and mental hygienic activity was recognized as early as 1837 by the Worcester State Hospital, then known as the Worcester State Lunatic Hospital, whose annual report for that year stated (29, p. 7), "Employment is one of the most successful means of cure resorted to in this institution. Few patients are indisposed to engage in any useful occupation, and most esteem it a privilege." In addition to the therapeutic aspects of employment, satisfying work has a profound preventive mental hygienic influence. To carry it still further, adequate vocational planning has significant value in preventing maladjustment. We have no way of estimating to what extent confusion about his vocational future may be affecting the adolescent's current adjustment. The anxiety experienced by the vocationally confused youngster can attain extreme proportions. Many instances of schizophrenic withdrawal in the teen-ager may be in response to anticipated difficulties in meeting the responsibilities of adulthood. One of these responsibilities is the choosing of a life's work that will be profitable and satisfying.

For most persons choosing a vocation is the most important decision they will make during their lives. Yet it is only comparatively recently that leaders in education, industry, and psychology have come to realize that this choice should be made in a careful and scientific manner. The present educational system does not in itself prepare one directly for a life work. Educational programs tend to stress the value of learning how to think, how to take one's place in society, and of various cultural accomplishments; these are all of value in themselves but the student who discontinues schooling after graduating from a general high school or even from a liberal arts college is rarely ready to earn his living. For the most part, only those who receive commercial or technical training at the high school, college, or graduate level are specifically prepared to do so. It is true that many of the larger industrial organizations, recognizing this need for specific training, have set up on-the-job training programs of their own. They are even doing a certain amount of vocational counseling through their college recruitment programs. But in the school systems, even those who receive vocational training ordinarily receive little or no guidance regarding the choice of the vocation for which they are being trained. A tragically small proportion of those receiving technical training have any comprehensive idea of the nature of the vocation they have chosen. This lack of information may even extend to the amount and kind of training necessary for it. An excellent example of this lack of information was seen recently when a fourth-semester university student reported at a clinic to which he had come for personal counseling that he hoped to receive his degree in psychiatry in about two years. He stated that he had always planned to be a psychiatrist and that he had to come to the university where he was in attendance because his father had been graduated from it. Although an academic adviser had had the wisdom to place this student in a premedical curriculum, no one had ever explained to him that medical training preceded psychiatric training, that medical training would require somewhat more than four years, and that since the university where he was currently enrolled had no medical school, he would have to go elsewhere for this training. This is a rather extreme illustration but it actually happened.

A sound vocational choice is best made by means of study, direct observation, and thorough acquaintance with the demands, required training, and the ultimate possibilities of the occupation or profession. This does not mean that vocational choices made by other means are always wrong—a choice arrived at by drawing a card out of a hat could, of course, result in a highly successful and happy outcome, but the chances are decidedly against it. A son following blindly in his father's footsteps often finds himself doing work for which he has little taste or ability. Even at the present time, the great majority of young people choose their vocations because of what their parents, teachers, or friends think, or in imitation of some respected elder. Relatively few make their own choices. Such vocational choices typically show lack of foresight, information, and scientific guidance. The student who, using both his own resources and those available through the guidance of a vocational counselor (or some other qualified person), finds out all he can about the requirements of various vocations and matches his capacities and interests with these requirements is much better able to choose a vocation in which he will be both successful and happy.

Even more tragic than the cases in which the wrong vocational decision is made, are those in which the individual is unable to make any decision at all. Persons with no preferences, and, even more extreme, with no technical or special preparation other than a general education, must take their chances at "getting a job" from almost anything that turns up, regardless of its nature. Many students have come to college just to come to college, bringing with them no specific interests or information on the basis of which to make a choice of vocation. Lack of information—and, because of this, no basis for any interest—is the most common pattern we see in the youngster who "doesn't know what he wants to be." In the grade school or even high school student we can expect this lack of information. Perhaps it is one of the guidance functions of school years to provide the student with some knowledge. At the adult level, in college or elsewhere, the person with little or no information about possible occupations presents a difficult and distressing problem. Most counselors would much prefer to counsel with the person with ten vocational objectives than with the individual who has none.

Confused and indefinite—or complete lack of—vocational planning is not limited to students in schools, colleges, and universities; it is, unfortunately, a problem often presented in clinics, hospitals, welfare agencies, employment offices, and other settings. Many clients presenting themselves to public and private agencies are suffering from debilitating illness or injury that may force them to change their work, but probably an even larger number have no vocational interests, preferences, or qualifications. Many of these clients have been unable to hold positions, or have held different jobs in different types of work. Careful, sensible vocational counseling offers the best solution to this growing problem. Education has come to realize this but we are still floundering as regards providing helpful guidance for all youngsters. We have only made a beginning in educational and vocational guidance. We have even made some errors; at times we have probably stepped backward by emphasizing authoritative counseling and overselling supposedly "quick, easy, and fool-proof" test procedures. We can hope that eventually real progress will be made in the area of preventive guidance. Ideally, the guidance workers should do such a successful job that there would be no business in this area for the counselor or therapist.

Among the institutions and agencies that are recognizing the importance of sound, constructive vocational planning is the Veterans Administration, which has become concerned about the number of veterans who have "found a home with the Veterans Administration." The Veterans Administration believes that the most significant reason why individuals fail to leave a Veterans Administration installation or to stay out when they do leave is their inability to find, hold, enjoy, and competently pursue some kind of work; counseling psychologists have been charged with the responsibility of attempting to deal with the problem. In institutions or agencies such as hospitals, clinics, employment bureaus, and welfare centers, the emphasis must change from vocational placement to total (vocational, personal, educational, etc.) counseling. A colleague told us recently that he had got at least five jobs for a hospital patient; the patient had lost them all and in each instance he had returned to the hospital. Our colleague's conclusion from this experience was that "there is very little for vocational counseling to offer." Actually, he had not even tried vocational counseling; he had merely served as a placement agent. Altogether too little real vocational counseling has been integrated into the total counseling process by psychologists up to the present time. We have been preoccupied with treating personalities and not persons, attempting to cure defects rather than rehabilitating people, educating minds rather than preparing youth for the practical as well as the aesthetic aspects of living. There are, of course, notable exceptions to these generalizations.

WHAT IS VOCATIONAL COUNSELING?

A somewhat vague answer to this question has already been given but at this point we should be somewhat more specific. Donald E. Super (24, p. 2) has defined vocational counseling as "the process of helping the individual to ascertain, accept, understand and apply the relevant facts about himself to the pertinent facts about the occupational world which are ascertained through incidental and planned exploratory activities." Definitions offered vary from this rather elaborate one to the simple statement that vocational counseling involves helping the individual choose, prepare for, and embark upon an occupation. The field of vocational counseling has been quite thoroughly described by writers such as Milton E. Hahn and Malcolm S. MacLean (11), Edward S. Borden (6), Harold B. Pepinsky and Pauline N. Pepinsky (19), and many others (2, 4, 9, 10, 12, 13, 14, 16, 17, 20, 21, 26, 27). The reader who wishes an elaborate treatment of the field of vocational counseling is referred to sources such as these. In this chapter we are going to keep our discussion brief and at a simple level.

Williamson (28, pp. 57–8) has described six steps in clinical counseling with students:

> These steps are analysis, synthesis, diagnosis, prognosis, counseling (treatment), and follow-up. *Analysis* refers to the collection from a variety of sources of data which provide for an adequate understanding of the student. *Synthesis* refers to the summarizing and organizing of the data from analysis in such a manner as to reveal the student's assets, liabilities, adjustments, and maladjustments. A case history or cumulative record form may be used to summarize the mass of data about the student's life, and test scores are summarized on a profile or psychograph. *Diagnosis* refers to the end result of diagnosing; it is the clinician's conclusions concerning the characteristics and causes of the problems exhibited by the student. *Prognosis* refers to the clinician's statement, or prediction, of the future development of the student's problem; whether he will readjust or what will be the probable outcome of a choice of a particular course of study. Prognosis is a statement of the implications of the diagnosis. *Counseling* refers to the steps taken by the

student and by the counselor to bring about adjustment and readjustment. The final step in clinical work, *follow-up*, includes what the clinician does to assist the student with new problems, with recurrences of the original problems, and what is done to determine the effectiveness of counseling. In actual clinical practice these steps do not necessarily follow in sequence; moreover, the counselor proceeds at a different pace for each problem exhibited by the student. He may be counseling a student's emotional problem at the same time that he is diagnosing a vocational problem. In other cases a vocational problem may "clear up" through the counseling of an associated emotional problem. Obviously the clinician uses a flexible procedure rather than adhering rigidly to a sequence of procedures. Every student must be dealt with in that way which produces the optimum results. The clinician has so immersed himself through experience in the techniques of his art that he uses them as resources to be utilized in terms of the way the case "breaks." [1]

We quoted this passage for two reasons. First, because it provides an excellent summary of important points in clinical counseling and, second, because it shows that the point of view of a counselor of students, not a clinical psychologist, does not differ significantly from the point of view presented in this text. All counseling involves the steps mentioned by Williamson. The primary purpose of all evaluative procedures is to plan for the end products of this counseling process.

The fundamental principle underlying the ideal approach to vocational guidance and counseling is to allow the individual to find his own vocation. This has sometimes been described as negative counseling. We can advise the boy (or girl), client or patient, that conditions to be met in certain occupations or professions are not such as to enable him to function at the highest level of efficiency of which he is capable. We can suggest that the characteristics of a particular vocation might not allow him to enjoy himself at work as much as his personality or interests would allow under conditions of a proper choice of a vocation. We do not, however, engage in positive guidance by telling the individual that his particular abilities, personality, and interests indicate that he should become a lawyer, a salesman, or a bricklayer. We must allow the inclination toward a specific occupation to originate within the individual and then aid him in determining his suitability for it. This is not to suggest that we cannot help the individual gain information that will allow him to "lean" in one direction or another. In fact, the counselor must assess (with the

[1] By permission from *How to Counsel Students*, by Edmund G. Williamson. Copyright 1939 by McGraw-Hill Book Company, Inc.

help of various tools) the client's interests as they exist and help him to clarify these interests. Of prior importance to the assessing of interest is the provision of occupational information, as without it interests can hardly become directed. Information about occupations should include the requirements and benefits of the occupation. The counselor can help the individual to evaluate himself insofar as the requirements are concerned, and he can assist in the interpretation of the benefits.

It frequently happens that an individual wishes to take up some occupation or profession because he enjoys dealing with a few of its elementary components. He may build a radio set and forthwith decide to become a radio engineer. His interest in this occupation may be reduced or may vanish when he learns that to prepare for it he would have to study for several years, learning advanced theories of alternating and direct current, of magnetism, of the properties of vacuum tubes, coils, and condensers. Learning all these advanced technical theories and facts is an entirely different proposition from carrying on a little random experimentation in which neither constructive effort nor a high degree of intellectual efficiency is required. Likewise, other aspects of a job may not be just as the person expects. He may not realize the various hardships involved in a certain work, such as extremes of heat and cold, odors, hours of work, or certain kinds of unpleasant duty. Steadiness and permanence of work are other factors that should be taken into consideration. The daily earnings of bricklayers and plasterers may attract a great deal of comment, but it may not be generally known that these workers frequently do not work a full week, sometimes they go through an entire winter season without work, suffering layoffs at other times. Furthermore, the amount of training and apprenticeship necessary before a novice can do independent work and earn full wages may far exceed expectations.

By far the best way for an individual to learn whether his interests, abilities, and personality coincide with the demands of a particular vocation is for him to actually go through the operations to make sure that most of the duties are pleasant and none are prohibitively unpleasant. There are routine and unpleasant duties in any occupation, but these will not appear unduly large in proportion to the pleasant aspects if a person's interests and abilities are genuinely in line with the demands of the work. Of course the practice of trying out all the occupations that a person might consider is out of the question from a practical point of view. Who would wish to train for a line of work and then work long enough to decide whether or not it is satisfactory? Rather a person must attempt to make up his mind before training and then spend the necessary time in preparation. Our present era is one of specialization and to become a specialist in one field takes so much time and money that no one wants to specialize in several lines of work just to try them out. Some application can be made of the trying-out principle, however. Although an individual cannot usually learn enough about an occupation from reading a job description, from an interview, or from a single visit to a business or industry, he can make frequent visits, perhaps work with someone else for a short time, and take vacation jobs and try-out work when this is possible. A few generations ago the youth who followed in his father's footsteps may have made a sounder decision than the same youth makes today, as in the nineteenth and early twentieth centuries the youth probably had a better idea of what his father did. Because parents frequently had their businesses and shops at home, the sons and even the daughters were much closer to the everyday operations. In other ways, too, families were closer, and the youth either knew that he did or that he definitely did not want to adopt his father's occupation.

In the hospital situation the trying-out principle can be applied in medical rehabilitation programs, in in-service work programs, and in member-employee programs. Perhaps the day will come when someone with ingenuity will design some model or sample work situations that can be used in out-patient vocational counseling. There are a few schools that provide students with opportunities for trial work experiences in various occupations and vocations. In general, this is a fine idea but the scope of such plans is of necessity limited as it is impossible to offer experience in the highly specialized vocations and professions. The colleges and universities allow the student some limited opportunity for trying out certain occupations by studying about them. The student has the opportunity to sample a subject by taking basic courses in it and to evaluate occupations through discussion with teachers, reading, etc.

Even if we could organize procedures so that our clients could "go through the motions" of various occupations, there would still be a need for counseling to narrow down the field of possibilities. It should be noted also that no matter how good an individual's vocational choice may appear to be, it should be regarded as tentative. If the client tries out an occupation and does not like it, he should feel free to withdraw from it and try something related or even very different. We must respect the individual who has the courage and common sense to withdraw from one occupation, even after much training, and undertake another if he cannot enjoy the first. We would hope, however, that this would not happen often, at least not to the same individual.

FACTORS TO BE CONSIDERED IN VOCATIONAL COUNSELING

The task of vocational counseling is to aid the client first in gaining information about occupations and then in matching facts known about himself with those known about the occupation, keeping the following points in mind:

1. GENERAL ABILITY. A person must have sufficient general ability to meet at least the minimum requirements of a particular occupation. Before deciding to enter a vocation, the client should consider his ability to meet its demands, and in order to do this he must have some idea of the level of his general ability. Consequently, in many instances the vocational counselor finds it useful to administer and interpret intelligence tests. These may not be infallible but they give some idea of the general ability of the individual. This knowledge can be matched with what is known about the requirements of different vocations and the ability necessary to complete training programs for them. Just as inadequate ability should serve as a deterrent to entrance into certain occupations, too high or exceptional general ability can also disqualify a person for happiness in certain kinds of work. Many jobs are boring and monotonous to the person with high ability, and as a consequence he may be careless and even incompetent in such jobs. Another point to consider is whether a person might be wasting his talents on certain kinds of work, and whether he might not be more effective and happier, and make a greater contribution to society, in a more demanding vocation.

2. SPECIFIC ABILITIES. Some occupations require certain special abilities; and if the client is lacking in these, it may be impossible for him to pursue these occupations. A minimum amount of such specific skills or abilities makes adjustment simpler in many occupations. Extreme proficiency in a particular skill may contribute to significant achievement on the part of the client, giving him extra satisfactions.

3. PERSONAL TRAITS. Persons of equal intellectual ability are not equally well fitted for the same types of work. One man will succeed as a supervisor or superintendent while another of equal intellectual ability will become prominent as a research worker. The former may be able to deal with people, while the latter, who rather shuns society, works best when dealing with abstract concepts. Certain traits of personality may be needed to sell and others to become an artist. We do not mean to suggest that vocations be typed from the standpoint of personal traits, but some consideration of traits is important in matching the man with the occupation.

4. LIKES AND DISLIKES. The individual's interests and preferences, their absence, or negative feelings regarding a vocation constitute another significant aspect of the person's choice. If a person likes the types of problems which the doctor or engineer meets, he is more likely to

be happy and to succeed in one of these professions than is a person who has equal ability but whose interests are elsewhere. Some people like manual work, others outside work; some prefer detailed machine work, others office work. We must make sure that expressed interests are genuine, not a reflection of suggestion on the part of parents and friends.

5. PHYSIQUE. This is an important attribute in some vocations although it is probably of less consequence than it was some time ago. The matter of strength must be taken into consideration in a few crude manual-labor positions where minimums may be required. Health, however, is a crucial matter in many occupations since a person must be fairly robust to stand specific types of work over long periods of time. Some occupations may be hazardous for persons with certain conditions of health. Conversely, there are some vocations that are suited to handicapped people. Traditionally, we have recognized that the watchmaker or the fine assembly worker can be hunchbacked or lame so long as he possesses manual dexterity. Some industrial concerns reserve positions to be filled by persons who are deaf, blind, undersized, or have other special handicaps. It has been found that handicapped persons may actually be more efficient in some kinds of work. For example, we find piano factories employing blind individuals because it is believed that they possess keen sensitivity to tone.

All these factors must be considered together and weighed against one another. When a client gives due consideration to his vocational future, it appears likely that he reduces his chances of dissatisfaction and unhappiness. Vocational counseling as discussed in this section is ordinarily woven into the total process of evaluation and rehabilitation.

OCCUPATIONAL INFORMATION

We have already mentioned several times the importance of information about occupations. The question arises as to where the client, or the counselor for that matter, is going to acquire this information. This question is of course too extensive to be answered in the present discussion. One-semester university courses are devoted to this topic, and psychological counselors are urged to take them. Textbooks by Max F. Baer and Edward C. Rober (3) and by Carroll L. Shartle (22) have been prepared for use in these courses and for reference by the counselor. These books contain some descriptive occupational information but are primarily devoted to sources of information and the means of collecting information when sources are not adequate.

Perhaps the best source of occupational information is the *Diction-*

ary of Occupational Titles (8). This publication was first made available in 1940 after several years of research conducted by the United States Employment Service. The first edition contained definitions of more than 18,000 occupations. An illustration of the changing times and rapidity of new developments is the fact that a second edition, published in 1949, contained 22,000 job definitions. The second edition consists of three volumes. Part I is entitled "Definitions of Titles" and contains the definitions and code numbers of the occupational titles with the titles listed alphabetically. Part II, called "Occupational Classification," gives the classification structure of the Dictionary. In this volume occupations are broken down into major groups and subgroups. Part IV classifies fields of work for entry job-seekers. Originally, there was a Part III but it, a temporary volume, was a conversion table between the classification structure previously used by the United States Employment Services Offices and the *Dictionary* classification that replaced it. Franklin R. Zeran (25, pp. 3–4) enumerates several uses of the *Dictionary* as follows:

(1) To aid in making a local occupational survey.

(2) To learn in which industrial field a job belongs.

(3) To learn the variety of jobs to which the same job title is applied in various industries.

(4) To learn what work is performed in any given job.

(5) To acquaint students with the vast number of ways to earn a living.

(6) To prepare pupils for field trips to industrial establishments.

The *Dictionary* has other uses as well, and counselors must familiarize themselves with it.

The counselor will also want to familiarize himself with many other publications in the field. Organizations such as Science Research Associates and The Institute for Research publish occupational briefs and monographs describing pertinent information about different occupations. These are constantly revised and brought up to date. Walter J. Greenleaf (18) has prepared a monograph entitled "Occupations," which is designed as a basic course for counselors and summarizes the task of the vocational counselor in a systematic fashion. The appendix, which lists source materials for occupational information, is a useful part of this monograph.

THE USE OF TESTS IN VOCATIONAL COUNSELING

In vocational counseling we use the same tests as those to be described in Part IV. We use the history and the interview as well, and the task of evaluation for vocational counseling is not substantially different from that used in planning any other aspects of counseling. In addition to these instruments there are a few that have been used more extensively for vocational counseling than for other purposes. We will describe some of these shortly, but first let us discuss the general philosophy underlying vocational testing. The central theme of this philosophy is to stress *negative* rather than *positive* guidance.

As applied to the use of tests the counselor employing positive guidance or counseling would in all probability give a battery of tests and match the profile of scores on these tests with the requirements of certain occupations. After he had found the best fit, he would be inclined to indicate directly or indirectly to the client that the best-fitting occupation should be his first choice, other things being equal. If other things (physical requirements, educational demands, etc.) were not equal, then the positive, authoritarian, directive vocational counselor would turn to the second-best fit, and so forth, until a vocation had been selected for the client. This procedure would be fine except for the dubious validity of many tests, lack of complete and exact information about the requirements of various occupations, the fallible judgment of the counselor, and, most important of all, the subtle personal factors that are not reflected in the tests. Not many (if any) reputable counselors follow the extreme procedure described above, although there are many who are relatively directive. They may not write a prescription of a vocation but they make a decision and strongly influence the client in the direction of their decision.

It is difficult to evaluate the extent to which a counselor should bias a client in the choice of an occupation. The counselor, because of his training and experience should be in a good position to offer advice; in the last analysis, however, it is best that the client make the decision. There are exceptions such as in the case of incompetent individuals. It has been assumed that patients in mental hospitals are incapable of making such decisions. This is a doubtful assumption and it may explain why the placement of some mental patients has not been successful. Some mental patients may be given vocational prescriptions, but it is hoped that this would be done as a last resort and that the prescriptions would be offered as tentative, pending some trying out. Among young people, particularly, it is imperative that the client have a major part in decisions that are made. Ideally, the test information and the knowledge about the client gained by the counselor from his other observations should all be regarded as personal information to be matched *by the client* against occupational information. Thus, the counselor's primary function is to help the client to gather together enough information both about himself and about occupations so that he (the client) can solve his vocational problem for himself. To this very slight degree the vocational counselor's use of tests differs somewhat from their use in general counseling. He may do more reporting and interpreting to the client. Some clinicians do a great deal of such interpreting in all counseling. Psychological evaluation data can be used as an integral part of the counseling process as well as in planning for it. However, it should be re-emphasized that tests are to be used as a basis for providing information and to aid in eliminating some vocations—in other words, they should be used in a negative rather than a positive fashion.

The tests that are used more frequently in vocational counseling than in other counseling are the interest inventories, the aptitude tests, and the achievement tests. Various attitude scales are also used directly or adapted for use in vocational counseling. Since tests are a topic so wide in scope, we are going to refer our readers again to the excellent vocational counseling texts mentioned earlier [2] and to the excellent measurement texts by Lee J. Cronbach (7) and Anne Anastasi (1). Here we will simply mention a few of the more widely used interest tests and give an example or two illustrating the use of aptitude and achievement tests.

First, let us go back to our statement that in vocational counseling we use all the tests and evaluative techniques ordinarily used in counseling. For the purposes of vocational planning we can ask ourselves the same questions we would ask in any planning situation. What are the potentialities and resources of the client? This may involve a study of his general ability through the use of intelligence tests. It may require a survey of special abilities including the client's ability to deal with problems. The approach on the Rorschach Test may suggest the client's approach to other problems. More specifically, we might ask how much aptitude does the client have for things mathematical or mechanical? We are interested in his present functioning ability as well as in his potential for development. We must appraise his ability to control this potential and to direct it into useful channels, and thus we begin the process of attempting to answer our questions from the results and observations based on personality tests of various kinds. We consider for purposes of vocational counseling, just as for any other purpose, the client's typical modes of response and his unique personality traits. Finally, we are interested in the motivation of the client. How much drive does he have and how is he specifically motivated? By the use of personality measures and with the help of interest and aptitude tests in addition, we hope to answer this question. So we can plan best if we study the "what," the "how," and the "why" of a given client's behavior.

Several inventories have been widely used in vocational counseling. The first that we will consider are Edward K. Strong's (23) Vocational

[2] *See* p. 253.

Interest Blanks. The Blank for Men was published in 1927 and revised in 1938. The Blank for Women was standardized in the early 1930's and revised in 1947. The Blank for Men, in particular, has been the most popular of all interest inventories and has been the subject of much research. It can be scored for 39 occupations (with some special additional keys not ordinarily used), and these occupations are arranged into the following six occupational groups:

(1) Artist, psychologist, architect, physician, and dentist
(2) Engineer, chemist, mathematician, and physicist
(3) YMCA physical director, personnel manager, YMCA secretary, social science high school teacher, city school superintendent, and minister
(4) Accountant, office worker, purchasing agent, and banker
(5) Sales manager, realtor, and life-insurance salesman
(6) Advertising man, lawyer, and author-journalist

In addition, the blanks are scored for nonoccupational interests. These are:

(1) Interest maturity
(2) Masculinity-femininity
(3) Occupational level
(4) Studiousness

The interest scales are fairly self-definitive. *Interest maturity* is a measure of the extent to which the interests are more like older than younger men's interests. *Masculinity-femininity* attempts to measure the interests of males and females, and is based on the assumption that some occupations are more typically masculine and others feminine. *Occupational level* indicates the extent to which interests resemble those of the business or professional man, in contrast to those of the workman. The *studiousness* scale is not fully developed but is supposed to reflect the interests that contribute to grades other than general ability. The inventory consists of 400 items. No time limit is set for doing the test, and ordinarily it requires at least 30 minutes. The first 100 items consist of 100 occupations, alphabetically arranged. The subject is asked to indicate whether he likes, dislikes, or is indifferent to each of them. In the same way, the subject reacts to 36 school subjects, 49 different amusements, 48 activities, and 47 statements of peculiarities of people. The next part lists four sets of 10 activities. In each set the subject picks the three enjoyed most and the three enjoyed least. In the next part the subject compares 40 pairs of activities, and in the last part he rates 40 statements concerning his present abilities and personal characteristics. The scores on the

Strong Test are usually reported in letter grades: A, B+, B, B−, C+, and C. When a person achieves a score of A in a particular occupation, this means that he has indicated that he enjoys or likes the same kinds of activities as are checked by persons who are successful in that occupation. C+ or C scores indicate little communality of interest, and the other grades are intermediate steps.

The other interest test that has seen wide usage since its publication in the late 1930's is the Kuder Preference Record (15). It has one distinct advantage over the Strong in terms of the scoring. The Strong requires the use of many keys and the hand scoring is laborious. Since the subject answers the Kuder by making pinholes in appropriate circles, it can be scored by simply counting the pinholes in the circles arranged for the areas covered in the test, thus securing the score for each area quite directly. Ten vocational areas are covered in the scale. These are:

(1) mechanical
(2) computational
(3) scientific
(4) persuasive
(5) artistic
(6) literary
(7) musical
(8) social service
(9) clerical
(10) outdoor

A V-score (verification score) is also included in the last revision of the test. If the score on V falls outside the 38–44 range, the results of the entire test are considered questionable, and the counselor should proceed with caution. The V-score item has, of course, been added to test the reliability of the answers given and thus the conclusions to be drawn from the test. The basis of this V-score is arrived at by comparing the individual's answers on certain items with those of a typical group. A "too-low" or "too-high" V-score may be indicative of several things: the individual may have misunderstood the directions; he may have been careless or may have answered the questions insincerely; he may have "skipped" items with a resulting "too-low" score, etc. The actual test consists of 169 triads of statements of different activities. The subject pierces holes in circles next to two statements in each grouping of three statements. He checks the one liked most and the one liked least. The scores are converted into percentiles, and a percentile of 75 or better is considered significantly high. The manual lists many occupations that fit the various areas and combinations of areas.

It must be stressed that scores on interest tests have no direct relevance to aptitude or ability. They are better indicators of satisfaction in a given occupation than success. The results of these scales as well as of those of values and attitudes must be used carefully and must never be confused with aptitude or ability. The results may be used to suggest possible vocational areas to be considered, but these areas should be carefully evaluated from many other standpoints. In general, interest scales are designed—as are aptitude and achievement tests, which we shall not discuss specifically—to provide supplementary kinds of information for use in the counseling process.

SOME EXAMPLES OF VOCATIONAL COUNSELING PROBLEMS

Early in the first chapter we introduced the case of the business-machine statistician who was involved in an automobile accident, after which he appeared unable to continue in his previous vocation. A discussion of this man's problems will illustrate several vocational counseling ideas described above. One is the impossibility of planning for an individual without careful psychological assessment and evaluation. The use of psychological tests in planning for this man was of particular importance, as an accurate appraisal of his resources was needed. His behavior, the psychological testing, and the neurological examinations all pointed to the existence of rather extensive brain damage. His educational and vocational history suggested that prior to the accident he had been an exceptionally intelligent man with a particular brilliance in the use of mathematical concepts and high facility in abstract thinking. His post-accident performance suggested that his over-all intellectual potential was only slightly higher than the average for the general population. This essentially average over-all ability was not as meaningful as an analysis of his more specific abilities and his qualitative performances. The most striking decrement in performance was in the area of abstract and conceptual thinking. His range of information was still quite extensive; his vocabulary remained almost intact although he exhibited some difficulty in formulating definitions of certain abstract terms. Despite this, his word use was excellent, and he could spell words that he could not define. His memory for both immediate and remote events appeared to be good. It is true that in the testing situation he had some difficulty in repeating digits in a reverse order, but his performance on memory items was generally above average. He could perform mathematical operations quite efficiently when concrete problems were placed before him. He did not appear to be able to derive formulas, or even to substitute values into a formula, but when given a problem, he could solve it even when some complex operations were involved. It seemed evident that he could not perform at his old level, but the appraisal of his performance in mathematical operations suggested that there were a number of activities related to his previous vocation that he could still perform.

The client had taken the Strong Vocational Interest test a few years earlier (before his accident), and the results of this test were available. He was retested on this inventory, and, as one might expect, his interest pattern had not changed significantly. His highest scores were in the group including such categories as accountant, office worker, purchasing agent, and banker. His next highest scores were in such activities as that of mathematician and physicist. On both pre- and post-test his scores were also quite high in the sales occupations. A study of his interests suggested strongly that he should be encouraged to plan for work in the same general area as that in which he had previously functioned. As he was not capable of doing the same work, it was necessary for him to accept something similar, but in all probability at a lower occupational level. However, this brought up a rather serious problem in that the only important change in his interest test results was his occupational level score, which was higher on the second administration. This was regarded as resulting from one or both of two factors. First, he had worked for several years as a high-level professional worker after taking the pre-test. Second, his realization of the results of his accident appeared to increase the attractiveness of higher-level activities.

The issue of his acceptance of his disability and of the limitations that it imposed on him became vitally significant. If he could accept his limitations, he could perhaps be trained for office work of a general and less professional nature. The physical rehabilitation workers believed that he could be taught to type. We knew that he could operate a comptometer and could go through the mechanical operations required in using some other business machines. But the question of whether he would accept this level of work still had to be answered. Counseling along this line was initiated with him. (We have already described [3] how he had profited from an opportunity for emotional release.) He was informed of the exact nature of his injuries, and he was able to lower his level of aspiration. A by-product of this counseling was his expression of interest in sales activities. He wondered whether he might not sell office equipment and machines. This was not completely ruled out, but careful investigation revealed that most machine salesmen are required to demonstrate complex operations. The client knew certain operations but both he and his counselor had doubts that he could be adaptable enough to demonstrate to prospective buyers how machines could be used for unusual purposes.

Other factors to be considered were the client's irritability, his short attention span, and his tendency toward distractibility. His irritability

[3] *See* p. 124.

gradually diminished as he became accustomed to some of his new limitations and regained confidence in himself. As he practiced typing and other clerical skills, it became clear that if the work was simple and mechanical, he could maintain his application for rather long periods of time. The entire counseling program required over a year, but this client was eventually placed in an office position where he does typing, filing, and routine computational work as secretary to a statistician. He still has periods of depression but these are not extreme and he is functioning effectively in a work situation. He hopes to improve the level of his work, and it is quite possible that he may become an office manager. He has surprised his counselor by learning some simple bookkeeping. If he is able to improve his status and his earnings, he should become happier.

This illustration emphasizes the overlap between environmental treatment and vocational counseling as well as the close relationship between all aims of counseling. The story might be almost duplicated with other handicapped persons. The problems of the chronically ill are also quite challenging. In the case of the tuberculous patient we see the necessity of changing vocations, but the situation may be complicated by a variety of personal reactions to the idea of morbid illness. With patients with heart disease and cancer, we are frequently faced with rehabilitative counseling and vocational training. With all handicapped persons, the problem of acceptance of the disability is of prime importance.

At times, of course, vocational counseling must be applied to the family as well as to the client. We have referred several times to the young stock showman. His mother was exceedingly anxious for her son to attend college and to study for a profession. That he should be allowed to do the kind of work he enjoyed, and in which he actually excelled, was difficult for her to accept. This attitude of attaching prestige to professional work, which is characteristic of many parents, is entirely understandable, but it indicates the need for widespread public education to promote the acceptance of many subprofessional occupations; often these are more desirable than the professions from the standpoint of an individual's welfare.

Perhaps more important than rehabilitative counseling is the field of developmental vocational counseling. A multitude of examples could be cited. Exceptionally bright children and those of average ability can profit from assistance in making vocational choices. Our last example will concern a youngster of ability somewhat below average. This young man fifteen years of age had failed two grades in school and had quite probably been advanced several other times when he actually had not done adequate work. He lived and attended school in a small community that had relatively few organized resources. There were no special education teachers, and there was no trade school available to him. He was unhappy in school, simply enduring it until the time when he could quit school and go to work; however, he had little idea as to what kind of work he might do. He worked in the evening setting pins in a bowling alley. His mother and an interested teacher were quite concerned that he might form undesirable associations if he were not in school. The teacher had referred him to a clinic, hoping that he would be encouraged to stay in school.

Interviews with the parents revealed that both parents had completed the eighth grade. Two older brothers had left school to join the Navy and had seemingly stayed in school until they were eighteen only because they had some athletic skills. No one in the family background was reported to be mentally retarded, but no one was above average. The school had taken the point of view that they should do as much for the client as possible in the more academic subjects and had not emphasized shop work or agriculture. Our general psychological evaluation indicated that he was basically a well-adjusted boy, but frustrated because of his inability to keep up with others in school. His verbal and conceptual abilities were decidedly below average, but his nonverbal or performance abilities were average for his age. He had better-than-average ability on both mechanical assembly and comprehension tasks. The results of interest tests were meaningless because of a severe reading deficiency, but when some of the test items were used in an interview situation, he showed a distinct preference for mechanical and outdoor activities, and a rather striking interest in musical activities. He said that he really wanted to stay in school but was tired of failing. He thought he might like to do a number of things such as automobile repair, house painting, electrical wiring, carpentry, or farming, but he had never had a chance to try any of them.

At the suggestion of the clinic the school "custom-made" a curriculum for him. He was allowed to take a double load in shop and agriculture courses (meeting with both the 9th- and 10th-grade groups); he was encouraged to engage in 4-H club work and was allowed to attempt the drums in the school band. (He became quite proficient with the drums, so proficient that the music teacher was unhappy when he finally dropped out of school two years later. Since he has been working, he has been able to continue this interest as a hobby, as a member of a civic orchestra.) In addition to the special curriculum, the counselor urged the teacher who was particularly interested in the client to talk with a number of the people in the community to arrange a series of part-time jobs for him. He worked for a few months successively in a garage, with a painter, a carpenter, an electrician, on a farm, and with a roofing company. Although he showed aptitude in several of these jobs, the activity that he most enjoyed was painting. He left school for a steady job as a painter and appears to be happy with his work.

This is a simple story but it illustrates how a community can mobilize its resources to provide a counseling and vocational training program without sacrifice on the part of anyone. In fact, the program for this young man has provided a pattern through which several other boys in the same community have been helped.

SUMMARY

We have included this chapter on vocational counseling to stress the importance of occupation in the total adjustment of the client. Vocational counseling is not regarded as a special or separate skill or trade. We do not feel that personal counselors and vocational counselors are different kinds of psychological counselors. Rather, in the practical working situation, vocational and personal counseling are so intertwined as to be indistinguishable. We must *never* neglect the vocational aspects of adjustment. The vocational counselor must always be mindful of the total adjustment of the client. In the history of counseling those interested in vocational work have seldom been mindful of it. And many psychological and psychiatric counselors have neglected the work adjustment of their clients. This is unfortunate, and it is hoped that the emphasis on vocational counseling in this chapter will mitigate the perpetuation of this omission. The most important criterion of adjustment is efficiency of behavior. In our culture this certainly involves successful, gainful, and happy employment. To repeat, vocational counseling is not a separate process; it cannot and should not be separated from the total rehabilitation program of any client.

BIBLIOGRAPHY

1. Anastasi, A., *Psychological testing*. New York: Macmillan, 1954.
2. Arbuckle, D. S., *Student personnel services in higher education*. New York: McGraw-Hill, 1953.
3. Baer, M. F., and Rober, E. C., *Occupational information: its nature and use*. Chicago: Science Research Associates, 1951.
4. Berdie, R. F. (ed.), *Concepts and programs of counseling*. Minneapolis, Minn.: Univ. of Minnesota Press, 1951.
5. Blum, M. L., and Balinsky, B., *Counseling and psychology*. New York: Prentice-Hall, 1951.
6. Borden, E. S., *Psychological counseling*. New York: Appleton-Century-Crofts, 1955.
7. Cronbach, L. J., *Essentials of psychological testing*. New York: Harper, 1949.
8. *Dictionary of occupational titles*. Washington, D. C.: U. S. Government Printing Office, Parts I, II, and IV, 1939, 1949.

9. Erickson, C. E., *A basic text for guidance workers.* Englewood Cliffs, N. J.: Prentice-Hall, 1947.

10. Forrester, G., *Methods of vocational guidance.* Boston: Heath, 1951.

11. Hahn, M. E., and MacLean, M. S., *Counseling psychology* (2nd ed.). New York: McGraw-Hill, 1955.

12. Humphreys, J. A., and Traxler, A. E., *Guidance services.* Chicago: Science Research Associates, 1954.

13. Kitson, H. D., and Newton, J. B., *Helping people find jobs.* New York: Harper, 1950.

14. Knapp, R. H., *Practical guidance methods.* New York: McGraw-Hill, 1953.

15. Kuder, G. F., *Revised manual for the Kuder Preference Record* (5th ed.). Chicago: Science Research Associates, 1953.

16. Little, W., and Chapman, A. L., *Developmental guidance in secondary schools.* New York: McGraw-Hill, 1953.

17. Myers, G. E., *Principles and methods of vocational guidance.* New York: McGraw-Hill, 1941.

18. *Occupations: a basic course for counselors.* Federal Security Agency, Washington, D. C., 1951.

19. Pepinsky, H. B., and Pepinsky, P. N., *Counseling: theory and practice.* New York: Ronald, 1954.

20. Recktenwald, L. N., *Guidance and counseling.* Washington, D. C.: Catholic Univ. of America Press, 1953.

21. Sanderson, H., *Basic concepts in vocational guidance.* New York: McGraw-Hill, 1954.

22. Shartle, C. L., *Occupational information: its development and application* (2nd ed.). Englewood Cliffs, N. J.: Prentice-Hall, 1952.

23. Strong, E. K., Jr., *Vocational interests of men and women.* Stanford: Stanford Univ. Press, 1943.

24. Super, D. E., *Appraising vocational fitness.* New York: Harper, 1949.

25. *The occupational dictionary as a tool in vocational guidance work.* Federal Security Agency, Washington, D. C., 1940.

26. Tyler, L. E., *The work of the counselor.* New York: Appleton-Century-Crofts, 1953.

27. Warters J., *Techniques of counseling.* New York: McGraw-Hill, 1954.

28. Williamson, E. C., *How to counsel students.* New York: McGraw-Hill, 1939.

29. Worcester State Lunatic Hospital, *Annual report of the trustees.* Boston: State Printers, 1838.

Special Counseling Techniques

IN THIS FINAL CHAPTER ON COUNSELING PROBLEMS AND TECHNIQUES we will review some of the approaches and considerations pertinent to the education and rehabilitation of individuals with specific disabilities and handicaps. The counseling approach with children and adults who present special disabilities or handicaps is fundamentally the same as that with any other clients. Within this over-all philosophy, the well-grounded counselor should be prepared to meet and deal with specific problems that are peculiar to clients with special disabilities. He must be sufficiently familiar with remedial techniques to be able to coordinate his efforts with those of remedial specialists.

Our basic philosophy in counseling with children is to stress the promotion of over-all development rather than the remedial treatment of specific defects. The child is regarded as a developing organism. During the preschool and elementary school years his development is continuous and rapid. Although much of this development occurs as physiological growth and maturation, an even greater percentage occurs through learning and the assimilation of experience. Not only is there the important area of direct experience or direct learning of facts about the world around him but, even as related to physiological maturation, learning is important. Physiological maturation does not take place in a vacuum, and its results become functional only to the extent that they are integrated with a body of experience so that responses are altered in ways that experience indicates to be desirable.

When a child suffers from a defect, whether it is a sensory deficiency, a motor incapacity, an emotional disturbance, a physiological imbalance, or whatever, he suffers a depreciation of experience as long as the defect exists. Some of the developmental experiences that he should be absorbing are being denied to him. These missing experiences, which are essential to performance on the higher developmental levels to which he has chronologically progressed, in turn interfere with his future performance. If we remove the defect by special therapeutic procedures, we have removed the barrier to experience but we have not supplied the missing experiences. Since the child has in the meantime progressed to a still higher chronological level, he will not, in the usual course of events, be presented with these missed experiences which he needs, and as a result he will become increasingly retarded in his total development as the missed experiences become essential to more and more activities.

Special remedial clinical procedures are directed toward remedying or alleviating defects; the particular type of procedure employed in an individual case will depend upon the area in which the child is defective. In instances where the defect can be wholly or largely removed, this is an essential first step, but it is also necessary to supply the experiences that have been missed or distorted due to the existence of the defect. We must recognize that when the defect is "cured," the individual is not yet normal until the developmental effects of the defects have been treated. Treatment should, most advantageously, be an integrated and co-ordinated process. Rather than thinking of remedial counseling and re-educative procedures as separate stages in the total rehabilitative program, we should consider them as all going on together. This means that the well-prepared counselor must concern himself with the total process, co-ordinating all aspects of the program.

In instances where the defect cannot be removed or can be only slightly improved, the rehabilitative or enablement program (in dealing with children or handicapped adults, enablement may be a more meaningful term) should be concerned with presenting experiences in such a manner that their essential elements can be absorbed in spite of the defect. We must recognize that the child who has an irremediable defect still needs certain essential experiences and that it is usually possible (depending upon the nature and extent of the defect) to supply a greater number of these experiences through an integrated program than would ordinarily be supplied without one. There are numerous children (and adults) who are in need of a program that will supply these necessary developmental experiences. These needs may have arisen from inadequate opportunity for normal experience, barriers to experience resulting from defects in the organism (congenital or acquired), and losses in experience resulting from the effects of defects that no longer exist. Fundamentally, a counseling program that seeks to provide for these needs is an educational or training program supplementing the remedial or healing program.

In addition to the individuals who have missed experiences for reasons already cited, many children become retarded in their over-all development because of the environment (home, school, etc.) in which they live. The environment may not have presented the child with certain experiences that he is assumed to have had before he enters school or at some later stage of development, or these experiences may not have been presented in a manner in which they could be absorbed by the child. Perhaps the school or community assuming a normal background of experience has placed the individual in activities beyond his abilities. Such a procedure leads to increased losses of experience, with the individual dropping further and further behind. To summarize, therefore, a desirable total counseling, rehabilitation, or enablement program is designed to supply the individual with experiences necessary to development which for one reason or another he has not been able to absorb.

Since a developmental program of this kind requires considerable time for its completion, the program is ideally accomplished in the client's home community. In most communities the necessary facilities for implementing such a program either are or can be made available. The principal problem is the discovery of available services and securing their co-operation toward a common goal. The task of co-ordinating these facilities falls upon the psychological counselor, who organizes the total over-all plan for a client and calls upon and integrates the work of other necessary agencies. An example of such planning was described in the previous chapter.[1]

When the client is referred to the clinician, he should receive a thorough evaluation. This evaluation includes a complete history; a study of the potentialities and resources of the client, including factors of motivation and control; a search for defects in the organism which may be contributing to his difficulties (referral for appropriate examinations including pediatric, hearing, vision, etc.); emotional adjustment; and an evaluation of the specific areas of poor achievement or performance (reading, arithmetic, perceptual organization, speech, etc.). If specific disabilities or handicaps are discovered, the clinician will lay out a protocol for treatment and training. This protocol may involve one or all of the areas included in the evaluation. The client will then return to his community (at Purdue University and in some other centers extension clinics operate right in the community so that the client never leaves the community), where the developmental program will be undertaken under the supervision of the psychological co-ordinator. The client should be re-evaluated periodically so that necessary revisions in the program can be made.

The basic concepts underlying our philosophy of dealing with developmental problems are those of enablement, habilitation, and rehabilitation rather than of therapy or treatment. A developmental program must be conducted within the individual community by parents, classroom teachers, special remedial therapists, physicians, and other person-

---

[1] *See* pp. 267–8.

nel in the community. Persons cannot be rehabilitated adequately in hospitals or in situations foreign to their normal lives. They may have to be referred to a special facility for specific treatment, but the developmental program must be integrated with the special treatment program, and insofar as possible it should be structured within the usual home and community environment of the client. The psychological clinician or counselor serves as a co-ordinator and consultant rather than as a therapist. We believe that it is within such a framework that the psychologist of the future will make his greatest and most unique contributions.

COUNSELING WITH THE PHYSICALLY HANDICAPPED AND DISABLED

Let us turn now to the adjustment implications of various physically handicapping and disabling conditions. We are concerned here not with disabilities but rather with persons who have experienced disablement. We do not think of that "spastic" in the children's hospital, or that "cardiac" in Ward B, or that "amputee" on the street corner; rather, we think of them as people just like ourselves and realize that it is only by fortuitous circumstances that we, ourselves, have not experienced disability. Perhaps with this perspective we can better understand the impact of their disability upon their attitudes, their behavior, and the satisfactions that they are able to get out of life. Their problems of adjustment are no different in *kind* or *quality* from those experienced by anyone else. They may differ in *amount* or *quantity* of particular kinds of problems presented, but the actual nature of the problems presented by all persons is remarkably similar.

There is one aspect of the adjustment of disabled persons that is relatively constant for all disabled persons, whether they are deaf or hard-of-hearing, paralyzed, or blind, whether they have respiratory or cardiac ailments, or some other disablement. They can hardly escape from a feeling of being different—they may feel incomplete or inadequate as well, but they cannot avoid looking upon themselves as different. This feeling inevitably leads to behavior that is compensatory and that attempts to "make up" for this feeling of difference. Some compensatory behavior is constructive and motivated by a frank, objective, conscious acceptance of the disability. This, we would most often view as good or healthy compensation. In other instances behavior reactions to the feeling of difference may not be so constructive. The reactions may reflect a denial of difference, a rebellion against being different, or even a passive, dependent acceptance of the difference, with the attitude, "I am disabled so you must take care of me." These latter forms of adjustment are not those for which we strive in counseling disabled persons.

Elsewhere we (29) have pointed out that there are many studies which suggest that certain kinds of disablement predispose the individual toward specific types of behavior and attitudinal reactions, thus presenting problems that interfere with the individual's rehabilitation. On the other hand, for almost every report of a study suggesting behavior reactions characteristic of a given group of disabled persons, we can find another report which denies that the reaction is common to that particular group. Whereas one report may suggest constellations of maladjustment that are associated with deafness, others will call attention to the excellent adjustment and employment records of deaf workers. Another report may indicate fundamental psychological differences among those with different kinds of cerebral palsy. Still other studies show no relationship between the crippling condition and specific personality characteristics. Some writers have discounted the importance of personality problems in the mentally defective; and other studies make a lot of the disturbances resulting from the differences between the level of aspiration and the potential capacity of the mentally retarded person. All sorts of personality characteristics have been ascribed to hypertensive persons, individuals with rheumatic heart disease, or those suffering coronary occlusions. Studies have been made of the "tuberculous" personality, and it has been suggested (26) that a person could even find "gout" personalities, asthma personalities, and perhaps tonsil and adenoid personalities if he were to look for them. This line of discussion brings us back to the point that while some individuals present severe reactions to their disabilities which interfere with their rehabilitation, others take their disability in stride and make satisfactory adjustments.

It appears that the one unique problem involved in counseling with disabled or handicapped persons is that of helping them to avoid inefficient reactions to their feelings of difference. How can we promote an acceptance of their disabilities? We do not want to achieve a passive acceptance or a surrender to the disability; nor do we wish to encourage a negative acceptance or refusal to recognize that a handicap exists. What we want to promote is *an ordered arrangement of the individual's life that recognizes the presence of the handicap or disability and yet allows the individual to mobilize his energies to meet the situation in spite of the handicap or to direct these energies into activities in which he is not so thwarted.* The well-adjusted individual is one who meets his needs with the resources available within his environment. The fact that a person has suffered a disability of a particular kind does not mean that satisfactory resources are not available to him. If the aim or goal of psychological acceptance of a disability is accomplished, the problems of counseling become those that are characteristic of counseling with all other clients.

The achievement of the goal is not a simple task, and no ready-made solution can be suggested. The Office of Vocational Rehabilitation (U.S. Department of Health, Education, and Welfare) and the National Council of Psychological Aspects of Physical Disability cosponsored a symposium on this topic at the 1953 meeting of the American Psychological Association, and the Office of Vocational Rehabilitation (5) prepared the papers presented at this meeting for publication. Excellent reviews of the problems of the deafened (Irving S. Fusfeld), the blinded (Louis S. Chalden), the cerebral palsied (James F. Garrett), and the mentally retarded (Samuel A. Kirk) are included in the pamphlet. Another useful source is the text edited by William M. Cruickshank (6) entitled *Psychology of Exceptional Children and Youth.* The education of the exceptional child is quite extensively covered in the Forty-Ninth *Yearbook* of the National Society for the Study of Education (17); and Alfred A. Strauss and Laura E. Lehtinen (32), Strauss and Newell C. Kephart (31), and others have discussed the problems of the brain-injured and the mentally retarded. Merle E. Frampton and Elena D. Gall (12) have edited a three-volume work, containing contributions by seventy professional authors, which discusses the general problems encountered in the special education, the rehabilitation, and the counseling of exceptional and handicapped persons. The coverage of this work is extensive, including discussion of over twenty kinds of handicaps. A particularly important aspect of this work is the compilation of source materials and special research studies on the counseling of the exceptional. All of these sources agree on the difficulties to be encountered in developing a counseling program for the handicapped or disabled person. It is certainly to be admitted that acceptance of disability is not easy for the cerebral palsied child who may present a grotesque appearance with a spastic paralysis of one side of the body, facial grimaces with inability to retain saliva, and a pronounced speech disability, and yet who may be of normal or superior intelligence. However our experiences have shown us that through the use of group and individual counseling procedures, re-education and re-training, and various aspects of environmental therapy, in combination with special treatment by many specialists, the job can be partially or completely accomplished.

In counseling with a severely handicapped individual it is of particular importance to counsel, also, with family, friends, teachers, employers, and the public at large. The public's prevailing attitudes of pity, of wanting to help handicapped people, and of occasional stigmatizing, all combine to make a frank objective acceptance of disability somewhat difficult. When family and friends can treat a client's disability objectively, his battle is half won. The other half depends on the client, but he can be helped by ingenious, carefully planned programs.

SPECIAL PROBLEMS WITH THE SPEECH–DEFECTIVE CLIENT

Speech therapy in the strictest sense should be conducted by the clinician who has had specialized training in the remedial procedures involved. Ordinarily the psychological clinician will not have had the training and the supervised experience that should accompany it to qualify as a speech therapist. There are frequent exceptions to this general picture in that more than a few clinical and counseling psychologists have had training in remedial speech. It is also not uncommon that a speech correctionist may have had considerable training and experience in clinical or counseling psychology. Regardless of whether in a given case a clinician handles the special remedial procedures as well as the total aspects of counseling, or whether two or more individuals are involved, it is essential that the remedial and rehabilitative aspects be closely co-ordinated. Exceptions to this rule are seen in certain unusual instances in which the speech habits of the client exist as isolated symptoms with little relationship to the total adjustment of the individual or in which the speech is only a symptom of a more basic emotional or behavioral disturbance. Either of these alternatives would appear to be indeed rare; even in the latter instance the speech problem usually constitutes a habit and the individual must be retrained even when the underlying problems are solved.

This section will concern itself only very briefly with speech therapy per se. We will discuss instead *speech hygiene*,[2] which encompasses some consideration of psychological factors that may be related to the cause and/or the aggravations of defective speech, as well as elementary treatment procedures.

The common speech problems can be grouped under three broad headings: voice disorders, articulation disorders, and stuttering. Disorders of voice are recognizable in that the voice does not conform to standards of volume, pitch, and quality. The person may speak too low or too softly; the pitch of his voice may not be natural for his age and sex; or his voice may be hoarse, nasal, or harsh. (These are just a few examples; the speech pathologist would isolate and describe many other aspects of voice.) Disorders of articulation are characterized by the omission, substitution, addition, or distortion of sounds. These disorders constitute the vast majority of speech problems. The prevention and

[2] In an article in a bulletin published in 1943 by the Association of Childhood Education and entitled "Learning to Speak Effectively," (25) we attempted to discuss this topic. The present discussion is based upon this article, with some revision as to the manner of presentation and point of view. Other articles in this bulletin should also be of interest to the psychological clinician, particularly if his interest is with children. By permission of Editor, Childhood Education.

correction of defective articulation and production of sounds, as well as voice problems, will be considered from the standpoint of five factors essential to the development and production of normal speech. If one or more of these factors is absent or disturbed, the development of normal speech is less apt to occur. The job of the counselor and the specialist in remedial speech is to correct factors or to supply missing factors.

One of the first prerequisites to the development of average or normal speech is a reasonably *normal speech mechanism*. Relatively few children have physiological systems so atypical as to make normal speech impossible, but many possess physiological structures that make normal speech difficult. Examples of the more serious organic problems are the cleft palate, various types of paralyses, hearing defects, and anomalies of the nasal passages and teeth. Wherever possible, the organic condition should be corrected as soon as possible so that bad speech habits are not developed. Once the habits of speech have been formed, retraining is more difficult. In the instance of paralyses, possible serious speech differences may be prevented or at least moderated if physiotherapy is initiated early. Deaf and hard-of-hearing children need special attention, and this should be provided as early as is practical. Often a person can learn to talk adequately in spite of some organic condition if sufficient motivation and stimulation are provided. When organic factors that have contributed or may contribute to poor speech habits are present, it is the counselor's responsibility to encourage medical or surgical treatment and/or physiotherapy so that the speech mechanism is in good physical condition as early in life or as soon after injury as possible. At the same time efforts should be made to promote adequate speech in spite of the handicap if such speech is possible.

A second essential prerequisite to normal speech is what we may call *speech readiness* or sufficient mental and physical maturation for the acquisition of speech. Attempts to force a child into perfect speech before this growth is complete can result in difficulties that may be manifested in several ways. Sometimes the child may react against the pressure and refuse to talk. In other instances continued correction because of the clumsy production of a sound may either serve to stamp in the error or make the child sensitive and even hesitant because he fears making a mistake. A mother's wish for her child to keep up with the timetable in the "book" may result in her explicit or implicit anxiety's directly handicapping the child.

The third prerequisite is that of *adequate stimulation*. The term "adequate stimulation" should be interpreted both quantitatively and qualitatively. Let us first consider the quantitative aspect. Many parents appear to feel that since children cannot understand them, it is unnecessary or even silly to talk to them. Consequently the child's speech may develop to the "babbling" stage and proceed no further. The deaf child will progress only to this stage unless he receives special instruction. We recently saw a mute youngster who was believed by his parents to be mentally retarded and to whom they seldom talked. When the child was tested, his performance on nonverbal tasks was above normal, and when he was normally stimulated, he learned to talk within a short period. We also know a bright boy who did not learn to use any words until he was over two years of age, and then he talked very slowly. His mother had placed him in a play pen all day and seldom talked to him. A "must" prescription for a baby from the day he is born is that he have large and frequent doses of good speech bombarding his ears.

A common cause of nonorganic speech defects is the quality of stimulation. Too frequently mothers, brothers, sisters, fathers, and teachers think it cute to talk "baby talk" with children. Some people seem to feel that this is the only kind of speech the baby can understand. Since much of speech is learned through stimulation, the child is almost sure to learn to speak as he hears others speak to him. Whole classrooms of children have been observed to have certain speech mannerisms characteristic of the teacher. Many children pick up their speech patterns from a nurse or a maid. One child, who simply "grew up" on the river front, spoke a mixture of many languages and styles of profanity. Another child presented speech that was the product of his mother's lisp, a cousin's tongue-tied, and his own bad teeth. Parents, teachers, and clinicians should make certain that children have an opportunity to hear the kind of speech they are expected to produce.

A fourth prerequisite is *motivation* to good speech. A child who receives no reward for speech and who is able to satisfy his needs without speech will probably be retarded in speech development. By the same token, the child who is able to satisfy his wants with defective speech, or who gains a little extra attention because of it, has little incentive to change. It should not be implied that one should penalize or "nag" poor speech, but the child should not regard the acquisition of poor speech as an asset. Furthermore, the asset characteristics of good speech should be reinforced. In some instances individuals find poor speech rewarding and as a consequence become attached to their particular deviations. One example is that of a college girl who achieved popularity almost overnight because it was discovered that she said, "I wove oo ten-doo-we"; another example is that of a high school girl who achieved notoriety and fame singing, "Red Shails in the Shun Shet."

A final essential to good speech is a necessary degree of *intellectual maturity*. Mentally retarded children are frequently retarded in their speech development. This is often complicated by lack of physical maturation, poor stimulation, and low motivation. The clinician can frequently assist the speech development of the retarded child by providing for more and better stimulation and for added motivation for speech, but he must expect this child's speech to be somewhat slow in development.

The recognition and prevention of articulatory and voice disorders of speech is best allocated to the specially trained speech correctionist. However all teachers and clinicians will find some training in speech correction helpful in distinguishing between the handicapped and the dull, and in carrying out the recommendations of the specialist. Several different general methods of therapy or treatment are prescribed by different authorities. Some of these are especially well adapted to the specific needs of certain clients, and all are probably effective in the hands of those with specific training and experience. For the inexperienced counselor or teacher the stimulation method [originally described by Lee Edward Travis (33) and later elaborated by Charles Van Riper (35)] will usually produce the best results with the least possibility of damage to the individual who has a reasonably adequate physiological structure. Wendell Johnson, et al. (22) have an excellent general text on speech problems of the school child. Other texts include one on special procedures for the child with cerebral palsy by William M. Cruikshank and George M. Raus (7); on the cleft palate by Muriel E. Morley (28); on the aphasic by Joseph M. Wepman (37); and on voice and articulation by Grant Fairbanks (10) and Elise Hahn, et al. (14).

The common element in all defects is a lack of proper integration of the speech mechanism as a whole. Some methods of treatment place the emphasis upon dealing with a narrow group of muscles or articulators. The teeth and tongue have been considered quite independently of other parts. We believe that a sound cannot be broken up into its component parts; that is, into lip movements and tongue movements. When the person has learned to produce the wrong speech sounds, he has learned wrong speech sound patterns, not wrong lip movements. Consequently, except where special organic limitations are present, we believe that drills should stress speech sound patterns rather than the manipulation of isolated groups of muscles.

Probably the most dramatic of all difficulties of speech is that usually described as stuttering. It is sometimes amusing, nearly always tragic, and of great concern to the client, his teachers, and his parents. It would only be confusing to attempt to outline all the various theories regarding the cause of stuttering or to attempt to define just what stuttering is. Although no two "stutterers" will "stutter" in the same way, they all regard themselves as "stutterers," they all fear speech, they all expect to have difficulty, they all make hard work of speech, and they all think they are different from "normal" speakers. As Katherine M. Cobb (3) has suggested, the etiology of stuttering remains controversial. Many accept the theory held by Wendell Johnson (20), that it is the result of anxiety engendered in early childhood by setting standards of speech too high. Various theories and therapies have been reviewed by Eugene Hahn (15). One theory that has received a great deal of attention is the laterality theory—that stuttering is produced by changed handedness. Gertrude H. Hildreth (18, 19) has reviewed the literature on laterality and finds little evidence for changed handedness as a causal factor. Characteristic of the search for a possible organic basis for stuttering is a study by John L. Boland (2), who interviewed the mothers of stutterers about the conditions attendant to delivery. He found that a higher percentage of these mothers reported instrumental delivery than that usually reported for the general population. He assumed that faulty memory reduced the number of instrumental deliveries reported by mothers of stutterers and corrected his data by one-third, thus producing a statistically significant difference in the direction of more instrumental deliveries for stuttering children. This correction would appear to be highly questionable, and it seems safe to conclude that we have no dependable evidence that birth injuries are actually a significant cause.

Upon the basis of all present evidence, attempts to find a constant difference between the normal-speaking child and the stuttering child have failed. There is no method at present by which we can predict in the very young child whether or not he is going to be a stutterer. However from our study of the development of stutterers, we know a few principles that can help us to prevent its inception. We know, for instance, that stuttering is always aggravated, if not actually caused, by someone "doing too much." In the early stages of speech a child is almost certain to repeat, pause, and prolong, especially if he feels that he must hurry or must try to speak well. This should be considered as normal; in fact, there is considerable danger in labeling it abnormal. The period from the first stages of connected speech until speech is firmly established is the time for exceedingly great tolerance on the part of parents and other listeners. This means that parents and teachers should refrain from constant coaching and that they should give no visible indication of being disturbed when the child struggles to produce words. Some children are a great deal more fluent than others and we should regard this as natural. The most important consideration is to make sure that the child does not become unduly concerned or alarmed about his speech. Children must never be made to fear that their speech is different or that they themselves are different. If a child has difficulty with speech, he should not be helped to label himself as a stutterer by such remedies as "take more time," "stop and think what you're going to say," "speak slowly so you won't stutter." Consciousness of "difference" or labeling may frequently occur when the child is rushed in speech situations or made to compete with others for attention. Children should not be forced to "show off" in situations that are obviously difficult for them. Little speeches, recitations, and similar activities can easily be deferred until the child is old enough and mature enough to handle them. This does not mean that a child should be excused because of his speech, but it does mean that he should not be forced to attempt situations before he is sufficiently mature physically, socially, and emotionally to deal with them. We have no idea how many stutterers are created in "show-uncle-how-well-you-recite" situations. Frequently, an individual finds that stuttering has profitable or asset characteristics that are difficult to deal with. Sometimes children can attract attention only by stuttering, just as some children can attract attention only by temper tantrums or "meanness" in school. This type of behavior must be avoided, first, by paying no attention to the speech; and, second, by giving the child sufficient love and attention at all times so that such roundabout tactics are not necessary.

Instead of making direct attacks upon a child's "speech problem" there are a number of procedures that can well be followed by those who have charge of stuttering children. These procedures are indirect but not all of them are don'ts. The following list may be helpful:

(1) Every child should have a clear conception of what is expected of him. All demands made upon him should be consistent.

(2) Assure good physical health. Every child should have plenty of rest and wholesome food.

(3) Children should be kept free from family tensions and quarrels.

(4) Indirectly try to prevent or at least do not encourage unsuccessful competition.

(5) No special favors should be granted a child because of his speech defect.

(6) If speech is discussed, refer to it in terms of exactly what is done. *Avoid such labels as "stuttering" or "stammering."* If the child pauses, call it pausing; if he repeats, call it repeating; and so on with holding breath, prolonging, or straining.

(7) Help the child to experience fluent speech as much as possible. This should be done very indirectly, and does not imply supplying words but does imply indirect encouragement in easy situations and equally indirect careful encouragement in difficult situations.

(8) Treat all speech, good or bad, with complete lack of anxiety. That is to say, some children need dental braces, some glasses, some have red hair, some are plump, some have a little trouble with speech.

(9) Set a good example of unhurried, effortless speech.

(10) Encourage the child to carry his share of conversation and schoolroom recitation. The stuttering child in the classroom should be treated as any other child.

(11) Never let the child think that he must stutter or that he always will stutter.

(12) Give the child sufficient responsibility so that he has some feeling of independence.

(13) Give the child sufficient attention, love, and affection.

(14) Give sufficient time for all speech attempts.

(15) Discourage the development of any mechanisms—finger waving, licking lips, stamping feet, blinking eyes—which may seem to make speech easier.

The above list of procedures has to do with the prevention of stuttering. Once the child begins to feel that he is a stutterer, all of the obvious aspects of so-called "stuttering" speech develop rapidly. Once he begins to strain, force, or struggle with his speech, stuttering truly develops. Once this behavior has developed, a competent speech correctionist should be consulted. The development of the secondary reactions to nonfluencies of speech have been excellently described by Van Riper (35); and Johnson (21) has described the development of stuttering in a young girl, presenting psychological evaluative data concerning this client. Assuming that stuttering is learned behavior and that an aspect of this behavior is anxiety, George J. Wischner (38) presents one of the constructive approaches to understanding stuttering. He reviews the published research data and, applying learning theory to this data, he comes to the conclusion that stuttering fulfills an expectancy and reduces tension although it does so at the price of normal speech. This should be recognized as an application of Hullian learning theory to the problem of stuttering. Research and therapy-planning along such a theoretical line appears to be promising. Specific procedures of therapy vary from clinician to clinician but all appear to attempt improvement in the client's mental hygiene. The efforts of the counselor and the speech specialist should be co-ordinated along this line.

COUNSELING AND READING

Clinical and counseling psychologists are frequently consulted about reading problems. Psychologists who are employed in the educational setting (elementary school, high school, or college) are often called upon to counsel with students who, among other problems, have difficulty in reading efficiently enough to adequately prepare their general assignments. Consequently, it seems appropriate to survey some of the methods used by reading specialists to improve reading.

There are two approaches to the improvement of reading ability, applicable to both children and adults, with which we should familiarize ourselves. The first of these is ordinarily known as developmental reading and the second as remedial reading. Developmental reading programs consist primarily of teaching reading skills with the use of equipment specifically designed to increase the speed of reading. Instructional techniques and procedures have been developed which, for the average person, will be effective in substantially increasing reading speed without any loss in comprehension. These methods have been described by Russell Cosper and Bariss Mills (4) and by Everett W. Kinne (23). Developmental reading programs are helpful to the individual who does not have special barriers to the achievement of reading skills. However reading deficiency in many individuals is traceable to factors such as general emotional maladjustment, specific dislike of or other negative attitudes toward reading, poor attention span arising out of emotional problems or physiological limitation, defects in symbolization, perceptual disorders, intellectual inadequacies, and a host of other problems that ordinarily cannot be materially overcome by the mere practice and perfection of the skills and techniques of reading. The approach to these latter problems is more properly described as remedial reading. Frequently it is necessary to remedy one or more of these conditions before the problems of reading can be approached; in fact, in many instances the problems can best be dealt with by a general counseling program rather than a remedial program. Of course, the person who has not learned to read because of some factor such as an emotional block against reading must be taught to read as the emotional problem is being ameliorated. Consequently there is a considerable overlap between some of the techniques used in remedial and in developmental reading programs. The resemblance is mainly in the techniques since the philosophies are quite different. The remedial-reading specialist must be clinically oriented and is more concerned with the unique problems affecting an individual, while the developmental reading specialist is concerned with the individual as a special problem.

There are a number of different remedial reading procedures, and various specialists stress different aspects of reading. Methods vary from the kinesthetic method as described by Grace M. Fernald (11) to the primarily psychotherapeutic approach of Beulah K. Ephron (9). Various other approaches to the problem of reading have been presented by Emmett A. Betts (1), Donald D. Durrell (8), Arthur I. Gates (13), William Kottmeyer (24), Marion Monroe and Ollie Backus (27), and Frances O. Triggs (34). The clinical and counseling psychologist is likely to feel that the text by Albert J. Harris (16) is more clinically oriented and broader in scope than most of the other references.

The clinician first makes a complete evaluation of his client to isolate various factors or conditions that may be affecting his general adjustment and particularly his reading. In some instances reading may appear to be a symptom of some more general disturbance, in others a primary problem. If the disturbance is general, attention to reading may be secondary to more global counseling objectives, whereas if reading is the primary problem, we may wish to concentrate on reading skills. In any case, there are several relatively simple activities that may contribute to improvement of reading ability. In this text we are concerning ourselves only with the person who has some reading ability since the task of teaching the nonreader or the severely handicapped individual is a special field of its own.

(a) Practice against time. Most people read less rapidly than their capacity permits. Some people are dawdlers when they read; they trifle with irrelevant thoughts instead of reacting to the material before them. By keeping a record of their speed of reading and practicing for a brief period each day, they can usually raise their speed considerably without impairing comprehension. In fact the dawdler can usually improve his comprehension in this manner. One method of self-help is to estimate the number of words on the pages of an assignment in a particular course and note the amount of time necessary to read a given unit. Then the student can consciously attempt to reduce the time required to read units of equal length. The number of words read per minute can be computed and a record of improvement kept.

(b) Read silently. One of the most serious causes of slow reading is excessive vocalization. Lip movement or inner-speech, which approximates reading aloud, is slower by far than the visual recognition of words. Some persons almost speak the word aloud, others only use lip movements, and others simply read by word but silently. In some instances specific drills may be necessary to change the habit of reading aloud, but, quite frequently, calling it to the client's attention followed by experimentation on his own will allow him to begin to break the habit. Ordinarily it is a carry-over from the oral reading of early reading instruction. Occasionally, it may be due to a limited perceptual span, which necessitates more detailed remedial attention.

(c) Extend word knowledge. Much of the inefficiency of reading is due to vocabulary limitations. The client should be encouraged to extend his vocabulary by keeping a list of words to be defined, used in writing and speaking, and eventually assimilated into the client's vocabulary.

(d) Learn to skip wisely. A good reader "hits the high spots." The poor reader must learn to skip phrases, sentences, and even whole paragraphs when he is sure he has caught the core of meaning. Often one needs only the first and last sentences of a paragraph to get the entire thought. The opening sentence or sentences can be cast into a question, and then one can read only what one feels is necessary to answer the question.

(e) Make a preliminary survey. Before reading a chapter in detail, one should attempt to discover what the chapter is all about. Rather than starting right in with the first sentence and plunging on through unexplored territory, the good reader will spend some time in surveying the chapter so that he will have a background that will help him to assess the importance of the details. Many persons get so lost in details that they spend much more time than is necessary. Many textbook writers place a summary statement at the end of each chapter. When this is done, the reader might wish to read it first. Perhaps the writer may help by placing such a summary at the beginning of each new chapter.

(f) Notice type carefully. The different kinds of type used in printing the headings will usually tell you what the author regards as important and what as subordinate. The student should attempt to see how the author puts his chapter and book together. This is helpful for outlining but, more important, if the reader can actually discover how the author has organized his material, he has probably mastered the material.

(g) Read graphs, drawings, and tables. These materials are included because they are important. Many facts and relationships can be summarized by figures in a small amount of space. If a table or graph can be correctly interpreted, this may save pages of reading.

(h) Learn technical terms. It is especially important to watch for technical terms and to be sure one knows the meaning of these terms.

(i) Recite. The poorest way to understand is to read without reciting. The student should learn to ask himself questions and, in effect, to recite to himself.

These simple suggestions may prove helpful to the poor reader, particularly the high school or college student. If no progress can be made in line with them, it is likely that more specialized procedures are indicated.

STUDY–HABIT COUNSELING

Our final topic on miscellaneous counseling procedures is included for the guidance of the counselor who is working in an educational or academic setting, although the ideas presented may have some relevance for other situations. For example, the client who is learning a new job or some of the details involved in a new procedure may find that he is unable to apply himself to his task. Even though more basic problems may be interfering, time will not allow the postponement of the immediate problem until the others have been worked through. Consequently some of the superficial techniques to be described may be helpful.

First, the student must recognize that study does not consist simply of sitting or lying down and reading words. Study should not be confused with the mechanics of following printed words across the page. Study does not necessarily involve reading at all. Too many people think they have studied a lesson once they have read the twenty-three pages assigned. On the contrary, it is possible that some of our most valuable study comes either before or after we read an assignment. Study is *work*, *labor*—intellectual work or labor. It involves solving problems, thinking through questions, or mastering methods of doing certain operations. To learn to work in this manner is far more important than the acquisition of particular bodies of information. It is true that we need information in order to do this work. The knowledge we gain from reading is ordinarily the tool that we use in our study or intellectual work. We need to know the definition of certain terms and we need certain facts before we can study psychology. We need to know certain theories before we can study geometry. We may need to know many facts before we can study animal husbandry. And just as the carpenter must know how to use his saw and the athlete his physical strength and agility, the student must know how to use his facts and knowledge.

By intellectual work, then, we do not mean that we work hard and read our assignments over three, four, five, or fifty times, but that after the lesson has been read, we think about it, we work it over, trying to figure out what the writer was talking about and to use the knowledge he has presented. In other words, we do not get very far by simply listening to a lecture or reading a few pages and hoping that the material will sink in. The counselor's job, then, is to talk with the student about how to read, how to take notes, how to outline, and, in general, how to gather information. This will do relatively little good unless the student can learn to puzzle out ways of using the information he has gathered. Such suggestions as the following may help:

(1) After listening to a lecture or attending a class, spend a half hour or so thinking about what was said. Review notes and attempt to reproduce the class period or lecture.

(2) Get an overview of each assignment before reading it carefully. Skim through the assignment or read the summary and then go back and do it carefully.

(3) Frame questions while reading. Ask questions and then try to answer them from the assignment.

(4) After reading an assignment, think about it and, as with lectures, attempt to reconstruct it.

One of the most important requisites of effective study is motivation—there must be some drive or need to study. A good student not only wants to learn but is willing to work in order to learn. He has intellectual curiosity. He is willing to spend time and energy in order to understand. This curiosity is not a native attribute, it is learned. Probably the first necessary condition is to have some interests in the specific area of learning or study. Most people are interested in something or other. Some are interested in a great number of areas, others in only a few.

Some study materials are definitely interesting to an individual, others are not. In order to attempt to develop interest in uninteresting areas, we should:

(1) Work at the subject. If we really think about or work with a subject, it may appear more interesting than we originally expected it to be. A certain amount of disinterest arises from lack of acquaintance with a subject. Furthermore, we sometimes develop a bias against a certain area because friends have commented that material is dry or that they dislike it. Earlier experiences often prejudice us so that we do not give ourselves a chance to develop interests.

(2) Acquire information about the subject, about the author of the text, and about the teacher of the class. Some people have interest in the area—where did they get it? A little knowledge may open up interests that are unsuspected.

(3) Tie the new information to bodies of old information.

(4) Make the information personal and attempt to relate it to ourselves, our family, our friends, etc.

In addition to interest factors, we are frequently poorly motivated to study for other reasons. Grades are not satisfactory goals for most people. The future use of knowledge in one's profession or career is a pretty remote goal. The counselor should strive to find means of more immediate motivation for the client. These means will undoubtedly be different for each client and must be custom-made for each individual.

To study effectively, most students find it necessary to plan for the efficient use of their time. Many are poorly prepared for college work or for independent study. Up to the time they enter college, too many young people have had their activities supervised by parents and teachers. Daily recitations in grade school and high school check the tendency to put off study, and supervised study periods foster study that is reasonably well distributed. Release from these directive influences often occurs very suddenly at the college level. The novelty of having to direct all one's activities is accompanied by a lack of skill in using time effectively, and this is further complicated by situations that are conducive to wasting time. The student's classes are scheduled intermittently, and unless he is careful, time between classes will be spent not in study but in conversation and loafing. There are a great number of social activities that may crowd out study time, create agitated attitudes, and prevent concentrated effort. Added to all of this, the college curriculum is usually more difficult, requiring more time in study, than previous curriculums.

Of course, every student must decide upon his primary objective in being in school. If he has come for a good time or if she has come to find a husband, it is, perhaps, the counselor's task to help the student plan time accordingly! For most students the primary objective is to secure an education; that is, to broaden and refine comprehension so that he will be better prepared to make wide and varied adjustments in later life. For many students this is synonymous with scholarship. If a student's primary objective is to learn in an academic sense and to enjoy as many of the social aspects of school life as he can, then he must budget his time. If he is interested in nothing but "book-larning," he probably does not need any time budget; but if his purpose is to get a well-rounded experience, the budget will be helpful.

The counselor can aid the student in preparing a schedule or budget. The first step is usually the making of an inventory of how time is being spent. This inventory can be made up by keeping a detailed record for a short period indicating how much time is spent on study for each course, in sleep, meals, class and laboratory, outside work, campus activities, leisure time, social time, and wasted time. After the inventory has been made, a tentative plan can be set up. This plan should be based upon a careful analysis of the importance of different time expenditures to the individual. Certain activities will be retained in terms of the student's interests. The amount of time spent on each course should be examined, and if too little is being spent on disliked or difficult courses, the time on these should be increased. Frequently the student will find that he is spending more time on easy and interesting courses than on difficult courses. This may, of course, be one reason why the easy courses are easy and interesting, and the time spent on them should not be drastically changed, but usually some adjustments can be made. The new plan should take into consideration the specific hours that were followed in the past, because the previous system was based, at least in part, on convenience. Insofar as possible, weekly study time for each course should be distributed rather than concentrated. If it can be arranged, some study time for each class should be allowed for as soon as possible before recitations and lectures, and some immediately after. A review period for each subject should be scheduled in each week. Social events and work that are fairly fixed should be scheduled. Every schedule should contain about an hour a day for leisure or loafing. Unexpected events arising during the day can be postponed to this time, when the student is free to do as he pleases. Finally, the schedule should have some flexibility, especially for evening study. The student may want to have a very special date or to do extra work on a particular night. The schedule would allow for a minimum of moving activities around to allow for such emergencies. These latter points are important since a schedule is of no use unless the student will follow it. Finally, the schedule should be tried out, discussed with the counselor, and altered until it can be followed.

The most common reason given by students for failure in school is their inability to concentrate. Many students come to the counselor with the hope that they can be taught to concentrate. Certainly, effective study does demand attention and concentration; but basically this is not an ability, it is rather a condition arising out of surroundings and internal conditions. To be absorbed in study is to be oblivious to everything else. Consequently, learning to concentrate is learning to overcome distractions. There are at least three kinds of distractions that must be overcome. These are:

(1) Distractions in the surroundings
(2) Distractions arising in one's body
(3) Distractions in the form of irrelevant ideas

Many distractions, particularly those arising from surroundings, are best dealt with by elimination. This usually involves choosing a study place that is as free as possible from noises, conversations, moving objects and people, glaring lights, bright colors, varied or novel objects, and other disturbing features. Study place habits are as important as study time habits. The student should have a place to study where he does not ordinarily do other things. As an example, a study desk should not contain magazines or books that are read for fun. On the side of bodily distractions, the student should attempt to study when he is not unduly fatigued or hungry. Sound health and bodily vigor must be maintained and digestive disturbances and eye strain are to be avoided. A good study place provides comfortable conditions of light, heat, and ventilation. The large class of distractions consisting of ideas and thoughts are sometimes difficult to deal with. These may be thoughts of other duties, of disturbing problems, emotional conflicts, financial worries and even of things one would like to do if he did not have to study. Many of these problems can be dealt with by postponement but often they require personal counsel. Not all distractions can be done away with, so the student must learn to concentrate in spite of them.

One of the basic problems is that of getting started on work or study. The student can be encouraged to start studying the moment he sits down at his desk or study table. As soon as he is seated, he should begin to go through the motions. Frequently the person who claims inability to concentrate will find himself absorbed in study once the effort is initiated. Many students work out ways of giving themselves immediate rewards for application and concentration. Perhaps the work can be divided into segments, with the student disciplining himself to cover one segment at a time. When he feels that he has mastered a particular segment, he can have a cigarette, a cup of coffee, stroll around the room, or take a brief break. Then he goes back to the second segment and applies himself industriously until he has covered it before taking another break.

This section on study-habit counseling should not be closed without some mention of note-taking, review, and preparation for examinations. We feel that these are individual matters to be worked out between the student and the counselor. Some students, for example, profit from extensive note-taking both while reading and while listening to lectures. Others may be distracted from the main ideas if they attempt to take notes, and can profit best by allowing time to reconstruct content after the lecture, period of reading, etc. Methods of review and preparation for examinations also vary in effectiveness for each student. The counselor can encourage experimentation and can usually help the student to improve his study efficiency.

SUMMARY

This final chapter on counseling procedures has merely sampled some of the special techniques and problems that will be encountered by the clinical and counseling psychologist. We have not attempted, either in this chapter or in the entire section (Parts II and III) to cover all the special or general problems that will be met by the professional psychologist. In this chapter the discussion of the role of the clinician and counselor in dealing with special defects in general, with the physically handicapped, the speech defective, the poor reader, and the ineffective student is designed primarily to illustrate a philosophy concerning the functions of the psychologist. In some instances the discussion has been quite general, giving references to other source materials, and in other instances rather specific suggestions have been made. The intent throughout has been to emphasize the psychologist's role in promoting total developmental adjustment, and to argue against the segmentation of the remedial or rehabilitative process into a number of separate "treatments."

The sections on counseling and psychotherapeutic functions have been intended to present an overview of theories and techniques so that the reader will have gained a certain familiarity with these concepts and procedures. It is certainly not assumed that the reader will be a qualified counselor after a study of these chapters, rather he should be prepared to enter upon his preparation. The entire portion is written with the strong conviction that one learns to be a counselor by doing and not by reading or talking alone. Some information is necessary before one can talk or discuss issues arising in the actual counseling situation, and perhaps some background has been supplied to this end. Theories have been presented rather completely; and insofar as the author's biases will allow, they have been presented within the framework of the theory itself. The intention has been to neither encourage nor inveigh against the student's belief in any particular theoretical position. Even though our general approach may appear directive at times, it is hoped that the tenor is always client-centered. Furthermore, we have repeatedly emphasized our interest in the *total* client, not in his inhibitions, his personality, his education, or his job, but in the entire developmental and adjustive process as it applies to his personal happiness, his family relationships, his education, his work, and his functioning in his twenty-four-hour-a-day social milieu.

BIBLIOGRAPHY

1. Betts, E. A., *The prevention and correction of reading disabilities.* Evanston, Ill.: Row, Peterson, 1936.
2. Boland, J. L., "Type of birth as related to stuttering." *J. Speech Hearing Disorders*, 1951, 16, 40–3.
3. Cobb, K. M., "Special disabilities." In *Annual Review of Psychology*, Vol. IV. Stanford: Annual Reviews, 1953.
4. Cosper, R., and Mills, B., "Reading comprehension and speed." *School and Society*, 1953, 77, 359–62.
5. *Counseling for psychological acceptance of disability.* U. S. Department of Health, Education, and Welfare, Office of Vocational Rehabilitation, Washington, D. C., 1953.
6. Cruickshank, W. M. (ed.), *Psychology of exceptional children and youth.* Englewood Cliffs, N. J.: Prentice-Hall, 1955.
7. Cruickshank, W. M., and Raus, G. M., *Cerebral palsy: individual and community problems.* Syracuse, N. Y.: Syracuse Univ. Press, 1955.
8. Durrell, D. D., *Improvement of basic reading abilities.* Yonkers-on-Hudson, N. Y.: World Book, 1940.
9. Ephron, B. K., *Emotional difficulties in reading.* New York: Julian, 1953.
10. Fairbanks, G., *Voice and articulation drillbook.* New York: Harper, 1940.
11. Fernald, G. M., *Remedial techniques in basic school subjects.* New York: McGraw-Hill, 1943.
12. Frampton, M. E., and Gall, E. D. (eds.), *Special education for the exceptional.* 3 Vols. Boston: Porter Sargent, 1955.
13. Gates, A. I., *The improvement of reading* (rev. ed.). New York: Macmillan, 1935.
14. Hahn, Elise, *et al., Basic voice training for speech.* New York: McGraw-Hill, 1952.
15. Hahn, Eugene, *Stuttering: significant theories and therapies.* Stanford: Stanford Univ. Press, 1943.
16. Harris, A. J., *How to increase reading ability.* New York: Longmans, Green, 1941.
17. Henry, N. B. (ed.), The forty-ninth yearbook of the National Society for the Study of Education. Part II. *The Education of the exceptional child.* Chicago: Univ. of Chicago Press, 1950.

18. Hildreth, G. H., "The development and training of hand dominance: IV. Developmental problems associated with handedness." *J. Genet. Psychol.*, 1950, 76, 39–100.
19. Hildreth, G. H., "The development and training of hand dominance: V. Training of handedness." *J. Genet. Psychol.*, 1950, 76, 101–44.
20. Johnson, W., "A study of the onset and development of stuttering." *J. Speech Hearing Disorders*, 1942, 7, 251–7.
21. Johnson, W., "A college freshman with a stuttering problem." In Burton, A., and Harris, R. E., *Clinical studies of personality*. New York: Harper, 1955.
22. Johnson, W., Brown, S. F., Curtis, J. F., Edney, C. W., and Keaster, J., *Speech handicapped school children* (rev. ed.). New York: Harper, 1956.
23. Kinne, E. W., "Reading improvement for adults." *College English*, 1954, 15, 222–8.
24. Kottmeyer, W., *Handbook for remedial reading*. St. Louis: Webster, 1947.
25. Mayforth, F. (ed.), *Learning to speak effectively*. Bulletin of the Association for Childhood Education, Washington, D. C., 1943.
26. Menninger, K., *The human mind*. New York: Alfred A. Knopf, 1930.
27. Monroe, M., and Backus, B., *Remedial reading*. Boston: Houghton Mifflin, 1937.
28. Morley, M. E., *Cleft palate and speech* (3rd ed.). Baltimore: Williams & Wilkins, 1954.
29. *Rehabilitation of the emotionally and mentally disabled veteran: the impact of disability upon the personality*. Marion, Ind.: Veterans Administration Hospital, 1955.
30. Sarason, S. B., *Psychological problems in mental deficiency*. New York: Harper, 1953.
31. Strauss, A. A., and Kephart, N. C., *Psychopathology and education of the brain injured child, vol. II: progress in theory and clinic*. New York: Grune & Stratton, 1955.
32. Strauss, A. A., and Lehtinen, L. E., *Psychopathology and education of the brain injured child, vol. I: fundamentals and treatment*. New York: Grune & Stratton, 1951.
33. Travis, L. E., *Speech pathology*. New York: Appleton-Century-Crofts, 1931.
34. Triggs, F. O., *Remedial reading*. Minneapolis, Minn.: The Univer. of Minnesota Press, 1943.
35. Van Riper, C., *Speech correction: principles and methods* (rev. ed.). Englewood Cliffs, N. J.: Prentice-Hall, 1943.
36. Wallin, J. E. W., *Education of mentally handicapped children*. New York: Harper, 1955.
37. Wepman, J. M., *Recovery from aphasia*. New York: Ronald, 1951.
38. Wischner, G. V., "Stuttering behavior and learning: A preliminary theoretical formulation." *J. Speech Hearing Disorders*, 1950, 15, 324–5.

Part Three

✳ ✳

EVALUATION AND
ASSESSMENT

CHAPTER

13

The Philosophy
of Clinical Evaluation

T HE ULTIMATE TASK OF CLINICAL AND COUNSELING PSYCHOLO-
gists has been described as that of promoting the efficiency of
function and the happiness of their clients. In Parts I and II a
number of theories, practices, and techniques of psychological counseling were reviewed, and the emphasis throughout this discussion was on
planning. The basic assumption underlying this emphasis is that persons,
their environments, and the unique interactions between the persons and
their environmental fields all differ. If counseling is to be intelligently
planned, planning must be based on knowledge of the individual. Although the counseling objectives represent the ultimate goals, we cannot begin to plan for these goals, much less work toward them, until we
have carefully assessed or evaluated the behavioral situations that we
hope to modify in a constructive manner.

Part III is concerned with the assessment procedures that are designed to give clinical and counseling psychologists the information they
need in order to plan constructively with their clients. Since we believe
that it is necessary to plan carefully for the mediate aims and objectives,
as well as for the long-range objectives, we placed the discussion of
counseling aims such as insight, emotional release, support, relearning,
socialization, environmental modification, and a number of more specialized objectives and techniques ahead of our examination of methods
for evaluation and assessment. It is hoped that we now have some understanding of the ends for which we must plan and that our assessment
activities can be consistently oriented toward them.

In Chapter 3 [1] we presented a field-theoretical approach to psychological counseling. We mentioned at that time that we must have a clear

[1] *See* pp. 49–51.

knowledge of a system before we disturb it in any way. The positive ad-vantages of such knowledge for the formulation of constructive plans should not require elaboration. However we must also realize that nega-tive effects can result from the application of certain techniques without knowledge of the checks and counter-checks inherent in the behavioral situation of any client at any particular time. In the case of the client with the intense anxieties and the hypersensitivity to certain voice char-acteristics, emphasis upon insight without support and the opportunity for release would have been traumatic. In a similar vein, retraining and vocational counseling with the brain-damaged business-machine operator had to be accompanied by constant support and encouragement, and quite probably had to be integrated with the understanding of his assets and limitations. In some instances the application of a particular pro-cedure may increase the strain on the system; in others it may reduce it until motivation would be reduced; and in still other instances stress on certain objectives may be ineffective, or even dangerous, because of lack of resources, lack of control, or lack of motivation. The assessment pro-cedures provide us with information about the client's resources and the manner in which the client is capable of directing and controlling them.

WHAT THE PSYCHOLOGIST EVALUATES

The psychologist is primarily concerned with behavior. He is con-cerned with the total behavior of the entire organism as it functions in its unique, complicated, and constantly changing environment. We are not basically interested in personality, intelligence, motivation, emotion, learning, or perceptions as such; we are interested in them as constructs that help us to understand and describe certain aspects of behavior. We are interested in other aspects of behavior as well. For example, we are interested in the attitudes of the client toward his environment, toward his job, toward other people, and of course toward himself. Attitudinal adjustments may be far more intrinsic than physical reactions, but the difference may be seen as relative. In the functioning individual a degree of intrinsic and extrinsic behavior is seen in all his reactions to the com-plex environment. It is these behavioral and attitudinal adjustments that we wish to understand and predict. Such concepts as personality or in-telligence, even though we use personality and intelligence tests as tools for evaluation, are best regarded as qualities or characteristics of be-havior and not as specific entities in themselves. All evaluation is con-cerned with the individual and the behavior of the individual. A report of a psychological evaluation should draw a word picture of a person that is such that the individual reading the report sees a person, not a mass of difficult-to-interpret abstractions based on a group of psychological tests.

The criterion of a good clinical report is the adequacy with which the client and his behavior is presented in a meaningful, useful fashion and the accuracy with which predictions for future behavior can be made from it—not necessarily the accuracy with which labels can be applied or how well these labels agree with those applied by someone else. Molly R. Harrower (1, p. 12), in her discussion of the evolution of a clinical psychologist, points up this last thought:

> The psychologist is entitled to the epithet "clinical" when he ceases to consider himself as the infallible psychodiagnostician —God's gift to the psychiatrist! Or, on the other hand, when he is past the stage of thinking of himself as "successful" only in terms of the number of times when his diagnoses equate with those of the psychiatrist, being elated when his batting average rises, plunged in the depths of despair as his "diagnoses" differ.[2]

The psychologist is concerned with furthering his knowledge or that of the clinical team relative to the dynamic formulation of a client's present behavior, attitudes, or symptoms so that something can be done about them. This, then, is the meaning of clinical evaluation as it is conducted by the psychologist.

Harrower goes on to suggest that the word "psychodiagnostician" might advantageously be dispensed with, since in the sense that it is generally used (as referring to one who applies a label), it is somewhat pretentious and inaccurate. It may be gratifying to the psychologist and reassuring to the psychiatrist to be able to confirm a particular diagnosis or label; but either the psychiatrist or the psychologist, if he has a complete knowledge of the clinical picture, can ordinarily attach an accurate label without benefit of projective and other tests. The psychologist should emerge to a more positive role. Harrower suggests that he can become an explorer of the individual's potentialities and resources, the assessor, surveyor, or map maker of the dimensions and depths of personality. The psychologist's function should be not merely to report that the patient is neurotic or psychotic, but rather to prepare a description of the person and the ways in which particular symptoms find expression. The actual label is a small part of the battle.

The following caricature of a comedy of errors illustrates what too often happens (1, pp. 14–15):

> The scene is laid in any hospital in which the psychologist is attempting to find his place without having clearly before

[2] This and a quotation that follows by permission from Harrower, M. R.: "The Evolution of a Clinical Psychologist." *Training in Clinical Psychology*, M. R. Harrower, Editor. Trans. First Conf. Josiah Macy, Jr. Foundation, 1947. Copyright 1947 by Josiah Macy, Jr. Foundation.

him his goal, his responsibilities, a knowledge of his place on the team. The intern, who has been asked to have the patient examined psychologically, translates these instructions into, "I want an IQ on this patient; they're going to discuss him on ward rounds." Since the intern has had no training in psychology, this vagueness is inevitable. The psychologist takes this request at its face value, and reports correctly, but in this case, misleadingly, "IQ, 100," without explanation of the all-important additional fact that "there is a considerable amount of scatter between the subtests."

The intern, ignoring the last sentence, reports at ward rounds, "The patient is normal; psychological examination negative." A psychiatrist in the group may look skeptical and ask if a Rorschach has been done. The intern (this is in the days before the famous film, "The Dark Mirror"!) makes a note to "get a raw something done" or alternatively, "one of those shock tests." The psychologist administers the Rorschach, and again, speaking in his foreign language, reports, "This patient shows W, 20%; D, 20%; Dd, 60%; F—, 50%; no M or FC; color shock on Card II." This technical monstrosity is read off by the intern next day, and, needless to say, no one is any the wiser.

At this point, two psychiatrists may disagree with regard to the patient's relationship to reality, and the psychologist is asked point blank to pronounce him either neurotic or psychotic. On the spot, and feeling grossly insecure, he remembers Rorschach's pronouncement that when color shock is found in a record, there can be no question of a psychosis. He makes a blind stab and pronounces the patient neurotic. When the patient several days later is transferred to a psychiatric hospital, the intern feels justified in remarking, "I certainly can't see any point in getting a patient psyched; first, they say the man is normal, then he's neurotic, and all the time the guy's nuts!"

Such a situation as this results when both the medical specialist and the psychologist are confused as to their roles. As silly as the above may sound, such incidents do occur. They would be much less apt to happen if all workers involved were preoccupied with understanding the individual so that recommendations could be made for his treatment, rather than being engrossed in applying a label to him.

William C. Menninger (4, p. 9), in discussing the relationship between psychology and psychiatry, gives his conception of the diagnostic functions of a psychologist. His description is an excellent summary of the diagnostic aims to be achieved if concrete plans are to be made for the individual. He says, "Today when, as a psychiatrist, I ask for a psychological test study of a patient, I do not particularly want to know the IQ or the Sum M to Sum C Rorschach ratio. I expect to receive a diagnostic appraisal of a total personality, with discussion of the nature of the illness, character structure, strengths or weaknesses of ego defenses, characteristic modes of adaptation, likely course of the illness and amenability to treatment." [3] This, then, is the basic purpose of evaluation in clinical psychology. It would seem to matter little whether the psychological test study is done by a psychologist for a psychiatrist or for the psychologist himself, for the aims and purposes should be the same, and they are the same wherever he works—in hospital, school, prison, or industry. Description is only a part of the psychological test study. Labeling may be a by-product, but it is not of basic importance. Understanding of the client's behavior is necessary, but even this, in itself, is not sufficient. It must be possible to make predictions of behavior from the study so that therapy can be planned or recommendations made concerning the individual's family, school, work, or recreational activities. The purpose of psychological diagnostic evaluation is to know the behavior of the person. Consequently the psychologist evaluates behavior.

IS THE PSYCHOLOGIST CONCERNED ONLY WITH THE PERSON?

In the larger sense this question has already been answered, as we have said many times that we are interested in the behavior of the person. We must remember that the person does not exist in a vacuum. He lives in an environmental field, the importance of which is so obvious that it is frequently overlooked. This field is composed of an almost infinite number of factors that separately and together have a profound effect upon the behavior of the individual. Most of these field factors are social in that they have to do with people, but we must not disregard the physical environment, the economic situation, or even such meteorological conditions as climate and weather. Although in theory most clinicians will admit to the importance of field factors, in actual practice these are too frequently by-passed in favor of the analysis of intrinsic motives. Recently one of our colleagues, who regards himself as an individual psychotherapist, was unable to see any good reason for referring a client to a vocational counselor. As he expressed it: "Anybody can tramp the streets and find this chap a job. It doesn't make much difference what he does if we can work through his feelings toward his mother." Some

[3] From "Relationship of Clinical Psychology and Psychiatry," by William C. Menninger, *American Psychologist*, 1950, 5, 3–15. By permission of the American Psychological Association.

vocational counselors go to the opposite extreme; they plan for the client's future with utter disregard for his personal needs and desires, giving major attention to the physical and economic aspects of his employability. These examples point up one of the principal reasons why we have consistently linked clinical *and* counseling psychology, rather than referring to clinical *or* counseling psychology. Too often the clinical psychologist emphasizes the person, and the counseling psychologist the environment. We believe that the person and the environment cannot be separated, that the functions of clinical and counseling psychology must be merged so that the psychologist deals with the interaction between these two elements in the total behavioral situation.

This is all in a direct application of Kurt Lewin's (3) statement that behavior is a function of the interaction between the person and his environment. If we accept this philosophy, it follows that the psychologist must employ tools for the evaluation of the physical and social environment of the client as well as devices for describing and assessing the personal determinants of behavior. The job of the psychologist is to identify as many as possible of the forces acting, both from within and without, upon the person, so that the resultant behavior can be plotted and predicted. This will be illustrated in a discussion of case study materials in Chapter 14. We must consider the organization of the family, the community, the church, and even the governmental structure within which the client lives. The final objective will always be to understand the influences of these factors upon behavior. We must consider the adequacy of vocational adjustment, the client's satisfaction with his work and the efficiency with which he performs it. We must know the people who interact with our subject. We must know their motives and goals and their desires for the person under study. We must know their values, their philosophies, and their temperaments. We must know the position of our client in this socal milieu. We must see all these influences in an interacting dynamic and developmental perspective as well as in the present force field.

THE ASSESSMENT TOOLS OF THE PSYCHOLOGIST

The tools of the psychologist include the anamnesis or the history, the interview, and the various psychological tests. The case history should include data from many areas such as the family history, developmental history, educational history, vocational history, and sociological history. This historical material is the most important source of information *about* the client. The case history, which will be described in Chapter 14, is broadly conceived and includes as much information as can be accumulated. Although we have many theories as to the cause of behavior disorders, our present store of knowledge is still too inadequate for us to streamline the amount of information that is needed for an understanding of the dynamic formulation of a particular pattern of behavior. We have no a priori basis upon which to decide what may or may not be important, and we must crossvalidate historical information by collecting data from as many sources as possible.

The history is conceived of in this text as including the complete life history of the client from conception to the present; in fact, in the family history we are even interested in the preconception history of the person. Analysis of the present situation is also a part of the total evaluation. Since information concerning the present is included, we should perhaps refer to the total knowledge about a client as the *case study* rather than as the *case history*. These terms are used by many workers interchangeably with the term "anamnesis." We will use the term "case history" or "anamnesis" to include the gathering of information about a client and the term "case study" to include *all* the information gathered, including interview and test data. The case study includes past and present information; indeed, to the degree that we may inquire of parents and teachers about plans for a client, it may even project somewhat into the future.

We will consider the diagnostic interview in detail in Chapter 15. In the philosophy of diagnosis to be described, great importance is attached to interview information. Of the many clinicians who have minimized the importance of the interview and the case history in favor of test data, Edward S. Jones (2, p. 162) has written, "They would apparently rather record a neurotic inventory score taken from a test, even though they do not know what the test really measures, than to note that a boy was clumsy in his oral expression and that his nose kept twitching as he talked, data that may have obvious social implications." Even though at times case history and interview data may have low reliability and validity, it has face validity, whereas test data has, in most instances, only inferred validity. Case history and interview information reveals behavior in the real-life situation, whereas test information emerges from artificial situations. This is not to suggest that we intend to do away with psychological tests as tools in psychology. Actually, we have to depend heavily on them, for in many instances case history data is so meager and interview information so questionable that the entire burden of evaluation is necessarily placed on tests. This, however, is no argument for placing them in a position of primary importance. When adequate direct information can be obtained concerning a client's past behavior, present behavior, and attitudes, this is far more valuable than the indirect inferences drawn from a test protocol. To reduce this problem to a simple level, we might consider an actual example.

Let us suppose we are presented with a young man who has successfully completed high school and two years of college. This fact has been substantiated by interviews with his teachers. The report of a psychological test indicates that he is of borderline intelligence and should not be capable of finishing grammar school. Which information would you accept as the more meaningful? The psychological examiner in this incident insists to this day that we must be talking about two different people. Another example concerns a man who is described by a test report as too disorganized in his thinking ever to hold a position of any kind; this man is today earning more money as president and active executive of a large business than most of the readers of this book, its author, or the psychological examiner will ever earn. One may, of course, question the adequacy of earnings as a criterion of adjustment, but in this instance careful study of the occupational history would suggest that the test was not a valid measure of the man's potentialities and resources. Psychological test data should supplement and complement other information but it cannot supplant it. By and large, we should use tests to confirm or deny hypotheses that have been formulated from the historical and clinical picture, to fill in gaps that may exist in the clinical picture, and in general to assist us in rounding out or substantiating our evaluations so that we can make predictions with the maximum of confidence.

It is clear that the contributions of psychology to the field of diagnosis have been substantially in the realm of testing. Even in the realm of research tests are effective tools, but the limitations of tests must be kept constantly in mind, and their results must not be overrated or used uncritically as substitutes for the *real* data or the actual behavior. Several forthcoming chapters (16-20) will be devoted to the description, evaluation, and use of psychological diagnostic devices. Specifically, we will discuss intelligence tests, tests of intellectual deficit, objective tests of personality, unstructured personality tests, and partially structured personality tests.

THE CONTRIBUTIONS OF PSYCHOLOGICAL TESTS

To give the reader a perspective of the total problem of psychological evaluation, we will now consider the contributions of psychological testing under functional headings. For purposes of the present discussion, psychological tests will be considered under:

(1) Evaluation of potentialities and resources
(2) Descriptive diagnostic techniques
(3) Evaluation of dynamics of behavior

In a sense psychological tests can be thought of as techniques for discovering the *what, how,* and *why* of a person's behavior. The history and interview both give information relative to all three of these questions. At the moment, however, we will limit our discussion to test devices.

1. Evaluation of Potentialities and Resources. *What* the client can do, *what* his potentialities and resources are, can be evaluated with the help of a number of test techniques. The first tests that come to mind are the various measures of intellectual functioning. The principal use of such tests should be to evaluate the potential and resources of the client which might be utilized if properly directed. The history of clinical psychology closely parallels the development of measures of intelligence.[4] Thomas W. Richards (5) designates diagnostic techniques in this area as measures of capacity. His concept of capacity is closely related to our concept of potential and resources although it differs from it; whereas we are interested in the individual's potentiality for using his capacity, Richards is concerned with the total potential capacity of the individual and discusses the evaluation of motivation and the evaluation of control as other aspects of the total diagnostic procedure. David Wechsler (7), too, has discussed human capacities and has summarized much of the knowledge regarding individual differences; he also appears to be concerned more with the problems of the limits and range of human capacities and perhaps somewhat less with the utilization of capacity although it is true that his global concept of intelligence does include motivational factors.

When we talk of potentialities and resources, we are concerned not only with the individual's total potential capacity, but also with his potentialities and resources for directing and controlling this capacity. We are not interested in the evaluation of capacity per se, but rather in evaluating a person's potential for making a particular kind of adjustment. We may be concerned with an estimate of the probability that a person will finish secondary school or that he has the necessary general and specific aptitudes for success at a particular kind of work. These examples represent rather traditional applications of capacity measures, but, to carry our discussion further, we may be interested in the extent to which a person can use his capacity to gain insight into complex behavioral dynamics and thus profit from psychotherapy. It may be necessary to determine whether a person has enough motivation to apply even borderline capacity, or to evaluate his potentialities for controlling and directing his capacity so that he can make the most of his resources. The concept of the evaluation of potentialities and resources involves an appraisal of the interaction between motivation, control, and capacity. While we are not primarily interested in appraisal of a person's present capacity, we do want to evaluate the limits and the probability as to where he will operate between them.

[4] *See* p. 12.

In the evaluation of this potential the clinician is seldom satisfied with one test, but compares various kinds of test performance with the history and current status of the client. A single score on a test is seldom, if ever, sufficient, and it is ordinarily advisable to study the pattern of performances within a test. Many qualitative observations are also significant; in fact, in some instances they are more significant than the quantitative observations. Furthermore, appraisal of potentialities and resources cannot usually be made from intelligence test data alone. In order to properly predict a client's potential performance, observations must also be made of aptitudes, interests, and personality characteristics. Techniques for personality appraisal may allow us to estimate the individual's present *functioning* intelligence as compared with his capacity. The ability to organize percepts, to gain insight into a complicated arrangement of detail, to approach a situation in a systematic, orderly fashion, to be original, and to maintain control over thinking are just a few examples of characteristic modes of behavior which can be estimated from the various kinds of psychological tests that will be discussed later.

2. DESCRIPTIVE DIAGNOSTIC TECHNIQUES.   Several varieties of psychological tests are concerned primarily with describing *how* a person behaves, *how* he thinks, and *how* he feels or has felt at a particular time. Most of these tests are of the inventory type with channelized responses of the "Yes-No" variety, and they are regarded as essentially of descriptive value. Many tests of this kind are available. The particular test used may depend on the type of trait the clinician wishes to describe or measure. Most of these tests give trait or category subtest scores. Seldom will the actual category scores be particularly useful in making specific plans. However these scores may be of value if the clinician wishes to investigate problems such as the amount of preoccupation with bodily functions, the degree of guilt feelings, the degree of impulsiveness, tendency toward neuroticism, or kinds of values and interests. These descriptive techniques are useful in evaluating the degree to which particular traits may characterize a person. Descriptive tests of personality are probably most frequently used for screening purposes; and interest and value scales, for vocational advisement or personnel selection purposes.

3. EVALUATION OF THE DYNAMICS OF BEHAVIOR.   A group of psychological test devices are designed to give information concerning the *why* of adjustment. These devices, when they can be used, are of the greatest value in understanding behavior and in making recommendations and plans for the individual. Although they are of value in planning therapeutic procedures, they are not often used with clients who are in poor contact with reality. They can be used except with the with-

drawn or nonco-operative client, but it is sometimes difficult to appraise the degree of distortion involved in the responses. It is possible, however, to use even distorted material for therapeutic purposes. Freud certainly did so in his use of dreams.

The following list gives areas in which information can be gained through the use of such partially structured tests as sentence-completion tests. It is illustrative of the kind of data that can add to an understanding of the dynamics of behavior (6, p. 47):

    (a) Family: attitude toward the family unit and toward each parent.
    (b) Past: attitude toward the past, reactions, to previous frustrations and failures, and the effect of past experience on present behavior.
    (c) Drives: the primary motivating factors.
    (d) Inner states: the feelings experienced most frequently and the nature of the situations that arouse such feelings.
    (e) Goals: the ends toward which a person is striving.
    (f) Cathexes: objects, activities, or ideas which a person desires and for which he is willing to make sacrifices.
    (g) Energy: the energy level of a person and how this energy level is affected by stress and frustration.
    (h) Time perspective: attitude toward the past, present, and future.
    (i) Reactions to others: attitudes toward inferiors, equals, and superiors.
    (j) Reaction of others to the person: a person's impression of how others feel toward him.[5]

This list is intended to be suggestive only. In the evaluation of dynamics we are interested in any or all aspects of motivation, frustration, and learned patterns of adjustment which may contribute to a person's behaving as he does. There is no one kind of test that includes all these aspects. Descriptive tests, techniques for the evaluation of resources, case history material, interview data, and still other qualitative and quantitative observations may contribute to an understanding. In general, however, the most useful devices for this purpose are the so-called partially structured projective devices.

    [5] Adapted from "The Use of a Sentence Completion Test for the Diagnosis of Personality," by Morris L. Stein, *Journal of Clinical Psychology*, 3, 1947, 47–56. By permission of the *Journal of Clinical Psychology*.

STRUCTURE IN A TEST

The terms "structured," "partially structured," and "unstructured" will be used rather often in this text. Briefly, a structured test is one in which the response is channelized or structured by the test item or test situation. Most intelligence-test items are structured, since they require a specific kind of answer. Another example of a structured test is the personality inventory that requires a "yes" or "no" answer to a specific question. In unstructured tests the answer is left completely open. The subject may be presented with an inkblot or a cloud picture and asked to tell what he sees in the picture. Anything he sees is regarded as a projection since what he sees certainly depends on the individual's own perceptions and not on any characteristics of the stimulus. Partially structured devices, such as were referred to in connection with the evaluation of behavior dynamics, fall between these extremes. The subject's attention is directed toward certain areas of adjustment or certain topics, and then he is left on his own to respond as he desires. Examples of such techniques are sentence-completion tests, story-completion tests, pictures about which stories are told, doll play, and other similar tests and situational observation procedures.

SUMMARY

In this chapter we have attempted to present the philosophy of evaluation which underlies the discussion of psychological evaluation throughout Part IV. Our philosophy includes several facets, all of which are vital and fundamental if clinical and counseling psychology is to be a profession instead of merely a technical skill: We should always be attempting to understand the person so that we can plan or make recommendations for his future. Tests are not given haphazardly; they are carefully selected to give the most information relative to a particular client. We see our client in a particular environmental field, and if we are to understand his behavior within that field, we must study forces acting upon him as well as those from within him. We depend greatly on the case history and on situational observational data for information that will help us to understand these forces.

Finally, this chapter included some cautions against the uncritical use of tests as they apply to the individual case, and a description of the kinds of information which can be gained from psychological tests. We will now turn from the general to the specific and discuss the various components of the job of the psychologist, remembering always that the clinical method of evaluation is more than the sum of its parts.

BIBLIOGRAPHY

1. Harrower, M. R., "The evolution of a clinical psychologist." In Harrower, M. R. (ed.), *Training in clinical psychology*, Transactions of the First Conference, March 27–8, 1947, New York City. New York: Josiah Macy, Jr., Foundation, 1947.
2. Jones, E. S., "Subjective evaluations of personality." In Hunt, J. McV. (ed.), *Personality and the behavior disorders*. New York: Ronald, 1944.
3. Lewin, K., *A dynamic theory of personality*. New York: McGraw-Hill, 1935.
4. Menninger, W. C., "The relationship of clinical psychology and psychiatry." *Amer. Psychologist*, 1950, 5, 3–15.
5. Richards, T. W., *Modern clinical psychology*. New York: McGraw-Hill, 1946.
6. Stein, M. I., "The use of a sentence completion test for the diagnosis of personality." *J. Clin. Psychol.*, 3, 1947, 47–56.
7. Wechsler, D., *The range of human capacities* (2nd ed.). Baltimore: Williams & Wilkins, 1952.

14

The Anamnesis

THE WORD "ANAMNESIS" REFERS TO A REPRODUCING IN MEMORY or a recollection. The adjective "anamnestic" pertains to the aiding of recollection. In clinical psychology the term "anamnesis" is used to describe collectively the various areas of information which comprise the complete case history. The term is employed in this text because the original meaning of "anamnestic"—"aiding the memory"—implies one of the important functions of the case history which is sometimes neglected. Its function is to serve as an outline of questioning and prompting, a system of signposts pointing out pathways to be followed, a map of unexplored territory. It tends to prevent superficiality and snap judgment during individual evaluation. When used by the trained examiner who is cognizant of its weaknesses and limitations, but alert to follow up any significant leads that appear, it gives a picture of the individual which is of inestimable value. Although the anamnesis or case history as an instrument for exploring another human being's life and typical modes of behavior is incomplete, often unreliable, and unsatisfactory in many ways, we believe that no adequate substitute for it has ever been found.

HOW TO USE THE CASE HISTORY

One of the first steps in the clinical method is the gathering of background and historical information; it is by gathering such data that the clinician begins to approach the problems of his client scientifically. By using the anamnesis as a starting point, the psychologist can deduce hypotheses that will later be tested with the aid of the other diagnostic tools and observational procedures in which he is skilled. The case history has many limitations, however, and these must be recognized and compensated for if we are to be truly scientific in our clinical work.

The case history is generally acknowledged to be an integral part of the study of an individual's behavior; and for a full understanding of behavior it is considered necessary to have data on the individual's development. C. M. Louttit (9) states that in dealing with primary behavior disorders, it is always necessary to investigate experiences in the child's past history as well as in the present in order to understand more completely the problem that is presented. Edward B. Greene (3) stresses the importance of case histories and biographies in providing useful records for evaluating long-term trends in a person's development; through these records an attempt can be made to show how long-term trends are dependent upon environment, and how they are related to each other. Greene, who is best known as a test and measurement specialist, maintains that the most accurate predictions are to be made on the basis of careful case histories combined with test data; this is also our point of view.

The importance of this developmental or longitudinal approach has been emphasized by representatives of the psychobiological school of psychiatry. For example, Leland E. Hinsie (4) comments that before psychiatric treatment is initiated, a longitudinal survey must be made of the patient's life; it should cover all available aspects of the client's activities from the period of birth up to the age period at which he appears for therapy. The value of the case history is recognized by many other psychiatric writers. Nolan D. C. Lewis (8, p. 14) writes:

> In the study of psychiatric patients, a good account of the previous history of the patient, the physical and mental development, and the manner in which the disorder began is very important. Without this information, it will be quite impossible in many cases to understand the nature of the disorder or to make a satisfactory diagnostic grouping or to outline treatment.

Edward A. Strecker, Franklin G. Ebaugh, and Jack R. Ewalt (14) also stress the importance of the case history and present an extensive outline for the history. The case history is the basic tool of and principal contribution from the field of social work. Still another discipline, speech pathology, has devoted a great deal of attention to the case history. Writers such as Lee Edward Travis (16), Wendell Johnson *et al.* (5), and Charles Van Riper (17) describe its usefulness. In his textbook on principles and methods of speech correction Van Riper has outlined what is probably one of the most extensive and detailed case history forms ever published.

G. Wilson Shaffer and Richard S. Lazarus (13) have reviewed a number of discussions on the uses and techniques of the case study:

Gordon W. Allport (1) has been a strong advocate of the method. John Dollard (2), too, has come to the defense of the life-history technique and has established some tentative standards for its use. Lewin (7) describes the case-study technique as fundamental to a non-Aristotelian science of behavior. Edmund G. Williamson and John G. Darley (18) plead for longer and more comprehensive history methods for use in guidance work. In educational and vocational guidance and counseling, record keeping and the accumulation of historical materials have long been regarded as important tools.

From these views, which are quite typical of the major portion of psychological opinion, we can see that the case history is widely advocated in psychological literature. There is, however, a school of thought somewhat in opposition to the taking of a formal case history. This opposing view is held by representatives of the nondirective or client-centered philosophy of clinical practice. Carl R. Rogers (12), although granting that a full case history is highly significant for a complete and satisfactory diagnosis, maintains that in the true counseling process the counselor gradually accumulates knowledge of the genuinely dynamic forces in the client's experience; and it is his belief that the individual is more likely to reveal these experiences in a counseling situation than in an interview for the purpose of collecting information. He acknowledges that without the case history there may be large gaps in the counselor's knowledge of the superficial and outward events in the client's life but he contends that gathering a suitable history interferes at times with the treatment process. Rogers states his view of case-history taking as (p. 81):

> When the counselor says in effect, "I should like to have you tell me about your problems and yourself, your background and your development, your education and your medical history, your family experiences and your social environment," he also implies the additional assurance, "and then I can tell you how to solve your problems." [1]

We should realize that it is quite possible, in fact probable, that information disclosed during the counseling process, when the client is ready to relate it, may be more valid than information gathered in an intensive interview situation. However, under some circumstances we may be required to make certain recommendations concerning a client and time may not always allow us to establish a counseling relationship before we search for historical information. In these situations, if in no others, we will need to secure an extensive history.

One of the factors that tends to discourage the use of the case his-

[1] By permission from *Counseling and Psychotherapy*, by Carl R. Rogers, published by Houghton Mifflin Co. Copyright 1942 by Carl R. Rogers.

tory is the amount of time involved in securing a complete history. Often the time available for working with the client does not seem to allow for gathering extensive data. The question of how much data should be collected is pertinent to this time problem, and there does not seem to be any categorical answer. Ideally, and for the purpose of research, it may be desirable to have extensive and identical kinds of information about every client. Practically, the nature of the task to be done necessarily imposes certain limits. It would seem that information should be limited to that which will enable the clinician to come to some adequate conclusions concerning the client and his problems within the limits of the availability and dependability of the sources of information. The limitations may be set by the availability of historical information or of persons who can give the information. If the information is available, there seems to be no excuse for not gathering it. Time limitations are not seen as sufficient excuse for omission or curtailment of the case history.

Another obstacle in the use of the case history is the difficulty of reconstructing the history of the individual. It is sometimes not easy to get a valid record of events that occurred several years ago. This is attributable to the rather vague memories of the client, his friends, his parents, and his teachers. The case history is not always a reliable document and cross-checking with other sources of information is necessary in order for it to contribute to the understanding of behavior with a maximum degree of significance. Furthermore, on this same point of reliability, Greene (3) has noted that case histories on the same person taken by two different investigators sometimes differ in very significant aspects. Lawson G. Lowrey (10) warns that in using the rather detailed outline of the usual case history, there is a tendency to use it too rigidly; this results in a stereotyped approach to the patient and to the recording, which eventually becomes sterile, failing to give a picture of the patient as a living, functioning individual. Van Riper (17) points out that when the case history is used by a poor examiner who merely asks questions and records the answers, assembling a mass of irrelevant information, it loses much of its significance. We cannot deny the importance of such comments. However they should be regarded as criticisms of the ways in which the case history may be collected or used, not of the method itself.

In planning for the future and making recommendations for the client, one of the most important limitations to be kept in mind is that the case history may not always be sufficient as a basis for arriving at conclusions about the client and for working out counseling and therapeutic programs for him. It provides, however, a first orientation and serves as a powerful adjunct to the other clinical methods at the disposal of the clinician. While the case history usually does not, of itself, provide a basis for complete understanding or for recommendations for the future, it does have important implications for planning. One of the more significant would seem to be that the gathering of complete data pro-motes an accurate evaluation of events leading up to the present and pre-vents superficiality and snap judgment. Furthermore, the case history provides the basis for hypotheses about the client that can be checked by other observations based on interview and test data.

Frederick C. Thorne (15) notes that the use of the history tends to reduce the number of errors in diagnosis which are due to the examiner's reaction to superficial appearances, to reasoning from false premises and inadequate evidence, to superimposing preconceived theories that have no valid application, and to faulty corroboration of facts. In addition, Thorne notes that in a situation in which different etiological factors may produce an identical result, or in a situation in which one etiological factor may bring out different personality reactions in different individ-uals, it is essential to secure enough of the history to show the develop-mental sequences involved in each particular case. In evaluating, making recommendations, or planning counseling or therapy, it seems logical that the approach be based on facts presented by the client rather than on facts the examiner sees which may support the theory of his own in-doctrination. A complete case history should permit the facts of the case to be viewed more discriminately and thus assist in a more scientific methodology. Thorne points out its usefulness in determining the truth in instances in which problems of interpersonal relationships result in con-flicting accounts that confuse the picture. He would attempt, through use of the complete case history, to check all significant facts from as many impartial sources as possible.

Lowrey (10) observes that the family history often throws light on hereditary factors involved, and frequently the health history of the fam-ily, carried back at least to the grandparents, reveals important factors regarding the biological stability of the client. An adequate history enables us to recognize the relevance of health factors and to trace out their etiological significance. Along this same line, the history may clarify the situation in which there is doubt regarding the functional or organic nature of the client's complaints by determining the nature and time of the onset of the disorder. If the symptoms have been present for years without material change in the condition of the client, the findings would tend to indicate a functional origin; whereas sudden or abrupt person-ality changes may suggest a rapidly developing organic lesion. An ac-tual situation is not usually as simple as this illustration, but it is pre-sented to show that the clinician will make use of the case history in this type of decision as well as in other differential diagnostic decisions.

Paul W. Preu (11) discusses the obvious but sometimes ignored fact that a record of the client's actual behavior in the past indicates more or less clearly what may reasonably be expected of him in like situations in the future, provided, of course, that no radical or significant influences have altered the pattern of behavior. The case history should include a record of such influences, and the diagnostic worker can then still make a prediction of future events in the light of past behavior, therapeutic activities engaged in, and resultant developments. Thorne, on this same point, calls attention to the experience of neuropsychiatric examiners engaged in selective service and Army induction work; he believes that it points to the conclusion that an adequate case history is the most reliable source of information upon which reliable predictions of future behavior can be made.

The case history is also of value in uncovering or identifying multiple causation and constellations of contributing factors. Another important point is that test data in combination with historical data allows the clinician to consider factors that may not be evident or even suggested in test information alone; the interpretation of test protocols is usually made richer when integrated with the case history and the suggestions of dynamics coming from it.

The above discussion indicates some of the diagnostic implications of the case history. It furnishes leads and indicates points of departure for the detailed study of the client's behavior, his problems, and his environment, and these leads may appear at any point in the history. The history also provides information of value in predicting future behavior when the degree to which the present illness deviates from the client's usual functioning is seen by contrasting his present with his past adjustment. A complete listing of the uses of the history is impossible since each client differs and the contribution that historical data can make varies from client to client.

SOURCES OF INFORMATION

There are three primary sources of information for the case history which the clinician should consider: interviews, formal records, and agency reports. While these sources will probably not all be fruitful, and they are not the only sources to be considered, they offer the best general opportunities for obtaining the amount and kind of information the examiner is seeking.

The interview is the most common source of information for the case history. Interviews are held not only with the client himself, but with members of his family, his neighbors, friends, teachers, employer, and others. We must remember that information gathered in these interviews is likely to be colored by the bias of the individual being interviewed. This coloring may be unconscious or it may be deliberate, but the clinician must be alert to notice discrepancies, contradictions, and other signs of bias. Reports of one individual should be weighed against those of another in order to make the best evaluation of the validity of the information gathered. Caution must also be exercised to qualify certain information in terms of the possible inadequacy of the memory of the informant. Cross-checking is an important control. The adjustment of the informant must be considered, as well as such factors as rapport in the interview situation and motivation of the interviewee to protect himself, his interests, or the interests of the client—the last often playing a part in situations in which pensions or other compensations are involved. Many other reasons for conservatism in acceptance of interview information exist. It is important to validate all information and weigh it in terms of the total picture.

Available formal records can also furnish information. Developmental-history data can probably be obtained more accurately from a carefully kept developmental record or baby book than from incidents recalled by a parent. Medical records, when available, give a long-range picture of the physical development and health which can be regarded as reasonably objective. School records give much information concerning subjects, achievement, promotions or failures, teacher evaluations, extracurricular activities, and the like. Unfortunately there are wide variations in grading standards, and most schools do not keep as complete records as we might desire. Samples of school work are often revealing. Records from the court and police, truant officers, hospitals, and many other sources all serve to round out the history.

Agency reports provide a further source of information. If the client has been known to a social welfare agency, it is usually possible to obtain a report from the agency on the individual's socioeconomic environment. When the client has been referred by some other agency, such as the Veterans Administration, the referral is often accompanied by a report, or one can usually be secured.

These are, of course, not the only sources of information. All possible sources should be canvassed, and none should be ignored.

COMPLETENESS AND FORM OF THE CASE–HISTORY RECORD

The procedure for gathering case-history material varies from the extreme of using a diagnostic form, with a number of items which are to be completed or checked by the clinician in a formal fashion, to that of simply noting whatever historical information may be voluntarily proffered by the informant without any prompting questions whatsoever. A number of possibilities exist between these extremes. For example, the history may be collected in narrative fashion with the clinician asking certain leading questions relative to general areas of information. Biographies are sometimes collected from the parent, or autobiographies are written by the client. There does not appear to be any hard and fast rule about the systematization or formality involved either in collecting or recording case-history information.

The case history should be as complete as possible, with the formality of its collection dependent on a number of factors which will be discussed. All available information should be collected, even though at the time it may not seem to have relevance to the problems under evaluation. In the working situation the psychologist seldom has a basis for deciding in advance what will be important, and unless the approach is very broad, significant information may be completely neglected. This may of course result in the collection of information that appears to have no relevance to the problem. George A. Kelly (6) has emphasized the necessity for the clinician's constantly forming "little hypotheses" and following them up in order to test them. This procedure would presumably result in his exploring areas that are relevant to the hypotheses— a selective procedure rather than a broad general collection of all available information. The clinician should constantly attempt to form hypotheses. However, he should never take the chance of omitting certain information that might permit of alternate or complementary, or even higher-order hypotheses simply because his selective procedure leads him in a very specific direction.

We have no completely adequate explanation of behavior, since all personality and behavior theories are tentative maps of unknown territory. Consequently, if we are to be completely objective and scientific in our diagnostic procedure, we must gather together all the facts and background data so that we will be able to see unique, complex, interacting, etiological, and developmental factors. In other words, we need to survey the total territory and then determine the direction to follow. Otherwise we may find ourselves taking the first road that seems clear and following it to a dead end, then coming back to find another, etc., before we eventually find the one that leads to a particular destination which may, in turn, be only one of several that might have been reached. Thorne (15, p. 135), again, summarizes this nicely by saying, "Instead of trying to find the facts to fit some preconceived theory, it is necessary to find a theory to fit the facts."

The formality and completeness with which case histories are collected and recorded depend on a number of practical and realistic problems. Keeping in mind that our intention is to be as comprehensive as possible, we will turn to a consideration of these practicalities.

1. THE EXPERIENCE OF THE CLINICIAN. It would seem clear that, the more experienced the clinician is, the less need he should have for dependence on a questionnaire, a checklist, or other guides for the col-

lection of historical information. As a matter of fact his checklist will probably be in his memory, and he will systematically cover the areas which he knows from experience are important. The experienced clinician is more apt to think in terms of interaction and multiple causation than single causation. His experience has equipped him with a particular method or procedure which in his hands is often more efficient and effective than any standardized form. Often he can direct the interview more freely and establish a better relationship without having a form before him. He may even prefer not to take notes during the interview. To the extent that professional judgment enters into the situation, he is undoubtedly better qualified than the less experienced clinician to operate without any formal outline or form.

The danger of omitting valuable data necessitates that the less experienced clinician follow definite guides. These may be systematically mapped out on a form to be completed either during or after the interview, or the clinician may use a systematic outline with which he is so familiar that he implicitly checks off items as he proceeds with the interview. Our own preference in the instance of the beginning clinician is for the use of an outline that he completes in the interview situation; with practice, he will place less dependence on it and eventually he will be able to dispense with the physical form, writing up his findings in a systematic fashion for record purposes immediately after the interview. The use of a form or outline facilitates the problem of record keeping.

It is sometimes said that the use of an actual form in the interview situation interferes with the interpersonal relationship. It is our experience that this is a minor problem which can be handled by most clinicians with most clients. Clients, and particularly the parents and teachers who may be informants, usually appreciate a businesslike, systematic approach, seldom objecting to the use of forms or to note taking. In fact, individuals have been known to ask why the clinician does not take notes and to question the clinician's ability to remember everything that is said. Even though experienced clinicians are better qualified than the less experienced to dispense with the actual forms of outlines, many continue to use them. The issue becomes, then, for the experienced clinician one of individual preference and efficient operation, but the novice should always use systematic guides.

2. THE WORKING SITUATION. The character of the working situation and its policies often determine the characteristics of the case history. In a clinic or hospital where a number of persons co-operate in collecting information, or where one person collects certain parts of the history and another integrates or reviews it, the use of systematic forms of outlines is most efficient. It is discouraging to have to search through a mass of information for specific data. A synchronized system, followed

by all who work together, is helpful. We have already suggested the advantages of having systematic, complete information for research purposes.

The clinician in private practice or working relatively independently of other professional personnel, assuming that he has a procedure that he himself can follow and understand, can be more flexible in his adherence to a definite procedure. Even though the person not working closely with others or in a formal agency has somewhat more choice, he should always proceed on the basis of optimum service to the client. Although there are those who argue that a violation of personal confidences is involved, most clinicians agree that it is advantageous, and probably ethically desirable, that records be kept. The clinician, of course, will follow the policies of the place in which he works, but when several professional workers co-operate, or when an agency engages in follow-up procedures, systematic and organized records are necessary.

3. THE PURPOSE OF THE EXAMINATION.   The purpose of the evaluation varies, and it may determine the procedures to be followed. If the history is taken as a part of a total examination to which several contribute, or if the purpose is to furnish a report or recommendations to other people, the procedure will usually be quite systematic and direct. Since the need in both cases is to get the maximum information in the minimum time, a degree of organization and formality is necessary. On the other hand, if the client is referred for counseling or therapy or has referred himself, the period for collecting historical information can be less formal. The client who is quite anxious and has referred himself to a counselor may not be appreciative if discussion of his most important problems is set aside for a time while a number of questions are answered about his family, his school, and his occupation. This is not to deny the importance of historical information for therapy planning. We are only suggesting that taking the history when the client himself is asking for help may be distributed over the first several interviews; it need not necessarily be concentrated in one period. Many counselors structure the first few interviews as therapy planning sessions and fill in the case history by directive questions woven into the discussion of the presenting problem. However some clients may wish to present as much information as possible early in the period, and they should be allowed to do so.

These remarks apply only to the taking of the history from the client himself. Insofar as it is possible, the client permitting, we should supplement information given by the client through interviews with others. Such interviews present a different problem, and completeness and systematization would seem to be indicated. When a responsible person refers himself or is referred to a clinician or clinic, we should never attempt to gather information about him from other sources without his permission. To summarize, when the purpose of the examination is diagnostic or when early therapy planning is desired, an immediate formal history is suggested, or if time permits and a series of conferences is scheduled, case-history material can be gathered as a part of the early interviews.

4. THE AGE OF THE CLIENT.   Extensive systematic case-history data is easier to gather when the client is a child than when the client is an adult since parents are more often available, as are also teachers and other sources of information. With a child the purpose of the evaluation is usually to make recommendations or to plan treatment, and systematic information must be gathered in a minimum of time. It is also important to note that case-history information is generally much more dependable when the client is a child. This is due to the freshness of memory as well as to the availability of informants. On the contrary, in dealing with adults, supplementary anamnestic information may not be available; in this case the client must give all the information that the clinician is to have. The diagnostic personality interview, which will be discussed in Chapter 15, may have to be the source of historical material. Some clinicians prefer to have the adult client write an autobiography. This is a satisfactory procedure if the client is capable of such spontaneous expression. In our experience it is usually necessary to give the client some guidance for his autobiography. In order to insure that important areas of information or time segments are not omitted, topics for him to write on can be suggested, or he can be given an outline to follow.

Complete and systematically collected case-history records are necessary for a scientific approach to the client's problems. The less experienced the clinician, the more organized the working situation, the younger the client, and the greater the need for early diagnostic information, the more necessary is the formal record; and any deviation from systematization in these instances should be made with caution.

THE REGISTRATION

Whenever an individual applies to a psychologist, social service agency, mental hygiene clinic, or any other individual or organized agency for professional help, he should be registered. This also holds true when a parent or teacher refers the client to any clinic or clinician; in both cases the responsible person should register the client. Registration data (whether it is called by this or some other name) is important for reasons that will be clear when the content is discussed; at this point we are considering its importance for reasons other than content. Ethically, we must not assume the responsibility for another person unless that responsibility is delegated to us. We have no right to enter another person's private world unless permission has been given to us. The registration serves the purpose of formally giving that permission and delegating that responsibility.

The registration may be very formal, with a trained social worker or receptionist actually taking specific interview information from the client or from the person responsible for him; or it may be quite informal and consist only of filling out a card or taking certain information on the occasion of the first interview. The bias in the present discussion is for the more complete registration. A sample registration form is presented as Figure 1. It is similar to the one we have used for many years and in a number of different working situations. Occasionally information is purposely omitted or is not available, but the basic outline is followed with each client, child or adult, diagnostic or counseling, private or clinic. This form is more extensive than the usual registration form as it is designed to serve several purposes. It can be used as a guide to the interview or as a record form, or both. It is constructed for a clinician's or clinic's use. It is not a report form, since a report sent to another clinician or agency, or used for presentation to a staff conference, is made up of an organized summarization of pertinent information, not of a collection of facts. The case report should describe the person and not simply contain a collection of data. Such forms as the registration form and others to be described in this chapter, then, are tools and not ends in and of themselves.

The registration form (Figure 1) comprises what might be regarded as intake interview information. It includes some information that may be covered on other forms, such as the educational history and the family history, and it will be useful for the assignment of a clinician or clinicians, for making decisions about psychometrics, and for other plans for the diagnostic or counseling procedures. The reason for including some of the items on the form may not be immediately evident. As important as it would seem to be always to note the exact date upon which information is recorded, many instances occur in which this is not done. Sometimes only the day and month are recorded. The director of a clinic can feel helpless and somewhat embarrassed when he receives an inquiry about a client several years after the client has visited the clinic and discovers that the date of registration was not recorded, or that it was recorded as "March 15." He does not know whether it was 1945 or 1950. *All information on all records should be dated—exactly dated and fully dated.* Even a scrap of paper bearing a note about the client should be dated. The name of the clinician who registers the client should be recorded; there are many reasons for this, but often this is useful when there is some lack of clarity in the record—the person who recorded the

Figure 1

PURDUE UNIVERSITY PSYCHOLOGICAL CLINICS
REGISTRATION

Date _____   Registered by _____

1. Client's Name _____ Sex _____ Birth date _____
   Address _____ Telephone _____
   Race _____ Religion _____ Birthplace _____
   Nationality _____ School _____ Grade _____
   Dependents (sex, age, relation) _____
   _____

   _____
   Present activity _____
   If a student, encircle appropriate
   year level   1 2 3 4 5 6 7 8 9 10 11 12
                          College   1 2 3 4 5 6 7 8
   If not, encircle highest level
   completed   1 2 3 4 5 6 7 8 9 10 11 12
                          College   1 2 3 4 5 6 7 8
   If in grade or high school
      Name of principal _____
         Mailing address _____ Telephone _____
      Name of most interested teacher _____
         Mailing address _____ Telephone _____
   If in college or ex-college, Major _____ Minor _____
      Name of adviser or major professor _____
         Mailing address _____ Telephone _____

2. Name of parent or guardian _____
      Mailing address _____ Telephone _____

3. Name of person referring _____
      Mailing address _____ Telephone _____

4. Name of informant _____
      Mailing address _____ Telephone _____

5. What are the problems prompting the referral? _____
   _____

   _____

6. When were these problems first observed? _____
   _____

   _____

7. What conditions are aggravating? _____
   _____

FIGURE 1 (*continued*)

PURDUE UNIVERSITY PSYCHOLOGICAL CLINICS
REGISTRATION

8. When least noticeable? _____

_____

9. What corrective measures have been or are being taken? _____

_____

10. What changes have come with treatment or the passing of time? __

_____

_____

11. Date of most recent medical examination _____
    Results of this examination _____

_____

_____

Name of Physician _____
Mailing address _____ Telephone _____
Is permission given for the clinic to request information from
this physician? Yes _____ No _____

12. Other information, clinician's impressions, etc. _____

_____

_____

13. Disposition _____

_____

_____

information may be able to reconstruct his meaning. All records should be made as specific and clear as possible, but when a record is vague it is important to attempt reconstruction.

Item 1 includes identification data. The sex as well as the name should be indicated, since not all names convey the sex of the client. The birth date is requested—this gives more information than a mere statement of age. The clinician may have to perform a little mathematics to figure the age, but, in the interest of space saving, we record only the birth date. Address and telephone number require no explanation Noting of race, religion, nationality, occupation, birthplace, marital status, and dependents is done for various reasons; some items are important for identification purposes only, others to give some cue to cultural factors, and all are important if we are to describe and plan adequately for the client. We record present activity as a person may have an occupation but temporarily be working at some other kind of job, going to school, unemployed or even in the military services. These items, as well as those concerning school level and names of teachers, advisers, etc., will not apply to all clients, but they are important insofar as they do apply. Occasionally a student will resist giving the name of an adviser. To forestall this at the Purdue Clinic, we reassure the client that we will not contact or give information without permission, and we do not push him for information if he does not wish to give it. (Incidentally, in a college or university clinic, it is enlightening to discover the number of clients who are not able to give the name of their academic adviser.)

Item 2 includes the name and address of the parent or guardian. Reasons for this information may vary from client to client. With students and children, the name of parent or guardian is necessary for several reasons, such as for emergency contact and for making appointments. With an adult, this information may be needed by the social worker in completing the case history. In the outpatient setting the client's permission is always requested before any contacts are made, and the client may be reassured of this. With hospital patients, permission for making contacts is usually given or implied upon admission.

The *person referring* pertains to direct referrals such as by the physician, the school teacher, the adviser, the welfare worker. In direct referrals a report is usually required and identification data is necessary. Adults may refer themselves, and in such instances the word "self" is inserted. Clinics sometimes inquire as to whether anyone suggested that the person come to the clinic. The principal reason for this would seem to be curiosity or to evaluate how well informed the clientele may be concerning the clinic services. This is not a referral and should be recorded as "self, suggested by. . . ." The name of the informant is important in all forms. The informant is the person supplying information. He (or she) might be a parent or a teacher, and occasionally may be the client himself. Bias is inevitable and the degree of familiarity with a client's problems varies. The teacher's appraisal may vary from that of the parent and vice versa. The informant, in the case of adults referring themselves to outpatient services, may well be the client and the form should so indicate.

The statement of the problem is not expected to be detailed but simply to give the character of the presenting difficulty. If the client himself wishes to go into detail, he should be allowed to do so. Also, if the registering clinician is the counselor who will continue with treatment, the statement may be quite detailed. In any organized agency where the mental hygiene team is functioning, it is necessary that the client make a frank statement of problem. When the registering is done by a receptionist or secretary in a counseling center or for a clinician in private practice, the client may not be urged to make a complete statement if he does not wish to. In the Purdue Counseling Center the practice is to say, whenever there is reticence, "Shall we say the problem is personal? You can talk it over with your counselor."

If there is no reticence, the person registering the client can go on to Items 6, 7, and 8. No discussion of these items would appear to be necessary. Items 9 and 10 are important, both in providing information for planning and as a matter of professional principle. If several persons are working with the client or have seen him, their efforts should be co-ordinated. Although this form does not provide a space for so indicating, the client may be requested to give permission for the clinic to ask for a report from other clinicians or agencies with whom he has worked. For example, many clients at the Purdue Counseling Center have previously been to the Vocational Guidance Center or are being advised by personnel at that Center. In these instances permission is requested before asking for a report from the Guidance Center.

Item 11 is regarded by the majority of clinical psychologists as of major importance. The only way a clinical psychologist can avoid "playing doctor" in the event that there are health implications is by requiring routine physical examinations. If the client has not had a recent examination or if a report of the examination is not available, the clinician should request that he have one, either by the physician of the client's choice or by the medical consultant associated with the clinic or clinician. The statement of results of medical examination given by the informant is not considered a statement of final diagnosis and is always corroborated by a medical report, but it is useful as tentative information pending verification.

"Other Information" may be used to record any data gathered at this time that is not included under other headings. It is impossible to anticipate the extent of such information since many unique and valuable topics may be discussed.

The registering clinician's impressions should always be recorded and designated as clinical observations to differentiate them from the data given by the informant. Such notations as "very anxious," "disorganized," "needs immediate attention," "very defensive," "seems to have considerable insight," "poorly groomed and careless about appearance," "mother very emotional," "teacher extremely co-operative" are just a few of the appropriate remarks that might be placed here. The alert clinician will nearly always have considerable material to record. "Disposition" refers to the immediate disposition of the client's case by the registering clinician. Notations should be made of further appointments, arrangements for preliminary or treatment planning staffs, referral to other agencies, and the like.

This form is presented for purposes of illustration only. Clinics and clinicians will have their own preferences for organization of registration information. Most agencies will have special kinds of data which they will want to gather. Certain information included in this form would not be of interest to a child guidance clinic. Other items would be of no interest to clinic dealing only with adults. It is important to remember that a registration form should not be used as a questionnaire, but rather as a guide to the interview and a recording tool. No attempt has been made to suggest the manner of asking questions; the clinician must learn to phrase his questions in the manner which best suits his own personality and which will be understood by the interviewee. Skill of this nature comes through supervised practice in interviewing. More will be said later about techniques of interviewing, but the most important rule about interviewing is that the clinician be completely familiar with the purpose of his interview.

Registration data is just as confidential and restricted as is any other material concerning any client. This point cannot be taken too seriously. Care must be taken to guard the confidentiality of this material. Most clinics require that it be kept in locked central files and removed only by authorized personnel, who must return it as soon as they have finished with it.

During an oral registration it is a common experience to have the client or the informant ask questions concerning the efficacy of corrective measures to be taken, the probable diagnosis, or the competence of the professional workers in the clinic. For example, a parent may ask, "Do you think my child is feeble-minded?" or "Do you think they will say that my child should go to a special school?" Instead of offering false reassurance to the parent by saying, "Oh, of course not!" or "I doubt it!" the clinician or worker registering the child should say, "Our examination will cover that point and whatever our opinion may be, it will be discussed with you quite frankly." An adult may say, "A friend of mine got a great amount of help here. Do you think they will help me?" Again, the worker must not either over-reassure or appear discouraging but must answer in such a way as to postpone the answer. The worker may answer by saying, "Many persons are able to gain help from psychological services. I'm sure we will do all we are able to do to help you solve your problems." Such answers are not intended to be entirely evasive but if parents or clients are over-reassured at the time of registration, the clinician is placed in an embarrassing position if unfavorable results must be reported at a later date. Such over-reassurance may also encourage withholding morbid but valuable information that might otherwise be volunteered. In fact, one parent, when told by the social worker that she doubted if a child was feeble-minded, instead of returning to the clinic for scheduled examinations, reported to the school that the clinic had told her that the child was of normal intelligence. Another adult client described his problem as a reading difficulty and asked the registering clinician whether she thought this reading problem could cause all the trouble he was having academically. Because the clinician answered that it certainly could, the client withheld information concerning a traumatic and chronic source of anxiety from his counselor for more than six months. When the anxiety-producing topic was finally broached and the client asked why he had not mentioned it earlier, he said, "That other clinician said my poor reading was causing all my difficulty, and I saw no reason for bringing up all of this other stuff." The problem of over-reassurance is not unique to registration; it applies to all clinical interviewing, both diagnostic and therapeutic.

EDUCATIONAL HISTORY

The educational history of children is usually completed in an interview with a representative of the school, preferably the classroom teacher. Quite frequently school records that provide quantitative and qualitative information can be made available to the clinic. If a school representative is not available, the parents may be able to give the information desired; however, for several reasons — such as lack of information, bias, or the possibility that behavior in school is at variance with that at home — it is best to get some report from the school, especially if the child is in elementary or secondary school. Data concerning preschool or nursery school life can usually be ascertained in the sociological interview or can be made the basis of a special report.

With college students and adults, information will probably be gathered from the client himself. It can be verified to some extent, if this is thought necessary, by securing school records, transcripts of credit, and the like. The social worker collecting data on the hospitalized patient often searches out school records and gathers as much information as possible from the family concerning his educational history. Outpatient clients should always be asked to give this information, and they may even have to request that records be sent to the clinic since most colleges do not release transcripts except at the request of the student or former student. This information, too, is confidential material, and the clinic must respect this. All the information that can be gathered is important. Educational information is particularly valuable as an index of past ability in cases of organicity, psychotic behavior, or in any instance where it is important to compare present with past performance. With the child, school is such an integral part of his present life space that it is naturally necessary to study his behavior in the educational setting.

Figure 2 is an Educational History form. It is another illustrative record form presented merely as a guide or outline for discussion. The importance of date, name of interviewer, as well as the name of the client,

FIGURE 2

PURDUE UNIVERSITY PSYCHOLOGICAL CLINICS
EDUCATIONAL HISTORY

Date _____   Interviewer _____

1. Name of Client _____ Age _____

2. Name of Informant _____ Relation to Client _____
   Mailing Address _____ Telephone _____

3. Date of beginning school _____ Age at beginning school _____
   Level (kindergarten, 1st grade, other) _____
   School _____
   Reaction to first school experiences _____
   _____

4. Present school level, if in school
   (encircle one)   1 2 3 4 5 6 7 8 9 10 11 12
                             College 1 2 3 4 5 6 7 8
   Highest level attained, if not in
   school   1 2 3 4 5 6 7 8 9 10 11 12
                             College 1 2 3 4 5 6 7 8

5. Have any years been repeated? Yes ____ No ____
   If so, which years? _____
   Reasons _____

6. List different schools which have been attended (continue on reverse
   side if necessary)

	Years Attended	Average Achievement
Elementary		
1. _____	_____	_____ _____
2. _____	_____	_____ _____
3. _____	_____	_____ _____
4. _____	_____	_____ _____
Junior High School		
1. _____	_____	_____ _____
2. _____	_____	_____ _____
High School		
1. _____	_____	_____ _____
2. _____	_____	_____ _____
College		
1. _____	_____	_____ _____
2. _____	_____	_____ _____
3. _____	_____	_____ _____

FIGURE 2 (*continued*)

PURDUE UNIVERSITY PSYCHOLOGICAL CLINICS
EDUCATIONAL HISTORY

Graduate or Professional
1. _____   _____ _____
2. _____   _____ _____

7. Recently studied subjects

Liked Subjects	Grade	Disliked Subjects	Grade	Difficult Subjects	Grade	Easy Subjects	Grade
_____	____	_____	____	_____	____	_____	____
_____	____	_____	____	_____	____	_____	____
_____	____	_____	____	_____	____	_____	____
_____	____	_____	____	_____	____	_____	____

8. Vocational plans _____
_____

9. Vocational training _____
_____

10. Avocational training _____
_____

11. Number of years of further schooling expected _____
Difficulties _____

12. Number of absences per month _____ Reasons _____
_____

13. Organizations belonged to   Offices held
_____   _____
_____   _____
_____   _____

14. Avocational interests   Proficiency
_____   _____
_____   _____
_____   _____

15. Describe parental co-operation with school by rating the following items

	(Circle) High	Low
Conferences	1 2 3 4 5	
Insight	1 2 3 4 5	
Pressure	1 2 3 4 5	
Stability	1 2 3 4 5	
Faultfinding	1 2 3 4 5	

Comment _____
_____

FIGURE 2 *(continued)*

PURDUE UNIVERSITY PSYCHOLOGICAL CLINICS
EDUCATIONAL HISTORY

16. Listed below are a number of attitudes which may be characteristic of the client. Rate the client on the continuum represented by the trait.

Dependent–Independent	1 2 3 4 5
Lazy–Industrious	1 2 3 4 5
Noisy–Quiet	1 2 3 4 5
Disinterested–Interested	1 2 3 4 5
Quiet–Talkative	1 2 3 4 5
Interest Narrow–Broad	1 2 3 4 5
Quarrelsome–Friendly	1 2 3 4 5
Rebellious–Co-operative	1 2 3 4 5
Tired–Energetic	1 2 3 4 5
Restless–Relaxed	1 2 3 4 5
Distracted–Calm	1 2 3 4 5
Cries easily–Mature	1 2 3 4 5
Follower–Leader	1 2 3 4 5
Unpoplar–Popular	1 2 3 4 5

Comments _____

_____

17. Other information _____

_____

his age, and the name and address of the informant have been discussed with respect to the registration, and the same rationale applies for this form. Age is recorded here, as well as on the registration, for ease of referral and interpretation. Items 3 and 4 are self-explanatory in that they simply include specific facts that are necessary for the evaluation of progress. The question regarding reaction to first school experiences should not be omitted regardless of the age level of the informant. Item 5 refers to any grades repeated and the reasons, if known. The reason for repeating is often other than failure, for example, changing schools, illness, or even parental desires. We must not confuse such reasons with failures, and the reasons themselves may be important in the over-all evaluation of the clinical picture. Listing of schools attended has several significant applications since it may give an indication of the stability of the home and family organization. Frequently it is well to inquire about the reason for the change and to make some notation of it. The continuity of education is certainly affected by school changes. Certain subject difficulties can sometimes be traced to gaps in training due to these changes. Also of considerable significance is the effect on the child's personality due to the breaking up of friendships and the making of new adjustments in new schools.

The informant and the client (if the informant is another person) can be queried concerning reactions to recently studied subjects. Answers can be forced somewhat by asking for listing of liked, disliked, difficult, and easy subjects; this tends to eliminate the response that they are all liked or that they are all difficult. Usually there is unevenness in difficulty and in interest, and this is diagnostically significant. The terms "liked" and "disliked" are used here instead of "interesting" or "uninteresting." The adult will tend to make more meaning out of the word "interest," but since we are desirous of getting something of the feeling aspects of the client's reactions to the subject-matter areas, we use the terms "liked" and "disliked" in order to elicit more information.

Vocational plans may have to be interpreted in terms of the identity of the informant. Teachers will usually give the client's plans, but parents frequently give their own plans for the client and for this reason they should probably be queried as to how the client reacts to these plans. Specific vocational training should be noted. Trade school and on-the-job training is certainly important. The major study of the college student may be applicable. Avocational training refers to music, dancing, drama, recreational training, and the like. The number of years of further schooling expected and difficulties that might be encountered is also a question that may be answered differently by parent, teacher, and client. If we have all points of view, we may see interesting comparisons. The difficulties that may be anticipated often vary from lack of ability or money to a host of other problems.

The attendance record of a student is revealing and should be ascertained fairly exactly. Typical reasons given for absences are valuable. Social activities, popularity, and leadership experiences are suggested by Item 13 concerning organizations belonged to. Because there are such vast differences between schools in the number of organizations to which a person can belong, a notation should designate the number of organizations belonged to as high, low, or average. The client's avocational interests are listed under Item 14. Item 15 concerns parental co-operation with the school. The clinician should ask about the teacher's estimate of the insight of the parents, the degree of pressure at home, the stability of the parents, the amount of criticism directed toward the school, and the number of conferences held and then rate the responses on the rating scale. Qualitative observations should be recorded, since in many instances these are more important than the ratings. Ratings will be based on the clinician's evaluation of the teacher's report. This item, of course, has meaning only for the school-age child. Item 16 also is relevant only for the school-age child. The teacher should be asked to describe the child in terms of each of the characteristics given. The clinician can, with practice, learn to assign a quite meaningful rating to the child. This list is fairly exhaustive, but other characteristics are almost always mentioned; these should be recorded under "comment." The last item simply provides a blank for recording other information. This may indicate tests taken by the client in school. If test results are recorded, the date of the test and the name of the test should be recorded. School records frequently contain other observations about the student that are valuable to the clinician.

It must not be assumed that information gathered in any one area of the case history is sufficient in itself. In fact, it is seldom, if ever, possible to feel that we have an adequate understanding of any client without data other than the historical information. This reminder is offered at this time because it is relevant to an example we will now discuss of material gathered in an interview with a teacher concerning the problems of a fifth-grade boy. This boy began school in the first grade (there was no kindergarten) when he was five years, six months of age. The school regulations were to the effect that the child's sixth birthday should be on or before January 1 or, in other words, that the child should be at least five years, eight months of age before entering, but the parents of this child had brought pressure to have him admitted at the slightly younger age. He was regarded as immature by the school at this time. There was a report that his mother brought him to school each morning and that he was frequently tearful. Apparently, at least for the first few weeks, he did not want to come to school. His teacher for the first six months was a permissive person who allowed the children to do about as they desired, maintained little discipline, and did not require high standards of performance. This teacher was pregnant and left the school before the year was out. Under this teacher the client came to like school but apparently spent most of his time in play.

The teacher who replaced the first teacher, and who was his teacher during the remainder of the first grade and the entire second grade, was an older person and a strict disciplinarian. She required the children to sit erect in their seats at all times, with their feet firmly placed on the floor. They were punished for leaving their seats, or for almost any noise they made. Apparently discipline was her most important goal, and although she made definite assignments and lectured to the students a great deal, it does not appear that she checked upon individual progress frequently or systematically. The client became again negative about school and was frequently brought into the building by force, screaming and kicking the while. During this period the only grades given were "satisfactory" or "unsatisfactory" and the client received satisfactory ratings.

In the third grade he had a new teacher, and at the same time the grading standards were changed. This teacher was the informant and the interviewer received the strong impression that she disapproved of both of the earlier teachers. Now specific letter grades were assigned to performance in each subject area, and at the end of the first six weeks a report card was sent home indicating that the client was doing failing work in all subjects. The school was immediately visited by the mother, who insisted that the teacher did not understand her child, that he had been doing satisfactory work and if he were not now doing it, this was the fault of the teacher, not the child. There were frequent conferences such as this throughout the year because the client continued to receive failing marks. As a consequence, he was held over in the third grade. Despite the parents' threats to move him into a different school, he repeated the third grade under this same teacher.

On the basis of a preponderantly "C" and "D" record, he was promoted to the fourth grade, where he had a new teacher. During this year he received mostly "B" and "C" grades and was promoted to the fifth grade. The informant was sure that he could not have accomplished passing work, since he was so "stupid," but explained the passing marks in terms of the leniency of the teacher and the fact that the client's mother was president of the Parent Teachers Association.

When the client entered the fifth grade the informant, who in the meantime had been transferred from the third- to the fifth-grade room, again became his teacher. He promptly received failing grades in the first marking period, and after a stormy conference between the mother, teacher, and principal, the mother agreed to leave him in school for another six weeks and announced that she planned to tutor him at home. At the end of this six-week period he was seen in the clinic. During this period his oral work had improved, but he did not do well on examinations that he had taken, and received barely passing marks. It was reported that he liked arithmetic, but disliked all other subjects. He had not expressed any vocational plans to the teacher, but the mother had indicated to the teacher that he was going to be a lawyer. She had three boys, and she and the father had decided that one was to be a doctor, one a lawyer, and the third a priest. He was taking music lessons and reportedly was doing well with the piano, but disliked to perform in school programs. He was frequently absent from school with severe digestive difficulties. He belonged to no organizations and had little interest or proficiency in sports. In school he always seemed to be tired, cried easily, was very quiet, was dependent on others, and was generally restless and nervous.

This was the over-all picture as derived from the teacher. Not all this information was specifically or directly queried for, but it all came out as a result of taking the history. This information by itself did not offer many explanations, but it provided the basis for the formation of a number of hypotheses which the clinic was able to explore. This is not the time for a complete discussion of this case, but the clinician obviously wanted to know more about the home situation, the child's general ability, his emotional adjustment, his reading ability, and the adequacy of his teacher who was our informant. After talking with the mother and father, he gathered the distinct impression that they were highly intelligent people who were dissatisfied with their own role as farmers and had extremely high ambitions for their children. There seemed to be a great amount of pressure placed on the children to succeed in school, with serious criticism for failure. The other two boys were doing well in school. When the mother tutored the client, she read all his lessons to him and quizzed him orally. He was always able to give her the right answers and she could not understand his failure at school. They worked (during the last six-week period) about three and a half hours every evening. The father had promised the client a pony if he raised his grades. On an intelligence test, with both verbal and nonverbal items, he performed at an average level on items not requiring reading or verbal proficiency and knowledge, and at a distinctly below-average level on verbal items. His reading ability was at less than the second-grade level. His present teacher was highly regarded in the school and well liked by other children and parents. In fact, she was well liked by the client. He appeared, both in interview and personality tests, to be a very tense, anxious, emotionally upset youngster.

Taking this entire picture into consideration, the clinician concluded that because of immaturity at the beginning of school, his extreme dislike of school in the early years, poor instruction, or all of these things taken together, he had not learned to read, and that this inability had resulted, at least in part, in his subsequent academic failure. Remedial reading was recommended. It was also concluded that he was being placed under tremendous pressure to succeed and that this was largely responsible for his nervous, tense state, which, in turn, did not in any way help his school work. An attempt was made to explain this situation to the mother in the hope that her attitude toward the boy would gradually change in some respects. Although his ability level appeared to be no more than average, it seemed to have been depressed on the test because of his extreme tension while taking it. No recommendations were made about the parents' ambitions except that they let the client have a chance to decide for himself some time in the future. Other recommendations and suggestions were made both to the family and to the school, but they will not be discussed here, since it would seem that we have adequately illustrated the uses, both direct and indirect, that can be made of educational history material.

FAMILY HISTORY

The family history is designed to be made up by the clinician in conference with a parent. The interview will ordinarily be most successful if only one parent is interviewed at a time. There is no particular preference as to which parent should be interviewed for the family history. If both parents are available, since much of the material in other areas can usually be best given by the mother—and unless there are special reasons to the contrary—the mother is usually interviewed first. If the father is available, he will be interviewed subsequently and perhaps asked some questions about which the mother was not clear. It is of value to attempt to ascertain whether attitudes reported by one parent are typical of both or whether there is conflict. The family history is frequently difficult to complete because parents are unable to see its bearing on the client's problems. In interviewing parents it may be helpful to make certain remarks at the outset. The clinician may say, "There are a great many questions that we always ask before giving any advice or suggestions concerning a child. Some questions may pertain to your child and some may not. We must ask them all so that we will not omit something important. Let's work rapidly and get all the information before us that we can."

The family history, as described in this section, can be regarded as both a family history and a description of the family-life situation. Some clinics discuss the family-life material under a separate heading or occasionally under the heading of the sociological history. Regardless of the headings, it is important that the clinician get to know the client's family as if he were a member of it. If the client is an adult, information in the family history may be difficult to obtain. The clinician may have to consult several sources in addition to the client himself. All such sources should be identified on the record.

A few additional comments concerning techniques of interviewing are pertinent before we begin our discussion of the remaining historical areas. The clinician must never show surprise, disapproval, censure, or over-reassurance by word, expression, or gesture, no matter how morbid or unusual the information given may be. This is not to suggest that he should be cold or unfriendly. One can be pleasant and friendly and still be impersonal and business-like. Delicate questions should be posed directly and frankly, never with apology or evasion. Questions touching on sensitive areas should be phrased in such a way as to make affirmative or significant responses easy, never in such a way as to encourage negative answers. As a negative example, the clinician would hardly say, "Of course, your child does not masturbate!" Such a question makes it difficult for the parent to indicate that the child does masturbate.

Figure 3 presents a suggested outline for the family history. The

FIGURE 3

PURDUE UNIVERSITY PSYCHOLOGICAL CLINICS
FAMILY HISTORY

Date _____   Interviewer _____

1. Name of Client _____ Age _____ Race _____

2. Informant's name _____ Relation to Client _____
   Mailing address _____ Telephone _____

3. Names of members of immediate family

	Age (if living)	Age (at death)	Cause of death	Educ.	Occup.
a. Mother					
b. Father					
c. Mat. Gr. Par.					
d. Pat. Gr. Par.					
e. Brothers					
f. Sisters					

4. Other family members
   a. Ages of maternal aunts _____
   b. Ages of paternal aunts _____
   c. Ages of maternal uncles _____
   d. Ages of paternal uncles _____

5. Which of the above live in the home with the client? (Indicate by initial as, M for mother, F for father, S1 for oldest sister, PGM for paternal grandmother, PU2 for second paternal uncle, etc.) _____

6. Which individuals in Items 1, 2, and 3, have any of the following conditions?

Illegitimacy	_____	Tuberculosis	_____
Suicide	_____	Epilepsy	_____
Blindness	_____	Feeble-mindedness	_____
Deafness	_____	Insanity	_____
Speech defects	_____	Narcotism	_____
Nervousness	_____	Criminality	_____
Headaches	_____	Venereal disease	_____
Alcoholism	_____	Other	_____
Convulsions	_____		_____
Paralysis	_____		_____

7. Indicate any divorces or separations in immediate family in terms of age of client at the time _____

   Comment _____
8. Indicate remarriages in the immediate family _____

   Comment _____

FIGURE 3 (*continued*)

PURDUE UNIVERSITY PSYCHOLOGICAL CLINICS
FAMILY HISTORY

9. What is the general economic status of the family? _____

Indicate any exceptions to this general status _____

10. Which of the immediate family were foreign-born? _____

11. Describe the nationalities and racial characteristics of the family members

12. Describe the religious background of the family _____

13. What are the principal sources of family tensions? _____

Reaction of client _____

14. What are the principal taboos or prohibitions? _____

Reaction of client _____

15. Describe the family organization _____

16. How does client compare with other siblings? _____

17. What are the family aspirations for client? _____

18. What are the recreational activities of the family? _____

Client's participation _____

19. Describe other pertinent psycho-social conditions in the home which are regarded as important _____

20. Other information _____

clinician should record the names of the immediate family, including those closely related to the client and extending beyond those who live in the home. It should be noted who lives in the home (Item 5). The entire list should include maternal and paternal grandparents, father and mother and siblings. The form does not call for the names of aunts and uncles, but they should be identified by age in Item 4 and listed in order of age; if any are deceased, this should be designated in some way. The parents should be included in this sequence under Item 4; this can be done by inserting F or M in the sequence. The age of each of the members of the immediate family is noted; for those who are deceased, the age of death and cause of death is recorded. Occupational and educational data for the immediate family is important.

An estimate (Item 9) of the general economic status of the home should be made. This can be done by inquiring about home ownership, automobile ownership, income, debts, home furnishings, and the like. Some clinicians like to have such data about all family members. Our preference is to indicate any exceptions to the general economic status. Nationality, race, foreign birth, and religion are all important. Marital status and marital history should be carefully studied and reported. In addition to divorces and remarriages in the immediate family, separations and the reasons for them should be recorded, with a notation of the client's age at the time. The clinician should also check on the incidence in the family of illegitimacy, suicide, insanity, feeble-mindedness, criminality, and all the other items listed in Item 6. This information can usually be gathered with reasonable reliability and validity by asking the informant to tell you if any of the items you are about to name apply to anyone in the family, then reading the list slowly and carefully.

Principal sources of family tensions, such as finances, recreation, religion, jealousy, gambling, and the like, are usually discussed quite frankly in reply to a question such as, "What are some of the things you quarrel about in your family? What is the principal bone of contention?" Taboos or prohibitions within the family should be noted since they, too, are apt to affect the client. The type of family organization refers to the control or direction of the family. Is it a patriarchal or matriarchal family? Who disciplines the client or has exerted control over him in the past? Parental comparisons among the children are frequently pertinent. How does the mother (or father) feel the client compares intellectually, emotionally, and socially with the other children? Family aspirations for the client are to be investigated and compared with those of the teacher and of the client. Recreational activities of the family often provide certain interesting leads. What is available at home in terms of books, magazines, hobbies, radio, or television? Recently a child was seen who could only be described as emotionally depleted and physically exhausted. The parents had left the child at the movies four to five evenings a week while they went "night-clubbing." She seldom got to sleep before midnight and, from eight o'clock in the evening until retiring, went from one emotional "binge" to another. Her only family life was with the screen figures and they tended to lead strenuous lives. Other psychosocial conditions, such as competitive and dominance-submission relationships, crushes, rejections, ignoring attitudes, and the like, are all of interest to the clinician.

The family history can be flexible in terms of methods of gathering information but the area should be covered comprehensively. It is important that the clinician's impressions be carefully described since the value of the interview may be largely in the observations that the clinician makes concerning the family members. To a degree, this interview provides a vehicle for observation; this is not to deny the importance of facts, but the situation should not be reduced to a routine itemizing of them.

The use of family history data is illustrated by the following somewhat extreme example. A seven-year-old first-grade child was referred to the clinic by the school because of her inability to learn. She could talk very little and could write only a part of her name; she even seemed confused as to what her name really was. The mother was the informant, but since there was reason to doubt the validity of the mother's report, all information was checked, insofar as possible, with other sources. The mother was 38 years of age and had left school when she was 16 without finishing the eighth grade. She claimed to have finished high school and to have gone to business school, but this was apparently untrue. The age and whereabouts of the client's father was unknown; he had been a soldier at the time of her mother's marriage to him and members of the community remembered him as a sergeant who was presumably an instructor at an Army camp near the present home of the client. Nothing was known about the paternal relatives, but the maternal grandmother had died in a state mental hospital where she had spent most of the last twenty years of her life. She had been a teacher in her earlier life and was described as a very bright woman when she was "right." The maternal grandfather died shortly before the child was referred to the clinic at the age of 60, after a life of alcoholism, criminality, and vagrancy. The mother said that he had died of "softening of the brain," and other reports suggest that he may have been paretic. The mother had two younger sisters both unmarried but each with two children. These sisters had been graduated from high school and were earning a satisfactory living as waitresses. The mother had an older brother who was currently in a state prison serving a sentence for robbery; he had completed high school and a few years of college. He was described as a prosperous-appearing person with no known or visible source of income.

Living in the home at the time the child was seen were the mother, the client, her stepfather, two stepbrothers, aged 16 and 14, and three half brothers, aged 4 years, 2 years, and 3 months. The mother had been married three times and the client was the only child of the second marriage. There were three older children by the first marriage, but the mother claimed to have lost contact with them; according to the social welfare department, she had deserted them when she went away with the father of the client. The first husband had previously divorced the mother for infidelity and had left her and the children with no support. These children had been placed in an orphanage but had all been adopted; they were described as bright, attractive, healthy children.

The father of the client apparently left the mother soon after the child was born. The mother moved in with the stepfather almost immediately, and although she described an elaborate wedding, the social worker did not believe that they were legally married. The family lived in a small two-room hut with practically no furniture except a television set. The client slept on a blanket on the floor with her stepbrothers. The one bed was occupied by the mother and sometimes by the stepfather. They drove a late-model automobile, and the stepfather had an income of about $80 a week from his work in a furniture factory. The mother said that he earned about $30 a week and this was apparently all that she saw. The mother described the home life as happy and serene, but the neighbors complained of frequent quarrels and reported that the client was often heard to scream for periods of from thirty minutes to an hour. The mother reported on one occasion that they sat at home every night watching television, and at another time she said that her husband was seldom home. The social worker believed him to be living with another woman in another town at least half of the time, and the mother was thought to have frequent male visitors.

The only reported recreation of the family was television. The mother said that there was no reading matter in the home because her husband could not read and flew into a rage if anyone spent money on newspapers or any other kind of reading material. No other information about the family history or family life could be secured. It was the interviewer's impression that the mother was grossly psychotic and that the client was almost completely neglected.

We see here an area of historical information suggesting hypotheses to be followed up in order to provide explanations of the client's present behavior. The several alternate hypotheses considered by the clinic group were: (a) that the child was mentally retarded; (b) that she was completely confused and disorganized because of the lack of stability in her life; (c) that she was so neglected that she had had no opportunity to learn; or (d) that a combination of these circumstances was operating. The first hypothesis was difficult to evaluate as the child was practically untestable by standard intelligence tests due to her lack of speech and her distractibility. Some of her performances, when her attention could be gained, were indicative of average or above-average potential ability but little could be concluded. The validity of the developmental history taken from the mother was questionable but there seemed to have been an average rate of physical maturation. The mother did report that the child's father once told her the child would never be "bright," but she could not report why or when he had said this. She talked vaguely about a Vitamin C deficiency in the child and reported that she had had irregular medication. At least one doctor had apparently told her that the child needed glasses. The clinic had no evidence of poor vision in their observations but comprehensive general medical and special medical examinations were recommended. All the half brothers, both by the first and third husbands of the mother, were of at least average ability, as the mother and father of the client were judged to be. Mental deficiency due to brain damage or other physiological conditions was difficult to rule out. The child's development since her referral to the clinic has verified the tentative assumption that she is of average potential ability. A complete discussion of the follow-up on this child is not appropriate at this time, but, to satisfy the reader's curiosity, it can be said that both the second and third hypotheses seem to have been verified by subsequent events. The child was taken from the home and placed in a foster home where she has received a great amount of attention. In this situation her development and general adjustment have been so remarkable that the foster parents have indicated their desire to adopt her.

As in the illustration on the use of educational data, it was not the history that directly determined the course of action as much as it was the indirect suggestion of ideas which could be examined in the light of other data. Still, one cannot avoid being impressed by the family history of poor adjustment and instability, as well as the deprived, if not depraved, nature of the current family setting.

DEVELOPMENTAL HISTORY

When the client is a child, the developmental history, like the family history, is most advantageously collected in conference with a parent. In the typical family the mother is the best informant. Records such as baby books, developmental records, and health histories are valuable aids in reconstructing development. With an older client such sources of information are of the utmost importance; some check on the memory and objectivity of the informant is always in order and parents should be urged to bring with them any records they have. Occasionally the parent may be asked to write a biography of the client for the clinic. Writing the biography may have therapeutic value to the parent and may provoke serious parental evaluation of developmental sequences that are of value to the diagnosis. Ordinarily the clinician will follow an outline, such as that presented in Figure 4, and collect the information in interview. In taking the developmental history, there is often some difficulty in keeping the interview under control. Occasionally the parent will discuss one topic at great length; in such a situation the interviewer should not interrupt if pertinent information is being given, but when the trend appears to drift from the purpose, he should have a question ready. A parent may stop the clinician to say, "My child has had none of those things!" The clinician can then explain that while few children have many of the

FIGURE 4

PURDUE UNIVERSITY PSYCHOLOGICAL CLINICS
DEVELOPMENTAL HISTORY

Date _____   Interviewer _____

1. Client's name _____ Age _____

2. Informant's name _____ Relation to client _____
   Mailing address _____ Telephone _____

3. Birthdate _____ Mother's age at birth ___ Length of pregnancy ___
   Health of mother during pregnancy _____
   _____
   Attitude of mother during pregnancy _____

4. What was the length of delivery? _____ Where delivered _____
   Any complications of delivery? _____
   _____

5. Weight at birth _____   At four weeks _____   At six weeks _____

6. Any unusual conditions at birth? _____
   _____

7. Has client experienced any injuries? Note age, kind, and severity
   _____
   _____

8. List diseases and illnesses which client has had:

Condition	Age	Duration	Severity	Temperature
a.				
b.				
c.				
d.				
e.				
f.				

9. At what age did client cut first tooth? _____ When was client
   weaned from breast? _____ bottle? _____ any difficulty? _____
   _____ When did client achieve bowel control? _____
   bladder control, day _____ night _____ At what age did client sit alone? _____ walk? _____ say words? _____ talk in
   sentences? _____ open doors? _____ lace shoes? _____ tie
   shoes? _____ use spoon? _____ cup? _____
   Comment on general rate of development _____
   _____

10. What sex instruction has been given? _____
    _____ When? _____

FIGURE 4 (*continued*)

PURDUE UNIVERSITY PSYCHOLOGICAL CLINICS
DEVELOPMENTAL HISTORY

Age of puberty _____ Any sex problems such as masturbation, exhibitionism, sex play, sex irregularity, etc.? _____

11. What are sleeping habits? _____

Sleeping companions _____

12. Indicate which of the following developmental problems have been present (circle and comment on age and measures taken in space below):

Nervousness, restlessness, worry, phobias, sleeplessness, sleep-walking, nightmares, timidity, shyness, seclusiveness, stubbornness, rudeness, disobedience, temper tantrums, quarrelsomeness, fighting, jealousy, running away, truancy, stealing, lying, swearing, smoking, drinking, thumb-sucking, nail-biting, sadism, masochism, constipation, enuresis, vomiting, fainting, headaches, exhaustion, tics, awkwardness, convulsions, chorea, mirror-writing, stuttering, other speech defects.

Comment _____

_____

_____

_____

13. Other information _____

_____

_____

problems, most have some of them, and it is important to know which few may have been met with. Because developmental information is extremely important, every effort should be made to elicit complete and accurate information.

It is frequently said that development begins with conception. Insofar as the developmental history is concerned, this is certainly true. Development begins with conditions or complications of pregnancy, including the general health and nutrition of the mother. The mother's attitude during pregnancy may be important; that is, whether the child was wanted or unwanted, whether the mother felt ashamed or limited in her activities. To the psychologist, both health and attitude factors are important, primarily in terms of the effect they may have upon the mother's feelings toward the child. Next, we are interested in the birth. Complications such as unusual presentation, instruments used, or injuries of any kind should be recorded. Facts pertaining to the length of the period of labor, whether the child was born at home or in a hospital, are noted.

The condition of the infant at birth is relevant. Birth weight and rate of growth in the first few weeks and months give us some indication of the early health of the child. The condition of the nose, throat, mouth, as well as any difficulty in initiating breathing or circulation should be carefully noted. Evidence of birth injury or malformation of any kind at birth, and any treatment or corrective measures employed, are other factors intimately related to the client's start in life.

Any injuries and illnesses that have occurred since birth should be carefully noted. Careful record is made of any injury, its seriousness and effect, particularly injuries in which there have been or could have been complications of a neurological nature. The height of temperature, the duration of high temperature, respiratory and circulatory conditions are all checked. Attention is obviously not to be limited to contagious diseases or childhood illness. Evidences of convulsive behavior and such conditions as diabetes and rickets are just a few illustrations of possible health conditions to be evaluated.

Our typical or sample form moves now to an appraisal of the rate of development of the child. Ages of first sitting, walking, talking, and other such performances may give us a rough approximation of the extent to which development proceeded at a relatively normal rate.

The kind of sex instruction given, how it was received by the client, and how the parent felt about it may suggest hypotheses. Problems of sexual development and, most particularly, the parents' reactions to these so-called problems are to be considered. Item 11 concerns sleeping habits and should include notations not only of amount of sleep, but of whether client sleeps alone, or has a sleeping companion. Whether this companion is a parent, a brother, a sister, or someone else is of interest. Does the client have his own room, and how long has he had such privacy? Item 12 lists a large number of problems that some children present. This list is rather extensive and not many of the problems will apply to any given child. The parent should be given a chance to react to all of them; and in the event that she associates one with the child, the age at which it occurred and the measures that may have been taken are discussed, and her comment is recorded. Other developmental factors may be important and all information that can be gathered is to be considered a part of the developmental picture.

No single case could begin to illustrate the use and value of a complete developmental history. In general terms, its importance is twofold: a careful study of developmental factors may suggest the presence of organic limitations in the functioning of the client, or it may suggest the impact of emotional reactions to injuries, illnesses, or anomalies of development. Quite commonly brain damage is suggested by mention of a long and difficult delivery, the use of instruments, unusual presentation, or evidences of difficulty in initiating breathing or circulation. If these conditions are noted in the birth history and followed by indications of retarded development, it certainly behooves the clinician to evaluate carefully the potentialities of the client for education and/or training. Serious injuries or illnesses after birth may be followed by change in the rate of development, or the emergence of behavioral reactions not originally noted.

Brain damage may be suggested by the developmental history and corroborated by testing, although testing alone might not indicate it. There are an almost unlimited number of effects that can result from different kinds and degrees of brain damage. Many of these effects would not ordinarily be identified by minor variations in a test performance, but they would be quite clear when the clinician had been alerted to them by the historical material. Brain damage may be much more common than it is ordinarily thought to be. The histories of many of the difficult-to-understand children referred to us by school personnel indicate the possibility of birth or early-life injury. These children are difficult to understand because they appear to be in good physical health. Even neurological examinations may not reveal any gross involvement of the nervous system, yet their performance is uneven, their attention span is short, or their learning potential is affected in some other way. A young man was recently seen who could solve computational problems in arithmetic with the greatest of ease, but he could not perform reasoning or story problems, even when the same quantities and operations were used. He could spell proficiently, but could not recognize words spelled correctly when they appeared in sentences or in other meaningful contexts. The results of the psychological tests did not suggest any possibility of brain damage to the examiner until they were carefully analyzed following the discovery that the young man had been a breech presentation, and that his mother had had an extremely long and difficult time at his birth.

The clinician must guard against the tendency to jump to the conclusion that brain damage is a certainty simply on the basis of significant historical data. Before we decide to understand and recommend for a client as if he were brain-damaged, we must have validating evidences from performance on tests or in other situations. Not long ago we saw a boy who all his life had been regarded as brain-damaged. His delivery had been quite unusual and statistics suggest that over 50 per cent of the children of such deliveries are mentally retarded. The parents, who were aware of this figure, had been extremely apprehensive; when the child was examined by a specialist, who took the history and made a cursory examination of the child, their fears were supported. This child

Figure 5

PURDUE UNIVERSITY PSYCHOLOGICAL CLINICS
SOCIOLOGICAL HISTORY

Date _____   Interviewer _____

1. Name of client _____ Age _____
   Mailing address _____ Telephone _____

2. Name of informant _____ Relation to client _____
   Mailing address _____ Telephone _____

3. Indicate interpersonal and social relationships with the following (note such factors as punishment, nagging, quarreling, fighting, domination, submission, love, protection, inseparable relationships, likes, dislikes, etc.):
   a. Members of the household _____
   _____
   b. Neighbors _____
   _____
   c. Teachers _____
   _____
   d. Companions _____
   _____

4. Are companions older or younger, same or different sex, noisy, quiet, etc? Discuss _____
   _____
   _____

5. What groups does the client belong to? What is his position in these groups? _____
   _____
   _____

6. List love affairs indicating age, age of other, termination, and dedree of intimacy _____
   _____
   _____
   _____

7. How does client express affection? _____
   _____
   _____

8. What escapades has client been involved in? _____
   _____
   Measures taken _____
   _____

FIGURE 5 (*continued*)

PURDUE UNIVERSITY PSYCHOLOGICAL CLINICS
SOCIOLOGICAL HISTORY

9. How much spending money? _____ Earned? _____
   How _____ Reaction _____

10. What belongings does client have? _____
    _____
    Own or shared? _____ Reaction _____

11. Does client have pets? _____

12. Does client have hobbies? _____

13. How are evenings typically spent? _____
    _____

14. What kind of literature is read? _____
    _____

15. Describe religious participation of client and family _____
    _____

16. Discuss social structure of home, community and position of client
    and family in this structure _____
    _____
    _____
    Reaction _____

17. Other information _____
    _____
    _____

was treated as a retarded child for five years, but when carefully studied prior to his admission to a school for retarded children, no evidence of any disturbed function could be noted. The child was actually found to be of well above average capacity, and it was concluded that if he had suffered any limitation of function, it was insignificant for his future education.

In many instances changes in the client's behavior may follow injury or illness without any organic involvement. We see frequent examples of preoccupation with bodily functions, dependency reactions, and regressive behavior following a period of invalidism. Traumatic injuries of the nervous system may be followed by paralysis long after the peripheral nerves have repaired themselves. One child presented a puzzling speech defect that developed after a severe bruising of the face while the child was learning to talk. The speech mechanism was found to be intact, and we could only conclude that the abnormal speech was one result of the compensations necessary to avoid pain while the child was learning to talk. It had apparently been very painful for the lips and facial muscles to be used, and the habit of talking with a frozen, immobile face had persisted. Fears often develop as a result of operations, accidents, and even from the delirium of illness, and may affect a person's adjustment for years.

SOCIOLOGICAL HISTORY

The information contained in this segment of the complete anamnesis is ordinarily compiled in conference with the parents and/or any others who can substantiate or add to the data. Figure 5 suggests some of the areas of relevant sociological information. This information is most often collected by the social worker, but in the absence of a trained social worker the psychological clinician may gather the information. It is not to be assumed that the areas mentioned in Figure 5 or in this discussion present a complete description of the sociological report, for there are other kinds of information unique to a particular client.

The sociological history is particularly concerned with the relations between the client and others. Special attention is paid to members of the immediate family, relatives, friends, neighbors, and teachers, but other relationships may also be of significance. We are especially curious about strong attachments, dominance-submission relationships, rejections, quarrels, fights, likes and dislikes, punishment and fears. Are companions older or younger, boys or girls, quiet or noisy or rough? To what groups does the client belong? What love affairs has he or she had? (Very young children sometimes report love affairs or strong attachments.) How much spending money does the client have? How is it spent, and how is it acquired? Does the client have personal belongings, pets, or hobbies? How are evenings spent? What literature is available, and what is read? A general description should be made of the social, economic, and religious milieu, noting the position of the client and his family in this social structure. This is, at least, a partial description of the scope and extent of the sociological history.

OCCUPATIONAL HISTORY

With adults, a chronological list should be made of jobs held; it should include length of time each job was held, average earnings, relationships with fellow workers, reasons for leaving, general success, likes or dislikes of different kinds of work, and any other material having to do with the efficiency with which the person is functioning, or has been functioning. Vocational training is included in the educational history, but both vocational and avocational training should be elaborated on here if further data is available. No illustrative form is suggested here, largely because none is necessary, since an itemization of jobs and discussion is all that is desired.

An adult who has done military service presents special problems, and the period of military service must be studied intensively. In addition to noting the client's progress and efficiency of functioning, attention should be given to the degree of stress he endured, reactions to this stress, extent of injuries, and results of and reactions to these injuries. Most military and veteran clinical facilities have their own ways of summarizing, reporting, and recording this information.

SUMMARY

Since much specific information has been given in this chapter, a detailed summary would be repetitious and unnecessary. We have attempted to present the elements of a complete case history by giving an extensive cross-section of the data with which a clinician is concerned, and which, under optimal conditions, is available.

Collection of this data is not necessarily the job of the clinical psychologist. In a well-staffed clinic this information may be collected by the social worker. Actually, it matters little who collects the information, but it is important that it be available so that an adequate diagnosis can be made. It is largely through case-history study that the evaluation of the client becomes dynamic and longitudinal, rather than static and cross-sectional. The collection of case-study data is not to be regarded as a simple stockpiling of bits of information; the goal should be toward building a complete story and to aid us in seeing a complete person functioning in his environmental field.

BIBLIOGRAPHY

1. Allport, G. W., "The use of personal documents in psychological science." *Soc. Sci. Res. Coun. Bull.*, No. 49, 1942.
2. Dollard, J., *Criteria for the life history*. New York: Peter Smith, 1949.
3. Greene, E. B., *Measurement of human behavior*. New York: Odyssey, 1941.
4. Hinsie, L. E., *Concepts and problems of psychotherapy*. New York: Columbia Univ. Press, 1937.
5. Johnson, W., Darley, F. L., and Spriestersbach, D. C., *Diagnostic manual in speech correction*. New York: Harper, 1952.

6. Kelly, G. A., "Where do little hypotheses come from?" Midwestern Psychological Association symposium: The role of theory in training clinical psychologists; F. J. Shaw, Chm., 1952.

7. Lewin, K., *Principles of topological psychology.* New York: McGraw-Hill, 1936.

8. Lewis, N. D. C., *Outlines for psychiatric examinations.* Albany: N. Y. State Dept. of Mental Hygiene, 1943.

9. Louttit, C. M., *Clinical psychology.* New York: Harper, 1947.

10. Lowrey, L. G., *Psychiatry for social workers.* New York: Columbia Univ. Press, 1946.

11. Preu, P. W., *Outline of psychiatric case-study* (2nd ed.). New York: Hoeber, 1943.

12. Rogers, C. R., *Counseling and psychotherapy.* Boston: Houghton Mifflin, 1942.

13. Shaffer, G. W., and Lazarus, R. S., *Fundamental concepts in clinical psychology.* New York: McGraw-Hill, 1952.

14. Strecker, E. A., Ebaugh, F. G., and Ewalt, J. R., *Practical clinical psychiatry* (6th ed.). Philadelphia: Blakiston, 1947.

15. Thorne, F. C., *Principles of personality counseling.* Brandon, Vt.: *J. Clin. Psychol.*, 1950.

16. Travis, L. E., *Speech pathology.* New York: D. Appleton, 1931.

17. Van Riper, C., *Speech correction principles and methods.* New York: Prentice-Hall, 1947.

18. Williamson, E. G., and Darley, J. C., *Student personnel work.* New York: McGraw-Hill, 1937.

The Diagnostic Interview

URING THE PAST FEW YEARS PSYCHOLOGISTS HAVE BECOME BET-
ter and better equipped to contribute to the appraisal and understanding of behavior through the use and refinement of psycho-
diagnostic tests. Clinicians have come to rely heavily upon "projective"
tests; in fact, we suspect that many psychologists tend to depend so con-
fidently upon the data to be inferred from them that they sometimes ignore the direct information that can be gathered in an interview. While
the value of tests such as the Rorschach, the Thematic Apperception
Test, and many other of these so-called "projective" devices is undis-
puted, they have limitations. It is not enough to have a Rorschach record
or even the results of a battery of projective tests. These present only a
segment of the complete psychological picture of the individual; in order
to understand thoroughly the meaning of the responses, it is necessary to
consider them in relation to other knowledge about the individual being
tested. The tasks of understanding the development of presenting problems and of planning for the future of the client cannot be adequately accomplished without direct data from him.

Consequently, in addition to historical material discussed in the
previous chapter and the use of diagnostic tests (to be described in subsequent chapters), the complete case study should include an interview
with the client, oriented toward a direct discussion of various attitudinal
and behavioral topics. This chapter will present an outline and description of such an interview. An interview of this kind should not be expected to lead automatically to a categorical diagnosis. We would fall
far short of our goal of planning for the future of our client if this were
its only accomplishment. Our purpose in the interview is to explore dynamic areas that will, to some extent, make clear the psychological or
personality factors of importance in understanding the behavior of the

client. Knowledge of these factors can lead, incidentally, to a categorical diagnosis when this is required.

STRUCTURING THE INTERVIEW

The first task is to create what Rogers (10) has called a warm and permissive atmosphere. To put it another way, we want to establish a comfortable and mutually co-operative relationship. This relationship we call "rapport." Rapport depends on many factors: on the personality of the clinician, the experience of the clinician, and of course the attitude of the client. Since at the stage of evaluation we can do little about the client's attitudes, we must concentrate on the clinician. Although no complete formula or recipe can be given for establishing rapport, there are some "do's" and "don'ts" that may affect the degree of rapport achieved.

The clinician should be friendly, but impersonal. When a client is ushered into the office, greetings may be exchanged, and the clinician should smile with cordiality. However no joking or wisecracking should be indulged in. Many interviewers seem to proceed on the assumption that the way to "break the ice" is to tell a funny story. In psychological interviewing nothing could ordinarily be further from the professional attitude. It is probably a truism that the client would not be there if his problems were laughing matters. The client is shown to a chair, and a businesslike attitude is maintained. The clinician should be cheerful and optimistic, but not effusive and flamboyant; neither should he be stern or forbidding. In other words, the clinician's manner should be serious and businesslike, but still friendly and cheerful. There is no reason for the clinician to touch the client except to shake hands unless the client is feeble, or for some other reason is in need of physical support. Recently a female client called on us in our capacity as director of a clinic, complaining that a clinician had been "familiar" with her. This seemed rather incongruous since we knew the clinician very well, but it was learned after questioning that the clinician had a habit of laying his hand on the back of the client as he opened the door to usher her into his office. This is just one example pointing up the fact that we can never predict just how another person may interpret any form of physical contact. Although the client's attitude in this situation was certainly of diagnostic importance, she was so upset that she could not feel comfortable in the clinician's presence, and this, of course, made rapport impossible.

After all necessary preliminaries of introduction and seating are accomplished, the clinician should relax and make himself comfortable. Such activities as settling back in the chair (not lying back with feet on desk!), perhaps lighting a cigarette (if the clinician smokes and it is known that the client will not mind) may contribute to the ease of the situation. The interviewer should always behave with dignity. Certainly not at the first interview, nor in those that follow, should he carry relaxation too far. For example, many persons seem to feel that the purpose of a desk is to provide a resting place for feet. Rapport is not encouraged if the client and the clinician must peer at each other around the feet of the clinician. In a slightly different vein, there is the example of the psychologist who could apparently feel comfortable only without shoes. The situation was ameliorated somewhat by the fact that it was a female psychologist, but the mannerism was distracting, and certainly detracted from rapport in at least one situation. The psychologist, an excellent clinician, was identified by a client as "that nice lady with the pretty feet," and he reported that he could not keep his eyes and thoughts off her feet.

Other habits of the clinician may also be distracting. The writer spent several years of his professional life in Utah and discovered belatedly, and much to his chagrin, that his habit of smoking was disturbing and probably even repulsive to some of his Mormon clients who did not approve of the practice. One of our colleagues who is not a habitual smoker will in certain interview situations light a cigarette in order to give the impression of relaxation and permissiveness. Since he is not accustomed to smoking, he almost always coughs and chokes, holding the cigarette in a stiff, unnatural manner. These illustrations indicate that while the clinician should give the appearance of being comfortable (in fact, he should *be* comfortable), he should take care that his comfort and relaxation are not disturbing to the client. On the other hand, if the clinician is obviously uncomfortable, the client will have difficulty relaxing in the conference. The clinician should carefully study his own personal characteristics and attempt to eliminate all nervous mannerisms and other disturbing or offensive bits of behavior. He can, of course, carry any of this too far—a dead-pan, cold, or lackadaisical attitude will not encourage the client to divulge personal problems.

The student clinician must first of all familiarize himself with the purposes of the interview. Such familiarity and the self-confidence that it engenders are valuable adjuncts to establishing and maintaining rapport. The clinician should appear to know what he is about. He should inspire confidence. Fumbling for words, for papers, and other signs of indecision, lack of self-possession, or self-confidence will have negative effects on the comfort of the client. Experience tends to develop self-assurance, but even if we lack self-confidence and experience, this lack should not be apparent to the client.

If there is any reason to suspect that a client is concerned about the confidentiality of the situation, he should be reassured. Some clinicians offer reassurance as a matter of routine. This is not always necessary as some clients expect the clinic to maintain the strictest confidence, and probably would not have presented themselves had they not felt secure in this respect. We should always be alert to signs of doubt, however, and attempt to allay fears of this nature. Many clients openly state that they have come because they know what they have to say will not be quoted. Ordinarily, we should take this as a question—not as a definite statement of conviction—and offer reassurance by agreeing with the statement. Much more telling than words is the behavior of the clinician. We should never hold telephone conversations about one client in the presence of another. We should use caution in discussing one client's problems with another merely to illustrate a point. Certainly, one client should never be identified to another, and no chance should be taken of identification. Papers concerning other clients should not be in evidence during an interview. Clinicians should never talk between themselves concerning client material in halls or waiting rooms where they may be overheard.

Recently a client reported that he felt a little uneasy after talking with a particular clinician because he was afraid that the clinician had discussed his case in a class. The clinician had actually not done so. The case discussed in class, to which the client was referring, had been a hypothetical one, but the client had apparently seen something of himself in the description. When assured that he had not been discussed, he was still apprehensive, saying that he could not help but wonder, for if cases were discussed, how could he be sure that his own would not be? The situation of the clinician who is also a teacher is rather difficult, and problems of this kind cannot be completely avoided, but the teacher-clinician must lean over backward to avoid suggesting in any way that he would ever discuss the private data of the client.

If at all possible, it is advantageous to establish a regular time and place of meeting. If a series of interviews is to be held, the clinician may set aside a regular time that the client can regard as his own. Appointments should be specific as to time and place. Since the client will quite naturally look forward with anticipation to the appointment, only in the event of very unusual circumstances should he be disappointed. Appointment arrangements should be concise and well understood, and the clinician must be careful to fulfill his obligation. (Although these remarks and those that follow are directed primarily toward scheduling a series of appointments in the diagnostic interviewing situation, they are equally applicable to counseling and therapeutic interviewing.)

The meeting place should be an office or interview room obviously used for the purpose of interviewing. Meeting in a home, a hotel lobby, or places usually used for other purposes is not ordinarily conducive to a good rapport relationship. Meetings on the golf course and at other places of recreation may conceivably contribute to the development of relationships of benefit to the client, but they are seldom the relationships that we would ordinarily associate with a professional diagnostic interview. The meeting place should be reasonably private. Partial partitions and screens are poor substitutes for walls, which appear, at least, to be soundproof. The arrangement of chairs and desk in the room should be such as to reduce outside noise to a minimum. Frequently, clients have expressed their feelings by saying, "We can hear them in the next room. Do you think they can hear us?" Two clinicians recently discovered that their clients were relieved when their desks were moved away from a common partition between their offices. The arrangement in which a single partition separated the desks allowed the clients to hear a murmur of voices from the adjoining room. Moving the desks to the outside walls reduced the sound to the degree that it was not distracting. Such problems would be avoided if all clinic rooms were soundproofed, but since this is idealistic at the present time, many clinicians have to make the best of poor physical arrangements. If a series of interviews is to be held, it is helpful if the meeting place is the same each time. Familiarity with the room and its appurtenances encourages relaxation and comfort on the part of the client.

There is no essential type of furniture. Ordinarily a desk or table and two chairs are all that are necessary. The chairs should be comfortable, but do not have to be lounge chairs; in fact, if the client is too comfortable, it is conceivable that he will relax so much that he may not be completely alert and attentive to the interview or counseling situation. There is a certain amount of prestige value in attractively furnished surroundings; however the furnishings should be reasonably consistent with those to which the usual clientele is accustomed. Clients may be overawed and ill at ease in lush surroundings. The lighting should be adequate, but under no circumstances should the client be placed in the brightest light. If there is an unavoidable focus of light, the clinician should be in that circle of light with the client on the periphery. At no time should a client be forced to stare into a bright light, whether it is natural (such as sun through the window) or artificial (such as that from a bright desk lamp.) Attention should also be given to conditions of temperature and ventilation. In every way possible, a comfortable, relaxed interview situation should be arranged.

Psychological counselors have little or no use for couches or examination tables. The interview is almost always conducted in a face-to-face situation. The client and clinician should always be placed so that they can see each other easily. The face-to-face situation produces a more natural and human situation than does the traditional analytic client-on-couch situation, which overemphasizes the passive role of the client. Any arrangement in which face-to-face contact is not possible makes it too easy for the client to shut himself off from the interview situation. Occasional exceptions may be made if the client can talk more easily while looking at a blank wall or a window, but, as Alfred C. Kinsey, *et al.* (7, p. 48) have said, "People understand each other when they look directly at each other."

PRINCIPLES OF INTERVIEWING

There are several good references on techniques or procedures of interviewing which the clinician should study carefully before attempting either case-history or diagnostic personal interviewing. The standard reference is Walter V. Bingham and Bruce V. Moore's (2) text *How to Interview*. Harry Stack Sullivan (11), too, has described the interview and the implications of its use by psychologists, social workers, and counselors. A brief text by Annette Garrett (4) provides insight into what happens in interviewing and suggests answers to practical questions concerning procedure in the interrogation and the interpretation of information and observations. Both Garrett's book and a discussion of interviewing procedures by Anne F. Fenlason (3) present several sample case studies and interviews. Wendell Johnson, Frederic L. Darley, and Duane C. Spriestersbach (5) also have suggestions helpful to the interviewer. Several of their suggestions form the basis for the discussion that follows:

1. SET THE RIGHT TONE.   Johnson and his coauthors summarize their point of view and the importance of this concept as follows (p. 3):

> Experienced interviewers have learned and repeatedly confirmed that the atmosphere most conducive to the successful elicitation of information is one of mutual respect. The informant and interviewer are by no means on equal grounds, for the former has come for help which the latter is in a position to give. It is to be expected that most of the questions and the guidance of the interview will issue from the interviewer, while most of the information will come from the informant. And yet, you, as the interviewer, cannot afford to be aloof, superior, critical, moralistic, God-like, rigid, intolerant, disdainful, or amused. You must show a liking for the person and sincerely try to understand his behavior and his problems; you must refrain from ridicule or condemnation. Rapport grows only as you show thorough acceptance (not necessarily expressed ap-

proval)—an acknowledgement of what is reported, an attempt to fit it in with other bits of information, a clearly implied assurance to the informant that you will still like him no matter what he says.[1]

These authors have quoted Kinsey *et al.* (7, p. 42) on this last point as follows:

One is not likely to win the sort of rapport which brings a full and frank confession from a human subject unless he can convince the subject that he is desperately anxious to comprehend what his experience has meant to him. . . . Histories often involve a record of things that have hurt, of frustrations, of pain, of unsatisfied longings, of disappointments, of desperately tragic situations, and of complete catastrophe. The subject feels that the investigator who asks merely routine questions has no right to know about such things in another's history. The interviewer who senses what these things can mean, who at least momentarily, shares something of the satisfaction, pain or bewilderment which was the subject's, who shares something of the subject's hope that things will, somehow, work out right, is more effective though he may not be altogether neutral.[2]

2. GET THE INTERVIEW OFF TO A GOOD START. One of the first tasks, in fact, obligations, of the clinician is to make sure that the client understands the purpose of the interview as clearly as he is capable of understanding it. He should be prepared for the kind of questions that will be put to him. Most clients submit quite readily to questioning if they know that the answers are necessary and that the clinician will treat the information in a responsible and professional manner. The original remarks or questions by the clinician should be quite directive and assume that the client has a problem and expects help from the clinic or clinician. Of course, this may not always be the case, as some clients may have been referred without a full explanation; this is not an ideal situation and should be avoided if possible. It is hoped that in most instances the client has come of his own free will, with an adequate understanding of why he has come. In any case, we must be sure that the reasons for the interview are explained in as much detail as is possible and

[1] This quotation and the following adaptations by permission from *Diagnostic Manual in Speech Correction*, by Wendell Johnson, Frederic L. Darley, and Duane C. Spriestersbach. Copyright 1952 by Harper & Brothers.
[2] By permission from *Sexual Behavior in the Human Male*, by Alfred C. Kinsey, Wardell P. Pomeroy, and Clyde E. Martin. Copyright 1948 by W. B. Saunders Company.

necessary. This entire point is, of course, an application of one of the basic rules of practice that no client should be seen unless he has been made to understand, as clearly as he is capable of understanding, the purposes for which the clinical examination is made.[3]

3. Frame Questions Clearly, Economically, Naturally. As Johnson, *et al.*, suggest, the clinician can save himself much time and secure more reliable information if he takes a lesson from the experienced public-opinion poll taker who words his questions carefully. The interviewer should be familiar with the purpose of the questions to be asked and should state them simply and concisely. Questions should not be stated in such a way as to bias or suggest any particular answer.

4. Adjust the Sequence of Topics to Be Discussed to the Anxiety Level of the Informant. Some anxiety is to be expected in any personal interviewing situation, and, as a matter of fact, some anxiety undoubtedly stimulates the client to talk. On the other hand, if he experiences too much anxiety, he may not be able to express himself easily or he may be so threatened that he will not be co-operative. Consequently, we should ask questions in such a sequence as to allow for the building up of rapport, without frightening the person by the premature introduction of emotion-laden material.

5. Move Rapidly Through the Interview. In personal interviewing and, even more important, in case-history interviewing a rapid-fire technique may result in greater reliability. We must realize that in the personal interview the person may have to take his time and present material in his own way, but we should always be ready to move on with new questions and topics as rapidly as is possible.

6. Record Information at the Time of the Interview. Johnson, *et al.*, advise the taking of notes on the spot. (The reader may wish to refer to their techniques for note taking.) We discussed this problem in connection with the case history and suggested that the formality of recording information depends on many factors.[4] In the case of the personal interview we favor the recording of information immediately after the interview rather than during the interview. However it is true that some clients feel more at ease and are reassured if the clinician is "doing" something and if they can feel that an accurate record is being made. If the clinician has this impression of the client, notes should certainly be taken during the interview.

[3] *See* p. 602.   [4] *See* pp. 315–18.

At this point it is of interest and importance to examine the results of a study by Thomas A. Wickes (12). This study was designed to examine the effect of the behavior of the clinician upon the responses that are made by the subject of a psychological examination. A series of thirty inkblots were designed that were similar to but not identical with the Rorschach inkblots. The subjects were asked to report what they saw in these blots. Each time the subject gave a response from which movement of humans could be inferred, the response was recorded. For example, if the response was "two Negroes dancing," "soldiers dueling," or "Indians beating a drum," the response would be written down. Three groups of subjects were used. In the first group, all thirty inkblots were shown, and the human-movement responses were recorded with no further activity by the experimenter. In the second group, the procedure for the first fifteen cards was exactly the same as in the first group. However for the second fifteen cards the experimenter not only recorded responses from which movement of humans could be inferred, but each time they were given he said either, "Good," "Fine," or "All right." In the third group, the procedure for the first fifteen inkblots was again the same, but for the second fifteen he either nodded his head three times, smiled, or leaned forward in his chair to record the response whenever a human-movement response was given. The subjects were not aware of the kind of response being noted. However groups two and three both gave more human-movement responses to the second fifteen cards than to the first fifteen, whereas group one did not increase the frequency of such responses. The most dramatic gain was in group three, where smiling, nodding, and leaning forward to write followed the response being observed.

This study is clearly of significance to psychological testing procedures, since it suggests that on projective or nonstructured tests the clinician may increase the frequency of certain responses by his interest in these responses, by his encouragement of the client, and by the manner in which he records responses. It seems likely that the same principles apply also to situations other than the testing situation. Especially when we are recording material in the interview situation, we, as clinicians, must be careful to respond in the same way, regardless of the kind of material reported. If the clinician leans forward in his chair or in other ways becomes especially interested at points of the interview, we may either encourage or discourage the reporting of certain kinds of information. A reproving attitude, an ill-timed gasp of surprise, a look of keen interest may cause the client to report material in a selective manner.

Some clinicians favor making electronic recordings of the entire interview. If the situation can be adequately structured and if the client is willing that the recording be made, there is no objection to such a procedure. However, under *no* circumstances should an interview be recorded without the permission of the client. Such a procedure is an unauthorized violation of the personal privacy of the client, and, as such, it is an unethical practice.

7. ASK "TICKLISH" QUESTIONS STRAIGHTFORWARDLY. As Johnson, *et al.* (5, p. 5), remark, "Having laid a solid foundation of rapport, mutual understanding and respect, it is best to ask the questions in a direct manner." Kinsey (7, p. 53) says to ask such questions "without hesitancy and without apology." He adds, "If the interviewer shows any uncertainty or embarrassment, it is not to be expected that the subject will do better in his answers. . . . Evasive terms invite dishonest answers."

8. CONSIDERABLE TACT AND SKILL MUST BE USED IN HANDLING PAUSES. We should not be too eager to make an answer for a client and should give him time to think through his answers carefully. On the other hand, we must not allow pauses to become so long as to become painful or awkward and thus make the client uncomfortable. Johnson, *et al.* encourage the interviewer to fight the impulse to break the pause. Rather than repeat the question or press the client, one can pass over the question at the moment and then come back to it later if the client does not refer to the topic himself. Another technique is to frankly recognize the embarrassment of the client by such a statement as, "This is hard to talk about, isn't it?" Questions can sometimes be rephrased. The question should not be answered for the client, and the person should not be forced into an answer or embarrassed by a too lengthy pause.

9. ATTEMPT TO GET BENEATH SUPERFICIAL ANSWERS. We should attempt to rephrase or ask additional questions when the client's answers are obviously superficial. This requires tact and skill, since we cannot attempt to force "confessions" or statements if the client does not want to make them. We should make it easy for him to give answers that are more than superficial but if he persists in superficiality we should simply note this behavior for its diagnostic significance.

10. NOTE DISCREPANCIES IN THE ACCOUNT AND CHECK THEM. When inconsistencies are noted, they should not be ignored, but should be checked as unobtrusively as possible without challenging the client's veracity.

11. HANDLE EMOTIONAL SCENES TACTFULLY. A moderate amount of crying, weeping, anger, or hostility is to be expected and is frequently a sign of good rapport. However it is the responsibility of the clinician to maintain control of the situation and not to allow it to get out of hand, or the client to become too depressed. The clinician must show

sympathy for the client's feelings but he must not exhibit personal feelings by losing control of his own emotions. If the client cries, the clinician does not weep with him, but ordinarily there should not be any attempt to keep him or her from crying. Perhaps it is good release and if the client is doing a satisfactory job, he should be allowed the emotional expression. Silence and waiting are probably the best ways by which the clinician can meet the situation. Occasionally the clinician may express some feeling for the client or reflect some feeling already expressed as the weeping abates. By and large, calm, impersonal, but not-reproving silence is the best therapy. The expression of emotion and feeling may become quite uninhibited and, especially if the purpose of the interview is for therapy or therapy planning, the client should be allowed any relief that he can gain from unburdening himself. Occasionally the clinician may have to stem the flow in the interests of saving time. This can usually be done tactfully by suggesting that there are other areas which you would like to discuss. Reassurance, redirection of the interview, summary of facts of an objective nature may all be used to control emotional scenes.

12. ENCOURAGE FREE EXPRESSION OF OPINION AND EMOTION, BUT KEEP IN MIND THE LIMITATIONS OF THE INTERVIEW SITUATION. No limits are placed on attitudes or emotions or the expression of them, but limits must be placed on behavior. There is no legitimate excuse for a clinician's failure to keep a client under control. Disciplinary problems arise only when there has been some question concerning the clinician's authority or ability to enforce instructions. The clinician is expected to take whatever measures are necessary to maintain control and to take them quickly. This discussion should not be taken to mean that the clinician should set himself up as an authoritarian figure. He should have prestige and that prestige should be recognized by the client. In other words, the problem of control will never arise if rapport has been well established.

13. BE PREPARED FOR QUESTIONS DIRECTED TO YOU BY THE INFORMANT.   If a warm relationship has been established, it is natural for the client to feel that he can ask you a question now and then. As Johnson, *et al.*, suggest, the clinician's answers will depend upon (a) his role in the clinic routine and (b) what his answer will mean in terms of helping or hindering the progress of the interview. Frequently a client will invite the clinician to concur in opinions such as those concerning "right" and "wrong," religion, or the behavior of friends. The opinion may have many motives insofar as the client is concerned. The clinician's concurrence may tend to repress a counter opinion in the client, and thus prevent subsequent discussion. Consequently, we recommend that the clini-

cian not express opinions of his own or concur in the client's opinion on personal or controversial matters. By the same token, we must tactfully avoid getting involved in arguments or denials of the client's point of view.

We will conclude these remarks on the principles of interviewing with one final comment. The clinical conference or interview requires the utmost alertness on the part of the clinician. At every moment mechanisms are revealed by the client that even the best of clinicians are likely to overlook. It is a great mistake for a clinician ever to assume that "nothing is happening."

PATTERN OF THE DIAGNOSTIC
PERSONAL INTERVIEW

The diagnostic personal interview is held with all clients who are capable of engaging in such an interview regardless of age or other factors. An attempt should be made to interview children as well as adults. Any child sufficiently mature and intelligent to carry on a conversation at any level of communication can be interviewed, and valuable information elicited. A personal interview can also be held with practically all neuropsychiatric patients. Only in the instance of the completely uncommunicative patient should the interview be dispensed with. Even with such a person, repeated contacts, until the patient becomes accustomed to the clinician, may result in a successful interview. Information from young clients, psychotic adults, clients of low intelligence, and clients who are unreliable for other reasons, may be limited, erroneous, or even bizarre. However, when considered in its proper perspective, any and all information is valuable. Information obtained directly from the client, even though it has its limitations, represents the client's point of view and should be regarded as indispensable.

The outline we are about to suggest is not presented as a checklist of questions to be asked of the client, but rather as a guide to be used by the clinician in his interview with the client. The presentation and discussion of the interview is closely patterned after material presented by Kelly (6),[5] with many alterations and revisions by the present writer. The topics for discussion are those that should be covered in any diagnostic personal interview. Specific questions are suggested for purposes of illustration and explanation, but no questions need be phrased exactly as suggested here. The clinician should be completely familiar with the pur-

[5] From "A Method of Diagnosing Personality in the Psychological Clinic," by George A. Kelly, *Psychological Record*, 1938, 2, 95–111. Adapted by permission of The Principia Press.

pose of the interview and structure his questions in a way most compatible with his own personality. By the same token, the order of the topics as given in this outline is only suggestive and need not be followed exactly. The individual clinician may wish to vary the order according to his own perferences, and certainly the order of topics will vary from client to client.

No specific record forms are recommended for the personal interview. Although Kelly has suggested the use of a record form, we feel that such a form encourages too great a degree of rigidity in interviewing and in the interpretation and reporting of interviews. In interviews for obtaining historical information, the use of forms was recommended, as the history contains much specific information collected from persons other than the client and, consequently, an organized systematic approach is desirable. It will be recalled that the forms suggested for historical information were not necessarily recommended as rigid checklists; rather, flexibility in the use of the forms was stressed. The personal interview must be even more flexible, and the outline should always be adapted by the clinician to the individual needs of the client. Much of the value of the personal interview lies in the qualitative observations that can be made concerning the behavior of the client in an interpersonal situation when his attention is focused on specific topics.

The remainder of the chapter will be devoted to the subject matter covered by a diagnostic personal interview. At times, specific questions to be asked of the client will be suggested, and it should be noted that in a series of such questions, those asked of children will always be listed first. The specific questions, as adapted from Kelly, are merely suggestions. However they have been tried repeatedly and have proved provocative of valuable responses. The terminology will vary with the age level of the client. The form of the questioning, too, will be somewhat dependent upon the intelligence, educational level, and general understanding of the client. It is important that the wording be such that the client comprehends the exact meaning of the clinician; on the other hand, good rapport is not established if the clinician implies condescension either by word or manner. The verbal techniques of the interview must be custommade for each individual client, and the following pages must be read with this in mind.

CONTENT OF THE DIAGNOSTIC INTERVIEW

STATEMENT OF THE PROBLEM.   It is always advisable that the client be given an opportunity at the beginning of the interview to state his problem as he sees it. This is wise for a number of reasons. The self-referring client—having perhaps come to the clinic after a long period of indecision as to whether to seek counsel—is in this way given an opportunity to unburden himself, and he will be more relaxed and at ease to continue with the interview. The referred patient, particularly if the referral is sudden and unexpected, is often especially benefited by this opportunity to "clear the decks." Frequently unanticipated referrals induce minor panics in persons already emotionally disturbed. Even the child or the psychotic adult who does not understand the reason for his being interviewed must be given the opportunity to talk about the presenting problem after the clinician has explained, to the best of the client's ability to understand, the reason for the referral. The client should be allowed to express his problems to a clinician with acceptant attitudes toward them. Expression of the complaints can make him feel more at ease about a situation which, at the outset, is threatening to him.

The client's mode of presenting his problems is of inestimable value for diagnosis. For example, the client may deny the existence of any problem, he may project the responsibility, he may present an elaborate systematization of causes, or he may attempt to rationalize the problem. Other clients exhibit a great deal of anxiety and may ask questions or in other ways solicit reassurance and help from the clinician. Of course many clients will indicate reasonable insight into the problem and discuss the situation frankly. Some clients will discuss the problem at length. Generally, such a discussion should not be interrupted or interfered with. After the client finishes, or when he finally says, "Well, that's my problem, where do we go from here?" or "I don't know any more to tell you," we should be prepared to continue with the interview. Whatever the reaction may be, whether a problem is described or denied, responsibility accepted or guilt expressed, the reaction is important and is a significant aspect of the evaluation process. Through all of this the role of the clinician should be that of outward acceptance, while at the same time "listening with the third ear."

COMMUNICATION. Insight may be gained into the client's ability to communicate and to discuss himself objectively by asking, "Tell me about yourself. Are you a good boy (or girl) or a bad boy (or girl)?" This will usually elicit some response, even from the very young child. Appropriate and similar questions may be asked of the adult. For example, the interviewer may ask, "Tell me about yourself. What sort of a personality do you have?" "Do you have a good personality, or are you rather disagreeable at times?" Or, "What sort of impression do you make on people?" The reaction of the client to such a question is always of diagnostic significance. He may give a brief answer and be uncommunicative, or he may be quite verbal in his response. His answer may be evasive. He may give a humorous or joking response, or he may plead ignorance. Still other clients may attempt to defend themselves or project to others. Many clients give objective, direct, frank responses that may be either favorable or unfavorable to themselves. The clinician is interested in the response, not only from the standpoint of content, but also in terms of the behavior mechanisms exhibited by the client.

Robert M. Martin (9) has studied the responses of neurotic and psychotic patients to such a question, and has listed several ways in which qualified persons seem to be able to differentiate with a high degree of agreement between these groups of patients. The specific task given to his subjects was: "I would like to ask you a question. It may seem difficult or it may seem easy, but I want you to do your best to answer it as fully and completely as you can. I'd like you to tell me what sort of person you think you are; not just the kind of person you may want other people to think you are, but the kind of person you really know yourself to be." The subject, when he had finished was asked, "Can you tell me anything more about the kind of person you think you are?" The reactions of the subjects to this question were described under eight categories. These categories and a discussion of each follow:

I. Responses indicating awareness of social status and/or social acceptance or nonacceptance. This includes patterns of social interaction and social techniques, successful or not.

Example: "I always try to be nice to people and get along with them."

This category presents, in a rather clear manner, a striking difference in the characteristic responses of the neurotic subjects as compared with those of the psychotic subjects. The neurotic subjects gave such responses more than three times as frequently as the psychotic subjects. The much more frequent reference to the social sphere by the neurotic subjects suggests that an important aspect of their self-concept is their relation to other people.

II. Responses in which the subject expresses a feeling of impotence as to answering the question.

Example: "I don't know."

Psychotic subjects were more apt (five times as often) to express an impotent feeling in regard to answering the question than were the neurotic subjects. This expression of impotence is especially interesting when contrasted with Category I, where it was seen that the psychotic subjects did not think of themselves in interpersonal relations as readily as did the neurotic subjects, and Category II would indicate that they are often unable to express a self-concept at all.

III. Responses in which the subject makes statements of how others see him and/or feel about him.

Example: "Other people think I'm stuck-up and don't like me."

This category of response was given five times as often by neurotic as by psychotic subjects and again reflects the stronger social orientation of the neurotic subjects.

IV. Responses in which the subject describes himself as self-conscious and/or sensitive to the slights of others.

Example: "I'm awfully easy hurt by people when they don't pay attention to me."

This category of response was given twelve times as often by neurotic as by psychotic subjects, and, whereas responses of Category III suggest that the neurotic is more aware of how others react to him, Category IV indicates that this is an area of special sensitivity and concern.

V. Responses in which the subject verbalizes an inability to look at himself or to judge himself and/or the need for an authority to do so for him.

Example: "It's wicked to think about yourself, but my old man could answer that for you."

This type of response was never given by a neurotic subject in Martin's sample, but it was given with moderate frequency by the psychotic subjects. This response suggests a highly submissive and dependent person, and it may reflect a great reluctance on the part of some of the psychotic subjects to commit themselves to a particular self-concept and the course of action it might imply.

VI. Responses in which the subject indicates a faultfinding attitude toward himself, giving a negative evaluation of himself and/or attributing "bad" or undesirable traits to himself.

Example: "Well, I'm too tactless for one thing, and I guess I'm sort of mean with people."

Although this kind of response occurred with moderate frequency in the psychotic group, it occurred almost three times as frequently in the neurotic group. Thus the neurotic exhibits the capacity to negatively self-evaluate himself more frequently than does the psychotic subject. It cannot be said, from the results of this study, that the psychotic cannot look at himself objectively or negatively, but it is apparently usual for the neurotic to do so.

VII. Responses in which the subject states that he is "normal," "average," "all right," "like everybody else," etc.

Example: "I'm just a regular fellow. I'm OK."

This category of response was given quite frequently by both groups, but nearly twice as often by the psychotic group. Apparently this group is not as aware of differences in thought, belief and behavior as is the neurotic group.

VIII. Responses in which the subject uses his illness or a symptom as an excuse or explanation of difficulties in social or economic roles.

Example: "Ever since I got so nervous I can't seem to get along with people at the factory."

This final category of response was given nearly three times as often by neurotic subjects as by psychotic subjects. It was used with only moderate frequency even by the neurotic subjects, and quite infrequently by the psychotic subjects.

Although the results of this study could be discussed at length in terms of the differences between the self-concepts of neurotic and psychotic subjects, our purpose is not to show how the question can be used to differentiate between these groups, but to demonstrate the variety of responses that might be given to it by a subject and information about the client that can be gained from it. The situation posed by this type of question provides information on the communicativeness of the client, and, also, if he answers at all, it may give an idea of his own concept of self. How does the individual perceive himself? Is he self-condemning, or does he feel that he impresses people favorably? Is the amount of confidence he has in himself in keeping with his apparent capabilities, or is his aspirational level too high or too low? In addition, it is valuable to know (when it is possible to infer this) just how accurate his own self-estimate is when compared with his behavior. Knowing, for example, that a patient thinks himself benevolent and thoughtful, even though it is known that he beats old women and small children is much more meaningful than just knowing that he feels himself benevolent and thoughtful.

INTERESTS. Still further appraisal of the productivity of the client and of his methods of thinking may be made, as well as specific information elicited, by questions about interests. It should be understood that the clinician must phrase all questions in his own style, and that specific as well as general questions will probably be necessary. It would be impossible to summarize all of the possibilities of questioning in this area, but for a child such a general question as "What are the things you like to do?" or "What do you like to play at?" or for the adult, "What are your principal interests in life?" may provide the clinician with information for his evaluation as well as leads for further questions.

The clinician will be interested in the varieties of interests suggested —studies, music, projects, dramatics, society, movies, gangs, athletics, mechanics, garden, pets, collections, toys, games, family, work. He will also note whether the interests are broad or narrow, whether the client is a participant in activities or an observer, whether he enjoys companionship or would prefer solitary activities.

SOCIAL PARTICIPATION IN RECREATION.   One specific follow-up of the above area might be in terms of recreational interests and social participation in recreation. The child should be asked about play, or what he does for fun, and who his playmates are. The adult client may be asked, "What sort of recreation do you get?" and "With whom do you usually take your recreation?" The client may indicate few or many activities, indoor or outdoor activities, social or individual recreational activities, planned or unplanned recreation, real or fantasy activities, and may be interested or bored by recreational activities. It is significant to note whether his companions are older or younger, of the same or different sex, parents, siblings, or friends; or whether he is indifferent to companions generally. Is he a leader or a follower in recreational and social activities? Is he aggressive or submissive? Is he aware of the needs of others or is all his behavior self-oriented? Is he so keenly sensitive to the feelings of others that he is a "milquetoast?" Does he show any ability to empathize with those he sees about him or does he ignore them? Is he capable of feeling sympathy? How does he feel about being with others —would he rather be out in the woods hunting? Does he belong to any groups or organizations that provide him with social contact and stimulation? Does he feel accepted by most of the people with whom he spends his time, or does he feel that they only tolerate him because, for some reason, they must? From what sort of activity does he derive most satisfaction? Does this activity require solitude, the company of a few friends or of large groups? If he is not comfortable in a social situation, can he explain his discomfort?

AMBITIONS AND ANTICIPATORY ATTITUDE TOWARD THE FUTURE. The clinician is interested in the client's ambitions, particularly in the vocational, marital, and family areas. In a more general sense, he is interested in the anticipatory attitude of the client. What does the future hold for him as he sees it? Does he expect failure or punishment? Does he feel that "fate has it in for him," or does he believe that things will work out constructively? If he has come for counseling or psychotherapy, does he feel that attention to his difficulties may lead to alleviation of his distress?

The child may be asked: "What do you want to do when you grow up?" "Did you decide that all by yourself?" or "Do you want to get married and have children of your own?" For an adult questions will be at a somewhat more advanced vocabulary level: "What are your ambitions?" or "What vocation are you going to prepare for?"

MOTIVATION. What are the primary motivations and strivings of the individual? What are his goals, and how might he be helped to set up goals? Is he well motivated, or do nihilistic attitudes predominate? Has he any motivation for changing his adjustment? Would he invite or accept counseling or therapy? If the order of the present outline is followed, the clinician may refer back to the ambitions and ask, "What is there about —— that you like so much?" "What is your reason for choosing that?" "Does that sort of thing mean a great deal to you?" "What are some of the other things that you want to get out of life?" "What would you say that life meant to you in general?" From these and similar questions, adjusted to the age level of the client, the clinician may note whether the client's principal motives fall into some of the following areas: exhibitionism, popularity, security, wealth, mastery, self-assertion, adventure, romance, escape, domination of persons, and the like.

INSIGHT INTO BARRIERS OR FRUSTRATIONS BEING EXPERIENCED OR ANTICIPATED. One of the more significant areas about which the diagnostician needs information concerns the barriers and frustrations that the client is experiencing or is likely to experience in the future. Equally important is the amount of insight he has concerning his needs and frustrations. Is there a suggestion that he may be attempting to introspect and understand his difficulties as they relate to his own behavior, or does he deny any connection between personal problems and his major complaints? Does he spontaneously volunteer information regarding interaction with parents, siblings, or coworkers? Does he seem intellectually capable of achieving insight even though none is expressed during the interview? If he is seriously ill, or institutionalized, does he realize that he is ill or even where he is?

If the client has not spontaneously volunteered information, or if the clinician wishes to pursue the subject further, he can frequently refer back to the ambitions and ask, "Is there anything that might keep you from doing that?" "Do you think you will achieve your ambition?" "What obstacle or obstacles stand in your way?" "What are some of the things you will have to overcome before you can achieve your ambitions?" In addition to evaluating the amount of insight and reality orientation revealed by the client's answers, the clinician should note the recognized barriers. These barriers may be in terms of factors such as intelligence, education, age, opposition from people, poverty, wife, children, parents, or other responsibilities.

DEPRESSING EXPERIENCES AND REACTION TO THEM. Most of the areas up to this point are not ordinarily very threatening or disturbing to the client. However the clinician must judge how fast the movement of the interview can be and govern its progress in terms of the client's reaction. Giving the client a chance to express himself about the depressing experiences he has had provides a reasonably good opening wedge to some of the more threatening areas. The client may be asked, "Has anything happened lately to make you feel badly?" "What are some of the things that make you feel unhappy?" "Have you had any serious disappointments in love, deaths in the family, or financial catastrophe?" The client may verbalize concerning disappointments, or describe depressing experiences arising from areas such as finances, health, education, social opportunities, personal recognition, deaths, love, or children. Notation of the areas is important, not only with reference to the disappointments themselves, but also in gauging the extent to which reaction is proportional to experience. The client's reaction as he describes these experiences is important. Is his emotion or feeling real, or is he flat and apathetic in describing the experience?

MOODS, AFFECTIVE STATES, AND TOLERANCE FOR EMOTIONAL RE-ACTIONS.   Does the client appear emotionally labile? Does he laugh or cry without reasonable provocation? Is there evidence that he is easily hurt? Does he seem easily discouraged? What is the nature of his extreme affective states? Although some cues to the individual's general affective state can be gained from posture and appearance, his general mood should be appraised also from the content of his verbalizations, as well as from his manner of speech. Does the future look gloomy, or does it hold hope? Is the optimism expressed based on reality or on fantasy; that is, does the future look bright because he is capable of meeting the environmental situations or stresses as they arise, or is there a "rose-colored" perception of tomorrow? If the mood is cheerful, is it best described as elation, exaltation, ecstasy, or euphoria? Are the negative aspects of the mood seen as depression, sadness, nihilism, apprehension, apathy, irritability, hostility, or anger?

Kelly suggests questions such as the following: "Are you a happy person, or are you a sad person?" "How happy do you feel?" "How sad do you feel?" "Do you ever feel you don't want to live any longer?" "Do you ever feel so happy that you just don't know what to do with yourself?" "Do you get the 'blues' frequently, or are you usually quite happy?" "How excited do you get when you are happiest?" "How do you feel at those times?" "How do you feel when you get the 'blues?' " "Do you feel sick and exhausted?" "Do you feel as if you want to kill yourself?" "How often do you feel that way? "Do those feelings come regularly?" "Do you frequently feel melancholy?" "Do your feelings of elation and depression come in regular cycles or at regular times?"

Answers to questions such as these should give the clinician information with which to clarify the nature of the client's "mood-outlook," and in addition they will give some indication of suicidal tendencies and cycloid trends. Some clients or patients may appear to exhibit morbid thought processes as a result of the suggestive nature of the questions used to elicit this material. The clinical judgment of the clinician may lead him to feel that in certain instances some of the questions suggested above should be omitted because of the danger of unduly disturbing the client. Although we must be cautious, it is likely that this danger is overrated. If the person has been considering suicide, for example, the questions will not suggest anything new to him; and if he has not, the questions will not be disturbing. Consequently, it is usually wise to approach sensitive and defensive points directly, after gradually and considerately leading up to them.

ANXIETIES AND WORRIES. The purpose of exploring this area is to learn the sources of anxiety and worry recognized by the client. Actually, many of the objects or subjects named by him may be façades—the anxieties recognized by him as acceptable substitutes for more basic anxieties that are repressed. In any case, it is important to know what he thinks or reports as the source of anxiety, and it is possible that some of the tensions and anxieties expressed are correctly associated with real sources of anxiety. In children, the named objects frequently have basic significance. Some suggested questions are: "When you feel sad, what do you feel sad about?" "When you feel unhappy, what do you think about?" "What do you worry about mostly?" "Do you worry in spite of your better judgment?" "Do you feel yourself compelled to worry even though you do not feel that there is any cause for worry?" "Is this just a temporary worry or do you have it frequently?" The typical responses to such questions may involve matters ranging from finances to dreams, from health to education, and may include social opportunities, personal recognition, death, love, pregnancy, castration, mates, parents, children, homosexuality, heterosexuality, masturbation, responsibilities, religion, philosophy, anger, accidents, or employment. It is useful to ascertain whether anxiety is chronic or temporary and to estimate its degree of superficiality.

FEARS AND PHOBIAS. Even though many of the recognized fears are, at times, substitutes for more basic sources of fear, the objects of fear which are reported should be noted, regardless of whether they are real or substitutes. The questioning may follow a line such as: "What are you afraid of?" "Are you afraid of the dark, or are you afraid of some people, etc.?" "Do you have any fears?" "What are your principal fears?" "Are you afraid of some things that you feel are not really dangerous?" "Do you have any unreasonable fears?"

It would be impossible even to attempt to list all the possible responses that might be given. Many names have been given to various phobias, such as nyctophobia, homophobia, monstrophobia, thematophobia, acrophobia, pathophobia, hydrophobia, agoraphobia, monophobia, neophobia, and the old familiar claustrophobia. It is not necessary to record phobias in such terms, and, in general, the everyday objects or subjects may be more meaningful than the technical names.

SOURCES OF CONFLICT.   It is especially valuable to talk with the client about the sources and kinds of conflict which he experiences. Are they mostly within the family? Are they centered around religion, morals, mores, or the law? Many conflicts are within the occupational area; and it may be important to identify the sources of conflict outside of the family or home in contrast to those within the family. Are the sources of conflict extrinsic, that is, outside the person, or are they intrinsic, such as conflicts with inhibitory ideas or moral codes?

Some suggested questions concerning conflict areas are: "How do you get along with your brothers and sisters?" "Are they nice to you?" "How do you get along with your mother and father?" "Do you like them?" "Do they like you?" "How do you get along with your girl friend?" "Are there sometimes tensions which arise at home?" "What is the nature of the difficulties at work?" "Do you have most of your difficulties with others?" "Who is usually to blame for your conflicts?" "Does your family stick together?"

The clinician should note carefully the number and kinds of conflicts reported. The actual number is not particularly important, but there is probably a difference in significance between the client's naming one item and discussing it extensively, and his listing many items. Particular significance might be attached to attitudes concerning the home such as: a marked tendency to defend members of the family, tendency to project upon members of the family, anxious attitude in the home, overt domestic tension, feelings of insecurity in the home, feelings of being unaccepted in the family and uncertainty regarding status in the family.

SOURCES OF ANGER AND HOSTILITY.   In addition to sources of conflict, we usually inquire about sources of irritation and anger. As with many of the topics discussed in this chapter, we are interested in the manner in which hostility is expressed, as well as to what or to whom it may be expressed. Inability to express anger or hostility may be as significant as the expression of it. Can the client express hostility toward figures of authority? What is the attitude toward parental figures in this regard? How does he feel toward past military service, or toward supervisors? Is he unable to criticize, or is he hypercritical? If he does not express hostility directly, how and toward whom is it displaced? Are his attitudes or his expressed feelings contradictory or ambivalent? Is the client able to perceive such contradictions?

Some suggested questions are: "Do you ever get mad?" "Are there people who don't like you?" "Did you ever get in a fight?" "Who won?" "Who stopped the fight?" "After that, what did you do about it?" "How do you feel about it now?" "What sort of situations irritate you or make you angry?" "What kind of people make you angry?" "Tell me about two or three of your enemies." Of significance to the clinician are situations that appear to arouse the client's anger, the people with whom he quarrels or fights, anxieties arising from anger or temper, self-contempt because of lack of self-control, projection of blame for conflicts, feeling of guilt because of anger, anger fantasies, and other pertinent kinds of information.

Likes and Dislikes.   This topic differs somewhat from the topic of interests, but it certainly overlaps with that area, as well as with others. Although likes and dislikes are important in and of themselves, the question is inserted here as a "breather" in the present order. Some of the items or questions have been rather directive and threatening; others that follow are perhaps more intimate, and possibly more disturbing. Even likes and dislikes are exciting to some clients, but in our experience we have found clients to be somewhat impersonal when discussing this topic. Although there is nothing magic about this order of questioning, in actual interviewing practice it proceeds quite smoothly. Regardless of the order followed, most interviewers will want to inquire about likes and/or dislikes.

Suggested questions are: "Tell me about some place you like to be." "What are some of the things you like (or dislike) very much?" "What kind of people do you like best?" "Who is your best friend?" "Do you know any other people who are as nice as that?" "Which of your belongings mean most to you?" "What places or situations are most attractive to you?" "What activities do you like (or dislike)?" "What kind of people do you prefer as companions?" The typical responses will concern objects, situations, activities, or people, and further discussion may reveal important characteristics or aspects of the responses.

Religious Beliefs.   An area of information all too frequently overlooked is that of religion. Attitudes and concepts regarding religion frequently play a dominant role in personal development and in the etiology of behavior disorders. The reasons for its importance are so obvious that they hardly need discussion. We presume that religion is sometimes neglected in interviewing because of the relationships between psychology and religion and the idea held by some that religion should be left alone by the psychologist. We believe that religion can be ethically discussed by the psychologist. Our only caution is that the psychologist should not take a personal position in his discussion of religion with his client.

Omission of this topic would leave a large gap in the "jigsaw puzzle" that the diagnostician is attempting to assemble, and an effort should be made to fill in this gap.

Some suggested questions in this area are: "Do you go to church?" "What church do you go to?" "Do you like church?" "How often do you go?" "Do you pray?" "What is there about church that you like?" "What is your attitude toward religion?" "Have you ever been converted?" "Do you feel or have you ever felt that you have a religious calling?" "What part of religion appeals to you the most?" When the clinician has knowledge of the religious affiliation or church membership of the client, some of the questions can be more appropriately phrased, but the attitudes of the client toward his church or religion in general should be explored. Typical responses may reveal items such as experience of conversion, mysticism, ritualism, taboos, fear, agnosticism, cynicism, pantheism, customary grace at table, regular prayers, number of Sunday school attendances per month, principal sources of religious influence, and similarity of or differences in beliefs between client and family or friends.

GUILT FEELINGS.   Guilt is difficult to evaluate but the clinician must attempt to make hypotheses about the presence or absence of guilt feelings and their relative importance in the client's adjustment. Almost certainly the evaluation of these feelings will not be complete from a single interview but a beginning should be made. The meaning of feelings of guilt and the significant bases for them may not be apparent with some clients until counseling has progressed. In any event, the clinician must ask himself: How much guilt is shown? Is it readily verbalized in statements that acknowledge responsibility for failure or deed, or is it inferred from apparent projection of guilt or from repression or blocking; what are the areas of the guilt; what is the attitude expressed if the responsibility is acknowledged—is it self-condemnation or promises for reform?

The clinician might ask, "Do you ever feel that you have been bad?" "What is bad about you?" "What do you feel guilty about mostly?" "Is it things that you think or things that you do that are bad?" "What have you been doing about it?" "What do you think you ought to do about it?" The client may express general or specific guilt feelings. He may express a felt need for expiation. He may report fear of contempt from others or self-contempt. He may rationalize, or report compulsive reactions or ambivalent attitudes toward his own behavior.

INHIBITIONS.   A discussion of inhibitory ideas or the controls that the individual may use consciously or unconsciously is still another area of extreme importance if the client can verbalize about it. In another sense the inability to verbalize any such inhibitory ideas may be equally diagnostic. The area may be tapped by such questions as, "What keeps you from doing naughty things?" "Does somebody watch you so that you will be good, or are you good just because you want to be?" "What is there to keep you from being bad?" "How is your life kept under control?" "Is it controlled by people who watch you?" "What is there to keep you from being immoral or bad?" "What kinds of things do you regard as immoral or bad?" "What kind of self-control do you exercise?" We may anticipate that the client will suggest that he is guided by hero worship, sense of duty, expected reward, by religion, by a moral code, or perhaps by other people, if he is aware of the source of his inhibitory ideas. Denial of any controlling principles or the denial of any inhibitions is as important from the standpoint of evaluation as the listing of many controls.

COMPULSIONS AND OBSESSIONS. Indications of frequent compulsive actions may be given spontaneously by the subject but more often it is necessary to elicit such material by means of questions. Activities such as repeated checking to make sure that the doors are locked or that fires in fireplaces or in ashtrays are out are examples of kinds of behavior suggestive of the individual's inability to rely on himself and are indicative of compulsive doubting. The kind of activity or thinking in which the person persists indicates much more than the fact that obsessive or compulsive behavior exists. The character of this activity may have definite diagnostic meaning. Questions can be quite directive: "Do you ever do things when you feel that you can't help doing them?" "Do you ever think things that you don't want to think?" "Do you sometimes find yourself doing things that you cannot help, for no reason at all?" "Do you have some ideas that seem to be forced upon you?" "Tell me about them." The possible responses are multitudinous, but samples of client reports include such topics as superstitions, destructive tendencies, compulsions to count, to lock doors, to expect accidents, sexual compulsions, etc.

DREAMS. Various approaches to the understanding of behavior dynamics, as well as approaches to therapy, differ in their emphasis on the use of dreams. However some use can usually be made of information about dreams and dreaming. Even though we may not be particularly interested in the content of dreams, we can make use of data concerning the frequency of dreaming, amnesia for dreams, frequency of nightmarish dreams, vividness of dreams, and special characteristics of the dreams. Our suggested questions concerning dreams include: "Do you dream?" "Do you have dreams that repeat themselves?" "Do you often have bad dreams or nightmares?" "Tell me about one of your dreams." In addition to recording the frequency and any other special characteristics of the dreams, the clinician may record one or more dreams reported by the client.

SLEEPING HABITS.   While inquiring about dreams, it is frequently convenient to cover sleeping habits by asking questions such as: "Is it easy for you to go to sleep?" "Do you go to sleep at the same time every night?" "How much sleep do you ordinarily get?" The client may respond by mentioning topics such as insomnia, tossing at night, somnambulism, unrested in the morning, regular sleeping habits, irregular habits, night terrors, or excessive sleeping.

FANTASY.   Since daydreaming or fantasy formation is regarded as a common form of compensation and is usually to some degree the result of frustrated motives, it follows that daydreams may be meaningful and significant. Even aside from the content, the amount of preoccupation with fantasy is suggestive of conflict in, and/or satisfaction with, present adjustment. Suggested questions for eliciting material in this area are: "What do you think about when you are all by yourself and there is nothing to do?" "Do you ever tell yourself a story or just play like things are happening?" "Tell me one of these stories." "Do you ever daydream or imagine things happening to you just for the fun of it?" "Do your daydreams ever come true?" We note responses such as continued daydream stories, repeated daydreams, systematized fantasy, bizarre daydreams, euphoric daydreams, self represented in daydreams, self represented as a conquering hero, few or many characters, and the conditions under which daydreams are most common.

HALLUCINATIONS.   Kenneth E. Appel and Edward A. Strecker (1) suggest approaching this topic by asking, "Is your hearing (or vision) good?" and then asking if the patient or client has ever thought that he heard or saw someone and then discovered that there was no one there. Our procedure is to be quite directive, and although there do not seem to be any obvious disadvantages in approaching the topic by first discussing sensory functions, we have not found this too helpful. Questions about imagination may elicit responses that indicate hallucination. Frequently the person who does hallucinate will be guarded about acknowledging the experience, but he may give himself away during the interview by turning suddenly and looking away (frequently up over his shoulder, in the case of auditory hallucinations), or by suddenly responding as if to another's statement, or by suddenly attending carefully to something of which the interviewer is not aware. However, simply noting that the patient or client hallucinates is not enough. An important aspect of hallucination, as far as a dynamic evaluation is concerned, is its content. We may sometimes learn the content of a hallucination by being acceptant of the fact that the client may hear voices even though the interviewer is unable to hear them. In some instances when it is quite apparent that the subject is actually hallucinating during the interview, we may ask, "What did you hear?" or "What did you see?" Some other specific questions that may be asked of the client are: "Do you ever think that you see things and then find that they are not really there at all?" "Do you ever feel things crawling over you?" "Do you frequently hear people talking to you when others can't hear them?" "Do you ever have visions that seem almost as real as actual events?" "Do you hear words or sounds that are difficult to account for?" We usually note whether hallucinations, if present, are visual, auditory, or in other sensory modalities, whether they are considered real by the client, the client's explanation of the event, value (such as prophetic) attached to the experience, whether voices or sounds come from within or without, and specific information such as voices coming from dead persons.

DELUSIONS.   If asked directly, the client will frequently deny delusional thoughts, and with many clients subtle questioning may be necessary when approaching this area. A simple question like "How are you getting along financially?" may gain entry to a whole delusional system if the interviewer is alert. When fixed delusions are reported, it is sometimes possible to spend some time discussing them. In this connection, many clinicians favor considerable caution, as delusions, particularly of a persecutory nature, may be strengthened if the interviewer seems to "know" about them. A few additional sample questions are: "Do you feel that people talk about you?" "Who are some of your enemies?" "Why are they enemies?" "Do you get along well with most people?" "Does everyone recognize you for what you are?" Typical responses to such questions include delusions of persecution, feeling of being watched or talked about, expressions of jealousy directed toward the client, belief of being wronged, influences used against the client, plans for revenge, delusions of grandeur, strength, power, wealth, noble birth. We note particularly the degree of bizarreness and systematization of the delusions.

HYPOCHONDRIA.   The client's concept of his own health and his preoccupation with health and bodily functioning is an area that should never be omitted from the personal interview. Actually, if hypochondriacal ideas are prominent, the clinician will not be able to avoid talking about this area. Hypochondriacal ideas are usually introduced by the client when he states the problem, and then referred to at every opportunity. Recently, a client who was being seen for the first time, massaged his adbomen throughout the entire interview with his hand beneath his trouser top. Before the interview was over, he had unfastened the top of his trousers and was massaging with both hands. With this client, the simple question, "Is your abdomen giving you trouble?" was sufficient to unleash a torrent of comment about his difficulties, his medications, and the general inadequacy of the medical profession in cases like his own. Clients often rub their eyes, hold their heads, or even take their pulse during interviews. It is not necessary to give examples of particular questions, as almost any inquiry about health will serve as a "primer" to stimulate the desired responses, even if no leads are suggested.

HETEROSEXUAL ADJUSTMENTS. It would not appear necessary to justify the need for questioning about heterosexual adjustments. They are important in the lives of most, if not all, clients. We do not need to subscribe to any particular theoretical frame of reference in order to ask questions in this area. Sexual conflicts and adjustments make up an area of behavior which should neither be neglected nor overemphasized. This area is best approached quite directly. Suggested questions for children and young people follow: "Do you have a girl (or boy) friend?" "How long have you had this friend?" "Do you sometimes like, and sometimes hate her (or him)?" "Do you love her (or him) and want to touch her (or him)?" (From now on, we will assume the alternate appropriate pronoun.)

"Are you afraid to talk to her?" "Did you ever do anything together that was naughty?" "What?" "Were you afraid?" "How do you feel about this?" "Are you happy with this friend?" "Do you hold each other real tight sometimes?" "Do you ever touch each other under your clothes?" "How close do you get to each other?" "How many times did you do that?" "How many girls have you done that with?" "Did you ever pay a girl for that?" "Did you ever see anyone else do that?" "Did any girl ever try to get you to have sexual relations with her?" Similar questions using more appropriate language and terminology may be asked of adults. It may not be necessary to ask many questions but the clinician should not make any assumptions about sexual adjustments, and even if the client is embarrassed, shocked, or offended, valuable information is gained by questions in this area. The clinician receives many different, but typical responses. We cannot list all the kinds of responses with which we might be concerned, but the following examples will illustrate the range of information that may be elicited: relationships with mate or lover, time love affair has lasted, ambivalent attitude toward opposite sex, erotic attitudes, inhibited attitudes, anxious attitudes, fearfulness, guilt, disgust, satisfaction with heterosexual status, number of kissing experiences, experience of petting, mutual masturbation, sexual intercourse, seduction, acceptance or offering of pay, etc.

HOMOSEXUAL ADJUSTMENTS. Many interviewers have difficulty in approaching the homosexual area and valuable information is frequently lost by default. Reticence on the part of the clinician is unjustified—the area can and should be approached frankly. Following discussion of heterosexual adjustments, one can ask, "Is it just as easy for you to like another boy as it is for you to like a girl (when the client is male)?" "Have you ever been in love with a boy (or girl)?" "Did you ever touch each other under your clothes?" "Or did you just feel like it?" "Has any other boy ever wanted to play with you sexually?" "How did you feel about it?" "When did you start playing with yourself?" We are interested in overt homosexual experiences, attitudes about such experiences and anxiety about such feelings, anxiety about masturbation, etc. If considerable anxiety is expressed following such questioning, the clinician should offer as much factual reassurance or support as is necessary to prevent aggravation of anxiety or the inducement of panic.

THE CLINICIAN'S OBSERVATIONS

The clinician should observe carefully the client's reaction to this examination. He may be depressed, anxious, may cry, may express hope or discouragement, or he may ask for a further appointment even though the interview was structured as diagnostic. The client may be relieved rather than disturbed, but at the end of the examination the clinician must realize that he has probably probed quite deeply into the intimate life of the client and that while the client may benefit somewhat from having a more objective point of view established, he is also likely to feel disorganized or fearful. Not infrequently he will feel that criticism was implied from the nature of the questions in the last part of the examination. It may be necessary to encourage the client to suspend judgment until the next conference. *If the client is depressed and no further conferences are in prospect, it is absolutely essential that he be reassured and left with a constructive point of view.*

The clinician should observe the appearance and activity of the client. Are his clothes in keeping with his economic and occupational level as inferred from other information? Are they dirty, ragged, sloppily worn, or is the individual overdressed, showing meticulousness that is suggestive of compulsivity? Notice his hands. What is done with them during the course of the interview? Are they noticeably moist and clammy? Are the nails bitten down beyond the quick, or are they carefully manicured? What was the impression gained from the handclasp at introduction? Was it firm and friendly, or was it limp? Did the client offer his hand readily and enthusiastically, or did he present it gingerly, held close to his body? What does he do with his eyes? Are they directed at the interviewer most of the time, or does his gaze wander about the room, out the window, or back over his shoulder? What can be observed about his facial expression? Does he frown frequently? Are extreme facial contortions, grimaces, or tics to be observed? Does he smile at logical times, or as if he perceives some cryptic meaning in the interviewer's remark or question, or not at all?

What is the general level of physical activity? Is there an overactivity or an apparent reduction in activity? Observe for stereotypy of movements, striking mannerisms, and sudden (impulsive) motor activity. Does the client relax and extend himself physically or does he give the impression of holding himself in, by keeping his arms, hands, and legs close to his body? Is negativism indicated by his movements in answer to suggestions such as "Won't you sit down?" What is his manner of speech? Is it steadily monotonous and infrequently punctuated, or is delivery accomplished by means of rapid spurts? Is there evidence of blocking, and, if so, in what area of content? Is there a suggestion of flights of ideas, or, on the other hand, does there seem to be a deprivation of ideas? Is the material presented relevant, or is it disconnected and incoherent? Indications of short attention span, divertibility of attention, and other disturbances of attention can usually be noted during the interview. Memory disorders can frequently be detected and such symptoms as amnesia for events associated with traumatic incidents, confabulation, retrospective falsification, and excessive recall of details are indicative of behavior that may be obvious, or at least inferred, from the discussion.

Finally, we should make observations of the orientation of the client. We may frequently be surprised to find that an individual who appears in other ways to be fairly well integrated shows lack of orientation. Traditionally, we think of orientation as being in the spheres of time, place, and person. In the rare instances when orientation is not apparent following the long interview, the clinician should ask the questions necessary to evaluate orientation. The point should be approached somewhat more subtly than by such questions as "What day is this?" "What is this place?" or "What is your name?" The inquiry should not be so threatening or ridiculous as to insult the well-oriented client. Questions such as "How long have you been here?" "How long since you finished school?" "What is your father's full name?" "Your full name?" etc., are usually more subtle than the unveiled questions sometimes asked.

It should not be assumed that the report or evaluation based in part on the interview should cover every point described. And it must be remembered that this is simply a guide for the clinician's observations and questions. The report of the interview will be most useful if it is narrative in form, describing the person as observed, in an integrated, meaningful fashion.

AN EXAMPLE OF THE USE OF AN INTERVIEW

A young man, whom we will call Ray, referred himself to a psychologist because he had a premonition that something terrible was going to happen to him. He could not describe what he expected, but he was constantly plagued by the feeling that some catastrophe was about to occur. He reported that he could not eat, that he perspired all the time, and that he had difficulty going to sleep, but when he finally fell asleep, he might sleep for fifteen to twenty hours at a time. Ray was a handsome, neatly dressed, clean-looking man of twenty-four. He was obviously tense, his hands were tremulous and moist, and he had difficulty in maintaining his attention. He was constantly glancing about, and he seldom looked the interviewer in the eye.

When asked what kind of a person he thought he was, he said that other people thought him silly. He went on to say that he did not want to think about this for fear he would "blow his top." His speech was jerky and limited mainly to incomplete sentences, although he occasionally burst out with a brief statement. He reported that he had been "beside himself" for about six months but that he had been "pretty tense" as long as he could remember. His interests were described as being quite broad. He listed a number of activities that he enjoyed, but hastened to inform the interviewer that he had not been able to take part in most of them because he was afraid of what might happen. Most of the interests he mentioned were intellectual in nature. He liked to read history, biography, and what he called "good" novels. He enjoyed music, art, and the theater. In fact, his interests seemed almost *too* broad, and the interviewer had the distinct impression that the client had made a deliberate effort to cultivate the "right" kinds of interests. Insofar as recreation was concerned, he described solitary activities, again mentioning music, art, good books, and similar interests that he pursued by himself. Vocationally, Ray mentioned his desire to be a pharmacist, but he was quite bitter about the fact that this required college training. He thought it silly to have to spend four years taking a lot of nonpractical courses just to fill prescriptions. This was one of the areas in which he burst out with several sentences, but he was reticent after his initial outburst. He said that he did not expect to attend college because he could not make the grades. He claimed to have been in college for two years and said that he had made all "A" and "F" grades. He never made any intermediate grades. He could see nothing in the future. Everything was sure to go wrong and he simply could not "see anything except trouble." Something would happen and he would (as he repeated several times) "blow his top."

In connection with this discussion of education, we discovered that he had "blown his top" at least once. When he was seventeen, he had been a student at a small and strict school. This was before he was drafted for military service. He had gone to school at his parents' request. He did not wish to attend school because he was sure he would be killed in the war and he wanted to enjoy himself while he could. The school did not allow him much opportunity for "living it up," and he had broken several of the regulations. Because of these difficulties and his grades, he was confident that he would be expelled. One night he was able to gain access to the main administrative offices of the school and within a few minutes raised havoc. He emptied all files onto the floor, turned over desks, mixed up index files, and, in general, turned things upside down. He was apprehended and immediately expelled.

He claimed to be continually depressed and related several occasions on which he had attempted suicide. The only reasons for these attempts were that he simply felt too badly to go on, that he was "nothing but trouble," and other vague explanations. Careful questioning about the suicide attempts led the interviewer to question whether they were sincere attempts. Ray took aspirin on several occasions. He took enough to make him ill, but his knowledge of pharmacy could hardly have allowed him to believe seriously that he would die.

When the question of depressing experiences was pursued, he related that he had been referred to a psychologist after the incident at the small school. The psychologist apparently felt that he should have psychiatric help and had referred him to a psychiatrist. Unfortunately, he misinterpreted the explanation of why he was referred. His reaction was to the effect that he was so sick that he was beyond the help of the psychologist. He reported that the psychologist had said, "I can't do anything for you." We have no idea whether this was actually said, but in any case he interpreted the remark as indicating the hopelessness of his situation. When the interviewer asked him about his fears and anxieties, further information was obtained about his "fear of insanity." This anxiety or fear had been much more general when he was younger. From the time he had begun school he had felt that he was different from other children. By the time of his second or third year in school, he began to be terribly afraid of physical conflict. He took no part in competitive games or sports. Later, as the thought of approaching military service presented itself he became preoccupied with the fear of fighting and the idea of death. At the time of the interview the fear of insanity was foremost, but he was also fearful of any form of physical conflict.

Ray was an only child. He at first reported no conflict with anyone. He said, "I get along fine with my parents." Further questioning along this line suggested that he was extremely dependent upon his parents. Apparently they had "done everything for him." Discussion of his health revealed that he had been a sickly child. At least his parents regarded him as such. He recalled that his first-grade teacher would carry him out to the playground where he would watch other children play while he sat in a swing. Presumably his mother had asked the teacher to do this. His parents picked him up at school and put him to bed soon after they got him home. Actually he saw relatively little of his parents, since they encouraged him to read quietly or to sleep. At the time of the interview he claimed to have no anxiety about his health. He insisted that he was strong, and he seemed to make quite a point of this. He exercised regularly and was quite preoccupied with physical culture. He insisted that he had never been angry with anyone. Certainly he had never had a fight.

Ray denied any feelings about religion. Then with further encouragement, he insisted that the only intelligent attitude was that of atheism. It was evident that he had done quite a bit of thinking about this. He also denied any guilt feelings. However it seemed significant that he took this opportunity to tell the interviewer more about his "fear of insanity." He said, "No, I don't feel guilty but I should tell you more about my mental health." After the psychologist had referred him to a psychiatrist, he had entered into a program of therapy in which he saw a psychiatrist three times a week. This was expensive and necessitated his living in a city some distance from his home. He obtained a job operating an elevator and saw his therapist for about ten weeks. Finally the psychiatrist told Ray that he did not want to waste his money and that he should discontinue treatment. Again, Ray interpreted this as a statement of the seriousness of his condition. Actually, the psychiatrist did not feel that Ray's problems were very serious (we have consulted the psychiatrist). On this occasion Ray decided to run away and he bought a motor scooter and started north. He did not know where he was going but felt he would go just as far as he could. He got tired after about a hundred miles and called his parents asking them to come and get him. After returning home he made his first "attempt" at suicide. He took a hundred aspirin tablets and tried to hang himself with a shirt, but the shirt kept tearing, and he finally wore himself out by frenzied efforts to do something to himself and called his parents.

Following this incident his parents placed him in a private hospital, but he ran away from the hospital and came home because he thought the other patients were "bad company." He could not elaborate on this at this point in the interview, but later when we asked about sexual behavior, it developed that some patient had made homosexual advances to him. After his return home, he enlisted in the Navy. His enlistment apparently followed his reading a letter from the hospital in which he was described as a "pre-schizophrenic" person. His period of initial training in the Navy was extremely traumatic and distasteful to him, and after a month he went to the dispensary to tell them he was a "schizophrenic." At first they laughed at him, but he insisted that they write to the various psychiatrists and the psychologist about him. After a few weeks he received a discharge and returned to his home. The interview under discussion was held soon after this time.

Ray did not appear ever to have experienced delusions or hallucinations of an unusual nature. He was constantly obsessed by his feeling of "impending doom," but his basic symptom appeared to be his generalized "free-floating" anxiety. Apparently he had had no contact with girls beyond talking with them, and even this had been very limited. He could not think of asking a girl for a date, and physical contact or sexual relationships were "unthinkable." He had seemingly experienced a severe panic reaction when a man at the hospital had put his hand inside Ray's shirt. He denied ever dreaming. He sometimes slept for long periods of time, but had trouble falling asleep.

All the above material was elicited in an interview lasting about fifty minutes. Actually, other information was elicited as well, but the above appeared most pertinent. The range of the material is quite extensive and should suggest some hypotheses to the psychologist. Our primary hypothesis was that basically Ray suffered from extreme feelings of physical inadequacy. These feelings seemed to have had their beginnings very early in his life. He had never been able, nor was he given a chance to find out whether he was able, to conduct himself physically as did other children. Subsequent information described him as a very awkward child who was late in learning to walk and who was weak and unsteady on his feet until he was five. This feeling of inadequacy had rapidly developed into a feeling of difference and a fear of physical conflict or competition. In grade school and high school he had compensated for this intellectually, but in college he could not excel (or at least thought he could not) in all study areas. He had adopted the idea that some subjects were worthwhile and others impractical. He concentrated on a few subjects and neglected the others. The interviewer was puzzled as to why Ray had not been able to compensate more adequately, but concluded that he was only slightly above average intellectually and that he was not able to excel enough to really satisfy himself. This was suggested by his limited verbal facility and naïve intellectualism. In one way or another Ray had been able to avoid physical conflict until the prospect of military service had come up. He had not seen any way of avoiding it and had simply given up, feeling that he had about two years to live. These factors, together with doubts about his masculinity (this was guessed at, but did come out later in counseling) and his continually repressed aggressive feelings, had resulted in his level of tension getting so high as to be uncontrollable. Consequently, he had wrecked the office of the persons from whom he expected criticism.

Following this episode, he had begun to think of himself as mentally ill. Perhaps he was aided by his misinterpretation of the comments of several professional people, but this now became the focus of his anxiety. He did not want to think this, but the idea was inescapable. Finally, he had determined to face his earlier fears of military service, but the physical activities and close personal associations with other people were difficult to handle. As a result he had used the excuse of mental illness to successfully escape from the military situation.

Once this had been accomplished he felt helpless and hopeless. He was a failure, he was a coward, he was mentally ill, and he had doubts about his masculinity. The episode at the hospital was quite significant in the light of later developments because being approached by another man confirmed vague doubts that he had been harboring for several years. The interviewer did not see this as repressed homosexuality but rather as repression of "sexuality," which Ray had interpreted as homosexuality when approached by the homosexual. Individual counseling was planned along this line with emphasis on insight or understanding of the development of his feelings and on encouraging him to express these feelings.

From impressions gained in the interview and from Ray's earlier school performance, the interviewer judged him to be intellectually capable of achieving such insight. He also believed him to be able to exert enough control to deal with his problems in an objective fashion, particularly if he was given support and an opportunity for expression. With this approach Ray relaxed rapidly and was easily able to understand and accept the way in which his feelings had developed. As this occurred, another facet of the situation presented itself which the interviewer had suspected earlier. This concerned his future plans. After his anxieties were reduced, Ray frankly stated that he doubted if he had the ability to complete college. He took several tests and was quite relieved when he was advised against college study. He took a position as a retail salesman in a drug store and is quite happy now as an assistant manager of his store. He has recently married and appears to be an adequately functioning person. The clinician's only recent contact with him was to briefly counsel with him about his young son, whom he appeared to be "pushing" too hard into athletic activities. He requested the interview, and, in reality, seemed to wish to confirm his own idea that he was too anxious to help his son avoid fears of physical competition.

This rather lengthy story should demonstrate the amount and kinds of information that can be gained from a diagnostic interview. In the process of counseling with Ray, the clinician learned that he had taken the Rorschach and other psychological tests while in the Navy awaiting discharge. The Rorschach record and report were secured. The record will not be presented since we have not as yet discussed the Rorschach method, but the summary is of interest. Ray was described as exhibiting a severe anxiety reaction, characterized by free-floating anxiety which he was attempting to repress. The Rorschach was described as being very constricted and guarded. Sexual conflict was inferred by his avoidance of any sexual percepts. Depressive features of the record were noted, and a retreat into neurasthenic-like behavior was predicted (we feel this was starting in his excessive sleeping). His intelligence was judged to be in the high-average range. No hypotheses were offered as to the dynamic formulation of his symptoms. In summary, it might appear that the interview in this example presented data that was valuable in planning counseling. Furthermore, the impressions gained from the interview were not far afield from the impressions gained from other sources.

A final consideration is the time required for the diagnostic interview. As in the case of many of our techniques, it takes more time to describe them than to use them. Usually, the more freedom there is from time restriction, the more significant is the material brought out. This is not a certainty, however, since many clients require direction, and a controlled interview may result in reduction of digression and still cover all the suggested items. There are no rules about time. The interview should be prolonged until information necessary to the evaluation of the client (if it can be obtained) has been elicited. It seems safe to observe that we too often attempt to cut corners; this can result only in incomplete evaluation, and with it inadequate planning.

BIBLIOGRAPHY

1. Appel, K. E., and Strecker, E. A., *Practical examination of personality and behavior disorders*. New York: Macmillan, 1936.
2. Bingham, W., and Moore, B. V., *How to interview*. New York: Harper, 1934.
3. Fenlason, A. F., *Essentials in interviewing: for the interviewer offering professional services*. New York: Harper, 1952.
4. Garrett, A., *Interviewing: its principles and methods*. New York: Family Service Assn. of N. Y., 1942.
5. Johnson, W., Darley, F. L., and Spriestersbach, D. C., *Diagnostic manual in speech correction*. New York: Harper, 1952.
6. Kelly, G. A., "A method of diagnosing personality in the psychological clinic." *Psychol. Rec.*, 1938, 2, 95–111.
7. Kinsey, A. C., Pomeroy, W. B., and Martin, C. E., *Sexual behavior in the human male*. Philadelphia: Saunders, 1948.
8. Lewis, N. B. C., *Outlines for psychiatric examinations* (3rd ed.). Albany: N. Y. State Dept. of Mental Hygiene, 1943.
9. Martin, R. M., "Self-evaluation in schizophrenics and neurotics." Purdue Univ.: unpublished M. S. thesis, 1951.
10. Rogers, C. R., *Counseling and psychotherapy*. Boston: Houghton Mifflin, 1942.
11. Sullivan, H. S., *The psychiatric interview*. New York: Norton, 1954.
12. Wickes, T. A., "Examiner influence on a movement variable in a testing situation." Purdue Univ.: unpublished M. S. thesis, 1955.

CHAPTER

16

The Evaluation of Intelligence

T
HUS FAR OUR EFFORTS HAVE BEEN DIRECTED TOWARD ACCUMULAT-
ing biographical and personal information that will enable us to
understand and know our client, his presenting problems, how they
have developed, and something of how or why he exhibits the behavior
that is characteristic of him. If we are to further complete our picture, we
must have some insight into what he is capable of becoming—insofar as
it is possible, we must evaluate his potentialities and resources, his inherent capacity and power for development and accomplishment. If we
are to thoroughly understand an individual and be able to make predictions about him, we must balance the scales, weighing his present behavior against his capacity for effective adjustment. All aspects of these potentialities and resources are closely interrelated and cannot be appraised
independently. In tapping this area, the psychologist has found that at
least three major factors enter into the picture: the individual's intelligence or capacity, his motivation, and his control. "Motivation," as used
here, refers to the drive or energy that the individual can mobilize in order to face and solve his problems of adjustment. The concept of "control" refers to the extent to which the individual can direct and use his
capacity and energy to function in an efficient, constructive, and happy
fashion.

We shall take up the concepts of motivation and control in later
chapters. Let us now consider the first of these overlapping areas: intelligence. What do we mean by intelligence? What tools are available to us
for its evaluation and measurement? How accurate and comprehensive
are these measures? These are all questions with which we must concern
ourselves as we consider the techniques that have been designed for the
evaluation of intelligence. None of these techniques measure any aspect
of the resources of the individual independent of the quality and degree

of his motivation and control. In other words, all that we can expect to glean from tests is a measure of present functioning ability, which Lee J. Cronbach (18, p. 113) has called "here-and-now behavior." However, to the extent that the clinician can administer an intelligence test under optimum conditions of motivation and control, certain inferences can be made about the potential ability of the client. By employing tests less structured than those used to measure intelligence, we can orient our inferences toward the amount and kinds of motivation and the manner in which this motivation is directed and controlled. Here again, we are observing the behavior of a person whose capacity to behave in a particular fashion must be reckoned with.

Before we discuss some of the definitions of intelligence that have been suggested by various psychologists, let us note that for the purposes of clinical evaluation, intelligence is regarded as a quality or characteristic of behavior. When we attempt to evaluate intelligence, we examine various bits of behavior, bits of behavior which the author of a specific test has decided is intelligent behavior, so that it is actually only by inference that we measure intelligence. On the basis of an intelligence test we cannot say that an individual has any particular amount of intelligence; we can say only that he *shows* so much in terms of the factors that the author of the test believes are indicative of intelligent behavior. Only to the extent that these factors are found to correlate or relate to other variables are we able from the test results to predict the client's behavior in other situations. Occupational success, school achievement, ability to learn new modes of behavior, and capacity to gain insight into complex dynamic adjustment problems are only a few of the variables that might be predicted by a knowledge of performance on an intelligence test.

DEFINITIONS OF INTELLIGENCE

Many authors have advanced more or less formal definitions of general intelligence. Some of these definitions are arranged chronologically below:

(a) In 1914 William Stern (84) defined intelligence as a general capacity to consciously adjust thinking to new requirements.

(b) The same author expanded the above definition to include memorial or perceptive activities that contribute to adjustment to new demands.

(c) "Intelligence means precisely the property of so recombining our behavior patterns as to act better in novel situations." Frederick Lyman Wells (103, p. 34) 1917.

(d) "Intelligence seems to be a biological mechanism by which the effects of a complexity of stimuli are brought together and given a somewhat unified effect in behavior." Joseph Peterson (53, p. 198) 1921.

(e) "Intelligence is the ability to learn." Burdette R. Buckingham (53, p. 273) 1921.

(f) "An individual possesses intelligence insofar as he has learned or can learn to adjust himself to his environment." S. S. Colvin (53, p. 136), 1921.

(g) "An individual is intelligent in proportion as he is able to carry on abstract thinking." Lewis M. Terman (53, p. 128), 1921.

(h) "We may then define intellect in general as the power of good responses from the point of view of truth or fact." Edward L. Thorndike (53, p. 124), 1921.

(i) Louis L. Thurstone (90), in 1923, characterized intelligence as a movement from trial and error toward increasingly abstract controls.

(j) "Intelligence may be regarded as the capacity for successful adjustment by means of those traits which we ordinarily call intellectual. These traits involve such capacities as quickness of learning, quickness of apprehension, the ability to solve new problems, the ability to perform tasks generally recognized as presenting intellectual difficulty because they involve ingenuity, originality, the grasp of complicated relationships, or the recognition of remote associations." Frank N. Freeman (30, p. 258), 1925.

(k) "Intelligence is the ability to learn actions or to perform new actions that are functionally useful." F. N. Freeman (31, p. 18), 1940.

James L. Mursell (62) in commenting on this list of definitions suggests that after reading the list one may very well feel that one still does not know exactly what intelligence is. Mursell feels that general intelligence is a loose and vague concept. To the extent that this is true, and it would certainly appear to be true as we examine the attempts at definition, the task of constructing a test of general intelligence is rather difficult and complex.

Frank S. Freeman (32) has attempted to classify definitions, such as those listed by above, into several groups. According to Freeman, one group of definitions places the emphasis upon the adjustment of the individual to his total environment. A second type of definition states that intelligence is the ability to learn, and still another group places the emphasis upon the ability to carry on abstract thinking. As Freeman indicates, these categories of definitions are not, and cannot be, mutually exclusive. It would appear that the ability to adjust to the environment, to learn, and to think abstractly are all involved in the various definitions that have been formulated and are all representative of the qualities or characteristics of behavior measured by intelligence tests.

In an effort to formulate a more comprehensive and global definition of intelligence, David Wechsler (97, p. 3) combined and extended the three types of definitions as follows: "Intelligence is the aggregate or global capacity of the individual to act purposefully, to think rationally and to deal effectively with the environment." In discussing this definition Wechsler suggests that "drive" and "incentive" enter into intelligent behavior. Freeman (32) doubts the validity of this. He acknowledges that effective utilization of intelligence depends on these factors but he prefers to set them aside as nonintellectual traits of personality. For our purposes, this would seem to be a rather academic argument, since our goal is to appraise *present functioning ability* so that we can make predictions about potential functioning ability. Whether traits such as drive, incentive, and intelligence are appraised by the same or different instruments, if we are to attain our goal, they must all be taken into consideration. George D. Stoddard's (85, p. 4) definition includes and goes beyond the three types of definitions already presented: "Intelligence is the ability to undertake activities that are characterized by (1) difficulty, (2) complexity, (3) abstractness, (4) economy, (5) adaptiveness to a goal, (6) social value, and (7) the emergence of originals, and to maintain such activities under conditions that demand a concentration of energy and resistance to emotional forces." In addition to the inclusion of drive and incentive to take specific cognizance of the concept of control, F. S. Freeman (32) discusses both Wechsler's and Stoddard's definitions at length. Our primary purpose here is to enumerate and note the extent of definitions and concepts of the meaning of intelligence rather than to discuss or describe them in detail.

Several psychologists have described different kinds of intelligence which should be distinguished one from the other. For example, Thorndike (89) has divided intelligent activity into three types—social intelligence, concrete intelligence, and abstract intelligence. Then, in an attempt to understand the structure of intelligence rather than the manner in which it functions, still other psychologists have attempted to analyze intelligence to determine its underlying factors or components. Their method has been that of factor analysis. After giving a large number of separate tests and computing the correlation coefficients between each test and every other test, the extent of communality and independence is determined between the tests. The use of such statistical procedures has resulted in a number of theories as to the nature of intelligence. These theories are of several types, and the most representative will be discussed briefly:

(a) The multifactor theory. According to this theory, there is really no such factor as general intelligence, but rather a number of separate factors operating together. Actually, even to Thorndike (89) who advances a multifactor theory, the important aspect of the theory appears to be that many of these factors actually work together in any mental or intelligent act.

(b) The two-factor theory. At the opposite extreme from the multifactor theory is Charles Edward Spearman's (83) two-factor theory. Spearman conceived of a general factor common to all mental activity possessed by all individuals in varying degree. He also postulated a number of specific factors, each of which is important to a particular form of activity. According to this theory, a test of general intelligence would be one that would measure the general factor.

(c) The group-factor theory. Thurstone (91, 92, 93) holds that intelligent activity is neither an expression of a number of specific factors nor an expression of any general factor, but that there are a number of groups of factors. Each group has a primary factor that gives the group its cohesiveness. Thurstone has identified six primary factors but believes that the entire number of possible factors is as yet undetermined. The six already identified are the number factor, the verbal factor, the space factor, the word-fluency factor, the reasoning factor, and the rote-memory factor. Two other possibilities, a perceptual factor and a deductive factor, have been suggested.

We have enumerated definitions, kinds, and factors of intelligence, in order to point up and make apparent the need for caution in the evaluation of intelligence and use of intelligence test results. The wide range of concepts concerning intelligence makes it evident that no single test could give any more than a rough approximation of the various attributes of what has been described as intelligence. In the same vein, certainly no single test score should be expected to be descriptive of intellectual ability, although single test scores may have validity for the prediction of specific achievement or particular bits of behavior. Such test scores, when validated by appropriate research, may be useful in personnel selection, vocational guidance, or even educational guidance, but they contribute to evaluation of only a fraction of the potentialities and resources of the individual. Consequently, the clinical or counseling psychologist is never satisfied with a single test or test score. He is anxious to appraise as many factors, kinds, and aspects of intellectual functioning as possible. He will usually give two or more tests that are presumed to measure different attributes of intellectual functioning, and he is always interested in the patterning of performance within a given test.

The psychologist should never describe a client or report a test result without reference to the particular test upon which the evaluation is based. To say that a client has an intelligence quotient of 100, or that his performance is at the fiftieth percentile, has little meaning unless this report is accompanied by a statement of the specific test upon which this performance was made and the population with which the client is being compared. The conditions under which the test is administered, the previous background of the subject, the comparison between this performance and that on other tests, and the distribution of relative performance throughout the test items are just a few of the supplementary facts that are considered indispensable to the clinician. We have too many reports such as that by Ralph M. Dreger (25), which suggests that different I.Q.'s for the same individual may be associated with different intelligence tests, to accept the I.Q., just any I.Q. on any test, as a meaningful fact by itself.

THE CONSTANCY OF INTELLIGENCE

In some of the introductory texts in psychology and other subject matter areas the student may find discussion of a topic called "the constancy of the I.Q." This concept maintains that a person's intelligence quotient remains stable throughout life, and supporters of the concept either state or infer that the intelligence quotient is a measure of native capacity. While no test can separate the effects of experience from innate, native, or inherited capacity, the idea that intelligence is hereditary and that tests can reflect this trait has created considerable confusion during the past thirty years. On the basis of our present knowledge, it seems safe to say that progress in the area of evaluation of potential and resources has been retarded many years by the stubborn adherence to the concept of "constancy of the I.Q."

The question of whether intelligence is inherited, although provocative of discussion and argument, is unanswerable. Every individual exists in an environment which modifies or affects all that is brought to it. As John E. Anderson (3, p. 213) has said, it is never "heredity *or* environment" but always "heredity *and* environment." Even though the theoretical problem is unanswerable and it seems a definite mistake to assume that heredity and environment are separate, or that either can completely explain what a human being does, it is necessary that the psychologist assess the relative proportions of influence that these two factors have upon the performance of a given individual. For this reason, it is important that we briefly review some of the evidence that intelligence has both hereditary and environmental origins.

There are at least four lines of evidence stressing the role of inheritance (adapted from Anderson (3, pp. 214–19):

(a) Familial resemblance. When members of the same family and their close relatives are given intelligence tests and the correlations between the intelligence of relatives are compared, we find that the degree of correlation is proportional to the closeness of the family relationship. For example, identical twins show the most resemblance (typical $r = .90$); fraternal twins, the next (typical $r = .70$); siblings show moderate resemblance (typical $r = .50$); cousins less resemblance (typical $r = .30$); and orphans and unrelated children show no resemblance to one another. Whereas the correlation between the intelligence of parents and children is approximately .50, the correlation between grandparents and grandchildren is about .15. Results such as these, which have been confirmed many times (78), suggest that there is a hereditary factor in intelligence.

(b) Influences of education. When the feebleminded child is given usual educational advantages, relatively little change occurs in his level. When bright children are given advantages, they seem to acquire as much or more than is presented to them. In fact, normal children seem to learn in spite of their schools and teachers but retarded children seldom do. Differences in intelligence persist in spite of education.

(c) Relationship between the intelligence of children and the occupational status and intelligence of their fathers. The relationship between the intelligence of the father and his occupational status and the relationship between the intelligence of young children of different ages and the occupational status of the father is approximately the same. If environment were dominant, the relationship would be high for the father and low for the young child, since the child has had less exposure to the environment. Since the relationships are much the same, it is suggested that something within the person determines the level of functioning.

(d) Studies of foster children. After several years of adoption, foster children seem to resemble their true parents in intelligence more than they resemble their foster parents.

On the other hand, there are several lines of evidence which stress the role of environment in the determination of intelligence.

(a) Effects of culture on intelligence test scores. Mandel Sherman (81, 82) studied several communities in Virginia that were separated from civilization in various degrees. Some of them were among the most backward in the United States. The average schooling in these backward areas was about one year and there were no doctors or nurses. There were no roads, and horses were used for travel. Other communities were somewhat more accessible, and the level of schooling was higher. At the other extreme, were communities with good roads, good schools, radios, and automobiles. In these various districts, intelligence tests were given to the very young children and the average scores for these young children were found to be very similar. However, when the children ten years of age or older were tested, average scores for those in the communities nearest to civilization were much higher, indicating that the stimulation of the better environments had something to do with the test scores. Similar results have been found by H. Gordon (44), who studied canal boat-children in England, Nathaniel D. M. Hirsch (49), and Sidney L. Pressey and J. B. Thomas (71).

(b) Effects of nursery school attendance on intelligence test scores. A group of studies have measured the effects of nursery school attendance upon intelligence quotients. Although the results are not dramatic, there appear to be consistent indications that the I.Q. can be raised by a stimulating environment.

Other evidence could be presented concerning the variability of the intelligence quotient, but taking all the evidence together, it appears clear that while we must assume an inborn potential, tests measure only present ability, and present ability is affected by both innate factors and experiences. The psychologist must, therefore, evaluate the tested performance of the individual in terms of the cultural and educational advantages that have been present, and then compare this evaluation with evidence concerning the intellectual level of the parents. Such a careful global appraisal should allow us to estimate the extent to which we might expect the intelligence of the client to be constant. After all, that is the clinician's purpose: to predict how the person may perform in other behavioral situations. If the client has had educational advantages and has not profited from them, what is the reason? Is it because he has low native intelligence as reflected by the occupational, educational, or economic status of the family; is he emotionally blocked in some way; or has he suffered some traumatic injury or disease? If the child's performance is superior to that which might have been predicted from the family history, how much further development can be expected? Thus, the problems of the constancy of intelligence and the relative contributions of heredity and environment are important to the psychologist, but largely as they affect his evaluation of the individual.

CAUTIONS CONCERNING THE USE OF INTELLIGENCE TESTS

All test scores are influenced by the subject's personal and emotional habits. Cronbach (18, p. 117) lists such factors as shyness with strange adults, lack of self-confidence, and dislike for "schoolish" tasks. In discussing this problem, he remarks as follows:

> A self-critical person may say, "I don't know," because he is dissatisfied with the best answer he can formulate; a person less sensitive to niceties may give an answer which is passable. A pedantic urge to accuracy may make it relatively easy to per-

form on memory tasks. Inhibition and fear of being incorrect may cause failure on tasks requiring insight and imagination. No matter how careful a tester is, there is some danger that a child may fail an item even though he could have passed. One should, therefore, always bear in mind that the final test score shows how well the child functioned in comparison with others, in his present state, which may be markedly affected by emotional complications.[1]

Emotional factors such as general depression, anger, or resentfulness, fear, sheepishness, or a feeling of shame, shyness, embarrassment, general nervous excitement, lack of confidence, and combinations of these or other factors may all contribute to the kind and level of performance. We have no way of knowing from the test alone whether the child's reaction is stable or transient; whether the client is always shy or fearful or whether this is related to the current testing situation. We must, therefore, compare all our observations before coming to a conclusion about capacity.

Language difficulties of the client frequently contribute to low scores, particularly on tests with verbal components. It is obvious that the child who speaks a foreign language is at a distinct disadvantage if he is expected to understand directions in English. This may be regarded as an absurd example because one might argue that no one with "common sense" would expect to test a child in other than his own language. Fortunately, few clinicians would be so absurd. Still, the child whose understanding of language is retarded in development is at a disadvantage because of this handicap. The speech-defective child may not be understood by the examiner, and the hard-of-hearing child may be limited in his understanding of the test situation. Paper and pencil or group tests almost always require reading ability, and the child with a deficiency in this skill may perform in a manner more indicative of his reading ability than his general ability. A child was recently referred to us who was performing poorly in school. The first-grade teacher had reported him to be very bright, but the third-grade teacher described him as dull and stupid. The school had given intelligence tests in the first and third grades. As extreme as this may seem, his recorded I.Q. in the first grade was 120 and his I.Q., on the basis of the third-grade tests, was 60. The test used in the first grade was essentially nonverbal and required no reading ability (most kindergarten, first- and second-grade tests do not), while the test given in the third grade required that questions and problems be read before they could be answered. Our hunch, on the basis of this evidence, was borne out by more careful evaluation of the child's functioning in

[1] By permission from *Essentials of Psychological Testing,* by Lee J. Cronbach. Copyright 1949 by Harper & Brothers.

different test situations. As we had surmised, the child could not read at all. Since language behavior is an inherent part of many tests, the psychologist will almost always require a measure of the person's performance in nonverbal or nonlanguage situations as well as verbal situations. By comparison of nonlanguage with language performance, a better understanding of the individual's functioning can certainly be gained.

An individual's performance on a test is often influenced by his physical state of health. Tests taken when the subject is tired or ill, when under the influence of sedation or medication, are just a few examples of conditions conducive to error in measurement. Physical distractions in the form of interruptions, distracting noises, visual stimuli, and the like, may also contribute to spuriously low performance. Perhaps the most serious single source of error in intellectual measurement can be described under the general heading of motivation in the test situation. This general heading subsumes many of the factors already mentioned, but includes in addition the possibility of deliberate deception, recalcitrancy, lack of seriousness, and lack of desire to perform well. The examiner's personal manner and attitude, his personality, and his training may be factors in the motivation of a client to do his best to co-operate in the testing situation.

All the factors so far described—including the extent to which the test measures what we are interested in measuring; the influence of education, cultural and environmental factors versus innate factors; the emotional, physical, and motivational state of the client—and many other factors should contribute to caution on the part of the psychologist in the use of intelligence tests. Since in the evaluation of intelligence we are looking at only one facet of the individual, we cannot be overly conservative in the use of such measures. Although intellectual evaluation is only a part of the total evaluation of the person, we should not discard these procedures because of their limitations. Any observation of behavior has value as long as we are aware of the factors that may affect it. Most of the factors described above will contribute primarily to the lowering of our estimates of potentiality. Frequently we are concerned with whether a person has the necessary minimum potentialities for some purpose. The examiner, then, should keep in mind why he is testing and what specific predictions he will make. We may not be as interested in the ultimate potentiality or the maximum possible potential and consequently can use with confidence even our most conservative estimates.

The dynamically oriented psychologist is interested, not so much in single test scores or performances on single tests, as in an evaluation of the profile of the client's performance in a variety of situations so that he can integrate these observations with all other information at hand concerning the individual under consideration. Armed with this global evaluation, he is able to predict and recommend for the client's future training or education and for a variety of other specific purposes.

CLASSIFICATION OF TESTS OF INTELLIGENCE OR CAPACITY

The various tests and measures that are used to evaluate intelligence can be conveniently classified in several ways. In the first place, they can be classified according to age. The tests that are ordinarily used with adults differ in certain respects from those used with children, just as those for children differ in certain respects from those used with infants. In discussing tests for children and infants, we will begin with tests primarily designed for use with children and then discuss the modifications or downward extensions of these tests designed for use with infants.

Secondly, tests can be classified in terms of whether they must be given individually or can be administered to a group of persons simultaneously. Individual tests are given by one clinician to one client at a time, while group tests are constructed so that one examiner can test several persons at a time. Group tests are usually of the paper and pencil variety; and although some involve language ability and verbal understanding, and some are nonlanguage tests, most require the ability to respond on a paper form with a pencil or stylus. Group tests are designed for use with both children and adults. Several of these tests will be named but there will be little discussion of them in this text. Clinical and counseling psychologists do not use group tests often, since when the evaluation of intelligence is sufficiently important for the clinician to administer any test, it is usually important enough to indicate the necessity for an individual test. Group tests ordinarily do not provide the clinician with any information other than a score or group of scores. In a group testing situation, motivation is hard to maintain and the effect of special disabilities may be difficult to appraise. When group tests are given, the results are usually used for screening. If the client apparently possesses adequate ability for our purposes as reflected by a group test, we may be satisfied with group-test results. If the score is low, however, it must be checked by other evaluations.

Thirdly, tests are also classified in terms of the role of language in the test situation. Some tests definitely require language comprehension and expression. These are called verbal or language tests. Others place less premium on language, and still others can be administered and taken without the use of language. These will be called nonlanguage, nonverbal, or performance tests; they are available both for children and for adults, but are most commonly used with children. Other tests are constructed with both verbal and nonverbal items. Our procedure will be to discuss first verbal tests, verbal-nonverbal scales, and performance scales as used with children; and then tests that combine verbal and nonverbal items and that are used primarily with adolescents and adults. Certain group tests will be mentioned at both child and adult levels.

THE STANFORD–BINET

The historical background of the Stanford-Binet test was described in Chapter 1.[2] Our discussion here will concern the 1937 Terman-Merrill Revision (88) of the original Stanford revision of the Binet-Simon Intelligence Scale. Although there were several American revisions and translations of the Binet-Simon scale, the revision that had the widest field of usefulness was the 1916 Stanford Revision (87). From the time of its publication in 1916, it became the standard clinical method for the evaluation of intellectual status. By 1937 it had become somewhat dated, and because of this and other limitations, Lewis M. Terman and Maude A. Merrill collaborated to bring out a more modern revision.

The Stanford-Binet (the new revision unless otherwise designated) is an individual intelligence test, largely verbal and classified as a verbal or language test. It is most frequently regarded as a test for children. It has certain limitations for use with adults, but it was the standard individual intelligence test for use with both children and adults until the publication of the Wechsler-Bellevue (to be described later). The Stanford-Binet consists of 122 items and 7 alternate items. The items are arranged in 20 age-level groups. There are six items in each age-level group except the average adult level, in which there are eight items. The test is scored in terms of mental age credits from which an intelligence quotient is computed by dividing the mental age credits (in months) by the chronological age. The age-level groups are arranged in six-month steps from ages two to four inclusive, in year steps from five to fourteen, and in larger units beyond that level. Figure 6 gives the age levels, number of items at each age level, months covered by each age level and the number of mental-age-month credits for each item in each age level.

The scale devised by Binet had 54 items and the 1916 revision contained 90 items. These 90 items were arranged into age-level groups with tests at each yearly age level from 3 to 10, a twelve-year level, a fourteen-year level, an average adult level, and a superior adult level. In devising the 1937 revision, the authors took cognizance of several faults of the 1916 revision. For example, the original scale was especially defective at both extremes, several subtests were unsatisfactory because of low validity, and there was only one form so that retesting was subject

[2] *See* pp. 12–13.

FIGURE 6

THE TEST ITEM ORGANIZATION OF THE
STANFORD-BINET

Age Levels	Number of Items	Months Spanned	Mental-Age Credits for Each Item
II	6	6	1
II–6	6	6	1
III	6	6	1
III–6	6	6	1
IV	6	6	1
IV–6	6	6	1
V	6	12	2
VI	6	12	2
VII	6	12	2
VIII	6	12	2
IX	6	12	2
X	6	12	2
XI	6	12	2
XII	6	12	2
XIII	6	12	2
XIV	6	12	2
Average Adult	8	16	2
Superior Adult I	6	24	4
Superior Adult II	6	30	5
Superior Adult III	6	36	6

to practice effects. The new revision contains two scales, Form L and Form M, which differ almost completely in content but appear to be equivalent. These scales cover a wider range, are more accurately standardized, and provide a better sampling of performance than the older scale. The test items include such kinds of tasks as analogies, opposites, comprehension, vocabulary, similarities and differences, verbal and pictorial completion, absurdities, drawing designs from copy and from memory, memory for meaningful material, and memory for digits. These tasks are not grouped together but are distributed throughout the test. Obviously not all kinds of tasks appear at any given age level, but several are repeated at different age levels with different scoring and performance requirements.

In administering the test to a particular client, it is necessary to determine at what age level of the test to begin, and several factors must be taken into consideration. We want to begin at a point where all of the tests at a given level can be passed. The clinician will take into account the chronological age, the grade placement, and other information in deciding on the starting point. It is usually good practice to start just below the chronological age if the client is regarded as average. In any case, even if we have to go back, we want to establish the *basal age level*, which is the highest level at which all of the tests are passed. The examination should be carried up the scale until an age level is reached in which all the tests are failed. In order to find the mental age, we must add to the basal age all credits achieved above the basal age level. It is to be remembered that the tests at each level cover the preceding period of mental development. To be credited with a basal mental age of six years, a child must score *plus* on all six of the tests listed under heading Year VI. Terman and Merrill (88, p. 67) present the following illustrations of mental age computations:

Suppose a child, aged four years and two months (written 4–2), passes all of the tests at Year III, five at year III–6, three at year IV, two at year IV–6, two at year V, and one at year VI. The total credit earned is as follows:

	Years	*Months*
Year III, all plus, basal year level	3	–
Year III–6, 5 tests passed, credit 1 month each	–	5
Year IV, 3 tests passed, credit 1 month each	–	3
Year IV–6, 2 tests passed, credit 1 month each	–	2
Year V, 2 tests passed, credit 1 month each	–	2
Year VI, 1 test passed, credit 2 months each	–	2
	3	14 or

Mental Age score, 4–2

Suppose in the case of an older subject the distribution of successes and failures has been as follows: six tests at year XIII were passed, four at year XIV, four at A.A., three at S.A. I, two at S.A. II, and two at S.A. III.

	Years	*Months*
Year XIII, all plus. Basal year level	13	–
Year XIV, 4 tests passed, credit 2 months each	–	8
Year A.A., 4 tests passed, credit 2 months each	–	8
Year S.A., I, 3 tests passed, credit 4 months each	–	12
Year S.A. II, 2 tests passed, credit 5 months each	–	10
Year S.A. III, 2 tests passed, credit 6 months each	–	12
	13	50 or

Mental Age score, 17–2

An adult subject who has passed all the tests at the A.A. level, five at S.A. I, all at S.A. II, and three at S.A. III, is scored as follows:

	Years	Months
Credit presupposed	14	–
Year A.A., 8 tests passed, credit 2 months each	–	16
Year S.A. I, 5 tests passed, credit 4 months each	–	20
Year S.A. II, 6 tests passed, credit 5 months each	–	30
Year S.A. III, 3 tests passed, credit 6 months each	–	18
	14	84 or

Mental Age score, 21–0 [3]

The I.Q. is computed by dividing the mental age by the chronological age. For example, in the first illustration given above, the I.Q. would equal four years, two months, divided by four years and two months, or fifty divided by fifty which equals one. In order to make for easy expression, this is then multiplied by 100 to make the I.Q. in this illustration equal 100. In the second example above, let us assume that the subject is twelve years and two months old. The I.Q. would then equal 206 divided by 146 multiplied by 100 or 141. The only time when confusion is likely to arise is in the case of subjects over 13 years of age. It is obvious that if we continued to use the actual chronological age, then after a point the person's I.Q. would decline as he grows older. In the 1916 revision, any chronological age above sixteen was disregarded in computing the I.Q. In the 1937 revision, the authors do not cease counting chronological age at a specific point, but taper it off by degrees. Tables are provided to make the computation simple but what the authors have actually done is to use as the chronological age of a subject between 13 and 16, 13 years plus two thirds of the additional months he has lived. The chronological age of a person actually 14 is counted as 13–8; of 15 as 14–4; of 16 as 15–0. The highest division that is ever used in the computation of an I.Q. on the 1937 Stanford-Binet is 15–0.

Although the Stanford-Binet is a very popular test and at least until recently has been the best individual verbal test available, it does have several decided limitations, one of which is that it provides only a single index of intellectual functioning, failing to give information concerning different kinds of functioning. It would be helpful if we could divide the test into different parts and obtain separate scores in areas such as reasoning, memory, vocabulary, information, etc. Quinn McNemar (58) factor-analyzed scores on various items and found that the factor of general intelligence accounted for about half of what the average item

[3] By permission from *Measuring Intelligence*, by Lewis M. Terman and Maude A. Merrill. Copyright 1937 by Houghton Mifflin Company.

measures. The other half of the variation is accounted for by miscellaneous factors. A particular factor is seldom found in more than one or two items. Therefore, it does not appear practical to attempt to break the total score down into separate factor scores. This is very unfortunate, since our philosophy of evaluation leads us to insist on a knowledge of the strengths and weaknesses of the subject.

Other disadvantages are inherent in the age-level groupings of the items. First, the method is inefficient since we must test at one level and then go on to the next level, etc. It would save a great deal of time if we could give all items of a particular kind, then go on to those of another kind, etc. Another disadvantage is the pass-fail scoring at each age level. As Cronbach (18, p. 134) has pointed out, there is a difference between a person who gets two absurdities correct and one who gets none, yet the person may be failed unless he gets three correct. As he comments, we may "throw away information." A point scale would seem to have advantages.

Max Hutt (52) has experimented with varying the test order with each subject, alternating easy and hard items, thus reducing the effect of failure at the end of the test. He reports that normal, well-adjusted children gave similar I.Q.'s to those obtained by the usual orders when his method was used, but poorly adjusted children obtained I.Q.'s with the adaptive method that were 4.5 points higher. Arden N. Frandsen, Betsey R. McCullough, and David R. Stone (29) suggest that the clinician can use the Terman-Merrill norms for serial (administering items in order of difficulty, grouping like items) testing since no significant differences have been found between serial and consecutive testing.

The Stanford-Binet is quite inappropriate for persons over 14 or 15 years old; the standardization population was largely composed of children, and thus the I.Q.'s obtained have doubtful meaning for adults. Other criticisms have been leveled at the Binet, all of which emphasize the fact that the results of the test should always be interpreted with qualifications. In spite of Stoddard's (85, p. 116) statement that ". . . over the years, the Stanford revisions have offered not very reliable measurements of functions not very close to intelligence," many of the limitations are limitations of the interpreter and not those of the test. The test is not valid unless a large number of assumptions about the subject are satisfied.

The test is heavily loaded with verbal items and tasks influenced by educational experience. Although some may regard this as a limitation, it does mean that the test has a considerable validity for the prediction of school success. Eldon A. Bond (12) found that the results of the test correlated .73 with reading comprehension, .59 with English and history grades, .54 with biology grades, .48 with geometry grades, and .43 with reading speed. These correlations are not spectacular but they do indicate that the Binet has some validity for the prediction of school success, in fact, as much as or more than most tests.

THE WECHSLER INTELLIGENCE SCALE FOR CHILDREN

The Wechsler Intelligence Scale for Children (79, 80, 99, 100) (which hereafter will be referred to as the WISC) was published in 1949. This scale has been developed from the Wechsler-Bellevue Intelligence Scales used with adolescents and adults (97, 98). There is considerable overlap in items between the WISC and the Wechsler-Bellevue but Wechsler emphasizes that the WISC is a distinct test in its own right, entirely apart from the Wechsler-Bellevue, and is independently standardized.

Since the WISC is a relatively new scale insofar as tests are concerned, we do not have extensive clinical experience by which it can be evaluated, but it was designed to overcome some of the disadvantages that have been attributed to other individual tests of intellectual functioning. A description of the organization of the scale and the methods of administration, scoring, and interpretation will serve the purpose of pointing up the differences between the WISC and the Stanford-Binet as well as familiarizing the reader with the scale.

The WISC consists of twelve tests that are divided into two subgroups. These subgroups are identified as verbal and performance scales. Thus the WISC yields verbal and performance scores as well as total scores, and the clinician can compare the person's ability in these two areas from the single testing procedure without supplementing the test by a performance test as is necessary with the Stanford-Binet. Although these groups are labeled "verbal" and "performance," they do tap factors that cut across the groups and thus make pattern analysis possible. In addition to analyzing the test performance into categories, the clinician can look at the subtest scores themselves and study a profile of performances. The construction and standardization of the scale allows for more meaningful predictions than can be made from the Stanford-Binet since the subject's performance is compared with a composite age group and not with the scores earned by individuals in any single age group.

The I.Q.'s on the WISC compare quite closely with the I.Q.'s from other scales such as the Stanford-Binet, and are convertible into percentile ranks. So far no attempt has been made to define the clinical, social, or practical significance of any given I.Q. In the first place, not enough clinical experience and statistics have been accumulated with different kinds of groups to make this possible. Secondly, the scale is expected to demonstrate its usefulness not merely as a tool for arriving at an I.Q., but more generally as a vehicle for making many qualitative and quantitative observations of the subject. An I.Q. may have very limited significance, and in fact may obscure other important kinds of information. The WISC by arrangement of the test items into subtests would appear to be a more efficient instrument than the age-level tests. Other advantages could be described and will be apparent as experience is accumulated. Undoubtedly, disadvantages and limitations will develop, but at the present stage the WISC, with the global concept of intelligence inherent in it, gives promise of being a valuable instrument.

Judith I. Krugman, et al. (55) have studied the relationship between the WISC and the Stanford-Binet and have reported correlation coefficients as follows: WISC Verbal Scale and Stanford-Binet, .74; WISC Performance Scale and Stanford-Binet, .64; and Full Scale and Stanford-Binet, .82. In general, the Binet yielded higher I.Q.'s and this difference was most marked at the higher levels. Several other authors have found similar results (28, 63, 102).

To illustrate the use of the WISC, let us consider the case of Lois, who was twelve years two months old and in the seventh grade when she was referred to the clinic because of nervousness, poor school progress, and lack of interests. This discussion will show the integration of test findings with other assessment data. Lois was the oldest of three children. Her two sisters were eleven and nine years of age. One was in the fifth grade and was described as an average student. However this sister had repeated the third grade. The other sister was in the fourth grade and was said to be an "A" and "B" student. It is possible that a miscarriage at two months preceded Lois. The mother was thirty-four years of age, had completed the tenth grade, and had worked in a factory as a machine operator for five years. The father was thirty-five, had completed the tenth grade, and was a farmer.

The mother's health was apparently good during her pregnancy with Lois, who was born approximately two weeks after she was expected. She was a breech presentation and was delivered with her knees folded up against her chest. The mother was in labor for thirty-six hours although the pains were not severe until twenty minutes before the actual delivery. The mother did not think that instruments had been used. Lois weighed six pounds, five ounces at birth and gained normally during infancy. She presented no feeding problems and was described as a very active child. The mother claimed that Lois walked at nine months of age. However she frequently fell and lost consciousness for a few seconds when she fell. She often hit her head against the floor or wall until she "raised knots on her head." The mother also reported that Lois used words before she was one year old and that she used two-word sentences at a very early age. She was the first grandchild in the family in thirteen years, and since the relatives lived close by, she received a tremendous amount of attention. Her early physical development was described as being advanced over that of her sisters. It was noteworthy that all the children were breech presentations and that the mother was in labor for sixty hours with the youngest child, who was born with a "club" foot. When Lois was about twenty-four months old, she developed a very high temperature. When she was taken to the hospital, her temperature was 105 degrees. This illness was not specifically diagnosed, but the physician was apparently quite concerned lest some brain damage result. Shortly before she was referred for psychological evaluation, she had been hospitalized for ten days with scarlet fever. She had had other childhood illnesses but none were severe. She had become quite nervous and irritable after the early fever. The mother had noticed particularly that she was easily startled.

The mother claimed that Lois had been a good student in the first grade. She was reported to be extremely distractible, but still made "A's." When she was in the second grade, she was referred to a person who was described as the "school psychologist." Lois had been misbehaving in class, disturbing other children, and often tearing up her books and papers. The teacher who referred her at that time believed Lois to be intelligent, but commented that she had a very short attention span and lacked perseverance. The mother said that her sleep was restless, that she frequently cried out and twitched in her sleep. The "school psychologist" reported to the school that Lois had an I.Q. of 98 and that she was "normal." The mother reported that Lois had not done passing academic work since the third grade. Arithmetic was described as her hardest subject, but English was also difficult for her. The mother had repeatedly talked with the school about Lois and her work. On every occasion the school had told her that they could not understand the situation since Lois was average in ability. Their suggestion had usually been that she must be emotionally disturbed and that there must be something in the home situation which was disturbing to her. The mother was extremely impatient with Lois' interest in outdoor work and wanted her to work in the house. The parents had discouraged her interest in 4-H Club work since she needed more time for her studies. The mother impressed the clinician as a flighty, nervous woman of low-average general intellectual ability.

Lois was an attractive, co-operative, and talkative child. She said that she did not like school "awfully well." She indicated that arithmetic and English were her hardest subjects. Fractions were described as particularly difficult and she added, "I don't get the catch to English." Apparently she was reading library books and enjoyed reading. According to testing at this time, she read at the sixth-grade level. On the WISC she achieved a Full Scale I.Q. of 99. This I.Q. seemed remarkably similar to her previous I.Q., which was probably derived from her performance on the Stanford-Binet. The examiner could have concluded that her ability was "average" or "normal." In this instance, it was his opinion that the over-all score was almost meaningless as a measure of her special capacities and weaknesses. Lois was administered ten subtests of the Wechsler Scale. (Ordinarily only ten of the twelve subtests are used.) The Digit Span subtest in the Verbal group and the Mazes test in the performance group were not given in this instance. (This is fairly common practice.) When the five subtests involving language and verbal abilities were considered alone, her Verbal Scale I.Q. was 94. The other five subtests yielded a Performance Scale I.Q. of 104. This spread suggested something of Lois' difficulty but did not completely describe her intellectual functioning. For this reason, both qualitative and quantitative aspects of her responses to the various subtests were carefully studied.

The Information subtest involves the knowledge of facts and general information. An average scaled score would be 10 on this and other subtests. Her score was 12. Apparently she had been able to learn facts such as are included in this test. On the Comprehension subtest her scaled score was 9. This is approximately average, but the score itself did not describe her behavior. Some of the items are relatively concrete "what-to-do" questions, whereas others are more abstract. In general, Lois did well on the concrete items but poorly on the abstract items. The same kind of qualitative observations could have been made concerning her behavior on the arithmetic test. Her scaled score was 9, but the more complicated and the more abstract the problems, the poorer was her performance. She had particular difficulty with problems involving division. The Similarities subtest, which involves the formation of concepts, was the one on which Lois made her poorest performance (her scaled score was 7). This pattern of abstraction loss was also revealed in the qualitative analysis of her responses to the Vocabulary subtest. Her scaled score on this test was 8 (10 is average) but this score was attained almost entirely by her definitions of words like "bicycle," "knife," and "donkey." She could not begin to define words like "join," "brave," or "fable." She could define words that stood for objects (referents) but not words that had no concrete referents. In the performance area her scaled score was 12 on the Picture Completion subtest. This test involves finding what is missing in the pictures of common objects. She was very good at this. In the Picture Arrangement subtest she achieved a scaled score of 13. She worked quickly and did surprisingly well. The Block Design subtest requires the subject to copy designs with a number of blocks that have solid colors on some sides and two colors, divided on the diagonal, on the other sides. This test involves visual-motor skills and some concept formation. Lois achieved a scaled score of 9, but did the test almost entirely by rapid trial-and-error performance. Her performance on the Object Assembly subtest was also interesting. Here again, she worked rapidly, easily completing the assembly of two objects when she was told what she was to make. On the other two assembly tasks, the subject is not told what is to be assembled; she did poorly with these and her resulting scaled score was 10. Likewise, her score on the Coding subtest was only 9. On this subtest she was never able to comprehend the idea behind the task and had to depend on copying the samples.

This description of test performance illustrates the value of analyzing qualitative performance and the advantage of a test yielding subtest scores. Certainly the above discussion presents a more meaningful picture than the statement of the Full Scale I.Q. In fact, the performance is quite characteristic of the brain-damaged child and is consistent with suggestions from the history. The clinician was impressed during the interview and the testing situation by Lois' short attention span and her distractibility. His evaluation of her personality from the interview and certain projective tests was that she was a very hyperactive but basically emotionally healthy child who was beginning to become easily frustrated. These observations were a further indication that her poor school performance was the result of her handicap in abstractionability, and not necessarily due to emotional disturbance. The clinician had the strong impression that too much pressure was being placed on Lois to accomplish tasks beyond her capabilities. He suspected that she had been exposed to ridicule at school. Her mother wanted her to plan for business college. Lois' ambitions were to work in a factory. She also wanted to participate in Future Farmers of America, but the mother would not permit it.

As a result of the clinician's total assessment, which considered history, interview, and results of intelligence test and personality tests, he made the following recommendations (these were discussed with the parents and the teachers more completely than they are presented here):

> In the school situation and at home, we must relieve the "pressure." When she achieves adequately, she must be praised and rewarded, but nothing is to be gained by criticizing or even calling attention to her poor performances on tasks for which she has little capability. We should try to formulate a curriculum for her that will minimize her liabilities as much as possible. Home economics, agricultural subjects, shop, art, history, and other subjects involving her performance ability and memory should be stressed. Advanced mathematics requiring symbolization and reasoning should be minimized in her curriculum. This is not to say that we should not attempt to teach her more arithmetic, but we should let her work out her own pace and not push her. She can learn English usage but we doubt if she can do well in the understanding of grammar. Everything must be reduced to concrete terms. Above all, we must accept

her as she is. She has become somewhat adverse to speed. If she comprehends, she is very quick, but if she does not, she becomes nervous and blocks. Her attention span is so short that she can best function by shifting frequently from one activity to another.

We believe that a decision should be made in the middle of the spring term (possibly in March) as to her advancement to the eighth grade at the end of the year. It will be better to retain her one year in the seventh grade than to let her go ahead unless she does adequate seventh grade work. Her chances of completing the advanced grades will be improved if she is more nearly prepared for advanced work. We would not demote her in grade this year, but would retain her next year unless her achievement improves quite remarkably. Actually, she should have been retained in one or more of the earlier grades. We believe that her behavior problems are related to her short attention span and her failure to comprehend some school work. Her lack of interest in some areas is certainly related to the above.

If she can be properly understood as a handicapped child of average general ability, then the emotional problems which are developing can be diverted. This child presents an interesting challenge. With removal of pressure, encouragement in practical skills and as much alteration of the curriculum as is possible, she should be able to become a useful and productive citizen. She will probably not study beyond high school. Even business college seems a doubtful objective. Most of the things which her mother wants for her appear to be untenable. Above all, we repeat that we must take off the pressure in all possible settings.

PERFORMANCE SCALES

Before the development of the WISC it was nearly always considered necessary to supplement the Stanford-Binet with some nonverbal measure of intellectual functioning. Because of this recognition that certain children might be definitely handicapped on a preponderantly verbal scale, a number of different kinds of performance items and performance scales were developed. Even with the WISC, occasions will frequently arise when some additional observation of a subject in a nonverbal or performance situation will be required. For example, the WISC is rather unsatisfactory with very young children and with low-grade mentally deficient persons. Of the many different tasks and scales, we will mention a few that are of historical interest and/or are commonly used by clinicians at the present time. These are tests that require the subject to "do something" rather than to make a verbal response. The subject may solve a maze, fit cutouts into the appropriate holes in a form board, assemble a pattern of blocks, assemble and put together pictures presented part-wise on pieces of board or card, etc. Such items did appear in the Binet and several were described in the WISC, but we will now consider only those tests in which the purpose is to get away from verbal ability or disability. Such tests are particularly applicable to those who cannot use English readily or are handicapped in some way in the understanding or use of language. Some of these tests are wholly nonlanguage with instructions conveyed by demonstration. Often a performance test includes items not unlike those in a test of mechanical or manual aptitude, but its purpose is very different. We are not interested in the ability to manipulate, but in the extent to which intelligence can be inferred from the manipulative performances of the subject.

1. PINTNER–PATERSON SCALE OF PERFORMANCE TESTS. The earliest elaborate battery of performance tests was developed by Rudolf Pintner and Donald G. Paterson (67) in 1914. They standardized several tests devised by William Healy and Grace M. Fernald (48) and added some devised by themselves and other psychologists. The final scale consisted of fifteen tests that can be presented without the use of language and do not require the use of language on the part of the subject. The subtests in the scale are as follows:

(1) Mare and Foal Form Board. Of the picture-puzzle type, this is a colored picture board of a mare and foal. Sections of the board are removed and the subject must replace them correctly. Score is based on time required and number of wrong moves.

(2) Sequin Form Board. This is a form board in which ten common geometric shapes are to be placed. Score is based on the shortest time required in three trials.

(3) Five-Figure Board. There are five geometric figures, each of which is divided into two or three parts. The pieces are to be fitted into their appropriate places. Score is based on time required and number of errors made.

(4) Two-Figure Board. There are two geometric figures, one cut into four sections and the other into five. These are to be correctly placed in two spaces. Score is based on time required and number of moves.

(5) Casuist Board. This form board consists of four spaces in which twelve sections have to be fitted. Score is based on time required and number of errors made.

(6) Triangle Test. Four triangular pieces are to be fitted into the board. Score is based on time required and number of errors made.

(7) Diagonal Tests. Five variously shaped sections have to be fitted into a rectangular form. Score is based on time required and number of errors made.

(8) Healy Puzzle A. This consists of five rectangular sections that are to be fitted into a rectangular frame. Score is based on time required and number of moves made.

(9) Manikin Test. Wooden legs, arms, head, and body are to be put together to make the form of a man. Score depends on quality of performance.

(10) Feature Profile Test. Wooden sections have to be put together to form the profile of a man's head. Score is based on time required.

(11) Ship Test. This is a picture of a ship cut into ten sections, all of the same size and shape, to be inserted properly into a rectangular frame. Score depends on quality of performance.

(12) Healy Picture Completion Test I. This is a large picture from which ten small squares have been cut out. The missing parts are to be selected from among forty-eight squares identical in size. Score depends upon the quality of completion within a limit of ten minutes.

(13) Substitution Test. A page of rows of geometric figures (five different shapes) which have to be marked with appropriate digits, to correspond with a key at the top of the page. Score is a combination of time and errors made.

(14) Adaptation Board. This is a form board having four circular blocks and holes; three are 6.8 cm. in diameter, while the fourth is 7 cm. The subject is shown that one block fits the larger hole. He is then required to keep his attention fixed and to fit this larger block into the correct space when the board is moved into four different positions. Score is based on the number of correct moves.

(15) Cube Test. Four cubes (one inch) are placed before the subject. With a fifth cube they are tapped in a specified order by the examiner. The subject is asked to imitate the order of tapping. The sequence becomes longer and more complex. Score is the number of sequences correctly imitated.[4]

The age range is from four to fifteen years but not all tests have discriminative value throughout this range. Three methods of scoring are provided by the authors. These are median mental age, point score, and percentile rank. Median mental age based on the median of an individual's M.A. on each of the several subtests is the commonest measure used.

Since many of the Pintner-Paterson subtests are used in other scales,

[4] From *A Scale of Performance Tests*, by Rudolf Pintner and Donald G. Paterson. Copyright, 1917, D. Appleton and Co. Adapted by permission of Appleton-Century-Crofts, Inc.

either in their original or in a similar form, some evaluation is in order. Such tests are susceptible to practice effects and chance successes are more frequent than with verbal tests. Consequently, the reliability coefficients may be low as compared with verbal tests. The scale is more useful with young children and with mentally deficient or retarded adults than with normal older children and adults. Donald A. MacMurray (57) compared the Stanford-Binet performances of fifty children at above 130 I.Q. on the Stanford-Binet and fifty children with I.Q.'s from 75 to 90, with their performances on the Pintner-Paterson scale. The resulting mental ages on the Pintner-Paterson were spuriously high for the bright group and spuriously low for the dull. Predictions of academic achievement were very poor. Performance tests of the Pintner-Paterson type correlate poorly or only very moderately with verbal tests when the group being studied is limited with respect to age or range of ability, but with wider ranges of ability and age the correlations increase. This suggests that although there may be little correspondence between the abilities measured by performance and verbal tests, both kinds of ability do increase with age. Charles M. Morris (61) factor-analyzed results obtained on thirty-four commonly used performance tests and reported that the principal factors measured by the performance tests and by verbal tests should be used to supplement each other but are not interchangeable.

2. THE CORNELL–COXE PERFORMANCE ABILITY SCALE. A test that contains few of the form boards so prominent in other performance scales was introduced by Ethel L. Cornell and Warren W. Coxe (17). This scale consists of the manikin and profile assembly tests that have already been described; the Koh's Block Designs; a picture-arrangement test different in subject matter but similar to the WISC and the Wechsler-Bellevue tests; a memory-for-designs test similar to that used in the Stanford-Binet in which the subject is asked to reproduce each design after it has been shown for ten seconds; a cube-construction test in which the subject is asked to duplicate models of cube construction; and a picture-completion test that may be substituted for the picture-arrangement test—the Healy Picture-Completion Test II, which is similar to the Picture Completion I already described, is used. Of the above tests, all are scored for accuracy and time except picture arrangement (or completion) and the memory for designs. Since this scale has not been found to be as satisfactory as the Arthur Point Scale at upper levels of development, we will not discuss it in any further detail.

3. ARTHUR POINT SCALE OF PERFORMANCE TESTS. In 1930 Grace Arthur (4, 5, 6) introduced a restandardization of eight tests of

the Pintner-Paterson battery and added two new tests. This scale, which is known as Form I, consists of the Cube Test, the Sequin Form Board, Two-Figure Form Board, Casuist Form Board, Manikin, Feature Profile, Mare and Foal, Healy Picture Completion I, Porteus Maze Test, and the Koh's Block-Design Test. The Porteus Maze Tests were presented by Porteus (68, 69, 70) as a "supplement and corrective" for the Binet; they consist of a series of mazes of increasing difficulty, and the subject is required to trace, with pencil, the course from entrance to exit. Form II of the Arthur Point Scale (7) consists of the Cube Test, the Sequin, the Porteus Maze Tests, the Koh's Blocks, the Triangle Test, the Five-Figure Form Board, and the Healy Picture Completion II. This form, constructed primarily for retest purposes, is commonly used by some clinicians in place of Form I. The scoring of the Arthur Point Scale, as the name implies, is in terms of a raw score determined by the number of successes, time required, or errors which are converted into weighted score points. The total of these points may be converted into a mental age.

The scale was devised primarily as a clinical instrument to be used as a substitute for verbal tests of the Binet type in cases in which a verbal scale is inappropriate. Arthur believes that the basic capacities required by her tests and the Binet tests are essentially the same. Actually, the coefficients of correlation between Binet I.Q.'s and I.Q.'s on Arthur tests are unusually high as compared with those between other tests. However the agreement in individual cases and at certain age levels is not sufficient for the tests to be used interchangeably. In actual clinical practice the results of both kinds of measurements should be compared with all other information available on the individual case and the interpretations based on the interrelationship of all data.

4. OTHER FORM-BOARD TESTS. Several other form boards have been experimented with and used occasionally in clinical practice. Among these are the Ferguson Form Boards, first described in 1920 (26), but restandardized by Louise Wood and Edythe Kumin (106) in 1939. They consist of a series of six form boards that progress in difficulty. Standardization data is available on 364 subjects ranging from grade one to college seniors. The Kent-Shakow Form Boards (54) were designed primarily for adult use. A modification of these form boards by William R. Grove (45) was standardized on a male adult prison population. Still another form-board test is the Carl Hollow Square Scale (15) which consists of a wooden panel in which is cut a $4\frac{1}{2}$ inch square hole, and 29 blocks of varying straight-line geometric forms, each having both straight and beveled edges. The problem is to fill the hole with sets of blocks in a series of several tasks of increasing complexity and difficulty. Arthur (8) has modified and restandardized the Lieter International

Performance Scale and has presented new norms for the three-to-eight year age group. This scale is growing in popularity with clinicians and is frequently used with language-handicapped children.

5. The Goodenough Drawing Test.   Rather widespread clinical use has been made of this test as a nonverbal supplement to other scales. Florence L. Goodenough (42) reviewed the literature and research on the drawings of young children as well as of persons of different races and cultures.

The test and standardization procedures were developed from the conclusions of this survey. The task is simple; the child is given a sheet of paper and a pencil and is asked to make a picture of a man. The productions are scored by assigning points of credit for various aspects of the drawing. In evaluating the drawings, artistic standards are entirely disregarded, and every effort has been made to eliminate the subjective element in judgments. As finally developed, the scale consisted of fifty-one points or units of measurement. Several illustrations will indicate the method of scoring. Any clear method of representing the head is credited with one point. Features alone, without any outline for the head itself, are not credited. Any method of representation clearly intended to indicate the legs is credited. The number must be correct; two should be portrayed in full-face drawings and either one or two in profile. Similarly, arms must be present and the trunk must be indicated. Additional points are given if the trunk is longer than it is broad, if shoulders are definitely shown, if arms and legs are attached to the trunk, if neck is present, if eyes are present, if nose is present, and so on through all the points outlined in the manual. The scores so obtained can be transmuted into mental age equivalents based on the standardization sample. The test is intended for ages three and a half years to thirteen and a half years. The reliability coefficients are satisfactory, but the drawing test does not correlate well with other types of tests used in the evaluation and measurement of intelligence. It does, however, provide another situation for the observation of a client, and certain personality factors may also be inferred from the drawings. More will be said about this later.

A shortened Goodenough scale consisting of the scoring of twenty items has been developed by Ralph F. Berdie (11). The results that can be expected from the use of this scale, as well as the original scale, are suggested by Gunzburg (46). He found that the correlation between the short form (Berdie Scale) and the nonverbal Wechsler was quite high (r = .73) when "nonpathological" drawings were considered. On the other hand, when drawings described as "pathological" or "doubtful" were studied, the correlations were much lower (r's = .36 and .46). He utilized a group of mental defectives and reported the agreement of his judges was high for classifying the drawings in terms of pathology. This, of course, suggests a qualitative use of the test situation which clinicians probably depend on more than they depend on the quantitative scores.

SCALES FOR INFANTS AND PRESCHOOL CHILDREN

There are several scales that have developed to measure or estimate the mental development of children from birth to six years or more. One group of tests or scales is similar to intelligence tests already discussed, while other types provide scales for evaluating the physical and social development of the child.

1. GESELL DEVELOPMENTAL SCHEDULES. Based upon his systematic study of infants and young children, Arnold Gesell first published his developmental schedules with norms at various age levels in 1925 (34). Revised schedules have been based on further investigations (35, 36, 37, 38), and the present infant scale lists a number of items of behavior which are scored plus or minus, depending on whether the infant manifests the behavior. The infant's "distinctive" level of behavior is observed, and from this level, responses showing greater or lesser degrees of maturity are added or subtracted. Thus, an algebraic sum of deviating responses from this distinctive level results in a rating of the infant in the following categories: postural behavior, prehensory behavior, perceptual behavior, adaptive behavior, and language behavior. The preschool scale extends from fifteen months to six years. Schedules for the preschool age levels provide for the observation of motor behavior, adaptive behavior, language behavior, and personal-social behavior. The preschool schedules are not scored quantitatively, but are used as guides to estimate the development of a given child.

The schedule for infants has clinical value since it provides a means for estimating a child's development during the first year of life. It is about the only such scale, and it is a well-standardized scale for use with this age group. Gesell makes no attempt to claim any predictive value for his schedules. They simply indicate the relative level of development when applied to a particular case.

2. CATTELL DEVELOPMENTAL AND INTELLIGENCE SCALE. Psyche Cattell (16) used the Gesell tests as a point from which to build. The items from the Gesell schedules were arranged in an age scale similar to that of the Stanford-Binet. In order to make the scale as much of an intelligence test as possible, over one hundred items that were thought to be related to home training or muscular control were eliminated. These were replaced by other items, some from the Stanford-Binet, and the resulting scale runs from two to thirty months.

The Cattell test has been constructed to constitute a downward extension of Form L of the Stanford-Binet Tests. The method of scoring is the same as with the Stanford-Binet. Groupings are provided at each month from two to twelve, at two-month intervals in the second year, and at twenty-seven and thirty months. There are five items at each age level. The correlations between Cattell scale I.Q. ratings in infancy and Stanford-Binet I.Q. ratings with the same children at thirty-six months are low, in fact negligible for tests given during the first nine months. As the age increases, the coefficients increase and are superior to those found with other scales. With the assistance of the Cattell test the clinician can usually identify children who are widely deviant, even at the young ages. It is probably the most widely used of the infant and preschool schedules.

3. OTHER INFANT OR PRESCHOOL SCALES.   There are several other widely used infant or preschool scales. Among these is the California First Year Mental Scale (10) consisting of 115 items for children between the ages of one and eighteen months; the Merrill Palmer Scale of Mental Tests (86) consisting of 93 items arranged in level of difficulty for use with children of from twenty-four months to sixty-three months of age; and the Minnesota Preschool Scale (43) in two forms, including twenty-six tests designed for use with children from eighteen months to six years.

4. VINELAND SOCIAL MATURITY SCALE.   The first formulation of the Social Maturity Scale was published by Edgar A. Doll (21, 22) in 1935. The scale presents a slightly different method for the evaluation of the functioning of the young child. Doll (23, p. 1) says, "The scale provides a definite outline of detailed performances in respect to which children show a progressive capacity for looking after themselves and for participating in those activities which lead toward ultimate independence as adults." The items of the scale are arranged in order of increasing average difficulty and represent maturation in such areas as self-help, self-direction, locomotion, occupation, communication, and social independence. The scale is said to be particularly useful for research and is believed to afford the following kinds of information (23, p. 2):

(1) A standard schedule of normal development which can be used repeatedly for the measurement of growth or change.

(2) A measure of individual differences and, consequently, of extreme deviation which may be significant in such problems as mental deficiency, juvenile delinquency, child placement or adoption.

(3) A qualitative index of variation in development in abnormal subjects such as the maladjusted, the unstable, the psychopathic, the epileptic.

(4) A measure of improvement following special treatment, therapy and training.

(5) A schedule for reviewing developmental histories in the clinical study of retardation, deterioration and rates or stages of growth or decline.[5]

We have included the scale among infant and preschool scales but it is standardized for use at age levels from birth to 25 years. Doll (24) describes its use with a wide range of subjects in considerable detail. There are 117 items in the scale and each has been given a categorical designation such as self-help general, self-help eating, self-help dressing, self-direction, occupation, communication, locomotion, and socialization. The items are arranged in order of average norms and all are separated into year groups.

One unique aspect of this scale is that the information is gathered from an informant or informants who are usually not the subject of the examination; however it may be practicable under favorable conditions to gather the information from the subject. The total score can be converted to an age score by interpolation according to the year-score values on the record sheet. The Vineland Social Maturity Scale is a useful clinical instrument that provides another approach to the evaluation of resources, particularly in the area of social adjustment. It does not, however, measure all aspects of that adjustment. One caution must be indicated regarding its use and this caution pertains to the dependence that can be placed on the reports of the parents or others who supply the information necessary for the clinician's ratings. An interesting controversy has arisen recently concerning a particular situation, which shows the danger of overdependence on the Vineland ratings. Since this situation also illustrates several other principles referred to in this section on intellectual evaluation, we will describe it in detail.

Two children from the same family were referred to the clinic for evaluation because they had not been able to adapt to the usual instruction in a public school setting. The older child, a girl, was nine years of age, and the younger, a boy, was seven. Both were in the first grade, the girl repeating the grade and the boy entering school for the first time.

When the older child had entered school, she had presented a picture of extremely low maturity. She had been unable to run and play with other children because of extreme awkwardness and retarded physi-

---

[5] By permission from *Vineland Social Maturity Scale: Manual of Directions,* by Edgar A. Doll. Copyright 1947 by Educational Test Bureau.

cal development. She became lost on the playground, and in the classroom she huddled in a corner whimpering most of the time. She did not speak at all and was extremely dirty and poorly groomed. She had not attained bowel control, and on one occasion had chased a group of boys (who had teased her) about the classroom attempting to hit them with her soiled panties, which she had removed after having had a bowel movement. After this episode the school officials had come to the conclusion that she did not fit into the usual school routine and had excluded her from school. The parents, wishing their child in school, had taken her to an institution for the mentally retarded for outpatient evaluation. Since the girl could not speak and could not be separated from her parents for what was regarded as adequate testing, the Vineland Scale was administered by the parents. According to the responses given to them, she was rated as having a Social Quotient of 85 and upon this basis it was recommended that the child be retained in the public school. It was recognized that this rating might be somewhat high because of the desire of the parents to present the child in a favorable light, but in spite of a Stanford-Binet I.Q. of 42 and an approximate I.Q. of 45 based on performance on several form-board tasks, it was still felt that the child would profit from placement in the public school.

When the girl and her brother were seen approximately one year later, the following general picture was pieced together. The mother gave the clinical impression to the staff of a severely retarded acromegalic adult, and it appeared quite clear that the validity of information received from her would require considerable checking. The mother had stayed in school until she was sixteen and at that time had been doing fourth- or fifth-grade work, a level of performance which was judged to be above her present level of functioning. The father, although definitely below average in general ability, had completed the eighth grade and was successfully holding down a relatively skilled position in a furniture factory. According to reports from others, mental retardation characterized many of the members of the mother's family, although most of them were not as low in potential as the mother appeared to be.

From a careful evaluation of the information available, it appeared that the girl's development had been extremely retarded, but the brother two years younger did not appear to have been nearly as slow; in fact, in most respects he had surpassed his sister when he was three or four years of age. Psychological testing suggested that the girl had a mental age of about 4 years, with very little variation in performance. Her performances on nonverbal tasks were approximately those of a three- or four-year-old child and the same was true of her performance on the somewhat more verbal tasks in the Stanford-Binet. Good co-operation and motivation was gained on the Minnesota Preschool Scale, and here again her mental age was about four years. I.Q. equivalents could not be derived for her on this last test since the norms do not go beyond a chronological age of five years eleven months, but all indications led to the conclusion of a level of intelligence which was less than that represented by an I.Q. of 50. Her drawings were only scribblings and were not scorable. Even though the history suggested a familial basis for low capacity, she appeared to be functioning at a lower level than that which might be expected. Because of her general poor health and the report of occasional convulsive behavior, the clinic's strong recommendation was for institutional care.

In the instance of her younger brother the picture seemed somewhat different. When he was with his sister, his behavior was quite similar to hers, with the sister exerting a sort of dominating dependence on him. When separated from the sister, he was able to perform at a much more mature level. In fact, on performance items he occasionally exhibited an above-average performance. On the WISC his verbal I.Q. was 76, his performance I.Q. 116, resulting in a full scale index that was essentially average. His drawings were about what would be expected from a seven-year-old, and from various observations he appeared to have a considerable amount of manual skill and concrete ability. He appeared to be performing, or at least showing the potential for performance, considerably higher than the family history would suggest to be likely. In any case, his potentiality appeared to be higher than that of his sister or mother. The clinic recommended strongly that he be kept in the public school, much to the teacher's surprise. She had assumed him to be much like his sister. The clinic could not predict that his academic success would be too outstanding, but it was believed that he would gain some basic education, and that later, with vocational training, he would be able to earn his living and take care of himself.

This rather simple example illustrates not only the danger of uncritical acceptance of parents' reports of information rated on the Vineland Scale, but also the importance of observing behavior in various test situations and of integrating and comparing these obervations against a background of historical information.

THE WECHSLER–BELLEVUE

The Wechsler-Bellevue Intelligence Examination for Adults (97) was first published in 1939 because of the need for an individual adult intelligence test. The Bellevue scale was devised to eliminate some of the shortcomings of the Stanford-Binet which we have already described in our discussion of the Binet and the Wechsler Intelligence Scale for Children. The use of subtests with items grouped into subtests and arranged in order of difficulty, the discarding of the mental age concept, and other innovations were discussed when we described the children's scale, which was published several years after the adult scales. As Wechsler (97) has pointed out, the great bulk of standardization data on earlier intelligence scales had been derived through the examination of school children. This was true for several reasons. In the first place, the usefulness of intelligence tests for the prediction of school success was apparent very early; secondly, children are more available; and, finally, it is easier to devise children's tests than tests for adults. In addition to their application to the school situation, tests were used very early for the diagnosis of mental deficiency. Up to the time of the publication of the Wechsler tests, the tests standardized for children were used with adults with little questioning of their applicability.

It is true that the 1916 Stanford Revision of the Binet included tests for adults but apparently these tests were standardized on only 62 adults, and testing of soldiers of the U.S. Army showed that these norms were unsatisfactory. The Terman-Merrill Revision also included tests for adults, but, again, these tests were not adequately standardized on adults. In spite of the fact that there were no adequate standardization norms, such tests as the Stanford-Binet were used for adult testing until 1939 or 1940, and, in fact, are still used by some.

Wechsler reports several other limitations of earlier tests which he attempted to correct in the Bellevue Scales. For one thing, the test materials did not appeal to an adult; for another, the materials placed the emphasis on tasks somewhat "schoolish" in nature; and still another limitation was the emphasis on speed in many tests standardized on children. Older subjects tend to do progressively worse on "speed" tests, and consequently are penalized by them. In addition to these reasons is the fact that adult intelligence cannot be evaluated in the same terms as child intelligence. The concept of mental age does not seem to have too much meaning when used to define adult capacity.

The Wechsler-Bellevue Scales were published in two forms (97, 98), each of which consisted of ten subtests—five "verbal" and five "non-verbal"—and a vocabulary test to be used as a supplement or an alternate. Form I has been revised (101) and is described as the Wechsler Adult Intelligence Scale (WAIS). The test items will not be described in detail because of their resemblance to items already described in the WISC and other tests. The subtest items and the mental processes presumably tapped by them are listed and described in Figure 7. Solomon Diamond (20) investigated the vocational guidance value of the test. He found certain subtests weighted heavily with a linguistic factor, others with a clerical factor, and still others with a spatial factor. He concluded that the Wechsler-Bellevue is of value to the vocational counselor, but that it is not adequate as a measure of vocational aptitudes unless taken together with other tests. Benjamin Balinsky (9) factor-analyzed

Figure 7

MENTAL PROCESSES IN WECHSLER-BELLEVUE SUBTESTS[6]

Subtests	Mental Processes
Vocabulary	Recall of previously acquired verbal meanings. Responses require some organization and formulation of ideas. Variation in quality of ideas and mode of expression revealed.
Information	Range of previously acquired (remote memory) everyday knowledge. Reflects alertness to world about person, his social circle, educational background. Answers in 1 or 2 words, no immediate learning or problem-solving effort required, and very little formulation and organization of responses needed.
Comprehension	Measures utilization of past experience (practical information) in problem solving; but does not require efficiency under time limit or invention of unusual solutions. Requires judgment, choice of appropriate alternative in deciding how to meet a situation.
Similarities	Abstract conceptual thinking. Discrimination in selecting fundamental from superficial similarities or concrete formulations. Reveals qualitative differences in level, evenness, and erraticalness of S's logical thinking. Verbal concept formation.
Arithmetic	Arithmetic reasoning. Previous training and experience (7th grade or ordinary business transactions) used in reasoning under stress of time limits. Scores affected by fluctuations of attention and emotional reactions. Concentration.
Digit Span	Attention, concentration, auditory receptivity, immediate recall and rote memory. Requires concentrated effort and freedom from distractions of anxiety and other stimuli.
Digit Symbol	Perceptual speed; memorizing: learning to associate unfamiliar symbols with familiar numerals under obvious pressure of time limits;

[6] Adapted from unpublished material provided by Arden N. Frandsen.

FIGURE 7 (*continued*)

MENTAL PROCESSES IN WECHSLER-BELLEVUE
SUBTESTS

Subtests	Mental Processes
	continuous shifting of mental sets; persistent effort and attention. Poor motivations, tendency to confusion from anxiety, etc., lowers score. Visual-motor co-ordination and psychomotor speed.
Block Designs	Involves ability to perceive and analyze patterns and ability to comprehend abstract units in multiple relationships (analytic and synthetic abilities). Requires persistent effort under time limits, shifting, autocriticism necessary. Visual-motor co-ordination.
Object Assembly	Initiative in seeking and achieving an unknown goal. Conception and perception from incomplete parts of a familiar configuration. Speed, persistence, shifting, autocriticism necessary. Visual-motor co-ordination.
Picture Completion	Utilizing past experience, it measures (perceptual and conceptual) abilities to comprehend picture as a whole and to analyze and differentiate essential from unessential details in determining the missing part from functions. Admits wide range of inaccurate but plausible choices and presents no self-contained criteria of accomplishment.
Picture Arrangement	Ability to comprehend (perceive and conceive) to size up a total situation: sequence of events, social in content. Involves anticipation, planning, and organizing in logical sequences. Visual organization and planning.

subtests scores based upon cases aged nine to sixty and found that different factors emerged at different age levels. In addition, the same subtests did not always contribute to a given factor when different age groups were considered. Cecil H. Patterson (64, 66) has suggested abbreviated scales and factors involved in them.

Because of the possibility afforded by the different subtest scores, workers have attempted to discover particular patterns of responses which are characteristic of certain clinical groups. There have been sev eral ways in which the differential analysis of performance has been used. One way is to look for certain signs that are thought to be indicative of a particular pathology or behavior disorder. Wechsler (97) has reported the Verbal I.Q. to be higher than the Performance I.Q. in organic brain damage, schizophrenia, and neurosis but lower for adolescent psychopaths and mental defectives. Wechsler also lists several signs of schizophrenia such as relatively high information and vocabulary, average to superior digit span and block design, average to poor arithmetic, and low object assembly and digit symbol. Wechsler describes the patterns of deviation for neurotics as relatively high in information, comprehension, similarities, and vocabulary; average to low in arithmetic; average in picture completion and block design, and relatively low in digit span, picture arrangement, object assembly, and digit symbol.

A slightly different approach which overlaps to some extent with the "sign" or profile approach is the study of scatter or variability in subtest performance. A. R. Gilliland (40), using samples of psychotics and normals, concluded that intertest variability was approximately 35 per cent greater in a psychotic group than could be predicted from Wechsler's standardization data. Subsequently, the same author (41) found no statistically significant results. Albert I. Rabin (72) devised a "schizophrenic ratio," which was a scatter index to differentiate schizophrenics from normals, neurotics, and manic depressives. Wilse B. Webb (95), however, demonstrated the questionable value of Rabin's ratio by applying it both to schizophrenics and normals from David Rapaport's (75) experimental and control groups, where he found the ratio to be somewhat normally distributed. Rapaport made a detailed statistical analysis of scatter patterns of selected psychotics, neurotics, and normal control groups and felt that they demonstrated statistically reliable differences between these groups with regard to intertest variability. Jack J. Monroe (60, p. 110) in commenting on research in this area has stated, ". . . no single problem in the area of clinical research has been so widely studied as has that of psychometric scatter, and few have yielded more inconsistent results." In an effort to clarify some of the conflicting findings, Monroe designed an exploratory analysis of variance in which the main effects of adjustment, intelligence, and geographic location upon intraindividual scatter were studied. He computed individual standard deviations on the Bellevue scale for 352 subjects (144 schizophrenics, 136 neurotics, and 72 well-adjusted normals). He utilized Rapaport's groups (from Kansas) and an approximately equal group from Indiana. The intelligence variable was broken into three factors by ordering I.Q. equivalents into low, medium, and high intellectual levels. He has summarized and discussed his results as follows (p. 113):

A Kansas sample of subjects seemed to be more variable on the Bellevue Scale than did a similar sample of Indiana subjects.

There was a strong indication of the presence of interaction between the adjustment and intelligence variables as influences of Bellevue scatter.

Extreme scatter on the Bellevue Scale is characteristic of only those schizophrenics with low intelligence. There was no strong indication that differences in scatter exist between neurotics and well-adjusted normals; and those schizophrenics with medium or high intelligence are no more variable on the Bellevue scale than any other adjustment types studied in this project.

The finding that scatter differences which seem to characterize Rapaport's experimental groups does not hold for a similar group of Indiana subjects is rather baffling at first glance, primarily because the "locality variable" is poorly defined. Obviously, the fact that one sample was drawn from Kansas and the other from Indiana offers no psychological interpretation of the differences that were found. These differences were, nevertheless, found; it is an empirical fact, and the absence of an adequate psychological label, while somewhat disturbing, does not alter the facts. Whatever the psychological variables are which account for these differences between the Kansas and Indiana subsamples, the variable, as defined in the present set of experimental designs is a systematic one and cannot rightly be attributed to error. By controlling the variable in this study the investigator was provided a more accurate estimate of experimental error by which to test the main effects of the adjustment and intelligence variables. The psychological "meaning" of this difference must await future research, but, in the meantime, caution seems indicated in accepting at face value scatter indices for the Bellevue test which have been arrived at under conditions different from those which govern the group upon which those indices are to be supplied.

Statistically, the interaction between the variables of adjustment and intelligence indicates that they are not independent as influencers of scatter. Clinically, this will mean that the impact of both variables is felt by the clinician who used the Bellevue scattergram as an aid in diagnosis. The fact that only certain schizophrenics show excessive scatter will obviously limit the use of the scattergram in detecting psychosis. The rather widespread clinical assumption that "excessive variability (on the Bellevue Scale) is the most ominous sign of maladjustment" should doubtless be reinterpreted in the light of new knowledge.[7]

William A. Hunt and Iris Stevenson (51, p. 29) have criticized standard mechanical diagnostic schemes that would eliminate "clinical judgment" as follows:

Two things are wrong with this picture. In the first place all the statistical procedures involved in test validation are group procedures. They are based on a group tendency and allow for a margin of error which expresses itself as a dispersion around the central tendency. Ideally, this margin is never large for many cases. The statistician therefore writes it off as statistically unimportant, and the psychologist interested in group testing writes it off as operating expense. The clinical psychologist, however, is not dealing with groups, but with individuals, and they are individuals who usually come from the deviant group, the atypical persons to whom a group validated test does not do justice. In handling these deviants, any standardized testing procedure frequently will yield erroneous results which can only be corrected by the psychologist's clinical evaluation. In the second place, the goal of perfection has not been even approximated in many testing fields. Whatever dangers are inherent in applying group techniques to an individual are accentuated by the imperfection of most of our present techniques. The fact that psychometrics has perfection as its goal may satisfy our super-egos, but it should not blind us to the practical fact that this goal is far away at present.[8]

Studies by Louis S. Levine (56), William D. Altus and Jerry H. Clark (1), J. Richard Wittenborn (105), Francis M. Gilhooley (39), Lawrence S. Rogers (77), and others (19, 33, 47, 50, 65, 96) all show conflicting results concerning the sign and scatter analysis approaches to Wechsler-Bellevue interpretation; this makes the utility of such approaches doubtful for individual diagnostic use.

Although the strictly empirical approach has not resulted in consistent group trends satisfactory for clinical diagnosis, the clinician can use the subtest distribution in a functional fashion to good advantage. By the study of the total clinical picture and the specific responses and approach to the test, many important observations can be made from the Wechsler-Bellevue or from the WAIS. It must be noted that in usual

[7] From "The Effects of Emotional Adjustment and Intelligence upon Bellevue Scatter," by Jack J. Monroe, *Journal of Consulting Psychology*, 1952, 16, 110–14. By permission of the American Psychological Association.

[8] From "Psychological Testing in Military Clinical Psychology: I. Intelligence testing," by William A. Hunt and Iris Stevenson, *Psychol. Review*, 1946, 53, 25–35. By permission of the American Psychological Association.

practice the clinician reports his observations of a client in terms of the total evaluation, and separate reports on different tests are seldom written. However, in an effort to illustrate some of the observations that can be made from Wechsler-Bellevue data, examples of the analysis of the results from testing are submitted.

A fifteen-year-old boy was referred for intellectual evaluation and for recommendations concerning further education. The pattern of his scaled scores on the various subtests follows:

Information	4	Picture Arrangement	7
Comprehension	8	Picture Completion	7
Digit Span	3	Block Design	11
Arithmetic	4	Object Assembly	12
Similarities	5	Digit Symbol	8
Vocabulary	6		

The Full Scale I.Q. was 80, the Verbal I.Q. 72, and the Performance I.Q. was 93.

The distinctly higher Performance I.Q. (93) than Verbal I.Q. (72) indicated that the subject was much more competent in dealing with practical, perceptual-motor activities than he was in dealing with words and verbal concepts. Following Diamond's and Patterson's groupings of the subtests (on the basis of factor analysis) into suggestive aptitudes, the following pattern appeared:

Mechanical (perception and management of spatial relations)	10.0
Visual-motor manipulation (similar to mechanical above)	10.3
Reasoning	7.5
Linguistic	5.7
Clerical	5.0

This pattern is consistent with the above-mentioned difference between verbal and performance parts of the scale. The subject was found to be relatively good in some mechanical aptitudes (equal to the norm average of 10). His reasoning ability was low, and he was distinctly low in both linguistic and clerical aptitudes.

Even more specifically, it was noted that the subject's range of information was distinctly low, indicating lack of alertness to the world about him and very limited profit from academic school experience. He did not know such things as the number of pints in a quart or the number of weeks in a year. He did not know the location of London or of Egypt, or what were the capitals of Italy or Japan, and he did not know who wrote *Hamlet*. He did, however, show fair ability to utilize experience in meeting practical, verbally presented situations. The very low digits and arithmetic scores may have been indicative of anxiety distractions, although anxiety was not clearly indicated in other ways during the examination, except in slight uncertainties in some responses ("I guess," "I imagine," and a self-reference to "getting worse (bad) yourself"). In dealing with Similarities, Vocabulary, and to some extent Comprehension, his reasoning was on a very concrete level; he showed limited ability for abstraction or generalizing in his thinking. For example, to the question, "How are dog and lion alike?" his concrete level response was, "They both have hair." His most adequate performances occurred clearly in perceptual-motor behavior. On the Block Designs test, taking an integrated, unified approach, he exhibited relatively good ability to perceive and to analyze patterns into multiple relationships and to resynthesize these patterns. His good ability in this sphere was corroborated on the Object Assembly Test, which also requires the seeking and achieving of an unknown goal.

Since this subject had been apprehended for sexually molesting a feebleminded girl, we were interested in his attitude toward controls of conduct. His attitude, which was one of restraint because of fear of consequences, was projectively suggested in answers to two Comprehension items: "Why should we keep away from bad company?" to which he answered, "So you won't get any worse yourself"; and "Why are laws necessary?" to which he responded, "If there wasn't no laws, you could take somebody's land or house, tell them to get, or kill somebody."

As for further schooling, the measures of aptitude indicated that some such curriculum as performance level mechanics, manual semiskilled industrial work, or practical farming might well be emphasized. In high school a specialized curriculum in practical vocational training on a semiskilled level was suggested to replace the usual emphasis upon English, science, and social studies. It seemed that the subject could profit somewhat from further individualized training in reading, arithmetic, etc., but that this aspect of the curriculum should probably be minimized. His further training in moral and social codes was continued on the concrete level that he had apparently accepted. It was believed that he would do what was right (or wrong) in the main for the concrete rewards or to escape from punishment, rather than to conform to abstract ethical ideals.

Another case report still further indicates how the Wechsler-Bellevue can be utilized in planning counseling and therapy with a client. This client was a thirty-year-old adult mental hospital patient. He achieved the following subtest scaled scores:

Information	12	Picture Arrangement	10
Comprehension	15	Picture Completion	11
Digit Span	14	Block Design	11
Arithmetic	8	Object Assembly	8
Similarities	9	Digit Symbol	7
Vocabulary	14		

His Verbal Scale I.Q. was 116, his Performance Scale I.Q. was 103, and the Full Scale I.Q. was 112.

Intellectually, the patient performed at a level termed "bright normal." Material in the verbal sphere was handled appreciably better than the performance portion of the test. The deterioration loss was computed and found to be negligible. Despite the fact that no deterioration was apparent, certain findings were not wholly contraindicative of organicity. However the patterning was not a far cry from that presented by the authors of the test as designating schizophrenic ideation. It was felt that test results were not optimal, and that disturbances of thought processes resulted in a discrepancy between tested intelligence and the examiner's estimation of intellectual endowment. High comprehension and vocabulary suggested that the patient had benefited from cultural contacts, still had the ability to evaluate past experiences, possessed a degree of social maturity, etc. High digit span contraindicated, to some extent, severe organic involvement. It appeared that, to a certain extent, the patient had lost some of his ability to discriminate between essentials and superficial likenesses (similarities). A decline in abstract thinking and ability to shift (block design) was indicated. The low subtest score on Digit Symbol hinted at difficulty in concentrating for any length of time. In general, although no bizarre responses were forthcoming, there appeared to be indications that a psychotic personality core was taking its toll, in part in the intellectual spheres.

A general indication from the Wechsler-Bellevue of use for therapy was the patient's I.Q. scores (verbal, performance, over-all). They gave indication that he had the capacity to work at and to comprehend some of his problems. His high score on the Comprehension subtest was a specially favorable indication. Behavioral signs were also favorable in that he presented an unusual degree of striving and desire to do well. This also pointed out some dynamic aspects of his personality—namely, the feelings of insecurity and inferiority and a tendency toward idealism and perfectionism.

A liability, so far as therapy was concerned, was indicated by his relatively low score in Similarities. The patient had apparently lost some of his ability to discriminate between essential and superficial likenesses, and this was borne out during therapeutic contacts. In talking about his various experiences, for example, he had difficulty in seeing and abstracting the essential likenesses and differences from them.

The relatively low scores on Block Design and Digit Symbol suggested two other aspects for therapy. One was his difficulty in changing "set." It was subsequently noted in the therapeutic sessions that when he started talking about a certain area (e.g., flying), he tended to stay on this subject for a good length of time; sometimes he carried a subject over from one session to another, repeating previously covered material.

This suggested that during therapy, as he met new concepts, it would probably take him a fair amount of time to learn and to integrate them. This was related to his apparent loss in abstract reasoning. As therapy continued, it was noted that he had difficulty in applying a concept or abstraction to different contexts. It seemed necessary for him to discuss each situation rather concretely, although a previously covered abstraction may have had a good deal of application.

There was a fair amount of intratest variability on the Wechsler-Bellevue which suggested anxiety, a "fading" phenomenon, or both; this produced symptoms that he discussed at some length during the therapy sessions. He complained of periods of "grogginess" and tightness at the back of the neck and in other muscle groups.

In general, the Wechsler-Bellevue suggested a good many assets to be utilized in therapy and the areas of difficulty mentioned were adequately dealt with. The test supported other test material in indicating a "good" prognosis.

Research concerning the Wechsler-Bellevue has been reviewed by Rabin (73) and Rabin and Wilson H. Guertin (74). Other discussions of its reliability and validity have been presented by Robert I. Watson (94) and Cronbach (18). As Cronbach has stated (p. 159) "Whether the Wechsler test is better or worse than the Stanford-Binet for ages under 16 is at present a matter of personal preference." However, at the present time it is the only systematic test designed and standardized for use with adults, and, as such, it is a necessary part of the clinician's repertoire.

GROUP INTELLIGENCE TESTS

As suggested by Hunt and Stevenson (51), group tests are group standardized, and the clinician who is primarily interested in the understanding of individual behavior will ordinarily not find group tests too helpful. However group test information is sometimes available concerning a client, and requires interpretation by the clinician. On other occasions the problem may be simply that of screening, and a group test may suggest whether an individual test or tests are necessary. Furthermore, some group tests have special validity or predictive value for specific purposes, and their use may be indicated. In any case, we must devote some attention to a few commonly used group tests so that the clinician will have a background for their use. Since we will simply identify or list some commonly used tests, the reader who desires more information should refer to such texts as those prepared by Anne Anastasi (2), Cronbach (18), F. S. Freeman (32), and Mursell (62).

1. GROUP VERBAL TESTS. Figure 8 describes several representative group verbal tests. Several other tests that are not in this table

FIGURE 8

GROUP VERBAL TESTS

TEST AND PUBLISHER	AGE OR GRADE LEVEL	SPECIAL FEATURES
ACE Psychological Examination (Educ. Testing Service)	High school, college	L (linguistic) and Q (quantitative) scores. Primarily for college guidance.
Army Alpha: First Nebraska Edition (Sheridan)	High school, adults	Revision gives verbal, number, and relationships scores.
Army General Classification Test (Sci. Res. Assoc.)	High school, adults	Used in World War II. Norms for vast number of adults.
California Test of Mental Maturity (Calif. Test Bureau)	Kindergarten-1, 1–3, 4–8, 7–10, 9–adult, various short forms	Yields diagnostic profile showing M.A. in separate tasks. "Language" and "nonlanguage" I.Q.'s.
Henmon-Nelson (Houghton Mifflin)	Grades 3–8, 7–12, college	Easily administered 30-minute test. Quickscoring.
Kuhlmann-Anderson (Educ. Test Bureau)	Overlapping forms, grades 1–12	Variety of test materials, scaled over continuous range. Relatively hard to administer.
National Intelligence Test (World Book)	Grades 4–9	Adaption for school children of group tests developed for Army recruits.
Ohio State University Psychological (Sci. Res. Assoc.)	Grades 9–college	Unspeeded test of verbal abilities.
Otis Quick-Scoring (World Book)	Grades 1–4, 4–9, 9–college	Easily administered 30-minute test.
Pintner General Ability Tests: Verbal Series (World Book)	Kindergarten-2, 2–4, 4–8, 9–college freshmen	Early tests are pictorial, later ones require reading. Semi-self-administering.
Selective Service Qualifications Test (Educational Testing Service)	College	Equal emphasis on verbal ability and quantitative reasoning material from major academic areas.
Terman-McNemar (World Book)	Grades 7–12	Measures verbal comprehension. Includes seven subtests.

should be mentioned. Among them are the Chicago Tests of Primary Mental Abilities (93) for ages eleven to seventeen and the Miller Analogies Test (59) which is becoming widely used as a scholastic aptitude test at the graduate level.

2. GROUP NONVERBAL TESTS. Figure 9 gives information on several representative group nonverbal tests. Several of these can be ad-

FIGURE 9

GROUP NONVERBAL TESTS

TEST AND PUBLISHER	AGE OR GRADE LEVEL	TYPICAL TASKS
California Test of Mental Maturity (Nonlanguage Tasks) (Calif. Test Bureau)	See Figure 8	See Figure 8.
Cattell Culture-Free Test (Psychological Corporation)	M.A. 12 to superior adult	Classification, figure series, etc. Nearly unspeeded. Supposedly free from school influence. Range covers superior groups.
Chicago Nonverbal (Psychological Corporation)	Age 6 to adult	Digit symbol, block counting, etc. Can be used with pantomime directions.
Pintner General Ability Tests: Nonlanguage (World Book)	Grades 4–6	Paper folding, reasoning with forms, etc. Pantomime directions possible.
Revised Beta (Psychological Corporation)	Age 16–60	Maze, digit symbol picture completion, etc.
SRA Nonverbal Form (Sci. Res. Assoc.)	Adolescents and adults	Picture classification.

ministered almost entirely without the use of language and may provide much useful information. Although many other group tests could be described, this section will be closed with mention of only one additional test. The Progressive Matrices Test (76) is a nonverbal series prepared in England by John C. Raven. It appears to be especially applicable to persons who have verbal handicaps or disabilities and those with cultural disadvantages. The test can be administered to groups in booklet form or individually as a form board. It is intended for all ages beginning at approximately three years. Each item in the test consists of a large meaningless figure called a "matrix of relations" from which a section is missing. The subject is required to choose from six to eight alternatives the one that will correctly complete a given matrix. There are sixty problems that become progressively more difficult. It appears to be a test with considerable utility and promise; it has not been used extensively in the United States, but it is worthy of further study.

Any group test can of course be administered individually, and several disadvantages of group testing procedure, especially the motivation difficulties, can be overcome by such individual testing.

We will not attempt to discuss various other tests such as aptitude tests and achievement tests. It should be apparent to the reader that aptitude tests are tests of resources and potentialities as well as special forms of capacity measures, and the well-rounded clinician should be familiar with a wide range of such tests. The necessity for such familiarity may be even more important in the case of the counseling psychologist, but space does not allow us to do justice to them in this presentation. Assuming that the client has had opportunity to learn, achievement tests are also indicators of the capacity of the client, and they are certainly valuable sources of further information concerning the potentialities and resources of a client. The reader is again referred for information concerning these areas of testing to the valuable texts by Anastasi (2), Cronbach (18), Freeman (32), and Mursell (62). The Mental Measurements Yearbook (13, 14) describes many tests and should be referred to for further information about tests of all kinds.

HOW TO SELECT A TEST

The complete answer to this question cannot be presented here. The various test and measurement texts referred to give a more comprehensive answer than we will attempt. We will pass over the important statistical problems of reliability and validity and concern ourselves with practical and clinical considerations. The clinician selects a test in terms of its fitness as a vehicle for observing the individual and completing his evaluation or confirming observations already made. Consequently, the test selected at any time will depend on the information desired or observations to be confirmed. We want to select reliable and valid measures, but in many instances the best evidence of validity will come from the clinician's experience. Such factors as convenience of administration, time, ease of scoring, expense, and other practical details are always of importance. The most important consideration is that the clinician have a wide range of familiarity with many tests so that he can easily select those that will be most useful in identifying and verifying the information that he requires.

SUMMARY

This chapter has been concerned with the evaluation of the capacity or the intelligence of the individual. The importance of this kind of evaluation was discussed and various ways of describing or defining intelligence were presented. It was concluded that no one measure could describe all of the characteristics variously described as intellectual, and, consequently, various kinds of measures were discussed and described. The field of intellectual evaluation was outlined in terms of verbal and non-verbal tests as well as tests indicating both kinds of behavior. Although the primary emphasis was placed on individually administered tests, some remarks were offered concerning group tests. Cautions in the use of tests were frequently mentioned and commonly used tests were described. The next chapter will continue with the same topic but will consider the specific problems of intellectual deficit and deterioration.

BIBLIOGRAPHY

1. Altus, W. D., and Clark, J. H., "Subtest variations on the Wechsler-Bellevue for two institutionalized behavior problem groups." *J. Consult. Psychol.*, 1949, 13, 444–8.
2. Anastasi, A., *Psychological testing.* New York: Macmillan, 1954.
3. Anderson, J. E., *The psychology of development and personal adjustment.* New York: Henry Holt, 1949.
4. Arthur, G., *A point scale of performance tests,* Vol. I. New York: The Commonwealth Fund, 1933.
5. Arthur, G., *A point scale of performance tests,* Vol. II. New York: The Commonwealth Fund, 1933.
6. Arthur, G., "A point scale of performance test." In *Clinical manual.* Vol. I (2nd ed.). New York: The Commonwealth Fund, 1943.
7. Arthur G., "A point scale of performance tests." *Manual for administering and scoring the tests,* Revised Form II. New York: Psychol. Corp., 1947.
8. Arthur, G., "The Arthur adaptation of the Leiter International Performance Scale." *J. Clin. Psychol.*, 1949, 5, 345–9.
9. Balinsky, B., "An analysis of the mental factors of various age groups from nine to sixty." *Genet. Psychol. Monogr.*, 1941, 23, 191–234.
10. Bayley, N., *The California First-Year Mental Scale.* University of California Syllabus Series, No. 243. Berkeley: Univ. of Calif. Press, 1933.
11. Berdie, R. F., "Measurement of adult intelligence by drawings." *J. Clin. Psychol.*, 1945, 1, 288–95.
12. Bond, E. A., *Tenth grade abilities and achievements.* New York: Teachers College, Columbia Univ., 1940.

13. Buros, O. K. (ed.), *The third mental measurements yearbook*. New Brunswick: Rutgers Univ. Press, 1948.

14. Buros, O. K. (ed.), *The fourth mental measurements yearbook*. Highland Park, N. J.: Gryphon Press, 1953.

15. Carl, G. P., "A new performance test for adults and older children: the Carl Hollow Square Scale." *J. Psychol.*, 1939, 7, 179–99.

16. Cattell, P., "The measurement of intelligence and young children." New York: Psychol. Corp., 1940.

17. Cornell, E. L., and Coxe, W. W., *A performance ability scale*. Yonkers-on-Hudson, N. Y.: World Book, 1934.

18. Cronbach, L. J., *Essentials of psychological testing*. New York: Harper, 1949.

19. Derner, G. F., Aborn, M., and Canter, A. H., "The reliability of the Wechsler-Bellevue subtests and scales." *J. Consult. Psychol.*, 1950, 14, 172–9.

20. Diamond, S., "The Wechsler-Bellevue Intelligence Scales and certain vocational aptitude tests." *J. Psychol.*, 1947, 24, 279–82.

21. Doll, E. A., "The clinical significance of social maturity." *J. Ment. Sci.*, 1935, 81, 766–82.

22. Doll, E. A., "Preliminary standardization of the Vineland Social Maturity Scale." *Amer. J. Orthopsychiat.*, 1936, 6, 283–93.

23. Doll, E. A., *Vineland Social Maturity Scale: manual of directions*. Minneapolis: Educational Test Bureau, 1947.

24. Doll, E. A., *The measurement of social competence: a manual for the Vineland Social Maturity Scale*. Minneapolis: Educational Test Bureau, 1953.

25. Dreger, R. M., "Different I.Q.'s for the same individual associated with different intelligence tests." *Science*, 1953, 118, 594–5.

26. Ferguson, G. O., "A series of formboards." *J. Exp. Psychol.*, 1920, 2, 47–58.

27. Frandsen, A. N., "Interpretation of intelligence test data." Unpublished mimeographed material.

28. Frandsen, A. N., and Higginson, J. B., "The Stanford-Binet and the Wechsler Intelligence Scale for Children." *J. Consult. Psychol.*, 15, 236–8, 1951.

29. Frandsen, A. N., McCullough, B. R., and Stone, D. R., "Serial versus consecutive order administration of the Stanford-Binet Intelligence Scales." *J. Consult. Psychol.*, 1950, 14, 316–20.

30. Freeman, F. N., "What is intelligence?" *School Review*, 33, 1925, 253–63.

31. Freeman, F. N., "The meaning of intelligence." *39th Yearbook, National Society for the Study of Education*, I, 1940, 11–20.

32. Freeman, F. S., *Theory and practice of psychological testing*. New York: Henry Holt, 1950.

33. Garfield, S. L., "A preliminary appraisal of scatter patterns in schizophrenia." *J. Consult. Psychol.*, 1948, 12, 32–6.

34. Gesell, A., *The mental growth of the preschool child*. New York: Macmillan, 1925.

35. Gesell, A., *Infancy and human growth*. New York: Macmillan, 1928.

36. Gesell, A., and Amatruda, C. S., *Developmental diagnosis* (rev. ed.). New York: Hoeber, 1947.

37. Gesell, A., *et al., The first five years of life*. New York: Harper, 1940.

38. Gesell, A., and Thompson, H., *The psychology of early growth*. New York: Macmillan, 1938.

39. Gilhooly, F., "Wechsler-Bellevue reliability and the validity of certain diagnostic signs of the neuroses." *J. Consult. Psychol.*, 1950, 14, 82–7.

40. Gilliland, A. R., "Differential functional loss in certain psychoses." *Psychol. Bull.*, 1940, 37, 439.

41. Gilliland, A. R., Wellman, P., and Goldman, N., "Patterns and scatter of mental abilities in various psychoses." *J. Gen. Psychol.*, 1943, 29, 251–60.

42. Goodenough, F. L., *Measurement of intelligence by drawings*. Yonkers-on-Hudson, N. Y.: World Book, 1926.

43. Goodenough, F. L., Maurer, K. M., and Van Wagenen, M. J., *Minnesota Preschool Scales, Forms A and B* (rev. ed.). Minneapolis: Educational Test Bureau, 1940.

44. Gordon, H., *Mental and scholastic tests among retarded children*. London Bd. Educ., 1923.

45. Grove, W. R., "Modification of the Kent-Shakow Formboard Series." *J. Psychol.*, 1939, 7, 385–97.

46. Gunzburg, H. C., "Scope and limitations of the Goodenough Drawing Test method in clinical work with mental defectives." *J. Clin. Psychol.*, 1955, 11, 8–15.

47. Hamister, R. C., "Test-retest reliability of the Wechsler-Bellevue." *J. Consult Psychol.*, 1949, 13, 39–44.

48. Healy, W., and Fernald, G. M., "Tests for practical mental classification." *Psychol. Monogr.*, 1911, Vol. 13, No. 2.

49. Hirsch, N. D. M., "An experimental study of the East Kentucky mountaineers: a study in heredity and environment." *Genet. Psychol. Monogr.*, 1928, 3, 182–244.

50. Holzburg, J. D., and Deane, M. A., "The diagnostic significance of an objective measure of intra-test scatter on the Wechsler-Bellevue Intelligence Scale." *J. Consult. Psychol.*, 1950, 14, 180–8.

51. Hunt, W. A., and Stevenson, I., "Psychological testing in military clinical psychology: I. Intelligence testing." *Psychol. Rev.*, 1946, 53, 25–35.

52. Hutt, M. L., "A clinical study of 'consecutive' and 'adaptive' testing with the Revised Stanford-Binet." *J. Consult. Psychol.*, 1947, II, 93–103.

53. "Intelligence and its measurement: a symposium." *J. Educ. Psychol.*, 1921, 12, 123–47, 195–216, 271–5.

54. Kent, G. H., and Shakow, D., "Graded series of formboards." *Personnel J.*, 1928, 7, 115–20.

55. Krugman, J. I., Justman, J., Wrightstone, J. W., and Krugman, M., "Pupil functioning on the Stanford-Binet and the Wechsler Intelligence Scale for Children." *J. Consult. Psychol.*, 1951, 15, 475–83.

56. Levine, L. S., "The utility of Wechsler's patterns in the diagnosis of schizophrenia." *J. Consult. Psychol.*, 1949, 13, 28–31.

57. MacMurray, D. A., "A comparison of gifted children and of dull-normal children measured by the Pintner-Paterson Scale as against the Stanford-Binet Scale." *J. Psychol.*, 1937, 4, 273–80.

58. McNemar, Q., *The revision of the Stanford-Binet Scale: an analysis of the standardization data.* Boston: Houghton Mifflin, 1942.

59. Miller, W. S., *The Miller Analogies Test.* New York: Psychol. Corp., 1947.

60. Monroe, J. J., " The effects of emotional adjustment and intelligence upon Bellevue Scatter." *J. Consult. Psychol.*, 1952, 16, 110–14.

61. Morris, C. M., "A critical analysis of certain performance tests." *J. Genet. Psychol.*, 1939, 54, 85–105.

62. Mursell, J. L., *Psychological testing.* New York: Longmans Green, 1949.

63. Pastovic, J. J., and Guthrie, G. M., "Some evidence on the validity of the WISC." *J. Consult. Psychol.*, 1951, 15, 385–6.

64. Patterson, C. H., "A comparison of various 'short forms' of the Wechsler-Bellevue Scale." *J. Consult. Psychol.*, 1946, 10, 260–6.

65. Patterson, C. H., "The Wechsler-Bellevue Scale as an aid in psychiatric diagnosis." *J. Clin. Psychol.*, 1946, 2, 348–53.

66. Patterson, C. H., "A further study of two short forms of the Wechsler-Bellevue Scale." *J. Consult. Psychol.*, 1948, 12, 147–52.

67. Pintner, R., and Paterson, D. G., *A Scale of performance tests.* New York: D. Appleton, 1917.

68. Porteus, S. D., "Mental tests for the feebleminded: a new series." *J. Psycho-asthen.*, 1915, 19, 200–13.

69. Porteus, S. D., *Guide to the Porteus Maze Test.* Vineland, N.J.: Training School, 1933.

70. Porteus, S. D., *Qualitative performance in the Maze Test.* New York: Psychol. Corp., 1942.

71. Pressey, S. L., and Thomas, J. B., "A study of country children in (1) a good, and (2) a poor farming district by means of a group scale of intelligence." *J. Appl. Psychol.*, 1919, 3, 283–6.

72. Rabin, A. I., "Test score patterns in schizophrenia and non-psychotic states." *J. Psychol.*, 1941, 12, 91–100.

73. Rabin, A. I., "The use of the Wechsler-Bellevue Scales with normal and abnormal persons." *Psychol. Bull.*, 1945, 42, 410–22.

74. Rabin, A. I., and Guertin, W. H., "Research with the Wechsler-Bellevue Test: 1945–1951." *Psychol. Bull.*, 1951, 48, 211–48.

75. Rapaport, D., Gill, M., and Schafer, R., *Diagnostic psychological testing,* Vol. I. Chicago: Yearbook Publishers, 1945.

76. Raven, J. C., *The Progressive Matrices Test.* London: H. K. Lewis, 1938. Rev. ed., Scotland: The Crichton Royal, 1947.

77. Rogers, L. S., "Differences between neurotics and schizophrenics on the Wechsler-Bellevue Scale." *J. Consult. Psychol.*, 1951, 15, 151–3.

78. Schwesinger, G. C., *Heredity and environment.* New York: Macmillan, 1933.

79. Seashore, H. G., "Differences between verbal and performance I.Q. on the Wechsler Intelligence Scale for Children." *J. Consult. Psychol.*, 1951, 15, 62–7.

80. Seashore, H. G., Wesman, A., and Doppelt, J., "The standardization of the Wechsler Intelligence Scale for Children." *J. Consult. Psychol.*, 1950, 14, 99–110.

81. Sherman, M., and Henry, T. R., *Hollow Folk*. New York: Crowell, 1933.

82. Sherman, M., and Key, C. B., "The intelligence of isolated mountain children." *Child Develpm.*, 1932, 3, 279–90.

83. Spearman, C., *The abilities of man*. New York: Macmillan, 1927.

84. Stern, W., *The psychological methods of testing intelligence*. Trans. by G. M. Whipple. Baltimore: Warwick & York, 1914.

85. Stoddard, G. D., *The meaning of intelligence*. New York: Macmillan, 1943.

86. Stutsman, R., *Mental measurement of preschool children*. Yonkers-on-Hudson, N.Y.: World Book, 1931.

87. Terman, L. M., *The measurement of intelligence*. Boston: Houghton Mifflin, 1916.

88. Terman, L. M., and Merrill, M., *Measuring intelligence*. Boston: Houghton Mifflin, 1937.

89. Thorndike, E. L., *et al.*, *The measuremnet of intelligence*. New York: Teachers College, Columbia Univ., 1927.

90. Thurstone, L. L., "The nature of general intelligence and ability." *Brit. J. Psychol.*, 1923–24, 14, 243–7.

91. Thurstone, L. L., "Primary mental abilities." *Psychometr. Monogr.*, No. 1. Chicago: Univ. of Chicago Press, 1938.

92. Thurstone, L. L., and Thurstone, T. C., "Factoral studies of intelligence." *Psychometr. Monogr.*, No. 2. Chicago: Univ. of Chicago Press, 1941.

93. Thurstone, L. L., and Thurstone, T. G., *The Chicago Tests of Primary Mental Abilities, Manual of Instruction*. Chicago: Science Research Associates, 1943.

94. Watson, R. I., *The clinical method in psychology*. New York: Harper, 1951.

95. Webb, W. B., "A note on the Rabin ratio." *J. Consult. Psychol.*, 1947, 11, 107–8.

96. Webb, W. B., and DeHaan, H., "Wechsler-Bellevue split-half reliabilities in normals and schizophrenics." *J. Consult. Psychol.*, 1951, 15, 68–71.

97. Wechsler, D., *The measurement of adult intelligence*. Baltimore: Williams & Wilkins, 1944.

98. Wechsler, D., *The Wechsler-Bellevue Intelligence Scale, Form II*. New York: Psychol. Corp., 1946.

99. Wechsler, D., *Wechsler Intelligence Scale for Children*. New York: Psychol. Corp., 1949.

100. Wechsler, D., "Equivalent test and mental ages for the WISC." *J. Consult. Psychol.*, 1951, 15, 381–6.

101. Wechsler, D., *Wechsler Adult Intelligence Scale*. New York: Psychol. Corp., 1955.
102. Weider, A., Noller, P. A., and Schramm, T. A., "The Wechsler Intelligence Scale for Children and the revised Stanford-Binet." *J. Consult. Psychol.*, 1951, 15, 330–3.
103. Wells, F. L., *Mental Adjustments*. New York: D. Appleton, 1917.
104. Wells, F. L., *Modified Alpha Examination*, Form 9. New York: Psychol. Corp., 1941.
105. Wittenborn, J. R., "An evaluation of the use of Bellevue-Wechsler subtest scores as an aid in psychiatric diagnosis." *J. Consult. Psychol.*, 1949, 13, 433–9.
106. Wood, L., and Kumin, E., "A new standardization of the Ferguson Form Boards." *J. Genet. Psychol.*, 1939, 54, 265–84.

CHAPTER

I7

The Evaluation of
Intellectual Efficiency

IN THE PREVIOUS CHAPTER WE WERE CONCERNED PRIMARILY WITH the evaluation of intellectual capacity. We will now go on to consider the evaluation of the efficiency of intellectual functioning. These areas are closely related; in fact, they may be two aspects of the same problem. However, the concept of efficiency involves certain aspects of intellectual functioning not always involved in the concept of capacity.

We approach the evaluation of the intellectual efficiency of our client with a twofold purpose; first, to examine his behavior for indications of functioning that is characteristic of brain damage or other intellectual deterioration; second, to facilitate the planning of counseling, therapy, or rehabilitation. The psychologist is frequently called upon to conduct psychological tests from which inferences regarding brain damage or intellectual deterioration can be made. Although such tests certainly cannot conclusively demonstrate the existence or absence of organic brain damage, they are of definite use in evaluating behavior that may be typical of, or resemble that of a person with, neurological abnormality. David G. Wright (101) has described a patient in whom the physician had no basis for suspecting the presence of brain damage from either psychiatric or neurological symptoms, but it was suggested by findings on the Rorschach and Wechsler-Bellevue tests. He described another case in which suspected organicity was ruled out by test findings. Such diagnostic conclusions are based upon inferences made from controlled observations of the patient's behavior, and not from any direct signs. The psychologist cannot be expected to perform any absolute tests. He can only suggest that the client behaves as an organically handicapped person might behave.

The efficiency of intellectual functioning is of the utmost importance in planning for a person without organic brain damage, as well as in planning for a person in whom such damage exists. It is significant whether the treatment is the re-education of an aphasic patient, vocational rehabilitation, occupational therapy, or personality therapy. In all cases the limitations and the efficiency of functioning must be recognized. The ability of the client to think abstractly or concretely, to conceptualize and to organize or synthesize his thinking must be taken into consideration.

We must ascertain the amount of re-education which will be necessary to enable the client to care for himself in both personal and economic spheres. Our goals of re-education must be tempered by our predictions of how much retraining will be possible. What about vocational guidance and training? Will it be necessary for the client to change his vocation? If so, we must consider what will be practical and feasible. The question of the advisability of occupational or physical therapy can be partially answered by the psychologist. How much has the client declined? How much visual-motor disturbance is involved? Is his attention span short, or does he perseverate and show a difficulty in shifting attention? Is his memory affected; and, if so, how and to what degree? Is his organizing and synthesizing ability something to be adjusted for? What about general problem-solving abilities and approaches? Does he use a whole approach or does he have difficulty relating discrete events and stimuli into an organized pattern? Does the client have reasonable self-confidence, or has he lost such confidence. How strongly is he motivated? How severe are his emotional reactions to frustration? Is he discouraged or confused when pressure for speed of performance is applied? Are his perceptual skills intact, or does he show some confusion in the formation of percepts, particularly in differentiating figure-ground relationships? Factors related to language and symbolic activity are certainly essential to the planning of various kinds of programs. These are just a few of the questions to be answered and factors to be considered in the evaluation of the efficiency of intellectual functioning. We have already seen how some of these items were involved in the planning of counseling for our business-machine operator and our young stock showman. In the previous chapter, the case of the girl called Lois illustrated the use of historical and test data in arriving at the conclusion that she should be regarded as a minimally brain-damaged child.

Deficiencies in the efficiency of intellectual functions are ordinarily associated with organicity, but variations in these functions occur in all persons. Consequently, although our point of departure here will be that of the organically brain-damaged person, the reader must constantly have in mind that the results of tests indicating the efficiency of intellectual functioning are important for planning of counseling and therapy for any person.

EVALUATION OF DEFICIT FROM INTELLIGENCE TESTS

One of the early cues to the presence of brain damage in an adult comes from evidences of deficit as suggested by the intelligence test results. There are many definitions of deterioration, and deterioration as evidenced by decline in intellectual functioning may be due to any of several factors; one of these factors is brain damage. Deterioration implies that the patient has undergone some decline in intellectual efficiency from an earlier level of performance. Deterioration is considered to be quite characteristic of aged patients—as a matter of fact, Wechsler (94) expects some deterioration on his test after the age of 30. Deterioration is also supposedly characteristic of patients with convulsive states and persons exhibiting schizophrenic behavior. The evaluation of deficit is a topic that pertains to the older child or adult and to the person who has suffered some psychological or physiological trauma after he has had some opportunity for learning. The topic is meaningless when applied to the brain-damaged child, especially to the birth-injured child.

If we could have repeated tests on an individual over a period of years, it would be rather easy to demonstrate deterioration. However results of repeated intelligence examinations over a period of time are seldom available. Rapaport and Webb (80) and Aaron H. Canter (17, 18) report experiments in which pre- and post-measures were used, but such data are rare. Consequently, it is usually necessary to arrive at some estimation of deterioration from observation at a given age level. Arriving at such an estimate involves several distinct tasks: (a) the measurement of the individual's actual or present functioning ability; (b) the evaluation of his previous functioning level; (c) the expression of the difference between the two in meaningful terms. Wechsler (94) has developed a differential test-score method of solving the above problems. He makes use of the fact that some abilities decline relatively little during adult life and others decline to a considerable extent. The ratio between these abilities is assumed to be a relative degree of deterioration. On the Wechsler-Bellevue, scores on certain test items have been found to decline rapidly and others more slowly. It may be assumed that this is also true on the WAIS. These tests have been designated "hold" and "don't hold" tests, and have been separated into two groups roughly matched as to verbal or performance ability.

Hold	*Don't Hold*
Information	Digit Span
Comprehension	Arithmetic
Object Assembly	Digit Symbol
Picture Completion	Block Design
Vocabulary	Similarities
	(Picture Arrangement)

The normal expected deterioration with age has been determined empirically, and it is therefore possible to define deterioration in the pathological sense. An individual may be said to show signs of possible deterioration if he shows a decrement greater than 20 per cent of that allowed for by the normal decline with age. On the basis of a review of the literature, C. V. Jackson (57) has concluded that deterioration indices based on weighted scores are invalid, and that Vocabulary and Information scores provide the best base line for scatter analysis. He describes a technique in which the testee's scores are compared with the mean scores for his age. A difference of more than one sigma score between "hold" subtests and any "don't hold" subtest is considered to indicate impairment on that subtest. John R. Schlosser and Robert E. Kantor (88) have questioned the statistical significance of the deterioration index in differentiating schizophrenics from neurotics. No statistically significant differences were found between the deterioration scores of psychoneurotics and those schizophrenics among whom deterioration might be expected (simple, catatonic, and hebephrenic types); nor were there significant differences between the scores of paranoid schizophrenics, where deterioration might be least expected, and the residual schizophrenic group. This emphasizes the limitations of scatter analyses, as discussed in the previous chapter, for making group differentiations. In the case of deterioration index we also find a considerable amount of conflicting evidence in studies by several investigators (1, 2, 3, 4, 26, 34, 56, 64, 84, 85).

Although research on the Wechsler deterioration index is about equally divided between positive and negative evidence, somewhat more encouraging results have been found with other indices that combine subtests of the Wechsler with other measures. One of these is the Hewson index. Louise R. Hewson (52) developed a series of ratios based on different combinations of the Wechsler-Bellevue subtest scores and a special method of administering and scoring the Woodworth Wells Substitution Test. Brigette Gutman (35) compared the Hewson ratios, Wechsler's signs of organic brain damage, and Walter R. Reynell's (84) index on the test records of 30 carefully diagnosed brain-injured patients and found the Hewson ratios to be the best. Even so, the method yielded

17 per cent false positives and 40 per cent false negatives. John I. Wheeler and Walter L. Wilkens (98) attempted to validate the Hewson ratios, and although some trends were found, they concluded (p. 165): "The Hewson ratio method of differential diagnosis, while one of the most sophisticated methods yet devised, is not valid enough for clinical diagnosis of neuroses, functional psychoses, or normalcy."

The general conclusion would seem to be that the Wechsler is a satisfactory instrument if used as a vehicle for observing the individual's behavior, but it is certainly not sufficiently refined so that "short cuts" in the form of quantitative indices will give valid results without other kinds of data. For individual diagnosis the clinician will need to look carefully for clues within the test performance. The clinician should be alert to those qualitative symptoms of brain damage which may be observed from performance on the Wechsler-Bellevue. In general, brain-damaged patients exhibit the following symptoms: (a) visual-motor disturbances; (b) loss of shift; (c) memory defects; (d) organizing and synthesizing disabilities. These are particularly indicated on tests such as digit symbol, block design, arithmetic, object assembly, digits backward. Harry S. Beck and Robert L. Lam (5) reported fair results with the WISC in the prediction of organicity in children but did not find any characteristic pattern of responses for organics as a group.

To the extent that problem solving is involved in the therapeutic process, the predicted mode of attack in problem solving is quite relevant to the planning of psychological counseling. Frandsen (25) has listed modes of attack in problem solving and has suggested the types of information available from the Wechsler-Bellevue which might enable the clinician to predict the mode of attack to be expected with a particular client. He has also offered the following guide for evaluating modes:

1. A direct and systematic problem-solving approach. Ideally, this should include: acceptance of an interest in attacking the problem; analytical observation (analysis) of the situation—observing the data, both perceptually and symbolically, in varied relationships and under different mental sets (shifting); tentatively trying out (evaluating) the suggested hypotheses (syntheses which occur as controlled association); testing by application to the problem a probable solution; checking or critically evaluating solutions; generalizing. Much of this pattern must, of course, be only inferred; but responses to such subtests as Block Designs, Picture Arrangement, Object Assembly, Similarities, Arithmetic, and Comprehension suggest variations in the quality of this general process.

2. An integrated and unified (rather than piece-meal) approach, involving anticipation and planning ahead. Exam-

ples of revealing items are Block Designs, Picture Arrangement, and Object Assembly.

3. Careful, thorough *persistence* balanced with *variability* of attack; keeping the mind open to and seeking for different leads and avoiding both single-tracked persistence and perfunctoriness. Such items as Object Assembly, Picture Arrangement, and Block Designs may be especially indicative of success or failure on this aspect of problem-solving.

4. Application to the problem of an adequate and functionally organized background of experience—information (facts and principles) and basic skills (language, reading, arithmetic, etc.). Information, vocabulary and arithmetic are indicative of strength or weakness of this factor.

5. A set to learn, to be guided in improvement from experience in problem situations. The progressively better adjustment to the testing situation as a whole and improvement on any succession of items of increasing difficulty would indicate normal or superior "work methods" in this category; and plateaus or regressions would indicate distinct limitations in the trait and, consequently, need for guidance toward improvement. In the Digit Symbol test especially accelerated rate would indicate efficient use of learning.

6. Confident, self-reliant, adequately independent attack in the face of difficulty, willingness to try promising leads. "Refusals," persistence, especially on Digits Reversed, despite only partial success rather than giving up completely, trying again after initial failure observable on several items, degree of dependence on examiner for leads and approval, and spontaneous comments and questions about performance are all indicative of the quality of this factor.

7. Attempting to fully understand problem and to base attack on such understanding, so that guessing, random and impulsive "hunches," free associations, perseverations, and egocentric confabulations of the problem are not necessary and so that wrong mental sets or "directions" do not lead to faulty solutions. Arithmetic, Similarities, Comprehension, and Picture Arrangement offer possibilities.

8. Sufficient motivation and freedom from anxiety and other distractions so that active attention and concentration to stimulus patterns and directions are maintained throughout the successive stages of problem-solving. Digits, Arithmetic, Picture Arrangement, and Digit Symbol are pertinent here.

9. Satisfaction from using efficient problem-solving methods rather than over-concern with success and failure aspects

of problems. Information on this factor is revealed best in spontaneous comments on interest or distaste for the problems following obvious successes or failures, in questions indicating concern about outcomes, and in observations of/or comments on work methods.

Special hindrances to effective problem solving are indicated by:

10. Emotional responses to frustration (apparent problem solving difficulties): (a) negativism, sulking, anger, aggression, destructiveness; (b) "refusals," withdrawing, overdependence, insecurity, anxiety, crying, "nervous" laughing, excitement, panic.

11. Reacting to anticipated failure (apparent problem difficulties) with defense mechanisms: rationalization, overcompensation (pseudo-profundity) substitute activities (turning attention away from directions to something else, talking about, rather than trying to solve problem, etc.), identification, projection, regression to more immature levels of response, repression, sympathism, phantasy, and various combinations of these mechanisms also contra-indicate effective problem solving.

12. Other common deviations or "dodges" from a direct problem solving approach: (a) perseveration and failure to "shift," (b) free associative responses, (c) egocentric confabulations, (d) random guessing rather than to say "I don't know," or to reason, (e) uncriticalness, (f) special disabilities in abstracting, analyzing and synthesizing.[1]

It is of interest to return briefly to a discussion of certain results obtained from tests administered to the business-machine statistician mentioned earlier. This man was given two WAIS tests, one administered about a month after his accident and the other about five months later. His performance on these tests and the comparisons between them added substantially to the clinician's understanding of his assets and liabilities for rehabilitation. On both the first and second tests his Information and Vocabulary subtest scores were high. These tests apparently reflect old learning, and since he was functioning at a high level prior to his injury, his performances on these subtests were expected to be high. On several other subtests he showed definite improvement between the first and second test administrations. In all instances his scores on these subtests were lower than on Information and Vocabulary subtests, and, except for one or two instances on the second test, they were below average. His score on the Comprehension subtest increased markedly, as did his score on

[1] By permission from unpublished material provided by Arden N. Frandsen.

the Arithmetic subtest. Definite gain was apparent on the Picture Arrangement subtest and the Object Assembly subtest. Some slight improvement appeared on the Digit Symbol subtest. It was concluded that after five months he presented a more direct and systematic problem-solving approach, a more integrated approach to problems, more ability to plan ahead, more persistence, more confidence, and that he had become better able to try to understand problems rather than to approach them by trial and error. In general, on the second test he showed less anxiety, less confusion, and was better oriented. There were some subtest areas in which he demonstrated very little change in his performance. His Digit Span subtest scores were about the same on both tests. This suggested that his memory for immediate material did not improve measurably. The Similarities subtest score, which is a measure of abstraction ability, did not improve on the second test. The Picture Completion subtest involves a relatively concrete task, and yet it does involve an element of concept formation and abstraction; this subtest score remained about the same on the second administration as on the first. His performance on the Block Design subtest remained about the same for the two tests. To the extent that performance on this test reflects visual-motor disturbance and some concept formation, it must be concluded that his abilities in these areas remained about the same.

In general, this man was considered a good prospect for rehabilitation. We have already described the plans for his retraining and some of the results of these plans. The gains made with the passage of time were encouraging, as were his performances on the Information and Vocabulary tests. As will be recalled, the most negative indication for his rehabilitation was the loss of abstract abilities which made continuance in his former occupation quite difficult.

In the example of our statistician we see that with the exception of the Similarities subtest and the Digit Span subtest, his achievements on verbal tasks were relatively high or showed some improvement, whereas on the performance tasks his achievement was somewhat poorer. This tendency will usually be noted in the case of adults who have suffered an injury after they have had an opportunity to learn certain basic facts and to develop a vocabulary. Birth-injured persons, on the other hand, can be expected to exhibit a somewhat different picture. This will be illustrated by another case later in the chapter.

TESTS OF INTELLECTUAL DEFICIT

Several other tests utilize the concept described by Wechsler to diagnose intellectual deficit. The Babcock-Levy (6) scale for measuring intellectual efficiency yields an efficiency index that is the ratio between scores obtained on the Stanford-Binet vocabulary test and on a series of nine tests arranged into three groups. These groups and the subtests are:

(1) Repetition (memory)
    (a) Digit span forward
    (b) Digit span backward (similar to Wechsler, except 10 forward and 10 backward, two series for each level, separate subtests with different scales)
    (c) Sentence repetition (23 sentences of increasing length)

(2) Learning (recent)
    (a) Story recall
        Immediate recall
        Delayed recall
    (b) Symbol Digit Subtest of Army Alpha
    (c) Paired Associates

(3) Motor group (speed)
    (a) Symbol digit
    (b) Timed writing of a sentence
    (c) Timed tracing of a maze

Older persons and those with toxic disorders or brain damage, as contrasted with schizophrenic or control subjects, tend to score higher on vocabulary than on efficiency tests. Although not all psychologists agree that the authors of the test are measuring the functions they believe they are measuring, and regardless of the precise functions measured, the Babcock-Levy tests have demonstrated their usefulness for clinical purposes, especially when the numerical index is supplemented by an analysis of specific impairment and qualitative observations.

The Shipley-Hartford Institute of Living (89) scale measures deterioration in terms of a discrepancy between scores on vocabulary tests and scores on tests requiring the patient to reason abstractly. Vocabulary and abstraction scores are derived, and the conceptual quotient is regarded as an index of intellectual deficit. As would be expected from the WAIS results, the brain-injured statistician gave a conceptual quotient indicative of drastic deficit. Ann Magaret and Mary M. Simpson (73) found that neither the Shipley-Hartford nor the Wechsler deterioration index correlated significantly with psychiatric ratings or with each other. Other evidence concerning the scale, which gave some suggestion of its validity both as a diagnostic instrument and as a scale of mental ability, has been presented by M. Erik Wright (104) and by Robert J. Lewinski (65). The Shipley-Hartford test is poorly standardized and not widely used by psychologists; it is offered here as an example of a simple screening scale.

Another more widely used test of brain damage is the Hunt-Minnesota devised by Howard F. Hunt (53, 54, 55). The test battery consists of the 1937 Stanford Vocabulary Test, which is relatively insensitive to brain damage, nine interpolated tests, and six tests sensitive to brain deterioration. If carefully interpreted, it is a useful test, and, in general, the experimental data confirms its usefulness. Although one study by Harriet M. Juckem and Jane A. Wold (59) with normal subjects found 60 per cent who exceeded Hunt's critical score, this group was made up of college students whose vocabulary scores were high. This shows that the tester must take into consideration the life history, intelligence, and clinical status of his client. A recent study by Don L. Winfield (100) points up the principle that in brain damage it is new learning that suffers primarily. He found that a battery of tests, including the Progressive Matrices Test, the Wechsler-Bellevue Digit Symbol, Associate Learning on the Wechsler Learning Scale, and the SRA Primary Abilities Test would discriminate between epileptics with known brain damage and those with no demonstrable damage.

Considerable speculation and research has been devoted to the problem of localization of the kind of injury which produces intellectual defects. Ward C. Halstead (36) tends to believe that the frontal lobe is of major importance. Donald O. Hebb (42, 43) has criticized the control groups used by Halstead and has discussed the necessity of securing adequate control group data, not only from normal groups, but from groups with lesions in other areas. For example, if one wished to show that frontal-lobe damage is more important than damage elsewhere in the brain, he would use two groups, a frontal group and a parietal-temporal-occipital group. Hebb believes that only two studies, Gösta Rylander (87), and Theodore H. Weisenberg and Katherine E. McBride (95), have utilized adequate control groups. The studies appear to stress the importance of the frontal lobes, but Hebb (43) emphasizes that we have no proof that any single higher function depends on this part of the brain alone. All in all, then, the question of localization of injury resulting in deterioration of higher functions is still unanswered.

EVALUATION OF THE THINKING PROCESS IN BRAIN INJURY

Kurt Goldstein (29) has shown that brain injury gives rise to certain symptoms that are more or less independent of the site of injury. One of the effects of injury is to raise the threshold of excitation. This causes the patient to be adversely affected by speed. He can succeed only if he has plenty of time. The second effect of injury is a tendency toward perseveration. Having once achieved a solution, the patient keeps trying to repeat this solution on new tasks (loss of shift). A third characteristic is disturbance of attention. The patient is either easily distracted or his attention is fixated on some one stimulus.

Goldstein attaches a great deal of importance to a fourth symptom. This is described as a blurring of the boundaries between figure and ground. He describes a test developed by Heinz Werner and Alfred A. Strauss devised especially for brain-injured children. This test consists of a marble board having 100 holes in ten rows. Marbles are placed in the holes to make a figure. The child is given an empty board and marbles and asked to copy the design. Brain-injured children, in contrast to normal children or even mentally retarded children without brain damage, are unable to distinguish figure from ground, and place their marbles in a random disarranged pattern. Even if they copy the design, they do not realize that there was a design in the stimulus.

Another symptom described by Goldstein is loss in the ability to think or behave abstractly. This particular symptom appears to be one of the more characteristic of the symptoms of generalized brain damage. In many instances the patient will even go to great lengths to circumvent the abstract and reduce the problem to concrete terms. Fernald (23) describes a 38-year-old woman who could not tell how much two apples would cost if three cost nine cents. She was given nine pennies and three apples. She carefully arranged the apples in a row, then shifted pennies around until she had an equal number near each apple. She counted the pennies near two of the apples and announced that the answer was six. Another patient (a 12-year-old boy) was asked, "If there are three brothers, and their father gives them each two cents, how much do they have altogether?" He caught sight of a box of pennies and another filled with beans. His face lighted up. He put the big red bean out for the father, and three white beans for the brothers. Then he gave each white bean two cents. Finally he counted and arrived at the answer. Robert W. White (99) tells of a patient who shows great skill in throwing balls into boxes located at different distances from him, but is unable to say which box is farthest away, or how he manages to aim differently. Another patient can count numbers on his fingers or in other roundabout ways and come up with results that look like good arithmetic, but he cannot state whether seven is more than four.

Shortcomings in the capacity for abstraction become apparent in tests that involve sorting. Strauss and Werner (reported by Goldstein and Martin Scheerer, 29) have used the technique of confronting children with fifty or more small objects, instructing them to put those things together "which go together, which fit together." The objects can be classified by function (key with padlock), or they can be grouped on the basis of form or color. Brain-injured children give more farfetched and peculiar solutions. Strauss and Werner have also devised a picture-object test. Two pictures are put up, one showing a house on fire, the other a boy struggling in water. The patient is then asked to put in front of each picture the toy objects that go with the picture. A brain-injured boy of twelve put some appropriate objects, such as a fire engine, in front of the house on fire, but also added some peculiar items: a wrench and pliers were supplied to repair the car, in case it was burned; a "slow" sign was put up to keep people from running into the fire; a black train was introduced to match the black suits of people watching the fire; a fork was added because one of the witnesses thought he saw food in the burning building; an envelop was put in place so that the firemen could read the address and find their way to the fire.

The Gelb-Goldstein-Weigl-Scheerer Object Sorting Test has been used rather widely as a measure of abstraction ability or concept formation. It is described with slight modifications of content and administration by Rapaport (79). A large group of relatively common items are presented to the patient. Goldstein and Scheerer (29) recommend three phases of administration: (a) the subject groups objects with articles that he himself has selected, and then with one or more that are selected by the examiner; (b) the subject groups all of the objects he thinks belong together; (c) the subject is asked to arrange all articles in still another way. If he does not do this, he is presented with new groupings and asked by the examiner why the articles are grouped as they are, and whether he can accept the new groupings.

Rapaport suggests two parts to the test. Part I consists of seven items. In each item the subject is given an object and asked to find what belongs with it. The first item is selected by the patient, others by the examiner. Part II has twelve items. In each item the patient is asked to explain why certain groups are placed together. Groupings and verbalizations are recorded completely. The test is interpreted in terms of (a) adequacy of sorting (relevancy, commonness, intelligibility); (b) inadequacy of sorting; (c) adequacy of verbalization; (d) inadequacy of verbalization; (e) conceptual level of sorting (functional, concrete, abstract-conceptional); (f) concept span (loose, narrow).

A test that has been widely used experimentally, but upon which there are few practical norms, is the Vigotsky (92) or the slightly modified Vigotsky, called the Hanfmann-Kasanin (39, 40, 61, 62). This test consists of 22 blocks in five different colors, six different shapes, two different heights, and two different widths. The problem is to discover how these blocks can be divided into four kinds. The solution is tall-narrow, tall-wide, low-wide, and low-narrow blocks. The blocks have numbers (in the Vigotsky nonsense syllables) on the back. One is turned over to begin with, and after each grouping another is turned over to indicate the error and to furnish a new clue. The test is usually scored on time and number of clues. The Vigotsky Blocks have been used in a number of ways and for a variety of purposes. One of the most interesting and useful applications (74) has been to study the method of thinking displayed by the subject. Knowledge of the way a person thinks in dealing with the complex problem presented by these blocks can be applied to clinical evaluation and the planning of counseling or therapy.

A relatively new test for the diagnosis of organic brain damage is the Grassi Block Substitution Test (33). Five different designs are presented to the subject, and he must construct twenty patterns—for each design four, representing simple concrete performance, complex concrete performance, simple abstract performance, and complex abstract performance. The analyses of the test results are based on a time and accuracy score, behavior and intellectual level. The maximum score is thirty. A score of twenty or more is supposed to be indicative of the absence of intellectual impairment. A recent study (79) utilizing the Grassi Test and comparing it with the Wechsler-Bellevue in the diagnosis of organic brain damage resulted in the Grassi failing to classify 25 per cent of a group of known organics correctly. The Wechsler-Bellevue mistakenly classified 50 per cent of the known organics as having no deterioration. The Grassi classified no normals as having severe deterioration, while the Wechsler-Bellevue indicated that 10 per cent had definite deterioration. The Grassi indicated 30 per cent of the normals as having moderate deterioration. In spite of this lack of perfection in the application of definite scores for classification purposes, the qualitative performance of the organic subjects was quite indicative of interference with their performance. An individual with suspected organic pathology was recently examined who achieved a score of twenty-two on the Grassi test. In spite of this score, which would be indicative of only slight impairment, the subject's manner of dealing with situations that he perceived as being too difficult for him was of definite interest. Rather than performing the tasks conceptually as required, he resorted to the use of mechanical aids. For example, he could not substitute color in the complex abstract designs without writing down which color was interchanged with which other color. This appeared to be a compensatory device for a perceived inability. This same subject displayed a great amount of effort on all tests. Such observations as these frequently give the clinician more information than actual scores on the tests. There is no substitute for the ingenuity and experience of the clinician. Tests are, at best, tools that the clinician can use as the basis for making clinical judgments.

Many other similar concept-formation tests have been developed. The Goldstein-Scheerer Cube Test (29) utilizes the Koh's blocks. The designs are somewhat more complicated than those presented in the Wechsler. This test taps visual-motor skills and the ability to recognize figure-ground relationships. The Gelb-Goldstein Color Sorting Test (29) consists of a variety of woolen skeins that are to be sorted according to color concepts. The Weigl-Goldstein-Scheerer Color Form Sorting Test (29) is made up of twelve figures consisting of four triangles, four squares, and four circles. In each set of four figures there is one that is red, one green, one yellow, and one blue. The reverse sides of all blocks are white. The subject is asked to group them. After one grouping is accomplished (for example, by color) he is asked to group another way. If the first grouping was by color and the patient cannot find another way, the blocks can be turned over so that color is not a factor. This test measures ability to shift as well as concept formulation and visual-motor skill. The Goldstein-Scheerer Stick Test (29) is designed to test whether the subject is able to copy figures composed of sticks and reproduce them from memory. Still other tests, such a word-sorting test by Harold A. Rashkis, Jane Cushman, and Carney Landis (77) and a geometric form-sorting test by Robert W. Zaslow (105) have been constructed.

The concept of disturbance in visual-motor function has been capitalized on in several other tests. One of them is the Bender Gestalt or Visual-Motor Gestalt Test standardized by Lauretta Bender (9). She has taken a group of figures known as the Wertheimer figures and asks the patient to copy them. Deteriorated patients tend to reproduce the same kind of figures which have been found to be characteristic of children prior to the maturation of psycho-motor function.

A test long used by psychiatrists is the Serial Sevens Test. A study by Max Hayman (41) suggests that this test correlates well with the Shipley-Hartford and the Babcock. Hayman feels that the test is a sensitive indicator of deterioration. Leon A. Pennington (77) has correlated results on this test with Wechsler results and finds little correlation. He suggests, however, that with persons of average or above-average intelligence, and of seventh- or eight-grade level, the data indicate some value for the Serial Sevens Test in detecting defect.

Although in the Rorschach the general approach to testing is quite different, similar behavioral characteristics are used to formulate a diagnosis of brain damage on the basis of this test. Zygmunt A. Piotrowski (78) has listed the following signs of organicity:

1. Total of R's (responses) less than 15.
2. Average time per response of more than one minute.
3. Not more than one movement response.
4. At least one color-naming response.
5. F+ (good form) percentage of less than 70 per cent.
6. Less than 25 per cent popular responses.
7. Repetition of same response for several blots.
8. Giving of response in spite of the fact that patient realizes it is inadequate.

   9. Distrust in patient as to his own ability.

   10. Presence of automatic phrases.

Five of these ten signs should be present for the diagnosis of organic involvement. The most important signs are color naming, perplexity, impotence, and automatic phrases. Since we have not discussed the Rorschach in its broader applications, the meaning of some of these signs may not be clear until we have discussed it in greater detail. However, even without a complete knowledge of this test, the reader can see some common elements between these signs and Wechsler's signs (visual-motor disturbances, loss of ability to shift or perseveration, memory defects, organization and synthesizing disabilities), or the Goldstein signs (raise in threshold of excitation or adversity to speed, perseveration, disturbance of attention, blurring of figure and ground, loss of abstractionability).

   Turning again to the statistician subject, we are able to make some rough comparisons between a pre-injury Rorschach test and a post-injury test that was given at the time of the second WAIS (about six months after his accident). Unfortunately, the pre-injury test was given by a student who used the client as a subject for practice testing, and the only record we have of the test is a summary sheet of the test responses as they were scored by the student. This scoring may have been crude, and we do not have the actual responses so that qualitative comparisons can be made. However, the total number of responses on the first test was seventy-six. On the second test the total was nineteen. This total is higher than fifteen, which was Piotrowski's cutting score, but the reduction in the number is quite dramatic. The average time per response was less than one minute on the post-injury test, but, even so, it was three times as long as on the pre-injury test. Likewise, the client gave ten movement responses on the pre-test and only three on the post-test. On the post-test he gave three color-naming responses and none on the pre-test. The F+ percentage was 60 on the post-test and 85 on the pre-test. He gave about the same percentage of popular responses on both tests: on the first test he gave eight and on the second he gave only two.

   On the second test he perseverated by giving several responses to two different cards, and he gave the response "butterfly" to three cards. We have no record of perseveration on the first test. On the second test he found fault with his responses on most cards and repeatedly said, "I just don't think I can give you what you want." Thus, we have post-test results that are quite consistent with what is expected from a brain-damaged subject, and the post-test is even more significant when compared with the pre-test.

   Halstead (36) is currently experimenting with a large number of tests and indicators that may give us more aid in the problem of evaluation of organicity. At the present time, however, we have many different tests, but too little information concerning the relationship between them.

It would appear likely that one reason why none of our various tests appear to have high validity for the identification of brain damage is to be found in the complexity and variability of brain damage. The brain is a complex physiological structure, and it is difficult to see how we can expect all brain-damaged subjects to respond in the same or even similar ways. The location of the injury and the extent of the injury are tremendously complicating variables, but more important still is the state of the organism when injury or damage occurred. The most variable factor is the age of the person when injured. The person injured at birth or soon after birth will exhibit more general handicap in performance than will the person injured at an older age. The younger person has had little opportunity to learn, and although the location and extent of the injury may affect learning in a selective way, the end result without special education will tend to be general retardation. When the injury occurs later in life, more specific functions will appear to be disturbed since the effects of the injury will be superimposed on a background of already learned behaviors. As a consequence of these considerations, the diagnosis as well as the evaluation of the effects of brain damage, especially that suffered at birth and early in life must depend upon many qualitative observations of behavior in a variety of test situations.

Brain-damaged children present a serious problem of evaluation and education. Purdue University offers a psychological clinic service to school systems in Indiana. Children are referred who present special educational problems, and we endeavor to evaluate these children and offer specific and concrete recommendations for their training and education. More will be said about this service later, but we mention it now to point out that at least a fourth of the children seen by us exhibit behavior that is suggestive of some early-life brain damage. This should not be surprising when we realize how difficult it is to understand the behavior of these children. No two of them show the effects of their presumed injuries in the same ways. Wechsler was quoted in the preceding chapter as suggesting that on the Wechsler-Bellevue, brain-damaged persons ordinarily have a higher verbal I.Q. than a performance I.Q. In contrast to this, the last ten children whom we have seen with a definite history of birth injury or early-lift trauma to the brain, all had higher Performance I.Q.'s than Verbal I.Q.'s on the WISC. In all of these cases, there was no extensive motor involvement and the specific performances involved were those verbal, reasoning, and abstract functions that were more characteristic of the verbal items. This trend should not be accepted as established because it is quite likely that in the next several children we see with a history of birth injury the manipulative and visual-motor skills may be interfered with. Evaluation of the effects of organic brain injury is and probably will continue to be a task that requires the total study of the unique behavior of each individual. Data from the various history areas must be considered since the age of injury, the developmental picture, and the evidences of areas of success and failure in school subjects may all be of interest. The indications of potential capacity as evidenced by the educational and intellectual status of the family must also be considered. It seems likely that the effects of injury on a child of low endowment would be different from the effects of a similar injury on a child of high endowment. This area of evaluation is one in which extensive research and investigation remains to be done.

The minimumly brain-damaged child also presents a serious educational problem for which our schools must frequently make adjustments if such children are to be adequately prepared to find a place in society. The importance of a careful assessment of the efficiency of intellectual functioning can be seen from a description of the clinic's evaluation of, and recommendations for, a sixteen-year-old (fifteen years ten months) girl whom we will call Jean. Jean was referred by her principal because of poor achievement in the first year of high school. She was the youngest of three children. She had a brother who was twenty-three; he was married and had a good job in a steel mill. He had graduated from high school and was described as having been an average student. He had been in the Army and his present position was that of a semiskilled worker. Another brother was twenty; he had also graduated from high school with average marks, and worked in a steel mill. The mother was forty-nine, a high school graduate, and appeared to be of average intelligence. The father was fifty-two; he had left school after completing the eighth grade to go to work. He had worked for the Farm Bureau until two years before Jean was seen, when he suffered a "stroke." He did not appear to be very intelligent, but it was difficult to evaluate in the interview the extent of deterioration that he had suffered as a result of his illness. Observations led to the conclusion that the general level of intellectual ability of the family was approximately average.

The mother had been in good health during the nine months' pregnancy with Jean. The child was born at home with a doctor in attendance. The doctor remarked during the delivery that the umbilical cord was wrapped around the baby's neck. There was some difficulty in initiating breathing, but this was not regarded as unusual at the time. Jean weighed eight pounds at birth and gained normally after birth. She was reported to have walked and to have developed physically at about the same rate as her brothers, although she seemed to have been slow in talking. She had had mumps, measles, and chicken pox, but none had been severe illnesses. At two years of age, she had had a bad cold and "near-pneumonia," but, again, her illness had not been severe. She was left-handed, as was her oldest brother. For some unexplained reason, she did not start school until she was seven years of age. The mother was quite indefinite as to the reason for the year's delay. Jean had never been a good student, but was passed each year except when she was in the third grade, which she repeated. At that time she had begun to have convulsions and she had been kept out of school for several months. She has been on medication since that time and has had no convulsions for about four years prior to the time she was seen. She began to menstruate at thirteen but her menstrual periods had been irregular until shortly before the testing.

Jean was an attractive girl, who was quite well developed physically. She said she liked school but that some subjects, such as biology and mathematics, were rather hard for her. She reported that she had some difficulty in reading. She did not seem to have much insight into how poorly she had been doing in her school work. In the testing situation she worked hard and her attention was good. She was given a reading test on which she performed at about the fifth-grade level, but her vocabulary was poor. She was given the WISC and several other tests. On the WISC she achieved a Verbal Scale I.Q. of 82, a Performance Scale I.Q. of 97, and a Full Scale I.Q. of 88. Her scaled scores on the various subtests were as follows:

Information	6	Digit Span	7
Comprehension	11	Picture Completion	14
Arithmetic	6	Picture Arrangement	8
Similarities	7	Block Design	8
Vocabulary	6	Object Assembly	10
		Coding	8

Throughout the testing we were impressed by her difficulty with verbal expression and the extent to which she was bound to the concrete. On the Information Test she seemed to know more than she could tell, and, in spite of her low score, and she surprised the examiner by knowing some items. She missed others that might have been expected to be easy, and as a result her score was low. Among the verbal items she did best on the Comprehension subtest items. She knew all of the practical "what-to-do" questions and got some credit on most of the items. She might have done better if she could have expressed herself more adequately. In arithmetic her difficulty with any abstract problems, especially those involving division, was striking. She did poorly on Similarities and on the Vocabulary Test. Her difficulty in abstraction showed up in both of these areas. She had particular difficulty in repeating digits in reverse on the Digit Span subtest. The Picture Completion items appeared very easy, and her performance on the Object Assembly subtest was average. On the other performance items she was below average for her age level. Her greatest difficulty on the Block Design subtest was a tendency to reverse figure and ground. Several times she assembled the patterns correctly, except for reversing the red and the white portions of the designs. She appeared to learn well, however, and actually did better on the last design than she had done on the earlier ones.

Jean was administered several other tests, including a sorting test. She was able to sort objects according to use (eating utensils together, tools together, etc.) but could not sort them in a different way. In other words, she could not shift, and tended to perseverate. On a task involving the sorting of different colored yarns, she required many different categories. She could not comprehend that the yarns could be sorted into a few basic colors. On the Color-Form Sorting Test she grouped the figures according to color, but could not group them in any other way. Her drawings on the Bender Gestalt were more like those of a nine- or ten-year-old than those of a fifteen-year-old. We attempted to give her the Rorschach Test but she rejected half of the cards, saying, "It's red!" or "It's pink!" On several of the cards, she simply laughed and said, "Somebody spilled something."

To plan for this youngster, we had to keep in mind that although she was in the ninth grade, she was functioning much below that level. She was certain to have academic difficulties with school subjects in the ninth grade. At her age and level of maturity we could not place her back at the grade level at which she could succeed. It was regrettable that her difficulties had not been recognized at an earlier age so that special remedial procedures could have been utilized. She had been promoted regularly, and by the time she reached the ninth year she was so far behind that remedial procedures would not be very effective. As yet, she had not developed negative reactions to her inability to compete. Her ability would probably have been, at best, little more than average, even if she had developed normally. She liked to sew, she wanted to be a nurse, and enjoyed most concrete activities. We suggested that she be continued in school for another year or so, or as long as she was able to make a satisfactory social adjustment. We urged that her curriculum be made as practical as possible and that both the family and the school be alert to possibilities for vocational training. It was felt that the regular curriculum of nursing education would be difficult for her and that some substitute would have to be found. The compromise was made (after much discussion and deliberation) for her to take training as a nurse's aid. This training followed a semester of a home nursing course in high school. She did well in this course and her interests appeared to be strong, so she left high school and took a short course in practical nursing. Subsequently she secured a position and is well liked by her supervisor. Since it appears likely that she will marry, her mother is continuing to prepare her for housekeeping work. Jean seems very happy, she is certainly leading a useful life, and apparently has avoided any serious reactions to her special handicap. The diagnosis might be "minimal brain damage," but such a label was much less important than the planning that resulted from the psychological evaluation.

RELATIONSHIP BETWEEN INTELLECTUAL PROCESSES AND PERSONALITY

To this point we have been discussing the organically injured individual. It must be recognized that emotional disturbances and personality disorders may also interfere with the thinking process, particularly with the ability to form abstract concepts. The purpose of the tests we have been discussing is not only to discover or identify organicity but to help the psychologist discover the extent to which a person's maladjustment (psychological or physiological) has impaired his conscious thinking, as revealed in his efforts to solve problems requiring the formation of concepts. Few adequate attempts to standardize tests have been made and scoring is largely qualitative. It seems apparent that there are huge individual differences in the ability to deal with concepts that may be related to intelligence, to personality disturbance, or to organic factors. Study of the relationship between the intellectual processes and personality is much needed and appears to be a fruitful area for research.

The ability to form concepts or to think abstractly has been investigated and discussed by a number of authors. One of the problems about which there has been a considerable amount of research is the role of conceptual thinking in schizophrenia. Glenn E. Wright (102, 103) has recently reviewed this literature and traced some of the change in thinking. Some of the ideas are of interest in connection with the present topic. The following are some of the definitions he cites of concept formation:

(a) "The *sine qua non* of concept learning is always response to relationships present in each member of a group of stimulus patterns, the stimulus patterns in question being classified as a group by virtue of the fact that they have certain relationships and perhaps certain characteristics in common." Kenneth L. Smoke (91, p. 277).

(b) Concept formation is seeing what belongs together or seeing "the common essential factor in a variety of things." Suzanne Reichard and Rapaport (83, p. 99).

(c) "Concept formation is the process through which the person manipulates and classifies the essential common features imbedded in a group of complex stimulus situations in order to arrive at a symbol which represents the common elements in the total range of stimuli." Leslie J. Briggs, as reported by W. Edgar Vinacke (93, p. 22).

(d) Goldstein employs the term "abstract or categorical attitude" instead of "concept formation." He suggests that in assuming the abstract attitude "we transcend the immediately given situation, the specific aspect of sense impression; we abstract common from particular properties; we are oriented in our action by a rather conceptual viewpoint, be it a category, a class, or a general meaning under which the particular object before us falls." Goldstein and Scheerer (29, p. 3).

(e) "The abstract attitude is the basis for the following conscious and volitional modes of behavior:

(1) To detach our ego from the outer world or from inner experiences.

(2) To assume a mental set.

(3) To account for acts to oneself; to verbalize the account.

(4) To shift reflectively from one aspect of the situation to another.

(5) To hold in mind simultaneously various aspects.

(6) To grasp the essential of a given whole; to break up a given whole into parts, to isolate and to synthesize them.

(7) To abstract common properties reflectively; to form hierarchic concepts.

(8) To plan ideationally; to assume an attitude toward the 'mere possible' and to think or perform symbolically." Goldstein and Scheerer (29, p. 4).[2]

One of the first persons to investigate conceptual ability in schizophrenics was L. S. Vigotsky, who stated (92, p. 1073), "While the normal mind has no difficulty in using given words metaphorically or figuratively, the same problem presents insurmountable difficulty for the patient with schizophrenia, in spite of the fact that he has retained from childhood the habit of using figures of speech, proverbs, etc." He went so far as to say that "The intellectual disturbance, as well as the disturbance in the fields of perceptions, emotions and other psychological functioning are in direct causal relationship with the disturbances of the functions of formation of concepts."

Eugenia Hanfmann (38) concluded that her study of 60 patients and 90 normal controls demonstrated that schizophrenic patients are at

[2] The passages from "Abstract and Concrete Behavior: An Experimental Study with Special Tests," by Kurt Goldstein and Martin Scheerer, *Psychological Monographs*, 1941, Vol. 53, No. 2 (Whole No. 239), 1–151, are quoted by permission of the American Psychological Association.

a disadvantage in concept formation. Jacob Kasanin and Hanfmann (39) have also found that concept formation is impaired in schizophrenic subjects although they suggest that this is true only in some varieties of schizophrenia; and in a later monograph (40) they changed their thinking somewhat and reported impairment in only one third to one half of the cases. In still another paper, Kasanin (60) presented a fivefold classification of schizophrenia: (a) neurotic type, (b) dissociative with fantasy elaboration, (c) old cases, (d) acute episodic psychoses, and (e) incoherent types. Most impairment of conceptual thinking is found in groups (c) and (e) with possibly some in group (d). Kasanin raises the question of the relationship between conceptual thinking and intelligence.

M. Marjorie Bolles and Goldstein (11) reported a study on schizophrenic patients using a variety of sorting tests and concluded that the difference between patients and normal individuals was that patients were not capable of showing abstract behavior at all. In later reports Goldstein became less positive. In 1943 he reported (27) that in certain schizophrenics there was a significant impairment of the attitude toward the abstract. At this time he suggested that some average individuals also show a preference for a concrete procedure. By 1949 (28) his thinking appeared to have undergone still further change in this same direction.

W. King (63) suggests that the general factor of abstract behavior may depend on other psychological factors. Vinacke (93, p. 27) following this idea, stated: "We do not really know for certain that there is an ability to conceptualize which might be distinguished from other perceptual and intellectual function." Both Smoke (91) and Rapaport (79, 82) describe a close relationship between conceptual skills and intelligence. Various studies reviewed by Glenn E. Wright (102, 103) emphasize the disagreement concerning the relationship between concept formation and schizophrenic processes. This disagreement and the confusion about the relationship led him to design a study to investigate the relationship between intelligence and concept formulation. In comparing a group of schizophrenics and normals matched on the Wechsler-Bellevue, he failed to find any differences on six concept formation tests, both verbal and nonverbal (102). In another study (103) he matched pairs of schizophrenic and normal subjects and also failed to find differences in concept formation when intelligence was controlled.

Elizabeth T. Fey (24) has compared the performance of young schizophrenics and young normals on the Wisconsin Card Sorting Test. She found that the schizophrenic subjects experienced greater difficulty with concept formation than did the normals, and that the discrepancy could not be attributed to differences in age, intelligence, or educational level. In view of the age range, it seems clear that the factors responsible for the deficiency in performance on the card-sorting test are present in the early stages of schizophrenic illness. Fey's analysis demonstrated that the performance of the schizophrenics showed perseveration, difficulty in maintaining set, and difficulty in responding to patterns as a whole. Although all these modes of behavior might, as Fey pointed out, be subsumed under such a concept as "loss of abstract attitude," it is doubtful that they have a single psychological "cause." Our knowledge of schizophrenic behavior would seem to be furthered by attempts to isolate and measure the specific characteristic aspects of behavior, and to study the conditions under which they occur in normal as well as abnormal behavior. Thinking, reasoning, problem-solving deterioration, and regression in schizophrenia have been studied by Norman Cameron (12, 13, 14, 15, 16). He has made some progress in the direction of reducing the observed deficiencies to the component factors, but still leaves several points unanswered.

It is interesting to speculate as to whether some adult schizophrenic patients may not actually have suffered brain damage at birth or at an early age. We cannot help but wonder what may happen to children like Jean, Lois, or our young farmer if their limitations are not recognized, and if they continue through life, never understood by others and frustrated in their attempts to achieve as do normal children. Many such children become discouraged and give up, others become rebellious and antagonistic, some run away, and still others may escape day-to-day problems in other, perhaps schizophrenic, ways. We strongly suspect that a number of them end up in hospitals or penal institutions. In other words, perhaps the lack of conceptual abilities comes first, and may in some instances be the cause, rather than the result, of schizophrenic withdrawal.

The discussion thus far has been concerned with the relationship between concept formation in abstract reasoning and the behavior disorder of schizophrenia. The question of what operates in schizophrenia has not been answered, and it will probably not be answered without the study of this and other aspects of thinking in other clinical groups and in normal persons. Studies have fairly well demonstrated that schizophrenic subjects differ from normal subjects, but we really do not know that they definitely differ from other clinical groups. Although we know schizophrenics differ from normals, there is a considerable degree of overlap (that is, some schizophrenics are able to form concepts), and we do not know the specific ways in which they differ.

Edna Heidbreder (44, 45, 46, 47, 48, 49, 50, 51) has done a series of studies on the attainment of concepts in normal subjects. She is particularly interested in the ease or facility with which concepts are formed and the regularity with which different levels of concepts may be formed. Her studies as well as a study by Priscilla E. Dottman and Harold E. Israel (21) suggest that perceptual factors have a definite relationship to the ease with which concepts are attained. A series of studies with the

Wisconsin Card Sorting Test (10, 24, 30, 31, 32, 72) is also concerned with the study of concept formation in normal as well as clinical groups. (Incidentally, one of these studies (72) suggests that feebleminded children can perform successfully on the Wisconsin Card Sorting Test.) Such studies as those by Heidbreder and at Wisconsin appear to be in the right direction. However, there is still a definite need for more research on the thinking process in subjects other than organics and schizophrenics and in relation to the interaction between emotional, personality, perceptual, and conceptual factors. Such research should be productive both for purposes of diagnostic evaluation and for the understanding of the theoretical basis of both normal and abnormal behavior.

An area of research somewhat related to this general topic is that on the concept of "rigidity." Abraham S. Luchins (66, 67, 68, 69, 70, 71) has noted certain deleterious effects of habituated behavior, when instead of individuals mastering habits, habits master the individuals. He calls this the formation of a mental set or an *Einstellung* mechanization. Luchins adapted a test using problems concerning measurements of water into various-sized jars to establish a set toward a particular solution and then tested the rigidity of this set by various extinction and criterion trials. He studied the ease or difficulty of breaking a set and found that most of his subjects were quite rigid; that is, when a set was established, it was difficult to change it. He found that neuropsychiatric military patients required more extinction trials than did normal subjects. He then hypothesized that rigidity, as measured by the jar test, might be tied up with neurosis. Luchins describes this *Einstellung* effect as the creation of a mechanized state of mind or a blind attitude toward problems in which one does not look at problems for their own merits, but is led by a mechanical application of a used method. Ernst G. Beier (8) found that when normal subjects were introduced into an anxiety situation, more rigidity and disorganization were found than in a control group. Emory L. Cowen and George C. Thompson (19, 20) found a significant correlation between rigidity and judges' ratings, based on Rorschach records, of such personality factors as diminished resourcefulness, inability to perceive complex relationships and to integrate constructively, tendency to "leave the field" when the going gets difficult, and a narrower sphere of functioning. This study suggests that rigidity is a general factor of personality, but that it is closely related to conceptual and abstract thinking. The above studies and others have been reviewed by Joan G. Bache (7). It is of interest to note that our veteran who was so disturbed by voices had little proficiency on abstract tasks; organicity did not appear to be indicated in his case. This was also the situation with the girl with the beautiful twin sister and the intelligent brothers. Emotional excitement or anxiety certainly do not facilitate conceptualization.

Edith Weisskopf-Joelson (96) has reviewed many of the dynamic factors influencing intellectual performance, and she emphasizes the importance of the effect of emotional factors upon thought processes. Her review summarizes many of the factors and relationships that require our continued study and investigation.

A study by Thomas F. Johnson (58) appears to suggest a considerable amount of relationship between concept-formation test results, rigidity measures, and certain personality traits as revealed by a paper and pencil test. Luchins found some relationship between concreteness of thinking and rigidity. Such studies as these will clarify many points, but in the meantime the evaluation of the thinking behavior of individuals would seem to involve study of rigidity of thinking. It is clear that there is a great overlap between intelligence test data, conceptualization test results, and rigidity, but all seem to be various aspects of thinking behavior which should be considered by the clinician. Finally, the relationship between these aspects of cognitive behavior and such behavioral processes as perception must be noted.

THE EVALUATION OF LANGUAGE AND SYMBOLIC ACTIVITY

Another aspect of intellectual behavior is that which is usually referred to as language or symbolic behavior. By the term "language" we mean all forms of symbolic stimuli and responses that are used by people to communicate with one another. Clifford T. Morgan and Eliot Stellar (75, p. 511) describe language as follows:

> Various sorts of signals and gestures fall within the scope of the term. So does arithmetic, algebra and higher mathematics. Any item of behavior may be called linguistic behavior if it is a symbol for some other behavior. And any stimulus may be called linguistic if it stands for some other stimulus. It is the symbolism that makes language a higher order memory function.

Morgan goes on to point out that language has various levels of complexity. These levels include alphabets to learn, words to spell, names to learn, and words to put together in sentences. We learn to understand language and to express ourselves in language. Individuals differ in their ability to use symbols in their language with facility. The clinician must observe and evaluate these differences in symbolic facility. To some extent, individual differences in language behavior are reflected by the differences in verbal and performance scores. These reflections are not always accurate, as many performance tests require the use of symbols, and people differ in the kinds of symbols they can use most effectively. Symbolic facility is also to some extent a function of what we call aptitudes. In general, there are no formal procedures for evaluating variations in symbolic skill among essentially normal individuals; this must be done from inferences drawn from the use of diagnostic tools designed to measure other behavior. However, there do exist several scales to be used in identifying different disorders in language that are designated as aphasia.

Disorders of language or in symbolic formulation and/or expression are called aphasias. A person may have both sensory and motor aphasias, and there are names for the various varieties of aphasic disability. Johannes M. Nielson (76) has discussed a wide variety of these names and presents a complicated classification system. He has described the observations of the patient in terms of type of disorder (aphasia or speechlessness, agnosia or loss of the function of recognition, apraxia or the inability to perform particular muscular movements), anatomical location of the associated injury, modality affected, and function affected. The loss of power to recognize letters by vision alone because of a lesion in the angular gyrus would be described as "agnosia, visual, angular, literal." His classification includes 87 different types. Weisenberg and McBride (95) classify aphasia into four groups: mixed expressive-receptive, predominantly expressive, predominantly receptive, and amnesic. Joseph M. Wepman (97, pp. 41–2) presents the following classification:

1. Expressive aphasia: symptoms predominantly motor productive in nature and consisting of an inability to express ideas through spoken or written language symbols.

2. Receptive aphasia: symptoms predominantly sensory or receptive in nature and consisting of a disturbance in the ability to comprehend language through spoken or written symbols.

3. Expressive-receptive aphasia: approximately an equal disturbance in both areas.

4. Global aphasia: all language forms seriously affected to the degree that it is impossible to use one of the preceding categories.

5. Agnosia: loss of ability to recognize objects or symbols through a particular sensory channel such as vision or hearing.

6. Apraxia: loss of ability to execute simple voluntary acts.[3]

[3] By permission from *Recovery from Aphasia*, by Joseph M. Wepman. Copyright 1951 by The Ronald Press Company.

Halstead and Wepman (37) have devised an aphasia screening test that can be used to identify and describe disabilities. The test consists of a number of tasks which the client is asked to perform and which will reflect difficulty in any of the language functions. These tasks are widely varied and include such items as reading orally, writing in response to spoken or written stimuli, spelling, using numbers in rote and problem situations, following simple commands, tracing forms, recognizing forms, naming colors, and many others. Another test or scale for the evaluation of aphasia has been presented by Jon Eisenson (22).

Aphasic symptoms are ordinarily due to cortical damage. They are to be distinguished from paralyses on the motor side, and from sensory handicaps on the sensory side. They are also to be distinguished from speech or hearing disabilities, which, of course, also interfere with communication. Since we are concerned with intellectual functions, we will not discuss speech problems except to note that the psychologist may be called upon to make a differential diagnosis. Aphasic-like symptoms of a transient nature may accompany emotional excitement or tension. The emotional blocking may be severe and the symptoms may resemble the consistent reactions due to cortical damage. We had been inclined to think that some of the symptoms presented by Jean had a functional, rather than an organic, basis until we discovered her history of convulsive disorders and learned the results of a neurological examination, which disclosed evidence of brain trauma.

In the instance cited above the results of a neurological examination disclosed evidence of organic brain damage which was not suspected from the psychological evaluation. Ordinarily this is not the case, since the psychologist is frequently able to infer brain damage which is not suspected from the neurological examination. In general, neurological tests are rather gross and may not reveal any evidence of organicity even when the psychological evaluation is suggestive that brain injury may have occurred. On the basis of historical factors, psychological test results, and behavioral observations, we frequently may infer that the client is handicapped by what might be very minimal damage which would not be revealed by neurological examinations. Even when the inferred damage is not positively confirmed, we must frequently recommend teaching procedures designed to compensate for possible handicap. The complete diagnostic appraisal should include both psychological and neurological examinations.

SUMMARY

In this chapter we have discussed some of the problems related to the efficiency of intellectual functioning. The effectiveness with which an individual utilizes his capacity is of prime importance in planning of treatment and in making recommendations for the education and rehabilitation of patients. The representative material has been presented and other studies have been referred to. This material suggests that our present knowledge concerning the evaluation of intellectual efficiency, deficit, and symbolic formulation leaves much to be desired; much theoretical and methodological research must still be done before completely adequate evaluations of functioning can be made. Research in this area must be concerned with the relationships between various aspects of personality and functioning dependent upon intellectual capacity.

Specifically, we have discussed the use of intelligence tests to estimate deterioration, the special tests of intellectual deficit, and the evaluation of certain aspects of the thinking process such as abstraction and conceptualization; the relationship between intellectual processes and personality has been examined especially with regard to schizophrenia, and, finally, we have touched on the disorders of language related to specific cortical damage.

BIBLIOGRAPHY

1. Allen, R. M., "The test performance of the brain injured." *J. Clin. Psychol.*, 1947, 3, 225–30.
2. Allen, R. M., "A note on the use of the Bellevue-Wechsler Scale mental deterioration index with brain injured patients." *J. Clin. Psychol.*, 1948, 4, 88–90.
3. Allen, R. M., "The test performance of the brain diseased." *J. Clin. Psychol.*, 1948, 4, 281–7.
4. Anderson, A. L., "The effect of laterality localization of brain damage on Wechsler-Bellevue indices of deterioration." *J. Clin. Psychol.*, 1950, 6, 191–4.
5. Beck, H. S., and Lam, R. L., "Use of the WISC in predicting organicity." *J. Clin. Psychol.*, 1955, 11, 154–8.
6. Babcock, H., and Levy, L., *The revised examination for the measurement of efficiency of mental functioning.* Chicago: C. H. Stoelting, 1942.
7. Bache, J. G., "Relationship between rigidity as measured by Luchin's Water Jar Test and performance on a stylus maze following frustration." Purdue Univ. M.S. Thesis, 1953.
8. Beier, E. G., " The effect of induced anxiety on some aspects of intellectual functioning: a study of the relationship between anxiety and rigidity." *Amer. Psychologist*, 1949, 4, 273–4.
9. Bender, L., *A visual motor Gestalt test and its clinical use.* New York: Amer. Orthopsychiatric Assn., 1938.
10. Berg, E. A., "A simple objective technique for measuring flexibility in thinking." *J. Gen. Psychol.*, 1948, 39, 15–22.
11. Bolles, M. M., and Goldstein, K., "A study of the impairment of 'ab-

stract behavior' in schizophrenic patients." *Psychiat. Quart.*, 1938, 12, 42–65.

12. Cameron, N., "Reasoning, regression and communication in schizophrenics." *Psychol. Monogr.*, 1938, Vol. 50, No. 1.

13. Cameron, N., "A study of thinking in senile deterioration and schizophrenic disorganization." *Amer. J. Psychol.*, 1938, 51, 650–65.

14. Cameron, N., "Deterioration and regression in schizophrenic thinking." *J. Abnorm. Soc. Psychol.*, 139, 34, 265–270.

15. Cameron, N., "Schizophrenic thinking in a problem solving situation." *J. Ment. Sci.*, 1939, 85, 1012–1035.

16. Cameron, N., "The functional psychoses." In *Personality and behavior disorders*, J. McV. Hunt (ed.). New York: Ronald, 1944.

17. Canter, A. H., "Direct and indirect measures of psychological deficit in multiple sclerosis," Part I. *J. Gen. Psychol.*, 1941, 44, 32–6.

18. Canter, A. H., "Direct and indirect measures of psychological deficit in multiple sclerosis," Part II. *J. Gen. Psychol.*, 1941, 44, 27–50.

19. Cowen, E. L., "The influence of varying degrees of psychological stress on problem-solving rigidity." *J. Abnorm. Soc. Psychol.*, 1952, 47, 512–19.

20. Cowen, E. L., and Thompson, G. G., "Problem solving rigidity and personality structure." *J. Abnorm. Soc. Psychol.*, 1951, 46, 165–76.

21. Dottman, P. E., and Israel, E., "The order of dominance among conceptual capacities: an experimental test of Heidbreder's hypothesis." *J. Psychol.*, 1951, 31, 147–60.

22. Eisenson, J., *Examining for aphasia.* New York: Psychol. Corp., 1946.

23. Fernald, G., *Remedial techniques in basic school subjects.* New York: McGraw-Hill, 1943.

24. Fey, E. T., "The performance of young schizophrenics and young normals on Wisconsin Card Sorting Test." *J. Consult. Psychol.*, 1951, 15, 311–19.

25. Frandsen, A. N., "Interpretation of intelligence test data." Unpublished mimeographed material.

26. Garfield, S. L., and Fey, W. F., "A comparison of the Wechsler-Bellevue and Shipley-Hartford Scale as measures of mental impairment." *J. Consult. Psychol.*, 1948, 12, 259–64.

27. Goldstein, K., "The significance of psychological research in schizophrenia." *J. Nerv. Ment. Dis.*, 1943, 97, 261–79.

28. Goldstein, K., "Frontal lobotomy and impairment of abstract attitude." *J. Nerv. Ment. Dis.*, 1949, 110, 93–111.

29. Goldstein, K., and Scheerer, M., "Abstract and concrete behavior: an experimental study with special tests." *Psychol. Monogr.*, 1941, Vol. 53, No. 2 (Whole No. 239), 1–151.

30. Grant, D. A., "Perceptual versus analytic responses to the number concept of a Weigl-type card sorting test." *J. Exp. Psychol.*, 1941, 41, 23–9.

31. Grant, D. A., and Berg, E. A., "A behavioral analysis of degree of reinforcement and ease of shifting to new responses in a Weigl-type card sorting problem." *J. Exp. Psychol.*, 1948, 38, 404–11.

32. Grant, D. A., Jones, O. R., and Talantis, B., "The relative difficulty of the number, form and color concepts of a Weigl-type thinking and reasoning problem." *J. Exp. Psychol.*, 1949, 39, 552–7.

33. Grassi, J. R., *The Grassi Block Substitution Test for measuring organic brain pathology.* Springfield, Ill.: Charles C. Thomas, 1953.

34. Greenblatt, M., Goldman, R., and Coom, G. P., "Clinical implications of the Bellevue-Wechsler Test with particular reference to brain damage cases." *J. Nerv. Ment. Dis.*, 1946, 104, 438–42.

35. Gutman, B., "The application of the Wechsler-Bellevue Scale in the diagnosis of organic brain disorders." *J. Clin. Psychol.*, 1950, 6, 195–8.

36. Halstead, W. C., *Brain and intelligence.* Chicago: Univ. of Chicago Press, 1947.

37. Halstead, W. C., and Wepman, J. M., *Manual for the Halstead-Wepman Aphasia Screening Test.* Chicago: Departments of Medicine, Surgery and Psychology, Univ. of Chicago, 1949.

38. Hanfmann, E., "Concept formation tests in schizophrenia." *Psychol. Bull.*, 1936, 33, 796.

39. Hanfmann, E., and Kasanin, J. S., "A method for study of concept formation." *J. Psychol.*, 1946, 3, 521–45.

40. Hanfmann, E., and Kasanin, J., "Conceptual thinking in schizophrenia." *Nerv. Ment. Dis. Monogr. Ser.*, 1942, No. 67.

41. Hayman, M., "A rapid test for 'deterioration' with comparison of three techniques." *J. Gen. Psychol.*, 1943, 29, 313–17.

42. Hebb, D. O., "Man's frontal lobes: a critical review." *Arch. Neurol. Psychiat.*, 1945, 54, 10–24.

43. Hebb, D. O., *The organization of behavior.* New York: Wiley, 1949.

44. Heidbreder, E., "The attainments of concepts: I. Terminology and methodology." *J. Gen. Psychol.*, 1946, 35, 173–89.

45. Heidbreder, E., "The attainment of concepts: II. The problem." *J. Gen. Psychol.*, 1946, 35, 191–223.

46. Heidbreder, E., "The attainment of concepts: III. The process." *J. Psychol.*, 1947, 24, 93–138.

47. Heidbreder, E., Bensley, M. L., and Ivy, M., "The attainment of concepts: IV. Regularities and levels." *J. Psychol.*, 1948, 25, 299–329.

48. Heidbreder, E., and Overstreet, P., "The attainment of concepts: V. Critical features and contexts." *J. Psychol.*, 1948, 26, 45–69.

49. Heidbreder, E., "The attainment of concepts: VI. Exploratory experiments in conceptualization at perceptual levels." *J. Psychol.*, 1948, 26, 193–216.

50. Heidbreder, E., "The attainment of concepts: VII. Conceptual achievements during card sorting." *J. Psychol.*, 1949, 27, 3–39.

51. Heidbreder, E., "The attainment of concepts: VIII. The conceptualization of verbally indicated instances." *J. Psychol.*, 1949, 27, 263–309.

52. Hewson, L. R., "The Wechsler-Bellevue Scale and the substitution tests as aids in neuropsychiatric diagnosis." *J. Nerv. Ment. Dis.*, 1949, 109, 158–83, 246–66.

53. Hunt, H. F., *The Hunt-Minnesota Test for Organic Brain Damage.* Minneapolis: Univ. of Minnesota Press, 1943.

54. Hunt, H. F., "A practical clinical test for organic brain damage." *J. Appl. Psychol.*, 1943, 27, 375–86.

55. Hunt, H. F., "A note on the clinical use of the Hunt-Minnesota Test for Organic Brain Damage." *J. Appl. Psychol.*, 1944, 28, 175–8.

56. Hunt, J. McV., and Cofer, C. N., "Psychological deficit." In Hunt, J. McV. (ed.), *Personality and the behavior disorders*, Vol. II. New York: Ronald, 1944.

57. Jackson, C. V., "Estimating impairment on Wechsler-Bellevue subtests." *J. Clin. Psychol.*, 1955, 11, 137–43.

58. Johnson, T. F., "The relationships between perceptual choice and rigidity in personality," Purdue Univ., Ph.D. thesis, 1953.

59. Juckem, H., and Wold, J. A., "A study of the Hunt-Minnesota Test for Organic Brain Damage at the upper levels of vocabulary." *J. Consult. Psychol.*, 1948, 12, 53–7.

60. Kasanin, J. S., "The disturbance of conceptual thinking in schizophrenia." In J. S. Kasanin (ed.), *Language and thought in schizophrenia*. Berkeley, Univ. of Calif. Press, 1944.

61. Kasanin, J. S., and Hanfmann, E., "An experimental study of concept formation in schizophrenia." *Amer. J. Psychiat.*, 1938, 95, 35–52.

62. Kasanin, J. S., and Hanfmann, E., "Disturbance in concept formation in schizophrenia." *Arch. Neurol. Psychiat.*, 1938, 40, 1276–82.

63. King, W., "Ability to abstract." In *Selective partial ablation of frontal cortex*, Columbia-Greystone Associates. New York: Hoeber, 1949.

64. Levi, V., Oppenheim, S. V., Wechsler, D., "Clinical use of the mental deterioration index of the Bellevue-Wechsler scale." *J. Abnorm. and Soc. Psychol.*, 1945, 40, 405–507.

65. Lewinski, R. J., "The Shipley-Hartford Scale as an independent measure of mental ability." *Educ. and Psychol. Measmt.*, 1946, 6, 253–9.

66. Luchins, A. S., "Mechanization in problem solving." *Psychol. Monogr.*, 1942, Vol. 54, No. 6 (Whole No. 248), 1–95.

67. Luchins, A. S., "Classroom experiments on mental set." *Amer. J. Psychol.*, 1946, 59, 295–8.

68. Luchins, A. S., "Proposed methods of studying degrees of rigidity in behavior." *J. Pers.*, 1947, 15, 242–6.

69. Luchins, A. S., "On recent usage of the Einstellung-effect as a test of rigidity." *J. Consult. Psychol.*, 1951, 15, 89–94.

70. Luchins, A. S., "The Einstellung test of rigidity: its relation to concreteness of thinking." *J. Consult. Psychol.*, 1951, 15, 303–10.

71. Luchins, A. S., and Luchins, E. H., "New experimental attempts at preventing mechanization in problem solving." *J. Gen. Psychol.*, 1950, 42, 279–97.

72. Magaret, A., Grant, D. A., and Berg, E. A., "A study of the performance of exogenous and endogenous feebleminded children on the Wisconsin Card Sorting Test." Unpublished.

73. Magaret, A., and Simpson, M. M., "A comparison of two measures of deterioration in psychotic patients." *J. Consult. Psychol.*, 1948, 12, 265–9.

74. Miller, E. O., "New use for the Vigotsky Blocks." *J. Clin. Psychol.*, 1955, 11, 87–9.
75. Morgan, C. T., and Stellar, E., *Physiological psychology* (2nd ed.). New York: McGraw-Hill, 1950.
76. Nielsen, J. M., *Agnasia, apraxia, aphasia.* New York: Hoeber, 1946.
77. Pennington, L. A., "The Serial Sevens Test as a psychometric instrument." *Amer. J. Orthopsychiat.*, 1947, 17, 488–99.
78. Piotrowski, Z. A., "On the Rorschach method and its application in organic disturbances of the central nervous system." *Rorschach Research Exchange*, 1947, 8, 23–40.
79. Ptacek, J. E., and Young, F. M., "Comparison of the Grassi Block Substitution Test with the Wechsler-Bellevue in the diagnosis of organic brain damage." *J. Clin. Psychol.*, 1954, 10, 375–8.
80. Rapaport, D., Gill, M., and Schafer, R. *Diagnostic psychological testing*, Vol. I. Chicago: Yearbook Publishers, 1946.
81. Rapaport, D., and Webb, W. B., "An attempt to study intellectual deterioration by premorbid and psychotic testing." *J. Consult. Psychol.*, 1950, 14, 95–8.
82. Rashkis, H., Cushman, J., and Landis, C., "A new method for studying disorders of conceptual thinking." *J. Abnorm. Soc. Psychol.*, 1946, 41, 70–4.
83. Reichard, S., and Rapaport, D., "The role of testing concept formation in clinical psychological work." *Bull. Ment. Clin.*, 1943, 7, 99–105.
84. Reynell, W. R., "A psychometric method of determining intellectual loss following head injury." *J. Ment. Sci.*, 1944, 90, 710–19.
85. Rogers, L. S., "A comparative evaluation of the Wechsler-Bellevue Mental Deterioration Index for various adult groups." *J. Clin. Psychol.*, 1950, 6, 199–202.
86. Rogers, L. S., "A note on Allen's index of deterioration." *J. Clin. Psychol.*, 1950, 6, 203.
87. Rylander, G., *Personality changes after operations on the frontal lobes: a clinical study of 32 cases.* London: Humphrey Milford, 1939.
88. Schlosser, J. R., and Kantor, R. E., "Wechsler's deterioration ratio in psychoneurosis and schizophrenia." *J. Consult. Psychol.*, 1949, 13, 108–10.
89. Shipley, W. C., "A self-administering scale for measuring intellectual impairment and deterioration." *J. Psychol.*, 1940, 9, 371–7.
90. Smoke, K. L., "An objective study of concept formation." *Psychol. Monogr.*, 1932, Vol. 42, No. 4 (Whole No. 191), 1–46.
91. Smoke, K. L., "An experimental approach to concept learning." *Psychol. Rev.*, 1935, 42, 274–9.
92. Vigotsky, L. S., "Thought in schizophrenia." *Arch. Neurol. Psychiat.*, 1934, 31, 1063–77.
93. Vinacke, W. A., "The investigation of concept formation." *Psychol. Bull.*, 1951, 48, 1–31.
94. Wechsler, D., *The measurement of adult intelligence.* Baltimore: Williams & Wilkins, 1944.

95. Weisenburg, T., and McBride, K. E., "Aphasia: a clinical and psychological study." New York: The Commonwealth Fund, 1935.

96. Weisskopf, E. A., "Intellectual malfunctioning and personality." *J. Abnorm. Soc. Psychol.*, 1951, 46, 410–23.

97. Wepman, J. M., *Recovery from aphasia*. New York: Ronald, 1951.

98. Wheeler, J. I., Jr., and Wilkens, W. L., "The validity of the Hewson Ratios." *J. Consult. Psychol.*, 1951, 15, 163–6.

99. White, R. W., *The abnormal personality*. New York: Ronald, 1948.

100. Winfield, D. L., "Intellectual performance of cryptogenic epileptics, symptomatic epileptics, and post-traumatic encephalopaths." *J. Abnorm. Soc. Psychol.*, 1951, 46, 336–43.

101. Wright, D., "Psychiatry and clinical psychology." In Pennington, L. A., and Berg, I. A. (eds.), *An introduction to clinical psychology*. New York: Ronald, 1948.

102. Wright, G. E., "An investigation of the relationship between concept formation and intelligence in schizophrenics and normals." Purdue Univ., M.S. thesis, 1951.

103. Wright, G. E., "The relation of vocabulary level to verbal concept formation in schizophrenia." Purdue Univ., Ph.D. thesis, 1953.

104. Wright, M. E., "Use of the Shipley-Hartford Test in evaluating intellectual functioning in neuropsychiatric patients." *J. Appl. Psychol.*, 1946, 30, 45–50.

105. Zaslow, R. W., "A new approach to the problem of conceptual thinking in schizophrenia." *J. Consult. Psychol.*, 1950, 14, 335–9.

CHAPTER

18

Structured Personality Tests

THE REPERTORY OF THE PSYCHOLOGIST INCLUDES A GROUP OF DIAG-
nostic devices variously described as structured personality tests,
objective personality tests, or self-report inventories. A structured
test is one in which the response of the client is channelized in a given
way. Items or questions that can be answered by "yes" or "no" limit the
subject's responses. On the other hand, if the subject is asked to tell what
he sees in a meaningless design or ink blot, the response is not channelized, and the task is described as unstructured. The use of the term "objective" describes the test in terms of the job of the interpreter. A list of
questions to be answered "yes" or "no" can be scored with a high degree
of reliability; that is, many persons can count up the total number of
"yes's" and "no's" and they will all come up with the same answer. On
the other hand, persons analyzing responses to an unstructured task may
differ greatly in their evaluations of the responses. Consequently, unstructured tests cannot be described as objective. Actually, structured
psychological tests of the kind to be discussed in this chapter are properly labeled objective only in the sense that the scoring is objective; clinicians may differ widely in their interpretation of what the total number of
"yes" and "no" responses on a given test means in terms of describing
the behavior of a given client. Consequently, in this text we will tend to
use the term "structured" in preference to the term "objective."

Another term used in connection with structured or objective tests
and inventories and one that is growing in popularity is "self-report."
This term implies that the subject reports his answers directly. It is used
somewhat in contrast to the term "projective," which implies that the individual reveals something of himself in his responses to a test situation,
particularly in an unstructured situation. In analyzing the responses to an
unstructured test, the clinician attempts to infer what the subject is re-

vealing about himself. It is assumed that the material revealed has more "dynamic" or unconscious meaning because the subject may not be aware of what he has revealed. Since the stimuli may be relatively meaningless, any meaning must be a function of the subject. Projective tests are believed to give us information as to the "why" of behavior. Structured psychological tests are believed to be useful primarily as descriptive procedures and to give us information as to the "how" of behavior. They are presumed to describe how the person thinks, behaves, or feels. To the extent that a test is valid—measures what it purports to measure—it can be used to characterize the client in terms of certain aspects of behavior.

Frank S. Freeman (37) has estimated that there are at least five hundred, and Stephen H. Pratt (75) suggests that there may be a thousand, structured personality tests and/or self-report inventories currently available, dozens of which are in common use at the present time. Structured personality tests are based on the idea that personality has various dimensions or traits. A trait may be defined as a tendency to react in a defined way to a defined class of stimuli (30). The construction of scales for trait measurement is based on several assumptions that have varying degrees of validity. Cronbach (30, p. 315) lists three assumptions (he calls them facts):

(1) Personalities possess considerable consistency; a person shows the habitual reactions over a wide range of similar situations.

(2) For any habit we can find among people a variation of degrees or amounts of this behavior.

(3) Personalities have some stability since the person possessing a certain degree of a trait this year usually shows a similar degree next year.[1]

WHAT PERSONALITY TESTS MEASURE

Personality is a construct denoting certain qualities and characteristics of behavior. Like intelligence, it should not be regarded as an entity but as a general term that is used to include a number of significant variations in behavior. The trait theory of personality assumes that behavior can be described in terms of a number of adjectives that are characteristic of the way a person behaves. The concept of personality should be broad enough to include covert as well as overt manifestations of behavior; the way a person feels, his attitudes, his opinions, and his values are all traits that may determine his unique mode of behavior. Most definitions of per-

[1] This and a quotation that follows by permission from *Essentials of Psychological Testing*, by Lee J. Cronbach. Copyright 1949 by Harper & Brothers.

sonality also include feelings about the environment which are unconscious as well as conscious. If we are to use the concept of personality to describe a given person in a way that differentiates him from other persons, we must hypothesize that the traits of personality which are present in varying amounts in different persons are organized in a dynamic and unique fashion in each person. The idea of dynamic organization also implies that these traits are interrelated and interact with each other as well as with the environment.

Keeping all these factors in mind, we might define personality as the unique and dynamic organization of feelings, attitudes, opinions, values, and traits of behavior, both overt and covert, conscious and unconscious, which are characteristic of an individual's typical and habitual adjustments to his environment. Such a definition is highly academic since it should be clear that we measure traits of behavior, not personality. Consequently, the evaluation of any test of personality must be made, not in terms of how well it measures personality, but in terms of the appropriateness of the traits that are being measured and the extent to which it measures the traits it purports to measure.

The concept of a trait is a broad one, and the appropriateness of a particular trait depends on how economically and accurately it describes certain variations in behavior. Gordon W. Allport and Henry S. Odbert (5), in what they called a "psycholexical study," went through the dictionary and found 17,953 adjectives describing personality traits. Although many of these adjectives are undoubtedly synonyms, describing identical or almost identical aspects of behavior, psychologists cannot go about measuring all traits; rather, they must try to decide which are most important and most basic to functioning in various spheres of activity.

Measures of almost anything can be and have been considered personality tests. A cursory survey of titles of tests and subtests gives a rough indication of the aspects of personality which personality questionnaires and inventories attempt to measure. Julius B. Maller (68, p. 186) presents the following partial list:

> . . . mental health, personality adjustment, home adjustment, health adjustment, social adjustment, emotional adjustment, self-control, social initiative, self-sufficiency, self-determinism, self-esteem, ascendance-submission, dominance-submission, cheerfulness-depression, introversion-extroversion, social introversion, depression-elation, cycloid tendency, neurotic tendency, mental instability, withdrawal attitude, personal inferiority, social inferiority, emotional maturity, happiness, anxiety, fears, frustrations, and many others.[2]

[2] By permission from "Personality Tests," by J. B. Maller in *Personality and the Behavior Disorders* edited by J. McV. Hunt. Copyright 1944 by The Ronald Press Company.

Such a list suggests that some progress (although of doubtful value) is being made in measuring many of Allport's adjectives.

Maller (68, p. 170) defines personality tests as "objective psychometric devices which purport to measure tendencies, habits, and a variety of distinctive characteristics other than those of physique and intellectual capacity." The concept of personality has a great deal in common with the concept of intelligence, and, in a general way, intelligence can be regarded as an aspect of personality. However, since we have tests of both intelligence and personality, it may be helpful to compare them, for both intelligence tests and personality tests are based on a limited number of responses that are considered representative of wider areas of behavior, and both use several subtests or scales in combination for more adequate measurement. They are objective, with prescribed administration and scoring, and usually some norms are provided or are available for the interpretation of scores. There are many ways in which intelligence and personality differ. Since intelligence is, relatively speaking, more innate and personality more acquired, there is a greater constancy in intelligence. Also, whereas mental abilities, in the main, show a more or less regular growth curve from infancy to maturity, a curve is not observable for many aspects of personality; for example, adults may have more information than children, but not necessarily greater honesty or more anxiety. There is no general "personality quotient" analogous to the I.Q. except, perhaps, for the idea of a place on an adjustment-maladjustment continuum. Mental abilities are usually placed on a linear continuum, that is to say, from smart, to smarter, to very smart, but personality traits on a continuum that allows for reversals (from the point of view of efficiency of function)—for example, courage may become foolhardiness, originality may become bizarreness, self-confidence may become conceit.

Among personality tests are included measures of character and morals, such as the tests by Hugh Hartshorne and Mark A. May (51, 52, 53) of good citizenship, of moral knowledge, and of other similar factors; and measures of attitudes and opinions—Thurstone's (85) scale of attitudes toward the Negro, the Chinese, war, the law, capital punishment, censorship, and other scales of attitudes on many topics, including Hermann H. Remmers' generalized attitude scale (77) and measures of values and interests such as Floyd H. Allport and Phillip E. Vernon's (3) study of values and the Strong Vocational Interest Blank (82). All these tests can give good insight into personality. For example, attitudes toward minority groups can tell us much about an individual; in this connection the work done on the California F-Scale is especially interesting (2). However for purposes of clinical evaluation we are somewhat more interested in measurements of temperament and adjustment—the standard personality inventories or psychoneurotic inventories.

These inventories are self-rating questionnaires, requiring the subject to answer questions dealing with overt behavior ("Do you bite your nails?"); with feelings about himself ("Are you often depressed?"); and with feelings about his environment ("Are most people dishonest?"). Various tests call for some form of "yes" or "no" answers as to whether statements apply to the subject, or how he feels about certain statements. Specific instruments have been devised for various purposes, ranging from those designed for quick neuropsychiatric screening on an adjusted-maladjusted basis, to complex tests that purport to give complete personality descriptions on the basis of several scores. In the present treatment we will discuss only a few of the many tests that have been devised, concentrating on those that are of most use to the clinician.

THE HISTORY AND DEVELOPMENT OF STRUCTURED PERSONALITY TESTS

A number of authors (30, 37, 40, 68) have traced the history and development of structured personality tests; for a comprehensive coverage of the literature, the reader is referred to their reviews. The first widely used scale was Robert S. Woodworth's Personal Data Sheet (96), which was used for screening recruits in World War I, and since that time innumerable inventories have appeared. Before we discuss some of these inventories, let us consider some of the methods involved in their construction and validation.

Three general methods, each of which has some variation, have been used in the construction of the various tests. These methods are:

1. A PRIORI PROCEDURES. Many of the early tests and some of the recent ones have been constructed by the selection purely by a priori definition of items that are *presumed* to measure certain *presumed* traits or dimensions of personality. This armchair procedure in selection may involve the use of an expert judge, or group of judges or raters, who decide what the answers to certain questions should mean, and the interpretation of scores may be based entirely on their judgments. Their judgments may reflect a wealth of experience, but armchair validation has come under so much criticism that it is rarely used as a sole criterion. In the construction of other tests a further step is taken; the author assumes that the test measures what he says it measures, and specific items are retained or rejected on the basis of the extent to which they correlate with the test as a whole. In this use of an item analysis of internal consistency, the supposed "traits" to be tested may be no more than a priori suppositions, but if the items designed to measure a particular trait are responded to in a consistent fashion, it is assumed that they are measuring

the same thing. Still other authors have standardized and validated their tests by correlating them with other items or tests that have been considered to be adequate measures of the hypothesized "trait" in question.

2. EMPIRICAL PROCEDURES. In the construction of some tests, items are selected and the total test is validated by checking the item or test against some external criterion such as clinical diagnosis, determining how well it distinguishes between clinical groups, discriminates between extreme groups, or is able to sort individuals on a variety of parameters. Woodworth in his original inventory used an emperical method of item selection by retaining only items that had been checked twice as often by known psychoneurotics as by normals. The Minnesota Multiphasic Personality Inventory (54, 55, 56, 57) and the Humm-Wadsworth Scale (60, 61) are current examples of empirical construction.

3. FACTOR ANALYTIC PROCEDURES. A few tests have been constructed on the basis of factor analytic studies of the test items. By this procedure the items are grouped into a number of categories, which in turn can be studied to gain some insight into what categories mean. This is a useful method for refining and describing objective personality tests. The factor analytic procedure goes a long way in the direction of overcoming Raymond B. Cattell's (25, p. 134) criticism that "clearly the natural unreliability of self-ratings questionnaire testing has here been still further exaggerated by the lack of clarity and critical insight in the designers themselves when setting up their 'unitary traits' or syndromes. Obviously, these categories of the market place cannot be accepted as the true functional unities."

One of the first important factor analyses of personality questionnaires was the study of John C. Flanagan (36) in which he analyzed the four Bernreuter subtests. He isolated three factors: Self-Confidence, Sociability, and Dominance. Guilford (41, 42, 43, 44, 45, 46, 47, 69) and Cattell (22, 23, 24, 25, 26, 27), in their pioneer work in developing an over-all factoral structure for inventories, sought always to use functional unities that were operationally determined. But even the extended studies of carefully defined tests that were used to detect these functional unities have thus far presented little evidence about the validity of the particular, refined tests.

VALIDITY

It seems appropriate to consider what is meant by "validity" in relation to structured personality tests before we discuss specific tests. Much of the material in this section is taken from an unpublished Ph.D. dissertation by Pratt (75), prepared under our direction. When we ask the question, "What is validity?" the stock answer is that validity is the extent to which a test measures what it is supposed to measure. This sounds simple enough, but on closer analysis we find that the question is actually quite complex, and that partial confusion on the part of some test constructors and validators has led to considerable obscuring of the basic issues involved.

It is all very well to epitomize validity as the capacity of an instrument to measure what it purports to measure. However we may not know exactly what we want to measure, or even if there is such a "thing" or "process" in objective reality. Assuming that we might know what we want to measure and the measurable dimensions thereof, we will want to validate these measures against some criterion. But do we know that this criterion represents what we want our test to measure? In these terms, is our criterion a reality at all? Still further, do we know any of the actual dimensions of our criterion, and can we measure any of these against which to check our test dimensions? This leads us to a consideration of the crux of the problem, the appreciation of which is relatively conspicuous by its absence in the literature. Rather than having validity or lacking validity, a test may have different levels of validity. A test may be quite "valid" at one level of interpretation and totally invalid at another. This last point and those leading up to it have resulted in endless irrelevant quibbling among psychologists as to the validity, or lack of validity, of their measuring instruments in general and of personality measures in particular.

With personality questionnaires, the validation criteria are usually internal or external; both are acceptable when they *are* criteria of what we intend to measure in objective reality. Regrettably, this has not usually been the case. Internally, we have the usual item analysis of "internal consistency." This avails us nothing if we do not know what fortuitous hodgepodge is being consistent, or what it is consistent with other than itself. Of what value is it to know something is internally consistent if we do not know what *it* is? This brings us to the ridiculous operational definition that intelligence is whatever intelligence tests measure. Apparently personality is whatever personality tests measure. This same logic applies when the test is "validated" by testing the ability of each item to differentiate between two extreme groups in the standardization population. This may be on total scores or part scores. The same question arises. Just what are we dealing with? Do these scores represent meaningful functional unities?

The use of outside criteria is usually equally suspect, and for the same reasons. For instance, "validation" against other equally suspect instruments is common practice. Often the outside criterion is considered as homogeneous and representative, yet it may be quite heterogeneous and unrepresentative. Criteria are usually treated as if they constituted simple entities or processes, whereas actually they may be complex or even combinations of several functional unities. This results in the validation of one unknown against another unknown. Pratt (75) urges the use of factorial methods to investigate the dimensions of "what is to be tested," the measuring instruments, and the criteria. Ultimately, of course, we must include all of these as well as various field or situational conditions in our factor matrix. We need to investigate factorially the questions as to what exactly are the functional unities in which we are interested, their dimensions, and likewise those of the criteria. Furthermore, we must ultimately determine the covariational relationships between particular test variables and particular criteria variables taken first in simple and then in complex relation.

Finally, let us return to the problem of levels of validity as it relates to structured personality tests. In short, we can consider that items, subtests, and tests may be used, interpreted, and validated at the following levels:

1. RESPONSES OR SCORES MAY BE TREATED AS OBJECTIVELY DIFFERENTIATING IN TERMS OF THE REACTIONS TO THE STIMULI. This is without regard to the item content per se or to the subjective mental processes of the subject. As Cronbach (30, p. 309) says, "Empirical uses of self-reports are necessarily valid. The report itself is a behavior report; one obtains a direct record of response to a standardized stimulus when he asks a verbal question." Cattell (25, p. 342), while inveighing against the construction, application, and interpretation of personality schedules in general, is very careful to emphasize that "the abuses practiced by those who typically seize upon the questionnaire are no argument, however, against its proper research use within the true limits of its validity." Charles I. Mosier (73, p. 265) also emphasizes the point as follows:

> It must be urged that the variables under investigation are not the presence or absences of certain objectively verifiable attributes, but rather items of behavior in the strictest sense—making a mark in one position rather than in another position when confronted with a printed verbal statement. The primary datum is not, for example, the answer to the question, "Does this man have stage fright?" but to the question, "Does this man say that he has stage fright?" This does not mean that it is not legitimate to generalize beyond that restricted interpretation, but it does mean that such generalization must be made with full realization of the exact nature of the data on which that generalization is based.[3]

[3] From "A Factor Analysis of Certain Neurotic Symptoms," by Charles I. Mosier, *Psychometrika*, 1937, 2, 263–86. By permission of *Psychometrika*.

Thus, items, subtests, and tests may have an empirical prima facie validity regardless of their validity at other levels of interpretation.

2. RESPONSES OR SCORES MAY BE INTERPRETED AS REVEALING ASPECTS OF THE SELF-CONCEPT OR MENTAL INTERIOR OR PERSONA (THE IMPRESSION THE SUBJECT WISHES TO GIVE). What a subject says is important to differential dynamics but the truth of his statement, also of interest, is quite another matter. As Cronback (30, p. 308) points out:

> One who wishes to consider himself healthy may overrate his health in answering, "Is your health better or poorer than the average for your age?" Another person with only minor ills may exaggerate them, perhaps without conscious intention, to get sympathy or justify self pity. This question would not obtain valid facts about health. But if it can be established that clinically diagnosed neurotics reply "poorer" more frequently than do normals, this answer may be diagnostic even when it is "untrue"—in fact, it may be diagnostic just because it is untrue.

Discussing this point, Paul E. Meehl (71, p. 9) in the same vein has said:

> . . . The verbal type of personality inventory is *not* most fruitfully seen as a "self-rating" or self-description whose value requires the assumption of accuracy on the part of the testee in his observations of self. Rather is the response to a test item taken as an intrinsically interesting segment of verbal behavior, knowledge regarding which may be of more value than any knowledge of the "factual" material about which the item superficially purports to inquire. Thus, if a hypochondriac says that he has "many headaches" the fact of interest is that he *says* this.[4]

And still another comment (43, p. 118):

> We must constantly remember that the response of a subject may not represent exactly what the question implies in its most obvious meaning. Subjects respond to a question as at the moment they think they are, with perhaps a lack of insight in many cases as to their real position on the question. They also respond *as they would like themselves to be and as they would like others to think them to be,* and as they wish the examiner

---

[4] From "An Investigation of a General Normality or Control Factor in Personality Testing," by Paul E. Meehl, *Psychological Monographs*, 1945, Vol. 59, No. 4. By permission of the American Psychological Association.

to think them to be. They also respond with some regard to self-consistency among their answers.[5]

Certainly levels such as these two overlap. We can interpret differential responses empirically, disregarding item content completely. We can investigate what a client or a nosological group says in its answers versus what other groups say, regardless of the "truth" of the answers. We can investigate what subjects say in terms of self-concept or persona, again regardless of "validity" in terms of how they "really" are in fact. In the sense of these first two levels of validity, structured personality tests may be assumed to have validity, or empirical validity may be established for certain differential diagnostic purposes.

3. THE PREDICTABILITY OF BEHAVIOR FROM SELF-REPORT. What is the correspondence between self-concept or *persona* on the one hand, and actual behavior on the other? Although structured tests are frequently used as if this level of validity had been established, there are few research studies that have demonstrated such validity.

4. THE ASSUMPTION THAT THE RESPONSES ARE EQUIVALENT TO ACTUAL BEHAVIOR. The level of validity in which one can predict behavior from test responses is, in general, a transitional level that leads us to the final level, that of accepting the self-report responses as representing *carte blanche* the person's actual behavior or personality. This is the level of validity which has been all too frequently assumed for structured personality tests as well as for other tests, but it has been infrequently established.

THE MINNESOTA MULTIPHASIC PERSONALITY INVENTORY

The Minnesota Multiphasic Personality Inventory (hereafter to be called the MMPI) (54, 55) is the most ambitious, the most complex, and the longest of the structured tests of personality, as well as the one most commonly used by clinical psychologists. It appears to be a promising test, and it is one on which much research has been done. It has about 550 items to be answered "true," "false," or "cannot say." These responses are scored on a number of different keys. The usual ones are: Hs—hypochondriasis; D—depression; Hy—hysteria; Pd—psychopathic deviate; Mf—masculinity; Pa—paranoia; Pt—psychasthenia; Sc—schizophrenia; and Ma—hypomania. In addition, there are keys that have been designed to control some of the errors common to self-report

[5] From "Personality Factors S, E, and M, and Their Measurement," by J. P. and Ruth B. Guilford, *Journal of Psychology*, 1936, 2, 109–27. By permission of the *Journal of Psychology*.

tests. These are the ?, L, K, and F keys. The ? key is simply the number of times questions were answered "cannot say." It is an index of evasion and helps the administrator to decide when other scores should be accepted. The L score is the lie score, based on a number of questions that are so extremely worded that a false answer to them constitutes prima facie evidence of lying. A high L score indicates that all the scores may be untrustworthy. The K score is designed to eliminate false positives. A low K score indicates severe self-description, without giving one's self the benefit of the doubt. The F (false) score is a count of replies given by a subject which are rarely given by others. It reveals carelessness, or misunderstanding, or lack of co-operation.

The scoring and validation of this test is empirical, based on records of clinical groups. Results of validation studies on this test, as on others, vary, although generally they are more favorable to this one than to others. Most studies show that groups of mental hospital patients can be readily distinguished from groups of normals, but there is doubt as to the ability of the MMPI to distinguish between different clinical groups. In providing a detailed self-evaluation by the client or patient, the test is useful as a clinical aid—and as a research tool. However, it has been grossly misused because of claims of simplicity, and the very names of the keys. One of its liabilities lies in its validation against psychiatric diagnoses, which are often inaccurate. Too, its reliability is not very high, and the test is much too long, almost always requiring more than an hour—sometimes up to five hours.

A great deal of research is being done on the MMPI and some pretty tall claims have been made: that it can distinguish between functional and organic backache (49); that it can distinguish between lesions of the frontal lobe and of the parietal lobe (6); that new scoring keys can measure dominance, responsibility, and status striving (39); that it can predict the outcome of therapy (35) (with reservations); that scales being developed will measure neuroticism (95) and schizophrenia (8); and that alcoholic (16) and multiple sclerosis (18) profiles are distinctly different from other profiles. Methods have been devised for coding scores and an atlas of case histories has been published, in which one can look up a profile similar to that of one's subject and find a case history to match (56). The latest trend is to avoid using the names of the keys by substituting their numbers. Thus, instead of characterizing a person as a hysteric with strong hypochondriasis, the authors now suggest that we speak of him as a "31" individual. A start has been made in describing the factorial composition of the test (73, 87, 92). This type of approach may be quite helpful to an understanding of what the test does measure and in supplementing the empirical validity studies upon which it was developed.

The MMPI is used with varying degrees of confidence and in different ways by different clinicians. In spite of the attempts to utilize the MMPI in a highly objective fashion, some workers (58) report that they can predict traits more accurately by scanning clusters of scores on the MMPI than by using a rigorous objective method for the same purpose. Brief screening procedures (19, 28, 31, 76) for psychopathological patients have been developed from the MMPI score patterning, and the test is frequently used for such screening. The experience of clinicians and investigators is contradictory insofar as the value of such scales is concerned. This may reflect the lack of validity of the test for such purposes or it may indicate the unreliability of psychiatric diagnoses. In any case, it does not appear that the MMPI is any substitute for the professional judgment of the clinician. The skilled clinician should be able to use the results of the test just as he uses other information available to him. In general, the test can be used with confidence as some might use an interview, and a consideration of why a person answers questions in a given way (validity levels 1 and 2 in preceding discussion) is helpful for diagnosis and therapy planning. However opinion is divided on the value of the raw scores for diagnostic and therapeutic purposes. The following case report from an administration of the MMPI may serve to illustrate both points—the relative sterility of the raw scores and some specific points that might be evaluated further.

The client was 30 years of age and had been referred because of repeated attempts at suicide. He claimed to "hate" his parents, and held that he had no good friends and could trust few people. He achieved ? and lie scores that were within the normal range. However his validity score was 80, which is above the limit for validity. This largely invalidates the scores obtained on remaining scales, but they are given here in order to outline the trends on the various scales:

Hypochondriasis Scale	70
Depression Scale	75
Hysteria Scale	73
Psychopathic Deviant Scale	93
Interest Scale	55
Paranoia Scale	88
Psychasthenia Scale	75
Schizophrenia Scale	88
Hypomania Scale	45

With the exception of scores on the interest and hypomania scales, all these are above the range of normality. Psychopathic deviate, paranoia, and schizophrenia scores are particularly high. With respect to the score on the psychopathic deviate scale, it should be noted that several of the statements that contributed to the high score are concerned with attitudes toward parents and siblings.

An examination of individual responses disclosed among the statements answered "true" the following that seemed most significant: "There is something wrong with my sex organs"; "At times I feel like smashing things"; "I have a daydream life about which I do not tell other people"; "Even when I am with people I feel lonely much of the time"; "At times I have enjoyed being hurt by someone I loved"; "I deserve severe punishment for my sins"; "Someone has it in for me"; "I am sure I am being talked about"; "I have had very peculiar and strange experiences"; "No one cares much what happens to you"; "I don't seem to care what happens to me"; "I am sure I get a raw deal from life"; "It does not bother me particularly to see animals suffer."

Among the responses placed in the "false" category, those that seemed most significant are: "I have never been paralyzed nor had any unusual weakness of any of my muscles"; "I seldom or never have dizzy spells"; "I have little or no trouble with my muscles twitching or jumping"; "I am not easily angered"; "I loved my mother"; "My mother was a good woman"; "My father was a good man"; "I have never been in trouble because of my sex behavior"; "My feelings are not easily hurt."

We had decided that some insight or understanding would be helpful to the client. Consequently, such responses as the above were used as topics for discussion in the individual counseling situation.

A report on the use of the MMPI with another client also suggests certain areas that might be considered in therapy. This client scored above normal limits on the schizophrenia, hypomania, and psychasthenia scales. His answers to many of the specific questions were enlightening. He reported having heard voices, feeling anxious about something or someone all the time, and enjoying hurting persons he loved. He was strongly attracted to members of his own sex, and would like to be a girl. He was bothered by thoughts about sex and would like to work with women. He had felt that someone was making him do things by hypnotizing him, that people could read his thoughts, and that he had had strange and unusual religious experiences. Although the validity score on this test made the results somewhat questionable, the client stated that he had answered the questions honestly and to the best of his ability. It was necessary to move very slowly, but the counselor was able to use the above responses as entering "wedges" to the discussion of certain deep-seated anxieties.

Although several persons (50, 72, 88) have proposed the use of the MMPI to aid persons in making vocational choices, the results of a study by Jerry H. Clark (29) suggest that the test should rarely be used for "counseling into" a college major and that it may also have a very restricted use in vocational counseling.

Since the MMPI and tests like it require, under usual conditions of administration, that the subject read in order to participate in the testing situation, it becomes pertinent to question the influence that reading ability may have upon test results. Utilizing reading-grade difficulty formulae, the reading difficulty of the MMPI has been established as being at the third-grade level (48). Although the MMPI appears to be one of the most readable of the current personality tests, the questions are sensitive to numerous interpretations by subjects who have had limited education.

One of the more interesting and useful of the various scales that have been developed by the use of MMPI items is the Taylor Manifest Anxiety Scale (83). Although it has been used primarily as a research instrument, some results (59) of its use suggest that it might also have sufficient validity for some kinds of clinical application.

OTHER STRUCTURED TESTS

1. THE PERSONAL AUDIT.   One of the tests more commonly used in the therapeutic or counseling situation is the Personal Audit (1). This test (the long scale) consists of nine parts, each with fifty items. Each part measures what is believed to be a relatively independent component of personality. The extremes of these nine traits are as follows: (a) seriousness-impulsiveness, (b) firmness-indecision, (c) tranquility-instability, (d) frankness-evasion, (e) stability-instability, (f) tolerance-intolerance, (g) steadiness-emotionality, (h) persistence-fluctuation, and (i) contentment-worry. Some bits of clinical evidence suggest that scores on several of these traits, especially the frankness-evasion component, may have some validity for predicting the successfulness of insight therapy. The use of this test from that point of view will require additional research.

2. THE CALIFORNIA MENTAL HEALTH ANALYSIS.   Another of the more promising of the objective or structured personality tests is the California Mental Health Analysis (84). This test is scored in terms of five traits making up a liability score, and another five traits making up an assets score. It may prove useful as a screening device, and some clients respond well to objective directive therapy oriented about the various assets and liability traits.

3. GUILFORD TESTS.   Joy P. Guilford (41, 43, 46) and Howard G. Martin (59) have developed several inventories for the measurement of variables of personality chosen on the basis of a factor analysis. One, the Inventory of Factors STDCR, covers the introversion-extroversion syndrome, the factors being: S—social introversion; T—thinking introversion; R—rhathymia; D—depression; C—cycloid. The second, the Inventory of Factors GAMIN, measures five traits operationally de-

fined as: G—great pressure for overt activity; A—ascendancy in social situations; M—masculinity in attitudes and interests; I—lack of inferiority feelings; and N—lack of nervousness and irritability. A third, the Personal Inventory, measures three traits of what is commonly called the paranoid syndrome; O—objectivity-subjectivity; Ag—agreeableness-belligerence; and Co—Co-operativeness. A fourth, the Guilford-Zimmerman Temperament Survey (47), has been developed from the other scales and results in measurements of ten traits designated as follows:

G—General activity
R—Restraint (opposite of rhathymia)
A—Ascendance
S—Sociability (opposite of "social introversion," formerly called traits of "cycloid disposition" and "depressive tendencies")
E—Emotional stability (opposite to a combination of the former "social extroversion")
O—Objectivity
F—Friendliness (former trait of "agreeableness")
T—Thoughtfulness (formerly called "thinking introversion")
P—Personal relations (formerly "co-operativeness")
M—Masculinity

This scale has been widely used as a research instrument and presents interesting possibilities for use in individual assessment.

The inventories of factors STDCR and GAMIN were administered to 280 psychotic patients by Pratt (75). These patients were selected from ten nosological categories. All but three of the ten factors were found to differentiate between sexes and clinical categories (either or both) at significant levels of confidence. This study suggests that the Guilford-Martin Tests may have more clinical usefulness than they have been previously considered to have.

4. The Bernreuter Personality Inventory.   This test (9) has 125 items—such as "Do you daydream frequently?"—with a method of weighted scoring, and it is designed to give a profile of such traits as self-confidence, sociability, etc., and a general index of neurotic tendency. Originally designed for use with college students, its use has been extended to include adolescents and older adults.

5. The Bell Adjustment Inventory.   This inventory (7) has 140 items designed for students and adults, and is intended more for use with normal groups than for clinical analysis. It gives scores for social adjustment, home adjustment, emotional adjustment, and health adjustment. When used for the purposes for which it was designed, that is, for

use in normal groups, it is a valuable indicator of specific areas of difficulty.

6. TEST OF PERSONAL ADJUSTMENT.   Carl R. Rogers' Test of Personal Adjustment (79), designed for use with children, is more complex than most of the others, yielding personality descriptions based on an analytic study of the items and the interrelations between different parts of the test. The questions are such as to interest and appeal to children. Results are not in terms of percentiles, but rather in terms of relatively complete descriptions. As Louttit (67) has indicated, this is one of the relatively few structured personality tests satisfactory for use with children.

7. THE INDEX OF ADJUSTMENT AND VALUES.   Robert E. Bills and others (15) have developed a form of self-rating scale which has been used in several research studies (10, 11, 12, 13, 14, 78) and which appears to have possibilities for clinical use. It is specifically designed to reveal the traits and values that the individual has accepted as definitions of himself. In other words, the index yields a measure of the "self-concept" of the person being tested. Specifically, the test consists of a list of 49 adjectives that the testee is asked to apply to himself. For example, if the adjective is "reckless," the testee first uses the term in a sentence as, "I am a reckless person." He then rates what proportion of time this statement is like him on a scale from one to five, with "one" indicating a rating of "seldom" and "five" indicating a rating of "most of the time." Then the subject is instructed to indicate by a rating how he feels about himself as described by the first rating. Again, the ratings range from one to five with "one" indicating "I very much dislike being as I am in this respect" and "five" designating "I very much like being as I am in this respect." Finally, the subject is instructed to use each of the adjectives in the sentence, "I would like to be a (an) ―― person" and to indicate how much of the time he would like this trait to be characteristic of him. The first rating samples the concept of self, the second measures the acceptance of self, and the third indicates the concept of the ideal self. The total of the discrepancies between the self-concept and the concept of the ideal self is supposed to be a measure of adjustment.

The purposes of the index of adjustment and values are similar to the Q Technique (81) where the subject is asked to sort self-referent statements in terms of whether they are more or less characteristic of himself. This technique might also be regarded as a structured attempt to secure a personality evaluation.

8. SCREENING TESTS.   For purposes of quick psychiatric screening, there are two tests that were the most widely used during World

War II and afterward in the armed forces and in industry. These are the Shipley Personality Inventory (commonly known as the P.I.) (80) and the Cornell Selectee Index (91). They are made up of direct questions on psychopathological symptomatology, calling for yes-no answers. Short and easy to score (the P.I. has 20 items, and the Cornell 32), the tests picked up between 50 and 90 per cent of the neuropsychiatric unfit, with a false positive rate of only 3 to 25 per cent. The questions closely approach the criteria. For instance, "Do you have frequent headaches?" The important thing, for purposes of military screening, is the existence of the headaches, rather than an individual's particular diagnosis. Such instruments may not aid in individual diagnosis, or in gaining an understanding of personality, but they certainly fulfill the important requirements of expediency. The Fort Ord Inventory (31) has been recently developed for use at Army induction stations. It is believed by its authors that whereas the P.I. and the Cornell scales measure primarily neurotic tendencies, this scale will also measure other psychiatric conditions. Preliminary data on the Fort Ord Inventory are encouraging.

9. Miscellaneous Scales.   Still other tests are the Gordon W. Allport and Floyd H. Allport A-S Reaction Study (4) presumably measuring ascendance-submission; the Allport-Vernon Value Scale (3); the Humm-Wadsworth Temperament Scale (61); and the Louis L. Thurstone and Thelma G. Thurstone Personality Schedule (86) yielding an index of neurotic tendency. Other inventories purportedly measuring more restrictive aspects of personality are: a test including items typical of schizophrenic behavior by James D. Page et al. (74); self-estimate of happiness by Goodwin B. Watson (90); symptoms of mental instability by D. J. Ingle (63); items dealing with persistence by Charles K. A. Wang (89); questions on depression-elation by Herbert H. Jasper (64); the psychosomatic inventory by Ross A. McFarland and Clifford P. Seitz (70); and a similar test by Max J. Freeman (38); temperament tests (20, 21) and others too numerous to list.

10. Interest Inventories.   Several of the interest inventories, although they are ordinarily used primarily in vocational counseling, may actually yield personality traits as well as indices of preferences. An example of such a scale is the Kuder Preference Inventory (66). The Krout Personal Preference Scale (65), which is composed of items that call for expressions of liking or disliking certain kinds of objects, activities, and relationships, is intended to estimate the extent to which a person shows tendencies reflecting the various stages of psychosexual development described in Freudian literature. Thus, in this test we have the interest or preference measurement technique deliberately used, not for vocational counseling, but rather as a pencil-and-paper personality test.

GENERAL EVALUATION OF STRUCTURED
PERSONALITY TESTS

In 1946 Albert Ellis (32) reviewed a few hundred studies of objective personality tests and characterized the results of these tests as positive (the test does what it is supposed to do), questionable, and negative. These studies involved many of the more widely known and used tests, including the Bernreuter P.I., Thurstone Personality Scale, Bell Adjustment Inventory, California Test of Personality, and others. Here are some of his findings (p. 425):

    (1) Of 9 attempts to validate personality questionnaires with groups of behavior problem children, 2 showed positive, 1 questionable, and 6 negative results.

    (2) Of 34 tests of validation against a diagnosis of delinquency—15 positive, 6 questionable, 18 negative.

    (3) Of 73 tests of validation against psychiatric or psychological diagnoses—36 positive, 7 questionable, 30 negative.

    (4) Of 44 tests of validation against teachers', friends', or associates' ratings—12 positive, 10 questionable, 22 negative.

    (5) Of 55 tests of validations against correlations with other personality questionnaires—9 positive, 18 questionable, 28 negative.

    (6) Of 42 studies of whether or not subjects overrated themselves on self-description instruments, 6 showed that they did not, while 36 showed that they did.[6]

All these studies were done on group tests, a category including most personality questionnaires. The box score for the MMPI, administered individually, is somewhat more encouraging. Of 15 studies of validation against clinical groups, the results showed 10 positive, 3 questionable, and only 2 negative. The reasons for these better results may lie in a better initial validation of the MMPI, or perhaps in the advantages of the rapport gained in individual testing.

    The results of all these studies raise serious doubt as to the actual value of some of these instruments, and arguments have been advanced on both sides. In a poll of clinicians reported by Ellis, most had little faith in paper-and-pencil tests of personality, although 15 per cent stated

    [6] From "The Validity of Personality Questionnaires," by Albert Ellis, *Psychological Bulletin*, 1946, 43, 385–445. By permission of the American Psychological Association.

that they found them quite satisfactory. Somewhat in contrast to the above review are the more promising results that Ellis and Herbert S. Conrad (34) report have been obtained with the use of personality inventories in military practice. In military practice, however, the tests are used for screening purposes and evaluated on group rather than individual results.

More recently Ellis (33) has surveyed the research reports on personality questionnaires that appeared in the literature between January 1946 and December 1951. He reports that during this six-year period far more research and theoretical papers were published on personality questionnaires than have been published in any equivalent period in the history of psychology. Ellis summarizes his survey by noting that the inventories give reasonably successful discriminations when used with neuropsychiatric, psychosomatic, alcoholic, age, sex, ethnic, and college groups. However the inventories do not seem to be measuring the independent traits they are supposed to measure. They do not appear to agree too well with each other or with the results of Rorschach and projective tests. They are easily faked. Furthermore, they do not discriminate successfully when used with vocational, academic, socioeconomic, and disabled and ill groups. Even more important is Ellis' observation that different experimenters keep obtaining directly contradictory results when using the same or similar inventories.

Among the limitations of the various researches analyzed by Ellis is the tendency of many authors to assume that because significant score differences have or have not been found, significant trait differences have or have not been proved. This appears to be an instance, as discussed earlier, of assuming a higher level of validity than has been demonstrated. As Ellis again suggests, such conclusions will not be warranted until it is conclusively shown that personality scores have a consistent relationship with the actual behavioral attributes of the traits presumed to be measured.

Ellis concludes that (33, p. 47) "although modern personality inventories, when employed for group diagnosis, have some degree of validity, scores obtained by individual subjects are partly or largely dependent upon (a) the subject's specific motivation at the time of taking the test; (b) the conditions under which he is tested; (c) his intelligence; (d) his degree of psychological sophistication; (e) his general test-taking attitudes; (f) his specific (conscious and unconscious) tendencies to lie to others and to himself; and (h) various other motivational and attitudinal factors." [7] When suitable correction and qualitative analytic procedures are devised for use with the inventories in order to cor-

[7] From "Recent Research with Personality Inventories," by Albert Ellis, *Journal of Consulting Psychology*, 1953, 17, 45–59. By permission of the American Psychological Association.

rect or identify these factors, the scoring and interpretation time becomes enormous. Ellis concludes his discussion with the following rather pointed statement (p. 48), "The clinical psychologist who cannot, in the time it now takes a trained worker to administer, score and interpret a test like the MMPI according to the best recommendations of its authors, get much more pertinent, incisive, and depth-centered personality material from a straightforward interview technique would hardly appear to be worth his salt."

In this vein J. Watson Wilson (94) has studied the predictability of performance on intelligence and personality scales through the use of a structured, clinical interview. He suggests that when the clinician follows a patterned interview with which he is familiar and uses tests with which he is familiar, he can predict with a fairly high degree of accuracy how the client will perform. Actually, the correlation between the clinician's prediction and the "score" was somewhat higher in certain instances than correlations between supposedly comparable tests.

To sum up the general question of structured personality tests, it can probably be agreed that the actual worth of these tests is somewhat less than what their authors claim. They have many faults, as well as assets. To dwell a little longer on the faults: The labels on the tests cannot be taken at face value. We cannot say that a high schizophrenic score on the MMPI or a high social introversion score on the STDCR means that an individual is schizophrenic. We cannot use any of these tests (either individual or batteries of tests) as a final criterion of mental health or of a particular personality parameter. Validity of most of them is shaky at best and often nonexistent. Laurance F. Shaffer (17, p. 26) sums up objections to them in his review of one.

> On the whole, the faults of the California Test of Personality are those of personality questionnaires in general. Such devices vainly seek the pot of gold at the end of the rainbow: a simple, cheap, foolproof method for studying human personality. Teachers, administrators, and school counselors who are tempted to consider the use of such devices would be benefited by a psychological insight into the fact that their own great need to do something about personality problems leads them to the delusion of accepting instruments of very low objective value.[8]

Interpreting personality on the basis of questionnaires reflects an adherence to an atomistic concept of personality, the view of personality

[8] From a review of the California Test of Personality by Laurance F. Shaffer in *The Third Mental Measurements Yearbook*, edited by Oscar K. Buros. Copyright 1949 by the Trustees of Rutgers College in New Jersey.

as a dynamic integration of many factors within and outside of the individual. Most tests do not pretend to provide such an interpretation, but some, such as the MMPI, do. However, with a realization of the shortcomings of paper-and-pencil tests, clinicians can use them to good advantage. While good scores do not necessarily reflect good adjustment, a poor score certainly indicates the need for further attention. The inventory has a better memory than the clinician—it asks all the questions all the time. It can elicit much information to be used in diagnosis, and it shows up areas that may profitably lend themselves to deeper study. Personality tests may provide a basis for structuring an interview around the results. Often a discussion of the results with the client makes it easier to direct the interview into productive channels and hasten the acquisition of insights. The testing situation itself has therapeutic possibilities. Filling out the questionnaire gives the subject an opportunity to become aware of and to assess certain areas of difficulty. Sometimes a client is more comfortable answering questions by making a check mark on a sheet of paper than in bringing up the points in an interview. William A. Hunt (62) goes so far as to suggest that group testing with group discussion of the results may have a useful place in group psychotherapy.

SUMMARY

In this chapter we have discussed the trait concept of personality, describing the structured personality tests based upon this theory. A rather extensive discussion of levels of validity was presented. Then several structured tests were described. It was suggested that, in general, structured tests are useful when we think in terms of rather basic levels of validity but that the assumption of higher levels of validity is quite dangerous and may lead to unjustified conclusions about clients.

BIBLIOGRAPHY

1. Adams, C. R., and Lepley, W. M., *The Personal Audit*. Chicago: Science Research Associates, 1945.
2. Adorno, T. W., Frenkel-Brunswick, E., *et al. The authoritarian personality*. New York: Harper, 1950.
3. Allport, G. W., and Vernon, P. E., *A study of values*. Boston: Houghton Mifflin, 1931.
4. Allport, G. W., and Allport, F. H., *The Allport A–S Reaction Study*. Boston: Houghton Mifflin, 1932.
5. Allport, G. W. and Odbert, H. S., "Trait names: a psycholexical study." *Psychol. Monogr.* 1936, Vol. 47, No. 1. (Whole No. 211), 1–171.
6. Anderson, A. L., and Hanvik, L. J, "The psychometric localization of

brain lesions: The differential effect of frontal and parietal lesions on MMPI profiles." *J. Clin. Psychol.*, 1950, 6, 177–80.

7. Bell, H. M., *The Adjustment Inventory*. Stanford: Stanford Univ. Press, 1938.

8. Benarick, S. J., Guthrie, G. M., and Snyder, W. U., "An interpretative aid for the Sc Scale of the MMPI." *J. Consult. Psychol.*, 1951, 15, 142–4.

9. Bernreuter, R. G., *Personality inventory*. Stanford: Stanford Univ. Press, 1938.

10. Bills, R. E., "Rorschach characteristics of persons scoring high and low in acceptance of self." *J. Consult. Psychol.*, 1953, 17, 36–8.

11. Bills, R. E., "A validation of changes in scores on the Index of Adjustment and Values as measures of changes in emotionality." *J. Consult. Psychol.*, 1953, 17, 135–8.

12. Bills, R. E., "A comparison of scores on the Index of Adjustment and Values with behavior in level-of-aspiration tasks." *J. Consult. Psychol.*, 1953, 17, 206–12.

13. Bills, R. E., "Acceptance of self as measured by interviews and the Index of Adjustment and Values." *J. Consult. Psychol.*, 1954, 18, 22.

14. Bills, R. E., "Self-concepts and Rorschach signs of depression." *J. Consult. Psychol.*, 1954, 18, 135–7.

15. Bills, R. E., Vance, E. L., and McLean, O. S., "An Index of Adjustment and Values." *J. Consult. Psychol.*, 1951, 15, 257–61.

16. Brown, M. A., "Alcoholic profiles on the Minnesota Multiphasic." *J. Clin. Psychol.*, 1950, 6, 266–9.

17. Buros, O. K. (ed.), *The third mental measurements year book*. New Brunswick: Rutgers Univ. Press, 1948.

18. Canter, A. H., "MMPI profiles in multiple sclerosis." *J. Consult. Psychol.*, 1951, 15, 253–6.

19. Cantor, J., "A brief screening scale for psychopathological patients developed from MMPI score patterning." *J. Clin. Psychol.*, 1955, 11, 20–4.

20. Cattell, R. B., "Temperament tests: 1. Temperament." *Brit. J. Psychol.*, 1933, 23, 308–29.

21. Cattell, R. B., "Temperament tests: 2. Tests." *Brit. J. Psychol.*, 1934, 24, 20–49.

22. Cattell, R B., "The description of personality: 2. Basic traits resolved into clusters." *J. Abnorm. Soc. Psychol.*, 1943, 38, 476–507.

23. Cattell, R. B., "Interpretation of the twelve primary personality factors." *Character and Personality,* 1944, 13, 55–91.

24. Cattell, R. B., "The principal trait clusters for describing personality." *Psychol. Bull.*, 1945, 42, 129–61.

25. Cattell, R. B., *The description and measurement of personality*. Yonkers-on-Hudson, N. Y.: World Book, 1946.

26. Cattell, R. B., "The main personality factors in questionnaire, self-estimate material." *J. Soc. Psychol.*, 1950, 31, 3–38.

27. Cattell, R. B., Saunders, D. R., and Stice, G., *Sixteen personality factor questionnaire*. Champaign, Ill.: Institute for Personality and Ability Testing, 1951.

28. Clark, J. H., "The relationship between MMPI scores and psychiatric classification of army general prisoners." *J. Clin. Psychol.*, 1952, 8, 86–9

29. Clark, J. H., "The interpretation of the MMPI profiles of college students: comparison by college major subject." *J. Clin. Psychol.*, 1953, 9, 382–4.

30. Cronbach, L. J., *Essentials of psychological testing.* New York: Harper, 1949.

31. Danielson, J. R., and Clark, J. H., "A personality inventory for induction screening." *J. Clin. Psychol.*, 1954, 10, 137–43.

32. Ellis, A., "The validity of personality questionnaires." *Psychol. Bull.*, 1946, 43, 385–445.

33. Ellis, A., "Recent research with personality inventories." *J. Consult. Psychol.*, 1953, 17, 45–9.

34. Ellis, A., and Conrad, H. S., "The validity of personality inventories in military practice." *Psychol. Bull.*, 1948, 45, 385–426.

35. Feldman, M. J., "A prognostic scale for shock therapy." *Psychol. Monogr.*, 1951, Vol. 65, No. 10 (Whole No. 327), 1–27.

36. Flanagan, J. C., *Factor analysis in the study of personality.* Stanford: Stanford Univ. Press, 1935.

37. Freeman, F. S., *Theory and practice of psychological testing.* New York: Henry Holt, 1950.

38. Freeman, M. J., "The standardization of a psychosomatic test: validation of a psychosomatic syndrome." *J. Pers.*, 1950, 19, 229–43.

39. Gough, H. C., McClosky, H., and Meehl, P. E., "A personality scale for dominance." *J. Abnorm. Soc. Psychol.*, 1951, 46, 360–6.

40. Greene, E. G., *Measurement of human behavior.* New York: Odyssey, 1941.

41. Guilford, J. P., *An Inventory of Factors STDCR.* Beverly Hills, Calif.: Sheridan Supply Co., 1940.

42. Guilford, J. P., and Guilford, R. B., "An analysis of the factors present in a typical test of introversion-extraversion." *J. Abnorm. Soc. Psychol.*, 1934, 28, 377–99.

43. Guilford, J. P., and Guilford, R. B., "Personality factors S, E, and M, and their measurement." *J. Psychol.*, 1936, 2, 109–27.

44. Guilford, J. P., and Guilford, R. B., "Personality factors D, R, T, and A." *J. Abnorm. Soc. Psychol.*, 1939, 34, 21–36.

45. Guilford, J. P., and Guilford, R. B., "Personality factors N and GD." *J. Abnorm. Soc. Psychol.*, 1939, 34, 239–48.

46. Guilford, J. P., and Martin, H., *An Inventory of Factors GAMIN*, (abridged edition). Beverly Hills, Calif.: Sheridan Supply Co., 1945.

47. Guilford, J. P., and Zimmerman, W. S., *The Guilford-Zimmerman Temperament Survey: Manual of instructions and interpretations.* Beverly Hills, Calif.: Sheridan Supply Co., 1949.

48. Hanes, B., "Reading case and MMPI results." *J. Clin. Psychol.*, 1953, 9, 83–5.

49. Hanvik, L. J., "MMPI profiles in patients with low back pain." *J. Consult. Psychol.*, 1941, 15, 350–3.

50. Harmon, L. R., and Wiener, D. N., "Use of the MMPI in vocational advisement." *J. Appl. Psychol.*, 1945, 29, 132–41.

51. Hartshorne, H., and May, M. A., *Studies in deceit.* New York: Macmillan, 1928.

52. Hartshorne, H., May, M. A., and Maller, J. B., *Studies in service and self-control.* New York: Macmillan, 1949.

53. Hartshorne, H., May, M. A., and Shuttleworth, K., *Studies in the organization of character.* New York: Macmillan, 1930.

54. Hathaway, S. R., and McKinley, J. C., *Manual for the Minnesota Personality Inventory.* New York: Psychol. Corp., 1943.

55. Hathaway, S. R., and McKinley, J. C., *Supplementary manual for the MMPI.* New York: Psychol. Corp., 1946.

56. Hathaway, S. R., and Meehl, P. E., *An atlas for the clinical use of the MMPI.* Minneapolis: Univ. of Minnesota Press, 1951.

57. Hathaway, S. R., and Monachesi, E. D., "The prediction of juvenile delinquency using the Minnesota Multiphasic Personality Inventory." *Am. J. Psychiat.*, 1951, 108, 469–73.

58. Hovey, H. B., and Stauffacher, J. C., "Intuitive versus objective prediction from a test." *J. Clin. Psychol.*, 1953, 9, 349–51.

59. Hoyt, D. P., and Magoon, T. M., "A validation study of the Taylor Manifest Anxiety Scale. *J. Clin. Psychol.*, 1954, 10, 357–61.

60. Humm, D. G., and Wadsworth, G. W., "The Human Wadsworth Temperament Scale." *Personnel J.*, 1934, 12, 314–23.

61. Humm, D. G., and Wadsworth, G. W., *The Humm-Wadsworth Temperament Scale,* Manual of Directions (rev. ed.). Los Angeles: D. G. Humm Personnel Service, 1940.

62. Hunt, W. A., and Stevenson, I., "Psychological testing in military clinical psychology: II. Personality testing." *Psychol. Review,* 1946, 53, 107–15.

63. Ingle, D. J., "A test of mental instability." *J. Appl. Psychol.*, 1934, 18, 252–66.

64. Jasper, H. H., "Measurement of depression-elation and its relation to a measure of extroversion." *J. Abnorm. Soc. Psychol.*, 1930, 25, 307–18.

65. Krout, M. H., and Tabin, J. K., "Measuring personality in developmental terms." *Genet. Psychol. Monogr.*, 1954, 50, 289–335.

66. Kuder, G. F., *Kuder Preference Record* (rev. ed.). Chicago: Science Research Associates, 1946.

67. Louttit, C. M., *Clinical psychology.* New York: Harper, 1947.

68. Maller, J. B., "Personality tests." In Hunt, J. McV. (ed.), *Personality and the behavior disorders.* New York: Ronald, 1944.

69. Martin, H. G., "The construction of the Guilford-Martin Inventory of Factors GAMIN." *J. Appl. Psychol.*, 1945, 29, 298–300.

70. McFarland, R. A., and Seitz, C. P., *P–S experience blank.* New York: Psychol. Corp., 1938.

71. Meehl, P. E., "An investigation of a general normality or control factor in personality testing." *Psychol. Monogr.* 1945, Vol. I. 59, No. 4 (Whole No. 274), 1–62.

72. Meehl, P. E., *Using the MMPI in counseling: a summary of selected new*

research results. St. Paul, Minn.: Veterans Administration Center, Fort Snelling, 1950.

73. Mosier, C. I., "A factor analysis of certain neurotic symptoms." *Psychometrika,* 1937, 2, 263–86.

74. Page, J. D., Landis, C., and Katzis, S., "Schizophrenic traits in the functional psychoses and in normal individuals." *Amer. J. Psychiat.,* 1934, 13, 1213–25.

75. Pratt, S. H., "The study of differential personality dynamics within and between various nosological groups and subgroups using objective type self report inventories." Purdue Univ. Ph.D. thesis 1952.

76. Quay, H., and Rowell, J. T., "The validity of a schizophrenic screening scale of the MMPI." *J. Clin. Psychol.,* 1955, 11, 92–3.

77. Remmers, H. H., and Silance, E. B., "Generalized attitude scales." *J. Soc. Psychol.,* 1934, 5, 298–312.

78. Roberts, G. E., "A study of the validity of the Index of Adjustment and Values." *J. Consult. Psychol.,* 1952, 16, 302–4.

79. Rogers, C. R., "Measuring personality adjustment in children nine to thirteen years of age." In *Contributions to education,* No. 548. New York: Bureau of Publications, Teachers College, Columbia Univ., 1931.

80. Shipley, W. C., and Graham, C. H., *Final report in summary of research in the personal inventory and other tests.* Applied Psychology Panel, Project N–113, Report No. 10, OSRD Rep. No. 3963, Publ. Ed., No. 12060. Washington: U.S. Dept. Commerce, 1946.

81. Stevenson, W. O., "A statistical approach to typology: the study of trait universes." *J. Clin. Psychol.,* 1950, 6, 26–37.

82. Strong, E. K., Jr., "A vocational interest test." *Educ. Rec.,* 1927, 8, 107–21.

83. Taylor, J. A., "A personality scale for manifest anxiety." *J. Abnorm. Soc. Psychol.,* 1953, 48, 285–90.

84. Thorpe, L. P., and Clark, W. W., *Mental health analysis.* Los Angeles: Calif. Test Bureau, 1946.

85. Thurstone, L. L., "The measurement of social attitudes." *J. Abnorm. Soc. Psychol.,* 1931, 26, 249–69.

86. Thurstone, L. L., and Thurstone, T. G., *Personality schedule.* Chicago: Univ. of Chicago Press, 1949.

87. Tyler, F. T., "A factorial analysis of fifteen MMPI scales." *J. Consult. Psychol.,* 1951, 15, 451–6.

88. Verniaud, W. M., "Occupational differences in the MMPI." *J. Appl. Psychol.,* 1946, 30, 604–13.

89. Wang, C. K. A., "A scale for measuring persistence." *J. Soc. Psychol.,* 1932, 3, 79–90.

90. Watson, G. B., "Happiness among adult students of education." *J. Educ. Psychol.,* 1930, 21, 79–109.

91. Weider, A., Wolff, H. G., Brodman, K., Mittelman, B., and Wechsler, D., *The Cornell Index.* New York: Psychol. Corp., 1948.

92. Wheeler, W. M., Little, K. B., and Lehner, G. F. J., "The internal structure of the MMPI." *J. Consult. Psychol.,* 1951, 15, 134–41.

93. Wiener, D. N., "A control factor in social adjustment." *J. Abnorm. Soc. Psychol.*, 1951, 46, 3–8.

94. Wilson, J. W., "Correlation of clinical estimates with test scores on mental ability and personality tests." *J. Clin. Psychol.*, 1954, 10, 97–9.

95. Winne, J. F., "A scale of neuroticism: an adaptation of the Minnesota Multiphasic Personality Inventory." *J. Clin. Psychol.*, 1951, 7, 117–22.

96. Woodworth, R. S., *Personal Data Sheet*. Chicago: C. H. Stoelting, 1917.

19

Partially Structured Personality Tests

IT HAS BEEN INDICATED THAT A DISTINCTION CAN BE MADE BETWEEN unstructured and partially structured tests based upon the extent to which the subject's responses are directed by the stimulus situation. In unstructured tests the stimulus is relatively meaningless or ambiguous, and anything seen and described or discussed by the subject depends largely upon his own perceptions. Partially structured devices present the subject with a stimulus which, although it may be somewhat ambiguous, has some meaning to the average person, and consequently the subject's response is at least partially structured by the stimulus situation. There can be all degrees of structuring and the various techniques vary on this dimension.

Since the term "projective techniques," commonly used by psychologists and other professional workers, is applied to both unstructured and partially structured devices, the reader should be prepared to associate the term with the techniques of individual evaluation described in both this and the following chapter. The various so-called projective techniques are methods of individual evaluation which leave the subject's responses much more to the subject than was true of the objective or structured personality tests described in the previous chapter. For purposes of description, we will follow the pattern of Max Hutt (44) and describe them in terms of the degree of structuring involved. The concept of projection has been bandied about, changed, enlarged, and limited by different individuals to such an extent that when it is applied to a specific technique, no particular meaning can be ascribed to it until the sponsor has stated what meaning it has for him. The concept of projection was originally used by Sigmund Freud (37), and it was given meaning in terms of testing methods by Lawrence K. Frank (36) in 1939. Various so-called projective tests have been described by several authors, and the reader should be aware particularly of excellent reviews by Harold H. and Gladys L. Anderson (7), Lawrence E. Abt and Leopold Bellak (1), and John E. Bell (11).

The task of the subject in taking an unstructured or partially structured test is one in which he attaches meaning to certain sensations, or, in other words, it is a perceptual task. The particular manner in which the subject perceives may tell us something about his unique manner of behaving. His unique mode of response may be thought of as resulting from particular experiences that he has had. It is believed that the less structured stimuli permit the diagnostician to get beyond the superficial level of behavior, enabling him to discover the inner workings and functions, the content, and the structure of personality in all its complexity more adequately than is the case with the highly structured tests. On the other hand, the less structured the stimulus situation, the more difficult is the problem of interpretation. Responses to the unstructured techniques depend entirely upon the frame of reference of the subject and may have meaning only for him. Consequently, the psychologist may gain little insight into the "why" of his behavior and can only infer what his potentialities for response may be and how he expresses these resources. For this reason, unstructured techniques are frequently thought to be most useful for the evaluation of the resources of the individual to organize, direct, and control his behavior. Partially structured techniques, since the stimuli are assumed to have meaning that can be shared by the clinician and the client, are frequently thought to be more useful for understanding the dynamics of behavior—for determining the "why" of behavior and planning treatment and rehabilitation procedures.

There are many assumptions underlying the use of unstructured and partially structured methods of behavior evaluation. The most important assumption (and perhaps a very tenuous one) is the validity of the procedures. Questions of validity arise at several levels. We can never be sure that the subject actually reports the perceptions he first experiences. At a fairly basic level of validity we can say that anything that he reports is important, and regardless of the priority of perceptions, any report has prima facie validity. It *is* what he said he saw and it *is* the manner in which he expresses himself. If we deal with the response at this level, we are certainly justified in making hypotheses concerning the meaning of a particular response.

The question of the validity of the interpretations that the clinician makes of the material produced by the client is much more complex, and it is far from being answered. It is the hope of the authors of the less structured procedures and of the research workers dealing with them that validation and reliability studies will be conducted and more exact scoring categories provided so that validity at this higher level can be demonstrated. In fact, considerable controversy exists between the point of view that these techniques should allow as much free expression as possible, and the belief that it is necessary to sacrifice some spontaneity in order to meet the demands of the more "rigorous, scientific school," that asks for careful standardization, validation, and high reliability. The philosophy in this presentation tends to favor the former rather than the latter point of view. We see the so-called projective techniques not as tests in the usual sense but as vehicles for observing the individual in a controlled and somewhat standardized situation. From this standpoint the devices have validity to the extent that they serve as the base for accurate predictions of individual behavior. In other words, the best index of the validity of these tests is the experience of the clinician and the extent to which he can use this experience to gain valuable information about his client. To put it still another way, we are not primarily interested in validity in the group-prediction and over-all statistical sense; we are interested in the "batting average" of a particular clinician as he uses the technique. Even this batting average may be difficult or impossible to compute since few adequate external criteria of prediction are available. In the last analysis, then, the value of unstructured and partially structured devices depends upon the skill with which the clinician uses them. Some of the techniques may be more adequate for certain situations, for particular purposes, and for given clients. However this adequacy will usually be a function of the kinds of information provided and the responsiveness of the client rather than a statistical index of validity or reliability.

In this chapter we will describe briefly a number of partially structured techniques or procedures. The discussion is intended to familiarize the reader with the procedures and some of their uses, and not in any sense to train him in their use. We will present, in some instances, indications of the general validity of the procedures and refer to pertinent research regarding them.

THE THEMATIC APPERCEPTION TEST

The Thematic Apperception Test (commonly called the TAT) is, at the present time, one of the two most frequently used techniques for individual personality evaluation in the United States. (The other, the Rorschach Inkblot Test, will be described in the next chapter.) The Thematic Apperception Test, which was introduced by Christiana D. Morgan and Henry A. Murray (56) in 1935, consists of a series of pictures which are presented to the subject one at a time with instructions to regard them as illustrations for stories. Robert W. White (83) reports that originally the subject was told to guess the probable facts represented in the picture; however he found in his own experience that much more of the personality of the subject was revealed by asking him to create a dramatic fiction. The current instructions imply, in words that can be adapted to the proper age and understanding of the subject, that the test offers an opportunity to use imagination. The third revision of the original set of cards distributed by the Harvard Psychological Clinic in 1936 appeared in 1943 (57). In this series of cards there are 31 pictures with eleven common to all subjects, seven for boys and men, seven for girls and women, one for boys and girls together, one each for females and males, one for males and females together, and one each for boys and girls.

Different test administrators use different procedures, and many vary the selection of pictures in terms of their knowledge about the subject. However, according to Murray's suggestions, each subject is presented nineteen pictures printed on white Bristol board and one blank card, calling for a total of twenty stories. These twenty cards are divided into two series of ten each, the pictures in the second series being more unusual, dramatic, and bizarre than those in the first. Approximately one hour is devoted to each series, the two sessions being separated by a day or more. The directions usually stress that it is a test of imagination and that the subject's task is to make up as dramatic a story as possible for each picture. The story should include what has led up to the event in the picture, the present situation, and the outcome. Approximately five minutes—this is very flexible—are allowed for each story.

The instructions can be varied according to the age and particular capacities of the subject. One of the procedures about which clinicians differ is the inquiry in which some may inquire as to the source of the story, and any lack of clarity. In the original use of the TAT an interview was held a few days after the completion of the test. In this interview the source of the story was sought by questioning, and free associations to the various elements of the stories were secured. Some administrators inquire immediately after each story, and others, such as Julian B. Rotter (63), emphasize the necessity of postponing the inquiry until all the pictures have been presented.

Practically all clinicians agree that the recording should be verbatim, that behavioral observations should be noted, and that if parts of the stories are omitted, the subject may be reminded of this by having the instructions repeated. Some examiners stress taking down the reaction time and the total time required for telling the story. With the several variations of administrative procedure that have been suggested, it is clear that the amount and kinds of material obtained will vary from clinician to clinician.

There are also many different approaches to the scoring and interpretation of TAT stories. In the 1943 manual Murray recommends that the successive events in each story be analyzed into the force or forces emanating from the hero and the force or forces emanating from the environment. First, the hero is identified; second, motives, trends, and feelings of the hero are noted; and third, the forces in the hero's environment, the outcomes, themata, interests, and sentiments are noted. This has been described as a "need press" system. Morris I. Stein (75) has developed a scoring system based on this concept of needs and presses. He stresses the following factors in the technique of clinical analysis and interpretation: the hero, the environmental stimuli, the hero's behavior, cathexes, inner states, the manner in which the behavior is expressed, and the outcomes. In addition to the content material Stein suggests that other factors should be studied: the client's behavior during the test, his reaction to the examiner, his reaction to the test situation as a whole and to each of the cards, the relationships between instructions and the sequence of events in the story, the client's use of the objective characteristics of the pictures, the sequence of reference to the stimuli in the pictures, the language used, and any use of symbolism in the stories.

Leopold Bellak (12) believes that TAT pictures are best seen psychologically as a series of social situations and interpersonal relations. His scoring categories include the main theme, the main hero, the main needs of the hero, the conception of the environment, significant conflicts, the nature of anxieties, the main defenses, the severity of the superego, and the integration of the ego.

Silvan S. Tomkins (78) attempts to tap the varying levels of abstraction in the hope that significant aspects will be detected in diverse protocols by the use of concepts ranging from a level of broad generality to a high degree of specificity. Four major categories are designed for this purpose: vectors, levels, conditions, and qualifiers. *Vectors* refer to the psychological direction characteristic of behavioral strivings, wishes, cathexes, and feelings. *Levels* involve the plane of psychological functioning indicated by the story. *Conditions* refer to any psychological, social, or physical state that is not itself behavior, striving, or wish. Finally, Tomkins uses *qualifiers* to refer to the more specific aspects of the other three (temporal characteristics, contingencies, intensity, negation, subsidiation, and causality).

Saul Rosenzweig (62) recommends the following steps to be used in the scoring procedure: (a) assimilation of the stories by several careful and complete rereadings; (b) descriptive analysis of productions; (c) statistical evaluations of responses with reference to available norms; (d) topic generalizations in which common elements of stories are abstracted; (e) composite generalizations in which relationships among topical generalizations are developed; (f) integration of composite generalizations with anamnestic and other test data to educe significant psychodynamic hypotheses.

Edith Weisskopf-Joelson (81) has proposed a quantitative measure of projection called the transcendence index. This index is computed from descriptions of pictures rather than stories about pictures. In fact, she asks her subjects to describe the pictures rather than to tell a story. The transcendence index of a picture is arrived at by counting the comments about a picture which go beyond pure description. Although this procedure lends itself nicely to research studies of various kinds, it is probable that the clinical utility of the concept has not as yet been completely developed.

The scoring and interpretation system of David Rapaport, Merton M. Gill, and Roy Schafer (60) and that of Rotter (63) are similar in general outline. These investigators analyze the formal characteristics of the stories, the compliance of the subject with instructions, and the intra-individual and inter-individual consistency of the stories. They also base interpretations on the content of the stories, which is divided into prevailing tone of the narrative, the figures in the story, strivings, attitudes, and obstacles or barriers.

And so we could go on and on describing various scoring schemes and the derived interpretations arising out of different theories of personality and of behavior. In general, the clinician's choice of a scoring system probably depends upon his personal orientation rather than his belief that the absolute truth will be revealed by one method rather than by another. The practical use of the TAT can best be illustrated by consideration of an actual application of the test in a school counseling situation. The following material has been adapted from a report by Arden N. Frandsen and Margaret Hunter (35) and indicates the kinds of stories which might be given to some of the pictures, an interpretation of them, and, finally, something of the use that is made of them.

This child was presented by her teacher as a problem of extreme aggression. To quote from her teacher's statement at the time:

"Jane is eleven years of age and is constantly involved in quarrels, and is very aggressive. She takes great pleasure in hurting or tormenting other children, and never passes up an opportunity to trip, poke, pinch, slap, or throw ink on other children. She will not let them work quietly and undisturbed. She apparently has no sense of fair play, tattles if other children retaliate, but lies and refuses to accept any blame for what she does herself. She is defiant and sullen with her teacher, and talks and mutters to herself a great deal. Other children do not pick on her—they are glad to have her join in games, but she often causes trouble. She seems to make no effort to win friends on her own account. Family background is poor. Her parents are separated and her mother lives in Michigan. She does not seem to know where her father is. Two older brothers are married and have homes of their own, and two younger children, a brother and a sister, live with the eldest brother in Detroit. Jane thinks they may live with their mother part of the time when they are not with the brother but she is not sure. Jane lives with foster parents in Indianapolis. These foster parents are friends of the family and they seem to be genuinely interested in her. She is kept clean and is always nicely dressed. However, she told her teacher that when she is twelve, she may go to live with her mother—seemed to look forward to it. She is slow scholastically, but does fair work."

The teacher, who has had considerable teaching experience, had been so disturbed at the constant turmoil Jane kept the class in, that she had gone to the principal with the demand that he take some action. He immediately called the foster mother, who came to school for a consultation. She expressed great distress at what had been going on and kept repeating that she just couldn't believe it—she was trying so hard to teach Jane to be a lady, and just couldn't believe that a girl who went to church would do those things. When called to the office, Jane admitted that she had done all the things she was accused of and said that she didn't know why, except "the kids are mean to me." The foster mother admitted she had a great deal of trouble in handling Jane herself. Later, the teacher found out from Jane that she was never permitted to leave for school before a quarter of eight and must report home by 3:30 P.M. That if she were to stay and help the teacher she must ask her mother in advance. She explained that "she says that way I can't get into any fights, 'cause I'll just have enough time to get to school." Evidently she had serious troubles out of school. "The visit by the foster mother helped for a day or two, but that was all," the teacher reported.

It seemed justifiable from the information at hand to explain Jane's sullen, resentful, and sometimes defiant attitude and extreme aggressiveness toward other children as a "case" of displaced aggression due to frustration she was experiencing from probable feelings of rejection by her own parents, from difficulty in establishing secure relations with the foster parents, from unsatisfactory adjustment to school, and from lack of feeling accepted and loved by her age-mates. And although an analysis of Jane's environment—home, school, and play relationships—revealed sufficient limitations to account for her maladjustment, it also appeared desirable for us to understand *how Jane perceived herself, her associates, and her problems.* To achieve such an "inside" view, the Thematic Apperception Test was administered.

The following 10 pictures were presented in the order of their listing here and Jane's stories for each are reproduced below:

#2. Picture shows outdoor scene. Man working in fields, woman leaning against a tree, a girl with books.

"The girl is going to school. Her mother is thinking how the garden will come out—if it will be a success or what. The girl is sad. Maybe they came on a place where there were Indians and maybe they killed someone in her family. The man is glad to plow his garden 'cause he wants to have something to eat. They might be trying to get rich. They are there because the Indians ran them away and the girl likes to go to school because when she grows up she'll get an education and be a school teacher."

#9GF Picture. Girl running along a beach. Another girl hidden behind tree, watching first girl.

"This girl is running away because she stole something—maybe she did something she shouldn't have done and the police are after her. The other girl heard about it on the radio and got a description of her and she is watching her. She is going to call the police and show them where she has gone. She stole because she wanted something real bad. They'll catch her with some hound dogs and carry her to jail. Her folks will feel bad and they wouldn't think she did it. She is happy now, but when they take her to jail she'll wish she hadn't done it."

#7GF Picture. Woman sitting beside child in living room. Is reading to her. Child is leaning against woman.

"This lady is reading to her little girl. Maybe the little girl's daddy died in the war and she is thinking about her daddy. The mother is reading to her to make her not think about her daddy so she will probably forget it. The little girl is looking outside and maybe she is forgetting for that day. They are going to be happy because she is going to get some presents and the little girl already has some new shoes."

#3GF Picture. Girl crying.

"Once there was a girl and her mother died. Then the girl went away to another house. She kept on going to school and she liked it at school. Someone beat her up because she called them a name they didn't like and now the girl is crying. The girl started it so her mother isn't going to do nothin'. They will send her to the Juvenile School and she will have to work. The kids talked about her and then she started calling other kids names that never bothered her and that's how she got into so much trouble. When she comes out of Reform School, then she'll work and be a secretary and get married."

#10 Picture. Woman crying.

"The lady is crying because some of her children have run away. Maybe they didn't like to go to school 'cause they'd get in lots of fights. Maybe 'cause they were poor and their mother and daddy didn't have enough money and they have to wear their clothes a long time and the kids say they're dirty. They wouldn't like that and start crying and then one day they ran away. And her husband says they'll try to find them. They found them a year later and they were living at a hotel with some of their friends, and they were happy. They said they didn't want to go back home because all the kids would make fun of them and they didn't want to be poor. They went back home and found that all the kids started liking them and then they wished they didn't run away."

#8GF Picture. Girl leaning against door. Thoughtful mood.

"She is thinking maybe she'll steal something and maybe not. She didn't have nothing and doesn't have a mother and daddy to help her and she don't want to work but has to clean up the house. So every time she goes to the store she steals a loaf of bread. Every time she goes she steals something and brings it home under her coat and eats it, except she don't have meat. Sometimes she finds things and sometimes she steals things and sells them and then she buys meat. She is thinking how can she steal something. Shall she wait till they close up at night time or steal something in the daytime? And that was how she made her living by stealing things. She didn't care if she steals things and finally the police caught up with her. They put her in prison all of her life, but she still doesn't care."

#1 Picture. Boy with violin on table in front of him.

"Once there was a little boy. He is reading the notes so he will learn to play. He wishes he was outside but he'd like to play the violin too. His mother makes him practice. He's seen

lots of more kids do it so he wanted one. Then when he got it
he didn't want to play it and wishes he didn't take violin lessons. He's going to keep on playing it till the year is over. Then
he won't take violin lessons any more but just go outside and
play. It is his fault so he don't blame his mother for it."

#17GF Picture. Girl leaning on railing of bridge looking
down at boats below. Dusky effect.

"The girl is looking into the sea. She is watching them
loading and taking boxes off the boats. It is going to rain and
she feels cold and scared. She is thinking she'd like to go to the
place where those people came from. Maybe they came from
New England and she'd like to see what it looks like. She's
thinking how could she get on the boat? She is going to run
away and see that land and next time when the ship comes back
she will come back home. But she falls in the water and drowns
because she couldn't swim."

(Tried #G-13 next but child said, "I can't tell a story
about that! I can't see anything to tell a story about!" Picture
was of a small child on circular staircase with light above. Saw
picture #5 underneath, which clinician hadn't chosen, and
said "I can tell one about that.")

#5 Picture. Woman is peering through partly opened
door into empty room.

"Maybe her little girl went outside and didn't do her work
and she is peeping in there and she's mad 'cause her little girl
didn't do her work. She calls her in the house and she can't
find her. She went to the little girl's friend's house and still
couldn't find her. So she went back home and she still didn't
hear nothing from her little girl—so she called the police. She
gave them a picture of her little girl and told them what kind
of clothes she had on. They found the little girl at her sister's
house in the next town. The mother whipped her and the little
girl never ran away again."

#16 Picture. A complete blank. Child told to imagine
what might be there.

"This is about a fish pond. Once upon a time there was a
fishing pond and there were some people living there. They had
a little girl and a little boy. One time the little girl and the little boy went to the pond to fish. The little girl, she stuck her
feet in the water. The little boy threw his fish pole in and she

got her foot caught on the fish pole. Her brother took her home and when her mother and father came out she was crying. They saw the brother carrying her and trying to carry the fish pole too. The daddy got a blanket and they laid her down and called the doctor. He had to take her to the hospital so they had an operation on her foot. They had to put stitches in her leg and a cast on it. And she couldn't go to school for a month. The brother brought her books home and she studied at home. She would always do her work and she went to school when the doctor said that she could. Some kids pushed her down because they didn't like her and she broke her leg. She got well and when she grew up she was a movie star."

SUMMARY INTERPRETATION OF STORIES

Identifications and interpersonal relations. Jane is obviously identified with an unhappy, anxious, aggressive, guilty, and unconfident "little girl," who feels rejected by both parents and playmates and who expects and accepts vague punishments. Other important characters projected into her stories are "mother" and "daddy," whose loss to her is keenly felt (7GF, 3GF, 8GF); a mother substitute (3GF) who is coercive (1), ever-ready to catch her in wrongdoing (9GF), lacking in sympathy and protectiveness (3GF), but also on occasion comforting to her (7GF); play and school mates whom she feels reject her, but whose friendship she wants intensely (3GF, 10); the police (5, 9GF, 8GF); and other vaguely-sensed hostile people (the attacking "Indians" in response to #2 picture).

Motives and goals. The dominant positive motives or needs in her life are for acceptance, love, security, status, mastery, and achievement. But because in these needs she is severely frustrated, she is pained with anxiety, feelings of inferiority and guilt. The deep, pervading nature of her anxiety is indicated especially by her reference to being "cold and scared" (17GF), by the need to have her mother read to her so she will *forget for a day* about her daddy who died (7GF), and very probably by her rejection (repression of a response) of Card 13 depicting a girl *all alone* on a long *bare* stairway (it was probably too anxiety provoking). Her feelings of inferiority and especially of guilt are frequently indicated (9GF, 3GF, 8GF, 1, 17GF, 5). She steals, she "calls other kids names that never bothered her," she is spied upon (9GF, 5). And when she tries to escape her difficulties, "she falls in the water and drowns because she couldn't swim" (17GF)—she is too inferior. Her status and mastery needs are indicated by her aspirations to be a teacher (2), a secretary (3GF), or a movie star (16). And her strong needs for love, solicitude, and sympathy, though referred to frequently, are most emphatically expressed in her projections to the blank card (16), wherein her brother, mother, father, and the doctor all care for her tenderly when she first gets a fishhook in her foot and then breaks her leg when the kids who didn't like her pushed her down.

Environment. The barriers to satisfaction of Jane's desires are perceived as (a) hostile people—police, a spying "mother" (5) and "other girl" (9GF), and children who "don't like her," "push her down," "talk about her," "call her dirty," and "beat her up"; (b) the loss of mother and daddy to love and care for her; (c) her own inferiority and lack of confidence; (d) being poor and lacking "meat" and "something you want real bad"; and (e) a somewhat unsympathetic (3GF), overcritical (5), and coercive (1) foster mother. But her environment is also supportive: even though school involves "lots of fights," she likes it and it will be a means to status and achievement; and her "mother," despite her limitations, sometimes comforts her (7GF), whips her so "she never ran away again," and since it was his own fault, (he) "don't blame his mother for it."

Modes of adjustment. Thus in the main thwarted, how does Jane try to adjust—achieve substitute or compromise satisfactions? Her modes of adjustment include wishes and half-hearted attempts to escape, repression, fantasy, aggression, appeals for sympathy, compromise, and self-improvement (getting an education) and work. Jane is preoccupied with escaping vaguely from her unhappy situations. At least four times the character with whom she identifies "runs away" (9GF, 10, 17GF, 5), but because of Jane's pervading anxiety and lack of confidence, they always come back and "wished they hadn't run away" or "never run away again." Some aspects of her life are so anxiety-provoking that they are repressed. She is read to so she will forget for a day, and Card 13 was rejected. Her resort to fantasy is indicated, in such frequently used expressions as "she is thinking" or "(he) wishes" (7GF, 8GF, 1, 17GF), by some unrealistically achieved happy endings and more specifically by stories (10, 5) in which her parents search persistently for her (her wish projected to her parents). Her aggression is revealed in stealing (9GF, 8GF), fighting other children, and calling them names. That Jane understands that at least part of her aggression is "displaced aggression" is indicated when she says "she started calling other kids names that never bothered her and that's how she got into so much trouble." Her ready acceptance of blame and punishment for her own wrong-doing ("They put her in prison all of her life, but she still doesn't care"), suggests that her aggression is also turned against herself and is related, of course, to her feelings of guilt.

In at least two instances Jane identifies with a character who attains her desires by appeals to sympathy (10, 16), but use of sympathy is most clearly revealed when because of her injuries she is showered with the love and attention of brother, mother, father, and doctor. She also compromises, first fulfills an unpleasant duty and then enjoys herself at play in (1). And in three instances she attains status eventually (becomes a teacher, secretary, or movie star) by study and work.

Outcomes. These latter two modes of attack upon problems indicate that Jane finds fair opportunities for achieving important motivational satisfaction by direct learning and problem-solving efforts, and that she is not yet bound by habits of escape, repression, aggression, and appeals to sympathy. But lacking opportunities, these are her present developmental trends. And although Jane feels guilty, lacks confidence, is resigned to or subconsciously wants (because of her guilt) punishment, and in one instance drowns because of the lack of ability, she seems not completely unoptimistic about eventual outcomes. In more than half her stories the endings were happy. She should, therefore, respond favorably to a school, home and play environment in which she could, in "give and take" relationships find satisfaction of her needs for acceptance, love, security, status, and achievement. And this development toward better mental health could also probably be promoted and hastened by a type of individual relationship therapy which would lessen her anxiety, increase her self-insight, and reorient her toward perception of a less hostile community of people. This diagnosis was developed in cooperation with Jane's teacher. The teacher had formerly reacted somewhat antagonistically to Jane's aggressive attitude and behavior; but now that she recognized her real motives and needs, the teacher immediately made an effort to provide for as many of Jane's needs as possible. Four ways of helping Jane were employed, including (1) counseling or modified play therapy, (2) promoting better relations between Jane and her classmates, (3) helping her to find more satisfaction in school work, and (4) helping Jane's foster mother to give her more acceptance and love. How this was done is told in excerpts from a report by the teacher.

TREATMENT

Situations were devised where the teacher and Jane could talk freely, with no interruptions. This had to be done after school when Jane was helping straighten the room, decorate, etc. The conversations were quite informal, since the teacher was trying to make Jane feel free, and comfortable enough that a relationship therapy could be developed, whereby she could express herself freely and what she said would be accepted with no reaction of surprise, disappointment, or shock. The teacher was anxious that Jane reach the goals of self-understanding in relationship to others, acquire greater frustration tolerance, become re-conditioned to respond with less enmity and guilt, have opportunities for releasing her tensions, hoping that they would eventually disappear and that she might with greater confidence and pleasure work toward attainable worthwhile objectives.

To Jane's complaint that "the kids pick on me," the teacher assured and interpreted that that often seemed to be true, and that yet, with some children, especially boys, teasing seemed to be just their funny way of getting acquainted and making friends. That learning to "take it" was just part of the fun. To this, Jane smilingly agreed. During these talks the teacher let Jane know that she loved her and that no matter what she did she would care for her, simply because she was Jane. When she corrected her it didn't mean she had ceased to love her, but just that she was anxious to help her attain her goal. Or, perhaps she (the teacher) was having a bad day, as everyone does, when things went wrong and she was maybe cranky and cross, but that friends learn to overlook those things in each other. For about three weeks Jane made some excuse to linger a moment after the others were gone, just to tell the teacher goodnight.

In the meantime, efforts were being made to improve relations with her classmates. Shortly after her first talk with Jane, the teacher mentioned to the class (Jane was out of the room), that she had noticed that Jane was trying hard to stay out of trouble. She suggested that it might be the kind thing to "give her a break" and show her that "we really like her" by overlooking any occasional outbreaks. Every opportunity was taken to give her deserved praise in the presence of the class. Since she is tall (it had been frankly commented on by the children when they were being weighed and measured) the teacher remarked on what a fine well-proportioned body she had, and how straight she stood. Her neatness in dress and appearance and the fact that she did her own ironing, even to the ruffles, were noted.

The other children never had been really antagonistic toward Jane. They had simply avoided her lest they be involved in a fight. They now began to make friendly overtures which were happily accepted. One little girl was especially nice to her and it wasn't long before Jane had a friend to walk to and from school with. Formerly, she had always been alone. About this time her lingering after school to say good-night ceased, as she had to meet Mary. She has been observed since on her way home and is seldom alone. Frequently she is with a group.

One day when she was talking with her teacher after school about some fun she had had at recess, she remarked, "You know, I used to shove the kids 'cause I was mad, but now when I do it, it's just for fun." Which showed a beginning of self-understanding. When the teacher reprimanded one boy for playing too rough, Jane said, "Oh, it's all right. He didn't hurt me. We were only playing." This was quite a change in the girl who would turn fiercely and fight if anyone accidentally brushed against her. As her frustration lessened, she began to acquire tolerance.

She was also encouraged with the comments that most of the things she did in her school work were correct and that she was increasing her speed. The teacher's first impression as to her being "very slow scholastically" has been somewhat altered. A great deal of her slowness is a matter of getting things down on paper—she is hampered by a very slow, cramped handwriting. And where at first she demanded a great deal of help, she now seems to have more confidence in herself and goes ahead on her own, which shows that she is getting nearer the goal of independence. She nearly always attempts a solution now, before asking for help. Also insists on finishing a task, regardless of how long it takes, showing a great gain in patience and less feeling of frustration.

Soon after, when report cards came out, the teacher enclosed a note to Jane's foster mother saying that she had once called her to school because of the girl's misbehavior, and she would now be very happy to have her come to visit any day she chose, to see how well she was getting along. She felt sure that the foster mother would be very proud of her.

A week later, although there had been no visit from the

foster mother, she apparently had reacted to the favorable letter with a change of attitude which was very helpful to Jane. The Monday after report cards came out, Jane came to school with some crepe paper flowers she had made for the teacher. She seemed to be quite pleased—said that her foster mother had bought the paper for her and had given her a needle and spool of thread and let her make what she wanted to. She was going to make a skirt for her little cousin out of part of the paper, and "my mother says pretty soon she is going to buy some of that stuff you make pretty towels out of and show me how to make them."

It has been a great satisfaction to her teacher to see the adjustments that Jane has made, and it has made for greater happiness for everyone with whom she comes in contact. The change has not come over night and there are still occasional bad days, but they are getting further and further apart. To the teacher, the speed with which she has made her readjustment in attitude is quite remarkable. (It has also been noticed by other teachers in the building.) She still needs reassurance, as her frequent question, "Am I doing better?" would indicate. The genuine liking of the class is shown by the fact that not long ago she was nominated for an office. While she didn't make it, she made a good run. She has practically no conflicts with class members any more. In fact, one of her best friends is a girl with whom she quarreled violently in the fall, and whose brother threatened her with a knife. While she still needs guidance, the goals mentioned earlier are becoming clearer to her and she has made great achievement in this line.[1]

The TAT has been described and discussed in considerable detail as an example of a partially structured personality test or evaluative technique. It has been demonstrated by many clinicians that the TAT pictures are useful stimuli for the elicitation of verbal material from a client. Whether we regard the material as fantasy or otherwise, trained and experienced clinicians can use the material to add to their understanding of their clients.

With a technique as widely used as the TAT we are constantly finding research problems both of a methodological and a theoretical nature that center about the procedure. This text will make no attempt whatsoever to characterize or summarize this research. Our purpose here is to familiarize the reader with the technique and to present it as an illustration of partially structured techniques. It is doubtful whether many training programs for clinical or counseling psychologists exist in which there is not a specialized course for the consideration of the TAT and related procedures. A more detailed examination of the theory and research data concerning the test will properly be considered in such courses.

THE CHILDREN'S APPERCEPTION TEST

The history of the Children's Apperception Test (CAT) is a very short one, as the manual (13) was only published in 1949. According to the manual, the original idea for the CAT was first offered by Ernst Kris in a discussion of theoretical problems of projection and of the TAT with Leopold Bellak. Kris pointed out that one can expect children to identify much more readily with animals than with humans (something known supposedly since the paper by Freud on the analysis of little Hans, "The Phobia of a Five-Year-Old"). It will be noted that this concept, broadened to a wider population in terms of age, is employed in the Blacky Test of Gerald S. Blum (15), to be described shortly, a test employing a family of animals. However, a more recent study by Mary Ann Smith Armstrong (8) throws some doubt on this hypothesis since she shows that children actually make more comments that go beyond pure description when human figures are used. In any case, Leopold and Sonya Sorel Bellak, after thinking the whole problem over for nearly a year, specified a number of situations fundamental to children which might conceivably be expected to expose the dynamic workings of a child's problems. It seemed that the TAT did not entirely fulfill the needs with young children, and, theoretically, Bellak and Bellak had reason to believe that animals might be preferred as identification figures for children from three years up to possibly ten. Thus they set out to create, pictorially, situations vital to this age range. A professional illustrator of children's books drew eighteen pictures, which were photostated. Some of them were used by the authors, and others were distributed to a number of psychologists working with small children. On the basis of experience with these pictures the number was reduced to the ten that had been found most useful, and the CAT resulted.

The CAT consists of ten pictures depicting animals in various situations. The pictures were designed with the hope of eliciting responses relative to feeding problems, oral problems, sibling rivalry, attitudes toward parental figures and the way these figures are perceived, the child's relationship to the parents as a couple (oedipal situation), the fantasies centering around aggression, acceptance by the adult world, the fear of being lonely at night, masturbation, and toilet behavior. After the examiner has established rapport with the child, he presents the ten cards in serial order. Whenever possible, the authors recommend that the test be presented as a game. If the child knows it is a test, the examiner explains that it is not competitive. It is suggested that the child be told that he and the examiner are going to engage in a game in which the child is to tell a story about pictures, that he is to tell what is going on and what the animals in the pictures are doing. At certain points in the story the child may be asked what went on in the story before and what will happen later. Responses are recorded verbatim, and after all the stories have been told, the examiner can go over each one asking for elaboration of specific points, and questions may be asked regarding the particular type of outcome of certain stories. If this is not possible immediately, the inquiry should be attempted as soon after administration of the test as possible. All side remarks and activities should be noted as they occur in relation to the story being told.

The authors have listed typical responses to each of the ten pictures, based on the records of approximately one hundred children between the ages of three and ten. In the interpretation, although the examiner should keep in mind that any individual response has unique meaning for the person giving it, he should compare the individual's responses with those of others. The authors of the test have also supplied a blank to be used in analyzing each story in terms of a number of variables. The summary sheet provided records the main themes and the main data, and the final report on the test consists of the summation of the salient facets of the personality as they reveal themselves in this behavioral situation.

THE MICHIGAN PICTURE TEST

A number of criticisms have been levied against the use of the TAT with children and adolescents. The pictures themselves, for one thing, have little face validity for use with children or with adolescents. Even the few pictures that appear to contain child or adolescent figures have relatively little appeal for the younger person. Furthermore, some of the TAT pictures are traumatic for the younger age groups, and the end result may be blocking or resistance to responding. The CAT is designed for the age range from three to ten years. Because there was no picture-story test specifically designed for older children, the Michigan Picture Test (6, 43, 80) was developed to investigate and measure the emotional reactions of children of from eight to fourteen years.

The test consists of twenty picture cards and one blank one. These are divided into two series of twelve pictures each, with some of the cards used in both series. In the standardization process, only one series was given to each child. The pictures portray reality situations such as those involving intra-familial conflicts, conflicts with authority figures, conflicts involving physical danger, sexual difficulties, conflicts arising out of school, feelings of personal inadequacy, confusions in the self-percept, conflicts involving aggressive drives, and feelings of social inadequacy. A scoring procedure resulting in a "tension index" has been developed. Although there has been but limited clinical experience with the scale, the following uses have been suggested:

(a) It may be used to assist in gaining a diagnostic appraisal of the child.

(b) The test may be used as a means of screening children in schools or other group situations so that those who most need clinical help may be selected.

(c) The test may be used as a cathartic agent to assist in the process of therapy.

THE BLACKY TEST

The Blacky Test (15) is a rather specialized kind of picture test which was designed to investigate the psychoanalytic concept of psychosexual development. However it is believed by the author (Blum) that it can also be used to discover other largely unconscious patterns of motivation within the individual. The results may also point toward clues that can be investigated in the progress of therapy. The test consists of twelve cartoon drawings that depict the adventures of a dog named Blacky. The first cartoon is an introduction to the cast of characters: Blacky, Mama, Papa, and Tippy who is a sibling figure. Each of the eleven subsequent cartoons is designed to portray either a stage of psychosexual development, such as the anal sadistic, or a type of object relationship within that development, such as positive ego ideal. The same cartoons are used for both male and female subjects, but when the subject is a male, Blacky is described as "son," and when female, "daughter." The cartoons are highly structured, and it is believed that they have face validity for the dimensions under scrutiny. For example, the oral eroticism cartoon depicts Blacky nursing on the mother.

The subject is asked to write vividly about how the characters feel, and each cartoon is accompanied by questions below the stories which are to be answered. The questions are mostly of the multiple-choice type, in which the subject is asked to pick the most applicable alternative, and there are also some direct questions requiring one or two sentences to answer. The client is asked to indicate whether he likes each cartoon, and to select the ones he likes best of all and write down the reasons. The same is also done for the most disliked. The subject is scored as being "very strong," "fairly strong," "weak," or "absent" on each of several dimensions that are characteristic of specific psychoanalytic concepts. On the basis of the scores and information relative to age and sex of siblings and age of parents, the author feels that interpretation of the psychosexual history and the status of development of the subject is possible.

THE MAKE–A–PICTURE STORY TEST

Since 1947 when Edwin S. Shneidman (71, 72) introduced the Make-a-Picture Story Test (MAPS), he and various other experimenters have studied its use with different subjects and groups of subjects (38, 73). This test, combining the features of a number of tests, consists of 67 cut-out figures, among which a six-foot human figure is represented by a cut-out that is five and a half inches high, and other figures are scaled proportionately. With few exceptions, the figures are standing. In the test the subject uses cardboard cutout figures as actors against a stage background to tell a story of his own devising. There are twenty-one backdrop pictures to be used as stages. They represent highly structured situations such as a bridge or a bathroom, and less structured situations such as a dream cloud or a blank card. The figures can fit realistically on any of the backgrounds. The task is a variation of the World Test, to be described next, in that materials are selected by the client and manipulated by him. In a sense, too, the task is a variation of the psychodrama in which the stage and cast are provided and the subject is left to project onto the stage whatever personnel in whatever action he desires.

Using the figures, which include human, mythological, and animal figures, the subject populates background pictures, one at a time, composing a story for each situation he has created. As each story is completed, the examiner conducts an inquiry regarding: (a) any important aspect of the instructions omitted in the stories, such as how it turned out; (b) any part of the story not clear to the examiner; (c) the age, sex, or personality of any of the characters in the story with whom the examiner feels the subject may be identifying; and (d) the title of the story. The examiner's tasks are two: to record verbatim the story related about a given construction, including all verbalizations, and to complete a figure location sheet as a permanent record of the figures used and their placements. Usually ten background pictures are given serially to each subject. Certain quantitative scoring categories have been proposed and suggestions have been made for qualitative interpretations, but no very exact scoring methods have been developed. The interpretation is usually based on the choice of figures, the interaction among characters, the description of characters, and the themes that persist in the stories. The test situation appears to have rather high subject appeal and to give definite support to timid subjects by giving them manipulative figures from which to choose.

THE WORLD TEST

The World Test, developed empirically by Margaret Lowenfeld (47, 48, 49) as an instrument to facilitate communication with children, consists of small toys representing houses, trees, fences, cars, people, animals, and the like, with which the subject is asked to construct whatever he wishes. Because it is semistructured in nature, it requires the subject to "project" in order to make a construction. He must organize elements of his experience in order to combine the materials in a way that has meaning for him, and in so doing he makes something that is uniquely his. In the construction of his World, the subject manipulates materials in somewhat the same way as materials are manipulated in play. For this reason we might expect some of the same principles to apply. These include the theory that play represents the individual's emotions, fantasies, and experiences on a nonverbal level, and that it may, in the case of the child, be an avenue for expression of experience that is preverbal. As the objects are manipulated in space, they become recognizable configurations to which language may become attached and they may therefore be dealt with on a verbal level.

Lowenfeld (48) stated explicitly in her first presentation of the test that it was based on no particular theory; her aim was that of a clinician who wished to devise a procedure that children could use to reveal their emotional and mental states without the intervention of an adult, either by transference or interpretation, and which would allow of a record being made of such a demonstration. She found that when a series of worlds was made, it seemed to display a connected line of thought, in which situations were elaborated on from day to day. The series might represent a fantasied situation or a real one. Although Lowenfeld found that the World materials contributed information that was helpful in diagnoses, prognoses, and treatment planning, she did not approve its use as a test from which conclusions might be drawn from a single observation. Specifically, she stated (49) that nothing of value could be learned from the first World, partly because the problem had not yet been completely presented and partly because the meaning of the items to the child had not yet been made clear to the clinician. Interest in the particular meaning of the materials to the subject and repeated administrations of the test are two uses of the test which differ from the use made of it by those who regard the technique only as a projective test.

Hedda Bolgar and Liselotte K. Fischer (17, 31) have done extensive work on standardizing World materials for adults. They devised scoring sheets and compiled norms for both clinical and normal groups. They found that the normal person makes a small village or town by building a "skeleton" using houses, bridges, possibly trees and fences, filling in details after the basic structure is developed. The normal person may use from 35 to 120 items from several different categories, and his construction has a two-dimensional quality, resembling an airplane view. Charlotte Buhler (24, 25) also standardized some of the performances and apparently is now in the process of making further standardizations, with emphasis upon establishing norms for clinical groups, mainly children. J. C. Michael and Buhler (55) found that the Worlds of neuropsychiatric subjects, both adults and children, were of the following six types, and that these types were indicative of maladjustment in a person's attitude toward life and were characteristic of different personality disorders: (a) aggressive Worlds, depicting fights, fires, attacking animals, etc., associated with open aggressiveness; (b) unpopulated Worlds which, though otherwise complete, had no people—these were found in subjects avoiding open aggression of the first type, but who had concealed hostility against or fear of people; (c) empty Worlds, containing less than fifty items, characteristic of mentally deficient subjects but also indicating lack of interest or inner emptiness; (d) closed Worlds, surrounded by fences, indicating fears or hostility, especially prevalent in the Worlds of children of four or five years of age; (e) disorganized Worlds, showing unplanned or poorly planned arrangements, indicating inner confusion; and (f) rigid Worlds, where things not usually in rigid arrangement were lined up in rows, indicating inner inhibitions and deep-seated conflicts.

Janet M. Lyon (53) has reported that the test appears to be valuable diagnostically for both adults and children. She feels that it is most useful in the way Lowenfeld has described, namely, as an instrument of communication in treatment. Children can apparently use the materials time after time, often each time narrowing down the selection of items, until only those that most specifically express the central conflicts are retained. With these the child attempts to work out his problems on a small scale. Lyon has experimented with the use of the technique with adult psychotic patients in much the same way. All the experience and evidence suggest that this technique, which offers a vehicle for nonverbal expression and serves as a facilitator for verbal expression, is an extremely promising procedure for use in evaluation and in counseling or therapy.

STRUCTURED DOLL PLAY

Before citing a specific structured or partially structured doll-play test, let us examine the use of play as an evaluative procedure. Play is the diagnostic or evaluative procedure particularly suited to the study of children, since it is their natural activity and not a new, frightening medium. As White (83) has stated, it is a complex activity, and its nature cannot be stated in a single formula. It may involve many motives and many needs such as wish fulfillment, the need for mastery, the need to escape from reality, and the need to escape from one's conscience. Play was first used for diagnosis and therapy by psychoanalysts who sought some substitute for free association. It was first used as an adjunct to therapy but it soon became apparent that it held certain remedial properties in its own right. So modern play techniques are framed for a twofold purpose —to understand and to treat—and in actual usage it is almost impossible to separate these two purposes.

Generally, the play technique consists of introducing the child to toys in a standardized situation designed to bring out some particular feature of importance to the child, or in a free situation in which the child plays as he wishes, limited only by the confines of the area, the toys, and at times a few very loose regulations. A great variety of materials has been used, and the procedures vary with clinicians, who also differ as to the amount and kind of interpretation they feel should be given in the play situation.

The Structured Doll Play Test (50, 51, 52) is described by David B. Lynn as a projective test particularly suitable for use by trained clinicians with children. The test seems most productive with children between the ages of three and ten. However, circumstances and the characteristics of a given child may indicate its use with children both younger and older than these limits.

The Structured Doll Play Test (SDPT) protocol is said to reveal a picture of family relationships, unique motivations of the child, and his methods of satisfying his needs, as well as the kind and severity of his conflicts. Thirty to forty-five minutes is usually required to administer the test, which consists of presenting the subject with a series of structured situations to which he responds as he sees fit. This approach has certain advantages over free play in that it allows a rapid evaluation of pertinent areas while retaining the spontaneous qualities of play. The test materials consist of four-inch, hard plastic mother and father dolls; two three-inch clothed, pliable, plastic girl dolls; one pliable plastic nude boy doll and one nude girl doll. The rest of the equipment consists of a double bed, single bed, crib, bathtub, toilet stool, potty chair, sink, a toy plate of food, nursing bottle, and cup.

The test is administered individually. In addition to the usual procedures for establishing rapport, Lynn has found that the dolls themselves can be used to advantage. This can be done prior to formal testing by structuring a situation in which a little child doll has come to see an adult doll. The examiner indicates to the subject that the little child doll was afraid at first but that all the big man (or woman) did was play with the little boy (or girl) and they had a wonderful time. Lynn has found that anxious children usually respond quite favorably to this procedure and then quickly enter co-operatively into the first formal test situation. Twenty different structured situations have been studied rather extensively. One of the situations and the instructions concerning it will be described in some detail to illustrate the nature of the test.

The materials are set up with the single bed and crib placed parallel, about two inches apart with the foot end of the beds nearest the subject. The child doll is held between and at the heads of the beds facing the subject. The examiner says, "Take the little boy (girl) in your hand. Now let's pretend this little boy (girl) has two places he can sleep. He can sleep either place he wants to. Show me and tell me what happens." Then the mother doll is held standing at the head of the crib and the father doll at the head of the bed. The subject is told, "Now, let's pretend the little boy (or girl) is in bed. Which one comes in—Mommy or Daddy?" After the choice is made, the non-chosen parent doll is removed, and the subject is instructed, "Now take Mommy (Daddy) in your hand and show me and tell me what happens." After completion of the response, the non-chosen parent is placed between the crib and the bed, and the subject is instructed, "Now let's pretend Mommy (Daddy) comes in. Take Mommy (Daddy) in your hand and show me and tell me what happens." All responses are recorded and may be interpreted qualitatively or in terms of scoring systems that are being developed by the Lynns (52).

DRAWING AND PAINTING TECHNIQUES

Investigators such as Anne Anastasi and John P. Foley (4, 5) have analyzed the drawings of different cultures and have also surveyed the literature on artistic behavior in the abnormal. There are other similar works that attempt to synthesize the data in the area, but, generally, the findings and information collected are diffuse—as diffuse as are the media, procedures, and interpretative systems. There are certain investigations, however, that represent careful attempts to arrive at the meaning of paintings and drawings as projective techniques. Among these is the research of Paula Elkisch (30), who studied 2,200 drawings and paintings done by twenty-five children over a period of five to eight years to gain "insight into the individual child's typical way of expressing himself in free art work." In her report the products of eight children were subjected to analysis, and it was found that categorization of the productions in terms of rhythm, rule, complexity, simplexity, expansion, and compression yielded measures that were in general agreement with the results of a sociometric study of these eight children. Another extensive investigation was that of Rose H. Alschuler and La Berta Weiss Hattwick (2), who studied easel painting and, in conjunction, work done in such media as crayons, clay, blocks, and dramatic play. One hundred and seventy children were studied over a period of about two years. The authors compared the children's work with individual case studies made of the individual children. The results suggested that there is a very general tendency for different individuals to express similar feelings, reactions, and problems in a comparable fashion. The likeness was evident in the choice of color and sometimes in the similarity of form, line, and space usage. From this, they concluded that just as creative activity appears to spring from some unexplained universal tendency, so the expression of universal experiences frequently takes on similar form.

It is probable that Florence L. Goodenough's (39) book and work served as an impetus to other studies not directly concerned with the measurement of intelligence. Karen Machover (54), in particular, was stimulated to study the personal differences expressed in the simple drawing of a figure. She has rather carefully outlined the administration procedure for a test she has devised with the directions that the subject is to draw a person, and later to draw a person of the opposite sex from that first drawn. Interpretative analysis, according to her scheme, concerns such features as: the breast, shoulders, hips, buttocks, waistline, joints, other anatomy indications, clothing, conspicuous buttons, pockets, tie, shoes and hat, as well as other presumed-to-be sexual symbols. Structural and formal aspects such as theme, action, succession, symmetry, size, placement, midline, stance, and perspective are studied carefully. Note is made of conflict indicators such as the differential treatment of male and female figures. The common criticism has been that no attention has been given to careful validation of any of the interpretations that Machover suggests can be made from characteristics of drawings involving the features she mentioned. Actually, use of the procedure is common because of the extreme ease of administration, the brief time required, and the ready availability of materials. Most clinicians make very qualitative interpretations of the productions, and the reliability of clinical judgments as well as their validity is certainly questionable. Richard H. Blum (16), for example, has found the validity of the Machover technique to be highly questionable.

Finger painting has been applied rather extensively for various purposes, and Peter J. Napoli (58) has discussed its use in diagnosis. He describes a standard kit for clinical use and explains a method for recording and interpreting systematic observations during the process. Research is also needed in the objective analysis of finger painting before we can use it in other than a very qualitative fashion.

One of the more fully developed drawing procedures is the House-Tree-Person technique (HTP) developed by John N. Buck (19, 20, 21, 22, 23). The HTP derives its name from the fact that the subject is requested to make freehand drawings of a house, a tree, and a person. After doing the drawing, the subject is asked to define, describe, and interpret the objects drawn and their respective environments. Finally, he is asked to associate to them. The specific steps involved are as follows:

(1) The subject is presented with a folded form sheet and asked to draw as good a house as he can, then a tree and a person. The time elapsing between instructions and the beginning of the drawing procedure is recorded. Other items recorded are the numbering of details as they appear, intra-item pauses, all spontaneous comments made by the subject, any emotion exhibited by the subject, and the total time consumed for drawing.

(2) This step is one of informal questioning as to what the subject has drawn. It is necessary in order to ascertain what specific meanings and connotations the drawings have for the subject so that the later qualitative and quantitative appraisal will be more accurate. At the conclusion of the questioning the subject is requested to draw a sun and a line representing the ground in each of the pictures in which he did not enter them spontaneously.

(3) The subject is asked to identify the colors of each of the eight crayons presented to him, and he is then asked to draw as good a house as he can, using the crayons. This is followed by the drawing of the other two figures. The same items are recorded as were recorded during Step 1.

(4) Again the subject is questioned to determine his intention. The objects should be identified and any conceptual differences between achromatic and chromatic productions explored.

(5) Next the examiner attempts to get the subject to identify any irrelevant details, account for the absence of essential details, the presence of bizarre ones, unusual proportions, and spatial or positional relationships. Then the subject is again asked to draw a sun and the earth line where they may be missing. The examiner writes a brief description of the weather conditions and notes whether the subject is right- or left-handed.

Buck believes the HTP to be a valid measure of adult intelligence as well as a technique that provides the basis for certain specific deductions concerning the subject's total personality and the interaction of that personality with its environment. Extensive qualitative and quantitative scoring and interpretative procedures have been developed. However it is doubtful whether we have sufficient evidence to regard either the qualitative or the quantitative factors as valid for the description and prediction of intellectual functioning. Additional normative studies must be made if the HTP is eventually to be regarded as a clinically useful tool. A substantial amount of such research is in progress, and a few of the reported results are worth mentioning. For example, Harry S. Beck (10) has studied a group of mentally handicapped children, both organic and nonorganic, comparing their performance with that of normal five- and six-year-old children. He reports results that confirm several of Buck's interpretations of certain aspects of house drawings and also some developmental data. This data suggests that great caution should be used in making interpretations of house drawings by children less than six years of age. In a study comparing HTP results with results on the Wechsler-Bellevue and using the Wechsler as a criterion, Harold Rubin (69) indicates that the HTP can be regarded as a valid measure of "intelligence." On the other hand, in this same study Buck's scoring patterns did not identify a group of psychiatric patients as maladjusted.

Indicators of positive and negative prognosis have been suggested by Emanuel F. Hammer (42), but here again there is no systematic validation data described. William Sloan (73) in his critical review of HTP validation studies, summarizes by saying that these studies are "characterized by lack of clear, logical statements concerning the concept of validation." As he suggests, clinicians should become aware of the fact that bland statements to the effect that "it works" cannot be accepted as satisfactory evidence for the validity of a technique. We need more studies of the kind reported by Murray Levine and Eugene H. Galanter (46) in which they test the theory that blemishes drawn on the tree are indicative of traumata that have occurred in the life of the person making the drawing. Buck has suggested that the ratio between the height of the traumatic indicator and the total height of the tree will yield the approximate age, plus or minus one year, of the occurrence of the trauma. Actually, this idea did not fare well in the results of the Levine and Galanter study. Such concepts must be systematically evaluated before they can safely be used.

THE SZONDI TEST

In 1930 Lipot Szondi, a psychiatrist in Hungary, began constructing a picture test with photographs of mental patients. The original purpose of the test was to prove experimentally his theory (28, 77) that the mental disorders of the persons in the photographs are of genetic origin and that the subject's emotional reactions to these photographs depend upon some sort of similarity between the gene structure of the patient photographed and that of the subject reacting to the photograph. In spite of the rather scientifically ridiculous, philosophical, biopsychological theory that resulted in the test, the test itself has had considerable application. During the years preceding World War II, Susan K. Deri (28) was one of the persons who worked with Szondi on the test; she came to the United States in 1941, and has continued to work with the test here. Considering it as a projective technique, she has developed a series of psychological assumptions from which interpretations can be derived. Deri does not believe that the use of the test depends on subscription to Szondi's theoretical formulations. In fact, she mentions them in her book only briefly, instead referring the reader to Szondi's original works. She draws heavily on Lewin and Freud to develop her theory, which conceives of personality as eight interdependent need-tension systems. Depending on the state of tension in each of the eight need systems, the pictures representing the corresponding needs will be chosen in various proportions; for example, a relatively large number of choices in one category means that the corresponding need is in a state of strong tension. Whether the particular types of pictures are chosen as liked or disliked depends on the subject's conscious or unconscious attitude toward that particular need. Consequently, projection in the Szondi means structuring the stimulus material in terms of positive and negative valences, remembering that valence in stimulus material depends on need-tension in the organism. Since the eight basic psychological tendencies have a wide range of potential manifestations, ranging from normal psychological phenomena to psychotic or autosocial symptoms, the interpretation of test profiles is a complicated process.

The test consists of six sets of pictures, each set containing eight photographs of mental patients. Each set contains a picture of the following: a homosexual (h), a sadist (s), an epileptic (e), a hysteric (hy), a catatonic schizophrenic (k), a paranoid schizophrenic (p), a depressive (d) and a manic (m). Thus each energy system is represented by six photographs. The series, each containing eight pictures, are presented to the subject consecutively, the cards of each series laid out in front of the subject in two lines of four pictures each. The subject's task is to choose from each series the two pictures he likes most and the two he dislikes most. These choices are repeated in each of the six series. Following the completion of the six series, the subject is asked to choose, from his twelve likes and twelve dislikes, the four most intense likes and dislikes in order of intensity. An optional part of the administration involves an association to the eight intense, or, if there is sufficient time, to all the twenty-four pictures chosen in the main experiment. It is recommended by Deri that the administration be repeated at least six, and preferably ten, times with an interval of at least one day between administrations.

The eight drives or energy systems, corresponding to the eight depicted clinical entities, are called "Factors." Each pair is considered as representing opposing tendencies in each of the basic motivational sources, called "Vectors." There are assumed to be four Vectors: S (sexual), P (paroxysmal), Sch (schizophrenic or ego), and C (circular or contact). Thus, each Vector is comprised of two factors; for example, the S-Vector is made up of the homosexual (h) and sadistic (s) factors.

Interpretation is complex and difficult, and no attempt will be made to describe it in this text except to say that a relative balance of Vectors and of Factors within the same Vector is considered essential for well-integrated functioning.

There are a number of criticisms that might be made of the technique. In the first place, the theories (both Deri's or Szondi's) underlying it make many assumptions. Furthermore, all the pictures used in the test were obtained from German texts in psychopathology, and include some of Hungarian patients and a few of Swedish criminals. Presumably, they portray a representative group of western European patients but it is doubtful what meanings they may have in other cultures. At best, the technique seems to be an empirical procedure, and many crucial experiments are needed to evaluate its validity, its predictive capacity, and the adequacy of its theory.

Harold L. Best and Etienne Szollosi (14) presented certain of the pictures to fifty psychiatrists, fifty psychiatric nurses, and fifty students of psychology. Each subject was asked to select the picture representing each of the deviant types of Szondi's system. It was found that a significantly large number of pictures were correctly identified but that there were no differences for the three groups selecting. Training in psychology or psychiatry does not seem to improve recognition. There was considerable inconsistency between sets and the accuracy of recognition, although significantly better than chance was not very striking. J. Flament (32) has also studied the extent to which a group of twenty-five psychiatrists could correctly identify the diagnostic categories. It is reported that correct identifications were made at significant levels for many of the cards. However, Flament concludes that his data do not necessarily support the theory of drives and that the test cannot be used as a scientific instrument. Martin Fleishman (33) studied the discriminative power of Szondi's syndromes by testing a normal group and six different types of psychopatholigical groups. Along with each administration of the Szondi, a control test consisting of 48 photographs of normal subjects was administered. Syndromes allegedly characteristic of particular clinical groupings did not predominate within the groupings of subjects. Chance furnished an adequate explanation for all the results. There was some trend for the syndrome signs reputedly correlated with homosexuality to show up in the homosexual group but this trend was not significant. Still another group of investigators (27) was not able to differentiate between overt homosexuals and epileptics on the basis of most of the signs proposed by Deri (28) and by Szondi (77). However, when the test profiles were submitted to clinicians for blind diagnosis, it was possible for them to distinguish between the groups to a significant degree. Other studies have been reviewed by Lloyd J. Borstelmann and Walter G.

Klopfer (18); these generally demonstrate a rather high degree of consistency but still leave interpretation "a tenuous process of undetermined validity."

SENTENCE–COMPLETION TECHNIQUES

Although a form of sentence-completion test to study mental capacity and reasoning ability was devised by Hermann Ebbinghaus in Breslau in 1897 (29) and was introduced into this country by Marion R. Trabue (79) and Truman L. Kelley (45) in the early part of the twentieth century for the same purpose, the first use of the test as a projective technique in personality study is credited to A. F. Payne in 1928 (59). The history of the technique and research on the procedure have been reviewed by John M. Hadley and Vera E. Kennedy (41).

Some sample items from a typical test are as follows:

"I like people who _____ "
"When people try to boss me _____ "
"As a child _____ "
"What worries me _____ "
"They _____ "
"The trouble with women _____ "
"I am _____ "
"Love _____ "
"The worst thing a man could do to a woman _____ "

The job of the subject is to finish the sentences in such a way as to make meaningful statements. Some tests contain as many as a hundred sentences, and others contain substantially fewer. Raymond B. Cattell (26) has pointed out that the trend, in what he terms "misapperception" tests, has been to go from the "inventive" to the "selective" type of misapperception test. In the list above, presumably he would term sentence stems such as "They . . ." "I am . . ." and "Love . . ." inventive items and the others somewhat more selective items. He differentiates between these two approaches on the basis that the "inventive," or at last the interpretation of responses to that type of item, is the more intuitive, and therefore the less meaningful one. This point of view has received some substantiation from Bertram R. Forer (34), who suggests that the more unstructured a sentence-completion test is, the less the amount of meaningful information that can be derived from it. On the other hand, less structured stems will maximize the production of the client and may increase the amount of projection. This is a point for speculation; sentence stems in different tests vary from those that are relatively unstructured to those that are relatively structured.

Scoring and interpretation of the sentence completions vary from highly qualitative and subjective evaluations to the more elaborate scoring procedures described by Rotter and his coworkers (64, 65, 66, 67, 68). Rotter recommends a rating procedure in which each response is scored in terms of the degree of conflict revealed by the responses. He describes sample responses for each rating and reports that when raters are trained there is a rather high agreement among them. The conflict score derived from the ratings of responses to the Rotter sentence stems appears to have satisfactory validity for screening purposes.

In addition to their use in screening, sentence-completion techniques and their elaborations into paragraph-completion and story-completion procedures have been used for a wide variety of other purposes. The interested student can find these elaborations and their uses described in a number of sources (70, 82, 86).

THE PURDUE MULTIPLE CHOICE SENTENCE COMPLETION TEST

Projective techniques have gained wide acceptance as methods of observing, evaluating, and understanding individual behavior. However, at the present time most of the projective procedures require some time to administer, are often difficult to score and interpret, and require skilled examiners. The Multiple Choice Sentence Completion Test (hereafter referred to as the MCSCT) was designed in response to the need for a projective technique that could be administered within a relatively short period of time and that did not require laborious, time-consuming, and subjective scoring procedures.

The underlying hypothesis in projective techniques is that an individual, given a neutral, ambiguous, unstructured stimulus, reacts by making something meaningful out of the stimulus in such a way that his unconscious needs, preoccupations, feelings, attitudes, anxieties, and values are called into play. In applying principles of projection to paper-and-pencil tests, Helen D. Sargent (70, p. 2) has made the following basic assumptions:

> A projective test is based on the theory that (1) when a subject is confronted with a neutral, ambiguous stimulus (2) which requires a response, (3) he will react in terms of his own individual personality, and therefore it may be assumed that (4) whatever meanings he finds are his own, and hence are highly revealing of his personal characteristics and experience. Furthermore, since (5) the subject is unaware of the purpose of the experiment, and cannot detect the factors on

which he will be scored, results are less apt to be distorted by an effort to choose the "right" answers. Finally, not only the content, but (6) the manner and form in which he perceives and organizes the material; his selective response to parts of the situation; and his voluntary and involuntary ways of expressing himself may all be regarded as potentially worthy of study.[2]

With the possible exception of the criterion of neutrality and ambiguity in the stimulus, it would appear that the traditional open-ended sentence-completion test fulfills these qualifications. Even in the instance of the stimulus it is possible to construct stems with varying degrees of neutrality and ambiguity. Although responses to verbal materials may be expected to be influenced more by meaning factors than those to less structured materials such as the Rorschach ink blots, these factors can also be expected to differ qualitatively and quantitatively from one individual to the next. In this vein Hutt (44) justifies the use of partially structured personality tests as projective techniques "because they elicit responses dependent in part upon the projection by the subject of his personal interpretation or interaction into the stimulus."

Most current structured inventories, rating scales, and questionnaires restrict the responses to what Hutt has called "channelized alternatives." Certainly the usual "yes-no" alternatives do not give the subject much choice or opportunity to reveal his wishes, fears, or affective attitudes. Furthermore, there appears to be little question but that the subject can easily falsify "yes-no" responses in order to obtain "good" or "bad" records or in order to answer in accordance with his own personal concepts of the "normal" personality. However the possibility that subjects may reflect certain of their needs in selecting alternatives that are not discernibly "right" or "wrong" seems worthy of investigation. While a multiple-choice test still restricts the responses of the subject, it does so to a lesser degree than does the "yes-no" type, particularly if four or five alternatives are provided. The forced selection of a particular item from several items, especially if the items were originally chosen to embody certain needs, may lead to significant findings concerning the behavior characteristics of the subjects.

The MCSCT has gone through a number of revisions [which we have described in detail (40) elsewhere], and the research has culminated in a final scale that is made up of 72 items, each of which contains a sentence stem with four alternative responses. The sentence stems, describing interpersonal situations with as much ambiguity as possible,

[2] From "An Experimental Application of Projective Principles to a Paper and Pencil Personality Test," by Helen D. Sargent, *Psychological Monographs*, 1944, Vol. 57, No. 5 (Whole No. 265), 1–57. By permission of the American Psychological Association.

serve as the stimulus for the subject's choice of response or expression of attitudes. These situations selected occur in such life areas as marriage, occupation, sex, family, and education, and were constructed with the purpose of sampling the kinds of problems that the "average" adult encounters in his everyday life and in which most adults can become emotionally involved.

Most of the stems were devised as a result of observations of people "in the field," and from a reading of newspapers, magazines, etiquette columns, and other syndicated articles dealing with problems of adjustment. For all items, each of the four responses describe a different mode of adjustment; these are withdrawal, aggression, passive dependence, and inaction. Research on the test is still in progress, and normative data is being accumulated but preliminary research and clinical experience thus far suggest that the test is very promising for screening, and for both vocational and therapeutic counseling.

WORD–ASSOCIATION TESTS

One of the last of the partially structured personality evaluative procedures to be mentioned is the word-association technique. It is undoubtedly the oldest of the projective procedures and the forerunner of all the others. The study of associations to stimulus words began with Galton in 1885 and has been used widely since that time. Because most readers probably became acquainted with this procedure in their first course in psychology, we will not discuss it in great detail here. However this lack of emphasis should not be interpreted to mean that its use is to be neglected. We feel that it is one of the clinician's most useful tools. It may also be the best standardized, the most valid, and one of the more reliable procedures. Its use is recommended for appropriate purposes by all clinicians.

Basically, the test consists of a standardized list of words, usually numbering between 50 and 100 items. Several lists have been widely used. Sometimes special lists are drawn up to meet the requirements of a particular case, or selected words are interpolated into one of the standard lists. The subject is instructed to respond quickly to the stimulus word spoken by the examiner with the first word that comes to his mind. A stop watch or timer is used to measure the reaction time. Reaction times and response words as well as peculiarities of speech and behavior are recorded. In analyzing the results, reaction times are considered and unusual associations are studied, with special attention to groupings of reactions that may reveal complexes. Besides noting the unusualness of content, we study other complex indicators such as the repetition of a previously given stimulus or response word, multiword reactions, and laughter or other signs of embarrassment. Lengthened reaction time and its extreme of complete blocking are regarded as signs of some emotional reaction to the stimulus word. For the student who wishes to learn more about this technique, source materials (1, 11, 62, 64) are available.

OTHER PARTIALLY STRUCTURED PROCEDURES

Finally, we will mention a few other tests that have been widely used or have potential for use. The Rosenzweig P-F Study (61) is a picture-frustration test in which the subject is presented with cartoons, each cartoon representing two persons who are involved in a mildly frustrating situation of common occurrence. The figure at the left of each picture is shown saying certain words that either frustrate the other individual or help describe what is frustrating to him. The subject is asked to examine the situations one at a time and write in the blank space the first reply that comes to his mind as likely to be given by the second figure. A detailed scoring procedure has been worked out, which presumes to describe the subject as turning his aggression out on the environment, as turning it inward upon the subject himself, or as turning it off. The nature of the barriers, the defenses of the subject, and his persistence are all taken into consideration in evaluating the test results.

A vocational apperception test (3) has been developed that is similar to the TAT but consists of plates portraying particular occupational situations, ambiguously drawn but clearly represented. The test, which is recommended for the clinical exploration of personal vocational difficulties, is designed for the projective determination of vocational attitudes and information.

A complete listing of all test devices would be almost endless. We will conclude by simply mentioning that auditory projective devices have also been utilized (9, 76, 84, 85), as well as devices that stimulate through the kinesthetic and tactile modalities (74).

SUMMARY

In this chapter we have summarized and described many of the better-known partially structured procedures for the evaluation of behavior, emphasizing their usefulness in revealing something of the "why" of behavior. In the main these evaluative procedures attempt to provide standardized stimulus situations to which the subject reacts, revealing, we hope, something of his characteristic modes of reaction and the reasons for them. In this way these procedures are useful for the planning of rehabilitative and therapeutic activities. The procedures described vary in their degree of structuring both within themselves and in relation to each other. No attempt has been made to compare them or their utility in a systematic manner. In general, the point of view has been that the ultimate test of a procedure's validity is the extent to which a given clinician can predict from it and use it to understand his client. All of these procedures apparently are useful to someone. No clinician can be expected to use all of them, nor would he want to. In the strictest sense our purpose has been to illustrate the wide variety of procedures that the ingenious and inventive clinician can develop. Our readers will probably develop even more, as well as add to the body of knowledge about procedures already developed.

We have described in a general way procedures that can be classified under the following headings: (a) picture-story tests; (b) drawing tests; (c) combinations of (a) and (b); (d) object arrangement and doll or object play tests, (e) picture preference tests, (f) completion techniques, and (g) association tests. In the next chapter we will describe a few of the more structured procedures, which persumably maximize the projection and freedom of response of the subject but may allow us to make more inferences about the "how" of behavior than the "why."

BIBLIOGRAPHY

1. Abt, L. E., and Bellak, L., *Projective psychology*. New York: Alfred A. Knopf, 1950.
2. Alschuler, R. H., and Hattwick, L. W., *Painting and personality*. Chicago: Univ. of Chicago Press, 1947.
3. Ammons, R. B., *Vocational Apperception Test*. Louisville: Southern Univ. Press, 1955.
4. Anastasi, A., and Foley, J. P., "An analysis of spontaneous drawings by children in different cultures." *J. Appl. Psychol.*, 1936, 20, 689–726.
5. Anastasi, A., and Foley, J. P., "A survey of the literature on artistic behavior in the abnormal: III. Spontaneous production." *Psychol. Monogr.*, 1940, Vol. 52, No. 6 (Whole No. 237), 1–71.
6. Andrew, G., Walton, R. E., Hartwell, S. W., and Hutt, M. L., "The Michigan Picture Test: the stimulus value of the cards." *J. Consult. Psychol.*, 1951, 15, 51–4.
7. Anderson, H. H., and Anderson, G. L., *An introduction to projective techniques*. New York: Prentice-Hall, 1951.
8. Armstrong, M. A. S., "Children's responses to animal and human figures in thematic pictures." *J. Consult. Psychol.*, 1954, 18, 67–70.
9. Ball, T. S., and Bernardoni, L. C., "The application of an auditory apperception test to clinical diagnosis." *J. Clin. Psychol.*, 1953, 9, 54–8.
10. Beck, H. S., "A study of the applicability of the H–T–P to children with respect to the drawn house." *J. Clin. Psychol.*, 1955, 11, 60–3.

11. Bell, J. E., *Projective techniques.* New York: Longmans, Green, 1948.

12. Bellak, L., *A guide to the interpretation of the Thematic Apperception Test,* revised form. New York: Psychol. Corp., 1951.

13. Bellak, L., and Bellak, S. S., *Children's Apperception Test.* New York: C. P. S. Co., 1949.

14. Best, H. L., and Szollosi, E., "Recognition as a criterion in the Szondi Test." *J. Clin. Psychol.,* 1953, 9, 75–6.

15. Blum, G. S., "A study of the psychoanalytic theory of psychosexual development." *Genetic Psychol. Monogr.,* 1949, 39, 3–99.

16. Blum, R. H., "The validity of the Machover DAP Technique." *J. Clin. Psychol.,* 1954, 10, 120–5.

17. Bolgar, H., and Fischer, L., "Personality projection in the World Test." *Amer. J. Orthopsychiat.,* 1947, 17, 117–28.

18. Borstelmann, L. V., and Klopfer, W. G., "The Szondi Test: a review and critical evaluation." *Psychol. Bull.,* 1953, 50, 112–32.

19. Buck, J. N., "The H–T–P Test." *J. Clin. Psychol.,* 1948, 4, 151–8.

20. Buck, J. N., "The H–T–P Technique, a quantitative and qualitative scoring manual." *J. Clin. Psychol.,* 1948, 4, 397–405.

21. Buck, J. N., "The H–T–P Technique, a quantitative and qualitative scoring manual, Part II." *J. Clin. Psychol.,* 1949, 5, 37–76.

22. Buck, J. N., "The use of the H–T–P test in a case of marital discord." *J. Proj. Tech.,* 1950, 14, 405–34.

23. Buck, J. N., "The quality and the quantity of the H–T–P." *J. Clin. Psychol.,* 1951, 7, 352–6.

24. Buhler, C., and Kelly, G., *The World Test: a measurement of emotional disturbance.* New York: Psychol. Corp., 1941.

25. Buhler, C., Lumry, G. K., and Carrol, H. S., "World Test standardization studies." *J. Child Psychiat.,* 1951, 2, 2–81.

26. Cattell, R. B., *A Guide to mental testing.* London: Univ. of London Press, 1936 (rev. 1948), pp. 196–210.

27. David, H. P., Orne, M., and Rabinowitz, W., "Qualitative and quantitative Szondi diagnosis." *J. Proj. Tech.,* 1953, 17, 75–8.

28. Deri, S., *Introduction to the Szondi Test.* New York: Grune & Stratton, 1949.

29. Ebbinghaus, H., *"Ueber eine neue Methode und Prüfung geistiger Fähigkeit und ihre Anwendung bei Schulkindern." Zeitschrift sur Psychologie und Physiologie der Sinnesorgane.* 1897, 13, 410–57.

30. Elkisch, P., "Children's drawings in a projective technique." *Psychol. Monogr.,* 1945, Vol. 58, No. 1 (Whole No. 266), 1–31.

31. Fischer, L., "A new psychological tool in function: preliminary clinical experience with the Bolgar-Fischer World Test." *Amer. J. Orthopsychiat.,* 1950, 20, 281–92.

32. Flament, J., "Contribution à l'étude expérimentale du test de Szondi." *Acta. Neurol. Belg.,* 1953, 53, 675–89.

33. Fleishman, M., "The discriminative power of Szondi's syndromes." *J. Consult. Psychol.,* 1954, 18, 89–95.

34. Forer, B. R., "A structured sentence completion test." *J. Proj. Tech.,* 1950, 14, 15–30.

35. Frandsen, A., and Hunter, M., "The 'TAT' in school counseling." *Utah Guidance Monogr.*, 1952, 3, 1–12.
36. Frank, L. K., " Projective methods for the study of personality." *J. Psychol.*, 1939, 3, 389–413.
37. Freud, S., "The anxiety neurosis." In *Collected Papers*, Vol. I. London: Hogarth, 1940.
38. Goldenberg, H. C., "A résumé of some Make-A-Picture Story (MAPS) test results." *J. Proj. Tech.*, 1951, 15, 79–86.
39. Goodenough, F., *Measurement of Intelligence by Drawings*. Yonkers-on-Hudson, N.Y.: World Book, 1926.
40. Hadley, J. M., "The Purdue Multiple Choice Sentence Completion Test." Unpublished manuscript.
41. Hadley, J. M., and Kennedy, Vera E., "A comparison between performance on a sentence completion test and academic success." *Educ. and Psychol. Measmt.*, 1949, 9, 649–70.
42. Hammer, E. F., "The role of the H–T–P in a prognostic battery." *J. Clin. Psychol.*, 1953, 9, 371–4.
43. Hartwell, S. W., Hutt, M. L., Andrew, G., and Walton, R. E., "The Michigan Picture Test: diagnostic and therapeutic possibility of a new projective test in child guidance." *Amer. J. Orthopsychiat.*, 1951, 21, 124–37.
44. Hutt, M. L., "The use of projective methods of personality measurement in Army medical installations." *J. Clin. Psychol.*, 1945, 1, 134–40.
45. Kelley, T. L., "Individual testing with the completion test exercises." *Teachers College Record*, 1917, 18, 371–82.
46. Levine, M., and Galanter, E. H., "A note on the 'tree and trauma' interpretation in the H–T–P." *J. Consult. Psychol.*, 1953, 17, 74–5.
47. Lowenfeld, M., *Play in childhood*. London: Victor Gollancz, 1935.
48. Lowenfeld, M., "The world pictures of children: a method of recording and studying them." *Brit. J. Med. Psychol.*, 1939, 18, 65–101.
49. Lowenfeld, M., "The nature and use of the Lowenfeld World Technique in work with children and adults." *J. Psychol.*, 1950, 30, 325–31.
50. Lynn, D. B., *Structured Doll Play Test*. Mimeographed, 1954.
51. Lynn, D. B., "An investigation of hypothesis basic to a concept of relative intensity of interaction." Purdue Univ., unpublished M.S. thesis, 1955.
52. Lynn, R., "A study of the responses of four and six year olds to a structured doll play test." Purdue Univ., unpublished M.S. thesis, 1955.
53. Lyon, J. M., "Communicability in schizophrenics as related to intervening projective activity." Purdue Univ., unpublished Ph.D. thesis, 1952.
54. Machover, K., *Personality projection in the drawing of the human figure*. Springfield, Ill.: Charles C Thomas, 1949.
55. Michael, J. C., and Buhler, C., "Experiences with personality testing in a neuropsychiatric department of a public general hospital." *Dis. Nerv. Syst.*, 1945, 6, 205–11.
56. Morgan, C. D., and Murray, H. A., "A method for investigating fantasies: the Thematic Apperception Test." *Arch. Neurol. Psychiat.*, 1935, 34, 289–306.

57. Murray, H. A., *Manual for the Thematic Apperception Test*. Cambridge: Harvard Univ. Press, 1943.
58. Napoli, P. J., "Finger painting and personality diagnosis." *Genet. Psychol. Monogr.*, 1946, 34, 129–231.
59. Payne, A. F., *Sentence completions*. New York: N. Y. Guidance Clinic, 1928.
60. Rapaport, D., Gill, M., and Schafer, R., *Diagnostic psychological testing*, Vol. II. Chicago: Yearbook Publishers, 1946.
61. Rosenzweig, S., "The picture frustration method and its application in a study of reactions to frustration." *J. Pers.*, 1945, 14, 3–23.
62. Rosenzweig, S., *Psychodiagnosis*. New York: Grune & Stratton, 1949.
63. Rotter, J. B., "Thematic Apperception Tests: suggestions for administration and interpretation." *J. Pers.*, 1946, 15, 70–92.
64. Rotter, J. B., "Word association and sentence completion methods." In Anderson, H. H., and Anderson, Gladys L. (eds.), *An introduction to projective techniques*. New York: Prentice-Hall, 1951, 279–311.
65. Rotter, J. B., and Rafferty, J. E., *Manual for the Rotter Incomplete Sentences Blank, College Form*. New York: Psychol. Corp., 1950.
66. Rotter, J. B., Rafferty, J. E., and Lotsof, A. B., "The validity of the Rotter Incomplete Sentences Blank: High School Form." *J. Consult. Psychol.*, 1954, 18, 105–11.
67. Rotter, J. B., Rafferty, J. E., and Schachtitz, E., "Validation of the Rotter Incomplete Sentences Blank for college screening." *J. Consult. Psychol.*, 1949, 13, 348–56.
68. Rotter, J. B., and Willerman, B., "The Incomplete Sentences Test as a method of studying personality." *J. Consult. Psychol.*, 1947, 11, 43–8.
69. Rubin, H., "A quantitative study of the H–T–P and its relationship to the Wechsler-Bellevue Scale." *J. Clin. Psychol.*, 1954, 10, 35–8.
70. Sargent, H. D., "An experimental application of projective principles to a paper and pencil personality test." *Psychol. Monogr.*, 1944, Vol. 57, No. 5 (Whole No. 265), 1–57.
71. Shneidman, E. S., "The MAPS projective personality test: preliminary report." *J. Consult. Psychol.*, 1947, 11, 315–25.
72. Shneidman, E. S., *The Make-A-Picture Story Test*. New York: Psychol. Corp., 1949.
73. Sloan, W., "A critical review of H–T–P validation studies." *J. Clin. Psychol.*, 1954, 10, 143–8.
74. Smith, F. V., and Madan, S. K., "A projective technique based upon the kinaesthetic and tactile modalities." *Brit. J. Psychol.*, 1953, 44, 156–63.
75. Stein, M. I., *The Thematic Apperception Test*. Cambridge: Addison-Wesley, 1948.
76. Stone, D. R., "A recorded auditory apperception test as a new projective technique." *J. Psychol.*, 1950, 29, 349–53.
77. Szondi, L., *Experimental diagnostics of drives*. New York: Grune & Stratton, 1952.
78. Tomkins, S. S., *The Thematic Apperception Test: the theory and technique of interpretation*. New York: Grune & Stratton, 1947.

79. Trabue, M. R., "Completion test language scales." In *Contributions to education*, No. 77. New York: Bureau of Publications, Teachers College, Columbia Univ., 1916.

80. Walton, R. E., Andrew, G., and Hartwell, S. W., "A tension index of adjustment based on picture stories elicited by the Michigan Picture Test." *J. Abnorm. Soc. Psychol.*, 1951, 46, 438–41.

81. Weisskopf, E. A., "A transcendence index as a proposed measure in the TAT." *J. Psychol.*, 1950, 29, 379–90.

82. Wexler, S., "An exploratory investigation of adolescent adjustment as measured by a forced-choice sentence completion test." Purdue Univ., unpublished Ph.D. thesis, 1953.

83. White, R. W., "Interpretation of imaginative productions." In J. McV. Hunt (ed.), *Personality and the behavior disorders*, Vol. I. New York: Ronald, 1944.

84. Wilmer, H. A., "An auditory sound association technique." *Science*, 1951, 114, 621–2.

85. Wilmer, H. A., and Husne, M., "The use of sounds in a projective test." *J. Consult. Psychol.*, 1953, 17, 377–83.

86. Witsaman, L. R., "An investigation of repressed hostilities toward family figures in schizophrenia." Purdue Univ., unpublished M.S. thesis, 1950.

Unstructured Personality Tests

THROUGHOUT THIS BOOK UNSTRUCTURED TECHNIQUES ARE DE-scribed as procedures in which the stimuli are ambiguous. Such stimuli can be interpreted to mean anything that the subject wishes them to mean, and presumably the responses that he makes are moti-vated by what they mean to him. Whereas structured tests prescribe the kind of response the subject is to make and actually limit the response to specified alternatives, and partially structured tests (depending on the degree of structuring) allow the subject considerable choice to respond to a stimulus that gives the direction of the area of response, unstruc-tured techniques allow the subject to respond in almost any way he sees fit. It is assumed that since the situation is unstructured, any response the subject makes is a projection. In other words, his response depends on his own selective perception and not on the characteristics of the stimulus.

In this chapter we will describe two techniques that most closely ap-proach the definition of an unstructured test: the Rorschach and the Mosaic tests. Actually, these procedures are not completely unstruc-tured. The responses of the subject are confined by the limits of the as-signment and the materials provided. In the Rorschach the subject is asked what he sees in a number of ink blots, and in the Mosaic tests he places different shaped and colored plastic pieces in a design. These are definite tasks or assignments. However, the ink blots, in and of them-selves, have no meaning, and the mosaic pieces are simple geometric forms; so within the limits of the assignment and the materials given, the subject responds in an unstructured fashion.

Although the projective hypothesis (that when presented with an ambiguous stimulus, the subject reveals himself by the characteristics of his response) has never been absolutely proved, it is quite generally accepted by clinicians. It is safe to say that the tests have had extensive clinical validation. Certainly, the trained and experienced observer can learn from them something of the subject's characteristic modes of response; but it must be remembered that it is possible for the subject to control his responses, to guard against making certain responses, or even to "fake" his responses in order to present himself in a desired light. Consequently, the subject's responses must be carefully interpreted, and the clinician's generalizations must be conservative. Even if the perceptions of the subject actually do reveal his characteristic reactions, we can never be entirely sure that he has reported or expressed those perceptions to us. If the clinician is constantly alert to simple and complex indications of poor co-operation or conflicting motivation, he can usually detect signs or indications of guarding, repressing, suppressing, or "faking."

Unstructured techniques for evaluation provide the clinician with an opportunity to make observations of the subject's characteristic mode of approach to complex problems. The partially structured procedures may be more useful for the determination of the "why," and many clinicians prefer the partially structured procedures when there is question of understanding the subject's motivation and the content of his associations. Consequently, it is frequently said that the dynamics of behavior are revealed by partially structured procedures and the structure of personality by unstructured procedures. Our point of view is quite similar to this. We regard unstructured tests as aids to the evaluation of potentialities and resources—the "what" of behavior as contrasted with the "how" (structured techniques) and the "why" (partially structured). It follows, then, that the uses of the Rorschach and the Mosaic tests are more akin to the uses of the measures of intelligence and of intellectual functioning than they are to the uses of the partially structured tests. Since they are unstructured, they are projective measures of potentiality and resources and can be contrasted with the more objective and structured tests of intellectual functioning.

It is important to realize that there is no magic in psychological evaluation. This is true when we consider any psychological procedure; it is just as true of the unstructured procedures as it is of any other technique or techniques. Much has been made of unstructured procedures, particularly the Rorschach test. Popular belief concerning "that ink-blot test" sometimes ascribes certain mystical and magical properties to it. Unfortunately, there are professional psychologists who act as if the test were some kind of psychological "pliers" that can be used to open the individual up and look inside—or perhaps as if it were a simple test or indicator such as litmus paper, or a scale like a thermometer or barometer that can be applied to the subject and certain automatic and objective signs noted or readings taken. These clinicians (or technicians) automatically apply unstructured procedures to all subjects and either neglect or disparage other data. Using these techniques as infallible tests is not deemed to be justified on the basis of our scientific information about them. However they can be viewed as additional means for observing a subject in a controlled situation. If the clinician takes this attitude and if he will view the observations from this situation against the background of all other information available concerning the subject, the unstructured techniques become exceedingly valuable tools for his use.

THE RORSCHACH TEST [1]

In 1911 Hermann Rorschach, a Swiss psychiatrist, became interested in the variety of responses he received when people were asked to report what they were able to see in ink blots. He related these responses to psychoanalytic theory and observed that schizophrenics, manics, hysterics, and other clinical groups had characteristically different ways of perceiving. In 1921, shortly before his death at the age of 37, he published *Psychodiagnostics*, describing his procedure and theory. The test, as used today, is almost identical with the test as he described it, and the responses are interpreted in substantially the same way as he outlined.

In the United States the early work with the Rorschach was done by David M. Levy. In 1930 Samuel J. Beck, who had been associated with Levy for three years, presented his doctoral dissertation, which was on the Rorschach test. The marked interest in the Rorschach in this country dates from a monograph by Beck appearing in 1937; another pioneer in the use of the method in America has been Klopfer, who has elaborated extensively upon Rorschach's original method. Others include Hertz and Piotrowski.

Materials for the Rorschach consist of ten cards or plates, on each of which is reproduced an ink-blot design. These blots are symmetrical laterally, and the simpler ones are similar to the result produced by folding vertically a paper on which a drop of ink has been placed. In fact, many years ago a parlor game called "Blotto" employed this same technique. Some of the blots are relatively simple and others complex. Five of the cards employ colored inks in addition to, or instead of black and white. Cards I and III utilize red as well as the black and white elements; Card VIII, pinks and oranges; Card IX is a vague mass of irregularly blended green, orange, and pink; and Card X, which is very compli-

---

[1] In this section we have departed from our usual procedure of supplying rather specific references concerning the topic under consideration. In connection with the Rorschach test this would be overly ambitious for the scope of this text. The literature easily contains two thousand published articles, and rather than present a partial list of significant references, we are simply suggesting that the reader familiarize himself with a number of general sources which are included in the bibliography (1, 2, 3, 4, 5, 6, 7, 8, 10, 11, 12, 13, 14, 16, 17, 18, 19).

cated, is a splashy mixture of bright colored forms. The other five cards are black and white with different degrees of gray shading in some.

1. ADMINISTRATION. The administration of the test is relatively well standardized. Most examiners prefer that the subject be seated so that both he and the examiner can simultaneously observe the cards, with the examiner's position slightly behind the subject so that the recording will not be obvious and distracting. Each card is given to the subject in order (Cards I to X). He is allowed to hold the card and turn it as he desires; while the subject is giving responses to a particular card, care is taken that the other ink blots are not exposed. Beck asks the subject to return a card to him when he is finished with it, while Klopfer suggests that the subject turn the card face down on the table. Most test administrators impose no time limit, allowing the subjects all the time they need to respond. Instructions to the subject are very simple, clinicians usually following Rorschach's example in asking, "What might this be?" Beck elaborates a little more by saying, "Look at each card, and tell the examiner what you see on each card, or anything that might be represented there. Look at each card as long as you like; only be sure to tell the examiner everything you see on the card as you look at it." Klopfer says, "People see all sorts of things in these ink-blot pictures; now tell me what you see, what it might be for you, what it makes you think of."

Some clinicians encourage the subject to give more than one response to a card, discontinuing this encouragement after the fifth card. Others avoid any suggestion or special prompting, allowing the subject to respond as he pleases. During the test the examiner carefully records the following observations:

(1) All verbalization of the subject.

(2) Each response or percept mentioned. The usual practice is to number these responses.

(3) The time up to the first response for each card. This is usually called "reaction time."

(4) The total time the subject holds each card, commonly referred to as "response time."

(5) The length of time during any long pauses between responses.

(6) The position of the card during each response.

(7) Behavior notes describing extraneous movement of the subject.

The above phase of the test administration is termed the "free association." After the completion of responses to all ten cards, the "inquiry" is usually conducted. The purposes of the inquiry are to clarify how the subject perceived the blot and to ascertain what aspects of the blot have determined the particular responses given. More specifically, the first purpose of the inquiry is to discover whether the subject has reacted to the formal characteristics of the ink blots, to the color of the blots, or to a combination of these factors. A second purpose is to locate the response, that is, to inquire which detail or portion of the blot prompted the response or whether the response was prompted by the entire blot. The inquiry may also give the subject an opportunity to add responses spontaneously.

An optional step in the test administration is "testing the limits." The information secured here is not scored but it is useful in interpreting the test material. The function of "testing the limits" is to explore the extent to which the subject can react to aspects of the blots not spontaneously reacted to in the "free association" or the "inquiry." For example, if the subject fails to respond with popular or frequently given responses, the examiner may directly question him as to whether he can see the percept when it is pointed out to him. Similarly, if the subject does not use the whole blot, the examiner may ask him if certain whole concepts can be seen. The limits can also be tested for the use of color and for specific areas of content. If a subject has not given any human responses or any sexual responses, the clinician may wish to question carefully to ascertain whether the subject is repressing the perception, or if, instead, the response simply did not occur to him.

There is a certain amount of variance among clinicians in evaluating the Rorschach. Although some make their evaluations primarily in terms of content and deal with the test in a very qualitative fashion, this is not generally regarded by psychologists as the most effective use of the test. In the hands of the trained examiner the most valuable observations concern the subject's manner of functioning in the controlled situation provided by the test procedure.

2. SCORING. In order to summarize and quantify observations, a careful scoring procedure is followed. To give the reader some understanding of the procedure, a rather detailed description is indicated. In scoring, each response is evaluated, and all responses are scored if, in any respect, the various requirements for scoring are met. Verbalizations are scorable only when they indicate a meaningful relationship to the stimulus properties of the ink blots. In scoring, a response is designated by the appropriate symbol or symbols (more than one symbol can be applied to a particular response). The principal scoring categories will be discussed briefly and the usual symbols introduced one by one.

Since the subject is free to react to the entire ink blot or to any portion of it, the possible responses fall into two broad categories—reactions to wholes and to parts. When the subject reacts spontaneously to the whole blot as an individual unit, this is an instant whole and is designated in scoring as a W response. For example, "bat" or "butterfly" are simple and common W responses given to the entirety of Figure V. Usually such responses are given quickly and without qualification. This simple W is often given in response to several of the cards. Because these are easy percepts requiring little analysis or synthesis, some writers have called them "lazy W's." They do not represent as much capacity as do W's that require more organizational activity. Although both kinds of whole responses are scored as W, interpretation of them differs.

Beck gives numerous examples of complex and simple W responses. To one card (VII) such a response as "pieces of stone, grown together . . . touched together; nothing else could be like that" is described by Beck as an example of an organized whole that gives meaning to the parts. This is the distinguishing characteristic—in the organized whole the percept requires synthesizing activity on the part of the subject. Rorschach himself distinguished between different varieties of organized W responses. He described the spontaneous organization mentioned above and also discussed the slower process of perceiving details separately and then putting them together to develop a whole percept. The latter have been termed "additive W's." Again, all wholes are scored as W responses, but the differences can be regarded as qualitatively important. Persons of lesser intelligence are more apt to give additive responses than are more intelligent, quick-thinking persons.

Rorschach also described primary and secondary W's. Primary W's are more often produced by persons in good mental health, whereas secondary W's may be found in persons with behavior problems. All W's except the additive W would be classed as primary W's and the additive W would be called secondary. Beck calls attention to the fact that additive W's can be produced by healthy people, and he describes the less healthy response as a DW or a DdW. In most instances these are contaminated responses in which a part of the figure suggests a percept, and the subject describes a whole even though only a part is seen. A simple example would be "a man . . . because of the face." Only the face is seen but the response of man is given in its entirety. Other examples to certain figures might be, "a cat . . . because of the tail," or "a rabbit . . . because of the ears." The worst kind of secondary whole is seen in certain responses that are almost entirely confabulated. Usually some detail reminds the subject of a more generalized concept, and this concept is given as a whole response. For example, a subject may see a bear but then describes the blot as "some sort of astrological symbol." A whole chain of association may lead up to the final whole response. Klopfer describes two additional whole responses. The "incomplete whole" is a response which suggests that certain minor parts or details have not been used. The "cut-off whole" is exemplified by the subject's criticizing some part of the percept, for example, "This is an animal skin but I don't know what these little things here might be."

When the subject uses less than the whole figure to determine his response, the scoring is usually described as a D or detail response. When some very tiny or infrequently given part is responded to, this is described as a Dd, or rare detail, response. Most D's are larger than the Dd's, but frequency of use is pragmatically the basis for scoring as D or Dd. In addition to reacting to the ink blot, the subject may see a percept in the white space either surrounding or enclosed by the outline of the blot. White space is always scored as D or Dd (actually Ds or Dds) with the vast majority being Dd. Beck has presented lists of the most frequent D and Dd selections, which can be used as examples for scoring. Problems of scoring D and Dd selections are multitudinous, and we will not attempt to describe them all since our purpose in discussing scoring is simply to indicate the rationale behind the use of the Rorschach.

Two Rorschach test factors are concerned with the balance and typical modes of response. In a Rorschach test record the presence of a specific response is of importance only as it is combined with and related to other responses. In other words, all Rorschach protocols must be evaluated totally. The ratio of one kind of response to another is more important than the number of responses of any particular kind. One of the two factors is the approach (Ap), which is the proportion of W, D, and Dd in any one record. In other words, Ap is a measure of the extent to which the subject distributes his attention between W, D, and Dd. We attempt to measure the extent to which a subject overemphasizes any of these modes of response. To do this, we must have some criterion as to what the normal expectancy of such proportions would be. Rorschach suggested that for thirty-four responses, an average or normal distribution would be 8 W, 23 D, and 3 Dd. We must always correct for the total number of responses (response total), and although clinicians may have somewhat different standards, normal expectancy for any response total would be roughly proportionate to this distribution. Beck feels that Rorscach's formula is overweighted by W and presents evidence that average individuals do not respond with quite as heavy an emphasis on W. He suggests that for thirty responses the normal expectancy would be 6 W, 20 D, and 4 Dd.

The second factor concerned with balance, sequence, is also based on the relationship between W, D, and Dd. Sequence (Seq) is the order in which Wholes, Details, and Rare Details stimulate the responses of the subject. There is no adequate formula for stating sequence, so it is usually based on inspection. There are usually three kinds of sequence which appear in different records. The order followed in the methodical sequence is almost always W, then D, and finally Dd. As Beck suggests, the subject makes a general survey of the problem, looks over the obvious elements, and then studies the minutiae. The confused sequence appears when there is no order or constancy in the subject's procedure. On one card he may start with D and follow it with W or Dd, and on another he may use an entirely different sequence. The irregular sequence falls some place between these extremes.

The form response, scored F+ or F−, is a response determined by the form or shape of the entire blot or portions of it. Whether a response is scored F+ or F− depends on the quality of the response; that is, whether the response is one that could readily be seen by most average or normal people, or whether it is unique, unusual, and hard to see. In this connection we frequently speak of good and poor form responses. The evaluation of form quality is not a simple matter, and in order to eliminate subjective appraisal, it is necessary to employ statistical methods. Although various workers differ slightly in the rules or guides they use in scoring F responses, the procedure of Beck is probably typical. He has provided lists of F+ and F− responses to serve as reference points for scoring. The F+ responses in his list are those frequently given by persons of good intellectual control who see their world accurately, and the F− responses are those given by persons who do not perceive their world accurately. Some persons of good control and intelligence may of course give F− responses, and similarly good responses can be given by a person of limited control. A very small percentage of responses are scored simply as F responses without any plus or minus. These are usually reactions to very rare detail and are given so infrequently that no frame of reference exists for their evaluation.

Beck believes that it is in the movement or M response that Rorscach made his most original contribution to personality study. A response is scored as M when movement is attributed to human content. Since the ink blots are static, any ascribing of movement within them or to them as a whole is believed to involve the projection of something of the subject's fantasy into the blot. The determinants for movement responses are within the subject and can be only partially referred to the shape or form or color of the blots. Movement responses, such as "two natives dancing" or "two children playing Peas Porridge Hot," are scored plus or minus (M+ or M−), depending on the form or shapes seen to be in movement. M is scored by the same standards as is Form (plus or minus depending on the frequency with which the percept is given by average or normal subjects), and it is actually the form that is scored. Most clinicians use Factor M to describe only human movement. There is some disagreement about this, but the rationale presented is that only human movement could be projected by the human subject. Klopfer sees significance in animal movement and scores it as Fm, while Beck does not score it except for the form determinants involved. Again, the problem of scoring becomes complicated and the intricacies will not be discussed here.

The individual who projects movement in his response is viewed as "intratensive" or as prompted by stimuli from within. Conversely, the person who is influenced by form is thought of as "extratensive" or as motivated by factors in the stimulus situation itself. A proper balance of these two traits is necessary for healthy functioning. In the Rorschach the person who gives very few F+ responses and many F− responses is not responding to the realities of the situation, at least not in the same way as do most healthy normal persons. This same person is also thought to be less influenced or more poorly controlled by the environment. If, on the other extreme, a person gives a very high percentage of F+ responses and almost no F− responses, he is seen as overcontrolled and as having little originality of thinking. Consequently, a range of from approximately 60 to 75 per cent of F+ percepts appears to be a good estimate of normal functioning.

The color response (scored as C) is presumed to be a measure of affectivity or feeling experience. Color responses are judged according to whether they are determined purely by color (scored C); by color and form together, with color dominant (scored CF); or by form and color together with form dominant (scored FC). In determining such scoring, the test administrator must lean almost entirely upon the reports of the subject during the inquiry. Again, in interpretation the balance or ratio of C responses is important. If a large proportion of the responses in a record are color determined, this is thought to indicate tension and over-emotionality. A lack or paucity of color-determined responses is interpreted as indicating flatness and dulling of feeling. The presence of some color-determined responses is healthy; too many or too few indicate disturbance.

Responses that are light determined are scored as Vista (V) responses when they have a three-dimensional characteristic, and as Y (for gray) when they are determined by the flat gray or shading aspects of the blots. Topographic maps and caves might be scored as V responses, while X rays, smoke, or cloud responses might be scored as Y. The scoring of such responses depends heavily on the inquiry. If Vista is seen, the scoring is V; but if the percept is determined largely by variations in blackness or grayness and seen without depth, the scoring is Y.

Seldom do we see pure V or pure Y since the form or shape usually influences the percept. Consequently, we score FV (seldom VF) or FY and less commonly YF. A pure V might be scored for a percept such as "mountains," if the only determinant was the impression of height. A pure Y might occur a little more commonly with responses such as "dark," "dreary looking," or "cold." In general, these responses are regarded as similar in meaning to the color responses in that they indicate an affective responsiveness. In contrast to color, which is usually thought to reflect elation, Y, in particular, is believed to be associated with depression. The V responses are a little more difficult to interpret since they may be given in response to the colored cards as well as to the black and white, and they sometimes indicate a considerable amount of intuition or intelligence.

Other types of scoring categories such as texture (for example, "fur") and position (Po) may be used. There are also blends in which the separate determinates merge, such as the coincidence of M and C in the same response. Since the reader is not expected to become a proficient examiner on the basis of this text, we will not discuss these diverse and blend determinants in any detail.

Some responses occur with such frequency that they can be classified as popular responses (P). Since they occur more frequently than other F+ responses they are all plus responses. Again, writers such as Beck have furnished us with lists of popular responses which may be used in scoring. The meaning of popular responses should be clear; the person giving a low number of P responses is not able to see what is commonly seen in the blot, while the person with a high number may be extremely conforming or even guarded.

The extent of content which may be represented in a Rorschach record is almost unlimited, but regardless of the possible breadth, the content usually falls into two areas: percepts of humans (H) and percepts of animals (A). When responses concern parts of human beings or animals, we score Hd and Ad. In addition to these two content-scoring categories, we score anatomy responses (An) and sex responses (Sex); still others are Abstraction (Ab), Art (Art), Clouds (Cl), Death (Dh), Music (Mu), Science (Sc), and Vocation (Vo).

Beck suggests a score for organization activity (Z). A response is given an organization, or Z-value, when two or more portions of the figure are seen in relation to each other, and when the meaning results from this organization. Numerical values are assigned by him to such evidences of organization, and a resultant Z-score is obtained for the subject. The Z-score is regarded as a measure of intelligence and effective functioning.

Using the scoring categories we have described, each response is scored in terms of location (W, D, Dd), determinants (M, C, Y, V, F, etc.), and content. The Rorschach summary is constructed on the basis of these categories and the calculation of certain percentages, such as the F+ percentage and A percentage, the white space (S) total, the total number of P responses, the approach, the sequence, the average time per response, the average time for the first response, and the response total. The interpretation may depend upon the calculation of still other percentages and ratios. These are too complicated to go into in a general discussion, but mention should be made of the experience balance (Exp). This is the ratio of movement to the total of color reactions. It is computed by assigning a value of one to each movement response and varying values (C, 1.5; Cf, 1.0; FC, 0.5) to each color response; and it is expressed in the form of a fraction or ration of movement over color.

3 INTERPRETATION. We believe that the chief purpose of evaluation is to plan treatment, and we regard this as far more important than the categorical classification of individuals into nosological groups. It is true that persons with similar patterns of behavior tend to behave in similar ways in doing the Rorschach, as in other behavioral situations. However, it is hoped that the reader will not use these similarities in behavior for classification but rather as guides for appraising the typical mode of response characteristic of an individual. Although some authors do present a standardized prescription, as it were, for interpretation of the Rorschach, it is more generally believed that the responses of the subject are so interrelated that conclusions drawn from a guide of this type would be misleading. We will discuss some illustrations of the use of the test in planning counseling or therapy, and present some of the general possibilities of interpretation.

Definite differences in Rorschach protocols do appear to exist between individuals exhibiting behavior usually described as neurotic and those whose behavior is described as psychotic. Let us examine first the types of response which are characteristic of persons exhibiting neurotic behavior. Such subjects quite commonly give indications of disturbance in response to color cards. This is sometimes described as color shock and is manifested in several ways:

(1) Increased reaction time on colored cards.

(2) Increased reaction time not only on card when shock occurs but on subsequent ones as well.

(3) Exclamations indicative of newly aroused emotions.

(4) Comment by subject indicative of newly aroused or old anxiety, tension, stress, newly mobilized defense mechanisms such as undue irritation, aggressiveness, passivity, etc. May be given during succeeding cards and referred to the cards that provoke them.

(5) Decline in total responses to color cards, especially the last three.

(6) Decline in equality of responses. F+ per cent may decline and quality of responses as to originality and complexity may be poor.

(7) Impoverished content—decline in richness, originality, expansiveness, and ingenuity. There is usually evidence of satisfaction with commonplace or indifferent responses (flight into security). This is particularly true of intelligent neurotics.

(8) Rejection of card (refusal to touch, or quick return to examiner).

(9) Irregular succession on color cards when succession on black and white cards is orderly.

(10) Decreased ability to see popular configurations when these are quickly seen on uncolored cards.

(11) Color shyness and absence of color-determined responses in an individual who shows ability to give them by verbal references to color but who is unable to use them to advantage in combination with form.

Color shock is usually interpreted to indicate some neurotic element in the patient's make-up. A second kind of shock is shading shock. This occurs as a reaction to shaded areas which is similar to color shock. It is likely to indicate a depressed or morbid tone. Shading shock often appears in conjunction with color shock and is manifested by increased reaction time, exclamations and comments indicative of anxiety, tension, horror, etc., a decrease in the number or quality of the responses, or rejection of the card in question.

In addition to color and shading shock we find other typical or characteristic modes of perceiving which are common to persons exhibiting so-called "neurotic symptoms." A few examples will illustrate the use of the Rorschach procedure in understanding the behavior of such subjects. Individuals who are extremely anxious and preoccupied with their worries and tension show considerable preoccupations with shading on the cards, and may give many YF, VF, and FV responses. They may give more than the usual number of movement responses; this may be indicative of the intratensive preoccupation with the actual physiological aspects of their anxiety. On the other hand, individuals who have found some expressive outlet for their anxiety, such as those manifesting conversion or obsessive-compulsive symptoms, show relatively little reaction to the shading elements of the cards.

Persons presenting conversion or hysterical reactions may fail to respond to the cards on the basis that the cards are silly. Such persons are usually sensitive and reluctant to expose themselves. They may, however, be persuaded to respond to the cards; whereas persons with organic problems and schizophrenic reactions will seldom respond to a card once they have refused. Conversion reactives will usually give a large number of pure C and CF responses, and they frequently show color shock. This is perhaps an indication of their egocentricity, uncontrolled affectivity, and dependence upon external influence. They may give good form responses, but, in general, form responses that are not as good as those given by the anxiety-reactive subjects or the obsessive-compulsive persons. The conversion reactives are extremely extravertive or extratensive, and since they are using a quite socially acceptable symptom to solve their problems, their Rorschach records show more preoccupation with form and color than with movement.

Persons with obsessive and compulsive behavior often show particularly profound color shock, and this may be emphasized by their remarks about the difficulty of the colored cards and their inability to use them. Their records frequently show a rigid sequence, a high animal percentage, and a large number of details (particularly small details); in general, they are as compulsive with the Rorschach task as with other tasks. They tend to give about as many M as C responses. A high F+ percentage and a marked degree of stereotypy appear in the protocol of the compulsive doubter, as well as a marked number of card rejections and indications of extreme perplexity.

Neurotic subjects, in general, tend to show a considerable amount of preoccupation with the quality of their responses. The diagnosis of neuroticism from a Rorschach protocol usually consists in first establishing the presence of neurotic behavior by noting indications of color shock, anxiety, and other signs mentioned above, and then eliminating the possibility of a more profound disorder by carefully scrutinizing the record for responses indicative of more disintegrative types of thinking and behaving.

Persons exhibiting psychotic behavior vary greatly in performance on the Rorschach. Using schizophrenic behavior as an example, let us look at some of the typical response characteristics. A schizophrenic subject will usually approach the cards in a confused manner. He will ordinarily give fewer whole responses than the average and many responses of the additive type. There will tend to be a number of confabulatory or DW responses as well as other indications of alogical thinking. In the same vein, we find much contamination in the responses. Rare details are frequent and may be significant qualitatively as well as because of their quantity. There will generally be few movement responses, although the person with paranoid thinking may give some M responses. The schizophrenic subject usually gives C and CF responses, but relatively fewer FC responses. One of the most significant aspects of the psychotic's record, particularly that of the schizophrenic, is the low F+ percentage. Among schizophrenic subjects this percentage will be highest in the records of persons with paranoid behavior and lowest in the records of those with regressive or hebephrenic behavior. Significant, too, is the variability of quality in response. The number of popular responses will be low with schizophrenic subjects. There will probably be blocking and rejection of cards, and perhaps a number of original responses. A more serious indication of this behavior disorder is believed to be the presence of an unusually large number of V and Y responses. Positional responses will probably be present as well as a number of abstract and personal references. The schizophrenic subject may perseverate, and the type of perseveration will differ from that of the organic or brain-damaged subject, who is unable to shift. Other responses will be in line with the schizophrenic's tendency to distort the world to fit himself and to see his own world rather than that seen by others.

In Chapter 17,[2] we described some of the Rorschach responses characteristic of persons with organic cortical or subcortical involvement. We will not repeat the discussion here, but as a final example of the diagnostic use of the test, we will consider some of the characteristics of records given by persons with convulsive reactions. The epileptic may tend to define blots rather than to interpret them. The average number of responses given by epileptic subjects may be greater than the number given by normal subjects, but the form responses are poorer. The reaction time for epileptic subjects is usually high. Their records show many color responses and human-movement responses; confabulation and perseveration is present and shading responses are frequent. These are just a few of the characteristics noted in the protocol of the epileptic subject, but, in general, he responds to the Rorschach situation much as one would expect an emotional, sometimes irritable, possibly brain-damaged person with uncontrollable aspects of behavior to respond.

The Rorschach testing situation can best be regarded as a controlled situation in which the examiner can observe the behavior of the subject. In the strictest sense, it should not be regarded as a test, but rather as a sample of behavior. If we observe (in the testing situation) a person behaving as an anxious person or as an epileptic person usually behaves, we may have leads for understanding the individual, leads that might otherwise not have been apparent. It is likely that all such observations could be made in other situations, but other situations often require more time and are less efficient in yielding results. In free observation of behavior most of the trends could be noted, but it often takes days of observation in a wide variety of situations to elicit all the aspects of perception and response which are revealed by the Rorschach protocol.

4. THE PLANNING OF COUNSELING. In planning counseling or therapy, the ultimate goal of evaluation, there are many test factors and constellations of test factors to be studied, and our concern is with the entire picture. Specific test factors often vary in their significance as the whole picture shifts. With this in mind, the person skilled in Rorschach interpretation can easily direct his attention to the planning of counseling, noting trends that might otherwise be ignored. In the process of planning from the Rorschach, or for that matter from any kind of evaluative information, there are at least two essential points to be kept in mind. First, we must look for positive constructive factors upon which we can build. Second, negative or pathological factors can be used to advantage. As an illustration of the second point, we can consider the simple example of a compulsive person who might make the most healthy adjustment in work of a detailed nature.

[2] See pp. 449–50.

As Beck points out, the Rorschach test indicates the degree or height of intelligence in several ways. The number of W responses is one index to the client's present functioning intelligence. The W score may be affected by many transitory factors. Insofar as planning for counseling or therapy is concerned, the present functioning intelligence is important. Some clinicians regard the estimate of present ability from the Rorschach as more significant to the counselor than the I.Q. as derived from other tests. It is probable that ability to gain insight into a unique, complicated constellation of etiological factors is better reflected from the ability to produce whole percepts than from many of the tasks making up standardized tests of intelligence. Furthermore, for purposes of treatment, we are also interested in qualitative differences among whole responses. For example, although the number of additive W's may be of import diagnostically, the presence of some degree of the more vigorous analysis-synthesis activity will point the way to a better prognosis. The presence of DW or DdW (discussing detail and finally coming up with a whole form) is common in most disturbed persons, and it is frequently dynamically related to the essential basis of maladjustment. The amount of this response may be positively related to the amount of difficulty experienced or expected in counseling. The organization or Z score will also give data of further significance to the counselor.

With regard to all Rorschach factors, importance is attached not only to the presence of certain factors, but even more to the balance *between* the factors. For counseling purposes the absence of D (detail) or Dd responses can be as significant as the absence of whole responses. Consequently, the counselor will pay special attention to the approach or emphasis as indicated in the distribution of responses between W, D, and Dd. When a person presents a good balance of W, D, and Dd, we usually contemplate a more favorable prognosis. On occasion the subject's approach may suggest a counseling aim that might otherwise have been neglected. Still further, the psychologist must be alert to the sequence of responses. Beck describes the function of sequence in neuroses and points out that the client who presents an orderly sequence (W, D, Dd) will probably be successful in coping with his conflicts. The client's effort to be methodical may, of course, go to extremes in some cases. On the other hand, serious or confused irregularity may indicate that the client will have difficulty in bringing his conflicts under control.

The client's ability to maintain control over his thinking shows itself best by the presence of accurate form responses (F+). The significance of F+ responses (such as those to color) is too complicated to discuss in this presentation. However it is well recognized that F+ is one of the most significant of the Rorschach test factors, particularly as an indication of personal stability. Counseling is often a disorganizing or disrupting influence for a time. Some clients may not be able to maintain sufficient control to survive therapy without developing an even more serious disorganization. The counselor must be alert to this situation when the emphasis of form percepts is F– rather than F+.

An individual who sees movement in static ink blots is exhibiting a high degree of originality, but the quality of the M (movement) response may vary. The M response, when found in combination with good form responses, reflects adaptability to change and creative thinking. The ability of the client to see and use color indicates energy and initiative, and these can be used in the solution of his problems. Again, however, there are qualitative differences in color responses, and we must take into consideration the manner in which color is combined with form and other determinants.

All these and other factors of the Rorschach protocol are helpful in planning counseling, and the interested counselor who is not already thoroughly familiar with the Rorschach must extend his study much beyond a cursory description of the test. Every Rorschach report should include evaluations of the person tested in terms of his therapeutic potentiality. An appraisal should be made of his functioning capacity, his emotionality, his control, his productivity, and his ability to perceive relationships.

A young married woman, 23 years of age, recently came to the clinic for personal counseling. She was a graduate student in one of the physical sciences, and her husband was an advanced graduate student in the same field. She described her problem as fear of taking certain qualifying examinations required by her department. She had postponed these examinations several times, and was now faced with the necessity of taking them very soon or she would be dropped from the department. She said she knew that she would fail them, that she was not prepared for them, and she expressed general feelings of unworthiness. The counselor felt quite sure that her depression was more general and involved than might be expected to result from the examination emergency, and that he needed much more information about the client before he could plan with her. However his only source of information was the client herself, and she was quite reticent about discussing anything except the examinations. The counselor was also somewhat reluctant to probe too much in an interview situation because of the client's apparent anxious, depressed state. The Rorschach was administered and some of the impressions gained from it illustrate its use in planning counseling.

In general, the record was that of a highly intelligent individual who was showing many signs of depression, morbidity, and a general intellectual letdown. She gave fifty-seven responses; she used movement to some extent and color quite considerably. Anxiety was indicated in her use of color and in the content of her responses. There were more color-form combinations than form-color combinations, suggesting emotional immaturity. The presence of anxiety signs, along with other aspects of the record, led the counselor to believe that no marked psychotic break had yet taken place. There were enough popular responses, the form quality was good, and the record did not seem to be that of a psychotic person. There was a strong emphasis on whole responses, and the balance between whole responses and movement suggested to the counselor that the individual, while highly intelligent, had probably been striving for goals that were, at least at the time when she was being tested, well beyond her functioning ability. Her intellectual efficiency seemed to be low, but her goals had not been modified to be consistent with it. She did not appear to be in any condition to take the qualifying examinations, yet she felt that she must take them; and she had not relinquished her objective of achieving a Ph.D. degree. Her interests and orientation had been toward science. Although persons in her field usually give Rorschach records with emphasis upon small details, she did not give even one such response. This suggested the tentative hypothesis that some change might be taking place in her typical modes of behavior reactions.

There was a total avoidance of sex responses. This suggested the necessity of exploring the area by other means. The lack of such responses was interpreted (when taken together with other observations) as indicative of conflict in the area, but it also suggested that the client had intellectual control over expression in the area of sex. This, again, indicated against the possibility that the client had retreated from reality to the point of a psychotic adjustment. The color responses were rather poorly controlled. The impression was that of a person with strong emotional reactions, who was irritable and who was not in control of mood swings. The experience balance (ratio of movement to total of color reactions) was near-ambigual, and this, combined with the depressed features, made the counselor suspect that suicidal fantasies had been indulged in frequently and that there was some risk of their being carried out in reality. There was a strong emphasis upon shading. These responses suggested great sensitivity and deep underlying disturbances of long standing. In some ways the responses were suggestive of reactive depression, but the total number of responses, use of movement, and use of color were against this. Rather, the counselor had the impression that current situations had brought to the fore conflicts of longer standing. Everything pointed to marked unhappiness and discouragement at the time.

Considering the degree of conflict in evidence and the intelligence of the client, the counselor believed that one of the most serious findings in the record was the lack of vista responses. This, coupled with other elements in the record, was taken to mean that there was currently no strong drive for self-appraisal. The client did not appear to be attempting to gain insight into her behavior or to relate herself to others in a constructive and realistic fashion. This was also borne out by the lack of human content. One response with human content was turned into a somewhat bizarre example of dehumanizing: "This pink part looks like sides of two hills, standing across these are blue parts, two persons, or go-rillas holding something across, sounds silly—gorillas because of large shoulders, sides of valley, hold on to something across." The suggested struggle of holding onto something was repeated in several responses. This struggle was believed to be symbolically important. In general, it was felt that the client was struggling to maintain control over her behav-ior and to avoid a psychotic break. The Rorschach record might have been interpreted as suggestive of a prepsychotic picture of an individual in transition to a psychotic state. However, there were evidences that no psychotic break had occurred. There were some withdrawal and regres-sive signs, and if a psychotic adjustment were adopted, it would probably be a hebephrenic or regressive reaction.

It must not be assumed that a Rorschach test administered by *any* examiner could reveal all the points made in the above paragraphs. First, the points made were only tentative hypotheses and could not be regarded as certitudes until supported by other observations. Second, we have mentioned excerpts from a record, and the counselor had the benefit of the total picture as well as face-to-face observation of the client. Con-sequently, the counselor was not engaging in "tea-leaf reading" to the extent that might be suggested from the above. Third, the counselor re-ferred to is a person of wide experience who is able, because of this ex-perience, to make penetrating and seemingly intuitive statements about the results of the Rorschach Test. The same insights can perhaps be gained from other types of observations of a subject if the clinician is suf-ficiently experienced.

It was judged from the preceding report that the first aim of treat-ment should be to offer support and to provide an atmosphere in which the client could feel comfortable. In other words, the clinician wished to help her in her struggle to maintain control over her behavior. After rap-port had been firmly established, the client was encouraged to ventilate and to relieve herself of pent-up emotional feelings. No attempt was made to examine any of the reasons for her present emotional state. It was felt that this might be too traumatic and might precipitate violent or bizarre behavior. After several interviews the client brought up problems attendant to her graduate study. The clinician spent a great deal of time helping her to plan her work and to reorganize her goals, thus making some progress toward the achievement of her advanced degree.

Specifically, she had been planning to earn a Ph.D. degree without first earning an M.S. This was permitted for exceptional students, but in order to earn a Ph.D. in this way, the candidate was required to pass the examinations which the client had been dreading and postponing. An alternate plan made it possible for the student to complete a Master's thesis and to be qualified as a candidate for the Ph.D. on the basis of the Master's research and examinations. After some deliberation the client decided that she might not want to work toward the higher degree. She had married only recently, and it became quite evident to her that she might actually be attempting to compete with her husband, who was brilliant and much more advanced in his studies than she. There was no reason for her to compete with him, and since she did not intend to work professionally, she decided that she might not continue beyond the Master's degree. This was consistent with the suggestion from the Rorschach that the interference from her emotional conflict was so great that her intellectual efficiency might be lowered below that which would be necessary for her to attain her goals. The clinician's aim was to bring her goals more closely in line with her functioning level. At this point he found it necessary to see the husband—thus employing environmental counseling —since the client felt that her husband was pressuring her to take the Ph.D. examinations and that he would be terribly disappointed if she failed. The truth of the situation was that he was extremely relieved to have her "lower her sights." He had no desire for her to do advanced work, and, perhaps selfishly, was happy with her changed plans since she might then show more interest in him. Since she had practically completed research work that would form the basis for a Master's thesis, she began to plan toward this objective, reserving judgment as to whether or not she would go further in school.

The client gradually gained some confidence in herself because of her professional achievements. Voluntarily she then brought up the traumatic marital problems that were actually basic to her depression. She told of having been assaulted when she was twelve years of age by a Catholic boy in her neighborhood. Her husband was Catholic, and her mother had bitterly opposed her marriage to him. In fact, she had had no communication with her family since her marriage. This was extremely important because she had always been exceptionally dependent upon her mother. Gradually, the picture began to evolve. She was quite apprehensive about both sexual intercourse and the possibility of pregnancy. Her fear of sexual relations seemed to stem from the earlier traumatic experience, and this fear was further intensified by the coincidence of her husband's religion. She had received little sexual education, and what her mother had told her about childbirth had stressed the pain and danger. She was horribly afraid, and she had no one to turn to. The sexual problems were so disturbing that she could not let herself think about them, and as a consequence she wanted to explain her anxiety in terms of the superficial and current problems related to her graduate study. At the same time she could not contend with the examinations and other requirements.

The clinician felt that in this instance a more direct or active attack in planning therapy would have been disastrous, for the client would have either reacted violently or rejected the counseling relationship. She simply could not face the situation in which she found herself. The Rorschach determined the strategy of therapy, as the clinical impression of the client was of a bland, sophisticated young woman who had no serious problems other than academic ones.

Before we leave the discussion of the Rorschach, we must call attention to the value of carefully studying the content of the associations. The limits of the individual and his capacity to deal with his problems in the counseling situation may be estimated from interpretation and interpolation of the test factors. However it is from the associational content that we get clues to personal needs, which are so important in planning counseling. Most of the responses speak for themselves, and we will not dwell on this point. It is suggested that the psychologist study carefully the actual protocol and make all possible use of any suggestions inherent in the content. In addition to supplying a wealth of information, the test often provides an opening wedge for establishing rapport, thereby getting the interviews under way. On occasion the psychologist may wish to use the test procedure for that express purpose. Finally, let us note again the necessity of evaluating the balance of Rorschach material. We must be alert to the positive factors which may point the way to constructive plans as well as to the negative elements which may serve as admonitions.

THE MOSAIC TEST

Until recent years the Mosaic Test (15, 20) was not widely used in the United States. It was developed in England by Lowenfeld in 1929, and it serves much the same purposes as the Rorschach. As Bell (8) points out, for clinical usage it bears the same relationship to the World Test as the Rorschach bears to the TAT—whereas the Mosaic reveals more of the personality structure, the World Test reveals more of the content of disturbing complexes. In terms of the differentiation of this text, the Mosaic gives us indication of the "what" of behavior (the potentialities and resources), and the World Test gives us more of the "why."

The materials of the Mosaic Test consist of small plastic pieces in different shapes and colors. A single set consists of 24 squares, 48 diamonds, 48 right-angled triangles, 36 equilateral triangles, and 42 scalenes. The pieces are in six colors (red, yellow, green, blue, black, and white) with one-sixth of each form group falling into each of the color groups.

Instructions for the test are simple: "Make anything you like out of the pieces." Most test administrators use a tray lined with a recording paper so that a permanent record can be made of the arrangements produced on the paper. Besides noting the subject's behavior during the test and his reaction to his production, the patterns produced are analyzed in a number of ways. Bell (8) lists the following twenty-three different observable characteristics of a Mosaic design:

1. The number of designs
2. The coherence or incoherence
3. Concreteness or abstraction
4. Harmony of the design as a whole
5. Completeness or incompleteness
6. Meaningfulness or emptiness
7. Simplicity or complexity
8. Compactness or looseness
9. Distinctness or configuration
10. Realistic or schematic nature of design
11. Static or dynamic representation
12. Configuration by pieces or by space enclosed
13. Position in reference to tray
14. Number of pieces
15. Choice of color
16. Choice of shapes
17. Emphasis on form or color
18. Production of simple geometric design
19. Appropriate choice of shapes for intention
20. Evidence of fixation in form, color, or piece put down
21. Symmetry
22. Repetition; stereotypy
23. Relation of design to what a subject says [3]

These characteristics of Mosaic productions, as well as a few others, have been utilized for both qualitative and quantitative analysis of the test. The research on the Mosaic Test has been summarized by Herbert Dorken (9); in general the test has proved to be a useful device when used by clinicians skilled and experienced in its use.

SUMMARY

Two tests have been described in this chapter as examples of the unstructured projective test. The Rorschach in particular was described in considerable detail, with emphasis on administration, scoring, and interpre-

---

[3] By permission from *Projective Techniques*, by John E. Bell. Copyright 1948 by Longmans, Green & Company, Inc.

tation. It was indicated that both the Rorschach and the Mosaic tests provide the subject with an unstructured and ambiguous stimulus situation in which the mode of response and method of dealing with the stimulus materials are believed to reveal the subject's typical manner of behavior, thereby allowing the clinician to make estimates concerning the subject's resources for dealing with other problems.

In Part III we have presented many different techniques and approaches to evaluation—all tools available to the clinician. The ultimate purpose of evaluation is the planning of counseling, educative, or therapeutic procedures.

BIBLIOGRAPHY

1. Abt, L. E., and Bellak, L., *Projective psychology*. New York: Alfred A. Knopf, 1950.
2. Allen, R. M., *Introduction to the Rorschach technique: manual of administration and scoring*. New York: International Univ. Press, 1953.
3. Allen, R. M., *Elements of Rorschach interpretation*. New York: International Univ. Press. 1954.
4. Anastasi, A., *Psychological testing*. New York: Macmillan, 1954.
5. Beck, S. J., *Rorschach's Test: I. Basic processes*. New York: Grune & Stratton, 1944.
6. Beck, S. J., *Rorschach's Test: II. A variety of personality pictures*. New York: Grune & Stratton, 1944.
7. Beck, S. J., *Rorschach's Test: III. Advances in interpretation*. New York: Grune & Stratton, 1952.
8. Bell, J. E., *Projective techniques*. New York: Longmans, Green, 1948.
9. Dorken, H. Jr., "The Mosaic Test: Review." *J. Proj. Tech.*, 1952, 16, 287–96.
10. Halpern, F., *A clinical approach to children's Rorschachs*. New York: Grune & Stratton, 1953.
11. Harrower, M., *Appraising personality*. New York: Norton, 1952.
12. Harrower, M. R., "Group techniques for the Rorschach Test." In Abt, L. E., and Bellak, L. (eds.), *Projective psychology*. New York: Alfred A. Knopf, 1950.
13. Klopfer, B., Ainsworth, M. D., Klopfer, W. G., and Holt, R. R., *Developments in the Rorschach technique*, Vol. I. *Techniques and theory*. Yonkers-on-Hudson, N. Y.: World Book, 1954.
14. Klopfer, B., and Kelley, D. M., *The Rorschach technique*. Yonkers-on-Hudson, N. Y.: World Book, 1942.
15. Lowenfeld, M., "The Mosaic Test." *Amer. J. Orthopsychiat.*, 1949, 19, 537–50.
16. Monroe, R. L., "The inspection technique for the Rorschach protocol." In Abt, L. E., and Bellak, L. (eds.), *Projective psychology*. New York: Alfred A. Knopf, pp. 91–145.
17. Phillips, L., and Smith, J. G., *Rorschach interpretations: advanced technique*. New York: Grune & Stratton, 1953.

18. Rorschach, H., *Psychodiagnostics*. Translated by Paul Lemkan and Bernard Hronenberg. Berne: Hans Boher, 1942.
19. Schafer, R., *Psychoanalytical interpretation in Rorschach testing*. New York: Grune & Stratton, 1954.
20. Wertham, F., "The Mosaic Test." In Abt, L. E., and Bellak, L. (eds.). *Projective psychology*. New York: Alfred A. Knopf, 1950, 230–56.

Part Four

✵ ✵

PROFESSIONAL ISSUES

CHAPTER

21

Qualifications of the Clinician

W HEREAS THE PREVIOUS CHAPTERS HAVE DEFINED AND DE-
scribed the professional field of clinical and counseling psychology, this chapter will attempt to define and describe the professional psychologist who works in that field. Students considering this
area of study as a possible career wonder whether they have the necessary personal and intellectual aptitudes for success as a clinician. The
general public and even members of other professional disciplines appear to have only a hazy idea as to the qualifications of the psychologist.
If psychology is to work with other professions in a constructive and co-
operative fashion, and it is to be utilized by the public to the fullest
advantage, a better understanding must be reached concerning the professional and personal qualifications of clinical and counseling psychologists.

The task of describing the personal attributes of a professional psychologist is a difficult one. Clinical and counseling psychologists must first
of all be psychologists. As psychologists they must utilize techniques of
investigation, of measurement, and of evaluation in an objective fashion.
Clinical and counseling psychologists must be scientific psychologists,
but they must be scientific psychologists who apply scientific techniques
to the benefit of their clients. To do this, they must have personal qualifications that are in some ways unusual. Individuals possessing quite different aptitudes and behavioral characteristics will undoubtedly function
equally well as professional psychologists. They may accomplish their
tasks in quite different ways, yet do their jobs effectively. Although any
description of qualifications is tentative and incomplete, we will discuss
some apparent trends in an effort to help clarify the various questions
that arise about the professional psychologist as a person.

The questions raised by prospective students and by members of other professional groups as well as by the general public are extremely varied, but perhaps the most common questions concern the amount and kind of training believed necessary before one can be regarded as professionally trained. Undergraduate students often elect psychology as a major area of study with no clear understanding of the graduate study and applied experience entailed if they are to secure employment as specialists in clinical and counseling psychology. Administrators of graduate training programs are impressed by the large number of applications for admission to graduate study from students who are either uninformed or misinformed about the nature of professional training in the area. Employers often decide that it would be a good idea to have a psychologist on their staff, yet have little accurate information about the training and experience that would make the psychologist most useful to them. Even more distressing is the situation of the unhappy, anxious person who, ignorant of the qualifications of a professional psychologist but intensely desiring help, takes his problems to poorly prepared and sometimes unethical individuals who represent to the public that they have psychological services to offer.

These are just a few of the reasons for including a discussion of the professional and personal qualifications of the clinical and counseling psychologist. In addition to describing the training and experience of the clinician and counselor, we will discuss some of the more personal attributes—intellectual capacity, mental health, interests and attitude toward work—of the competent and ethical psychologist.

THE TRAINING OF A PSYCHOLOGICAL CLINICIAN

To be adequately prepared as a clinical or counseling psychologist, one must have earned the Doctor of Philosophy degree in psychology with major training in the specific applications of psychology to clinical problems. This first requirement represents a minimum. It is true that many persons have held positions and have functioned as psychologists without this training. At the present time, however, there are few, if any, professional positions available to the person without the doctor's degree. State Civil Service Boards in some states may list positions that they call clinical psychology positions which do not require the doctor's degree, but by and large all positions that involve any professional responsibility require it. Positions open to persons with less training are basically technical in nature. Within the last few years the Veterans Administration has established the Doctor of Philosophy degree plus two years of experience as the basic requirement for their starting or journeyman grade of employment. With few exceptions other Federal government agencies have the same requirements.

The recently organized American Board of Examiners in Professional Psychology requires for certification a doctorate plus five years of experience and the successful completion of written and oral examinations. During the first few years of the board's operation, it accepted applications from, and granted certificates to, persons without the doctorate if they had had ten years of qualifying experience. This "grandfather clause" was designed to allow the certification of persons with extensive experience but with less education. Provision was also made for certification without an examination of persons who had received their undergraduate degrees prior to 1935, if they otherwise qualified. This clause has now expired, and in the future there will be no exceptions to the minimum educational requirements of a doctor's degree, experience, and examination. It would seem that ultimately all professional psychologists who hope to occupy responsible positions will wish to achieve certification by the American Board of Examiners in Professional Psychology.

Various states have passed laws concerning the practice of psychology. Whether these laws pertain to licensing or to certification, most of them do not permit a psychologist without the doctorate to call himself a psychologist or to represent that he offers psychological services. Exceptions have been made for the established psychologist, who may secure a license with less training if he has demonstrated himself to be competent. However, he must have demonstrated his competence by the time the law was passed. In most instances the person who enters the field at the present time must present the Ph.D. degree in order to be licensed or certified as a psychologist. Persons with less training may be given some legal status but they are usually designated as technicians or assistants. In view of this, beginning students must look forward to earning the Doctor of Philosophy degree if they wish to prepare for professionally responsible work in the field. As a matter of fact, many schools will not accept students for training as clinical or counseling psychologists if they do not expect to continue their education until they have earned the Ph.D. Schools that offer subdoctoral programs usually stress the value of these programs as preparation for employment as technicians.

The beginning clinician should realize that the higher requirements apply particularly to the practice of counseling or therapy. A doctorate plus substantial experience should be an absolute "must" for the person who expects to function as a counselor or as a therapist. Many schools have taken the position that preparation in therapy should be reserved for post-doctoral training. This position may be somewhat extreme, but it seems evident that all accredited schools agree that one is not qualified as a therapist until at least a doctorate has been completed.

The doctoral training programs for both clinical and counseling psychologists have been given a great deal of careful consideration. The

American Psychological Association created a committee on training in clinical psychology shortly after World War II. This committee has been replaced by a board on training which is studying all specialties and levels of training in psychology. Among the committees represented on the board are several concerned with university graduate training, as well as with internship training in clinical psychology. In the summer of 1949 the United States Public Health Service (2) sponsored a conference among leaders in the field of clinical psychology and related disciplines to study training problems in clinical psychology. A follow-up of this conference was held in the summer of 1955. A committee on training in clinical psychology has made a number of recommendations concerning the characteristics of desirable graduate training in this area (1). Approximately five years after the APA Committee on Training in Clinical Psychology published its report, similar reports (3, 4) were published by the APA Committee on Counselor Training. The similarity among all of these reports is dramatic. In view of the belief that counseling and clinical psychology are both applications of the same body of scientific knowledge, this should not be surprising. However, it is reassuring that committees made up of entirely different people should come to essentially the same conclusions after a five-year interval. It will be well to discuss several recommendations of these committees as representative of the attitudes held by most training institutions.[1]

(1) The committees stressed particularly that the clinician should be trained as a psychologist first and as a specialist only after he has been thoroughly trained in general and experimental psychology. He should be given an opportunity to acquire a core of basic concepts, tools, and techniques that should be common to all psychologists. This is consistent with the concept that the clinician applies the principles of general psychology. It would be just as incongruous for a Doctor of Medicine to specialize in obstetrics or pediatrics without first completing his basic training in medicine as for a psychologist to specialize in diagnostic or therapeutic procedures before he has had basic training in general psychology.

(2) It was emphasized that the program of education for the professional clinician should be just as rigorous and intensive as for the traditional doctorate in other fields. When we consider the full year of internship recommended by the committees in addition to the academic requirements, this means that the doctorate in clinical or counseling psychology should involve a minimum of four years of study beyond the bachelor's degree. Universities accredited by the American Psychological Association, with few exceptions, adhere closely to this recommendation. In the case of the exceptions, the internship is required after the doctor-

---

[1] The statements of the recommendations and the discussion are not necessarily those of the committees. We have taken certain liberties with their presentation and have combined the several reports.

ate but before the student is recommended for employment or is regarded as a fully trained professional psychologist. This procedure conforms with the typical practice of medical schools, but until some form of licensing of psychologists is provided by all states, most universities will probably require that the doctorate not be conferred until after the internship is completed.

(3) It was recommended that the academic preparation be broad and that it be directed primarily toward research and professional goals rather than toward technical goals. Training should be in the three functions of evaluation, research, and counseling or therapy with the special contributions of the research worker emphasized throughout. It should be clear from this and other recommendations that the emphasis is on training of a professional rather than a technical nature.

(4) To meet the above requirements, the committee felt that the program of study should include several areas. Although there are certain differences in minor details, most of the accredited universities organize their study programs around these areas:

(a) General psychology
(b) Personality organization and development
(c) Evaluation and appraisal of the individual
(d) Knowledge of social environment
(e) Counseling and therapy
(f) Research methods
(g) Related disciplines

(5) The program of graduate training should be organized around theory and practice. It was emphasized that a portion of the training should be supervised or guided experience. The recommended course of study included a minimum of a year's internship. In addition, however, practicum or supervised practice should accompany every course or course work area.

In order to insure that the student have contact with clinical material, both directly and indirectly, throughout the four years, the following progression was recommended:

(a) Laboratory
(b) Practicum
(c) Internship

As an example, at Purdue University [2] the first year of study includes laboratory courses in intelligence testing, observational and lab-

[2] This program is reported in some detail as an example of what a beginning student might look forward to. It is not necessarily regarded as a model [see also Hadley and Asher (6)].

oratory courses in child psychology, and clinical procedures with children, in addition to basic study in statistics, research methods, general psychology, physiological psychology, and personality theory. In the laboratory courses subjects are provided simply for practice purposes. No testing or interviewing is done with "real" clients. In the second year the student gains laboratory experience in projective techniques during the first part of the year, and as the year progresses he begins to receive practicum experience in interviewing and testing. This practicum experience consists of carefully guided work with "real" clients. However at this stage the supervisor, not the student, takes primary responsibility for the work and carefully criticizes all reports and results of the student's work. Also in the second year the student continues his study of general and experimental psychology, personality theory, and research methods. In this year, too, he begins a theoretical study of counseling or therapy and other remedial techniques. He may, in addition, begin to gain practicum experience in remedial counseling, vocational guidance, and counseling with minor adjustment problems.

The third year is ordinarily devoted to internship training. For the clinical psychology option, the internship must be approved by the university, supervision must be provided by psychiatrists as well as psychologists, and the discipline of psychiatric social work must be represented. The ideal internship is regarded as one in which the intern functions as a member of the mental hygiene team. (Although the counseling psychology major does not necessarily intern in a medical setting, he must also serve a year in an appropriate work setting.) It is hoped that in addition to gaining some experience in clinical work with "real" clients, the student will have an opportunity to participate in interdisciplinary seminars and to attend staff conferences. Research opportunities are provided and the student is encouraged to gather material for his own dissertation as well as to collaborate with other research workers. Some internships may provide experience with patients at different age levels presenting a variety of behavior disorders. Students who have fairly definite vocational plans may be guided to internships offering specialized training. The fourth year of the typical program is devoted to further experience, research, and elective courses.

(6) The Committee on Clinical Training has further commented on the desirability of utilizing representatives of various disciplines as teachers and on the need for the development of a feeling of responsibility for patients and clients. All through the recommendations there is emphasis on research implications. It is hoped that through research work clinicians will develop the habit of constantly asking "how?" "why?" and "what is the evidence?" Other points are mentioned in the committees' reports but this should suffice to give the reader a general conception of what comprises training.

The goal of the professional psychologist is to foster the psychological development of the individual. This includes all persons on the adjustment continuum from those who function adequately, or even at a superior level, to those who present severe behavior disorders. The psychologist who is working with persons in the normal range should utilize all facilities and personnel available to him. The psychologist should not "go it" alone, but should be acquainted with and use community resources for meeting educational, employment, health, social, and marital needs. Still another consideration is the development of awareness of the various administrative patterns characteristic of the working setting in which the psychologist may find himself. On the college campus he needs to understand the administrative structure of higher education, in the business or industrial setting he must understand the tables of organization involved, and similarly for all other working situations. The unique and most significant contribution that the psychologist can make is in the area of research. The entire heritage of psychology is experimentation, not diagnosis or therapy, and let us pray that this vital tradition can be maintained and that psychology will not be sold short.

PERSONAL ATTRIBUTES OF THE PSYCHOLOGICAL CLINICIAN

1. INTELLIGENCE.   Although it is absolutely necessary to insist that a certain level of training be completed before a person practices psychology, there are personal qualifications that are undoubtedly just as fundamental as training. Perhaps the most important qualification of a clinician is his intelligence. The recently completed study of the prediction of performance in clinical psychology by E. Lowell Kelly and Donald W. Fiske (7) reports the Miller Analogies Test (a test designed to measure aptitude for graduate study) to be the most useful in their battery of tests for predicting both academic and clinical performance. Other tests of intellectual abilities were found to be significantly related to many of their criterion measures. Although the Miller Analogies Test measures verbal and informational factors as well as native capacity, the results reported by Kelly and Fiske certainly indicate the importance of intelligence for competence in clinical psychology. It is quite reassuring that the standardization data on the Miller Analogies Test (9) indicates that graduate students in psychology scored as high or higher than students in thirteen other graduate and professional school groups on this particular test. The only group of graduate students that approached the psychology students were those in the physical sciences. Students in the fields of medicine, law, social work, education, engineering, and all other

groups tested scored considerably lower. This is emphasized as an indication of the generally high intellectual capacity of graduate students in psychology.

Each client presents a unique syndrome and constellation of causative factors which must be thoroughly understood by the clinician. In the solution of novel problems, there is no satisfactory substitute for native mental ability. The clinician does not have blueprints that can be applied to all the situations he will meet. One might compare the task of the psychologist with that of the bridge or chess player who is presented in each hand or game with a novel problem that has never been seen by him before or, in fact, has probably never been seen by anyone else. There are, of course, certain similar constellations of factors, just as there are similar types of bridge hands, but no two are exactly alike. As the problem is worked through, new variations appear, and these constantly present new situations with which the psychologist must deal. The intricacies of any human being's personal problems are far more complicated than the problems of bridge or chess, and the task of coping with them demands a marked degree of intelligence. As in the case of the bridge hand, there are similar patterns, and there are some general stratagems that may be effective in dealing with these patterns. Culbertson presented a system that has enabled poor or mediocre bridge players to develop into average players. His system will hardly make a master out of a "dub." Certain systems of psychology may aid the psychologist, but the systems will not do his job for him. It takes a certain amount of intelligence to learn and understand a system, and intelligence becomes even more necessary when the actual problem-solving situation evolves into new and different complications for which there are no rules. It is doubtful whether a system can make a good bridge player out of a stupid person. By the same token it seems highly unlikely that a keen, intuitive clinician depends entirely on the rules of the game or the precepts of any system or framework of psychology; rather he appears to use his ingenuity to a marked degree.

A great deal has been written and said concerning clinical intuition. In fact, clinical methods have been labeled by some as intuitive and hence unscientific. When the factor of intuition is carefully analyzed, it appears probable that intelligence is a major component. Most intuitive insights, at least in clinical practice, are the products of a keen, well-trained observer who responds to a total situation, including even some minimal cues, and achieves closure (organizes his perceptions in a meaningful fashion) from a set of stimuli that may seem entirely unrelated to the less intelligent or less experienced observer. It would seem more accurate to substitute the concept of professional judgment for that of clinical intuition. It will be clear to the reader at this point that professional judgment involves more than intelligence. It involves training and experience as well as other factors to be mentioned later, but "good" professional judgment is hardly possible without a minimum of general intellectual ability.

Finally, it is important for all beginning students of psychology to realize that the task or ordeal of completing a Ph.D. degree is quite selective. Mastery of much of the academic material, understanding of many elaborate personality theories, grasping of subtleties in the projective techniques, gaining of skill in application of statistical concepts, comprehension of the remarkable organization of the nervous system, the design and conduct of a research work, even the passing of language examinations all require a substantial degree of native capacity.

2. MENTAL HEALTH. A second qualification essential to the psychological worker is his own mental health. A clinician must be prepared to shoulder vicariously a great many difficult personal problems. If he is in a poor state of mental health or has only lately recovered from such a state, he may be overtaxed. It would seem unnecessary to elaborate this point.

Jorge J. Dieppa (5) asked a number of clinicians to rate the case history of a client using a rating scale consisting of 105 forced-choice paired comparisons. The items that made up these paired comparisons were fifteen "areas of adjustment" considered to be of importance in evaluating the personality of individuals. The clinicians were also asked to rate themselves using the same rating scale. In addition, the clinicians answered a questionnaire about their own personal characteristics, and these were rated by three judges according to the same scale. The results of the study seem to indicate that the similarity between the pattern of choices used by the subjects when rating themselves and when rating the patient is very strong. This suggests that they may be seeing their own problems in the patient material. However in some subjects there was a negative relationship between the self-ratings and the patient ratings. These clinician subjects were not able to see their own problems in the patient. The relationships between self-ratings and patient-ratings were not distributed by chance. In other words, the subjects either tended to see their own problems in the patient or resisted seeing them. It is unlikely that either extreme would result in a completely objective appraisal of the patient. Similar results were obtained when the judges' ratings of the clinician were related to the clinician's ratings of the patient. Several other interesting findings developed from this study, but those we have reported would seem to indicate that the personality conflicts or problems of the clinician are reflected in his evaluations of clinical material. The role of the clinician as a participant observer has been discussed in Chapter 1.[3] Recognition of this role underlines the importance of good mental hygiene for this observer.

[3] See pp. 18–19.

The prestige of the clinician is a matter of some importance. One of the main points to be considered in this connection is the behavior of the clinician both within and without the clinical conference. It is highly desirable that the clinician be a dignified and mature person. The behavior of the psychologist off the job as well as on it is of the utmost importance. As a matter of fact, psychological services would have wider public acceptance today if representatives of the profession were better examples of maturity and adjustment. Uninhibited behavior *may* be regarded by some as indicative of mental health, but, within our society, psychology will gain prestige if this lack of inhibition is not flaunted before actual and prospective clients. This serious point must not be taken lightly. The psychologist is still a human being, but his position is particularly vulnerable since he is generally expected to set an example of adjustment to reality.

Before completing his training, every psychologist should undergo psychological assessment and evaluation, and he should accept psychological counseling or therapy if it is recommended. The evaluation should be directed toward the potentialities of the prospective psychologist and not merely toward his current adjustment. It is entirely possible that one who has successfully solved personal problems may be a better clinician because of his experiences. He may have more sympathy and sensitivity for his client's problems. It is most important that the individual who hopes to become a clinician either have attained mental health or have the capacity for attaining it. An interesting situation presents itself insofar as the selection of psychologists is concerned. Many become interested in the study of behavior pathology because of a conscious or unconscious hope that by their study of such behavior they will improve their own adjustment. Fortunately, some achieve their goal. Unfortunately, many do not—at least not by their own efforts. The individuals who do not frequently provide the basis for jokes about psychology and make poor representatives of the field. Personal therapy should be sought by those psychologists requiring it, and if mental health cannot be achieved, it is the responsibility of the profession or of training agencies to guide them into other applications of psychology or perhaps even into other vocations.

One caution must be repeated concerning psychologists who have received therapy. The value of therapeutic experiences must not be minimized, but we must see that the psychologist receiving therapy, or who has had therapy, also has broad training in the techniques and applications of therapy. Many psychologists have a tendency to relive with their clients their own therapeutic experiences. We must guard against this tendency to look for our own patterns of behavior in others. After all, psychologists are human and are subject to all the weaknesses and vagaries with which they work. Finding our own problems repeated and repeated in others may be so comforting that we oversimplify our theory of behavior and behavior disorders. If, however, therapeutic experiences serve to make the psychologist aware of his own feelings, needs, and desires so that they may be directed and controlled, these experiences are truly helpful.

Psychoanalytic workers have recognized this problem almost from the beginning of their work in the late nineteenth century. They have felt that the answer was to be found in requiring that the analyst himself be analyzed before he attempt to undertake the psychoanalysis of a client. They believe that the analyzed clinician can distinguish his own personal feelings from those of the client being observed or treated, and as a consequence can guard against biases, recognized or unrecognized, that may influence the accuracy of his observations. Much is gained if the observer can view his own behavior, attitudes, and feelings objectively. Some may doubt, however, whether personality therapy assures unbiased observation. In addition to the possibility that the clinician may relive his own therapeutic experiences, it is possible that personal therapy may invest the clinician with certain higher-order biases. He may have a tendency to interpret his observations in terms of the theoretical system that assisted him in his own self-understanding. Frederick C. Thorne (12, pp. 461–2) has commented:

> Psychoanalysts in general are characterized by the blitheness and confidence with which they omnipotently assume the responsibility of reorganizing the personality of another human, and unbelievers may be forgiven if they express questioning doubt concerning the omniscience and psychiatric infallibility of the analyst who presumes to revise the works of God after communing briefly with the works of Freud.[4]

It is suspected that Thorne had his tongue in his cheek when he wrote this sentence, but although we may regard it as somewhat facetious, there is a lesson to be gained from it. Psychoanalysis alone—or, for that matter, any other variety of personal therapy alone—will not insure competence as a clinician. There are other attributes of the healthy clinician who deals in other people's quandaries and presumes to insert himself into the personal and intimate lives of other human beings. Personal counseling or therapy is certainly indicated if it will assure impersonality and objectivity on the part of the clinician, or if it will contribute to the maintenance of his adjustment. The person who assumes added responsibilities by his role as a clinician must be mentally healthy himself. There is no royal road to the achievement of mental health, and there is no one

[4] From "A Critique of Nondirective Methods of Psychotherapy," by Frederick C. Thorne, *Journal of Abnormal and Social Psychology*, 1944, 39, 459–70. By permission of the American Psychological Association.

kind of therapy which can be arbitrarily regarded as more satisfactory for either the clinician or the client.

The preceding discussion is largely based on clinical experience and professional judgment. Little definitive research data can be brought to bear on the problem. Kelly and Fiske (7) have reported correlations between each of the several scores on certain tests of personality and the criterion measures in their study of the prediction of performance in clinical psychology. Although only a small proportion of their correlation coefficients are statistically significant, most of them are in the expected direction. Furthermore, most of the significant values are for two scores, "Freedom from Cycloid Tendencies" and "Thinking Extroversion." Among other criteria in this study, supervisors and academic personnel were asked to rate the subjects in terms of their preferences for hiring, assuming that they were able to employ a clinical psychologist. The "Freedom from Cycloid Tendencies" score was the best single predictor of "Preference for Hiring." This would suggest that stability of behavior is an important attribute of the clinician.

3. INTERESTS.   Since it is probable that students enter the study of psychology for a variety of motives, it seems worthwhile to consider the interest patterns characteristic of those in the field. Graduate training institutions have been aware for some time that there appears to be a difference in the interests of clinicians and those of other students of psychology. Too frequently clinicians have been described as "do-gooders." Undoubtedly social service motives are strong in the clinician, but the question arises as to whether desire to help others is sufficient motivation for the study and practice of psychology. The research studies (7, 8) that have attempted to study the relationship between performance on interest inventories and clinical performance suggest that this interest in other people and desire to help others does contribute to the clinician's performance in counseling and therapy. However, it is exceedingly important to stress that an individual should not base his choice of psychology as a vocation on such service interests and motives alone. The clinician apparently must have an unusual interest pattern. In addition to interests in people, he must have interests in quantitative things since he must do research and deal with mathematical and statistical concepts. Furthermore, he must be interested in dealing with ideas as well as with people.

All this suggests that it is important that clinicians have quite broad interests. Few persons will possess interest in all the activities that make up a part of the clinician's job. At the same time, if the clinical psychologist is to be successful and happy in both research and service, he must have tolerance for these activities even if interest is not strong in both.

4. ATTITUDE TOWARD HIS WORK.   The fourth personal qualification which we are to discuss is that of the attitude of the clinician to-

ward his work. This is no less important than the qualifications of training, intellectual capacity, mental health, and interests, but the attitude of the clinician toward the responsibilities of his work is certainly much more difficult to evaluate. By the same token, it is also more difficult to describe. This qualification along with others comes close to being an ethical qualification. In another sense, it relates to certain personal values or philosophical frameworks that are evident more in behavior than in what is "speakable" or "printable."

It appears vital that the professional psychologist realize that his responsibility toward his client must transcend all other responsibilities. Illness, study, research, vacation, and all other personal interests and problems of the clinician must be considered secondary to the problems of the client. The psychologist cannot feel his responsibility too deeply. He cannot arrange his time and activities to his own personal convenience. He must realize that psychological problems may be, and perhaps generally are, more acute than those of bodily health. Of course, there are medical emergencies that require immediate attention but most medical problems are more chronic than acute. So it is with psychological problems: some may be emergencies and occasionally involve matters of life and death—suicide or murder; however our present consideration is concerned more with situations which might not be considered emergencies in the medical or survival sense but which, nevertheless, must not be taken lightly by the psychologist or psychiatrist just because life is not in danger. The clinician must realize the effect the anxieties of an adolescent, the doubts or suspicions of the wife, or the security needs of the child may have upon his or her entire life. A need for affection or acceptance that is not recognized early may result in anguish carried to the grave. All functional problems presented to the clinician are acute to the client, and at times only the client can judge how important they are. The clinician cannot feel his responsibility too deeply. He must be available when he is needed. Individuals who are unwilling to assume this attitude should not attempt to become clinicians.

The written word seems inadequate to express the importance of this point. The reader is urged to read and reread the above paragraphs and to ask himself, "Do I really want to be a clinician? Do I feel that way about another person or another person's problems? Am I that unselfish?" As a matter of fact, few people can honestly answer these questions with an unqualified "yes," but if the beginning psychologist sincerely believes that he or she can really behave as if the answer were in the affirmative, he or she probably possesses this very necessary qualification.

5. OTHER PERSONAL QUALIFICATIONS.   There are still other qualities or personality traits desirable in the clinician. Like the attitude toward his work, these qualifications are difficult to evaluate or describe—they

are more qualitative than quantitative. Not many persons can qualify in every respect. Perhaps there are few who can qualify in terms of all the personal and professional characteristics already mentioned. Some will have more of one characteristic and less of another. The person contemplating the study of psychology can take a personal audit of himself and weigh the assets against the liabilities. Some of the liabilities can be compensated for and some of the desirable characteristics can be developed or undesirable characteristics can be controlled. What then are some of the other qualifications that are desirable?

A vital personal characteristic which, in some ways, may overlap with other qualities is respect for others. Carl R. Rogers (11) builds his entire philosophy of client-centered therapy around this concept. His emphasis of this point is one of the most important contributions ever made to the field of clinical psychology. We once failed an examination in speech pathology because our entire paper made reference to speech *defects* instead of *persons with speech defects*. The teacher who scored the examination felt that the entire point of the semester's work had been missed if his students had not learned that they do not deal with psychological problems but with *people with problems*. These people have emotions, feelings, desires, ambitions, and motives. We do not diagnose or treat schizophrenia, but work with schizophrenic reactions or behavior as presented by a person. We must have respect for that person. Everything we do should be centered around this person or client—hence the term "client-centered." Any criticism directed toward the work and writing of Rogers is not, or at least should not be, directed toward this fundamental concept. Clinicians must be able to respect all clients as people with all the characteristics of human organisms. A psychologist recognizes his clients as having the rights and privileges of equals. He does not regard them as poor, unfortunate creatures to be herded around like animals or catalogued and filed like statistical reports—they might conceivably be our fathers, mothers, brothers, sisters, or even ourselves. Regrettably, this quality of respect for others is all too uncommon in our present culture. If it were more common, many interpersonal problems, indeed even international problems, might not exist.

The clinician must be relatively free from "control" or "power" motives. He should not enter the field of psychology consciously or unconsciously because of needs to direct or control the activities of others. Too many clinicians feel that they must do something *to* other people. They feel that they are not functioning adequately unless they can direct, control, prescribe, or actively treat their clients. No clinical psychologist or psychiatrist ever "cured" a functional or nonorganic condition, or for that matter any other condition. The client helps himself. The clinician may be able to make it possible for the client to help or even to "cure" himself; he may be able to encourage him and may frequently guide or direct his efforts, but his role is that of a catalyst, not a person who supplies the effort or rebuilds or even reorganizes the personality of the client. No psychologist should pick a vocation for his client or make other major decisions for him. The clinician attempts to make it possible for his client to help himself but must allow him the responsibility for his own behavior.

All of the clinician's relationships with his subjects are interpersonal or social in nature. Consequently, he must have a high degree of "social intelligence" or "tact." Some people are able almost instinctively to do or say the "right" thing. This is not to imply that this ability is unlearned or instinctual. It is a skill that is acquired through the social experiences that the person may have had. Many of the training experiences of the psychologist may contribute to this facility. On the other hand, social skills begin to develop very early in life, and four years of graduate training can hardly be expected to overcome twenty-plus years of interpersonal relationships of a negative kind. Tact is not something that can be put on and taken off like a coat. Consequently, tactful relationships with other people cannot be limited to the clinical interview or conference. Let us evaluate our ability to "get along" with others in all of our social relationships.

Earlier in this chapter the professional training of the clinician was discussed at some length. Some mention should be made of the general educational qualifications of the professional psychologist. The clinician cannot ordinarily select his clients from any particular occupational, educational, economic, ethnic, racial, or religious group. For this reason, if a mutually satisfactory relationship is to be established with all clients, it will be advantageous that some common knowledge be present. The clinician should have a broad general education. Knowledge of the requirements of various occupations, of sociology, of literature, of economics, of the tenets of various religious groups, of racial prejudices, or of "nationalisms" and "regionalisms," to mention a few, will help the clinician to function to advantage. Consequently, all beginning or prospective clinical psychologists are encouraged to study and read as extensively as possible.

Comment should be made on still another characteristic of the ethical professional psychologist. He must be able to "keep his mouth shut." This has two applications. First, a great deal can be learned by listening —a trained listener does not have to ask many questions in order to learn. The more crucial point concerns the ethics of the individual who is the recipient of intimate confidences. The temptation is great at times to entertain at a dinner party or to impress a friend, or even to demonstrate a point in a lecture, by describing some incident or situation divulged in a clinical confidence. *This temptation must never be yielded to.* The psychologist must lean over backward to avoid the violation of personal confidences. This may require great control, and it is this control that must be possessed by the clinician. The need to talk probably arises most frequently out of the personal adjustment of the clinician. Adequate mental health will ordinarily assure the clinician's maintenance of silence when it is necessary.

Still another characteristic of the successful clinician must be mentioned. The first task of the psychologist in any diagnostic or therapeutic situation is the creation of what Rogers (10) has called a "warm and permissive atmosphere." This would appear to be one way of describing the mutually co-operative attitudes of clinician and client which are technically described as "rapport." The ability to create rapport is a function, largely, of the attitudes and the behavior of the clinician. No definite instructions can be given as to methods of creating rapport. Much of this ability comes from the experience of the clinician. On the other hand, to a considerable degree success in establishing rapport may be intrinsic to the personality of the clinical psychologist. If we could devise a selection device that would identify and measure the traits of personality that encourage confidence, we would have one excellent device for the selection of clinicians. There are those who cannot take a ride on a train for more than an hour without learning the personal history of at least one of their fellow travelers. Of course, inherent in this situation are some of the impersonal aspects of the ideal clinical relationship. The casual association is impersonal, temporary; confidences are not apt to be violated, and if they are, it will probably make little difference—the recipient of these confidences is not apt to run home and tell mother, inform the dean, or otherwise cause the troubled person to be ostracized. Clinicians should carefully review instances in which rapport was not established in an attempt to discover what may have occurred that may have contributed to the failure. If consistent failure to achieve rapport appears to be a function of the personality of the clinician which cannot be remedied, then the person might consider other applications of psychology or other vocational interests.

SUMMARY

In this chapter we have attempted to review the qualifications of the clinician. Some minimum qualifications were described and some optimum qualifications were mentioned. The following points were made:

(a) A Doctor of Philosophy degree, including a year of internship, is the minimum of professional training.

(b) There is no substitute for a high degree of native intelligence for the tasks of evaluation or diagnosis with which the psychologist is faced.

(c) The psychologist must have adequate mental health or the capacity to gain mental health.

(d) The interests of the clinician are similar to those of other professional and scientific persons. They differ slightly on the basis of interests more characteristic of the professions which involve contact with people, social welfare, and persuasive activities.

(e) The clinician must be able to place his responsibilities to his clients before his responsibilities to himself.

(f) The clinician must have respect for others.

(g) The clinician must not be dominated by the need to control others.

(h) The clinician must be able to demonstrate tact in dealing with others.

(i) The clinician should have a broad educational background as well as the specific requirement of the doctorate.

(j) The clinician should be able to respect the confidences of others.

(k) The clinician should have those characteristics that encourage people to feel comfortable and at ease in his presence.

In the next chapter we will discuss the fields of application and the scope of clinical and counseling psychology.

BIBLIOGRAPHY

1. American Psychological Association, Committee on training in clinical psychology, recommended graduate training program in clinical psychology. *Amer. Psychologist*, 1947, 2, 539–58.
2. American Psychological Association, Conference on graduate education in clinical psychology, Boulder, Colo. Victor C. Raimcy (ed.), *Training in clinical psychology*. New York: Prentice-Hall, 1950.
3. American Psychological Association, Committee on counselor training, recommended standards for training counseling psychologists at the doctorate level. *Amer. Psychologist*, 1952, 6, 175–81.
4. American Psychological Association, Committee on counselor training, the practicum training of counseling psychologists. *Amer. Psychologist*, 1952, 6, 182–8.
5. Dieppa, J. J., "The influence of the personality of the participant observer upon his clinical judgements." Unpublished Ph.D. thesis, Purdue Univ., 1953.
6. Hadley, J. M., and Asher, E. J., "Clinical, counseling, and school clinical psychology at Purdue University." *Amer. Psychologist*, 1955, 10, 71–4.
7. Kelly, E. L., and Fiske, D. W., *The prediction of performance in clinical psychology*. Ann Harbor: Univ. of Michigan Press, 1951.
8. Kriedt, Philip H., "Vocational interests of psychologists." *J. Appl. Psychol.*, 1949, 33, 482–8.

9. *Manual for the Miller Analogies Test.* New York: Psychol. Corp., 1947.

10. Rogers, C. R., "Significant aspects of client-centered therapy." *Amer. Psychologist,* 1946, 1, 415–22.

11. Rogers, C. R., *Client-centered therapy.* Boston: Houghton Mifflin, 1951.

12. Thorne, F. C., "A critique of nondirective methods of psychotherapy." *J. Abnorm. Soc. Psychol.,* 1944, 39, 459–70.

CHAPTER

22

The Scope of Professional Psychology

THOSE AMONG OUR READERS WHO ARE CONTEMPLATING CAREERS IN psychology will be particularly interested in the places where, and conditions under which, the professional psychologist may expect to pursue the activities for which he is preparing. What are the applications of the individual approach to the study of behavior? What opportunities exist for careers in clinical, counseling, or school clinical psychology? Where or in what settings does the psychological clinician work? What functions does he perform in these settings? What are the limitations of the practice of psychology? What is the relationship between psychology and other disciplines? These are a few of the questions that our students raise about the scope of clinical and counseling psychology. In this chapter and the next we will discuss a number of these questions and some of the problems associated with them.

The professional psychologist may find employment and apply his training in many different kinds of situations. For convenience of discussion we can classify these into certain general categories. For example, throughout the past ten years a growing number of psychologists have accepted positions in various medical settings. The range of possibilities for such employment is broad. Psychologists are employed in federal, state, and private hospitals. They are employed in general hospitals, in neuropsychiatric hospitals, and in other specialty hospitals, such as those for tuberculosis, pediatrics, or orthopedics. The psychologist may work in mental hygiene clinics, child guidance clinics, or medical schools. Another broad area of application is that of education. Here, again, the range is broad. Psychologists work in public schools as school psychologists, in school psychological clinics, and engage in a wide variety of activities at the college and university levels. In colleges or universities the psychologist may work as a clinician in a clinic or counseling center, he may teach, he may conduct research, and frequently his work will combine all these functions. Still another area is that of industry, where the opportunities range from industrial mental hygiene clinics to the application of case study techniques to problems of personnel evaluation or interpersonal relationships. Finally, we find a few psychologists who are in private practice either independently or in collaboration with other professional personnel. Examples of the functioning of the psychologist in each of these settings will be discussed in detail. In addition, we will consider work settings that are borderline and not conveniently classifiable into the four areas of medicine, education, industry, and private practice.

Before we plunge into the specific description of psychology in these various settings, some general discussion of careers in psychology seems to be in order. As George A. Kelly (46) has pointed out, a career in psychology is much more than a succession of jobs and places of employment. It should be an actively pursued course of personal growth; or, as Kelly might phrase it, a development of a life role. Even though there are many different jobs available to the clinical psychologist, there is marked similarity in the professional responsibilities in these various work settings. Consequently, most training programs are not designed to train practitioners or specialists; rather they are oriented toward the development of professional psychologists who can apply their professional training and experience in a wide variety of specific places of employment. A trend is appearing for young psychologists to begin their careers in positions in which they are not specialists in any particular application of psychology but are general workers who are expected to be able to carry on a wide variety of activities. After a few years of general work they begin to specialize and develop a core of interests around which a psychological role can be molded.

As of January 1957 there are about 15,000 [1] members of the American Psychological Association. This membership is especially remarkable when we compare it with the 31 in 1892, 393 in 1920, 5,000 in 1948, and 8,600 in 1951. About 40.5 per cent of the membership in 1951 listed their primary interest as being in clinical psychology or in some aspect of work with the behavior deviations; 13.3 per cent listed their specialty as educational psychology, 5.5 per cent listed vocational psychology, 4.9 per cent listed social psychology, 3.5 per cent identified their interests as developmental psychology, and 2.9 as personality. It is a little difficult to interpret just what the respondents to the questionnaire

[1] This estimate is based on membership figures reported by Sanford (64) with additions based on subsequent new members. Other statistics in this section are also based on Sanford's report. In terms of this discussion Watson's (82) monograph on *Psychology as a Profession* is of interest.

meant by indicating a particular specialty, but it appears that between 50 and 75 per cent of the membership of the American Psychological Association are concerned with interpersonal and intrapersonal problems and the application of psychology to the study of individuals. Even if we consider the minimum figure, we can assume that at least 7,500 psychologists are currently working primarily as clinical and counseling psychologists. Before World War I there were probably fewer than thirty trained psychologists in the United States engaged in clinical practice. Between 1931 and 1940 the number of members of the American Psychological Association able to call themselves clinical psychologists increased 200 per cent. Since 1940 the rate of growth has been even more rapid. Psychologists are numerous and their number has been increasing rapidly, especially in the areas of clinical and counseling psychology.

It is perhaps of practical interest to prospective students of clinical and counseling psychology to learn that although there are many clinicians working in a variety of settings, the field is still growing. There are a large number of positions available in clinical and counseling psychology at the present time. Many factors are contributing to the demand for psychologists with professional training in the clinical and counseling areas. Hospitals of all kinds are rapidly increasing the size of their psychology staffs and asking them to take over broader and broader responsibilities; this in turn results in the need for more staff psychologists. All over the United States community clinics are being organized, creating new positions. Existing clinics are showing their worth, and new staff positions are being created. Industrial positions for the clinical and counseling psychologist are opening up at a rapid rate, and schools are demanding psychological services. These developments have been in progress for several years, but the rate of development appears to be accelerating rapidly. Along with this acceleration in the increase of non-academic positions, there is a rather sudden demand for psychologists in the academic setting. Since World War II enrollments in colleges and universities have been on the decline. Now, however, we are beginning an era of increased college enrollments which appears to be almost overwhelming. Educational and statistical prognosticators all over the country are predicting increases in college and university enrollments of from 100 to 150 per cent within the next ten to fifteen years. The babies born during the war years are beginning to hit the campuses, and at the same time a rapidly increasing proportion of young people are seeking college educations. This tremendous increase in the number of students will produce a demand for college teachers in all fields including psychology. Coincident with the increase in demand for psychologists, the smallest group of the past several years is graduating from college and entering graduate schools. As a result the supply will be low for several years. As of the present writing a rather alarming shortage of clinical and counseling personnel would appear to be developing, and this area of study should be one in which students can feel secure insofar as their future employment is concerned. It seems safe to predict that there are more than enough positions to accommodate persons now in training or likely to enter training in the next few years.

It may also be of practical interest to learn that psychologists are well paid. The median 1951 income reported by psychologists with the Ph.D. was $6,400. The median income for Ph.D.'s in chemistry was $6,900, while Ph.D. physicists earned $7,100. The median salary for clinicians is less than that for psychologists in most of the other specialties. At the same time the individual clinicians are younger than psychologists in any other specialty, except for experimental psychology; this may contribute to the lower average rate of pay. Salaries have increased markedly since 1951, and in the foreseeable future psychologists can certainly expect to earn a reasonable living wage. It is expected that the competition for trained persons will contribute to increased salary levels within the next few years.

THE PSYCHOLOGIST IN THE MEDICAL SETTING

Basic to an understanding of the functioning of the psychologist in a medical setting is the concept of the mental hygiene team. Laurance F. Shaffer (70), in describing the meeting of the committees appointed from the two APA's (the American Psychiatric Association and the American Psychological Association) to study the joint concerns of these professions, has discussed the rationale of the mental hygiene team. Psychiatrists lack a background in normal and experimental psychology, and are deficient in quantitative and research methods. Psychologists lack the medical training that is essential to the detection and understanding of physiological disorders that may underlie maladaptive behavior. One might argue that a new profession should emerge, requiring training in both psychiatry and psychology, but this would mean ten years of graduate study, which seems impracticable for most students. It must also be recognized that other professions have contributions to make. For example, the social worker contributes to the understanding of the whole individual, and it could be maintained that the thoroughly trained clinician should know social work as well as psychiatry and psychology. Then, too, we have the psychiatric nurse, the aide, the occupational therapist, the physical therapist, and many others, all of whom contribute their bit to the complete picture of diagnosis and therapy. On the basis of such reasoning, the joint committees from the two professional organizations came up with the following solution [as reported by Shaffer (p. 8)]:

Neither profession is adequate in itself. As a principle and an ideal, the joint committees recognize the mutual dependence of the two disciplines, in the complete description of human personality or diagnosis; in the handling of persons with deviations, or therapy; and in research on problems of human behavior. A full diagnosis of each person involves at least medical, psychological, and social contributions. The same basic considerations apply to the area of treatment. The interdependence of the professions is achieved most fully by emphasis upon the concept of team work, both in professional practice and also in training. This is the proposed solution: since neither is self-sufficient, the only possible course of action is to join forces, so as to provide the most effective and the most widely available services for human welfare.[2]

This blueprint or plan of the mental hygiene team has achieved rather general application. The job to be done is concerned with the health and welfare of people, not with academic disputes, and the strength of the clinic team—psychiatrist, social worker, and psychologist—lies in the checks and balances inherent in its composition.[3] The concept of the mental hygiene team is, indeed, a step toward our goal of scientific practice. The concept has achieved wide acceptance in many work settings, with the Veterans Administration and the United States Public Health Service leading the way.

Every team must have a quarterback who takes the responsibility for directing the team effort. For the mental hygiene team, this responsibility is ordinarily assigned to the medical or psychiatric representative on the team. In any medical setting a physician-patient relationship exists. Therefore, the legal responsibility for the total welfare of the patient is that of the physician. The physician may delegate this responsibility for a period of time and for specified purposes to nonmedical personnel, but he can never absolve himself from the ultimate legal responsibility for the patient's welfare. More will be said about the relationship between psychology and medicine in the next chapter, but for the reason mentioned here, as well as for several others that will be discussed later, the psychologist who works in the medical setting may have to reconcile himself to being "supervised" by the medically trained man in charge. In a sense the psychologist, by choosing to be first of all a scientist, condemns himself to the role of team member and not team leader. Actually, it would seem to be fitting and proper that the psychologist working in a

---

[2] From "Clinical Psychology and Psychiatry," by Laurance F. Shaffer, *Journal of Consulting Psychology*, 1947, 11, 5–11. By permission of the American Psychological Association.

[3] The functioning of the mental hygiene team has been described by many writers in the several professional fields (1, 11, 42, 56).

medical setting work under the direction of the physician or psychiatrist. The psychologist can hardly regard himself as qualified to take medical responsibilities. It is most important that the psychologist recognize, understand, and accept his role in the medical setting. The Ad Hoc Committee on Relations between Psychology and the Medical Profession (6, p. 151) states the following principle:

> In sharing their applied functions with members of other professions psychologists accept the obligation:
> (a) to abide by all applicable legal provisions surrounding the rendering of such professional service;
> (b) to know and conform to the traditions, mores and practices of whatever professional group or groups with whom they work;
> (c) to collaborate fully with all members of the professional groups with whom a service function is shared.[4]

1. THE CHILD GUIDANCE CLINIC. It was recognized in the 1920's that any program of mental hygiene must begin with the early recognition and treatment of the problems of children (73). To this end, between 1925 and 1929 the National Committee for Mental Hygiene, with the support of the Commonwealth Fund, organized and operated five experimental child guidance clinics. The child guidance clinic movement has developed very rapidly since that time. Recently the development of child guidance clinics has received definite impetus from the United States Public Health Service by its support and encouragement of community mental hygiene and child guidance clinics.

Although some child guidance clinics operate outside the medical setting, the typical child guidance clinic provides an excellent example of the functioning mental hygiene team. It has been recognized from the start that the child's needs are not efficiently met by one sort of specialist working alone, but rather that the psychologist, the psychiatrist, the psychiatric social worker, the pediatrician, and other personnel all have important functions in the child guidance clinic. C. M. Louttit (51) commented that Witmer's philosophy and the actual clinic organization in his pioneer clinic did not differ materially from the philosophies found in the modern child guidance clinic.[5]

There does not seem to be a clear delimitation of the psychologist's

---

[4] This and the following quotation from "Report of *Ad Hoc* Committee on Relations between Psychology and the Medical Profession: Psychology and Its Relations to Other Professions," *American Psychologist*, 1952, 7, 145–52, are printed by permission of the American Psychological Association.

[5] The role of clinical psychology in child guidance clinics has been described by Matthews (52), Carter (22), Brewer (14), Harms (35), and others (12, 62, 66).

function in the child guidance clinic. His duties appear to range from psychometry to full responsibility for diagnosis, research, and therapy. Whereas in the earlier stages of the history of such clinics the psychologist's primary activity was diagnostic testing, his contribution soon expanded to include primary responsibility for remedial procedures in speech, reading, and other educational skills. More recently it has become apparent that testing and remedial work cannot be separated from the total adjustment of the child, and the psychologist has become active in individual therapy, group therapy, play therapy, and parental guidance. The psychologist in child guidance activities has also begun to play an increasingly important role in community education, in research, and in a variety of other hygiene services.

2. THE MENTAL HYGIENE CLINIC.   The development of mental hygiene clinics, where, again, we find the typical mental hygiene team in operation, so overlaps the history and organization of child guidance clinics that it is difficult to draw a distinction between them. Such a distinction is based largely on the age of the client. Child guidance clinics commonly deal with children, their parents, and their teachers; while mental hygiene clinics may offer services either to adults alone or to people of all ages, in fact, many of these clinics are serving all age groups. Some clinics dealing with all age groups are called guidance clinics, some psychiatric clinics, and others mental hygiene clinics.

The development of the Veterans Administration mental hygiene clinic program should be singled out for special attention (2, 3, 21, 49). The basic staff unit of its mental hygiene clinics is the mental hygiene team. There are frequently several teams at a clinic, but each team operates entirely as a unit with the needs of individual clients determining the division of labor within the team. The intake interview is usually conducted by the psychiatic social worker, although it may be conducted by the staff member—whether he is psychiatrist, psychologist, or social worker—who is available when the client first comes to the clinic. An intake staff (meeting of the team to discuss the intake information) will be held in which decisions are made about the extent and nature of psychological testing required; the psychiatric, neurological, or other physical examinations indicated; and the social data needed. The client is then seen by the various team members, who collect all the information that was decided on at the intake staff plus additional information that each individual member may feel is necessary. Finally this information is brought to a therapy-planning staff. At this staff meeting treatment will be planned in terms of the needs of the client, and, ideally (in fact, quite commonly), the assignment of a therapist will be made on the basis of these needs, rather than on the basis of the specific profession of the therapist. The professional training of the staff members is considered.

If the client requires medical treatment, if he presents somatic or psycho-somatic complaints, or if the indicated therapy would seem to be intensive or analytic, the psychiatrist is usually the choice. If the indicated therapy is primarily environmental, or if frequent family and social contacts seem to be in prospect, the psychiatric social worker is the logical choice. The clinical psychologist is called on if educational or remedial techniques, vocational guidance, or other therapies developed by psychology are indicated. In the typical clinic there is much overlap in terms of the techniques of therapy which the various staff members are qualified to administer. Consequently, the personality qualifications of the clinician in relation to the requirements of the client is most commonly the primary consideration in the assignment of the therapist. Regardless of the choice of therapist, the team will continue to function as a unit throughout the course of treatment, with frequent staff consultations and occasional auxiliary treatment offered by team members other than the principal therapist.

This description of activities represents an ideal functioning of the mental hygiene team. It is to be noted that the clinical psychologist in such a team is a professional worker and not a technician with limited responsibility. Although there are some exceptions, most mental hygiene clinics, whether within the Veterans Administration or operating within other contexts, will have a psychiatrist as director. In view of the fact that the problems brought to mental hygiene clinics represent a wide variety of psychosomatic disorders, psychoses in remission, and organic disorders, as well as functional disorders, this direction would appear desirable.

3. THE NEUROPSYCHIATRIC HOSPITAL.   The entrance of clinical and counseling psychologists into the neuropsychiatric hospital as professional staff members is the most recent innovation in the development of psychology as a profession. This relatively new utilization of psychological services has grown out of the experiences of the military and those of the Veterans Administration (13, 15, 23, 39, 40, 41, 43, 60, 66). There are many functions that psychologists can and do perform in the neuropsychiatric hospital, and the trend is definitely in the direction of the psychologist playing an important if not indispensable role in such a setting. These functions include:

(1) Intake interview. The entering patient, with the possible exception of very disturbed patients who are assigned immediately to security wards, will have an early intensive contact with a psychologist. This interview will probably cover such areas as previous illnesses and hospitalizations, occupations and/or military history, family history, personal history, and presenting problem. On the basis of this interview the

psychologist will plan the psychological testing and make note of personal and social data that must be substantiated, clarified, or supplemented by the psychiatric social worker.

(2) Psychological evaluation. This will usually consist of a more intensive and personality-oriented interview, intelligence testing, personality evaluation, and the administration of any other psychological tests that may be indicated.

(3) Staff presentation. Information gathered by the psychologist will be presented at a preliminary staff meeting, preferably very soon after the patient's admission, and will then be integrated with that obtained from the psychiatric examination, the physical examination data, social service reports, and ward observations. On the basis of this integrated data the staff will plan the immediate care and treatment of the patient.

(4) Planning occupational, educational, and vocational therapy. At many hospitals the diagnostic information, supplemented by vocational and interest tests, will be evaluated in terms of plans made for the hospital activities of the patient.

(5) Individual therapy. The patient may be referred to a psychologist for individual personality therapy.

(6) Group therapy. There is a growing inclination in many hospitals to assign primary responsibility for group therapy to psychologists. Because of their background and training in educational activities, psychologists appear to be especially well prepared for group-therapy activities.

(7) Vocational counseling. Such counseling should be an integral part of the entire treatment program for the patient, and the psychologist usually has a specific responsibility to consider and plan with the patient concerning the adequacy of his vocational adjustment and objectives. Occupations may have to be changed, training programs inaugurated, schooling planned, and jobs secured. These activities are merely a part of the total job of the psychologist in aiding the patient to make a satisfactory transition from the hospital to the world outside.

(8) Trial visit and discharge planning. Psychology is almost always represented at staff conferences charged with the responsibility of making decisions for trial visits and discharge.

(9) Follow-up. Social work has the primary responsibility for follow-up but psychology is usually consulted, particularly when vocational planning or guidance is involved.

(10) Screening of personnel. In most hospitals the psychology department is called upon for advice and consultation concerning the personality evaluation of prospective employees. Psychiatric-aide screening is a highly important responsibility since psychiatric aides spend so much time in direct contact with patients.

(11) Training of personnel. The clinical psychologist is being used more and more as a teacher in the training of psychological interns, psychiatric residents, psychiatric aides, psychiatric nurses, and other professional personnel.

(12) Research. Most hospitals are beginning to realize the psychologist's potential contribution in the area of research. Not only are many research projects initiated by psychology departments but these departments are frequently called upon for consultation in connection with the design and statistical analyses of many research problems that may be only remotely related to psychology.

These and other functions are currently being performed by psychologists in neuropsychiatric hospitals. In a limited number of these hospitals responsibility for ward administration or even for hospital policy may be assigned to psychological personnel. This suggests a trend that may expand, although some psychologists entertain serious doubt as to whether administrative decisions should be made for or concerning patients by psychologists. It is our position that psychologists can contribute constructively to such decisions but that, in general, no one discipline should be solely responsible for administrative and policy matters.

A considerable degree of reliance is being placed on many psychologists in neuropsychiatric hospitals for leadership in the total program planning for patients. This relatively new development offers a tremendous challenge to the psychologist who functions in such a program as a co-ordinator and adviser to all departments of the hospital and certainly not just as a "tester" or a "treater." This program-planning task involves planning for each patient so that *all* of his activities will be constructive and beneficial. It certainly requires a broadly trained psychologist and not a specialist. Discussion of these program-planning activities was included in the section on treatment, and elaboration is not appropriate at this point, except to stress that these functions require the psychologist to conduct himself in a professional manner, using knowledge quite unique to psychology.

4. THE GENERAL HOSPITAL. An interesting trend can be seen in the utilization of psychology in general hospitals, both with and without neuropsychiatric wards.[6] This is by no means an established development, but the possibilities for useful service are many. The applications of psychology in general hospitals are still in the experimental phase. In the hospital with a neuropsychiatric ward the psychologist's function is

[6] The interested student should read a series of articles appearing in the 1944 September-October issue of the *Journal of Consulting Psychology* (9, 47, 61, 67, 68, 72, 76, 83, 85, 90) on the functions of psychologists in hospitals. Other reports (10, 36) have discussed the importance of psychology in a complete medical program.

similar to that which he holds in a psychiatric hospital. Frequently, he may have somewhat more responsibility for ward management and administration, and he is often called upon for consultation on other services.

Several psychologists have been employed in neurological centers, in tuberculosis hospitals, and in centers for the care and treatment of other ill or handicapped persons. The functions of psychologists in such settings have not crystallized but individual experiences have impressed representatives of medicine in general with the adaptability and initiative of professional psychologists. It will be interesting to see what develops as the psychologist works more closely in collaboration with internists on psychosomatic problems, with patients whose problems might be more properly described as somatopsychic (some true illness present to which there are psychological reactions), and with the disabled or the physically handicapped. In a general hospital the functions of vocational and readjustment counseling are extremely important.

THE PSYCHOLOGIST IN THE EDUCATIONAL SETTING

Psychologists have traditionally practiced their profession as school psychologists, in psychoeducational clinics, in remedial education clinics, in vocational and educational guidance clinics, in college and university psychological clinics or counseling bureaus, and in a number of other miscellaneous varieties of situations within the framework of education. It is the conviction of many psychologists that the psychologist can make his greatest contribution as a professional clinician in educational services. Prior to World War II definite progress had been made in school psychological services, but during and since the war the extension of psychological services has been in the direction of the medical rather than the school setting.

Although the medical profession, in general, has not felt that educational psychological functions overlap with the field of psychiatry or medical psychology, there are numerous instances in education when definite need for medical collaboration is just as acute as it is in the medical setting. Ideally, the concept of the mental hygiene team should be applied in educational institutions just as it is in other institutions and organizations. In contrast with the situation in the medical setting where the psychiatrist will almost always be the quarterback, in the educational setting the psychologist may co-ordinate the team activities. Since the aims in schools are educational rather than therapeutic in nature, the psychologist will ordinarily be best qualified to assume the responsibility for achieving these aims.

Although it is impossible to draw a distinction between psychotherapy and counseling, it is possible to view these processes as extremes of a continuum. The continuum proceeds from functions that are essentially medical, and involve treatment in the sense of procedures developed within the discipline of psychiatry, to functions that are essentially educational, and involve treatment procedures developed by education and psychology. In the medical setting the entire continuum is represented, and, similarly, all kinds of problems may present themselves in the educational setting. The distinction is quantitative and one of emphasis with relatively more therapy in the medical setting and more counseling in the educational setting. *Even though it would appear that the ideal solution to the service needs of patients or clients in both settings is the mental hygiene team, we must face reality—neither the profession of psychology nor the profession of psychiatry is able to staff both settings in any active fashion.* Consequently, we must compromise our ideal. This means that all disciplines may not be represented on the team in all working situations. This is apt to be true in the education setting where psychologists may have to work without the close collaboration of psychiatry. It must be emphasized that the psychologist who is working in this setting should seek the best qualified collaboration available.

1. THE SCHOOL PSYCHOLOGIST.   As the name implies, school psychologists are employed in school systems. Not only do they work with the pupils, but also with principals and teachers. For this reason a knowledge of educational procedures is essential. However, the functions of school psychology, or (as we prefer) school *clinical* psychology, are not to be confused with the functions of educational testing, curriculum building, or educational guidance. We are not discussing here the educational psychologist who is concerned with the broad aims of education, but rather the clinician who deals with the individual aims of education.

The activities and functions of the psychologist in the school system are diverse.[7] Ethel L. Cornell (26) surveyed the activities of school psychologists in the state of New York. She reports that the major activities of these psychologists include individual psychological examining, teacher conferences regarding individuals interviewed, contact with agencies outside the school, planning remedial instruction, and giving remedial instruction. One interesting aspect of this study concerns the number of school psychologists reporting each of the above activities. Whereas only 44 per cent reported giving remedial instruction, over 75 per cent reported engaging in all other mentioned activities. Apparently the school psychologists surveyed by Cornell performed diagnostic and advisory functions rather than direct remedial services. This appears to be rather characteristic of the activities of professional psychologists in most

---

[7] They have been described in a series of articles introduced by Symonds (8, 18, 38, 48, 55, 63, 74, 77, 91) and more recently by Courtney (29).

schools. For instance, the School City of Indianapolis recently employed four psychologists, each of whom has been placed in charge of a psychological unit serving a specific portion of the city. Each unit consists of the psychologist and approximately ten school social workers. Children are referred to the psychologist, who evaluates them and makes recommendations concerning their handling. These recommendations are then carried out by the social workers or by the teachers. The psychologist's time, therefore, is mainly occupied with diagnostic study and with consultations with social workers and teachers.

In Ohio, Douglas Courtney (29) served as chairman of a committee of psychologists, psychiatrists, school administrators, directors of pupil personnel, guidance personnel, and other related specialists which prepared a report to be submitted to the Ohio Commission on Children and Youth. This report offers a formulation of principles upon which a child study and guidance service might be provided to the public school.

The committee emphasized the concept that teaching is a function of the school, and defined the role of the specialist as a valuable accessory to the central purpose of education. Courtney goes on to point out that the special training necessary to be a specialist in this setting goes beyond the training of a teacher. He suggests that appointing a well-liked or older teacher to assume the duties of a "guidance counselor" or a "director of guidance" is a definite mistake. The specialist should have specific professional training. This is not to deny the advantage of having a specialist with teaching experience or educational experience, but this experience should not be regarded as a substitute for specialized training in child study techniques. It was urged that the services be applied to parent and teacher counseling as well as counseling with children. In some school systems the entire special service may be one person, and, paradoxically enough, the small system needs the more highly and broadly trained person. In large systems all special services should be under the direction of an administrator, who co-ordinates all special services. These principles define the setting in which the school psychologist must necessarily function. Courtney feels that it is conservative to predict that (p. 175) "within a few years the public school is going to provide a central platform from which clinical psychologists may make their most effective contribution to national mental health."

The psychologist within the public school system must be prepared to perform a number of functions,[8] some of which are as follows:

(a) Evaluation of intellectual level
(b) Evaluation of achievement
(c) Evaluation of personality
(d) Evaluation of "potential"

[8] These functions are in the main taken from Courtney's article, with some modifications.

(e) Evaluation of environmental forces
(f) Evaluation of school setting
(g) Evaluation of interpersonal dynamics
(h) Methods of recording evaluative information
(i) Individual and group therapy with children
(j) Therapeutic conferences with teachers, parents, and others
(k) Group conferences with teachers and administrators
(l) Utilization of community resources
(m) Manipulation of curriculum
(n) Provision and assignment of special classes
(o) Development of remedial programs in special academic skill areas
(p) Vocational guidance
(q) Appropriate referral to consultant specialists [9]

These are the functions of the school psychologist. Psychologists who plan to work in schools should have the same training and experiences (within broad limits) as those who plan to work in other settings. This training should include an internship providing experience with persons presenting behavior disorders. Even though the school psychologist is going to work with essentially "normal" behavior, he should have experience with "abnormal" behavior so that he can recognize any signs of deviant behavior in the school child. This training should be supplemented by educational experience.

Margaret E. Hall (34) and Mae P. Claytor (24) have surveyed the employment requirements and state certification requirements for public school psychologists and report that only about one fourth of the states have certification procedures for school psychologists. Requirements vary widely, but even the states with certification of school psychologists seem to have very low requirements in terms of training and experience. It also appears that some of the course work requirements are irrelevant to the functions outlined above. In states without certification requirements there is little protection for children from the services of specialists lacking vital specialty training. This problem is one that must be solved by training agencies. Adequate qualifications cannot be required until we have a pool of trained personnel to supply the need for school psychological services. This appears to be a most crucial need and psychology is challenged to meet it.

2. THE PSYCHOEDUCATIONAL CLINIC. There is much overlap between the functions of the psychoeducational clinic and the child guid-

[9] From "Clinical Psychology in Public Schools," by Douglas Courtney, *Journal of Clinical Psychology*, 1951, 7, 171-5. By permission of Frederick C. Thorne.

ance clinic. The term "psychoeducational clinic" is used here to describe the referral agency developed within an educational rather than a medical framework. Problems referred to the psychoeducational clinic are generally those that develop out of the educational setting. These problems may involve medical or psychiatric considerations, and the clinical psychologist in the psychoeducational clinic must be constantly alert to the need for consultation with, or referral to, the appropriate medical specialist.

A few psychoeducational clinics are operated by public school systems but most are connected with colleges, universities, and teachers' colleges. The clinic in the higher educational institution is designed for the dual purposes of service and training for teachers and specialists. The functions of the psychologist in these clinics are quite similar to those in child guidance clinics. The difference is one of basic responsibility in that psychoeducational clinics are ordinarily directed by psychologists. The School Psychological Clinic at Purdue University is an excellent example of a psychoeducational clinic. This clinic is under the direction of a psychologist and is staffed by psychologists. A psychiatrist and several pediatricians serve as consultants to the clinic. Most referrals to it are made by school systems, but some children are referred by pediatricians and a few by juvenile authorities. The psychologist in such a clinic interviews teachers, parents, and other persons who can contribute to the understanding of a given child. He utilizes a variety of assessment procedures, and on the basis of his evaluation attempts to formulate recommendations for the treatment and training of the child. These suggestions are carefully interpreted to the persons who have the responsibility for the client, and every assistance is given to aid them in implementing the recommendations.

3. THE COLLEGE COUNSELING CENTER OR MENTAL HYGIENE SERVICE. Most universities provide mental hygiene services and counseling services. The scope of these services ranges from guidance services concerned primarily with vocational and educational guidance [similar to the program described by Edmund G. Williamson (87, 88) and Williamson and John G. Darley (89)] to services that are basically psychiatric in nature. Some college services operate under the direction of psychiatrists, with both psychology and psychiatry staff members (80). The duties of the psychiatric team may be combined with vocational educational counseling (31). Other college services (53) are under the direction of psychologists, and still other universities maintain vocational and educational guidance services entirely independent of the psychological or psychiatric clinics.

In the guidance service emphasis is ordinarily upon test administration, interpretation, and the giving of information. In the psychological or psychiatric clinics we find less reliance placed on the use of tests and more on the use of short-term counseling. Both types of services should be available, as one cannot be considered a substitute for the other. By the same token, regardless of whether the clinic is under the supervision of a psychiatrist or a psychologist, it is essential that both disciplines be represented on the clinic team. In the college clinic the bulk of the clientele will be relatively "normal" persons. However facilities must be available for the recognition and disposal of psychotic, psychoneurotic, or psychopathic persons. In a sample of 200 cases studied at the University of Missouri, Fred McKinney (53, 54) found that in 39 per cent of the cases the problems centered around social situations, in 38 per cent motivational issues were present, and in 69 per cent emotional problems were prominent. Actually, there was great overlap and individuals presented multiple rather than single problems. Annette C. Washburne (80) has reported that in the Neuropsychiatric Service of the Department of Student Health of the University of Wisconsin, 865 out of 2,331 psychiatric cases were diagnosed as "tension states." Harriet E. O'Shea (58) has also indicated some of the problems of college students and has called special attention to the challenge of work in this area. She makes the somewhat dramatic but significant point that college students are the parents of the future. Of at least equal importance is the fact that they are the future leaders in business, science, education, and politics.

Donald L. Grummon and Thomas Gordon (32) have discussed various aspects of the organization of the University of Chicago Counseling Center where, in addition to the services offered to clients, they stress the functions of training and research which are an integral and important justification for their existence. Many psychologists find an opportunity within the university setting to combine the functions of teaching, counseling, and research. The importance and the extent of college adjustment services has led to the organization of an association of college and university psychiatrists and psychologists in the Midwest (59). This group is made up of psychologists and psychiatrists who are active in college and university mental health services. Meetings are held twice a year and attention in the meetings is focused directly upon the problems of the worker in this area.

PSYCHOLOGISTS AND CORRECTIONAL SERVICES

An area not directly classifiable under our main headings of medicine, education, industry, or private practice is the area within the framework of correction. A rather extensive discussion is included in order to point up what might be done in an application of psychology in this field, which has been somewhat neglected. In 1948 Arthur Burton (19) listed 78 names in his *Directory of Clinical Psychologists Engaged in Correctional Psychology*. He (20) has also reported that 79 per cent of these psychologists were employed by states and the rest by federal or municipal governments. In 1949 twenty-four states did not employ psychologists in their correctional institutions. At that time only one out of five psychologists listed research among his duties, and the principal activity reported was diagnostic or personality testing. Raymond J. Corsini (27, 28) has described the work of a psychologist in prisons as falling under the three broad categories of psychometric, guidance, and total evaluation. Studies of the functions of clinical psychology in correctional institutions, such as the above and that by Marshall C. Greco (33), paint a discouraging picture of the situation. According to Greco, the psychologist is often looked upon as an "I.Q. indicator" and the psychiatrist as the man who recommends institutional transfer for the psychotic. The situation has improved somewhat within the past few years, and some institutions are providing more valuable and responsible services than was true a short time ago. The correctional institutions should provide a challenge to clinical and counseling psychologists, and it is surprising that more do not attempt to secure employment in reformatories and prisons. We will describe a composite or ideal summary of the functions that psychologists might (or do) perform. This program is not in existence at any particular institution. Parts of the program are being carried out at one institution and parts at another, but the picture described here is a composite one.

The first contact that the psychologist may have with the new inmate is at the time of his admission. Most institutions, particularly reformatories or institutions for delinquents, have an assignment or classification board. The psychologist is, or should be, an important member of this board. The new inmate spends his first few days or weeks in a period of quarantine. This period of quarantine is either combined with or followed by a period of classification. If the objectives of the correctional institution are sincerely those of rehabilitating, reforming, or correcting the inmate, this is one of the most important periods in the inmate's term in the institution.

One of the most important functions that the psychologist can perform is to hold an intake interview with the new inmate. This interview should be both historical and evaluative. On the basis of this interview the psychological testing should be planned. From information obtained through interviews, the testing, the social history, the vocational history, the educational history, and the health examination, the classification board should be in a position to make general plans for the new inmate. During the period of classification or orientation the new inmate should participate in group conferences. Although the primary aim of such group sessions is that of information giving or orientation, they may also have therapeutic by-products. In order to maximize the therapeutic benefits, most institutions assign these orientation groups to psychologists or social workers.

The classification board should consider a variety of assignments for each new inmate. Actually, combinations of assignments are usually in order. If professional personnel are available, further mental hygiene diagnosis and/or therapy should be considered. Every new inmate might be considered for assignment to a "problems-of-social-adjustment" course. Ideally, again, although the objectives of such a course would be largely didactic, it would also have therapeutic benefits for some inmates, and, consequently, professionally trained psychologists or group therapists should handle such a course. The advisability of assignment to group therapy should be considered for each inmate. Group therapy might be conducted by different approaches but training and skill in group work on the part of a group leader would make it an invaluable experience for the inmate. The program described thus far places a great deal of emphasis on group work. The ordinary sequence for a new inmate would be orientation, social-adjustment class, and later group therapy. There are two reasons for the emphasis upon group work. One is the economy of staff time but the most important reason is the need of most inmates for controlled and directive social experiences. Group work must be planned very completely, and extreme care must be exercised in selecting inmates for the group activities.

The matter of educational and/or vocational training should be given careful thought, and unless the inmate has a definite and constructive occupation, he should be assigned for vocational counseling and guidance. The board must make a decision about the work assignment of the inmate. The experience of most correctional psychologists is that it is essential that the inmate be kept busy. The work activity should also be selected for its therapeutic benefits. If facilities permit, the assignment of cellmate, age range of companions, and degree of security should also be given consideration. All these plans should be tentative and flexible, and any contemplated changes should be evaluated by the board. The inmate and/or the staff should have the privilege of requesting changes in the plans, and the plans for each inmate should be re-evaluated at frequent intervals even though no request for change has been made.

The activities of the classification board have been discussed in great detail because its activities are important and because of the contributions that the psychologist can make on such a board. Psychologists can also contribute to the mental hygiene clinic staff, to the parole board, and in other ways. It is suggested that the mental hygiene team concept can be applied just as effectively in the field of correction as in others. For example, all individual therapy or intensive personality therapy should be a team function. Much can be accomplished by planning activities, group work, and educational programs. Individual therapy involves time investment that is disproportionate to the social reform accomplished, and probably should not be engaged in unless psychiatric collaboration is available and staff time is not at a premium.

The last, but (from a long-range standpoint) the most important contribution to correctional services which might be made by the psychologist is, as always, research. We know pitifully little about the rehabilitation of persons with character and behavior disorders who have failed to conform to our legal regulations. The rather speculative, composite program we have described is far from complete and may be impractical for some institutions, but it is suggested to illustrate the extent to which the skills of the psychologist can be utilized in the correctional setting.

Augusta F. Bronner (16) has underlined another function, undoubtedly the most vital function of psychologists in this area: the prevention of delinquency. Many courts have established behavior clinics whose primary purpose is the early treatment of young offenders. These clinics utilize the services of clinical psychologists in almost every case.

THE PSYCHOLOGIST IN SCHOOLS OR HOMES
FOR THE MENTALLY RETARDED

One of the landmarks in the history of clinical and counseling psychology has been the work of psychologists with the feebleminded. The Training School at Vineland has been and still is an important center for research and the application of clinical psychology. The present and future status of the psychologist in the field of mental deficiency has been discussed by John N. Buck (17). The excellent textbook dealing with mental deficiency written by Seymour B. Sarason (65) is an impressive demonstration of the applications of psychology which can be made in work with the mentally retarded. Psychological work at Letchworth Village in New York State has been reviewed by Elaine F. Kinder (46). Although this report was written in 1937, the general objectives have probably changed but little. She describes the activities of the psychologist as falling under the three headings of clinical service, educational activities, and research. The major service load in institutions has always been and will undoubtedly continue to be the examination of new admissions. Many students of psychology as well as mature psychologists are inclined to regard this examination in terms of the administration of an intelligence test. Intellectual evaluation is, of course, an integral part of the diagnostic examination; however personality evaluation is also a necessary function of the psychologist. Psychological examination at the present in most institutions is not for classification or statistical purposes alone, but is basically oriented toward planning training and treatment. The present trend is to make training schools what the name implies—*training* schools.

It is a little disappointing that educational activities in many institutions seem to be primarily preoccupied with the training of psychologists rather than the subjects of the institution. The principles of psychology can be and should be applied to educational and vocational training problems of the mentally deficient. Vocational guidance, training, and placement activities must be encouraged in these institutions. Many of the students in these schools are employable if they receive proper training and guidance. We need to train psychologists but this objective can best be accomplished as a concomitant of the primary function of the institution. In this setting the most fundamental principles of educational psychology can be put to crucial test. In the past, with a few exceptions, research at schools for the feebleminded has been oriented toward the methodological problems of testing and evaluating the low-intelligence subject. The trend at the present seems to be toward more theoretically oriented research.

THE CLINICAL AND COUNSELING PSYCHOLOGIST AND INDUSTRY

A rapidly expanding field of application for the individually oriented psychologist appears to be opening up in the realm of business and industry but because of the newness of this application, no specific pattern of activity exists. The services offered do fall under broad headings such as the following:

1. MENTAL HYGIENE SERVICES.   An example of the contribution of clinical and counseling psychology to industrial mental hygiene can be found in the program at the Caterpillar Tractor Company (71). This program has been outlined by Arthur Weider (84, pp. 309–10) as follows:

1) Selection and placement:
   a. Routine battery. To assure better selection and placement of new employees, a psychological test battery was introduced.
   b. Special battery. The battery of tests given routinely to all new employees was supplemented with additional tests for supervisory positions, e.g., College Trainees, Sales, and Service Departments.

2) Induction: An induction talk fortifying the individual against the stresses of industrial work was developed for new employees to insure good work adjustment.

3) Interviewing and counseling: Large-scale interviewing was introduced to discover each new employee's emotional status so as to prevent the aggravation of existing disturbances and/or the development of new ones. A counseling service was made available to all employees, especially those with emotional problems and personality disturbances.

4) Training of interviewers: A training course was designed to educate employment interviewers in the concepts of psychology in order to broaden their perspective, and to increase the efficiency of their interviewing techniques.

5) Training of supervisors: Procedures were innovated to train foremen in the recognition and management of minor emotional problems in persons under their supervision.

6) Mental hygiene education: Information concerning mental health was disseminated as a prophylactic measure and as a brief psychotherapeutic adjunct.

7) Social service: Employees were referred to outside community agencies in connection with counseling and readjustment.

8) Research: Studies to validate the above new features have been planned and will be seen through to fruition. New tests are being standardized and others further studied before being included as part of any battery.[10]

2. INDUSTRIAL RELATIONS. The utilization of psychology in dealing with interpersonal problems in the industrial setting is a relatively recent development. Morris S. Viteles (79) called attention to the growing concern of industrial psychologists with the factors affecting the interplay of people, and Ronald Taft (75) has mentioned the tendency within industrial psychology to utilize a more individual approach but with these exceptions relatively little has been published concerning the various activities that clinical and counseling psychologists are performing in industrial relations. The application of group conference or group counseling techniques to a problem of interpersonal relations in industry was made recently by a group of Purdue psychologists.

The president of a moderate-sized manufacturing concern consulted the department relative to his concern about tension between several of his top management personnel. It appeared that the friction had resulted from misunderstandings existing between the personnel and was further

[10] From "Mental Hygiene in Industry—a Clinical Psychologist's Contribution," by Arthur Weider. *Journal of Clinical Psychology*, 1947, 3, 309–20. By permission of Frederick C. Thorne.

aggravated because some of those involved were relatively unskillful in handling social and interpersonal situations. This lack of tact had produced something other than harmonious working relationships, and, to a degree, was being carried over to contacts with other businesses and to the public generally. Because these people were valuable to the industry, the president did not want to transfer or discharge them. Although it was never described as group therapy or counseling, a plan was designed to provide a situation in which certain therapeutic benefits might be expected. What was actually proposed was a series of seminar discussions on personal and social adjustment. All the top management personnel (approximately twelve), including the president, were expected to attend these group meetings. The seminar period consisted of about forty-five minutes of discussion by one of the seminar leaders followed by about the same amount of time spent in group discussion. At least two psychologists were present at each meeting. One of them presented certain topics for discussion and both participated in leading and directing the discussions. The seminars started out quite formally with the presentation of materials concerning early life development, learning, motivation, mechanisms of behavior, and consideration of behavior disorders. The group discussion was lively and the participants were interested even though the first few seminars were quite academic. After the first five or six sessions the group was encouraged to suggest topics for discussion, and the seminars became oriented toward personal problems. Eventually a considerable amount of personal and interpersonal feeling was expressed, and the sessions became the vehicle for very frank expressions of attitudes. It was possible to keep the seminar under adequate control, and many of the sources of tension were worked out. As a result of insights gained during the group meetings, several of the participants asked for and were given the opportunity for individual counseling.

It is difficult to evaluate quantitatively the benefits to be gained from such a procedure. No attempt was made to do so in this case. Qualitatively, it seemed to the psychological staff to have been a very profitable experience and numerous testimonials as to its short- and long-range effects, which seem to substantiate this belief, have been received. This is just one example of the application of psychology to industrial relations problems. Other applications can certainly be made if opportunities are given for psychology to deal with such problems. It seems safe to predict that these opportunities will eventually be forthcoming.

3. MANAGEMENT EVALUATION AND DEVELOPMENT. A third application of psychology to industrial problems which has been described by Charles D. Flory and J. Elliot Janney (30) involves the application of clinical or individual study procedures to the evaluation of key individuals in business and industrial organizations. These business leaders are

evaluated in terms of such factors as intelligence, emotional control, skill in human relations, insight into human behavior, and organizational ability. The procedure for evaluation utilizes detailed personal interviews, histories, situational observation, and appropriate testing. This evaluation service is paralleled by a development service in which therapeutic procedures are utilized to bring about maximum effectiveness.

4. PERSONNEL SELECTION. In spite of the extensive research and practical experience in the field of personnel testing there are still many kinds of jobs or positions for which success cannot be predicted from test batteries or other personnel techniques. Examples of these are executive and management positions. The need for selection techniques for executive and management personnel led to the development of the service described by Flory and Janney. However there are still other types of work which are not subject to systematic job analysis and in which success cannot be predicted by means of procedures in current use. David F. Kahn and John M. Hadley (44) have suggested the use of clinical devices such as unstructured or projective techniques and other individual study procedures as aids to selection of personnel for other types of work. Much research is indicated in this area, which is certainly another area of application for the clinically trained psychologist.

DO AND SHOULD PSYCHOLOGISTS ENTER PRIVATE PRACTICE?

The first part of this question is easy to answer. An increasing number of clinical psychologists have either part-time or full-time private practices. The answer to the second part of the question requires more extensive discussion and is related to the problems of interprofessional relationships which will be discussed in the next chapter. At the present early stage in the professional development of psychology no definite answer can be given to the question as to whether psychologists *should* enter private practice. We will discuss some of the issues involved and the student can formulate his own opinion.

There are, of course, various kinds of private practice and various degrees of independent application of the procedures of psychology. Some of the issues can be disposed of quite easily. For example, the clinical psychologist who enters private practice in collaboration with a qualified and competent physician or psychiatrist would seem to be on sound ethical and professional grounds. The clinical psychologist whose private practice consists of evaluation or assessment services is probably well within his professional rights providing he maintains ethical standards in taking referrals and making reports. It would appear highly important that careful consideration be given to the necessity of accepting referrals from and making reports to appropriate professional personnel. Evaluation reports based on clinical techniques should seldom be given directly to the client unless a program of counseling is to be entered into with the client so that constructive plans can be made on the basis of the reports. Reports may be made to professionally responsible persons in educational, medical, or industrial settings and occasionally to other persons, providing the psychological data is clearly interpreted. Extreme caution should be exercised to ascertain the use of reports. Furthermore, reports should be made in terms of the purpose for which they are requested. Some psychologists offer private research consultation services. This would not appear to offer many problems as long as the psychologist functions as a scientist and can maintain control over the interpretation and application of results.

Other psychologists are engaged in or plan to engage in the independent private practice of psychotherapy. Such practice by psychologists presents many serious problems. We must realize that we treat total organisms; not just biologic organisms but persons. Persons with essentially functional behavior disorders may be subject to illnesses of various kinds; they may possess organic pathology, and, more likely than not, will exhibit psychosomatic symptoms and complaints. If the psychologist were to accept only clients referred by physicians, or if he were to follow the precept of requiring routine physical examinations, he is still placed in a position of having the responsibility of recognizing organic pathology that may develop subsequent to the physical examination. The Ad Hoc Committee on Relations between Psychology and the Medical Profession (6, p. 151) has discussed this dilemma and has made the following statement:

> The committee is unanimously agreed that the interests of good practice are best met when psychologists work in close and intimate conjunction with other psychologists and with members of other professions. The best interests of the client, of society, and of the profession seem more likely to be achieved through the co-operative functioning, mutual stimulation, and reciprocal specialization made possible by team functioning whether the members of the team operate on a salaried or fee basis. For these reasons, the committee is strongly concerned that private independent practice does not represent the most desirable pattern of development for applied psychology. Any psychologist who assumes the tremendous responsibility which independent private practice entails is obligated to convince both himself and his colleagues that he is fully qualified to do so, both in terms of formal training and supervised experience.

In general, we find ourselves in agreement with this discouragement of the *independent* private practice of psychotherapy by psychologists. The private practitioner must have a continuing co-operative working relationship with the medical and psychiatric disciplines. From a practical standpoint, it must be recognized that there are many geographic areas that possess few, if any, psychiatrists. In certain kinds of practice, such as work with behavior-problem children, the number of qualified specialists (in this case, child psychiatrists) is exceedingly small. Since pediatricians are taking an increasing interest in the psychological aspects of children's difficulties, some psychologists have collaborating relations with pediatricians. In the event that psychiatric collaboration is not obtainable, we should use our best judgment to secure the best trained and informed collaboration available until psychiatric facilities are available. The most important consideration is the training of the person entering private practice. We must establish some standards of training and experience for those who plan to enter private practice. Membership in the American Psychological Association does not imply any certification of professional experience and competence. It is recommended that those who expect to enter private practice not do so until they have achieved sufficient training and experience to be eligible for certification in their specialty by the American Board of Examiners in Professional Psychology.[11]

RULES GOVERNING THE PRACTICE OF THE CLINICIAN

(1) The psychologist should never undertake responsibility for an individual who has not been referred to him for evaluation or counseling. Parents, teachers, physicians, and others who confer with the psychologist about cases but who do not present these cases must be made to understand that the responsibility is entirely their own. Recommendations in such instances must be limited to general rules of mental hygiene which may be applied safely in any case by any layman. It is even wiser to refuse to make evaluations or offer recommendations of any kind unless the case has been actually referred and seen. Mail order diagnoses and treatment should never be attempted.

This problem is one that is particularly acute and one that presents many complications. The psychologist—and just as often, the student of

[11] The Division of Clinical and Abnormal Psychology, Committee on Private Practice (7) has submitted certain recommendations concerning standards for the unsupervised practice of clinical psychology. These recommendations spell out in detail the kinds of experience which they consider as minimum for various kinds of practice. Some of these might be more rigid than required by the American Board of Examiners in Professional Psychology, while the total experience could be less. We feel that in addition to the specific qualifications, certification is also desirable.

psychology—is perpetually being faced with the proposition, "You are a psychologist; you can tell me what to do about my friend who is very unhappy." The question is put in many forms but the position of the psychologist must always be the same. He should not make recommendations unless the client has been referred and then *only if he is fully qualified to practice.* The psychologist himself must ever guard against his natural tendency to prescribe and recommend for his friends and acquaintances.

(2) No client should be seen unless he has been made to understand, as clearly as he is capable of understanding, the purpose for which the clinical examination is made and the general functions of a psychologist. The practice of seeing persons or making recommendations for them under false pretenses is never justified even in the most extenuating circumstances. No client should be administered therapy unless it has been specifically requested by himself or by those responsible for him and who present him.

(3) The psychologist treats directly only the problem presented and recognized by the client. Actually, we must consider the client's total personality and hope that as a result of counseling the client will do the same. We strive to help the client to see the interrelation between various aspects of his behavior. Stanley G. Law (50, pp. 10–11) gives the following example of this point:

> The patient may complain of symptoms caused by guilt over rejection of a child, and the doctor discovers incidentally that the patient habitually takes three cocktails before dinner, about which the patient is perfectly happy. The physician is overstepping the limitations of therapy if he attempts to cure the "alcoholism" which is not producing symptoms, desirable as this might be to the social and economic life of the patient. If there is any relationship between rejection of the child and the drinking, then, of course, it is a different matter, and the patient himself will decide what to do about it.[12]

(4) Unless the psychologist is working in a hospital, certain potentially violent or uncontrolled persons should not be seen any more than is necessary to effect their referral to a hospital. Any counseling must be limited to the completely supportive procedures. Psychotic patients should not be treated on an out-patient basis unless it has been firmly established that the behavior is well under control, in which case, of course, the individual would not be considered as violent and the psychosis would be in remission. This principle should be followed by all clini-

---

[12] By permission from *Therapy Through Interview*, by Stanley G. Law. Copyright 1948 by McGraw-Hill Book Company, Inc.

cians, psychological or otherwise. Persons addicted to uncontrolled or violent behavior will frequently require sedation or physical restraint. Since a psychologist *never* prescribes for or lays hands on a person, he should exert extreme caution in seeing clients who may require such treatment. We discussed earlier, in much detail, the use of diagnostic tools in planning treatment. The present point is, however, the strongest argument in favor of preliminary diagnosis; without preliminary diagnosis the psychologist may be surprised and chagrined when his client suddenly does damage to himself or others. In general, psychologists should be cautious in seeing any clients not in close contact with reality. This will exclude most psychotics.

Psychologists should be cautious about seeing adults who do not want help and who are satisfied with their current adjustment. This principle also excludes many psychotics. Children may be seen if their parents, or their teachers, or others responsible for them are ready to follow suggestions. However little progress should be expected in individual therapy when the client (child or adult) is satisfied with his current adjustment.

In general, most medical practice laws prevent anyone other than the duly accredited physician from treating the psychotic. Of course the psychologist may be consulted, and in that case he will not be subject to legal action if the physician retains the responsibility. The safest and only tenable ethical position is for psychotics to be seen only in the hospital and then in co-operation with psychiatrically trained personnel.

(5) The relation between the psychologist and client should always be impersonal. Consequently, the psychologist should not assume responsibility for his own friends, close acquaintances, or relatives beyond the usual responsibility of a friend or relative.

SUMMARY

In this chapter we have examined the various applications of clinical psychology in considerable detail. We have discussed the role of the psychologist in the medical setting, the educational setting, the correctional setting, the training school, in industry, and in private practice. A few rules of practice have been suggested. We have presented an extensive bibliography and have made many references to it in the text. It is hoped that this material will help the student of psychology to gain some conception of the scope of clinical psychology. In the next chapter we will discuss the relationships between clinical psychology and related disciplines.

BIBLIOGRAPHY

1. Ackerly, S. S., "The clinic team." *Amer. J. Orthopsychiat.*, 1947, 17, 191–5.
2. Adler, M. H., Valenstein, A. F., and Michaels, J. J., "A mental hygiene clinic: its organization and operation." *J. Nerv. Ment. Dis.*, 1949, 518–33.
3. Adler, M. H., Futterman, S., and Webb, R., "Activities of the mental hygiene clinics of the Veterans Administration." *J. Clin. Psychopath.*, 1948, 9, 517–27.
4. American Medical Association, "Licensure or certification of clinical psychologists." *J. Amer. Med. Assn.*, 1952, 148, 271–3.
5. American Psychological Association, Conference on graduate education in clinical psychology, Boulder, Colo. V. C. Raimey (ed.), *Training in clinical psychology*. New York: Prentice-Hall, 1950.
6. American Psychological Association, Report of *ad hoc* committee on relations between psychology and the medical profession: psychology and its relations to other professions. *Amer. Psychologist*, 1952, 7, 145–52.
7. American Psychological Association, Division of clinical and abnormal psychology, committee on private practice. "Recommendations concerning standards for the unsupervised practice of clinical psychology." *Amer. Psychologist*, 1953, 8, 494–5.
8. Baker, G. D., "What the public school needs from the psychologist." *J. Consult. Psychol.*, 1942, 6, 177–80.
9. Barten, M. B., "Psychometric methods in a mental hygiene clinic of a psychiatric hospital." *J. Consult. Psychol.*, 1944, 8, 286–90.
10. Bijou, S. W. (ed.), *The psychological program in AAF convalescent hospitals*. Washington: U. S. Govt. Printing Office, 1947.
11. Blain, D., "The psychiatrist and the psychologist." *J. Clin. Psychol.*, 1951, 3, 4–10.
12. Boyd, G., and Schwiering, O. C., "A survey of child guidance and remedial reading practices." *J. Educ. Res.*, 1950, 43, 494–506.
13. Braceland, F. J., and Hunt, W. A., "Psychology in a psychiatric program." In Kelly, G. A., *New methods in applied psychology*. College Park: Univ. of Maryland, 1947.
14. Brewer, J. E., "A community program of psychological services." *J. Clin. Psychol.*, 1951, 7, 357–60.
15. Brill, N. Q., "Psychology and psychiatry in the Army." In Kelly, G. A., *New methods in applied psychology*. College Park: Univ. of Maryland, 1947.
16. Bronner, A. F., "Behavior clinics." In Branham, V. C., and Kutash, S. B., *Encyclopedia of criminology*. New York: Philosophical Library, 1949.
17. Buck, J. N., "The present and future status of the psychologist in the field of mental deficiency." *Amer. J. Ment. Def.*, 1949, 54, 225–9.
18. Burnside, L. H., "Psychological guidance of gifted children." *J. Consult. Psychol.*, 1942, 6, 223–8.

19. Burton, A., "Director of clinical psychologists engaged in correctional psychology." *J. Psychol.*, 1948, 26, 19–23.
20. Burton, A., "The status of correctional psychology." *J. Psychol.*, 1949, 28, 215–22.
21. Campbell, H. M., "The role of the clinical psychologist in a Veterans Administration Mental Hygiene Clinic." *J. Clin. Psychol.*, 1947, 3, 15–21.
22. Carter, J. W., Jr., "The Wichita Guidance Center." *J. Consult. Psychol.*, 1944, 8, 27–30.
23. Challman, R. C., "The clinical psychology program at Winter VA Hospital, The Menninger Foundation and the University of Kansas." *J. Clin. Psychol.*, 1947, 3, 21–8.
24. Claytor, M. P., "State certification requirements for public school psychologists." *J. Psychol.*, 1950, 29, 391–6.
25. Combs, A. W., "A report of the 1951 licensing effort in New York State." *Amer. Psychologist*, 1951, 6, 541–8.
26. Cornell, E. L., "The psychologist in a school system." *J. Consult. Psychol.*, 1942, 6, 185–95.
27. Corsini, R. J., "Functions of the prison psychologist." *J. Consult. Psychol.*, 1945, 9, 101–4.
28. Corsini, R. J., "Psychological services in prisons." In Branham, V. C., and Katash, S. B., *Encyclopedia of criminology*. New York: Philosophical Library, 1949.
29. Courtney, D., "Clinical psychology in public schools." *J. Clin. Psychol.*, 1951, 7, 171–5.
30. Flory, C. D., and Janney, J. E., "Psychological services to business leaders." *J. Consult. Psychol.*, 1946, 10, 115–19.
31. Fry, C. C., and Rostow, E. G., *Mental health in college*. New York: The Commonwealth Fund, 1942.
32. Grummon, D. L., and Gordon, T., "The Counseling Center at the University of Chicago." *Amer. Psychologist*, 1948, 3, 166–71.
33. Greco, M. C., "Clinical psychology and penal discipline." *J. Clin. Psychol.*, 1945, 1, 206–13.
34. Hall, M. E., "Current employment requirements for school psychologists." *Amer. Psychologist*, 1949, 4, 519–25.
35. Harms, E. (ed.), *Handbook of child guidance*. New York: Child Care Publications, 1947.
36. Hawley, P. R., "The importance of clinical psychology in a complete medical program." *J. Consult. Psychol.*, 1946, 10, 292–300.
37. Heiser, K. F., "Certification of psychologists in Connecticut." *Psychol. Bull.*, 1945, 9, 624–30.
38. Hildreth, G., "The psychologist's role in pupil classification." *J. Consult. Psychol.*, 1942, 6, 212–17.
39. Holzberg, J. D., "Clinical techniques in an Army neuropsychiatric hospital." In Kelly, G. A., *New methods in applied psychology*. College Park: Univ. of Maryland, 1947.
40. Holzberg, J. D., Teicher, A., and Taylor, J. L., "Contributions of clinical psychology to military neuropsychiatry in an Army psychiatric hospital." *J. Clin. Psychol.*, 1947, 3, 84, 95.

41. Hunt, W. A., "Post-war clinical psychology in the Navy." In Kelly, G. A., *New methods in applied psychology*. College Park: Univ. of Maryland, 1947.

42. Hutt, M. L., Menninger, W. C., and O'Keefe, D. E., "The neuropsychiatric team in the United States Army." *Ment. Hyg.*, New York, 1947, 31, 103–19.

43. Hutt, M. L., and Milton, E. O., "Analysis of duties performed by clinical psychologists in the Army." *Amer. Psychologist*, 1947, 2, 52–6.

44. Kahn, D. F., and Hadley, J. M., "Factors related to life insurance selling." *J. Appl. Psychol.*, 1949, 33, 132–40.

45. Kelly, G. A., *New methods in applied psychology*. College Park: Univ. of Maryland, 1947.

46. Kelly, G. A., "A student's outline of graduate training in clinical psychology at Ohio State University." Columbus: The Ohio State Univ., mimeographed, 1950.

47. Kinder, E. F., "Work of the psychologist in a psychiatric unit for children." *J. Consult. Psychol.*, 1944, 8, 267–72.

48. Krugman, M., "The psychologist's role in pupil classification." *J. Consult. Psychol.*, 1942, 6, 205–11.

49. Kutash, S. B., "The psychologist's role in clinical practice." *J. Clin. Psychol.*, 1947, 3, 321–9.

50. Law, S. G., *Therapy through interview*. New York: McGraw-Hill, 1948.

51. Louttit, C. M., *Clinical psychology*. New York: Harper, 1947.

52. Matthews, W. M., "Scope of clinical psychology in child guidance." *Amer. J. Orthopsychiat.*, 1942, 12, 388–92.

53. McKinney, F., "Four years of a college adjustment clinic: I. Organization of clinic and problems of counselees." *J. Consult. Psychol.*, 1945, 9, 203–12.

54. McKinney, F., "Four years of a college adjustment clinic: II. Characteristics of counselees." *J. Consult. Psychol.*, 1945, 9, 213–17.

55. McNally, H. J., "Organizing school curricula to meet individual differences." *J. Consult. Psychol.*, 1942, 6, 200–4.

56. Menninger, W. C., "The relationship of clinical psychology and psychiatry." *Amer. Psychologist*, 1950, 5, 3–15.

57. Miles, W. R., "A year of state certification of psychologists." *Amer. Psychologist*, 1946, 1, 393–4.

58. O'Shea, H. E., "Mental health problems in college." *J. Consult. Psychol.*, 1939, 3, 41–8.

59. O'Shea, H. E., "Problems in college students' adjustment service." *J. Consult Psychol.*, 1940, 4, 210–15.

60. Pennington, L. A., and Timm, O. K., "Service and training in a clinical psychology unit in a Veterans Administration neuropsychiatric hospital." *Amer. Psychologist*, 1949, 4, 33–7.

61. Rapaport, D., "The psychologist in the private mental hospital." *J. Consult. Psychol.*, 1944, 8, 298–301.

62. Robinson, J. F., "Current trends in child guidance clinics." *Ment. Hyg.*, 1950, 34, 106–16.

63. Rosebrook, W. A., "Psychological service for schools on a regional basis." *J. Consult. Psychol.*, 1942, 6, 196–200.
64. Sanford, F. H., "Annual report of the Executive Secretary: 1952." *Amer. Psychologist*, 1952, 7, 686–96.
65. Sarason, S. B., *Psychological problems in mental deficiency*. New York: Harper, 1949.
66. Scheibel, A. B., Zehrer, F. A., and Chambers, R. E., "The establishment of a child guidance clinic in an Army general hospital." *Bull. U. S. Army Med. Dept.*, 1949, 9, 449–57.
67. Schott, E. L., "The psychologist in the general hospital." *J. Consult. Psychol.*, 1944, 8, 302–7.
68. Seidenfeld, M. A., "The psychologist in the tuberculosis hospital." *J. Consult. Psychol.*, 1944, 8, 311–18.
69. Seidenfeld, M. A., "Postwar clinical psychology in the Army." In Kelly, G. A., *New methods in applied psychology*. College Park: Univ. of Maryland, 1947.
70. Shaffer, L. F., "Clinical psychology and psychiatry." *J. Consult. Psychol.*, 1947, 11, 5–11.
71. Spears, E. M., "Mental hygiene of Caterpillar Tractor." *Conf. Bd. Mgmt. Rec.*, 1947, 9, 190–1.
72. Stevens, P., "The station hospital psychologist." *J. Consult. Psychol.*, 1944, 8, 319–22.
73. Stevenson, G. S., and Smith, G., *Child guidance clinics: a quarter century of development*. New York: The Commonwealth Fund, 1934.
74. Symonds, P. M., "The school psychologist—1942." *J. Consult. Psychol.*, 1942, 6, 173–6.
75. Taft, R., "The staff psychologist in industry." *Amer. Psychologist*, 1946, 1, 55–61.
76. Tallman, G., "The psychologist in a neurological hospital." *J. Consult. Psychol.*, 1942, 6, 181–4.
77. Thayer, V. T., "Psychological services needed in a private school." *J. Consult. Psychol.*, 1942, 6, 181–4.
78. Virginia Academy of Science, Psychol. Sec. The committee on training and standards, the certification of clinical psychologists in Virginia. *Amer. Psychologist*, 1946, 1, 395–8.
79. Viteles, M. S., "Postlude: the past and future of industrial psychology." *J. Consult. Psychol.*, 1944, 8, 182–6.
80. Washburne, A. C., "Seven-year report from the Neuropsychiatric Department, Student Health Service, University of Wisconsin." *Wisconsin Med. J.*, 1946, 15, 1–10.
81. Watson, R. I., *The clinical method in psychology*. New York: Harper, 1951.
82. Watson, R. I., *Psychology as a profession*. New York: Doubleday, 1954.
83. Wechsler, D., "The psychologist in the psychiatric hospital." *J. Consult. Psychol.*, 1944, 8, 281–5.
84. Weider, A., "Mental hygiene in industry—a clinical psychologist's contribution." *J. Clin. Psychol.*, 1947, 3, 309–20.

85. Wells, F. L., "Psychologists' functions in hospitals: introductory note." *J. Consult. Psychol.*, 1944, 8, 267–72.
86. Wiener, D. N., "The Minnesota law to certify psychologists." *Amer. Psychologist*, 1941, 6, 549–52.
87. Williamson, E. G., *How to counsel students*. New York: McGraw-Hill, 1937.
88. Williamson, E. G., "Coordination of student personnel service." *J. Consult. Psychol.*, 1940, 4, 229–33.
89. Williamson, E. G., and Darley, J. G., *Student personnel work*. New York: McGraw-Hill, 1937.
90. Wittman, P., "Psychological services in state hospitals for the mentally ill." *J. Consult. Psychol.*, 1944, 8, 291–7.
91. Zehrer, F. A., "The school psychologist as a mental hygiene specialist." *J. Consult. Psychol.*, 1942, 6, 218–22.

23

Professional Relations and the Public Interest

THERE ARE A NUMBER OF CHARACTERISTICS OF A GOOD PROFESSION, several of which have been discussed in a report by the Ad Hoc Committee on Relations between Psychology and the Medical Profession (6). This report is not limited to the relationships of psychology with the medical profession, but deals with professional relationships in general and should be read by all prospective professional psychologists. At least one significant characteristic of a mature profession is its ability to work co-operatively with other fields of service. In other words, a profession must fit into society. Psychology is well on its way to becoming a profession. If it is to continue to mature as a profession, it is essential that it work harmoniously with related disciplines. Psychologists must realize that any professional group can strive to work on a team without losing prestige as a profession. The characteristics of a good team member have been excellently described by a representative of the profession of nursing (21):

> To be part of a team means that one must be extremely prepared in his own field, that he must see himself in relation to the contribution of others, that he must sense constantly the changing needs of the individuals whom he and the group are serving, that he must accept the corresponding changes in his contribution and the contributions of the other team members to those needs, that he must have the courage to say what he can do and why he feels that he can do that thing better than another, that he must have the grace to give up what he likes to do if another can do it better. It means further, that he must learn to do things which do not come too easily if they can best

be done by him for the good of all. It means the will to pull with others and the integrity to withdraw from those parts of an undertaking which are not his. It means the enduring belief that together we can do things which none of us individually could do alone, and that the togetherness makes possible a concept of the job which is greater than the sum of the individual parts.[1]

This statement emphasizes among other things that good team work involves the surrender of the sovereignty of all team members. As Shaffer (37) has reminded us, in discussing the mental hygiene team, even if some of the sovereignty of psychology is surrendered, a certain amount of the sovereignty of psychiatry is also involved. Psychology as a profession must be very careful that the status needs of its members do not get in its way, preventing development as a profession. The psychologist who deeply fears that his contributions will not be heeded or his status as a Ph.D. (if he is one) not recognized usually ends up taking an M.D. degree, or perhaps wishing that he had done so.

Let us always remember that *psychology* is the profession—as Robert I. Watson (46) has stressed, not clinical psychology, not counseling psychology, not industrial psychology, but psychology. Counseling is not a profession; it is a technique used in many professions. Similarly, clinical methods of evaluation, assessment, and appraisal are not the earmarks of the profession. These techniques are used by psychologists other than clinical and counseling psychologists and by related professions as well. Certainly, psychological counseling and therapy are not professions. They, too, are tools to be shared with other professions. As Watson further emphasizes, there is room for specialization within the profession, but there is *one* profession, not several. The reader will recognize as we discuss specific relationships with other disciplines or professions that differences or conflicts between these disciplines are frequently based primarily, if not entirely, on the question of whether a given technique is the sole prerogative of a particular profession or whether it can be shared with others. This question may be important in and of itself, but we must not lose sight of the fact that we are dealing with techniques and that the status of the profession of psychology will not be seriously affected by the giving up of a technique or the sharing of one.

Students of clinical and counseling psychology as well as the representatives of these areas of application must be familiar with the issues involved in all interprofessional intercourse. Consequently, we shall risk

---

[1] From "The Nurse on the Healing Arts Team," an address given by R. W. Hubbard at the annual meeting of the Pennsylvania Nurses Association, Pittsburgh, Penn., Nov. 9, 1948. By permission of the Pennsylvania Nurses Association.

redundancy and proceed to discuss some questions that will enable us to look at the whole picture—the pitfalls, why they exist, and how they can be avoided.

PSYCHOLOGY AND PSYCHIATRY

Prior to World War II, although psychiatry and psychology were beginning to give attention to some of the same problems, there was little in the training and experience of either group to serve as a basis for communication with the other. Each may have been somewhat insecure and somewhat distrustful of the other, but the problems of conflicting interpersonal relationships were avoided by assigning a dominant role to the psychiatrists in mental hospitals and clinics and leaving the fields of remedial education, educational and vocational counseling, and industrial applications to psychologists. However, during World War II psychologists were assigned responsibilities usually reserved for persons with psychiatric training. Psychiatrists, psychologists, and social workers discovered that they were all carrying out similar functions.

Since the war there have been many events that have contributed to the overlap in the functions of psychiatrists and psychologists. The Ad Hoc Committee on Relation of Psychology to the Medical Profession (6) has discussed the intricate relations that have developed between psychology and other professional and scientific fields. The Veterans Administration adopted the concept of the mental hygiene team and established large-scale training programs for clinical and counseling psychologists. As time went on other events contributed to the psychologist's responsibility for participating in diagnosis, therapy, and research in the field of psychopathology.

Since psychology and psychiatry were engaged in a mutually cooperative enterprise, it seemed to be the mutual obligation of the two disciplines to clarify the areas of misunderstanding and disagreement with the greatest possible speed. It was to this end that the committees from the two A.P.A.'s were appointed to study the interrelations of psychiatry and psychology. These committees, meeting separately and together, worked out recommendations that they presented to the official bodies of the two associations. According to reports (37), they met in an atmosphere of mutual acceptance and good will. Even in respect to the difficult problem of psychotherapy they worked out at least a core of agreement regarding the psychologist's role in treatment. Although the psychiatrists (2) expressed themselves as being opposed to independent private practice of psychotherapy by psychologists, they did approve of psychologists' doing therapy in a medical setting. The psychologists (3) expressed the opinion that all psychologists engaged in diagnostic or therapeutic work "must maintain accurate, open channels for collaborative working relationships with physicians most qualified to deal with border-line problems which occur. . . . We are opposed to the practice of clinical psychology (and, in particular, to the practice of psychotherapy) that does not meet these conditions." The agreement in the two statements seemed to be quite encouraging, and basically there appeared to be little real differences between the two professions.

During the past few years several incidents have occurred which suggest that the relationships between psychology and psychiatry are not as good as we had hoped (33). The principal bone of contention has been and continues to be the problem of psychotherapy. Some psychiatrists believe that most psychologists are interested in nothing but therapy; and they are concerned with the qualifications of psychologists to engage in therapy. They doubt that psychologists are qualified to conduct independent therapy, and they are distrustful of the intentions of psychologists insofar as therapy is concerned. Even though psychologists may dislike admitting it, there are some instances in which this distrust has been earned. Whereas psychiatry will not endorse the independent private practice of psychotherapy by a physician who does not have at least three and preferably five years of supervised residency training in psychiatry beyond the M.D. and the general internship, many psychologists feel that they are qualified to treat after earning a Ph.D. Even the best of the doctoral programs provides no more than two years of clinical work comparable to that required of psychiatrists. We have the report (13)—and psychiatrists are also aware of this—that the "chief interest of a substantial proportion of the young psychologists is to treat rather than to test or teach or investigate." As a matter of fact, a substantial number of persons calling themselves clinical psychologists are practicing independent therapy without even having earned the Ph.D. degree. We give "lip service" to necessary qualifications for the psychologist who engages in therapeutic activities, and yet, until recently, we have had no adequate standard of professional competence which could be used as a criterion. It is possible that certification by the American Board of Examiners in Professional Psychology can be used as a criterion of competence within a few years, but at the present time, even with the awareness of the standards represented by such certification, we allow persons not eligible for certification the privilege of practice. We have clinical psychologists a year or two out of graduate school who presume to question the competence of psychiatrists to conduct therapy, others who insist that they are qualified to supervise therapy, and still others who, in public meetings, are tactless and brash enough to insist that psychotherapy is not a branch of medical science but of learning, and as such is a branch of psychology. Such a statement may be acceptable in principle, but until we develop techniques of psychological treatment based on psychological principles, and as long as these same psychologists continue to use techniques developed by psychiatry, statements of this kind can only be expected to create ill feeling. On every hand we find psychologists who contentiously and aggressively insist that they should be granted certain prerogatives because they have Ph.D.'s in clinical psychology.

All this, despite the fact that there are few major university psychology departments that purport to train psychotherapists. It is true that supervised experiences in therapy may be provided, but it is doubted whether any institution would endorse its graduates as competent for independent therapy. In fact, most university training departments place the emphasis upon research training, yet the graduates of these same universities neglect research and diagnostic duties in order to engage in therapeutic activities for which they are certainly not adequately prepared. Such events appear to be due to the ambitious striving of a young profession, and it seems safe to predict that as maturity is gained, the profession will set and enforce standards. Until this is done, it is little wonder that William C. Menninger (26, p. 11) can comment:

> From our experience in psychiatry, we have learned that many physicians who can do excellent clinical diagnostic work are not adept at prolonged or intensive psychotherapy. The probabilities are that in most instances, the present educational curriculum in clinical psychology does not provide sufficient controlled experience to indicate clearly to an individual his own capabilities or limitations to carry on psychotherapy. Therefore, when the Doctor of Philosophy in clinical psychology, upon graduation, sets himself up in private practice because of his interest in therapy, he has not had the experience or training which would permit him to recognize his own limitations. Nevertheless, many individuals do just this, and, for legal reason, call their attempted psychotherapy "counseling." Fortunately, the leaders in both of our professions fully disapprove of this practice. Unfortunately, a considerable number of individuals who classify themselves as clinical psychologists maintain a resistance toward the acceptance of this opinion.[2]

Even though we caution the psychologist to apply himself to those activities for which he is trained, we must ask whether there is really a marked difference between the practice of clinical and counseling psychology, and psychotherapy. Menninger goes on to point out that whether or not he practices formal psychotherapy, the clinical psychologist must of necessity be therapeutically minded since any contact with the patient has therapeutic implications. He urges that all psychologists, whether

[2] From "The Relationship of Clinical Psychology and Psychiatry," by William C. Menninger, *American Psychologist*, 1950, 5, 3–15. By permission of the American Psychological Association.

they are teachers, investigators, or clinicians, have an opportunity to develop a therapeutic attitude toward those with whom they work instead of one that is purely academic, didactic, or experimental. It would seem quite obvious that the research in psychodynamics and/or psychotherapy, which is so critically needed, could scarcely be conducted by one with little or no opportunity to gain experience in therapy. The fact that therapeutic influences are at work in all contacts with the patient, no matter how casual and incidental, has led Watson (45) to observe that no matter what the aim, the psychologist cannot help but be therapeutically oriented. At the same time psychologists should seriously question their personal motivation for therapeutic activities. Many are probably indulging themselves in their therapeutic work. Too, we must realize that all psychologists are not equally qualified as therapists; in fact, many who are academically qualified are certainly not qualified in terms of their own personal adjustment.

The student contemplating a career in clinical and counseling psychology should not be dismayed by this discussion. The profession of psychology is sufficiently broad in its scope for all persons who are capable of attaining a broad training in psychology to find satisfactory and constructive activities in which to apply this training. The point of our discussion is simply to emphasize that the major activity of psychologists does not have to be psychotherapy. At least it does not have to be therapy in the classical or psychiatric sense. It is quite conceivable that the concept of therapy is changing and that treatment procedures which are basically psychological are developing. It is hoped that students of psychology and young psychologists can devote themselves to the perfection of such procedures, which will maximize the contributions of psychology to the public welfare. Certainly these contributions are not to be furthered by contentious competition with an older, better established discipline. If we must compete, let us do so by the invention of more effective treatment procedures.

Many psychologists appear to be threatened by an indication that they work under the supervision of, or even in collaboration with, psychiatrists. In connection with this point it is well that we consider further the problem of a psychologist working in a medical setting.[3] The older professions (such as law, the ministry, medicine, and education) have developed conventions and practices designed to protect both the welfare of their clients and the status of their professions. When a psychologist elects to render services within the framework of another profession, he has moral, ethical, and practical obligations to adapt himself to the con-

---

[3] This discussion is based in large measure on a preliminary report of the Ad Hoc Committee on Relations between Psychology and the Medical Profession. This preliminary report was revised extensively and its final form (6) has been referred to on a previous occasion.

ventions and legal strictures of that profession. This need not involve any status implications whatsoever. The psychologist who elects to serve in a medical setting should realize and accept these obligations, just as certain conventions and conditions must be accepted if he joins the staff of a university or an industrial or business firm. The psychologist must recognize and accept the physician-patient relationship both intellectually and emotionally. The chosen physician, in accepting responsibility for the care of a patient, assumes the final moral and legal responsibility. By law, it is his responsibility to determine treatment, and to determine who shall administer it. This responsibility cannot be legally delegated to any other person. In order to serve the patient most effectively, the physician has the right and obligation to utilize all resources at his command, such as the assistance of psychologists or others. For all that happens to the patient in these ministrations, the physician in attendance bears the final responsibility, and consequently he must be free to direct the activities of his associates. The position of the psychologist is little different from that of other physicians who are asked to assist the chosen or prime physician. They, too, are supervised by the physician in charge of the specific patient.

When a psychologist is performing the functions of diagnosis and therapy in a medical setting, the relationships between the psychologist and the physician should be obvious. Nobody can reasonably question the primary responsibility of the physician insofar as these two functions are concerned. The physician can request services from the psychologist; he may even request a psychologist to perform therapy for long periods of time and give the psychologist responsibility for planning and carrying out the therapeutic measures. Such an arrangement does not diminish the responsibility of the physician one iota. The ultimate responsibility of the physician must not be forgotten by the psychologist. When the psychologist is conducting research involving the use of patients, he has a slightly different situation from that when he is doing clinical work. Although the physician must still determine whether a patient can be used as a subject in a research project, the ability and the competence of the psychologist should determine the responsibility he has for the planning, design, and actual conduct of the work in question. When the psychologist teaches in a medical setting, he acts (as does the physician who might be a teacher) as any other teacher and abides by the conventions and strictures common to education. He has complete freedom to plan and present the didactic aspects of his work, giving due consideration to the established objectives and purposes of the instruction for which he is responsible.

The important concept here is not so much the prestige of a profession or the status needs of the individual, but the priority of the physician-patient relationship in a medical setting. The psychologist who chooses to work in medical settings will by necessity function under the supervision of a representative of the medical setting. If he cannot accept this role, either he is poorly trained as a psychologist or he should not have elected psychology as a profession. In nonmedical settings the psychologist may find himself acting as a leader or taking primary responsibility, but there will always be times when he must, for the good of his client, accede to the advice of other disciplines.

Insofar as private practice is concerned, there should be no problem of interprofessional relationships if psychologists will simply abide by the resolution adopted by the Council of Representatives of the American Psychological Association at its Denver meeting in 1949 (4, p. 445):

> We are opposed to the practice of psychotherapy (not to include remedial teaching, or vocational or educational counseling) by psychologists that does not meet the conditions of genuine collaboration with physicians most qualified to deal with the borderline problems which occur (e.g., differential diagnosis, inter-current organic disease, psychosomatic problems).

At the Boulder Conference (31, p. 140) the following resolution was adopted:

> Because of: (a) the extreme complexity and variety of problems presenting themselves for solution, (b) the equally wide variety of skills and techniques required for the most effective service to the individual, and (c) the fact that the current training of any one profession cannot possibly insure mastery of all these techniques—we urge clinical psychologists to adopt, as a principle of practice, the establishment and maintenance of active and effective liaison with members of allied professions in all service functions.[4]

The psychologists' proposed code of ethics (5, p. 162) includes the following principle:

> Principle 3.51–1. In clinical or consulting practice, the psychologist must refer his client to an appropriate specialist when there is evidence of a difficulty with which the psychologist is not competent to deal.

More recently other statements (6, 8) have been made that are essentially similar to the above; they all stress the need for collaboration and the necessity that we avoid the practice of independent psychotherapy.

In the last analysis it must also be remembered that there are all kinds of personalities represented in psychology and psychiatry. It is the

[4] By permission from Raimy, Victor C., ed., *Training in Clinical Psychology.* Englewood Cliffs, N.J. Copyright, 1950, by Prentice-Hall, Inc.

responsibility of the psychological profession to clean its house and to be sure that professional psychologists are personally and professionally qualified. It is equally important that psychiatry screen its potential practitioners just as carefully. In the meantime there will continue to be interpersonal problems. Interprofessional conflicts can be resolved more easily than interpersonal ones. Actually, there are many indications of good working relations at the local levels. This is, of course, sometimes an indication of weakness: the relationship may be good merely because of the poor training of the psychiatrist or physician, who as a result turns all responsibility over to the psychologist; or it may be good because of the submissiveness of the psychologist to a dominating psychiatrist, who thereby relegates the psychologist to the role of a psychiatric handmaiden. Ordinarily the working relationships are good because the well-trained, well-adjusted professional team members learn to understand each other. Psychologists and psychiatrists must submerge their own needs to the needs of society. The two disciplines with their different backgrounds and widely divergent programs of training must work in close co-operation if the needs of society are to be met. David Shakow (38, 39), in his article entitled "Psychology and Psychiatry: A Dialogue," has presented an extremely frank exposition of the issues involved in the relationship between psychology and psychiatry. The keynote of his article can be found in his statement that most differences of opinion have arisen from (38, p. 191) "too many considerations based on the conscious and unconscious needs of the two professions and their professors, rather than the needs of the patient or the fundamental needs of society."

CLINICAL PSYCHOLOGY AND PSYCHIATRIC SOCIAL WORK

The third member of the mental hygiene team is the psychiatric social worker. Psychiatric social work is a subdivision of the broader field of social work. Psychiatric social workers have specialized in work with the mentally and emotionally disturbed, and since they bring another tradition to the team, they make an important contribution to its work.

The representative of the American Association of Psychiatric Social Workers at the Boulder Conference on Training in Clinical Psychology (31, pp. 150–1) presented a statement comparing the professions of clinical psychology and psychiatric social work. This is reproduced in summarized form below:

Social work has progressed from volunteer service, with its workers trained outside universities, to the graduate, professional level; with research included as a part of its training program. There is now a movement to train social workers to the doctoral level. The orientation of the social worker has always been service to people who have problems in social adjustment. Psychiatric social work is one of the many social work fields. It is distinguished from the others by the fact that the psychiatric social worker has had a sequence of courses and field experience with psychiatric orientation, and works (eventually) in a psychiatric setting. The following tabulation presents an oversimplified but not inaccurate comparison of clinical psychology and psychiatric social work:

	Clinical Psychology	*Psychiatric Social Work*
Base setting	Psychology-Science-Research	Social case work
Tradition	Academic-Scientific	Service
Training (a)	Four years	Two years plus
Training (b)	Research and clinical	Interviewing, Case material recording, Supervision
Therapy practiced	Wide variety of treatment measures	Case work treatment in a psychiatric setting
Language	Conceptual	Concrete and related to "case material"

The major differences between the psychiatric social worker and the clinical psychologist seem to be highlighted by the differences in attitude displayed in the clinical setting. The psychiatric social worker is trained to accept assumptions about human behavior whereas the clinical psychologist is taught to question almost any assumption.

Further discussion at the Boulder Conference of the relationship between the disciplines of psychology and social work brought out three major areas in which social workers criticize psychologists:

(1) The psychologist's attitude toward the patient is too often similar to his attitude toward a laboratory subject.

(2) The psychologist on the mental health team is likely to play the role of critic and thus create tensions in the team relationships.

(3) The broad field encompassed by the training program of the clinical psychologist creates a risk that he will be trained as a second-rate psychiatrist or second-rate social worker.

The fact that such criticisms exist underlines the need for more satisfactory mutual understanding of the functioning of the professions. The psychologist's lack of knowledge concerning the field of social work has been emphasized by Joseph Andriola (11), who points out the need for two-way communication between the two professions. He reports that although accredited schools of social work require their students to have at least a nodding acquaintance with psychology, he sees little evidence among psychology students or psychologists which would indicate even a minimal elementary knowledge of the field of social work.

It is not within the scope of this book to describe the field of social work, but it must be emphasized that students of clinical psychology should make it their responsibility to become familiar with it. In the functioning of the mental hygiene team, it is essential that each member understand the unique contributions that can be made by the others if the best possible service is to be offered to the client. Myra Bachman (12) describes the duties of the psychiatric social worker in a mental hygiene clinic as the initial contacting of the client, learning from the client what the trouble is as he sees it, the establishment of contact with parents of the client, and getting the client to the clinic. We might also include among these responsibilities the collection of case history material and the conducting of therapy with selected cases, particularly if environmental manipulation or adjustment is required. Other functions could also be mentioned but these are enough to illustrate our point. The clinical psychologist might insist that he is competent to conduct an intake interview or to contact parents or even to engage in therapies involving environmental adjustments. The psychiatrist might question the social worker's function in therapy and around we could go. The ideal working relationship is proposed by Fritz Schmidl (36), who describes how a specific clinic attempts to use the members of the clinical team on the basis of the needs of each individual client rather than on the basis of a theoretical conviction as to the functions of the professions represented.

To go back to the criticisms of psychologists which have been offered by psychiatric social workers, we must first realize that the history of social work has been integrated with psychiatry. It is true that the psychiatric social worker may tend to accept uncritically many assumptions about behavior, but, on the other hand, the psychologist is sometimes too prone to criticize working hypotheses. Such criticisms are frequently not accepted in the spirit in which they are offered, and tensions result. It is vital that the psychologist understand the relative absence of research orientation in the social worker and attempt to elicit the co-operation of his coworkers in significant investigations rather than antagonize by a perpetually questioning attitude.

Psychological and psychiatric supervisors have noted that psychology students are frequently relatively insensitive to the feeling aspects of a client's verbalizations. Too often, factual events are simply recorded without any appraisal of the reactions of the client to these events. Social workers are trained to observe and report many subtle aspects of a client's behavior in the interview situation, and unless the psychologist can regard the client as less of a laboratory subject and more of a feeling being, he will indeed be a second-rate social worker. From the most casual perusal of standard texts in psychiatric social work as compared with those in clinical psychology, it is apparent that the "case-study method" is one of the unique contributions of the field of social work. The clinical psychologist must appreciate the value of this approach, for it seems unlikely that diagnostic testing can take the place of case-history material. Medical examinations, case-history taking, and diagnostic testing are all interdependent functions, and regardless of who does what, all is best accomplished by the mental hygiene team.

This section cannot be closed without agreeing with Andriola that two-way communication is necessary, and we hope we can be pardoned if we suggest that it is doubtful whether most psychiatric social workers have very much knowledge of professional psychology. Inspection of their texts discloses few references to the field of clinical and counseling psychology, and although there is much discussion of the interrelationship between psychiatry and psychiatric social work, there is, since psychology is seldom mentioned, little discussion of the relationship between psychology and psychiatric social work. Therefore, it is suggested that social work also give consideration to its relationship with psychology so that we can effect the two-way communication so necessary for smooth operation of the team.

CLINICAL PSYCHOLOGY AND COUNSELING PSYCHOLOGY

Since this text is concerned with clinical *and* counseling psychology and not with clinical psychology or counseling psychology as separate or distinct fields, the reader may wonder at the inclusion of this section. Our point of view is that there is no basic difference between the training or the objectives of clinical and counseling psychology. However there are persons who call themselves counseling psychologists who would not call themselves clinical psychologists, and there are clinical psychologists who do not see themselves as counseling psychologists. Most counseling psychologists are active in the Division of Counseling and Guidance of the American Psychological Association, and most clinical psychologists are associated with the Division of Clinical and Abnormal Psychology. Furthermore, the American Board of Examiners in Professional Psychology offers a diploma in each of the areas of counseling and clinical psychology. So distinctions have apparently been drawn between the two fields of endeavor, although many of the functions as well as the general objectives of counseling psychology overlap with those of clinical psychology.

In 1952 the Veterans Administration announced a training program for counseling psychologists (28) which is administratively separate from the program in clinical psychology. The Education and Training Board of the American Psychological Association has developed a plan for accrediting universities to offer graduate training in counseling psychology which does not require that universities approved for training in counseling first be approved for clinical psychology.

The distinctions that some have made between these two fields of professional psychology can be pointed up by examination of the definitions and applications of the fields. The Committee on Counselor Training, Division of Counseling and Guidance of the American Psychological Association (7), has discussed the role and functions of counseling psychologists. Counseling psychology is defined as that discipline which fosters the psychological development of the individual. Like the clinical psychologist, the counseling psychologist works with persons all along the adjustment continuum, from those who function at tolerable levels of adequacy to those who are suffering from severe behavior disorders. However the counseling psychologist will spend the bulk of his time with individuals within the normal range of adjustment, while the clinical psychologist most often concentrates on persons outside this range. Although we do not agree with the division of functions or applications, the distinction which is often made is that counseling stresses the positive and the preventative rather than the remedial. Clinical psychology is interested in the positive and the preventative but, in terms of application, the major emphasis is probably on the remedial.

The above assumes that the clinical psychologist is ordinarily employed in the hospital or clinic setting and that the counseling psychologist finds his central setting to be within the educational framework. Clinical psychologists who do work within the educational framework will more frequently be found in clinics, while the counseling psychologist will be found in the guidance service, in vocational guidance centers, in student personnel work, or in administrative positions more concerned with the developmental phases of education than the remedial. In reality, counseling psychologists may work in hospitals, and clinical psychologists, as well as counseling psychologists, may be found in industry. The work of the counseling psychologist in the hospital is apt to be coordinated closely with that of the clinical psychologist. The differences appear to be in terms of application rather than of the specific activities engaged in. For example, the functions of the counseling psychologist in the Veterans Administration are described (28, pp. 684–5) as follows:

> Apply psychological principles, techniques and instruments to the evaluation, counseling and placement of hospitalized individuals.

Administer and interpret tests of intelligence, achievement, aptitude and personality.

Carry out group or individual counseling when requested by the patient and attending physician.

Confer with all professional staff members regarding individual cases under treatment.

Conduct research in the field of vocational counseling and placement as well as upon problems of evaluation, counseling and placement.

Evaluate and counsel individuals having disabling or handicapping conditions as related to possible employment.

Assist and motivate patients to accept vocational and rehabilitative goals.

Supervise and instruct trainees in the counseling field and collaborate in the orienting of other professional hospital personnel such as psychiatrists, physicians, social workers and nurses.

Plan, direct, and co-ordinate the vocational counseling program or perform other administrative duties.

Consult, when necessary, with universities, other agencies of the local, state, or federal government, and outside groups, upon problems involving any of the areas described above.[5]

Except for the use of the term "counseling" and the emphasis upon vocational counseling, this job description is very similar to the job description of the clinical psychologist. In general, activities and the training needs are similar except for those knowledges relative to vocational guidance.

The counseling functions in the hospital differ from the clinical functions primarily in the emphasis upon educational and vocational needs of persons who are regarded as relatively "normal," rather than upon remedial procedures with persons who are very disturbed. If a separation is to be made, the counseling psychologist is somewhat more apt to work with persons near the terminal phase of their hospitalization. He will work in tuberculosis hospitals and general medicine and surgical hospitals as well as in neuropsychiatric hospitals. Whereas the clinical psychologist (in the Veterans Administration) is attached to the Department of Neurology and Psychiatry and is supervised in his work by the chief of this department, the counseling psychologist is responsible to the chief of professional services at the hospital. An examination of

[5] From "The VA Program for Counseling Psychologists," by Bruce V. Moore and Lorraine Bouthilet, *American Psychologist*, 1952, 7, 684–5. By permission of the American Psychological Association.

the recommended training program indicates that the program for counseling psychology (7) follows the same pattern as that for clinical psychology, the primary differences being in terms of application at the practicum and internship levels rather than at the training level.

CLINICAL PSYCHOLOGY AND VOCATIONAL AND EDUCATIONAL GUIDANCE

The broad definition offered for the field of counseling psychology could apply equally well for the field of guidance. However we find that guidance stresses the developmental and educative functions somewhat more than does counseling psychology and certainly more than does clinical psychology. Educational and vocational guidance, as the name implies, goes beyond vocational guidance. Guidance services include many activities designed to help pupils with their life-adjustment problems and needs. They are concerned with the pupil's health, social and recreational activities, and extend into the vocational areas. Well-adjusted persons can be aided as well as those whose adjustments are less adequate. The guidance program might be conceived of as the process of helping each person as an individual and as a member of groups to make wiser choices and better adjustments.

Donald G. Paterson (29), in tracing the development of guidance from 1909 to 1938, regards educational and vocational guidance as a branch of student personnel work. Other branches of this general field are mental hygiene, student housing, extracurricular activities, financial-aid programs, and activities dealing with mores, morale, and morals of students. Paterson stresses that the modern guidance worker utilizes the clinical method. However he emphasizes that the clinical method of guidance is not, in his estimation, a direct outgrowth of the work of clinical psychologists. He comments that clinical psychologists all too frequently become arrested in their professional development on the level of the I.Q. We must remember that he was writing in 1938 and at that time many clinical psychologists *were* arrested at that level. He traces the manner in which the clinical method used by the guidance clinician originated in the research efforts of applied psychologists concerned with the psychology of individual mental differences and how the development of tests, testing procedures, and the statistical methods and statistical facts concerning the tests formed the basis for modern guidance.

So, too, it will be remembered that earlier we traced the origins of modern clinical psychology to the psychometric analysis of individual differences. We (17) have described elsewhere how clinical psychology and guidance have many aims in common. Theoretically, however, there is some distinction between the two areas of specialization. Whereas the clinical psychologist's efforts are primarily directed toward the changing of inefficient attitudes and habits of behavior in poorly adjusted persons, the specialist in guidance should direct his efforts toward the further development of efficient modes of adjustment in all persons. Both functions are closely related to the broad objectives of education. According to this differentiation, guidance is most clearly an educative process, while clinical psychology is oriented toward a remedial or therapeutic process, and counseling psychology may be thought of as lying approximately midway between these extremes.

Practically, there is considerable overlap, and it is usually impossible to decide whether a given activity should be engaged in or directed by a guidance worker, a counseling psychologist, or a clinical psychologist, but if representatives of these fields engage in long debates over who does what, it is doubtful if anyone will profit and the public will probably suffer. It is important, however, that the given activity be engaged in by those who are adequately trained and qualified. Relatively few guidance workers have training or experience with the abnormal modes of adjustment, and it is urged that they use extreme caution in dealing with problems of unusual behavior. Furthermore, the interpretation of many kinds of test data may be difficult or impossible without actual experience with the entire adjustment continuum.

To summarize, the scope and purpose of educational and vocational guidance is to provide organized developmental, preventive, and remedial services to assist students in developing their potentials through their educational experiences for making satisfying and socially useful adjustments, personally and vocationally. These purposes require the use of techniques for individual appraisal, the organization of group activities, the interpretation of curriculum content, and the co-ordination of school and community resources. Guidance practices are concerned chiefly with the orientation of students and their parents to the school; the adaptation of the curriculum to student needs; the guidance of students in the selection of courses and curricula in terms of interests, needs, and goals; the use of community resources to acquaint the student with the requirements and opportunities for various occupations; planning for student participation in social, civic, and vocational activities; and the provision of remedial services directly, or through referral, for students who, because of educational, personal, and vocational problems, are unable to make adequate progress through their educational experiences.

Careful examination of this description of the purpose and scope of activities of the educational guidance worker should emphasize the close relationship between guidance, and clinical and counseling psychology. It should also indicate that there is in guidance a field of service which is sufficiently unique in its application that it can be differentiated from psychology.

Positions in educational and vocational guidance appear to be of four general types: public school guidance personnel; the employment counselor; the counselor in various community agencies or institutions such as private and public social agencies, hospitals, and industries; and the college personnel officer. In public schools, colleges, and universities the positions are often combined with teaching. In larger institutions the position may consist chiefly of the organization and the administration of the services.

CLINICAL PSYCHOLOGY AND EDUCATION

We have discussed the role of the school psychologist and described the interaction between the functions of the school psychologist and the broader functions of education. In the discussion of educational guidance we suggested that clinical psychology in its broadest sense is an educative activity. If there is a distinction between clinical psychology and education, it is that clinical psychology places primary emphasis upon the individual aims of education, while education is more concerned with the broader aims of socialization and aiding the development of people in general.

The rapid rise of interest in psychometrics and guidance activities among educators has resulted in the development of an educational psychology that overlaps clinical psychology in several functions. The inevitable result of the introduction of psychometric and counseling activities into the school has been that many of these activities are conducted by improvised personnel who are considered poorly trained by professional psychologists. In comparison with psychological training the one-year or one-semester course in tests and measurements which comprises the training of many of these personnel may understandably be regarded as inadequate.

In this connection it is interesting to note the development and definition of the field of educational psychology. Educational psychology has been defined by a faculty committee at Yale University (51) as the selection, organization, and interpretation of psychology for its bearing upon the understanding and direction of education. Correspondingly, an educational psychologist is a psychologist with an interest in and knowledge of education which cause and enable him to serve and improve the work of education. This is a broad definition. There are specialized labels for parts of the work of the educational psychologist. The Yale Committee conducted a study of two hundred educational psychologists and found them teaching, rendering psychological services to individuals, engaged in research or in the direction of research, directing student personnel services, and administering some phase of the educational program.

The duties of the educational psychologist and the functions of education in general would seem to overlap many of the areas already described. Again, we do not wish either to stress the overlap or to attempt to differentiate sharply, but simply to emphasize the need for coordination of activities and the delineation of duties in terms of the training of personnel. It should be the responsibility of the fields both of psychology and education to insure that the service worker is adequately prepared for the kinds of responsibilities assumed by him.

CLINICAL AND COUNSELING PSYCHOLOGY AND INDUSTRIAL PSYCHOLOGY

Industrial psychology and clinical and counseling psychology have much in common in that, at least in part, both have grown out of the study of individual differences. Certainly, both utilize testing, interviewing, and other evaluative techniques. We discussed earlier the application of clinical or individual study techniques to industrial problems. We would be splitting hairs if we attempted to distinguish between the clinical and counseling psychologist and the industrial psychologist in terms of the techniques or tools employed.

Perhaps the principal difference involves the purposes for which the tools are employed. The industrial psychologist's function is to appraise the capacity, aptitude, and motivation of individuals and advise on problems of personnel selection, personnel advancement, job proficiency, efficiency, safety, and a large number of related problems so that the overall production and economic goals of the business or industry can be achieved. The industrial psychologist's primary allegiance is to the agency that employs or retains him. In a manner of thinking, the needs of the individual are secondary. No criticism of this is intended but it seems necessary to be realistic. On the other hand, the clinician puts the needs of the individual first and studies or evaluates the individual. No conflict between the purposes of clinical and counseling psychology and industrial psychology should ever exist as long as their functions are clearly separated. When the industrial psychologist interprets information to the individual and attempts to use information collected for another purpose to aid the individual, he should be properly trained for this individual application or he may do the individual much harm, and, in fact, would presumably be guilty of unethical practice. However, complete disregard for the welfare of the individual is certainly an exaggeration of the application of industrial psychology and is not to be encouraged.

Fortunately, the needs of the individual and the needs of industry usually coincide rather than conflict. It is not good individual mental hygiene for a person to be assigned work for which he has no aptitude or interest—or for which he is otherwise unqualified. Safety and morale are obviously related to individual mental hygiene as well as to industrial efficiency. In actual practice we seldom find examples of activities or practices which are in the best interests of industry that are not also in the best interests of the individual.

So far, we have stressed the similarities and have emphasized that both fields of work apply the principles of general psychology to the study of individuals. It must also be indicated that the similarities are more in principle than in practice. The clinician is most frequently involved with persons whose capacities, aptitudes, motivation, or control is atypical or abnormal. The industrial psychologist is most frequently dealing with persons whose behavior and behavior potential is relatively normal. However the industrial psychologist may have occasion to work with persons all along the adjustment continuum. Short, intensive, and cross-sectional evaluations are more characteristic of the work of the industrial psychologist, while long, extensive, and longitudinal evaluations are more typical of the work of the clinician. The industrial psychologist employs group-study techniques; the clinical or counseling psychologist, individual-study methods. Remedial or therapeutic activity is almost always more the function of the clinician than of the industrial psychologist.

Here again, little is to be gained by belaboring the differences between fields of work. Both are applications of psychology for specific purposes, and, in general, both disciplines are concerned with the promotion of efficiency of behavior. We should rather be concerned with the training and preparation of the professional worker for the responsibilities assumed by him or assigned to him. If he is adequately prepared, it makes little difference whether he is a clinical or industrial psychologist. For a comprehensive description of the typical activities of the industrial psychologist, the reader is referred to Joseph Tiffin's text *Industrial Psychology* (42).

CLINICAL PSYCHOLOGY AND THE LAW

The psychologist must maintain an attitude of helpfulness in all legal situations. Information, however, that is received in confidence by a psychologist acting in a professional capacity must be regarded as confidential. There have been a few instances when the position of the psychologist as a recipient of confidential information has created delicate legal situations. One situation has been described by Edward Joseph Shoben (40). Shoben had counseled with a young man who was subsequently charged with strangling his girl friend, and Shoben was served a subpoena to appear in court as a state witness. He was denied privileged communication by the court and required to testify as to the content of a confidential interview with the young man on trial. Shoben, in this case, decided to testify and presents his reasons for doing so in the reference mentioned above. This type of situation would seem to argue the need for legislation giving the right of privileged communication to psychologists. However there are many other facets and such legislation may not be forthcoming or even advisable. In any case, no legislation of this type exists at the present time except in a few states, and it is necessary that each psychologist, whenever necessary, resolve the conflict as best he can in view of all legal, ethical, and professional considerations. The professional psychologist, just as other professional workers, has multiple loyalties: loyalties to his client, to his employer, and to the society of which he is a part. A rough pattern for his professional practice might be made up from an evaluation of his relative allegiances. If the best interests of his client can be served without jeopardy to the interests or safety of others, it would seem that no problem exists; if, on the contrary, the health or safety of a larger portion of society beyond the client is endangered, the larger segment should be protected. Decisions of this kind are always going to be in the nature of professional judgments and, of course, are subject to the vagaries of human nature. The psychologist may be required to make decisions on legal matters, or more often concerning potential legal situations, without having any absolute rules to follow. He must make these decisions on the basis of the individual situation.

Except in the case of psychologists who are employed by the court or by some other agency of the law, or in those rare instances in which the psychologist may be called upon for expert testimony, the relationship between psychology and the law is the same as for any other citizen or group of citizens.

CLINICAL AND COUNSELING PSYCHOLOGY AND RELIGION

There is much to be said about the relationship between psychology and religion; however we will sum it up by saying that the clinician must recognize as belonging to religion all matters customarily thought to belong to religion. In general, this refers to considerations of the rightness or wrongness of behavior. It is not the function of the psychologist to judge or to pass upon attitudes possessed by a client.

This is not to say that the philosophies and beliefs of the client are not to be discussed with the psychologist. It is intended, however, to emphasize that the psychologist is not to interfere with these beliefs. It must be constantly realized that the influence of religion offers many persons security and support that cannot be replaced by psychology. Of course, conflict centering around religion is not uncommon. The psychologist must feel free to consider such conflict, but his function is to aid in the resolution of the conflict, and not to tamper in any way with the client's belief in the tenets of his particular faith.

Psychology has much to offer to religion and to the ministers and representatives of the various faiths. Many theological training institutions are teaching more and more psychology. This is a problem for their consideration, and psychology can best serve by maintaining again, as with the law, an attitude of helpfulness without obstruction, interference, or criticism. It is, furthermore, the right and privilege of each psychologist to follow the teachings of his own particular faith, but, as an ethical professional psychologist, he must respect his clients as individuals and recognize that it is also their right and privilege to believe as they wish.

PSYCHOLOGY AND LEGISLATION [6]

As psychologists have become engaged in activities that bring them more and more in contact with the public, they have, of necessity, become quite sensitive about the place of their profession in society. Along with this sensitivity, and as an aspect of it, psychology has developed an awareness of the need for a program of social control in psychology. One form of social control is legal, and the pros and cons of legal control as well as the current status of legal controls is the topic for our present discussion. Other forms of social control have been directly and indirectly alluded to in this and other chapters. The establishment of standards for the training of professional psychologists and the carefulness with which persons are screened for admission into, and graduation from, training programs is a fundamental aspect of control. If we could be completely confident of the adequacy of our selection and training, the need for other controls would be lessened. We must remind ourselves, however, that psychologists are human; they can make mistakes and are subject to perfectly natural inadequacies that necessitate added safeguards. The professional associations (national, state, local, and, to a lesser extent, regional) certainly exert a degree of control over the attitudes and behavior of psychologists. In some ways this is the most healthy, long-lasting, and far-reaching form of control as psychologists are influenced to conform their ideas and their conduct to a professional structure of which they are a part, and to which they can feel a degree of "belongingness."

[6] This topic has been the subject of much discussion in the literature (1, 9, 10, 14, 15, 16, 18, 19, 20, 22, 23, 24, 25, 27, 30, 32, 34, 35, 43, 44, 47, 48, 49, 50, 52). The most comprehensive discussion is the joint report of the American Psychological Association and the Conference of State Psychological Associations Committees on Legislation (9). This report was adopted as official American Psychological Association policy at its September 1955 meeting. The present discussion is closely modeled after this report, but is by no means an adequate abstract of it. The interested student should read the entire report.

Unfortunately, this influence is limited to the members of the associations, and not all persons who present themselves as offering psychological services are actively exposed to the effects of membership in professional groups. Furthermore, it is regrettably true that there are persons in the profession who are not affected by, or who even abuse the privileges of, informal social control. The development of a code of ethical standards for psychologists has done much to direct the behavior of psychologists, but it is more of a functional guide than a form of control which can prevent malpractice. The primary purpose of the American Board of Examiners in Professional Psychology is social control. This Board designates those individuals possessing superior qualifications for applied professional services in the fields of clinical, counseling, and industrial psychology. As the public becomes informed about the meaning of certification by this Board, it will be more inclined to turn to professionally competent psychologists for help. The setting of minimum employment standards is still another method of social control in psychology.

Psychologists as a group have discussed, debated, and studied the needs for social control and methods for attaining it and have reached the decision that over and beyond the informal controls there is need for some form of legal control of the practice of psychology. One of the basic purposes of legal controls is to protect the public against incompetent or unethical practices. There appears to be general agreement with the principle that the work of certain psychologists or of people who call themselves psychologists involves threat or danger to the health, safety, or welfare of the public. The fact that there are numerous quacks and near-quacks in existence suggests that informal social controls alone are not adequate for the protection of the public. In addition to protecting the public from quackery and incompetence, it is felt that legal controls will protect the profession of psychology as a whole from the irresponsible behavior of a small number of persons calling themselves psychologists. For these reasons, as well as others not specifically discussed here, legal control has been accepted as desirable. The next question for discussion is the kind of legislation that would most effectively accomplish this control.

Although legislative action must of legal necessity be at the state levels, the advantages of uniformity in legislation make it advisable that the entire profession deal with the problem on a national as well as a state basis.

Briefly, uniformity would seem to be desirable for at least two reasons:

(1) It is in the interest of both the public and the profession to have a clear definition of the nature and functions of psychological roles and services. We need to define in a general way the conditions of practice of psychology. If widely different titles and standards are used in the

different states, definition is going to be difficult to attain. Legislation already passed and in operation in several states provides for the following titles for practicing psychologists:

Psychologist
Certified Psychologist
Certified Clinical Psychologist
Applied Psychologist
Clinical Psychologist

Bills under consideration provide for titles such as qualified psychologist, licensed psychologist, consulting psychologist, and certified consulting psychologist. As Arthur W. Combs (15) suggests, one shudders to think what the list might be like if all forty-eight states had laws. It would seem obvious that we need a national policy as soon as possible to prevent further complications. This need is emphasized when we consider the different provisions of the laws and the different levels of competence covered by them.

(2) As a matter of convenience to individual psychologists and to examining boards, we need uniformity as a basis for reciprocity between states. Without reciprocity, psychologists will be faced with the necessity of repeatedly going through the process of becoming certified or licensed each time they move. Since psychologists move frequently, it would be helpful if one state would honor action taken in another state. This can be expected only if there are relatively similar standards from state to state.

Three general kinds of psychological legislation and several subtypes have been considered by the various professional groups. In the past we have been in the habit of thinking about "certification" and "licensure" and various kinds of each. Variation in the meaning of these terms is so great that currently the attempt is to categorize the various kinds of legislation in terms of titles and functions. As an example of the variation and confusion between these terms, we might look at their use in several of the states that have laws. The proposed mandatory certification bill in New York State would result in the issuance of a license. A certificate is issued under the Kentucky licensing law. The Georgia law and the Tennessee law both are described as licensing laws, but are really mandatory certification laws which, like the proposed New York law, adopt a midway position resulting in hybrid licensing-certification bills. Several states, for example, Connecticut, Virginia, Minnesota, Maine, and Washington, have certification laws that restrict the term "psychologist" or "certified psychologist" or some similar title to certain individuals.

The several types of laws, as described by the most recent report (9) on legislation, are as follows:

(1) Voluntary legislation. This is the type of legislation which has already been described by the many committees that have been interested in it as permissive certification. It restricts the use of a particular title (certified psychologist, for example) to persons who have met certain standards of training and experience set by an examining board. In this way, a group of well-qualified practitioners are designated but there is no provision for prohibiting anyone from practice so long as he does not use the prescribed title.

(2) Nonrestrictive legislation. This type of legislation may take several forms; these forms have in common the exemption of certain groups from the provisions of the law. There are at least three forms that this legislation may take:

(a) By title only. This kind of legislation applies to a larger group of persons than does voluntary legislation. It attempts to bring all members of the profession under the law by limiting and controlling the use of a more general title such as "psychologist" or other terms "tending to imply that such a person is practicing as a psychologist." Such a law requires that anyone purporting to be a psychologist must meet certain standards set by an examining board. It does not attempt to control persons applying psychological techniques under other names unless they hold out or imply that they are psychologists. Thus the law attempts to control psychologists but does not interfere with other professions such as psychiatrists, teachers, or ministers who might use certain psychological techniques.

(b) By title and function. This kind of legislation is very similar to Category 2a, except that it defines the practice of psychology. The definition may be very general or very specific. In the proposed New Jersey bill, the extreme of generality is represented by the statement that practice be described as "rendering services to individuals or to the public for remuneration." The other extreme appears in the following statement from the Georgia law: ". . . and renders to individuals or to the public for fees any service involving the application of recognized principles, methods and procedures of the science and profession of psychology, such as interviewing, administering and interpreting tests of mental abilities, aptitudes, interests and personality characteristics for such purposes as psychological diagnosis, classification or evaluation, or for educational or vocational placement, or for such purposes as psychological counseling, guidance or readjustment." An intermediate position between these extremes, and one that may have advantages, is illustrated by the following section from the proposed New York bill: ". . . and represents himself as being able to or undertakes to employ appropriate psychological procedures in dealing with any person, corporation or association." This kind of legislation does not prohibit the use of psychological techniques by unqualified persons unless they call themselves psychologists. Other professional personnel can use psychological techniques if they do not call themselves psychologists. If they call themselves psychologists, they must be qualified by an examination board.

(c) By title and/or function. This categoary is similar to what has been called nonrestrictive licensing. In a law such as this, the attempt is to define the practice of the profession and restrict practice to qualified persons. It is stronger than the other categories since, in this instance, regardless of what title is used, the practitioner comes under the law. Here again, practice is not made the exclusive prerogative of a particular profession. Instead, members of other professions who might legitimately use psychological techniques are exempted. This kind of a statute prohibits the use of psychological techniques by unqualified persons, no matter what they call themselves.

(3) Restrictive legislation. Such a statute would define a profession solely in terms of its functions. It would say that anyone doing certain specified things is practicing psychology, no matter what he calls himself, and because of his activities he comes under the law. This is the pattern of most medical practice acts that define the practice of medicine and deny all except licensed physicians the right to engage in this practice.

Psychologists have quite generally gone on record as being opposed to this kind of legislation. There are at least two reasons: first, it is felt that psychology certainly does not wish to interfere with the legitimate use of psychological methods by other professions; and, second, this type of law requires such a specific definition of practice that we might "freeze" psychology at its present stage of development. It may be dangerous to spell out the practice of psychology in legal terms. If the practice had been specifically defined before World War II, we would have a definition very different from that which we could write today. No one knows what we might wish to say in 1975.

The joint report of the legislative committees of the American Psychological Association and the Conference of State Psychological Associations also advises against voluntary legislation, and gives as an additional reason that it depends upon the psychologist's decision to apply for a certificate. It simply directs those of the public who are sufficiently informed to some of the qualified psychologists. It does not affect the charlatan or quack if he chooses to call himself by some name other than that specified in the law. Consequently, it is quite ineffectual in protecting both the public and the psychologist and is not preferred by most thinkers on the problem.

On the basis of the elimination of categories (1) and (3), we are left with the various alternates under category (2). It is felt by most psychologists that type (2c) is the preferred kind of legislative control, but the experience of those who have attempted to secure legislation is that other professional groups are distrustful of laws which control the title and/or the function, and have opposed such bills. It is hoped that in the future these problems can be solved because such statutes would appear to offer the maximum amount of protection to the public without restricting service. (Most psychologists seem to favor the issuance of a certificate rather than a license.)

Another problem has concerned the level of training and experience which should be covered by a law. It appears most important that we work toward certification at the doctoral level, plus one or two years of experience. The recommended title is that of psychologist. Two states (Arkansas and Tennessee) have two-level laws which offer a certificate to persons without the doctor's degree, but with some graduate training and one or two years of experience. When certification is given on two levels, the lower level should be designated by the use of the terms *"examiner," "assistant,"* or *"technician"* so that it will not be confused with the doctorally trained level. Some laws have been designed to apply to some specialty such as "clinical psychology." Again, the general agreement seems to be that it is psychology that should be controlled and not any particular specialty.

Still another aspect of most bills is the provision within the law for the right of "privileged communication." This means that a legally recognized psychologist cannot, under ordinary circumstances, be required to reveal or to testify to the content of any information divulged to him in confidence and in the practice of the profession of psychology. Some psychologists value this right quite highly. Although we do not question the value of this legal protection for our clients, we feel that the importance of this point may be overemphasized and that most situations covered by such a provision would be matters of ethics rather than legality.

In summary, it appears that in the various states laws governing the practice of psychology will be prepared and submitted to the state legislatures (at least nine are known to be in preparation). It is hoped that these laws will be relatively uniform and that they will follow the general pattern of certification of the doctoral psychologist, with at least a year's experience, to practice activities broadly defined as falling under the heading of psychological practices. It is hoped, furthermore, that with the exception of certain exempted professions, limits will be placed on the practice of psychological activities by those other than fully qualified psychologists, regardless of the title used by the practitioner.

Along with such a legal program we must continue all our informal controls, and, in addition, we must educate the general public as to the meaning and practice of psychology. No amount of legislation will accomplish our purposes unless we can inform the public so that they can protect themselves. It is certainly true that even the very restrictive medical practices acts are far less than 100 per cent effective in controlling quackery in medicine. There is a still more important reason for public education. In reality, in spite of our concern about unauthorized and unqualified personnel, the most critical problem is that the public does not utilize psychological services enough, or at least not to their fullest advantage. Legislation will help to present a public image of psychology, but other efforts designed to inform the public are also indicated.

A FINAL THOUGHT

Between the functions that are purely psychiatric, psychological, or educational there is a large borderline area in which adequately trained specialists from any one of these professions can operate effectively. The field of mental hygiene and preventative psychology is too broad to be dominated by any one professional group—there is no room for professionalism or factionalism. The goals of mental hygiene do not belong to any one profession. Indeed, much of the responsibility for effecting mental hygiene must be assumed by the clergy, by teachers, by social workers, and by community leaders; in fact, it is the responsibility of all people. The purposes of all are the same. The methods may vary but there is, of course, great overlap in terms of method as well as in the areas of application. Co-operation and mutual assistance should be the keynote, regardless of the base of operation—the hospital, the school, the church, or the community.

SUMMARY

In this chapter we have emphasized that psychology as a profession can best serve if it maintains co-operative working relations with other professions. The relationship between psychology and the disciplines of psychiatry, social work, vocational guidance, education, law, and religion have been discussed at length. Some attention has been given to relationships within the field of psychology. The issue of legislation for psychology has been extensively discussed. It is recognized that most of these issues are in constant flux. However, it will most certainly continue to be true that the public will be best served if there are close working relationships between all those who offer personal services.

BIBLIOGRAPHY

1. American Medical Association, "Licensure or certification of clinical psychologists." *J. Amer. Med. Assn.*, 1952, 148, 271–3.
2. American Psychiatric Association, *Report of the committee on clinical psychology*, 1949.

3. American Psychological Association, *Report of the committee on the relation of psychology to psychiatry*, 1949.

4. American Psychological Association, Proceedings of the fifty-seventh annual business meeting of the American Psychological Association, Inc., Denver, Colo. *Amer. Psychologist*, 1949, 4, 443.

5. American Psychological Association, Committee on ethical standards for psychology, Ethical standards in clinical and consulting relationships: Section 3, Parts II–V. *Amer. Psychologist*, 1951, 6, 145–67.

6. American Psychological Association, *ad hoc* committee on relations between psychology and the medical profession; "Psychology and its relationships with other professions." *Amer. Psychologist*, 1952, 7, 145–52.

7. American Psychological Association, Committee on counselor training, division of counseling and guidance, "Recommended standards for training counseling psychologists at the doctoral level." *Amer. Psychologist*, 7, 1952, 175–81.

8. American Psychological Association, *ad hoc* committee on relations between psychology and other professions, "Implications for legislation in the report of the *ad hoc* committee on relations between psychology and other professions." *Amer. Psychologist*, 1953, 8, 546–50.

9. American Psychological Association, Joint report of the APA and CSPA committees on legislation. *Amer. Psychologist*, 1955, 10, 727–56.

10. American Psychological Association, "Division of Clinical Psychology, The proposed legislative moratorium." *News Letter*, 1955, 8, 1–9.

11. Andriola, J., "Psychologists' Ignorance of Social Work, Comment." *Amer. Psychologist*, 1951, 6, 12, 690.

12. Bachman, M., "The psychiatric social worker in the Delaware Mental Hygiene Clinic." *Delaware St. Med. J.*, 1949, 21, 176–80.

13. Benton, A., "Round table on the psychologist in the clinic setting." *Amer. J. Orthopsychiat.*, 1948, 18, 507–11.

14. Combs, A. W., "A report of the 1951 licensing effort in New York State." *Amer. Psychologist*, 1951, 6, 541–8.

15. Combs, A. W., "Problems and definitions in legislation." *Amer. Psychologist*, 1953, 8, 554–63.

16. Ellis, A., "Pros and cons of legislation for psychologists." *Amer. Psychologist*, 1953, 8, 551–3.

17. Hadley, J. M., "What the guidance counselor should know about clinical psychology." Proceedings of the Fourteenth Annual Guidance Conference held at Purdue Univ., April 4 and 5, 1949. *Studies in Higher Education*, LXIX, 1949, 5–9.

18. Heiser, K. F., "Certification of psychologists in Connecticut." *Psychol. Bull.*, 1945, 9, 625–30.

19. Heiser, K. F., "The need for legislation and the complexities of the problem." *Amer. Psychologist*, 1950, 5, 104–8.

20. Heyns, R. W., "How many psychologists will be affected by legislation?" *Amer. Psychologist*, 1953, 8, 570–1.

21. Hubbard, R. W., "The nurse on the healing arts team." Address at annual meeting of the Pennsylvania State Nurses Association, Pennsylvania

League of Nursing Education, Pennsylvania Organization for Public Health Nursing, Pittsburgh, Pennsylvania, Nov. 9, 1948.

22. Jacobsen, C. F., "Clinical psychology as related to legislative problems." *Amer. Psychologist*, 1950, 5, 110–11.

23. Kelly, G. A., "Single level versus legislation for different levels of psychological training and experience." *Amer. Psychologist*, 1950, 5, 109–11.

24. Landsman, T., "Legislation in various states: Tennessee." *Amer. Psychologist*, 1953, 8, 580–2.

25. Macfarlane, J. W., "Interprofessional relations and collaboration with medicine and other related fields." *Amer. Psychologist*, 1950, 5, 112–14.

26. Menninger, W. C., "The relationship of clinical psychology and psychiatry." *Amer. Psychologist*, 1950, 51, 3–15.

27. Miles, W. R., "A year of state certification of psychologists." *Amer. Psychologist*, 1946, 1, 393–4.

28. Moore, B. V., and Bouthilet, L., "The VA program for counseling psychologists." *Amer. Psychologist*, 1952, 7, 684–5.

29. Paterson, D. G., "The geneses of modern guidance." *Educ. Rec.*, 1938, 19, 36–46.

30. Peatman, J. G., "The problem of protecting the public by appropriate legislation for the practice of psychology." *Amer. Psychologist*, 1950, 5, 105–06.

31. Raimy, V. C. (ed.), *Training in clinical psychology.* New York: Prentice-Hall, Inc., 1950.

32. Saffir, M. A., "Certification versus licensing legislation." *Amer. Psychologist*, 1950, 5, 105–06.

33. Sanford, F. H., "Across the secretary's desk: relations with psychiatry." *Amer. Psychologist*, 1953, 8, 169–73.

34. Sanford, F. H., "Across the secretary's desk: psychology, psychiatry, and legislation in New York." *Amer. Psychologist*, 1954, 9, 160–4.

35. Sanford, F. H., "Across the secretary's desk: relations with psychiatry." *Amer. Psychologist*, 1955, 10, 93–6.

36. Schmidl, F., "The dynamic use of the psychiatric social worker's services within the clinical team." *Amer. J. Orthopsychiat.*, 1950, 20, 765–75.

37. Shaffer, L. F., "Clinical psychology and psychiatry." *J. Consult. Psychol.*, 1947, 11, 5–11.

38. Shakow, D., "A dialogue, Part I." *Amer. J. Orthopsychiat.*, 1949, 19, 191–208.

39. Shakow, D., "A dialogue, Part II." *Amer. J. Orthopsychiat.*, 1949, 19, 381–96.

40. Shoben, E. J., "Psychologists and legality: a case report." *Amer. Psychologist*, 5, 1950, 496–8.

41. Super, D. E., *Appraising vocational fitness.* New York: Harper, 1949.

42. Tiffin, J., *Industrial Psychology* (3rd ed.). New York: Prentice-Hall, 1952.

43. Virginia Academy of Science, Psychology Section, The committee on training and standards, "The certification of clinical psychologists in Virginia." *Amer. Psychologist*, 1946, 1, 395–8.

44. Washington Legislative Committee, "Legislative activity in Washington." *Amer. Psychologist*, 1955, 10, 570–1.

45. Watson, R. I., *The clinical method in psychology*. New York: Harper, 1951, 779.

46. Watson, R. I., *Psychology as a profession*. New York: Doubleday, 1954.

47. Wendt, G. R., "Legislation for the general practice of psychology versus legislation for specialties within psychology." *Amer. Psychologist*, 1950, 5, 107–8.

48. Wiener, D. N., "The Minnesota law to certify psychologists." *Amer. Psychologist*, 1951, 6, 549–52.

49. Wiener, D. N., "Some legislative and legal problems of psychologists." *Amer. Psychologist*, 1953, 8, 564–9.

50. Wolfle, D., "Legal control of psychological practice." *Amer. Psychologist*, 1950, 5, 651–5.

51. Yale University Faculty Committee, "Preparation for the work of an educational psychologist." *Amer. Psychologist*, 1951, 65–7.

52. Young, F. M., "The licensing law in Georgia." *Amer. Psychologist*, 1952, 7, 477–8.

☼

CHAPTER

24

Research and Service

THE CONCEPT OF A PROFESSIONAL PSYCHOLOGIST IS CONSTANTLY changing. Within the brief history of clinical and counseling psychology we have seen the pendulum swing from one extreme to another and perhaps back again. The primary heritage of all psychology is experimentation. Psychology had its beginnings in the establishment of a laboratory. The first psychological clinic was established in 1896 as a part of the Laboratories of Psychology at the University of Pennsylvania. The definition of the function of this clinic included the application of laboratory methods to the problems of children. As time moved rapidly onward, the emphasis on the applied nature of clinical and counseling psychology became more pronounced. With World War I the emphasis upon development of tests and techniques became full blown, and through a tragically long period in our history most clinical and counseling psychologists concentrated on the development of new tests, new testing methods, and their application. While general and experimental psychologists continued to conduct basic research in an effort to discover regularity and predictability in the behavior of organisms, during this same period clinical and counseling psychologists devoted the larger portion of their time to applied and methodological research and to technical activities. Clinical and counseling psychologists earned for themselves the reputation of being "testers."

With World War II and events immediately following it the clinician enlarged his scope of application. He now began to be a "treater." He became interested in problems of therapy and began to occupy himself with "doing" therapy. During this phase a large proportion of his energy and time was also concentrated on receiving therapy. For a few years immediately preceding and around 1950 one had to be "analyzed" to attain status in clinical and counseling psychology. During this period of our short life, the role of the psychologist as a scientist was practically forgotten, certainly it was neglected, by clinical and counseling psychologists. The "tester" did a great deal of methodological research in the development and standardization of his tests. The "treater" did little research (there were laudable exceptions), simply accepting the teachings and precepts of other disciplines. For a time (and again with exceptions) he did little to develop his own techniques or to criticize the techniques he used. He was service-oriented—he was bent on "doing good" and "helping people." He concentrated on working in hospitals and clinics where he "tested" and "treated." Most of the time he even forgot he was a "tester" when he was a "treater." He quarreled with psychiatrists about his prerogative in using their techniques. He not only neglected his heritage as a scientist but seemed to forget that he was an academician, that he had grown up in an educational setting. He was concerned with nebulous concepts such as "personality reorganization," and he looked at his client (whom he usually called a patient) through the wrong end of the telescope excluding his social milieu.

Now we seem to be entering into a new era. We see the return of the scientist in the numerous attempts to study psychopathology and to discover uniformity in the development of behavior disorders. We see the emergence of psychological approaches to behavior change. We see the psychologist becoming interested in the total life of the client, including his occupational activities, and instead of treating the personality, he appears to be concentrating on working with the entire life situation. He does less treating and more teaching and co-ordinating. He works with other persons within the life situation of his client, as well as with his client, and attempts to get them all pulling together for his client's welfare. He finds satisfaction in group work, in administrative work, and sees himself quarreling less with other people who no longer see him as usurping their prerogatives.

Although he strives to make clinical methods and procedures as scientific as possible, the professional clinician must be more than a scientist. The scientist, at least the pure scientist, is interested in gaining knowledge. Sometimes this knowledge is seen as important only for its own sake. The scientist tends to be primarily concerned with the aims of his own science. Professional psychology goes beyond the aims of psychology and becomes concerned with the problems of a client or clients. Clients may be individuals, business firms, or institutions, but, in any case, the professional psychologist has responsibility for his client and thereby is called upon to help in achieving the aims of industry, mental hygiene, education, or possibly even government. As Walter V. Bingham (1) has pointed out in his address on psychology as a profession, the role of the psychologist as a scientist is primary. Perhaps we see here the evolution of a new kind of professional scientist. George A. Kelly (2, pp. 3–4) has expressed this as follows: "Science and society are on the march. Just as the concept of the witch doctor with supernatural authority had to give way to the concept of a professional man exercising authority by virtue of formalized training, so this latter concept must eventually yield to the concept of a professional man being first of all a scientist."

The central theme that appears to run through the wide variety of employment settings for the psychologist is the application of a scientific or research-oriented philosophy to the problems presented. Just as the psychologist must be more than a scientist, so must he be more than a practitioner. In effect, then, he is a practitioner-scientist but, as Bingham and Kelly have stressed, "first of all, a scientist." This emergence of the professional scientist is not limited to the field of psychology. It would appear to be the trend in other professions as well. The unique qualifications of the psychologist as a research worker should enable psychology to play a significant and indispensable role in the transition within the professions from practitioners to professional scientists. This transition, as Kelly has commented, will probably be resisted by many, both by those within the ranks of the professions who will insist that it is enough to learn the skills of the practitioner, and by those who have identified themselves as "scientists" and who will protest that research competence is a special gift that only a few dare claim. In spite of these objections Kelly urges that psychology emerge as a "new kind of profession . . . a genuinely scientific profession."

To be sure, our concepts of both research and clinical practice will have to be restructured within this new concept of the profession. However Kelly believes that it is time that this should be done anyway. A perusal of our journals, particularly the comment sections, suggests that both research and practice have been conceived too narrowly. On the research or scientific side the basic difficulty has been our failure to recognize that the most important and difficult stage of research is that which precedes and leads to the formulation of testable hypotheses. Research has too often been conceived as beginning with the testable hypotheses— a failure to recognize that in clinical and counseling psychology the best testable hypotheses arise out of the experiences of the sensitive, theoretically oriented clinician. At the other end of the scale is the "old-fashioned clinician, alert and responsive to the murmurings of nature but unmindful of the scientific implications of what he sees and hears." If the clinician can be taught to formulate his experience into tentative hypotheses and if the scientist can be given an appreciation of how new hypotheses come into being, we will strike a happy medium between these contrasts, and the new concept of the profession of psychology will continue to develop. This evolution most certainly seems to be in progress. If psychologists can accept this trend rather than fight it, we will develop as a scientific profession. We will be researchers as well as practitioners. It is predicted that the future will see a breaking down of the dichotomy between the scientific and the professional psychologist. A few years from now Watson (3) will have difficulty classifying psychologists into these two categories.

Now that we have started to make predictions, and since this last part of the book is concerned with the future of clinical and counseling psychology, let us take up the traditional functions of clinical psychology and make some predictions about each.

FUTURE DEVELOPMENTS IN THE AREA OF RESEARCH IN CLINICAL AND COUNSELING PSYCHOLOGY

The past few years have seen the embryonic development of the practitioner-scientist. The development will continue but not at the sacrifice of the service contributions of the clinician. The research-oriented clinician will make his contribution in several areas of research but the most significant of these will be in the area of psychopathology. That the psychologist must be the bellwether of research in this area would appear to be inevitable. Of all the specialty areas concerned with behavior disorders, psychology is best qualified to lead the research in this field. This is the unique contribution that psychology can make. There is no field in which research is more vitally needed than in psychopathology. To say that there is much more that we do not know than we do know about the causes and treatment of the behavior disorders is an understatement. As the psychological practitioner becomes curious, raises doubts, asks questions, formulates meaningful hypotheses, we will begin to scratch the surface in the development of scientific knowledge that may contribute to a better understanding of the behavior disorders. We will see less of research for research's sake, less looking for a problem to do (just any problem that will lead to publication), and we will see many more attempts to answer the questions that arise out of our experiences.

We will see an increase in the amount of empirical and inductive research. Research workers will come to the realization that in clinical and counseling psychology we do not have enough facts available upon which to build a completely adequate theory. The deductive research that will prove to be fruitful will be structured within the framework of existing psychological theory developed from our body of knowledge about the functioning of human animals in general. Learning theory, perception theory, and motivational theory will all be applied to psychopathology. We will realize that the results of much of the research on personality theory and on the etiology and dynamics of behavior disorders has been biased by the theoretical framework of the research worker, and we will repeat much of this research attempting to rule out this bias. The reader should not jump to the conclusion that we are predicting a trend away from theory or that the present discussion is antitheoretical. The value of theory is not denied. The importance of theory construction as an aspect of the scientific method has been well demonstrated in the history of science. We are simply predicting that the theories which will prove most useful in research are those which are buttressed by a fund of knowledge in general psychology. Until we can accumulate many more facts about the behavior of the atypical, these are the only theories that appear useful. In the past many workers in the field of psychopathology have been so shackled by their own biases that they were unable to entertain any ideas contradictory or inconsistent with them. If a person disagreed with a "believer," his arguments would be dismissed with "You just don't understand." We will also be told less frequently that we do not understand simply because we have not had the proper training or experiences. The belief that one must commune with some authority or disciple of that authority in order to understand human behavior will be finally and completely rejected by the research-oriented psychologist. In the past we have misused theory in designing experiments and have misinterpreted experimental results because of theoretical biases. These same theories have been adhered to in the absence of experimental verification, and at times even in the face of contradictory data.

We will realize that much of the theory of psychopathology on which we have been operating and which we have been accepting as fact is based on pretty shaky logical grounds, and on a vacuum insofar as experimentation is concerned. We will begin to concentrate on behavior both in our clinical research and in our clinical work. We will cease searching out inferences concerning some abstraction and then using that abstraction as a measure of the behavior of the individual. This will affect many aspects of the clinician's functioning. Not only will it change his approach to research but it will definitely change the character of many Rorschach (and other test) reports. We will see more basic observation of the behavior of subjects who present behavior disorders. We will study their social interaction, their perceptions, their problem-solving ability, their learning performances, their thinking, their motivation, and even their sensing. These are all basic aspects of behavior about which psychology has some data and some knowledge. This should help us to understand the behavior disorders. One of the most dangerous and unscientific aspects of the research that has appeared in psychological and psychiatric journals is the lack of control and/or comparison groups. One clinician in working with one, seven, or even fifty patients notes a characteristic theme that seems to run through all the subjects presenting similar behavior or bearing the same diagnosis. He writes an article, presents a paper, or authors a book describing his "findings." He develops a tentative theory about the etiology of paranoid reactions or the psychodynamics of essential hypertension, or even suggests the possibility of a universal growth process. Let us further assume that our clinician has a degree of prestige among his colleagues. Others read his words or listen to his lectures and are impressed. His audience or students then go back to their practices. They see a similar patient or client. They see the same phenomena. They then exclaim with reverence about the greatness of the teacher. His hypotheses have been proved! When their next client with this particular behavior disorder appears, they *know* what to look for; furthermore, they know what to do about it. They may even proceed to "do it" without actually observing the phenomenon they are treating. No one has bothered to question whether the phenomenon is characteristic of all patients who present the behavior disorder under consideration. No one stops to consider that selective factors which are characteristic of the authority's own clientele may be operating. No one questions the problem of selective perception. Even more basic, no one questions whether the observed phenomenon is a unique characteristic of the behavior reactions being studied or whether it is possibly characteristic of all human beings. Too often those who pose such questions are scorned for questioning the judgments of the "master" or are politely ignored for their naïveté.

The use of control groups is difficult, and consequently too much emphasis has been placed on the "findings" of studies using comparison groups from populations that differ radically from those of the experimental groups. For example, groups of hospital patients have been compared with groups of students from a college psychology class without consideration of differences in age, education, or socioeconomic background. In the future, studies will be designed utilizing adequate comparison and control groups. We will discover that certain factors may be uniquely related to specific syndromes of behavior. We will see less credence placed on research that is merely anecdotal and biographical. Observations that are published will be those which have been verified by controlled observation and experimentation. The principles of behavior which we observe will be tested by research, not therapeutic experience, and will be integrated and co-ordinated with knowledge from the social sciences, learning theory, and field theory.

The statistical treatment of our data will be much improved. We will see fewer studies utilizing product-moment correlation coefficients and other statistics that assume rectilinearity. Such an assumption in most of our clinical studies seems to be hazardous procedure. The very complexity of the behavior that we study should tend to dissuade the investigator from any preconceived assumption as to the nature of the distribution. The clinician who decides beforehand that a straight line will provide the best fitting curve and uses samples of less than fifty cases, where correlation coefficients are subject to some bias, must recognize the limiting aspects of his procedure. Research studies in the future will solve the problems of experimental control statistically. They will design studies so that factors can be allowed to vary and still be observed. Thus the research workers will recognize and study the interaction between experimental variables. We will see the use of larger numbers of subjects, ingeniously designed successive-sample studies, observations validated by the use of hold-out groups and cross-validation studies, and factor-analysis techniques extended, and we will undoubtedly see many innovations in experimental designs and statistical manipulations. The psychologist will play an even larger role than he is playing at the present as a consultant in research to other disciples. Carefully designed studies will test the effectiveness of physiological, surgical, and pharmaceutical forms of treatment.

These are just a few of the anticipated developments in the research field, and we have, of course, merely touched upon the scope of the research functions of clinical and counseling psychology. Entire textbooks could be written describing procedures, needed areas of research, reviewing examples of "good" and "poor" research, and stressing the importance of such effort. We have mentioned only a few sample areas and have taken the liberty of expressing a few opinions. Nevertheless, it is anticipated that the psychologists of the future will not persist in the desire to treat something they do not understand. By devoting just a portion of the time now spent in preoccupation with diagnosis and therapy to the design of scientific research, the psychologist of the future will truly enhance his prestige as a professional worker.

FUTURE TRENDS IN CLINICAL EVALUATION

Many of the future developments are already taking form. Basically, psychologists will be called upon to describe the behavior of total persons and to make predictions about the behavior of individuals. We will see less and less giving of tests without a specific purpose. Standardized batteries of tests will seldom be used and personality descriptions will rarely be written. The psychologist will choose evaluative materials with a view to answering specific questions involved in planning enablement and rehabilitation programs for his client. Evaluation reports will describe functioning persons and will be organized around possible or potential plans for the individual. These plans will involve practical and specific real-life activities designed to give learning experiences which can be generalized to other experiences, and which will contribute to the changing of attitudes and behavioral patterns so that the client can make a more efficient adjustment to his environment.

It is predicted that we will see a return to the use of historical and interview data, and that this data will be supplemented by situational observations. We expect that the fad of emphasis on projective testing will gradually pass and that projective tests will be partially replaced by situational tests and time-sample observations in model or real-life situations. Tests of general intelligence will be replaced almost entirely by special skill, aptitude, and achievement tests. Structured personality tests will give way to self-rating scales in which the individual attempts to evaluate his past, present, and anticipated behavior, as well as the attitudes that others have toward him. Role playing and participation in various activities on a trial or experimental basis will be utilized for evaluative purposes.

Thus the clinician will attempt to reduce the number of inferences which he is now forced to make about present and potential behavior and will strive for more and more face validity until he approaches the ultimate of prima facie validity. In this way he will become more and more accurate in his predictions. Moreover, he will take more and more time in the process of evaluation; this, however, will not disturb the clinician of the future since evaluation will be an integral part of the enablement and rehabilitation process.

THE FUTURE OF COUNSELING AND THERAPY

We predict that the future will see a de-emphasis on therapy in the classical or traditional usage of the term. This is not to say that no personal therapy will be conducted. There will certainly always be a need for counseling. What we do want to say is that the treatment process will be extended beyond the treatment of personality to the treatment of behavior. The change in emphasis will not appear to be drastic since the new approach will depend substantially upon interviews held with individual clients. Informal conversations and interviews will be held, but the clients will be viewed more as persons and not as "patients" or "cases." The purpose of the interviews will not be treating, reorganizing, or restructuring the personality, but rather planning for environmental alterations or experiments in real-life situations. There will be discussion of past, present, and anticipated behavior in order to understand the past and present, and to attempt to predict the future. There will be friendly supportive relationships with a counselor, and at times there will be opportunities for the release of feeling and the expression of anxieties and fears. The interview will be a miniature social situation in which ideas and ways of reacting or behaving will be tried out with the counselor. Most important of all, however, these will be consulting and planning interviews, in which the client is encouraged and aided in his attempts to experiment with his feelings and with his environment. Successes and failures in this experimentation will be analyzed, and new plans and programs worked out.

Perhaps the psychologist of the future will spend more time working with small groups of people than with individuals. These groups will serve much the same function as that served by the individual sessions described above, except that in the groups several persons will be participating in plans and discussions. Various points of view will be available, with the group itself serving as an additional supporting factor. The group, being made up of a number of persons, will provide more varied social experiences than are provided in individual sessions, and more complicated experimental behavioral situations can be arranged. A considerable amount of role-playing will be conducted in these groups, and the groups will take an increasing amount of responsibility for their own activities both collectively and individually. Most frequently we will see combinations of group and individual counseling, with the group members consulting with the psychologist individually, as occasions arise. However in both group and individual work the effort will constantly be to figure out what is best for the client in connection with a wide variety of problems ranging from sex to work and from reality testing to education.

When dealing with children, the amount of time the clinician spends in direct contact with the client will vary in proportion to the maladjustment and age of the client. Actually, it is our anticipation that the school clinical or child clinical specialist of the future will be occupied relatively little with direct formal treatment of children. Although he may spend time with individual children for evaluation, the larger part of evaluation will be based upon direct observation of children in the classroom, playground, or other situations. Once his preliminary evaluation observations are completed, his efforts will be directed primarily toward planning, with the parents, teachers, and other personnel, programs that will provide for the remedial educational and emotional experiences that he deems to be necessary. The evaluation procedure will continue throughout the remedial program, with the clinician remaining in a consultive relationship with the persons who are working with the child in a normal home or school situation. It is predicted that the utilization of the total environment for treatment purposes will prove to be far more effective than special individual or group therapeutic counseling. The latter may go on too but only for extreme problems, and it will be regarded as auxiliary treatment rather than primary treatment. Further, we see the psychologist evolving from a school consultant into a community consultant, serving as co-ordinator for the re-education and rehabilitation of individuals of all ages presenting a variety of problems. In the future we see more emphasis upon hygiene and prevention as a part of this consultive role. Communities will utilize clinical and counseling advice in planning recreational programs for persons of all ages, group discussion techniques to solve all sorts of community problems, adult education programs, and programs for the ill, the handicapped, and the aged.

In the hospital situation the psychologist is becoming and will become the co-ordinator for total treatment programs. Here, too, it is believed that individual therapy will be supplemented by hospital treatment and group work programs. Evaluations will be used to plan individual treatment objectives, and these will be implemented by all personnel who come into contact with the patient. Programs now regarded as supplementary treatment programs such as occupational therapy, physical therapy, educational therapy, manual arts therapy, corrective therapy, and special services will carry the burden of treatment, with their efforts integrated by the clinical and counseling psychologists. Nurses, attendants, and all other personnel will be mobilized in order to provide a therapeutic environment. Efforts will be made to prepare the patient as soon as possible for trial visits and discharge, with the community resources called into play to continue his rehabilitation. This phase, too, will be under the supervision of psychology.

The psychologist will continue and expand his role in hospitals other than the neuropsychiatric hospitals. He will work in close relationship with the appropriate medical specialists in tuberculosis hospitals, in orthopedic hospitals, and in all general medicine and surgery hospitals. He will be called upon to predict individual reactions to surgery or to debilitating illness and will assist in working out rehabilitative programs with patients presenting all kinds of illnesses. We already know of the employment of psychologists in obstetric and gynecology departments and in ophthalmology departments, as well as in neurology, pediatric, and orthopedic departments. The psychologist's role in such services is not that of a therapist but rather a consultant.

Psychologists will be found more and more in administrative positions in a multitude of settings in education, medicine, and industry. One development to be expected soon is that of the psychologist administering ward activities in many of the neuropsychiatric hospitals. The present patients in these hospitals are likely to be reclassified, and many of them will be regarded as people and not patients. Those requiring intensive medical, surgical, or pharmaceutical treatment will continue to be treated as patients in the usual sense, but the rest will be placed under the administrative jurisdiction of psychologists who, in reality, will be concerned with the development of educational and rehabilitation programs for them. Perhaps in other instances the psychologist may simply be concerned with providing a happy and even minimumly constructive environment for the person who has no prospect of discharge. Psychologists may even assume administrative functions, such as those of the manager or superintendent of many hospitals. We see the development of rehabilitation centers that will frankly not even pretend to be hospitals but rather intermediate and perhaps transient stations between the hospital and the community. The psychologist will be admirably qualified for the administrative supervision of these centers. Psychologists will be assigned administrative functions in domiciliaries and homes for the aged.

From our point of view, the most constructive trend anticipated for the future is the extension of the psychologist's role as a teacher. Not merely as a teacher in the college or university but as a teacher in other settings. In the elementary and secondary school he will offer in-service training to other educational personnel. The classroom teachers, remedial teachers, subject-matter teachers, and athletic coaches will carry the load of the treatment and training of emotionally disturbed and handicapped children. They are going to need preparation for this new facet of their job. In the schools more mental hygiene and social development courses will be taught. Psychologists will be called upon to teach these courses or prepare others to do so. This teaching function will extend to the community and into the hospitals. In-service training programs will be organized to prepare nurses, welfare workers, and probationary workers for their added responsibilities in group work with their patients and clients. Generally, the psychologist will devote more and more of his efforts to preparing persons in many walks of life to serve as counselors.

Finally, we see psychologists carrying the same evaluation-plus-consultation role into the correctional systems, into industry, and even into government. Thus, the traditional counseling and therapy role will gradually shift as the emphasis is placed on the total functioning of persons within their particular social and physical environments.

SUMMARY

Even though the content of this, our final chapter may read more as psychological fiction than fact, we firmly believe that many of the predictions will come true. We have not been discussing realities in every instance; however the reader is urged not to regard the predictions in this chapter as fantasy. We sincerely believe that the "handwriting is on the wall." To repeat a partially borrowed phrase, "Science and psychology are on the march." Psychology has left the confines of the ivy-covered walls of its ivory towers and is rapidly taking its place in society. If it does not take its place in the way described in this text, it will take it in some other equally or more constructive way. With the broadening of scope in psychological application, more and more psychologists will be needed—psychologists who will be trained to function as professional scientists; psychologists who will patiently and painstakingly further our present stockpile of basic knowledge regarding human behavior; psychologists who can forget their own status needs in a joint effort (with members of their own and other professions) to satisfy the needs of their clients; psychologists who can approach each task with humility, fully cognizant that they do not and can never know all the answers. When our profession can offer such representatives to society, then, indeed, will psychology be ready to serve.

BIBLIOGRAPHY

1. Bingham, W. A., "Psychology as a science, as a technology and as a profession." *Amer. Psychologist*, 1953, 8, 115–18.
2. Kelly, G. A., "A student's outline of graduate training in clinical psychology at Ohio State University." Columbus: The Ohio State Univ., Mimeographed, 1950.
3. Watson, R. I., *Psychology as a profession.* New York: Doubleday, 1954.

Glossary

ability. Power to make certain responses or to perform certain motor and intellectual acts.

abormal. Usually that which is widely divergent from the average or central tendency. In psychopathology, abnormal behavior is behavior that is ineffective or unsatisfactory.

abreaction. Discharging pent-up emotion by the reliving of emotional experiences.

abstract. That which cannot be directly perceived through the senses.

acceptance. A positive attitude toward some concept, idea, object, or person. Carl Rogers uses the term to describe the attitude a counselor should have toward a client.

acculturation. The process of acquiring a culture by learning or diffusion.

achievement. Proficiency in behavior, especially to the extent that the proficiency has resulted from learning experiences.

acting out. Translation of feelings, emotions, or attitudes into overt physical activity.

active therapy. Term used by Fisher to describe deliberate interference by the therapist with the client's activities outside the consultation.

activity-group procedures. As developed by Slavson, these procedures involve a maximally permissive situation in which the group members work together in various activities.

adaptive behavior. As used by Ruesch, refers to a change in social techniques. More generally, it refers to the ability to adjust to novel situations.

adaptive interaction. Term used by Shaw to describe learning to interact in social positions efficiently and in ways that are uniquely suited to an individual's own resources.

adjustment. Solving, harmonizing, and arranging the conflicts and problems that must be met in everyday life in order to maintain mental health. "Good" adjustment results in efficient and satisfying resolution of conflicts.

advice. The giving of suggestions or directions for the solution of problems.

affect. Generalized feeling tone, usually distinguished from emotion in that it is more pervasive and persistent and is not directly reflected in physiological reactions.

affect therapy. Treatment aimed at feelings, with little use of thought processes.

aggression. Behavior characterized by attacking or pushing forward rather than by avoiding difficulties.

agnosia. An aphasic disorder characterized mainly by inability to recognize objects or symbols.

agnosticism. The doctrine that nothing is understandable or explainable except experience. All knowledge is relative and uncertain. Commonly used as the denial of the existence of any supernatural power.

Alcoholics Anonymous. A nonprofessional organization established for the purpose of treating alcohol addicts by personal, religious, and social influences. Branches in many, if not all, large communities.

alexia. Impairment of understanding of written speech. Sometimes referred to as "word-blindness."

ambitions. The expectations and hopes that a person has for himself or others.

ambivalence. Simultaneous incompatible attitudes, such as love and hate for the same person.

amelioration. The act of making better or improving. In counseling, it refers to the reduction of symptoms.

American Psychological Association. The major professional organization for psychologists in the United States.

amnesia. Loss of memory or recall.

amplification. Jung's term for the enrichment of material from the collective unconscious by studying analogous ideas from folklore and mythology.

anal. In psychoanalytic terminology, a stage in psychosexual development when erotic interests and satisfactions are centered about the anus.

anal erotism. Refers to fixation of the libido at anal phases of development.

analysis. Separation into constituent parts or elements. The term is commonly used to describe the process of undergoing psychoanalysis.

analyst. One who analyzes. Commonly, the practitioner of psychoanalysis.

analytic psychology. The theoretical system of Jung.

anamnesis. The client's case history.

anamnestic analysis. The preliminary stages of therapy in the Jungian approach.

anecdotal. The method of study which is based on the recounting of stories or clinical anecdotes.

anima. Term used by Jung to describe the inner aspects of personality which are turned toward the unconscious.

anomaly. Any factor that is outside the normal range of probability.

anomie. Term used by Merton and others to describe a condition of normlessness in society. A culture such as the term describes has little to give but ambiguity, and is characterized by the absence of a strong, comprehensive, and insistent philosophy that would give the individual values by which to live.

anthropology. The science that investigates the human species.

anxiety. A state of tension arising during conflict or frustration situations. It is related to emotional excitement, but is usually more chronic and often related to symbolic rather than to real danger.

anxiety neurosis. A form of neurotic behavior characterized by continuous diffuse anxiety usually accompanied by the physiological concomitants of emotion.

apathy. Absence of feeling or emotion in situations that usually call up such reactions.

aphasia. Disorder of symbolic formulation and expression resulting in impairment of communicative functions with no difficulty in sensory or motor aspects of communication.

apperception. The attachment of meaning to a situation in terms of past experience.

apprehension. Anticipatory dread or fear of what is to come.

a priori validation. Items in a test are presumed to measure certain traits because they have been judged as valid by persons who are regarded as experts.

aptitude. Special ability or capacity to profit from a specific kind of training.

archetypes. Jung's concept of primordial trends of thought or emotion represented in the unconscious by object-images or memories that are inherited residues of the evolution of the human species.

Aristotelian. Pertaining to the philosophy of Aristotle. Most pertinent is the concept that the characteristics of any behavior are determined by the nature of the object or organism which produced the behavior. Contrasted with searching for explanation in the dynamic characteristics of the total field.

art. Practical application of knowledge, natural ability, skill, dexterity, facility, or power.

Arthur Point Scale of Performance Tests. A scale of performance of non-language tests. Two forms are available.

articulatory disorders. Speech disorders characterized by the omission, substitution, addition, or distortion of sounds.

assessment. The process of taking evaluative data and after careful analysis making predictions of behavior. Commonly used interchangeably with the term "evaluation" but may be regarded as the use of the results of evaluation for specific predictive purposes.

association. The establishment of relations between and among psychological events as a result of experience.

atheism. Denial of the existence of a God.

athetosis. Tentaclelike movements of the hands and feet associated with certain forms of brain damage.

attention. The process of focusing on certain aspects of experience so that these aspects are vivid.

attention span. The range of items which a person can comprehend and the length of time this attention can be maintained.

attitudes. Predispositions to react in a particular way.

authoritarian figure. A person or the concept of a person who is expected to exercise control and direction by virtue of his position.

autism. Fantasy formation, particularly involving self-preoccupation.

autonomic nervous system. The portion of the nervous system which regulates the glands, heart, and internal organs.

autonomous man. Fromm's concept of a spontaneous and responsible person who is flexible and tolerant of ambiguity.

avocational. Pertaining to activities that are not ordinarily related to a vocation but to the use of leisure time.

awareness. The state of knowing.

behavior. In general, the reactions of an organism. Overt behavior is directly observable. Covert behavior is that which can only be inferred. Extrinsic behavior is overt and measurable, and involves motor responses. Intrinsic behavior consists of attitudes, ideas, and feelings that are a part of the private world of the individual.

behavior disorders. Inefficient and unsatisfactory patterns of behavior. Behavior disorders are frequently referred to as psychopathological reactions.

barrier. Term used by Lewin to indicate forces or areas in the dynamic field which frustrate the person in his efforts to reach a goal area or satisfy a need.

Bell Adjustment Inventory. A structured personality test.

Bender Gestalt. A test requiring the subject to copy a number of figures. Reveals visual-motor co-ordination and visual perception.

Bernreuter Personality Inventory. A structured personality test.

bias. An attitude for or against a given proposition which prevents one from observing or judging objectively.

biographical. Refers to the life history or biography.

biological memories. According to Adler, these are memories derived from the personal experiences of the individual which are contained in the unconscious.

birth trauma. Term used by Rank to describe the experience of painful separation of the infant from intra-uterine bliss. This trauma was believed to produce immediate anxiety, and the search for substitutes for the uterine state in order to relieve the anxiety was thought to be the core of neurosis.

bizarre. Odd, extravagant, or eccentric. Involves striking incongruity with surrounding conditions of precipitating events.

Blacky Test. A picture test utilizing a family of dogs, with the central character a young dog named Blacky. Designed to investigate the psychoanalytic concept of psychosexual development.

blocking. Functional inhibition of recall, communication, or ideation.

brain damage. A general term that is applied to describe damage to the brain or brain stem which results in specific handicaps, including a variety of conditions that may be due to birth injury, either mechanical or caused by anoxia, and a wide range of postnatal trauma.

breech presentation. In general, any delivery in which the child is born feet or buttocks first.

California First Year Mental Scale. A scale designed for infants of from 1 to 18 months of age.

California Mental Health Analysis. A structured personality test.

capacity. Term used by Richards to describe the potential ability of an individual. It is a rough equivalent of intelligence.

Carl Hollow Square Scale. A test that uses a wooden panel with a square hole and a number of blocks having straight and beveled edges. The tasks involve filling the hole with different sets of blocks.

case history. Information gathered about a client, including family, developmental, sociological, educational, and vocational data. A slightly more specific term than "case study."

case study. All information gathered about a client. In addition to historical data, it includes test data, interview data, and the results of other examinations and observations.

case-study method. The method that utilizes the case study to gather necessary information. In research it may be contrasted with the experimental method, the statistical method, and other research methods.

castration. The removal of sex glands from either sex.

castration anxiety. The term has special meaning in psychoanalytic thinking, referring to what is conceived to be a reaction to intimidation regarding loss of genital organs or their function.

catatonic reactions. Extreme inactivity reactions in which the person does not take any responsibility for his own actions. He may refuse to react to stimuli or he may be extremely compliant but in either instance he does little on his own initiative.

catharsis. The release of unpleasant emotions through talking or some other form of behavior.

cathexis. Attachment of special significance or value to objects or ideas.

Cattell Developmental and Intelligence Scale. A downward-in-age extension of the Stanford-Binet that uses items from the Gesell Schedule.

cerebral cortex. The outer portion of the cerebrum or neopallium.

cerebrum. The main division of the vertebrate brain. Made up of three portions: (1) the olfactory brain or rhinencephalon, (2) the corpus striatum, and (3) the cerebral cortex or neopallium.

certification. A form of control of the activities of professional persons. It may be voluntary or mandatory. Voluntary certification is usually accomplished by professional organizations that issue certificates to persons they deem qualified to practice. Mandatory control is accomplished by legislation and requires that the practitioner have a certificate issued by some legally constituted board or agency. Certification differs from licensure in that the latter provides penalties for malpractice within the conditions of the law.

character. The moral nature of an individual. The more enduring traits of personality which have ethical and social significance.

character neurosis. Used by Horney to describe alterations in character structure which begin in early childhood and which take precedence over the external life situation.

child guidance clinic. Term generally used to describe the clinic that offers its services primarily to children and their parents. Such clinics exist both in medical and school settings.

Children's Apperception Test. A picture-story, partially structured, personality test designed specifically for children.

chorea. Spasmodic muscular twitchings that are involuntary, irregular, and jerky.

chronic. A persistent, continuing condition that is not directly amenable to treatment. Contrasted with "acute."

chronological age (C.A.). Actual time since birth. Obtained by subtracting the birthdate from the present date.

class theories. Theories which assume that events can be assigned to classes or categories and then explained in terms of the characteristics of the categories to which they are assigned.

claustrophobia. Morbid fear of closed places.

client. Term used to designate the person who applies to a clinician for service.

client-centered counseling. Refers to the therapeutic approach developed and described by Rogers which postulates that counseling or therapy should be regulated and guided by the client. It is assumed that the client has an inherent capacity for growth which will unfold if the counselor provides an accepting atmosphere. The term is currently used in lieu of the term "nondirective."

clinical psychology. The field of psychology which applies the methods of general psychology to the study of the individual case. In general the work of the clinical psychologist may be differentiated from that of the counseling psychologist in that the former is usually concerned with the more maladjusted extreme of the continuum of efficient and happy adjustment. The clinician is more often found in the hospital and clinic; the counselor, in the school, in industry, and in the guidance center.

coercion. The use of extreme authority to order or require that a client be have in a specific fashion.

cognition. The process of thinking, ideation, or knowing.

cognitive learning theories. These theories emphasize subjectively held hypotheses or expectations as the centrally held concept. Behavior is the function of the subject's expectations, and the role of reinforcement is to change these expectations. The first person to clearly formulate this concept was Tolman.

cognitive maps. A construct offered by Tolman to denote the subject's pattern of expectations and "sign gestalts" which comprise his knowledge of the goal, its position, and the "path" to it.

collective unconscious. Jung's concept that in an individual's unconscious are the archaic memories of all mankind.

color shock. A pattern of response on the Rorschach Test believed to be indicative of neurotic tendencies.

coma. Deep, unresponsive stupor.

communication. In general, the process of interchange of ideas and information. More specifically, the term is used to describe the extent to which a client can express himself to others.

comparative psychology. The branch of psychology which studies the relationships among different species with regard to their behavior.

compensation. A mechanism of adjustment whereby the individual attempts to make up for real or imagined feelings of inadequacy.

complex. A group of related ideas, attitudes, or affects.

compulsion. An act carried out in accordance with a persistent idea that anxiety will be avoided if the impulse to act is followed. An almost uncontrollable tendency to react in a particular manner.

concept. A mental process that refers to more than one object or experience, or to one object in relation to others. Concepts are the result of abstraction.

conceptual quotient. An index of intellectual deficit. Assuming that vocabulary holds fairly constant but that conceptual ability declines, the ratio or quotient between tests of these performances is presumed to be a measure of deficit.

concrete. Referring to real organisms, things, or phenomena—any objects that can be specifically denoted. Contrasted with "abstract" which refers to qualities for which specific referents are not available.

conditioning. The process of establishing conditioned responses. Such responses are acquired responses that were originally initiated by a certain stimulus but are now initiated by a second stimulus that had occurred earlier in connection with the first stimulus.

confabulation. The filling in of gaps in memory with fantastic, inconsistent, bizarre, or unusual accounts.

confidant. A person in whom another person confides.

conflict. The situation that exists when a motive is thwarted or when two or more opposing motives are in equilibrium.

congenital. Existing at birth, due to hereditary factors or environmental circumstances during embryonic life.

conscious. The state of being aware. In psychoanalytic theory, those elements of experience which have not been repressed.

constancy of the I.Q. The belief that a person's intelligence quotient remains stable throughout life. Supporters of the belief state or infer that the I.Q. is a measure of native capacity.

construct. The empirical equivalent of a concept.

control. The extent to which motives and capacity can be directed and utilized in an efficient manner.

control groups. In research, in order to know the meaning of events occurring in an experimental group, it is frequently desirable to have a comparison group from the same population which is not subjected to experimental manipulation.

controlled association. The procedure by which the subject is required to associate in a particular manner. Opposed to "free association."

controlled observation. Observation conducted under conditions that are designed to create objectivity and to reduce bias.

conversion. Unconscious adoption of physical symptoms to ease tension in conflict situations.

convulsion. Intense, involuntary muscular spasms usually involving large segments or all of the body.

Cornell-Coxe Performance Ability Scale. A scale of performance tests.

corrective emotional experience. Term used by Alexander and French as equivalent to abreaction or the working through of emotional experiences so that the traumatic effects of earlier experiences can be undone.

cortical. Referring to the function of the cerebral cortex.

counseling. Generally, the term refers to the process involved when persons talk with one another in order to resolve problems. Historically in psychology, it has been used in connection with vocational counseling. Recently it has come to be used in a wider sense that includes the concept of therapy and refers to much of the psychologist's service activities.

counseling psychology. The application of psychology which applies the methods of general psychology to the study of individuals. The field of counseling psychology overlaps extensively with that of clinical psychology. The counseling psychologist has traditionally been more concerned with vocational and educational psychological counseling than with therapeutic counseling. Recently the distinction has become less apparent; however counseling psychologists are more often employed in schools, industries, and various community activities, and clinical psychologists, in clinics and hospitals.

countertransference. The development of certain emotional attitudes toward the client by the clinician. Contrasted with "transference," which describes the client's emotional reactions directed toward the clinician.

cretinism. Congenital thyroid deficiency resulting in bodily deformities and usually in impaired intellectual functioning.

cross-validation. The technique by which validity is checked by gathering data from different sources.

cues. From the Hullian point of view, cues are associated with certain stimuli that are not themselves strong enough to act as drives. However, when these cues are associated with situations in which responses are rewarded, the connections between the cues and the reinforced responses are strengthened and cues can impel responses.

culture. The sum total of the attitudes, ideas, and behavior shared by members of a society, together with the results of such behavior.

cure. Removal of the symptoms of a disease and prevention of their recurrence. The term is used primarily in medicine and has little meaning for psychology.

cycloid. Characterized by alternation of moods.

cynicism. The doctrine that human conduct is motivated entirely by self-interest.

deduction. Inference or reasoning from premises or propositions to more concrete and specific conclusions.

deep therapy. The exploration and clarification of early memories and experiences. Sometimes used in the sense of dealing with basic, early, or childhood "levels" of the personality. The term "deep" connotes time more than anything else. Deep therapy goes back to childhood experiences, as contrasted with superficial therapy, which deals with the relative present.

defense. Unconscious protection against threatening ideas or affect.

definition of the problem. The first step in any scientific procedure. In counseling it is also important to attempt to define the problems with which we deal. Frequently, when a problem is once defined, the person can solve it with little help.

delirium. A clouding of consciousness with dreamlike, incoherent ideas.

delusion. Morbid false belief.

dependency reactions. The tendency to lean on other persons and to depend on others for help in initiating activity or in making decisions.

depression. Retardation of activity. Emotional depression involving despondency and hopelessness.

depressive reactions. The tendency to be retarded in activity, flat in affect, and generally nonreactive.

depth psychology. Term used by classical psychoanalysts, especially Freudian, to distinguish psychoanalysis from therapies that deal with superficial aspects of behavior.

deterioration. Degeneration or decline of intellectual capacities. Usually associated with cerebral disease or injury, or old age.

development. Changes in an organism which occur in its transition from origin to maturity.

developmental history. Contains data concerning the physical, mental, social and emotional development of a client together with an account of factors that may have facilitated or interfered with normal development.

developmental reading. Procedures designed to develop or improve a person's reading skills. It is assumed that the person has no special disability but has not learned efficient habits.

diagnosis. Determination of the nature, origin, precipitation, and maintenance of ineffective or "abnormal" modes of behavior.

dialectical process. A dialogue between two persons. As applied to counseling, it refers to a procedure in which the counselor participates to the same degree as the client.

Dictionary of Occupational Titles. Prepared by the United States Employment Service, it consists of definitions, classifications, and descriptions of fields of work.

Digit Symbol Test. A task appearing in several intelligence scales. Requires the subject to associate symbols with digits.

Diplomate. A board member in a particular specialty. The American Board of Examiners in Professional Psychology issues a diploma to persons who have a certain amount of experience and who can pass an examination.

dissociation. Inadequate integration of consciousness so that some ideas are inconsistent.

distraction. Anything that diverts attention or makes it difficult for attention to be maintained.

directive. As applied to counseling, it refers to the use of such procedures as advice, suggestion, reassurance, and coercion and similar active and direct techniques.

diversional therapy. Consists of suggestion or assistance given to the client for the beneficial use of activities. The aim is to focus the client's attention on specific activities so that he will be less preoccupied with problems.

Doctor of Philosophy Degree. A graduate degree requiring at least three years of graduate study and the preparation of a thesis or dissertation that must be an original research investigation. In clinical and counseling psychology a fourth year of supervised experience or internship is required.

dominance. The tendency of an individual to lead or take precedence over others in social situations. Neurologically, it refers to the concept that certain levels of the nervous system have control over other levels.

drive reduction. A concept developed primarily by Hullian learning theorists to describe the reduction in the intensity of basic drives. Such reduction is conceived of as reinforcing insofar as the activity resulting from the reduction is concerned.

drives. Basic motives of the individual. Usually conceived of as tissue needs. Sometimes a differentiation is made between primary drives (physiological states) and secondary or derived drives, which are ordinarily social in nature and are learned.

dynamics. The study of determinative space-time relationships.

eclecticism. The selection of features from a number of theories and the organization of these features into a comprehensive system.

ecology. Study of the manner in which organisms distribute geographically with reference to disease, species, and other factors.

ecstasy. Excessive and overwhelming feeling of rapture or joy.

educational history. An individual's complete record of educational progress, including direct school performance and activities in the school situation.

ego. Self, conscious experience, or awareness.

Einstellung. Luchins' term for mental set, or the adherence to a habit to the extent that it results in rigid behavior.

emotion. A mental state characterized by strong feeling and accompanied by autonomic activity.

emotional disturbances. Generally, the term refers to functional behavior disorders as contrasted with organic disorders. Specifically, it is the failure of control of emotional reactions.

emotional release. The process of ventilating, undamming, or relieving emotional tension.

empathic identification. The process by which the client-centered counselor assumes the client's internal frame of reference, and experiences with the client so that the growth process can be facilitated. In this way the clinician can clarify and reflect the client's feelings and attitudes.

empathy. The recognition of the nature and significance of another person's behavior at an objective level.

empirical validation. Tests are validated by checking the items, scales, or test as a whole against some external criterion. Applies to any situation in which theories, ideas, or hypotheses are tested against objective reality.

enablement. Used to describe the habilitation process in which an individual is aided in developing certain functional capacities that will enable him to find a place in society.

environmental factors. Forces or tendencies in the environment outside the individual which may influence his behavior.

environmental field. The sum total of factors or forces in the environment among which the individual functions.

environmental manipulation. Refers to definite changes brought about in the client's environment and usually involves complete removal to a new environment.

environmental modification. Stresses changes in some aspects of the client's life setting as it exists in the present. It may involve changing the attitudes of those surrounding him or changing the expectations others have for him.

environmental treatment. Any process designed to help an individual or a group of individuals to make desirable behavioral adjustments by inducing changes in the social or physical environment.

epilepsy. A group of reactions characterized by convulsive states.

erotic. Having sexual meaning.

essence. Ultimate or intrinsic nature.

ethics. Moral principles. Among professional workers the term refers to principles of practice.

etiology. The study of the causes or significant antecedents of given events or phenomena.

euphoria. Unwarranted feelings of comfort, well-being, or optimism.

evaluation. The process of individual study which combines case history, interview, test observations, and situational performances in order to assess the resources, motivation, and control of the client. The term "evaluation" is used almost interchangeably with "assessment" although assessment is sometimes regarded as a higher-order process.

exhortation. Language intended to incite and encourage.

experimental controls. Research procedures designed to keep constant all variables except the one being investigated. Thus any effects are presumed to be due to the variable not held constant.

extinction. The dropping out or decrease in intensity of a response when it is not reinforced.

extratensive. Tendency to be motivated by external pressures rather than by internal drives.

extrinsic. Pertaining to, or derived from, things outside.

factor analysis. A statistical procedure designed to determine the extent of communality and independence between tests or other measures of performance.

faculty psychology. A school or system of psychology based upon the classification of mental processes and performances under a small number of factors which are treated as entities, causes, or principles of explanation.

family history. Contains information about the family stock from which a client has come and the general family setting in which he has developed.

fantasy. Calling up imaginary scenes, events, or occurrences.

feelings. Affective experiences, especially of pleasantness and unpleasantness.

Ferguson Form Boards. Six form boards that progress in difficulty.

fetishism. Morbid sexual attraction and stimulation by some inanimate object, usually an article of clothing.

field. A complex of factors or forces.

field forces. The factors in the environment and in the field surrounding the individual which act upon him to influence the direction and nature of his activity.

field theory. A theory identified with Lewin. Its basic statements are that behavior can be derived from a totality of coexisting facts and that these facts have the character of a dynamic field, in that the state of any part of the field depends on every other part of the field.

figure-ground relationships. The concept that certain elements in our psychological perceptual field stand out in focus as figures and others remain simply as background. Some ambiguous figures result in shifting percepts, insofar as figure and ground are concerned.

fixation. The arrest or halting of development at some stage so that a portion of the behavior or emotional life of the individual remains at a level that was appropriate at an earlier age, but is now inappropriate.

fixed ideas. A general term for obsessions and delusions. Ideas that are adhered to in spite of evidence to the contrary.

flaccid paralysis. Paralysis characterized by lack of use of certain muscle groups. It is accompanied by atrophy and is caused by injury to lower motor neurons.

flexible therapy. Treatment that follows the principle of flexibility as described by Alexander. In general, it refers to the idea that treatment should be planned and designed to fit the individual and that all procedures should be flexible enough to account for individual differences and for changes in the individual.

force system. A dynamic system of forces or vectors interacting with one another which may combine to form a resultant vector of a particular strength acting in a certain direction or which may be in equilibrium.

forces. Any condition or set of conditions which brings about changes or maintains equilibrium among mental or social phenomena.

foreconscious. Mental processes of which an individual is not aware at a given moment, but which he is able to call to consciousness more or less rapidly. Sometimes called preconscious.

frame of reference. A particular set of beliefs or a personal philosophy by which an individual judges or evaluates events and experiences.

fraternal twins. Twins that develop from two fertilized ova.

free association. The process of associating ideas in the absence of limiting instruction or predisposing conditions.

frustration. Prevention of the satisfaction of needs or drives.

fugue. Episodes of automatic behavior, usually associated with the desire to run away from unpleasant situations, for which the individual has no memory.

functional disorder. A disorder in the manner in which an organism behaves or functions. Not a defect in the organism itself.

functioning intelligence. The level and quality of performance which the person exhibits. Contrasted with the concept of potential intelligence.

generalization. Forming a general idea, a judgment, or a response and applying it to an entire class of data or stimuli on the basis of a limited number of experiences.

genital. Pertaining to the reproductive organs. In psychoanalysis, it refers to
the stage of psychosexual development during which the individual's
erotic interest centers on the genital areas.

genotype. Refers to underlying traits that are the basic determiners to action.

Gesell Developmental Schedules. Norms are provided for scoring the appearance of a number of items of behavior in infants and children and thus
estimating developmental rate.

Gestalt. Configuration or organization of a total field.

global intelligence. The aggregate or over-all capacity to deal with the environment. Includes the concepts of drive and incentive.

goals. The achievements or areas of activity toward which persons strive in
order to attain satisfaction of their motives and gratification of their
needs.

Goodenough Drawing Test. A standardized scoring system developed for
evaluating performance on the task of drawing a man.

grand mal. A generalized convulsive seizure accompanied by a sudden
loss of consciousness.

Grassi Block Substitution Test. Utilizes the Koh's blocks and requires the
subject to reproduce designs.

gratification. A pleasant emotional attitude attached to the perception or experience of a situation.

grimace. A distortion of the face.

group counseling. Application of counseling, psychotherapeutic, or re-educational methods by a clinician to a group of individuals at the same time.

group-factor theory of intelligence. Intelligence is held to be an expression
not of a number of specific factors or of any general factors, but of a
number of groups of factors. Each group has a primary factor that gives
the group cohesiveness.

group tests. Tests that are so constructed that they can be administered by
one examiner to a number of subjects at the same time.

group therapy. Bringing individuals together in a group for the purpose of
changing individual behavior and improving interpersonal or intrapersonal relations. The term is used interchangeably with "group counseling." See definition above.

growth. Increase in size, complexity, efficiency, value, or any other kind of increase.

growth principle. One of the basic postulates of the client-centered approach
in counseling. It assumes that the client has an inherent power to develop, to enhance the self, and to organize experiences, and that he will
do so if given the opportunity.

guidance. Procedures oriented to facilitate the total development of the individual. When the term is used in vocational guidance, it is usually interpreted as the provision of information and direction so that the client
will be in a position to make a choice.

guiding fictions. Schemes of understanding and organizing experiences. Term
used by Adler.

Guilford Tests. A number of structured personality tests that have been refined by factor-analytic techniques.

guilt. Conscious or unconscious dread of retributive punishment, or the feeling of need for punishment.

habit. A constant, unconscious, learned, pattern of behavior.

hallucinations. A perception accepted as real by the subject but occasioned by no apparent external stimuli.

hebephrenia. A disorder of behavior primarily characterized by regression. Usually regarded as a type of schizophrenia.

heterosexual. Sexually oriented or attracted to members of the opposite sex.

hierarchy of response. A complex organization of responses in which responses of a higher order include, as components, responses of lower orders.

higher mental processes. The functions of cognition, of conscious reasoning, of imagination, and of verbalization.

homeostasis. Relatively constant internal environment maintained by the coordination of physiological processes.

homosexuality. Erotic interest or relations between persons of the same sex.

hostility. Tendency to be aggressive or antagonistic. It may be directed or it may be quite general.

House-Tree-Person Test. A drawing technique in which the subject is asked to draw a house, a tree, and a person. Detailed procedures are provided for questioning and evaluation.

human engineering. The study of the relationship between men and machines. It includes the designing of equipment for human use and the training of persons for the most efficient use of equipment.

hydrocephalus. Enlargement of the cranium because of pressure of cerebral-spinal fluid.

hydrotherapy. Treatment by various types of baths or the internal or external administration of water.

hyperopia. Farsightedness or the inability to focus on near objects.

hypnosis. A trancelike, passive state in which the subject shows increased suggestibility induced by monotonous suggestion of relaxation, sleep, or control by the hypnotist.

hypochondriasis. Excessive preoccupation with bodily functions, and the tendency to focus on symptoms and illness.

hypothesis. A preliminary theory, supposition, or assumption, provisionally adopted to explain certain facts and to guide in the investigation of others.

hysteria. Term used synonymously with "conversion" or sometimes in conjunction with it—conversion hysteria. Refers to the converting of psychological problems into physical ones by the assumption of bodily ailments to relieve tension in conflict situations.

id. Unconscious urges, motives, instincts, and drives.

idea. An experience or thought not directly due to sensory stimulation and having a symbolic function.

ideas of reference. Beliefs that one is constantly the object of thoughts and actions of others.

identical twins. Twins developing from the fertilization of one ovum.

identification. Adoption of the personality characteristics or identity of another person.

illusion. A misinterpretation of a sensory percept.

image. An element of experience that is centrally aroused but possesses most of the attributes of a sensation.

imagination. The process of calling up images from past experience and organizing them with new relations into an ideational experience.

impotence. Generally, the inability to make integrated responses and the expression of this inability, as in the response, "I don't know." Sexually, the term refers to the inability to perform normal coitus. In the male, it ordinarily refers to the inability to gain an erection.

impulse ego. Term used by Rank to describe the basic primitive drives of the individual.

Index of Adjustment and Values. A form of self-rating scale in which the subject rates certain adjectives as they apply to him.

individual counseling. The situation in which a clinician or counselor holds individual interviews or sessions with a single client at a time.

individual differences. The concept that traits or characteristics are possessed in differing degrees by different individuals. In general, it is expected that these differing characteristics will distribute themselves normally.

individual psychology. The psychology of Adler. The central concept is the study of individual differences in the manner in which persons strive for superiority.

individual-study approach. The main characterization of clinical and counseling psychology. The application of the methods of study of general psychology to the study of the individual case.

individual tests. Tests that are so constructed that one examiner can examine only one subject at a time.

individuation. Term used by Jung to describe the drive that persons presumably possess to achieve individuality or to be their "real selves."

induction. The process of reasoning from particular to general. Inductive theory starts with certain empirical data and organizes it into a general theory.

infant developmental scales. Scales developed and standardized to estimate the rate of development and probable ability of infants and preschool children.

infantile. Resembling the stage of infancy.

infantile conflicts. In psychoanalytic theory, it refers to conflicts at early stages of infantile sexuality which prevent the development of the individual to more mature stages, or are responsible for regression to these early stages when the usual outlets for the libido are blocked in adult life.

infantile sexuality. The concept that the infant has certain erotic interests. It is usually assumed that these center around anal and oral areas.

inference. The process of reasoning on logical grounds that certain factors are present or that events either will occur or must have occurred.

inferiority complex. Feelings of inadequacy or inferiority to which the person reacts by compensation.

inferiority feelings. Related to inferiority complex. Refers to the real or imagined belief or feeling of inadequacy.

informant. The person who gives information.

inhibition. The internal checking of a feeling, thought, or act.

initiating power. A drive that Rank believed was effective in guiding and integrating the self in assimilation of the outer world. This force was commonly referred to as the "will."

innate. Present in the individual at birth.

inquiry. A phase in the administration of certain projective tests in which the clinician attempts to determine just what aspects of the stimuli were effective in prompting the responses. An inquiry may also be used to clarify responses.

insight. A term with a wide variety of meanings, depending on the school of thought employing it. In psychoanalytic theory, it refers to the recovery of repressed memories. In learning theory, it is nearly equivalent to verbalization or labeling. In general, it refers to the conscious understanding and clarification of sequences of events.

insight therapies. Treatment procedures aimed at the understanding of sources of conflicts.

instinct. An innate, unlearned pattern of behavior. Historically, in psychology, the concept of instinct was used to explain many complicated performances. Today the concept is generally used as synonymous with basic drives.

institutionalization. The term used to describe the act of placing an individual in a hospital, a training school for the intellectually retarded, or some other type of public or private institution.

intake interview. The interview held with the client or the person responsible for him on the occasion of his admission to a hospital or clinic.

integration. The organization or arrangement of material into units of a higher order.

intellectual deficit. The extent to which a person is unable to perform at his previous level.

intelligence. A term with many meanings, but in general taken to mean the capacity of the individual to adapt, or learn to adapt, to novel situations.

Intelligence Quotient (I.Q.). A converted score based on performance on an intelligence test which expresses the individual's mental age (M.A.) in relation to his chronological age (C.A.). The formula for this relationship is $\text{I.Q.} = \dfrac{\text{M.A.}}{\text{C.A.}} \times 100$. The average I.Q. is therefore necessarily 100, since the average 10-year-old will receive an M.A. of 10, etc. For persons over 15 years, the formula is revised to $\text{I.Q.} = \dfrac{\text{M.A.}}{15} \times 100$.

interaction. A relation between two units of a force system, such that the activity of each is in part determined by the activity of the other.

interest. An attitude or set conducive to focusing special attention on certain content.

internship. A period during which a student works in a real service setting under supervision in order to gain experience and become qualified for independent work.

interpersonal. Refers to interactions between persons.

interpretation. The organization of data or experience into a meaningful system.

interview. The situation during which the clinician or counselor obtains direct information from the client or others in response to questions and discussion.

intrapersonal. Refers to interactions between factors within a person.

intratensive. The tendency to be motivated by pressures or motives from within rather than by those from without.

intrinsic value. The worth of a given object or activity regardless of its relation to others.

introversion. Turning to interests within. Frequently used in the sense of self-preoccupation.

intuition. Immediate comprehension or judgment of data, principles, or experience without preliminary cognition. In psychology, the tendency is to regard it as the final stage in the process of perceptive synthesis.

inventories. Devices that require the subject to answer a number of questions with channelized responses of the "yes-no," "agree-disagree," or "like-dislike" variety.

involuntary activity. Refers to a movement or direction of attention which takes place without any effort to initiate it and frequently in spite of efforts to inhibit it.

judgment. The application of a concept to a given situation or object.

Kent-Shakow Form Boards. A series of form boards designed primarily for adult use.

Koh's Blocks. A set of blocks approximately one inch square, with different colors on each side. Some sides are of one color and others of two colors meeting on the diagonal. The blocks are used in a number of performance scales, the task being to reproduce designs with them.

Kuder Preference Record. An interest or preference test that indicates the subject's relative preference for activities in certain general vocational and professional areas.

labeling. Term used by Dollard and Miller to describe the process of verbalization or symbolization of previously unconscious feelings and thoughts so that they are made conscious and subject to control by the subject's higher mental processes. The term is also used occasionally by workers in the field of semantics to describe the identification of a person with a word that becomes a label and in turn influences the person's reactions. The person may tend to behave in reference to the label.

lability of affect. Unusually changeable emotionality, often inadequately controlled.

laboratory. A room, building, or place designed to be used for scientific research.

language tests. Tests that require language comprehension or expression. Generally used synonymously with "verbal tests."

latent. Underlying, covert, not observable. As applied to anxiety, it refers to the covert aspects that are not reflected in overt bodily reactions. In dreams the latent content refers to the unconscious meaning behind the manifest content.

latent content. In psychoanalysis, the unconscious meanings of symbols as opposed to the manifest or superficially obvious content or meaning.

lay analyst. A person, not a physician, who uses psychoanalytic techniques.

learning. The modification of response as a result of previous experience.

learning theory. A general, descriptive term that refers to any one of several theoretical approaches that conceive of behavior change, especially in counseling or therapy, as resulting from learning phenomena.

lecture-discussion technique. An approach to group counseling which is quite didactic and consists essentially of brief lectures on pertinent topics of adjustment. These lectures are designed to stimulate group discussion and participation. The approach is identified with Klapman.

Leiter International Performance Scale. A performance scale recently re-standardized by Arthur. It is particularly well adapted to language-handicapped children.

lesion. Injury, or destroyed tissue.

leucotomy. Brain surgery in which fibers from the prefrontal lobes are severed or destroyed. Sometimes the term is used interchangeably with "prefrontal lobotomy."

level of aspiration. A subject's personal expectation or prediction as to the level or the quality of responses that he is capable of making.

libido. The energy of the sexual drive

licensing. A form of social control by which practitioners of a particular profession are required to hold a license to practice. Practice without a license, when such is required by law, is illegal.

life-space. Term offered by Lewin to describe the totality of the dynamic field in which a person exists at any amount of time. The life-space includes the person and the phenomenal field forces that interact to determine the resultant behavior.

life style. Term used by Adler to describe the manner in which an individual strives for security and adaptation to the environment.

lobe. With reference to the brain, the larger portions of the cerebrum are designated as frontal lobe, parietal lobe, occipital lobe, and temporal lobe. Other body organs, such as the lungs, are divided into large portions called "lobes."

macrocephaly. An abnormally large head.

Make-a-Picture-Story Test. Commonly known as the MAPS. Consists of figures that can be arranged against a stage background to tell a story.

maladjustment. concept of poor adjustment, or the situation in which inadequate and unsatisfactory problem-solving techniques are used.

malaise. Boredom, a feeling of not being able to go on, and a general sense of futility.

malingering. The deliberate simulation of a disease or an ailment.

management evaluation. A service offered by certain industrial consulting firms which uses psychological procedures to evaluate the ability of a person to function adequately in a particular kind of management position.

manic behavior. The tendency to be excitable, to react quickly to many real or imaginary stimuli. Characterized by flights of ideas, hyperactivity, and high emotionality.

manifest. Immediately observable or apparent. As applied to anxiety, it refers to the directly observable or reportable aspects of anxiety. In dreams, the manifest content consists of the obvious items or images experienced.

masculine protest. According to Adler, the superiority granted to the male in our Western culture, the subordinate position being held by women, carries with it feelings of inferiority in women against which is raised the "masculine protest."

masochism. Satisfactions gained by physical pain or by actions turned against oneself. Sometimes believed to have an erotic attribute.

masturbation. Erotic manipulation of one's own genitals.

maturation. Development that accompanies the process of cell differentiation and is not directly dependent on growth through use or experience.

means-end readinesses. In Tolman's system, these are broad orientational expectancies—or sets—that behaving in a particular manner in response to a known complex of stimuli will lead to certain patterns of activity.

measurement. The comparison of quantitative data with a standard. In psychological testing it involves the use of psychological tests and the comparison of a subject's performance with the performances of similar subjects on the same test.

megalomania. Delusions of grandeur.

melancholia. A morbid mental state characterized by depression, gloominess, or hopelessness.

memory. Pertains to the retention of material learned on some former occasion.

meningitis. A disease marked by inflamation of the membranes that cover the brain and spinal cord.

Mental Age (M.A.). A converted score based on performance on a mental test, and determined by the level of difficulty of the test items passed. Thus if an individual child, no matter how old he is, can pass only those items passed by the average 10-year-old, he will be given a mental-age score of 10. Because of the nature of the developmental curve, the M.A. unit is difficult to apply after the age of 13. *See also* Intelligence Quotient.

mental deficiency. Impairment or lack of capacity for intellectual growth and development.

mental disease. A commonly used but somewhat inaccurate term describing abnormal or psychopathological behavior. Most behavior so described is believed to be functional and not the result of any disease—not of disease as it is conceived of in the field of medicine.

mental hygiene. Term used to designate the development of optimal modes of personal and social behavior in order to prevent the development of behavior disorders.

mental hygiene clinic. A clinic organized for the detection and treatment of behavior disorders. Mental hygiene clinics, as contrasted with child guidance clinics, serve persons of all age groups.

mental mechanisms. Patterns of adjustment which are learned by the person as methods of easing tension in conflict situations. Examples are compensation, projection, repression, regression, conversion, etc.

Merrill Palmer Scale of Mental Tests. A scale of tests or tasks arranged for children of from 24 to 63 months of age.

Michigan Picture Test. A picture-story, partially structured, personality test.

microcephaly. An abnormally small head.

milieu. The complex of social and physical factors that surround us. When applied to therapy, it refers to these factors as manipulated and mobilized for the benefit of the client.

Miller Analogies Test. A widely used scholastic aptitude test for use at the graduate level.

Minnesota Preschool Scale. A scale designed for children of from 18 months to 6 years of age.

Minnesota Multiphasic Personality Inventory. Commonly known as the MMPI. A structured test of personality upon which much research has been accomplished. The responses are scored on a number of different keys, which are designated in terms of psychopathological symptoms.

mongolism. A congenital condition characterized by distinctive appearance and usually accompanied by mental retardation.

moods. The character of a person's affective states and the nature of emotional reactions.

morbid. An abnormal, disordered, or diseased state or condition.

mores. The traditional standards of a group.

Mosaic Test. Consists of different-colored plastic pieces to be placed in a design.

motivation. The concept of drives plus the mechanisms by which they are satisfied. The study of the incentives to activity.

motives. The forces energizing behavior. Primary motives are usually thought of as drives. Secondary motives are learned elaborations of basic drives. In general, a motive has both strength and direction, and is a higher-order concept than that of tissue needs.

motor incapacity. Disorder in the performance or co-ordination of motor acts. Examples include paralyses and gross disorders of co-ordination.

motoric activity. Refers to overt physical or motor activity, as contrasted with cognitive or implicit activity.

multifactor theories of intelligence. These theories maintain that there is no single factor of general intelligence; rather, a number of separate factors operate together.

multiple causation. The concept that a number of factors may contribute to the characteristics of an individual's behavior.

multiple personality. A dissociated state in which certain memories and ideas break off from the individual's normal awareness and assume independent existence. As a result, he may behave in a certain way on one occasion and in a different on another.

mutuality. A concept introduced by Shaw to describe a relationship between client and counselor that is conducive to the alteration of expectancies.

mysticism. The view that certain events are governed by some power other than known phenomena.

narcissism. The admiration or love of self. Sometimes narcism.

needs. Internal or personal motives. Implies some very basic requirement such as physiological need or tissue need, although sometimes used to describe very fundamental social needs such as the "need for attention."

negative vocational counseling. Allowing the individual to find his own vocation. The counselor may advise that certain occupations or vocations present difficulties but not specify that a particular vocation is indicated. A process of elimination and not of positive selection.

negativism. Stubbornness or obstinacy. Refusal to react or to respond.

neo-analysis. Term used to describe a variety of approaches that have varied from the classical approach of Freud. The principal variance is the substitution of the interaction of man with his cultural milieu for the mechanistic, biological, and instinctual interpretations of Freud.

neurasthenia. A syndrome of symptoms characterized by weakness and fatigability.

neuropsychiatric hospital. A hospital designed for the care and treatment of patients with behavior disorders.

neuropsychiatry. The branch of medicine which deals with both neurology and psychiatry. The term is commonly used synonymously with "psychiatry."

neurosis. A general classification of behavior disorders in which the person is in contact with reality but suffers from such symptoms as extreme anxiety, tiredness, psychosomatic symptoms, and conversion reactions. As contrasted with psychotic behavior, in which the person's reactions are personally oriented, neurotic behavior is socially oriented.

neurotic trends. Term introduced by Horney to designate the concept of strivings toward safety, which were substituted in her theory for Freud's instinctual drives.

nihilism. The delusional denial of the existence or the worth of any activity.

non-Aristotelian. Refers to philosophical principles that are opposed to those of Aristotle. Generally, these are principles that are labeled "post-Galilean." In contrast to the Aristotelian concept that the behavior of bodies is the result of the intrinsic nature of the bodies, post-Galilean concepts explain behavior as the result of forces acting upon and from within the bodies.

nondirective counseling. Refers to the therapeutic approach developed and described by Rogers, which postulates basically that the client has the inherent capacity for positive growth if the proper atmosphere is provided for this growth. The term has been replaced for most purposes by the term "client-centered."

nonlanguage test. Tests that can be administered and taken with little or no use of language. Sometimes called "nonverbal."

nonverbal tests. Tests that can be administered or taken with little emphasis on language comprehension or expression.

normal. Within the average range. When applied to behavior, it connotes efficient, satisfactory behavior.

norms. Standards based on the performance of a representative group of subjects.

nosology. The naming and classification of diseases.

nymphomania. Incessant, almost insatiable sexual desire or activity in women.

objective. The lack of personal bias or error. In connection with tests, the term describes a test from the point of view of the interpreter. An objective test can be scored with a high degree of reliability.

observation. The examination of events or phenomena as part of the process of investigation or evaluation.

obsession. A persistent, conscious idea.

occupational history. A record of positions the client has held and of his specific training and experience in various areas of work.

occupational information. A general term that includes the study of information about occupations, their potentialities, and their requirements.

occupational therapy. Treatment involving the use of constructive recreational or vocational pursuits. Usually involves manual activity.

oedipal wishes or strivings. Sexual or erotic feelings of the son toward the mother and antagonistic or aggressive feelings toward the father.

oedipus complex. Mother fixation on the part of the son, mother complex, or the state of having oedipal wishes or strivings.

operationism. Includes concepts whose meanings can only be understood in terms of the operations from which they are derived. Each operation is stated in terms of empirical standards that are consistent, repeatable under the same conditions, and definitely based on objective reality.

oral. In the region of the mouth. In psychoanalysis, the stage in psychosexual development which refers specifically to the sexual activity in nursing.

organic. Related to structural change in one of the bodily systems. Contrasted with functional.

organ inferiority. Innate constitutional inferiority. The term was originally used by Adler and later modified to include feelings of social inadequacy resulting from hereditary or environmental deficiencies.

orgasm. The height of erotic pleasure just preceding detumescence and relaxation.

orientation. Awareness of person, place, and time relationships.

overt. Easily seen or recognizable.

palliation. The reduction of symptoms, usually temporary, in order to make the client more comfortable.

panic. Extreme anxiety with flight or disorganization of behavior.

pantheism. The doctrine that the universe is God. There is no God but the combined forces and laws that are manifested in the existing universe.

paranoid reactions. The tendency to disregard reality by developing delusions to explain events that occur. Reality is not completely disregarded but is interpreted in terms of the individual.

parataxic. Term devised by Sullivan to describe the reaction to a current situation in terms of earlier experiences.

paresis. A behavior disorder caused by syphilitic infection of the brain.

partially structured tests. Tests that suggest the general nature or the area of response but do not set the limits very specifically, so that the individual has considerable latitude of response.

participant observer. Suggests the concept that no observer, not even a clinician, can completely divorce himself from the situation in which he is functioning. The clinical interview or testing situation is a social situation, and the clinician and the client are both affected by the interactions in that situation.

pathology. The study of disease. Most specifically, used to describe the study of physiological changes.

pattern analysis. An approach to the analysis of certain test performances in an effort to discover patterns that can be correlated with certain behavioral reactions.

pediatrics. The branch of medicine which treats of the hygiene and diseases of children.

penis-envy. In psychoanalytic theory, the unconscious longing of the female for male attributes.

percentile. A point on a distribution above which and below which a certain percentage of cases fall. The 40th percentile on a test performance means that 40 per cent of the standardization group made scores below the particular point and 60 per cent were above it.

perception. The awareness of objects or relations that depend upon sensation. Commonly defined as the attachment of meaning to sensations.

performance tests. Tests that require manual or visual-motor performance and do not require language comprehension or expression. The term "performance" is generally used synonymously with "nonverbal" or "nonlanguage" but sometimes to describe the specific visual-motor aspects of the tasks.

peripheral nerves. Nerves outside the brain and spinal cord.

permissiveness. Term used by Rogers and others to describe the attitude that a counselor should have toward a client and his behavior. The attitude should encourage the free expression of feelings. No limit is placed on the expression of feelings, and the clinician should maintain complete acceptance of whatever is expressed.

perseveration. The tendency to repeat responses and to have difficulty in shifting to new tasks or new areas.

persona. The impression the subject wishes to give of himself.

Personal Audit. A structured personality test.

Personal Data Sheet. The first widely used structured personality test. Constructed by Woodworth. Many personality inventories have been derived from it.

personality. A construct used to describe qualities or characteristics of behavior. It is used with a variety of meanings. In general, it is used to represent the sum total of behavior as it affects other people. Trait theories conceive of personality as consisting of a number of specific traits or variables.

personality integration. Refers to behavior that is well organized and consistent.

personality reorganization. According to "deep" therapists, this is the goal of counseling or therapy. Consists of helping the client to integrate or organize the disorganized aspects of his behavior.

personal orientation. The attitude of disregard for social pressures and the tendency to live in a very personal world. Characterized by intratension or introversion.

personnel testing. The selection and administration of psychological tests for the purpose of identifying the best-qualified workers for a particular assignment.

persuasion. The attempt to direct the client's motivations toward goals desired by the counselor.

phenomenal field. The private world of the individual which is composed of all his consciously perceived experiences and provides the reality to which he reacts.

phenotype. Characterized by the visible or obvious traits common to a group, in contrast to the underlying, individual determiners of action.

philosophy. The science that investigates the facts and principles of reality, of human nature, and of conduct.

phobia. A morbid dread or fear of an object, situation, event, or act.

physical handicap. A physical disability that places the individual at a disadvantage insofar as normal adjustment and competition are concerned.

physician-patient relationship. The legal, ethical, and moral relationship between the patient and the physician to whom responsibility has been delegated by the patient.

Pintner-Paterson Scale of Performance Tests. It consists of 15 tests and is the earliest elaborate performance battery.

positive vocational counseling. Telling a client that his particular pattern of interests and abilities indicates that he should enter a particular area.

postulate. A proposition that is taken for granted or put forth as axiomatic.

potentiality. The level of functioning which can conceivably be expected, assuming optimum conditions.

practicum. A situation in which a student is given supervised experience in professional work. Sometimes used to include internship experiences and sometimes to represent a learning situation more advanced than a laboratory experience but involving less responsibility than in internship.

prediction. That which is foretold. One of the goals of psychology and a special goal of clinical evaluation and assessment. Behavior must be predicted before counseling can be planned.

predisposition. The basis for and the tendency toward exhibiting a characteristic, trait, disorder, reaction, or disease.

prefrontal lobotomy. Surgical severing of the tracts connecting the frontal lobes of the brain with the thalamus.

pregenital. Term used in psychoanalysis. Refers to the stages in psychosexual development prior to the development of awareness of genital areas.

prenatal. Before birth.

preschool scales. Scales designed to estimate the physical and mental development of infants and preschool children.

pressure. The exertion of steady and persistent suggestion that a client behave in a specific fashion.

prima facie validity. The concept that responses to test items have meaning in and of themselves, regardless of the mental processes involved. For example, an answer of "yes" is an answer of "yes," regardless of why the answer was given.

primal. First in time.

primal impulses. Basic drives or primitive needs. Similar to id impulses.

primal scene. Designates a child's observation of coitus between its parents.

primates. In zoology, an order of mammals consisting of man and the apes, monkeys, etc.

principle of flexibility. A basic premise of Alexander and French that various therapeutic procedures and techniques must be adapted in a flexible manner to the needs of each individual client.

principle of planning. A basic principle of Alexander and French which emphasizes the necessity for a unique plan of treatment for each client, based on a careful appraisal or assessment of the individual. Such a plan is not to be firmly set and must be used with flexibility.

private practice. Offering service for a fee rather than working for a salary as a staff member of some organization such as a hospital or a clinic.

privileged communication. The legal right of workers in some professional areas, such as the law, the ministry, or in medicine, to regard information disclosed to them by their clients as confidential. As a consequence of this right, such professional workers cannot be forced to testify, nor can their records be presented as evidence.

problem-solving behavior. The process by which responses are adapted until the subject is able to adjust effectively to a conflict or problem situation.

problem-solving learning. Sometimes called solution learning. One of the two factors advanced by Mowrer to account for learning. Such learning follows the principle of reinforcement and is under the voluntary control of the central nervous system. It is the means by which we acquire tendencies to action. Contrasted with conditioning or sign learning.

profession. An occupation that involves a specialized education and certain intellectual elements. Contrasted with manual labor and commercial, mechanical, and agricultural activities which are not ordinarily regarded as professional. In general, professional workers serve people in a more or less personal way, and their activities are governed by ethical standards laid down by the profession itself.

prognosis. Prediction of the duration or course of a disease or disorder.

Progressive Matrices. A nonverbal intelligence scale developed in England. Particularly applicable to persons with special disabilities.

projection. The process of attributing characteristics of one's self to others.

projective hypothesis. The hypothesis that when presented with an ambiguous stimulus, the subject reveals himself by the characteristics of his response.

projective tests. Devices that present the subject with ambiguous stimuli that have little or no meaning in themselves. The subject is presumed to project his own percepts and thus reveal something of himself.

prototaxic. Term used by Sullivan to describe the undifferentiated wholeness of an infant's experience.

psychasthenia. Term applied to anxiety, compulsions, and obsessions.

psychiatric social work. An application of social work which has aligned itself with psychiatry and which is primarily concerned with persons presenting behavior disorders. In general, social workers are concerned with the family.

psychiatrist. Physician specializing in the diagnosis, care, and treatment of behavior disorders.

psychiatry. The division of medicine dealing with behavior disorders.

psychic energy. A seldom-used term of referring to the motivational state of the person. Specifically, it is used to describe the initiative, will, and drive of the person.

psychic totality. Term used to describe Jung's concept of the result of the client's awareness of the material in the collective unconscious.

psychoanalysis. A system of therapy, theory, and research largely propounded by Freud.

psychoanalyst. One who practices psychoanalysis.

psychobiology. A system of therapy, theory, and research outlined by Meyer.

psychodrama. Term used by Moreno to describe the technique of having a client act out his problems or conflicts in supervised relationships with others.

psychodynamics. Term used to describe the dynamics of psychological behavior. It has been most often used by psychoanalysts in referring to the long-range determiners of behavior.

psychoeducational clinic. A clinic primarily designed to evaluate and treat problems arising within the school or educational setting.

psychogenic. Resulting from psychological factors.

psychologist. A person who conducts scientific research bearing on psychological problems or who applies the knowledge of psychology. Usually possesses the Doctor of Philosophy Degree or the equivalent in training and/or experience.

psychology. The science of behavior. Its aims are the understanding, prediction, and control of behavior.

psychometrics. Psychological measurement.

psychoneurosis. Commonly used as the equivalent of neurosis. Occasionally used to designate forms of neurotic behavior with recent and superficial causes, as contrasted with "true" neuroses.

psychopathology. Term used to describe the study of behavior disorders.

psychosis. Refers to behavior that seems to have little basis in reality and that is personally oriented.

psychosomatic. Refers to somatic or bodily conditions that have their origin in emotional reactions to persistent conflict.

psychosynthesis. Term used by Freud to describe the reorganization and integration that was thought by him to accompany somehow automatically the uncovering and interpretation of repressed content.

psychotherapy. Procedures designed to influence behavior so that the person will be more efficient and happier with his adjustment.

qualitative. Connoting variation in kind but not in degree.

quantitative. The general character of phenomena which allows them to be measured or counted.

racial unconscious. Term used by Jung to describe archaic memories presumed to reside in the unconscious and to be derived from the accumulated experiences, habits, knowledge, and traditions of the race.

rapport. An interpersonal relationship in which there is mutual co-operativeness.

rational. Conscious, sensible, logical, and meaningful.

rationalization. The conscious justification of attitudes, concepts, ideas, or
acts.

reaction time. The time that elapses between the presentation of a stimulus
and the response by the subject.

reactive neurosis. Prolonged depression resulting from an actual event or
situation.

reality. The actual, observable environment surrounding the subject. A philosophical question may arise as to reality for whom. In psychology,
reality is often determined by consensual agreement of a number of
observers. Phenomenal reality describes reality as it is experienced by
the individual.

reality testing. The process of interpreting and verifying perceptual experience.

reasoning. Cognition, thinking, the manipulation of symbols.

reassurance. When used as a counseling technique, it consists of showing
respect for the client, reinforcing positive feelings, pointing out gains,
encouraging optimism, and in general deliberately influencing the client
to feel that he is capable of progress and that gains are going to be
forthcoming.

Recovery, Inc. An organization of recovered mental patients founded in 1937
with the purpose of enabling persons to help themselves and each other.

re-education. Retraining or relearning. Assistance to the client in his efforts
to regain efficient patterns of behavior which he has lost.

referral. The act of suggesting to an individual that he seek personal assistance, and/or making arrangements for the service.

registration. The formality by which a client indicates that he wishes a facility or a clinician to take certain responsibilities for his welfare. It
may include giving identifying data, stating the problem, and presenting
other general information.

regression. The resumption of, or the going back to, earlier modes of adjustment.

rehabilitation. The process by which an individual is helped to regain his
place in society and to function as an efficient person.

reinforcement. Any event or activity that rewards a response or strengthens
the connection between stimuli and responses. In the Hullian framework, reinforcement takes place through drive reduction.

reinforcement learning theory. This theory is identified with Hull and is also
referred to as stimulus-response theory. Learning proceeds as a result
of reinforcements that reduce the physiological drives activating behavior.

rejection. In the case of the individual, the term refers to his putting aside,
or turning away from, certain attitudes, ideas, or tendencies. In the social
setting, it refers to the situation in which a person is not accepted, or is
turned away, by others or by a group. In the testing situation, it refers
to the refusal of a task by the testee.

relationship. Any connection or mutual influence between two or more bits
of data or between two or more persons or events.

relaxation. Reduction of tension. To cease active contraction of a muscle or muscle group or to relieve oneself of mental strain.

relearning. When applied to counseling, it refers to the goal of altering the client's behavior or attitudes by means of principles of learning and constructs derived from learning theory.

reliability. The dependability of sources of information. The extent to which information gathered from one source, or at a given time, agrees with information collected from other sources, or at other times.

remedial reading. Special techniques designed to deal with specific disabilities and to aid the person in developing reading skills. If the person is not able to learn by ordinary procedures, it is assumed that remedial reading is necessary.

remedial treatment. Special procedures designed to remedy certain disabilities.

repetition compulsion. A pressing tendency to alleviate the anxiety of past traumatic experiences by re-exploring or re-enacting them in fantasy or in actuality.

repression. The denial and banishment of certain desires, feelings, or ideas from conscious awareness.

resistance. In psychoanalytic therapy, the mainly unconscious reluctance of the client to give up accustomed patterns of thinking, feeling, and acting in favor of new modes of adjustment. Sometimes has the more limited meaning that the ego refuses to accept insight into the unconscious.

resources. The capacity to utilize potential ability. Includes intellectual factors as well as the energy and control that the person can mobilize to utilize the potential ability.

response. A behavioral reaction to a stimulus that is strong enough to impel an adjustment by the subject.

restrictive legislation. Legal controls over the practice of a specialty which restrict the practice to those who are duly licensed.

resultant. The vector or the direction and strength of a force due to the interaction of a number of forces in a force field.

retarded child. A general term that is coming into common usage to describe the child who is slow in physical and/or intellectual development. Also used as a synonym for the feebleminded child.

retraining. The process of re-education or re-establishment of behavior patterns that have been discontinued.

rigidity. Tendency to be inflexible, to follow a prescribed or habitual approach without variance.

ritualism. The dependence and acceptance of an organized system of rites or ceremonies. Frequently applied with reference to the compulsive person who feels that he must do things in a precise manner.

role playing. A variation of psychodrama in which the client and the clinician take certain roles and practice or experiment with modes of behavior.

Rorschach Test. An unstructured test consisting of 10 ink blots that the subject is asked to react to. The blots are presumed to be ambiguous.

sadism. Pleasure derived from inflicting pain on others.

sample. A limited number of cases taken at random out of an entire group or population.

satyriasis. Intense, almost insatiable, sexual desires and activities in men.

scatter. The range of performances by the same person on different tests or by different persons on the same test.

schizoid. A personality type characterized by seclusiveness, lack of emotional attachment to others, diminished initiative, and preoccupation with fantasies.

schizophrenia. A general term that includes various mechanisms of withdrawal.

schizophrenic ratio. A scatter index developed on the Wechsler-Bellevue Intelligence Examination to differentiate schizophrenics from other groups.

school clinical psychology. The application of procedures of clinical psychology to the evaluation and treatment of psychoeducational problems.

science. Statement or classification of facts, laws, relationships, and causes, gained and verified by exact observation and logical thinking. Scientific methods are those that attempt to provide for exact and objective observation, systematic and logical thinking, and the application of these methods to the acquisition, classification, and statement of knowledge.

security operations. Term used by Fromm-Reichman as the equivalent of ego-defenses to illustrate the manner by which the client may protect himself against threatening or unacceptable material.

self. That part of the perceptual field which becomes recognized as "I" or "me," as contrasted with the objects or experiences that are not acceptable or are not incorporated by the individual.

self-assertion. According to Adler, the basic instinct. An inherent tendency in the organism to achieve superiority.

self-consciousness. Being overly aware of self and unduly sensitive to the reactions of others.

self-knowledge. Jung's term for insight.

self-realization. The equivalent of individuation.

self-report tests. Tests that require the subject to report his answers directly. Such tests are usually of the inventory or paper-and-pencil variety.

semantic. Pertaining to the science of the meaning of words.

sensation. A form of experience aroused from outside the nervous system.

sensory deficiency. Any handicap or defect in the sensory capacities of the individual. The most common examples are disorders of vision or hearing.

sentence-completion tests. Tests in which the subject is given a sentence stem or a beginning of a sentence and is asked to complete it. In personality testing, such tests are regarded as partially structured.

set. A predisposition to react in a certain way to a particular stimulus or complex of stimuli.

shock therapy. The use of insulin, metrazol, or electric shock as a therapeutic procedure.

sibling. A full brother or sister. Usually not used to refer to a twin.

sign learning. Learning by conditioning; governed by contiguity principles. It is mediated by the autonomic nervous system and is involuntary. This is one of Mowrer's two principles of learning. It is the avenue through which we acquire expectations, sets, and predispositions. Contrasted with problem-solving learning.

sign-significate expectancies. A construct offered by Tolman to describe the learned "cognitive map" of "what leads to what" in a pattern of behavior.

simple schizophrenia. A behavior disorder characterized by indifference, lack of judgment and foresight, tendency to avoid responsibility.

skill. Facility in the performance of acts. Usually employed in the sense of motor skill or skills.

social orientation. Awareness of social pressure, of the attitudes of other persons, and of the comparison of self with society. Characterized by extra-tensive or extravertive behavior.

social prescription. Term used by Thorne to describe specific instructions of the counselor that the client engage in certain social activities.

social technique. Term offered by Ruesch to describe all the methods used by an individual in approaching, managing, and handling other persons.

social worker. The professional person who ordinarily has the responsibility for gathering information about the social history of the client and for therapeutic activities that involve his social adjustment.

socialization. In a general sense, socialization is a life-long process through which the individual learns a culture or several cultures. From a counseling point of view, it involves the use of social experiences as proving situations in which the client can apply and experiment with new attitudes and responses.

sociological history. A record of the kind and quantity of social relationships a client has had with others.

somatic. Pertaining to the body.

somnambulism. Walking in a state of sleep, trance, or fugue.

sorting tests. Tests that require the sorting of objects or materials into different categories. A number of such devices have been constructed for the study of concept formation.

spastic paralysis. Paralysis characterized by tense, drawn musculature and caused by injury to upper motor neurons.

speech correction. The professional field of work which specializes in the diagnosis and treatment of speech disorders. The study of the causes of speech disorders is sometimes referred to as speech pathology.

speech disorder. Any one of a number of conditions that interfere with the production of understandable and efficient speech. May be distinguished from a language disorder, which involves the formulation but not necessarily the production of speech.

speech readiness. Sufficient mental and physical maturation for the acquisition of speech.

spontaneity. As used by Moreno, the making of adequate responses to new situations and adequate new responses to old situations.

Stanford-Binet Intelligence Test. The revision of the Binet scales that has had the widest use. The 1937 Terman-Merrill Revision of the Stanford-Binet is an age-level test that is individually administered, is largely verbal, and is the one most commonly used with children.

static. Bodies or forces at rest or in equilibrium. The opposite of dynamic.

statistical controls. The elimination or reduction of bias and the isolation of significant factors by the use of refined statistical procedures and adequate samples.

statistics. The branch of general mathematics which is applied to the evaluation and arrangement of data into meaningful categories.

stereotypy. Continued repetition of sounds, words, or movements.

stimulus. Energy external to a receptor which excites a receptor.

stimulus-response learning theory. A drive-reduction theory of reinforcement. Learning proceeds as a result of the occurrence of events, known as reinforcements, which reduce the drives activating behavior. The concept is ascribed to Hull.

Strong's Vocational Interest Blanks. This test or inventory is designed to reveal whether a person has interests that are similar to those of persons who are successful in a certain vocational pursuit.

Structured Doll Play Test. A mode of personality evaluation designed for use with children that is based on the use of play materials. Lynn has devised a scale in which situations are presented and the responses of the subject are studied.

structured test. A test in which the response is channelized or structured by the nature of the test items or test situations.

structuring the interview. The procedure of helping the client to understand to the best of his ability why and how the interview is to be conducted.

stuttering. A disorder of speech in which the smooth-flowing production or the rhythm of speech is disrupted. The secondary stutterer repeats, blocks, strains, and struggles with speech. Such reactions are sometimes regarded as avoidance reactions to the primary hesitancies and pauses.

subcortical. Refers to levels of the central nervous system below that of the cerebral cortex.

sublimation. The process of diverting frustrated motives into other channels. Ordinarily applies to undesirable motives that are diverted into socially acceptable activities.

submission. The tendency to give in, to follow, or to be influenced by others.

subnormal. Below average, inferior as compared with a normal group.

suggestion. In counseling, it refers to the use of the counselor's authority position in actively influencing the client to think or act in a particular manner.

superego. Conscience.

superficial therapy. Therapy dealing primarily with current problems and symptoms. Contrasted with depth therapy, which purports to explore the unconscious antecedents of present behavior.

superstition. A fixed, irrational idea or notion maintained in spite of, or in the absence of, scientific evidence to the contrary.

support. That which maintains or reinforces a person's self-confidence and feeling of well-being.

supportive therapy. Counseling procedures that are designed to strengthen the client's defenses, give him needed guidance, and sustain his confidence.

surplus energy. Term used by Alexander, and derived from Ferenczi, to describe the discharge of unused or undirected excitations within the organism. It is creativity and capacity for growth.

symbolic activity. Intrinsic behavior that involves the manipulation of symbols. Includes most, if not all, cognitive activity.

symbols. Words, names, alphabetical characters, hieroglyphics, numerals, signals, gestures, and the like, used as substitutes for things, ideas, or concepts. Most symbols are integrated into language, but some are used in science and art, which are not part of language as we usually think of it.

sympathetic system. One of two divisions of the autonomic nervous system.

sympathy. The compatible sharing of desire or feelings between two persons.

syndrome. A group or constellation of symptoms that group together to serve a common purpose and are likely to be related to one another in their origin and development.

synthesis. Combination of parts and elements to form a whole.

systematic delusions. Well-organized, consistent, and integrated delusions.

Szondi Test. In this test a number of pictures of mental patients are presented to the subject and his reactions studied.

taboo. A strict social prohibition.

talent. A natural aptitude for some specialized occupation or activity.

temperament. The general affective state of the individual.

tension. A state of readiness to react or a condition of strain and suspense.

tension reduction. The process of relaxation, unwinding, or decreasing tension.

tension states. As used by Lewin, the term refers to readiness for action. More generally, it is used to describe states of emotional excitement or anxiety, and these are felt to have disruptive effects.

test. Any controlled or standardized situation for studying the behavior of a subject.

Thematic Apperception Test. A partially structured test that consists of a number of pictures with varying degrees of ambiguity about which the subject tells a story.

theory. A general principle or set of principles designed for the purpose of explaining a set of phenomena.

therapeutic community. Term used by Jones to describe a highly structured situation in which all activities are planned to prepare patients for their eventual role in society.

therapy. Treatment. In psychology and psychiatry, it applies to the changing of the client's behavior in order to promote his efficiency and happiness. It is a somewhat broader term than psychotherapy but the terms are frequently used interchangeably.

threshold of excitation. Term used by Goldstein to indicate the degree of control present. Brain-damaged patients tend to be easily excited. In addition to other symptoms, they are frequently adversely affected by speed. These characteristics are said to indicate a raised "threshold of excitation."

tissue need. A basic physiological necessity if life is to continue.

total-push. A method of treatment in which every available means is used to energize or activate the subject.

trait. Tendency to react in a certain way to a defined class of stimuli.

transfer. In learning, it refers to the improvement of a function through training or practice of some related function, without direct learning experiences.

transference. A relationship between the client and the counselor in which dissociated emotions that were formerly directed toward other situations, persons, or objects are activated and directed toward the counselor or therapist.

transference neurosis. Unusually strong displacement of affect toward the therapist which must be worked through before the treatment process can proceed.

trauma. Any injury, physical or otherwise, that disrupts the functioning of the organism.

traumatic neurosis. Neurotic behavior characterized by acute anxiety, startle reactions, depression, frequent nightmares, and other symptoms, following exposure to extreme physical danger, physical depletion, and other traumatic situations.

tremor. Rapid shaking or trembling of small magnitude.

trial-and-error. A mode of learning in which the learner tries various methods in a somewhat random manner until a solution is found which is reinforced and consequently adopted by the subject.

two-factor theory of intelligence. Intelligence is conceived of as containing both a general factor common to all mental activity and possessed by all individuals in varying degrees, and a number of specific factors each of which is important to a particular form of activity.

two-factor theory of learning. A theory suggested by Mowrer and based on the premise that no single explanation of learning will cover the different varieties of learning experience. He suggests that problem solving and conditioning will account for most, if not all, learning.

unconscious. A condition of lack of awareness concerning an item of behavior.

unconscious activity. Activity that occurs with no awareness on the part of the person. Psychoanalysts attribute a dynamic quality to unconscious activity and believe it to be a powerful determinant of behavior.

uncovering therapy. Therapy designed to remove repressions and recover memories from the unconscious.

unstructured tests. Tests that present an ambiguous situation to which the subject reacts in any way that he sees fit.

valence. The premise that behavior is essentially determined by the value of various goal-objects in the field. The concept was employed by Lewin.

validity. The truth or reality of a proposition. In reference to tests or other observational techniques, validity is the extent to which we measure or observe that which we presume we are evaluating.

values. "Built-in" inner systems of beliefs, or ideas that we believe in, from which we can gain security or support.

vector. Term used to denote a line representing the strength and direction of a force.

ventilation. When applied to counseling, it ordinarily refers to encouragement of the client to talk freely and to express his feelings completely.

verbal test. A test that requires verbal responses. Term used interchangeably with the term "language tests."

verbalization. The expression of feelings in words and the process of "talking out."

Vigotsky Test. A test requiring the sorting of a number of different-sized, different-colored, and different-shaped blocks into categories. Requires concept-formation skills.

Vineland Social Maturity Scale. A rating scale of social development which can be administered in an interview with parents or others familiar with a child's development.

visual-motor disturbance. A handicap that shows up in tasks requiring visual-motor co-ordination.

vocabulary test. A measure of the ability of the subject to define or indicate the meaning of a sample of words, from which vocabulary skill can be estimated.

vocational counseling. Procedures designed to aid the client in choosing educational and vocational objectives. Super has stressed that counseling helps the person to ascertain, accept, and apply the relevant facts about himself to the pertinent facts about the occupational world.

voice disorders. Speech that does not conform to standards of volume, pitch, and quality.

voluntary activity. Refers to a movement or direction of attention which is preceded by the idea or the desire to accomplish it.

Wechsler Adult Intelligence Scale. Commonly known as the WAIS. A revision of Form I of the Wechsler-Bellevue. Contains both verbal and performance subtests.

Wechsler-Bellevue Intelligence Examination. This scale has both verbal and performance subtests and was designed in two forms for use with adolescents and adults.

Wechsler Intelligence Scale for Children. Commonly known as the WISC. It is a scale containing verbal and performance items, and was developed and standardized for children. There are 12 subtests that are separately administered. The items are arranged in order of difficulty.

Weltanschauung. A view of the world or a philosophy of life. Usually includes a value system. A viewpoint has to be very inclusive in order to be called a *Weltanschauung*. For example, a religion, democracy, communism, national socialism, is a *Weltanschauung*. Temperance is not, because it pertains to one area only, but it might be the result of a more comprehensive *Weltanschauung*.

will. A conscious drive or impulse by which the individual initiates and controls his activity. The term was used by Rank and believed by him to describe a power present in all persons and developed in his therapy.

will ego. Term used by Rank to describe the intellectual or cognitive aspects of the person.

will-to-power. Term used by Adler to describe the basic driving force of the individual to achieve security and to overcome inferiority.

Wisconsin Card Sorting Test. A measure of ability or skill in forming concepts.

word-association tests. One of the earliest forms of projective personality tests. Words are presented and the subject is asked to associate to these words.

working through. The process of discussing and analyzing feelings and emotional reactions, particularly transference reactions, in order that they may be objectively understood by the client.

World Test. Consists of a large number of small, toylike objects that can be arranged to construct whatever the subject wishes to make with them. The constructions are called "worlds."

Name Index

Page numbers given in **bold face** indicate that the name appears in a bibliography.

Aaron, Solomon, 229, **248**
Aborn, Murray, 422, **431**
Abt, Lawrence E., 496, 528, **529, 529,** 536 n, **555**
Ackerly, S. Spafford, 581 n, **604**
Adams, Clifford R., 482, **489**
Adler, Alfred, 47, 53, 73–5, 78, 116–17, 128–9, 134–5, 164, 654, 662, 664, 667, 670, 677, 682
Adler, Gerhart, 30 n, **40,** 73, **118**
Adler, Morris H., 583, **604**
Adorno, Theodor W., 472, **489**
Ainsworth, Mary D., 536 n, **555**
Alexander, Franz, 30, 35, 37, **40,** 42, 51, 57, **60,** 90, 91 n, 92–4, 116–17, **118,** 145, 151, **160,** 657, 661, 673, 679
Allen, Frederick H., 146–9, **160**
Allen, Robert M., 439, **463,** 536 n, **555**
Allport, Floyd H., 472, 485, **489**
Allport, Gordon W., 310, **347,** 471, 485, **489**
Almada, Albert A., 244, **247**
Alschuler, Rose H., 518–19, **529**
Altus, William D., 422, **430**
Amatruda, Catherine S., 412, **432**
Ammons, Robert B., 528, **529**
Anastasi, Anne, 261, **268,** 426, 429, **430,** 518, **529,** 536 n, **555**
Anderson, A. Lloyd, 439, **463,** 479, **489**
Anderson, Gladys L., 496, **529**
Anderson, Harold H., 496, **529**
Anderson, John E., 390–1, **430**
Andrew, Gwen, 512, **529, 531, 533**
Andriola, Joseph, 619–20, **636**
Appel, Kenneth E., **181,** 374, **384**
Arbuckle, Dugald S., 253, **268**
Armstrong, Mary A. S., 511, **529**
Arthur, Grace, 409–10, **430,** 666
Asher, E. J., 563 n, **575**
Axelrod, Pearl L., 242, **248**
Axelrode, Jeanette, 152, **160**
Axline, Virginia Mae, 101, **118,** 194, **199,** 241 n, 242–3, **245**

Babcock, Harriet, 443, **463**
Bach, George R., 244, **245**
Bache, Joan G., 459, **463**
Bachman, Myra, 619, **636**

Backus, Ollie, 283, **292**
Baer, Max Frank, 258, **268**
Baker, G. Durwood, 588 n, **604**
Balinsky, Benjamin, 250, **268,** 417, 430
Ball, Thomas S., 528, **529**
Barnard, Ruth, 219, **225**
Barten, Mildred Borst, 586 n, **604**
Bayley, Nancy, 413, **430**
Beck, Harry S., 440, **463,** 520–1, **529**
Beck, Samuel J., 536 n, 537, 539–41, 543, 548, **555**
Beers, Clifford W., 16
Beier, Ernest G., 459, **463**
Bell, Hugh M., 483, **490**
Bell, John E., 496, 528, **530,** 536 n, 553, 554 n, **555**
Bellak, Leopold, 13, **21,** 496, 499, 511, 528, **529, 530,** 536 n, **555**
Bellak, Sonya Sorel, 511, **530**
Benarick, Stanley J., 479, **490**
Bender, Lauretta, 137–8, 242–3, **245,** 449, **463**
Bensley, M. L., 458, **465**
Benton, Arthur L., 612, **636**
Berdie, Ralph F., 253, **268,** 411, **430**
Berg, Esta A., 459, **463, 464, 466**
Bernardoni, Louis C., 528, **529**
Bernreuter, Robert G., 483, **490**
Best, Harold L., 523, **530**
Bettleheim, Bruno, 211, **225,** 242, **245**
Betts, Emmett A., 283, **291**
Bierer, Joshua, 229, **246**
Bijou, Sidney W., 586 n, **604**
Bills, Robert E., 484, **490**
Binet, Alfred, 12–13, **21**
Bingham, Walter VanDyke, 354, **384,** 640–1, **650**
Birch, Herbert G., 66, **118**
Bisch, Louis E., 9, **21**
Blain, Daniel, 581 n, **604**
Blos, Peter, 31, **40**
Blum, Gerald S., 511, 513, **530**
Blum, Milton L., 250, **268**
Blum, Richard H., 519, **530**
Bois, J. S. A., 30, **40**
Boland, John L., 280, **291**
Bolgar, Hedda, 515, **530**
Bolles, M. Marjorie, 457, **463**

Bollinger, Dorothy M., 242, **246**
Bond, Eldon A., 400, **430**
Borden, Edward S., 253, **268**
Boring, Edwin G., 14 n, **21**
Borstelman, Lloyd J., 523–4, **530**
Bouthilet, Lorraine, 621, 622 n, **637**
Boyd, Gertrude, **604**
Braceland, Francis J., 233, **246,** 582 n, 584, **604**
Brenman, Margaret, 136, **142**
Breuer, Josef, 121, 128
Brewer, Joseph E., 582 n, **604**
Bridges, J. W., **22**
Briggs, Leslie J., 456
Brill, A. A., 128 n., **142**
Brill, Norman Q., 584, **604**
Brodman, Keeve, 485, **493**
Bronner, Augusta F., 595, **604**
Brown, Donald J., 244, **246**
Brown, J. F., 46–7, **60**
Brown, M. A., 479, **490**
Brown, Spencer F., 279, **292**
Buck, John N., 519–21, **530,** 595, **604**
Buckingham, Burdette R., 387
Buhler, Charlotte, 516, **530, 531**
Burnside, Lenoir H., 588 n, **604**
Buros, Oscar K., 429, **431, 490**
Burton, Arthur, 592–3, **605**

Cadman, William H., 244, **246**
Call, Annie Payson, 141
Cameron, D. Ewen, 131, 142, 163–4, 174 n, 179, **181,** 192–3, **199**
Cameron, Norman, 194, **200,** 458, **464**
Campbell, Helen M., 583, **605**
Camus, Jean, 230, **246**
Canter, Aaron H., 422, **431,** 438, **464,** 479, **490**
Cantor, Joel M., 480, **490**
Carl, George P., 410, **431**
Carrol, Helen Sara, **530**
Carter, Jerry W., 582 n, **605**
Cattell, James McKenn, 12–13, **21**
Cattell, Psyche, 412, **431**
Cattell, Raymond B., 474, 476, 485, **490**
Chalden, Louis S., 275
Challman, Robert C., 584, **604**
Chambers, R. E., 582 n, 584, **607**
Chapman, Alvan L., 253, **269**
Clark, Jerry H., 422, **430,** 480–1, 485, **491**
Clark, Willis W., 482, **493**
Claytor, Mae P., 590, **605**
Cobb, Katharine M., 279, **291**
Cofer, Charles N., 439, **466**
Cohen, R. Robert, 233, **246**
Colvin, S. S., 387

Combs, Arthur W., 99, 101, **120,** 147, **161, 164, 182, 605,** 629 n, 631, **636**
Conn, Jacob H., 176, **181**
Conrad, Herbert S., 487, **491**
Coon, Gaylord P., 439, **465**
Cornell, Ethel L., 409, **431,** 588, **605**
Corsini, Raymond J., 593, **605**
Cosper, Russell, 283, **291**
Courtney, Douglas, 588 n, 589 n, 590 n, **605**
Cowan, Emory L., 459, **464**
Coxe, Warren W., 409, **431**
Cronbach, Lee J., 261, **268,** 386, 392, 393 n, 400, 426, 429, **431,** 470 n, 473, 476, 477, **491**
Crow, Alice, 195, **200**
Crow, Lester D., 195, **200**
Cruickshank, William M., 275, 279, **291**
Cuber, John F., 175, **181**
Culbertson, Eli, 566
Curtis, James F., 279, **292**
Cushman, Jane F., 449, **467**

Danielson, Jack R., 480, 485, **491**
Darley, Frederic L., 309, **347,** 354, 355 n, 356, 358–9, **384**
Darley, John G., 310, **348,** 591, **608**
David, Henry P., 523, **530**
Deane, M. A., 422, **432**
DeHaan, Henry, 422, **434**
Dejerine, Joseph Jules, 230
Denney, Reuel, **160, 200**
Deri, Susan K., 521–3, **530**
Derner, Gordon F., 422, **431**
Diamond, Solomon, 417, 423, **431**
Dieppa, Jorge J., 567, **575**
Doll, Edgar A., 16, 413, 414 n, **431**
Dollard, John, 37, **40,** 102–6, 111, 113, **118,** 132, **142,** 166–7, 173, 178–9, **181,** 187, **200,** 310, **347,** 666
Doppelt, Jerome E., 401, **434**
Dorken, Herbert, 554, **555**
Dottman, Priscilla E., 458, **464**
Dreger, Ralph M., 390, **431**
Dreikurs, Rudolf, 175, **181**
Durkin, Helen E., 150, **160**
Durrell, Donald D., 283, **291**
DuVall, Everett W., 223–4, **225**

Ebaugh, Franklin G., 309, **348**
Ebbinghaus, Hermann, 13, **21,** 524, **530**
Edney, Clarence W., 279, **292**
Eisenson, Jon, 462, **464**
Elkisch, Paula, 518, **530**
Ellis, Albert, 486 n, 487 n, 488, **491,** 629 n, **636**
Emerson, William R. P., 230–1, **246**
Ephron, Beulah K., 283, **291**

Erickson, Clifford E., 253, **269**
Ewalt, Jack R., 309, **348**

Fairbanks, Grant, 279, **291**
Farrand, L., **21**
Feldman, Marvin J., 479, **491**
Fenichel, Otto, **118**
Fenlason, Anne F., 354, **384**
Ferenczi, Sandor, 91–2, 679
Ferguson, George O., 410, **431**
Fernald, Grace M., 283, **291**, 407, **432,**
446, **464**
Fey, Elizabeth T., 457–9, **464**
Fey, William F., 439, **464**
Fischer, Liselotte K., 515, **530**
Fisher, Vivian E., 213 n, **225**, 651
Fiske, Donald W., 565, 570, **575**
Flament, J., 523, **530**
Flanagan, John C., 474, **491**
Fleishman, Martin, 523, **530**
Fleming, Louise, 243, 244 n, **246**
Flory, Charles D., 599, **605**
Foley, John P., 518, **529**
Fontel, M. C., 233, **246**
Forer, Bertram R., 524, **530**
Forrester, Gertrude, 253, **269**
Fosdick, Elsie Sjostedt, vi
Foster, J. C., **22**
Foulkes, Sigmund Heinz, 228, 230, **246**
Frampton, Merle E., 275, **291**
Frandsen, Arden N., 400, 402, 418 n,
431, 440–1, 442 n, **464,** 500–9, 510 n,
531
Frank, Jerome D., 244, **247**
Frank, Lawrence K., 13, **21,** 243, **246,**
496, **531**
Freeman, Frank N., 387, **431**
Freeman, Frank S., 387–8, 426, 429,
431, 470, 473, **491**
Freeman, Max J., 485, **491**
French, Thomas M., **40,** 42, **60,** 90,
91 n, 92–4, 116–17, **118,** 657, 673
Frenkel-Brunswick, Else, 472, **489**
Freud, Anna, 149
Freud, Sigmund, 13, 15, **21,** 27, 47, 53,
68–83, 88, 90–1, 95, 100, 104, 106–
10, 115–16, **118,** 121, 127–8, 134–6,
148, 150, **160,** 164, 197, **200,** 305,
495, 511, 522, **531,** 669, 674
Frohman, Bertrand S., 74, **118**
Frohman, Evelyn P., 74, **118**
Fromm, Erich, 79, 87–8, 91, 197, **200,**
653
Fromm-Reichmann, Frieda, 79, 87–90,
116, **119,** 677
Fry, Clements C., 591, **605**
Fusfeld, Irving S., 275
Futterman, Samuel, 583, **604**

Galanter, Eugene, 521, **531**
Gall, Elena D., 275, **291**
Galton, Francis, 12, 13, 14, **21**
Gardner, Willard, 53, 54 n, **60**
Garfield, Sol L., 422, **431,** 439, **464**
Garrett, Annette, 354, **384**
Garrett, James F., 275
Gates, Arthur I., 283, **291**
Gesell, Arnold, **21,** 412, **431, 432**
Gildea, Margaret, 242, **246**
Gilhooley, Francis M., 422, **432**
Gill, Merton M., 136, **142,** 420, **433,**
467, 500, **532**
Gilliland, A. R., 420, **432**
Glass, Albert J., **142**
Glazer, Nathan, **160, 200**
Goddard, Henry H., 10, 13, 16, **21**
Goldenberg, Herbert C., 514, **531**
Goldenson, Robert M., 243, **246**
Goldman, Nathan, **432**
Goldman, Rosalie, 439, **465**
Goldstein, Kurt, 445–50, 456 n, 457,
463, 464, 680
Goodenough, Florence L., 411, 413,
432, 519, **531**
Gordon, H., 392, **432**
Gordon, Thomas, 592, **605**
Gorlow, Leon, 244, **246**
Gough, Harrison G., 479, **491**
Graham, Clarence H., 485, **493**
Grant, David A., 459, **464, 465, 466**
Grassi, Joseph R., 448, **465**
Greco, Marshall C., 593, **605**
Greenblatt, Milton, 439, **465**
Greene, Edward B., 309, 311, **347,** 473,
491
Greenleaf, Walter J., 259
Grove, William R., 410, **432**
Grummon, Donald L., 592, **605**
Guertin, Wilson H., 426, **433**
Guildford, Joy P., 434, 477, 478 n, 482–
3, **491**
Guilford, Ruth B., 434, 477, 478 n, 482,
491
Gunzburg, Herbert C., 411, **432**
Guthrie, George M., 402, **433,** 479, **490**
Gutman, Brigette, 439, **465**

Hadden, Samuel B., 244, **246**
Hadley, Ernest E., 79, 85, **119**
Hadley, John M., 34, **40,** 50, **60,** 274,
276 n, 524, 526, **531,** 563 n, **575,** 599,
606, 623, **636**
Hahn, Elise, 279, **291**
Hahn, Eugene, 280, **291**
Hahn, Milton E., 253, **269**
Hall, Margaret, 590, **605**
Halpern, Florence, 536 n, **555**

Halstead, Ward C., 445, 450, 462, **465**
Hambrecht, Leona, 222, 223, **225**
Hamilton, Gordon, 207, **225**
Hamister, Richard C., 422, **432**
Hammer, Emanuel F., 521, **531**
Hanes, Bernard, 482, **491**
Hanfmann, Eugenia, 447, 456–7, **465, 466**
Hanvik, Leo J., 479, **488, 491**
Hardwick, R. S., **22**
Harlow, Harry F., 66–7, **119**
Harmon, Lindsey R., 481, **492**
Harms, Ernest, 582 n, **605**
Harris, Albert J., 283, **291**
Harrower, Molly R., 297 n, 298, **307,** 536 n, **555**
Hartley, Ruth E., 243, **246**
Hartshorne, Hugh, 472, **492**
Hartwell, Samuel W., 512, **529, 531, 533**
Hathaway, Starke R., 474, 478–9, **492**
Hattwick, LaBerta Weiss, 518–19, **529**
Havighurst, Robert J., 198, **200**
Hawley, Paul R., 586 n, **605**
Hayman, Max, 449, **465**
Healy, William, 16, 407, **432**
Hebb, Donald O., 445, **465**
Heidbreder, Edna, 458–9, **465**
Heiser, Karl F., **605,** 629 n, **636**
Hendrick, Ives, **119,** 149, **160**
Henri, Victor, **21**
Henry, Nelson B., **291**
Henry, Thomas R., **434**
Herring, John F., 13, **21**
Hertz, Marguerite R., 536
Herzberg, Alexander, 37, **40,** 158, 212, **225**
Hewitt, Helen, 242, **246**
Hewson, Louise R., 439, **465**
Heyns, Roger W., 629 n, **636**
Higginson, Jay B., 402, **431**
Hildreth, Gertrude, 280, **292,** 588 n, **605**
Hilgard, Ernest R., **181,** 213, **225**
Hines, Ruth Baker, vi
Hinsie, Leland E., 128, **142,** 309, **347**
Hirsch, Nathaniel D. M., 392, **432**
Hobbs, Nicholas, 98–9, **119,** 229, 237, 238 n, 239, 245, **246**
Hoch, Erasmus L., 244, **246**
Holt, Robert R., 536 n, **555**
Holzberg, Jules D., 229, **248,** 422, **432,** 584, **605**
Horney, Karen, 79–80, 81 n, 84, 87–8, 95, 116, **119,** 655, 669
Horwitz, Selma, 243, **246**
Hovey, Henry B., 480, **492**
Hoyt, Donald P., 482, **492**
Hubbard, Ruth W., 609, 610 n, **636**

Hull, Clark L., 164–5, 657, 659, 675, 678
Humm, Doncaster G., 474, **492**
Humphreys, J. Anthony, 253, **269**
Hunt, Howard F., 445, **465, 466**
Hunt, J. McV., 439, **466**
Hunt, William A., 17–18, **21,** 422 n, 426, **432,** 489, **492,** 582 n, 584, **604, 606**
Hunter, Margaret, 500–9, 510 n, **531**
Husni, May, 528, **533**
Hutt, Max L., 400, **432,** 495, 512, 526, **529, 531,** 581 n, 584, **606**

Ingham, Harrington V., 122, **142**
Ingle, D. J., 485, **492**
Israel, Harold E., 458, **464**
Ivy, M., 458, **465**

Jackson, C. V., 439, **466**
Jacobsen, Carlyle F., 629 n, **637**
Jacobson, Edmund, 34, **40,** 141, **142**
Janet, Pierre, 121
Janney, J. Elliot, 599, **605**
Jasper, Herbert H., 485, **492**
Jastrow, Joseph, 13, **21**
Johnson, Thomas F., 460, **466**
Johnson, Wendell, 44–5, **60,** 279, 282, **292,** 309, **347,** 354, 355 n, 356, 358–9, **384**
Jones, Arthur J., 195, **200**
Jones, Edward S., 301, **307**
Jones, Maxwell S., 219, **225,** 680
Jones, Omer R., 459, **465**
Juckem, Harriet M., 445, **466**
Jung, Carl Gustav, 47, 53, 71–3, 75, 78, 116, 129, 134, **142,** 652–3, 656, 664, 674–5, 677
Justman, Joseph, 402, **432**

Kahn, David F., 599, **606**
Kantor, Robert E., 439, **467**
Kardiner, Abram, 136, **142**
Kasanin, Jacob, 447, 457, **465, 466**
Katzis, S., 485, **493**
Keaster, Jacqueline, 279, **292**
Kelley, Douglas M., 536 n, **555**
Kelley, Truman L., 524, **531**
Kelly, E. Lowell, 565, 570, **575**
Kelly, Gayle, **530**
Kelly, George A., vi, 49, 50 n, **60,** 155, 156, **160,** 315, **348,** 360 n, 361, 368, **384,** 578, **606,** 629 n, **637,** 640–1, **650**
Kelly, Robert L., 13, **21**
Kennedy, Vera E., 524, **531**
Kent, Grace H., 410, **433**
Kephart, Newell C., 275, **292**
Key, Cora B., **434**

Kinder, Elaine F., 586 n, 595, **606**
King, W., 457, **466**
Kinne, Everett W., 283, **292**
Kinsey, Alfred C., 354, 355 n, 358, **384**
Kirk, Samuel A., 275
Kirkpatrick, Edwin A., 13, **21**
Kitson, Harry D., 253, **269**
Klapman, Jacob W., 228 n, 229, 232–6, 245, **246,** 666
Klopfer, Bruno, 536 n, 537, 539, 541, **555**
Klopfer, Walter G., 244, **246,** 523–4, **530,** 536 n, **555**
Kluckhohn, Clyde, 43 n, 44, **61**
Knapp, Robert H., 253, **269**
Knight, Frederick B., vi
Kohler, Wolfgang, 65–6, 101, 164, **181**
Konopka, Gisela, 242, **246, 247**
Korzybski, Alfred, 45, **60**
Kotkov, Benjamin, 229, **247**
Kottmeyer, William, 283, **292**
Kraines, Samuel H., 136, **142,** 175 n, **181,** 191, 192 n, 199, **200**
Kraus, P. Stefan, 222, **225**
Kriedt, Philip H., 570, **575**
Kris, Ernst, 511
Krout, Maurice H., 485, **492**
Krugman, Judith I., 402, **432**
Krugman, Morris, 402, **432,** 588 n, **606**
Kuder, G. Frederic, 263, **269,** 485, **492**
Kuhlman, Frederick, 13, **22**
Kumin, Edith, 410, **435**
Kutash, Samuel B., 583, **606**

Laing, Louise D., 155, **160**
Lam, Robert L., 440, **463**
Landis, Carney, 449, **467,** 485, **493**
Landsman, Theodore, 629 n, **637**
Law, Stanley G., 29, 30 n, 35 n, **40,** 602 n, **606**
Lazarus, Richard S., 216, **225,** 309–10, **348**
Lazell, Edward W., 232, 234, **247**
Lefever, David W., 195, **200**
Lehner, George F. J., 479, **493**
Lehtinen, Laura E., 275, **292**
Lepley, William M., 482, **489**
Levi, V., 439, **466**
Levine, Louis S., 422, **433**
Levine, Maurice, 136, 139, **142**
Levine, Murray, 521, **531**
Levinson, Daniel J., 472, **489**
Levy, David M., 122, 133–5, 138, **142,** 536
Levy, John, 146, 150
Levy, Lydia, 443, **463**
Lewin, Kurt, 6, **22,** 45 n, 46, 50–1, 61, 164, 169–70, 178, **182,** 198, **200,** 300,

Lewin, Kurt (*continued*)
307, 310, **348,** 522, 653, 661, 667, 680–1
Lewinski, Robert J., 444, **466**
Lewis, Nolan D. C., 309, **348, 384**
Little, Harry M., 242, **247**
Little, Kenneth B., 479, **493**
Little, Wilson, 253, **269**
Lotsof, Antoinette B., 525, **532**
Louttit, C. M., 9 n, 17, **22,** 309, **348,** 484, **492,** 582, **606**
Love, Lenore R., 122, **142**
Low, Abraham A., 229, 233, **247**
Lowenfeld, Margaret, 14, **22,** 515–16, **531,** 553, **555**
Lowrey, Lawson G., 311–12, **348**
Luchins, Abraham S., 244, **247,** 459–60, **466,** 659
Luchins, Edith H., 459, **466**
Lumry, Gayle K., **530**
Lynn, David B., 517–18, **531,** 679
Lynn, Rosalie, 517–18, **531**
Lyon, Janet M., 516, **531**

Machover, Karen, 519, **531**
Macfarlane, Jean W., 629 n, **637**
MacLean, Malcolm S., 253, **269**
MacMurray, Donald A., 409, **433**
Madan, S. K., 528, **532**
Magaret, Ann, 444, 459, **466**
Magoon, Thomas M., 482, **492**
Maller, Julius B., 471 n, 472, 473, **492**
Malone, Thomas P., 219, **225**
Marsh, L. Cody, 231, **247**
Martin, Clyde E., 354, 355 n, 358, **384**
Martin, Howard G., 474, 482, **491, 492**
Martin, Robert M., 363–5, **384**
Maslow, Abraham H., 217, **225**
Masserman, Jules H., 207, **225**
Matthews, W. Mason, 582 n, **606**
Maurer, Katherine M., 413, **432**
May, Mark A., 472, **492**
May, Rollo, 198, **200**
Mayforth, Frances, **292**
McBride, Katherine E., 445, 461, **468**
McCann, Willis H., 230, 244, **247**
McCary, James L., 145, 159, **160**
McClosky, Herbert, 479, **491**
McCullough, Betsey R., 400, **431**
McDougall, William, 164, **182**
McFarland, Ross A., 485, **492**
McGeoch, John A., 66 n, 67, **119**
McKay, L. A., 233–4, **247**
McKinley, J. Charnley, 474, 478, **492**
McKinney, Fred, 591–2, **606**
McLean, Orison S., 484, **490**
McNally, Harold J., 588 n, **606**
McNemar, Quinn, 399, **433**

Meehl, Paul E., 474, 477 n, 479, 481, **491, 492**
Menninger, Karl, 274, **292**
Menninger, Willam C., 221, **225**, 298, 299 n, **307**, 581 n, **606**, 613 n, **637**
Merrill, Maude A., 13, **22**, 396–8, 399 n, **434**
Merton, Robert, 197, **200**, 652
Meyer, Adolf, 674
Meyerson, Abraham, 218, **225**
Michael, J. C., 516, **531**
Michaels, Joseph J., 583, **604**
Miles, Walter R., **606**, 629 n, **637**
Miller, Eleanor O., 448, **467**
Miller, Neal E., 37, **40**, 102–6, 111, 113, **118**, 132, **142**, 166–7, 173, 178–9, **181**, 187, **200**, 666
Miller, Wilford S., 427, **433**
Mills, Bariss, 283, **291**
Milton, E. Ohmer, 584, **606**
Misbach, Lorenz, 244, **246**
Mittelmann, Bela, 217, **225**, 485, **493**
Monachesi, Elio D., 474, **492**
Monroe, Jack J., 420–1, 422 n, **433**
Monroe, Marion, 283, **292**
Monroe, Ruth L., 536 n, **555**
Moore, Bruce V., 354, **384**, 621, 622 n, **637**
Moreno, Jacob L., 133, 135, **142**, 229, 232, 240–2, 245, **247**, 674, 678
Morgan, Christiana D., 14, **22**, 497, **531**
Morgan, Clifford T., 460, **467**
Morley, Muriel E., 279, **292**
Morris, Charles M., 409, **433**
Mosier, Charles I., 476 n, 479, **493**
Mowrer, O. Hobart, 37, **40**, 43 n, 44, 52, **61**, 106–14, **119**, 166–8, 173, 178- 9, **182**, 187, 197, **200**, 673, 677, 681
Mullahy, Patrick, 80, 83 n, 84–5, **119**, 128, **142, 182**
Murray, Henry A., 14, **22**, 497–9, **531, 532**
Mursell, James L., 387, 426, 429, **433**
Myers, George E., 253, **269**

Napoli, Peter J., 519, **532**
Newcomb, Theodore M., **200**
Newton, Juna Barnes, 253, **269**
Nielsen, Johannes M., 461, **467**
Noller, Paul A., 402, **435**
Nuttin, Joseph, 128 n, **143**, 198, **200**

Odbert, Henry S., 471, **489**
O'Keefe, Daniel E., 581 n, **606**
Oppenheim, Sadi V., 439, **466**
Orne, Martin, 523, **530**
Ort, Robert S., 189 n, 190. **200**

O'Shea, Harriet E., 592, **606**
Overstreet, Phoebe, 458, **465**

Page, James D., 215, **225**, 485, **493**
Pagniez, Phillippe, 230, **246**
Papanek, Ernest, 241, **247**
Parsons, Talcott, 197, **200**
Pastovic, John J., 402, **433**
Paterson, Donald G., 407, 408 n, **433**, 623, **637**
Patterson, Cecil H., 419, 422–3, **433**
Paunz, Arpad, 219, **225**
Payne, A. F., 524, **532**
Pearson, Gerald H. J., 176, **182**
Pearson, Karl, 14
Peatman, John Gray, 629 n, **637**
Pennington, Leon A., 449, **467**, 584, **606**
Pepinsky, Harold B., 194, **200**, 253, **269**
Pepinsky, Pauline N., 194, **200**, 253, **269**
Peterson, Joseph, 387
Phillips, Leslie, 536 n, **555**
Pintner, Rudolf, 407, 408 n, **433**
Piotrowski, Zygmunt A., 449, 455, **467**, 536
Pomeroy, Wardell B., 354, 355 n, 358, **384**
Porteus, Stanley D., 16, **433**
Powdermaker, Florence B., 244, **247**
Pratt, Joseph H., 229–31, 234, **247**
Pratt, Stephen H., vi, 470, 474–8, 483, **493**
Pressey, Sidney L., 392, **433**
Preu, Paul W., 312, **348**
Ptacek, James E., 448, **467**

Quay, Herbert, 480, **493**

Rabin, Albert I., 420, 426, **433**
Rabinowitz, William, 523, **530**
Rafferty, Janet E., 525, **532**
Raimey, Victor C., 616 n, 617, **637**
Rank, Otto, 75–8, 95, 116–17, **119**, 130, 135, **143**, 146, 148, 654, 664, 682
Rapaport, Anatol, 45, **61**
Rapaport, David, 420, **433**, 438, 447, 455, 457, **467**, 500, **532**, 586 n, **606**
Rashkis, Harold A., 449, **467**
Raus, George M., 279, **291**
Raven, John C., 428, **433**
Recktenwald, Lester N., 253, **269**
Redl, Fritz, 229, 242, **247**
Reichard, Suzanne, 455, **467**
Remmers, Hermann H., 472, **493**
Reynell, Walter R., 439, **467**
Ribback, Beatrice Barrett, vi, 65–118, 127, 146–50

Richards, Thomas W., 7, **22,** 303, **307,** 654

Riesman, David, 145, **160,** 197, **200**

Riggs, Austin, 177, 216

Rober, Edward C., 258, **268**

Roberts, Glen E., 484, **493**

Robinson, J. Franklin, 582 n, **606**

Rogers, Carl R., 15–16, **22,** 37, **40,** 95 n, 96–101, 102 n, 117, **119,** 136–7, **143,** 146, 193–4, **200,** 237, 310 n, **348,** 350, **384,** 484, **493,** 572, 574, 576, 651, 655, 670–1

Rogers, Lawrence S., 422, **433,** 439, **467**

Rorschach, Hermann, 14, **22,** 536 n, 537, 539–41, **556**

Rosebrook, Wilda A., 588 n, **607**

Rosenzweig, Saul, 12, **22,** 499, 528, **532**

Rostow, Edna G., 591, **605**

Rotter, Julian B., 153, 154 n, 160, **161,** 163, 170, 172, 173 n, 176, 178, **182,** 186–7, 199, **200,** 498, 500, 525, 528, **532**

Rowell, John T., 480, **493**

Rubenstein, Ben, 242, **247**

Rubin, Harold, 521, **532**

Ruesch, Jurgen, 187–8, **200,** 651, 678

Rylander, Gösta, 445, **467**

Saffir, Milton A., 629 n, **637**

Salter, Andrew, 132–3, 135, **143**

Sanderson, Herbert Z., 253, **269**

Sanford, Fillmore H., 578 n, **607,** 612, 629 n, **637**

Sanford, R. Nevitt, 48, **61,** 472, **489**

Sarason, Seymour B., **292,** 595, **607**

Sargent, Helen D., 525, 526 n, **532**

Saunders, David R., 474, **490**

Saxe, Carl H., 229, **248**

Schachtitz, Eva, 525, **532**

Schafer, Roy, 420, **433, 467,** 500, **532,** 536 n, **556**

Scheerer, Martin, 446–9, 456 n, **464**

Scheibel, A. B., 582 n, 584, **607**

Schilder, Paul, **143,** 230, 233, 239, **247**

Schiller, P. H., 66, **119**

Schlosser, John R., 439, **467**

Schmidl, Fritz, 619, **637**

Schott, Emmet L., 586 n, **607**

Schramm, Theodore A., 402, **435**

Schwartz, M. W., 220, **225, 226**

Schwesinger, Gladys C., 391, **433**

Schwiering, O. C., **604**

Seashore, Harold G., 401, **434**

Seidenfeld, Morton A., 586 n, **607**

Seitz, Clifford P., 485, **492**

Shaffer, G. Wilson, 216, **225,** 309–10, **348**

Shaffer, Laurance F., 48 n, **61,** 113–14, **119,** 121, 132, **143,** 488 n, 580, 581 n, **607,** 610–11, **637**

Shakow, David, 410, **432,** 617, **637**

Shartle, Carroll L., 258, **269**

Shaskan, Donald A., 228, **248**

Shaw, Franklin J., 37, **40,** 113–14 **120,** 170, 171 n, 172, 178, **182,** 187, 189 n, 190, 199, **200,** 651, 669

Sherman, Mandel, 391, **433**

Shipley, Walter C., 444, **467,** 485, **493**

Shneidman, Edwin S., 514, **532**

Shoben, Edward J., 37, **40,** 48, 52, **61,** 113–14, **120,** 627–8, **637**

Shuttleworth, K., 472, **492**

Silance, Ella B., 472, **493**

Simon, Benjamin, 229, **248**

Simon, Theodore, 12, **21**

Simpson, Mary M., 444, **466**

Slavson, Samuel R., 130–1, **143,** 229, 236 n, 237, 241–2, 245, **248,** 651

Sloan, William, 521, **532**

Smith, F. V., 528, **532**

Smith, Geddes, 582, **607**

Smith, Joseph G., 536 n, **555**

Smoke, Kenneth L., 455, 457, **467**

Snyder, William U., 243, 244 n, **246,** 479, **490**

Snygg, Donald, 99, 101, **120,** 147, **161,** 164, **182**

Solomon, Joseph C., 134, **143**

Spearman, Charles Edward, 389, **434**

Spears, Ethel M., 596, **607**

Spiegel, Herbert, 136, **142**

Spriestersbach, Duane C., 309, **347,** 354, 355 n, 356–9, **384**

Stanton, Alfred H., 220, **225, 226**

Stauffacher, James C., 480, **492**

Stegman, Erwin J., vi, 121–3, 127–41

Stein, Morris I., 305 n, **307,** 499, **532**

Stellar, Eliot, 460, **467**

Stern, William, 12, **22,** 386, **434**

Stevens, Peter, 586 n, **607**

Stevenson, George S., 582, **607**

Stevenson, Iris, 422 n, 426, **432,** 489, **492**

Stevenson, W. O., 484, **493**

Stewart, Kathleen K., 242, **248**

Stice, Glenn, 474, **490**

Stoddard, George D., 388, 400, **434**

Stone, David R., 400, **431,** 528, **532**

Strauss, Alfred A., 275, **292,** 446

Strecker, Edward A., 309, **348,** 374, **384**

Strong, Edward K., 261–2, **269,** 472, **493**

Stutsman, Rachel, 413, **434**

Sullivan, Harry Stack, 79, 83 n, 84–91, 95, 116, **120,** 148, 354, **384,** 671, 674

Sullivan, Louise A., 242 n, **248**

Super, Donald E., 253, **269, 637,** 681
Sylvester, Emmy, 211, **225**
Symonds, Percival M., 588 n, **607**
Szollosi, Etienne, 523, **530**
Szondi, Lipot, 521–3, **532**

Taba, H., **200**
Tabin, Johanna K., 485, **492**
Taft, Jessie, 146, 148 n, **161**
Taft, Ronald, 597, **607**
Talantis, Billie Sue, 459, **465**
Tallman, Gladys, 586 n, **607**
Taylor, Janet A., 482, **493**
Taylor, Joseph L., 584, **605**
Teicher, Arthur, 584, **605**
Telschow, Earl F., 244, **246**
Terman, Lewis M., 12–13, **22,** 387, 396–8, 399 n, **434**
Thayer, V. T., 588 n, **607**
Thomas, J. B., 392, **433**
Thompson, George C., 459, **464**
Thompson, Helen, 412, **432**
Thorndike, Edward L., 66, 387, 389, **434**
Thorne, Frederick C., 11, **22,** 56–8, **61,** 137, 139, 141, **143,** 150 n, 154–5, 157, 160, **161,** 190, 191 n, 199, **200,** 312, 315, **348,** 569 n, **576,** 678
Thorpe, Louis P., 482, **493**
Thurstone, Louis L., 387, 389, 427, **434,** 472, 485, **493**
Thurstone, Thelma G., 427, **434,** 485, **493**
Tiffin, Joseph, 627, **637**
Tillotson, Kenneth J., 218, **226**
Timm, Oreon K., 584, **606**
Tolman, Edward C., 168–71, **182,** 656, 667, 677
Tomkins, Silvan S., 499, **532**
Trabue, Marion R., 524, **533**
Travis, Lee Edward, 279, **292,** 309, **348**
Traxler, Arthur E., 253, **269**
Triggs, Frances O., 283, **292**
Turrell, A. M., 195, **200**
Tyler, Fred T., 479, **493**
Tyler, Leona E., 253, **269**

Valenstein, Arthur F., 583, **604**
Vance, Edgar L., 484, **490**
Van Fleet, Phyllis, 243, **248**
Van Riper, Charles, 279, 282, **292,** 309, 311, **348**
Van Wagenen, M. J., 413, **432**
Verniaud, Willie M., 481, **493**
Vernon, Phillip E., 472, 485, **489**
Vigotsky, L. S., 447, 456, **467**
Vinacke, W. Edgar, 456–7, **467**
Viteles, Morris S., 597, **607**

Wadsworth, Guy W., 474, **492**
Wallin, J. E. Wallace, 21, **292**
Walton, Ralph E., 512, **529, 531, 533**
Wang, Charles K. A., 485, **493**
Warters, Jane, 253, **269**
Washburne, Annette C., 591–2, **607**
Watkins, John G., 139, **143**
Watson, Goodwin B., 485, **493**
Watson, Robert I., 16 n, **22, 120,** 204, 208, 211, **226,** 426, **434,** 578 n, **607,** 610, 614, **638,** 642, **650**
Webb, Robert, 583, **604**
Webb, Wilse B., 420, 422, **434,** 438, **467**
Wechsler, David, 13, **22,** 303, **307,** 388, 401, 416–17, 420, **434, 435,** 438–9, 450, **466, 467,** 485, **493,** 586 n, **607**
Weider, Arthur, 402, **435,** 485, **493,** 596, 597 n, **607**
Weisenberg, Theodore H., 445, 461, **468**
Weisskopf-Joelson, Edith, 197, **200,** 459–60, **468,** 500, **533**
Weitzel, H. I., 195, **200**
Wellman, P., **432**
Wells, Fred Lyman, 386, **435,** 586 n, **608**
Wender, Louis, 230, 232–3, **248**
Wendt, G. R., 629 n, **638**
Wepman, Joseph M., 279, **292,** 461 n, 462, **465, 468**
Werner, Heinz, 446
Wertham, Fredric, 553, **556**
Wertheimer, Max, 164, **182**
Wesman, Alexander G., 401, **434**
Westburgh, Edward M., 17, **22**
Wexler, Samuel, 525, **533**
Wheeler, William M., 479, **493**
Wheeler, John I., 440, **468**
White, Robert W., 446, **468,** 497, 517, **533**
White, William Alanson, 79, 232
Wickes, Thomas A., vi, 357, **384**
Wiener, Daniel N., 481, **492, 494,** 608, 629 n, **638**
Wilkins, Walter L., 440, **468**
Willerman, Benjamin, 525, **532**
Williamson, Edmund G., 249, 253, 254 n, **269,** 310, **348,** 591, **608**
Wilmer, Harry A., 528, **533**
Wilson, J. Watson, 488, **494**
Wineman, David, **247**
Winfield, Don L., 445, **468**
Winne, John F., 479, **494**
Wischner, George J., 282, **292**
Witmer, Lightner, 16, **22**
Witsaman, Leslie R., 525, **533**
Wittenberg, Rudolf M., 243, **248**
Wittenborn, J. Richard, 422, **435**
Wittman, Phyllis, 586 n, **608**

Wolberg, Lewis R., 141, **143,** 158, 160, **161**
Wold, Jane A., 445, **466**
Wolfe, Alexander, 230, 239–40, 245, **248**
Wolff, Harold G., 485, **493**
Wolfle, Dael, 629 n, **638**
Woltmann, Adolf G., 243, **248**
Wood, Louise, 410, **435**
Woodworth, Robert S., 473, **494,** 672
Wright, David G., 436, **468**
Wright, Glenn E., 455–7, **468**

Wright, M. Eric, 444, **468**
Wrightstone, J. Wayne, 402, **432**

Yerkes, Robert M., 13, **22**
Young, Florene M., 448, **467,** 629 n, **638**

Zaslow, Robert W., 449, **468**
Zehrer, Frederick A., 582 n, 584, 588 n, **607, 608**
Zeran, Franklin R., 259
Zimmerman, Wayne S., 474, 482, **491**

Subject Index

ability, 387–8, 651
abnormal, 10, 651
abreaction, 70, 76, 92, 129, 651
abstract, 651; intelligence, 388
abstraction, 47, 446–9, 454–9
acceptance, 98, 651; of disability, 275
acculturation, 84, 188–9, 651
achievement, 651; tests of, 261
acting out, 69–70, 138, 242, 651
active therapy, 231, 651; through play, 134
activity-group procedures, 130–1, 236–7, 242, 651
adaptive, 388; behavior, 651; interaction, 189, 651
adjustment, 26, 44, 651·
advice, 50, 156–7, 651
affect, 651; therapy, 133, 651; reactions, 70, 368
agency reports, 314
aggression, 63–4, 68, 651
agnosia, 461, 651
agnosticism, 372, 651
Alcoholics Anonymous, 230, 233, 651–2
alexia, 652
Allport-Vernon Value Scale, 485
ambitions, 366, 652
ambivalence, 188, 376, 652
amelioration, 56–7, 652
American Board of Examiners in Professional Psychology, 561, 601, 620, 630
American Psychiatric Association, 580–1
American Psychological Association, 275, 652; Ad Hoc Committee on Relations between Psychology and the Medical Profession, 582, 600–1, 611–12; and the mental hygiene team, 580–2; Committee on Training in Clinical Psychology, 12, 562; Committee on Training in Counseling Psychology, 562, 621; Denver annual meeting, 616; distribution of membership in sections, 578–9; Education and Training Board, 12, 562; Section on Clinical Psychology, 10, 12, 621–2
amnesia, 184, 652

amplification, 73, 652
anal, 652; erotism, 652
analysis, 10–11, 652
Analytic Psychology, 30, 47, 71–3, 652
anamnesis, 300–2, 308–47, 652
anamnestic analysis, 72, 652
anecdotal, 652
anger, 370–1
anima, 46, 652
anomaly, 652
anomie, 197–8, 652
anthropology, 44, 80, 652
anxiety, 106, 113, 124–5, 369, 652; neurosis, 652; reaction, 13, 186
apathy, 652
aphasia, 460–2, 652
apperception, 652
apprehension, 652
a priori validation, 473–4, 652
aptitude, 653; tests, 261
archaic memories, 71
archetypes, 71, 653
Aristotelian, 45, 51, 653
art, 17, 653; vs. science, 53–4
Arthur Point Scale of Performance Tests, 409–10, 653
articulatory disorders, 276–7, 653
A–S Reaction Study, 485
assessment, v–vi, 295–6, 300–2, 653
association, 12, 67, 653
atheism, 372, 653
athetosis, 653
attention, 12, 653; disturbance in, 446; span, 405, 418, 653
attitudes, 7, 27, 41, 653
authoritarian, 653
autism, 85, 653
autonomic nervous system, 653
autonomous man, 197–8, 653
avocational, 327, 653

Babcock-Levy Scale of Intellectual Efficiency, 443–4
barrier, 169, 367, 653
basal age, 398
behavior, 59–60, 643–5, 653; changes in, v–vi, 5, 27, 41; conflict a component of, 44; control of, 8; defined, 6,

behavior (*continued*)
9–11, 655; disorders of, 653; evaluation of, 296–8, 645–6; field-theoretical aspects of, 6; functional aspects of, 43; in relation to field, 44; postulates concerning, 163–4; resultant of force system, 51; total, 27, 296–7
Bell Adjustment Inventory, 483–4, 653
Bender Gestalt Test, 449, 654
Bernreuter Personality Inventory, 483, 654
bias, 18, 654
bibliotherapy, 230
biographical, 654
biological memories, 74, 654
birth trauma, 75–6, 654
Blacky Test, 511, 513–14, 654
Boulder Conference, 616–18
brain damage, 343–5, 436–455, 654
breech presentation, 654

California First Year Mental Scale, 413, 654
California Mental Health Analysis, 482, 654
capacity, 303, 654
Carl Hollow Square Scale, 410, 654
case history, 300–1, 308–47, 654
case study, 19, 300–6, 349, 654
case-study method, 19–20, 310, 620, 654
catatonic reactions, 184–5, 654
catharsis, 31, 57, 122, 128, 655
cathexis, 305, 655
Cattell Developmental and Intelligence Scale, 412–13, 655
cerebral cortex, 462, 655
cerebral palsy, 274–5, 655
cerebrum, 445, 462, 655
certification, 561, 629–35, 655
character, 472, 655; neuroses, 80–3, 655; structure, 80–1
Chestnut Lodge Sanitarium, 220
child guidance, 207–8; clinics, 582–3, 655
Children's Apperception Test, 511–12, 655
chorea, 655
chronological age, 12, 398–9, 655
classification board, 593–5
class theory, 44, 51, 655; contrasted with field theory, 46–7
claustrophobia, 370, 655
client, 602–3, 655; -centered counseling, 16, 37, 52, 95, 238–9, 655; -centeredness, 7, 53, 572
clinical and counseling psychology, 655; activities and subjects, 8; aims of, 8,

clinical and counseling psychology (*continued*)
25; and education, 625–6; and industrial psychology, 626–7; functions of, 8–9; history of, 11–12; and interpersonal relationships, 620–3; knowledges of, 7; practical art, 17–18; and psychiatric social work, 617–23; qualifications for, 559–75; relationship to law, 627–8; relationship to religion, 628–9; scientific approach in, 18, 642–5; theories in, 19; training for, 560–5; and vocational and educational guidance, 623–5
coercion, 59, 157–8, 191, 656
cognitive learning theories, 165–74, 656
collective unconscious, 71–3, 656
color shock, 544–5, 656
coma, 656
communication, 131–2, 362–5, 656
comparative psychology, 65–8, 656
compensation, 37, 73, 273–4, 656
complex, 656
compulsion, 186, 373, 545–6, 656
concentration, 289
concept, 656; formation, 455–9
conceptual quotient, 444, 656
concrete, 446–9, 656; intelligence, 388
conditioning, 37, 107, 167–8, 656
confabulation, 544, 656
confession, 121, 136
confidant, 656
confidentiality, 324, 351–2
conflict, 44, 51, 70, 72, 370, 656
congenital, 656
conscious, 46, 656
consensual validation, 85
constancy of intelligence, 390–2, 656
construct, 105, 657
contiguity, 107, 167–8
control, 52, 140–1, 385, 572, 657
controlled association, 13, 63, 657
controlled observation, 18–20, 643–5, 657
conversion, 183–4, 545, 657
convulsion, 657
Cornell-Coxe Performance Ability Scale, 409, 657
Cornell Selectee Index, 485
corrective emotional experience, 92–5, 657
cortical, 460–2, 657
counseling, 657; and clinical psychology, 620–3; contrasted with guidance, 623; final goal of, 26–7; function of the professional psychologist, 563; in the Veterans Administration, 621–3; planning of, 54–6

countertransference, 112, 657
cretinism, 657
cross-validation, 19–20, 645, 657
cues, 66–7, 102–6, 166–7, 170–1, 187–8, 657
culture, 79, 183, 187–9, 197–8, 391–2, 657
cure, 28, 572–3, 657
cycloid, 550, 657
cynicism, 372, 658

deduction, 111, 642–3, 658
deep therapy, 31, 658
defense, 658
definition of the problem, 31, 41, 658
delirium, 658
delusion, 186, 375, 658
dependency reactions, 34, 658
depression, 186, 367–8, 658
depth psychology, 658
description, 302–4
desensitization, 131–2
deterioration, 436–40, 658
development, 309, 658; history of, 19, 300–1, 339–46, 658; in reading, 282–3, 658
diagnosis, 658; aim of, 38, 296–9, 615; psychodynamic origins, 12; psychometric origins, 12
diagnostic interview, 349–84
dialectical process, 73, 658
Dictionary of Occupational Titles, 258–9, 658
differentiation, 99, 101
Digit Symbol Test, 419–20, 423–5, 439, 441–3, 658
dilution therapy, 136
Diplomate, 561, 658
directive techniques, 56–8, 190–3, 659
dislikes, 371
dissociation, 109, 659
distraction, 289, 659
diversional therapy, 158–9, 659
Doctor of Philosophy Degree, 560–2, 659
doll play, 138, 176
dominance, 346, 659
drawing and painting techniques, 518–21
dreams, 69, 72–4, 373–4
drives, 128, 166–7, 187–8, 659; basic or primary, 79, 102–3, 107, 166–7; learned or secondary, 102–3, 107, 166–7; reduction of, 103–4, 165, 659
dynamic, 659; assumptions of theory, 43; evaluation of factors, 302–5; force system, 51, 169; recent trends in theory, 53

eclecticism, 659
ecology, 659
educational, 659; counseling, 59, 194–5; guidance, 194–5, 588, 623–5; history, 19, 300–1, 325–32, 659; psychology, 625–7
ego, 31, 37, 46, 57, 68, 73, 89, 91, 106–7, 659
Einstellung, 459, 659
emotion, 32, 130, 659; disturbances of, 183–6, 659; integration of, 90; release of, 32–4, 48, 56, 60, 121, 142, 223, 659
empathic identification, 98, 659
empathy, 84, 660
empirical validation, 474, 660
enablement, 271–2, 660
environmental, 18, 80; factors, 45, 660; field, 299–300, 660; manipulation, 50–1, 56, 151–2, 175–7, 204–24, 619, 660; modification, 60, 204, 646–7, 660; treatment, 29, 55–6, 184, 203–25, 227, 660
epilepsy, 547, 660
erotic, 376, 660
essence, 44, 51, 660
ethics, 599–601, 630, 660
etiology, 660
euphoria, 368, 660
evaluation, 5–6, 25, 41–2, 563, 585; definition of, 295–6, 660; descriptive, 302–5; future trends in, 645–6, 648–9; history of, 12–14; of dynamics of behavior, 302–5; of management in business and industry, 598–9; of mentally retarded, 595–6; of potentialities and resources, 302–4; philosophy of, 295–306; purposes of, 5, 25–40, 295–6
exercise, 33
exhortation, 50, 660
expectancy, 153, 167–74, 186–7
experimental, 51, 638–50; controls, 18, 660; neuroses, 207; psychology, 14–15, 564
explanation, 56
expressive therapy, 139–40
extinction, 37, 103–6, 132, 660
extratensive, 183–4, 660
extrinsic, 660
extroversion, 185, 570

factor analysis, 474, 660
faculty psychology, 46, 660
familial resemblance, 390–1
family history, 19, 300–1, 333–9, 660
fantasy, 84, 374, 661
"father of clinical psychology," 16
"father of individual differences," 12

fears, 369–70
feelings, 368, 661; of difference, 273; of inferiority, 74–5
Ferguson Form Boards, 410, 661
fetishism, 661
field, 44–5, 661; forces, 44, 49–51, 163–4, 169, 661; post-Galilean theory, 53; -theoretical view of behavior, vi, 59; -theoretical view of learning, 168–9; theory and counseling, 49, 59; theory, 44–5, 169, 295–6, 661; vs. analytical concepts, 46–9; vs. class-theoretical concepts, 46–8
figure-ground relationships, 99, 101, 446, 661
first psychological clinic, 16
fixation, 78, 661
fixed ideas, 661
flaccid paralysis, 661
flexible therapy, 93, 661
follow-up, 585
force system, 49–51, 59–60, 661
foreconscious, 46, 661
formal records, 314
Fort Ord Inventory, 485
foster home, 208–9
frame of reference, 19, 42, 661
fraternal twins, 391, 661
free association, 12, 63, 77, 82, 89, 98, 103, 136, 661; on the Rorschach, 537
Freudian analytical theory, 68–71, 127–8, 150–1
frustration, 367, 661
fugue, 184, 661
functional disorder, 183–6, 661
functioning intelligence, 386, 388, 548, 661

generalization, 104, 662
genetic approach, 88–90
genital, 662
genotype, 14, 662
Gesell Developmental Schedules, 412, 662
Gestalt learning theory, 65–8, 111
Gestalt psychology, 44, 65–8, 662
global intelligence, 388, 662
goals, 89, 102–4, 164, 169, 662
Goodenough Drawing Test, 411–12, 662
grand mal, 662
Grassi Block Substitution Test, 448, 662
group counseling, 36, 58, 60, 227–45, 585, 662; evaluation of, 244; in industrial relations, 597–8; in the future, 646–9; psychoanalytical, 239–40

group-factor theory of intelligence, 389, 662
group-study approach, 627
group tests, 395, 426–9, 662
growth, 44, 146–8, 662; principle, 96–102, 662
guidance, 26, 591–2, 662
guiding fictions, 128–9, 662
Guilford Tests, 482–3, 662
guilt, 63, 82–3, 109–12, 130, 372, 662

habit, 168, 663
hallucinations, 186, 374–5, 663
hebephrenia, 186, 663
hereditary factors, 312
heterosexual, 376, 663
hierarchy of response, 66, 663
higher mental processes, 105, 167, 663
homeostasis, 92, 663
homosexuality, 376–7, 663
hostility, 370–1, 663
House-Tree-Person Test, 519–21, 663
human engineering, 663
Humm-Wadsworth Temperament Scale, 485
Hunt-Minnesota Test for Organic Brain Damage, 445
hydrocephalus, 663
hydrotherapy, 141, 663
hypnosis, 136, 663
hypochondriasis, 375–6, 663
hypothesis, 20, 41, 641, 663
hysteria, 36–7, 128, 545, 663

id, 46, 68, 70, 106–7, 663
ideas of reference, 663
identical twins, 391, 663
identification, 144, 663
Illinois Institute for Juvenile Research, 16, 21
illusion, 663
image, 663
imagination, 12, 663
impotence, 664
impulse, 128, 130; ego, 130, 664
Index of Adjustment and Values, 484, 664
individual, 664; counseling, 7–8, 59, 585; differences, 12, 623–5; psychology, 73–5, 664; -study approach, 5, 6, 598–9, 627, 664; tests, 395, 664; totality, 71
individuality, 77
individuation, 71, 77, 148, 664
induction, 111, 664
infant developmental scales, 412–16
infantile, 664; conflicts, 68–71; sexuality, 69–73, 664

inference, 301, 664
inferiority feelings, 73–5, 664
informant, 318–20, 326, 331, 334, 340, 344, 664
inhibition, 372–3, 664
initiating power, 76, 664
innate, 664; ego motive, 73–5
inquiry, 537–8, 664
insight, 29–32, 60–118, 133–4, 149–50, 166, 205, 223, 367, 665; and problem solving, 56–7; as a curative power, 89; examples of, 63–5; in client-centered counseling, 95–102; in comparative psychology, 65–8; in Gestalt psychology, 30–1, 66–8; in psychoanalysis, 29–32, 68–95; not always desirable, 65; promotion of, 31, 62
instinct, 75, 665
Institute for Psychoanalysis, 90–5
Institute for Research, 259
institutionalization, 208–11, 665
intake interview, 38, 319, 583–5, 593, 665
integration, 44, 71–3, 665
intelligence, 47, 665; constancy of, 390–2; deficit in, 302, 438–45, 665; definitions of, 386–90; development of, 49; efficiency of, 436–63; evaluation of, 385–430; maturity of, 278–9; of the clinician, 565–7; quotient, 12, 389–93, 399, 401, 665; tests, 12, 261, 302–3
intensive therapy, 90
interaction, vi, 48, 83, 665
interest, 365–6, 570, 665; inventories, 261–4, 485
internship, 562–4, 665
interpersonal, 5, 573, 665
interpretation, 31, 69, 77, 82, 90, 104–6, 109, 665
interview, 301–2, 313, 349–84, 665; principles of, 354–60
intrapersonal, 665
intratensive, 185, 665
introversion, 185, 665
intuition, 566–7, 665

judgment, 12, 567, 666

Kent-Shakow Form Boards, 409, 666
Koh's Blocks, 409, 449, 666
Krout Personal Preference Scale, 485
Kuder Preference Record, 263, 485, 666

labeling, 104–6, 113–4, 666
lability of affect, 368–9, 666
laboratory, 563–4, 666
language disorders, 461–2, 666

language tests, 395, 666
latent content, 666
lay analyst, 666
learning theory, 44, 52, 59, 102–15, 131–2, 163–74, 642, 666; and socialization, 186–90; cognitive or expectancy, 165, 168–70, 174; in counseling, 37, 43, 52–3; monistic, 52, 107; reinforcement or stimulus-response, 165–74; two-factor, 57, 107
lecture-discussion technique, 234–6, 666
Leiter International Performance Scale, 410–11, 666
lesion, 445, 666
Letchworth Village, 595
leucotomy, 666
level of aspiration, 666
Lewin's formula, 48
libido, 71–2, 79, 106, 666
licensing, 561, 629–35, 666
life space, 666
life style, 74, 666
likes, 371
lobe, 445, 666
longitudinal approach, 309
loss of the abstract, 446–9
loss of shift, 440, 446

macrocephaly, 667
Make-a-Picture-Story Test, 514–15, 667
maladjustment, 667
malaise, 667
malingering, 667
management evaluation, 589–90, 667
manic behavior, 186, 667
manifest anxiety, 482, 667
masculine protest, 74, 667
masochism, 341, 667
masturbation, 333, 376, 667
maturation, 342, 667
means-end readiness, 169, 667
measurement, 10–1, 302–6, 667
memory, 12, 86–88, 668; defects, 440
mental age, 12, 398–9, 668
mental deficiency, 274–5, 668
mental hygiene, 567–70, 635, 668; and guidance, 623–5; and psychiatric social work, 619; in the industrial setting, 596–9; team, 580–4, 587, 593–5; team relationships, 609–25
mental mechanisms, 668
mental testing, 12
Merrill Palmer Scale of Mental Tests, 413, 668
Michigan Picture Test, 512–13, 668
microcephaly, 668
milieu, 198, 211, 668
Miller Analogies Test, 427, 565, 668

Minnesota Multiphasic Personality Inventory, 478–82, 668
Minnesota Preschool Scale, 413, 668
misery, 103
mongolism, 668
moods, 368, 668
Mooney Problem Check List, 198
morbid, 369, 668
mores, 668
Mosaic Test, 553–4, 669
motivation, 50, 52, 278, 367, 385, 669
motoric activity, 169, 669
multifactor theories of intelligence, 389, 669
multiple causation, 313, 669
music therapy, 206, 230, 243
mutuality, 172, 669
mysticism, 372, 669

narcissism, 669
National Committee for Mental Hygiene, 16
National Society for the Study of Education, 275
needs, 499, 469
negative vocational counseling, 254, 260, 669
negativism, 669
neo-analysis, 78–95, 669
neurasthenia, 159, 185, 214, 669
neuropsychiatric hospital, 384–6, 669
neurosis, 185–6, 544–6; Adlerian concept of, 74; Alexander's concept of, 91; character, 80; definition of, 669; Dollard and Miller's concept of, 102–3; Freudian concept of, 68–71; Horney's theory of, 78–83; Mowrer's concept of, 107; Rank's concept of, 75–8; situational, 80
neurotic trends, 79, 669
nihilism, 670
non-Aristotelian, 45, 670
nondirective counseling, 56–9, 96, 193–4, 670; with children, 241–2
nonlanguage or nonverbal tests, 395, 670
normal, 670
norms, 417, 670
nosology, 670
nursery schools, 392
nymphomania, 670

objective tests, 302, 469, 670
objectivity in counseling, 6, 18–20
observation, 6, 17, 82, 670
obsessive, 36–7, 186, 373, 545–6, 670
occupational history, 346–7, 670

occupational information, 258–9, 670
Oedipus, 36–7, 91, 95; complex, 79, 670; defined, 69
Office of Vocational Rehabilitation, 275
operationism, 670
oral, 670
organic, 437–8, 670
organ inferiority, 73–4, 670
organizing disability, 440
orgasm, 671
orientation, 378, 671
overt, 377, 671

palliation, 57, 155, 671
panic, 671
pantheism, 372, 671
paranoid reactions, 186, 671
parataxic, 85, 671; distortions, 89–90
paresis, 671
partially structured tests, 302–6, 495–529, 671
participant observer, 18–19, 86, 567, 671
pattern analysis, 419–22, 671
pediatrics, 671
penis-envy, 671
percentile, 671
perception, 671
perceptual field, 66
performance tests, 395–6, 401, 406–12, 671
permissiveness, 350, 572, 671
perseveration, 445–6, 450, 671
persona, 46, 477, 671
Personal Audit, 482, 672
personal counseling, 55–9
Personal Data Sheet, 473, 672
personality, 470–1, 672; a characteristic of behavior, 47; defined, 85; integration, 672; reorganization, 640, 672; tests, 469–555, 672
Personality Schedule, 485
personal orientation, 183–6
personal unconscious, 70–1
personnel testing, 599
persuasion, 50, 56, 672
phenomenal field, 96, 99, 672
phenotype, 14, 672
phobia, 62, 369–70, 672
physical handicap, 273–5, 672
physical world, 54
physician-patient relationship, 581–2, 615–17, 672
physiological psychology, 564
Pintner-Paterson Scale of Performance Tests, 407–9, 672
planning of counseling, 25, 38, 41–2, 54–9, 299, 311, 441, 585

play therapy, 134, 137
poison-pen therapy, 139
positive vocational counseling, 254, 260, 672
post-Galelian, 53
postulate, 672
potentiality, 302–4, 385, 672
power motive, 83–4
practicum, 563–4, 672
practitioner-scientist, 15, 638–50, 642–5
prediction, 6, 297–8, 672
predisposition, 672
pregenital, 36, 673
prenatal, 673
preschool scales, 412–16, 673
pressure, 157–8, 190, 673
prima facie validity, 477, 673
primal, 71–2, 673; anxiety, 75–6; impulses, 72; scene, 673
Primary Mental Abilities Tests, 427
primates, 66, 673
primordial images, 71–2
principle of flexibility, 93, 673
principle of planning, 93, 673
private practice, 599–601, 673
privileged communication, 627–8, 673
problem-solving, 56–7, 67, 170–1; behavior, 114, 205, 440–2, 673; learning, 107, 167–8, 673
profession, 609, 673
professional psychology, 10, 17, 559–60, 577–603; and correctional services, 592–5; and future developments, 639–49; and industry, 596–9; and legislation, 629–35; and private practice, 599–601, 612; and research, 586, 638–50; and the mentally retarded, 595–6; and training of personnel, 586; as preparation for administration, 586; demand for, 578–9; employment settings, 577–80; in child guidance clinics, 582–3; in educational settings, 587–92; in general hospitals, 586–7; in medical settings, 580–7; in mental hygiene clinics, 583–4; in the Veterans Administration, 583; professional relations, 609–35; rules governing, 601–3; salaries in, 580; training for, 578–9
prognosis, 673
Progressive Matrices, 428–9, 673
projective, 13, 495–6, 673; hypothesis, 13, 496, 525–6, 535, 673; tests, 13, 349, 469–70, 495–6, 646, 673
prototaxic, 85, 674
psychasthenia, 674
psychiatric social work, 152, 222–3, 564, 617–20, 674

psychiatry, 15, 27, 309, 564, 611–17, 674
psychic totality, 72, 674
psychoanalysis, 15, 44, 102–3, 674; contrasted with Mowrer's theory, 107–9; goal of, 69, 91; supportive element in, 150–1
psychobiology, 309, 674
psychodrama, 232, 242–3, 674
psychodynamic, 13–14, 674
psychoeducational clinic, 590–1, 674
psychogenic, 674
psychological counseling, 25–39; aims of, 25, 62; and guidance, 26, 249–68; and psychotherapy, 587–8; as a developmental process, 38–9; client-centered, 52–3, 95, 238–9, 655; compared with psychiatry, 27; concept of learning in, 52; course of, 37–9; defined, 26; directive client-centered, 52–3; elements of, 28, 37–9; emotional release in, 32–4, 121–42; environmental, 28, 55–6, 203–25; field-theoretical approach to, 49–51; functions of, 26–37; goal of, 26–7; group, 58–9, 227–45; individual, 58–9; insight in, 28–32, 62–118; orientation to, 25–40; relearning in, 36–7, 162–81; research needs in, 53–4, 642–5; rules governing, 601–3; socialization in, 35–6, 183–99; support in, 34–5, 144–60; theoretical framework for, 41–3
psychology, 674; and legislation, 629–35; and professional relations, 609–23; and psychiatry, 611–17; and the law, 627–35; applied to the individual case, 45–8; as a profession, 609–11; definition of, 6; general, 564; of interpersonal relationships, 15
psychometrics, 12–13, 625, 674
psychopathology, 183–6, 640, 642–3, 674
psychophysical methods, 14
psychosis, 74, 186, 544–6, 602–3, 674
psychosynthesis, 70, 674
psychotherapy, 674; contrasted with psychological counseling, 25–8, 587–8; history of, 15–16; in private practice, 600–1; overview of, 25–268; rights of the client in, 602–3
punishment, 187
puppetry, 243
Purdue Multiple Choice Sentence Completion Test, 525–7
Purdue University, 272; Psychological Clinic, 35, 320–1, 323, 326–8, 334–5, 340–1, 344–5, 591; Training Program, 563–4

qualifications of the clinical and counseling psychologist, 559–75

racial unconscious, 46, 675
rapport, 82, 675
reaction time, 13, 675
reality, 85, 675; testing, 85, 99
reasoning, 12, 675
reassurance, 56–7, 105–6, 152–6, 675
reconditioning, 114
recording information, 356–61
Recovery, Inc., 233, 675
recreation, 158–9, 206, 213–4, 366
re-education, 26, 36–7, 94, 114, 169–70, 174–7, 271–3, 675
referral, 318–20
registration, 318–25, 675
regression, 675
rehabilitation, 26, 271–5, 646–8, 675
reinforcement, 166–7, 675; learning theory, 52, 111, 114, 165–74, 675
rejection, 675
relationship, 146–50, 675
relaxation, 34, 50–1, 57, 141, 158, 676
relearning, 36–7, 79, 162–81, 676
release, 32, 50, 133–4
reliability, 429, 676
religion, 144, 371–2, 628–9
remedial, 676; education, 26, 51, 59, 271–4, 564, 676; reading, 59, 282–5, 676; treatment, 59
repetition compulsion, 69, 82, 88, 676
repression, 32, 68–71, 103–4, 106–7, 113, 676
repressive-inspirational therapy, 230
research, 14, 48, 51, 53–4, 563–4, 615, 638–50
resistance, 69–70, 676
resources, 52, 302–4, 385, 676
respect for the individual, 572
response, 6, 8, 166–7, 187–8, 676
responsibility, 571
rest, 158–9, 206
restrictive legislation, 633, 676
resultant, 49, 51, 676
retarded child, 676
reward, 114, 187–8
rigidity, 459–60, 676
ritualism, 372, 676
Rogers Test of Personal Adjustment, 484
role playing, 36, 647, 676
Rorschach Test, 14, 198, 261, 349, 436, 449–50, 534–53, 676; administration, 537–8; interpretation, 544–7; planning from, 548–53; scoring, 538–44
Rosenzweig P–F Study, 528
rules of practice, 601–3

sadism, 676
St. Elizabeth's Hospital, 232
satyriasis, 676
scatter, 420–2, 676
schizophrenia, 455–9, 677
schizophrenic ratio, 420, 677
schizophrenic reactions, 184–6, 546
school clinical psychology, 5, 587–90, 647, 677
science, 677; defined, 17; in research, 638–50; vs. art, 53–4
Science Research Associates, 259
scientific method, 20
scientific observation, 18–20
security feelings, 144–5
security operations, 89, 677
selective perception, 644
self, 84, 96–100, 677; acceptance, 97, 148–9; assertion, 677; concept, 363–5; confidence, 144–5; consciousness, 677; dynamism, 84–8; knowledge, 677; realization, 73, 194, 677; -report tests, 469–70, 677; representation, 241
semantic, 677
sensation, 677
sensory discrimination, 14
sentence-completion tests, 13, 524–5, 677
Serial Sevens Test, 449
set, 67, 169, 677
sexual drives, 68
Shipley Hartford Scale, 444
Shipley Personality Inventory, 485
sibling, 391, 677
sign learning, 67, 107, 677
sign-significate expectancies, 169, 677
situational neurosis, 80
social, 677–8; history, 19, 300–1, 346, 678; intelligence, 388, 573; learning therapy, 153; orientation, 90, 183, 677; prescription, 191, 678; psychotherapy, 193; technique, 187–8, 678; worker, 152, 208, 222, 309, 319, 346–7, 589, 678
socialization, 35–6, 162, 183–99, 230, 678
soliloquy, 241
somnambulism, 374
sorting tests, 446–7, 678
sources of information, 313–14
speculative philosophy, 53
speech, 678; correction, 309, 678; disorder, 276–82; hygiene, 275–82; readiness, 277, 678
spontaneity, 133, 678
spontaneous improvisation, 241
Stanford Binet Intelligence Test, 13, 396–401, 678

statement of problem, 361–2
statistics, 564, 678; control by, 18, 644–5, 678; methods of, 14–15, 623
stimulation, 277–8
stimulus-response learning theory, 165–74, 678
Strong's Vocational Interest Blanks, 261–3, 265, 678
Structured Doll Play Test, 516–18, 679
structured tests, 302–4, 306, 469–89, 646, 679
structuring, 679; the interview, 350–4; the situation, 31
study habits, 285–90
stuttering, 276, 279–82, 679
sublimation, 139–40, 679
submission, 344, 679
subnormal, 10, 679
suggestion, 50, 156–7, 679
summer camps, 242
superego, 46, 68, 106–10, 237, 679
superficial counseling, 56–7, 154–5, 679
superstition, 18, 679
support, 32, 34–9, 48, 50, 56–7, 60, 144–60, 205, 223; contrasted with dependence, 34; contrasted with transference, 150–1; defined, 34, 679; example of, 34–5; in reducing field forces, 50, 60; promotion of, 34; related to amelioration, 56–7
surplus energy, 92
symbolization, 113, 460–2, 679
symptomatic therapy, 154
syndrome, 679
synthesis, 72, 440, 679
systematic delusions, 375, 679
Szondi Test, 521–4, 679

taboo, 335, 380
tact, 573
technician, 634
temperament, 472, 680
tension, 33, 57; reduction, 32–4, 48, 50, 56, 121, 142; states, 680
tentative hypothesis, 20, 640–1
testing the limits, 538
Thematic Apperception Test, 14, 198, 349, 497–511, 680
theory, 680; application of, 26, 41–62, 642–5; in planning counseling, 42–4; requirements of, 43–4
therapeutic community, 219, 648, 680
therapy, 8, 15; and the psychologist, 611–17, 646; defined, 26, 680; environmental, 29; final goal of, 26–7; of interpersonal relations, 88–90; planning of, 54–6; superficial vs. deep,

therapy (continued)
56–7; total personality, 55; uncovering, 51
threshold of excitation, 445, 680
total-push procedures, 50, 195–6, 218–19, 680
training programs, 11, 560–5
trait, 470–1
transfer, 680
transference, 89, 92, 110; defined, 17, 77, 82, 680; neurosis, 69, 680; vs. support, 34
trauma, 680
trial and error, 66–7, 680
two-factor theory of intelligence, 389, 680
two-factor theory of learning, 52, 681

unconscious, 46, 68–73, 86, 104–5, 681
uncovering therapy, 51, 681
United States Army, 11
United States Public Health Service, 11, 562
unstructured tests, 302–4, 306, 464–70, 495, 534–55, 681

valence, 169, 681
validity, 474–8, 496–7, 681; a priori, 473; consensual, 85; empirical, 474; factor, 474; prima facie, 477
values, 198–9, 681
vector, 45, 49–50, 59–60, 681
ventilation, 57, 136, 685
verbalization, 48, 87, 104, 114, 132, 681
verbal tests, 395, 401, 681
Veterans Administration, 11, 252, 581, 583–4, 621–3
Vigotsky Test, 447–8, 681
Vineland Social Maturity Scale, 413–16, 681
Vineland Training School, 16, 595
visual-motor disturbance, 440, 449, 451, 681
vocabulary test, 397, 401, 417–18, 444, 681
Vocational Apperception Test, 528
vocational guidance and counseling, 17, 26, 59, 249–68, 564, 585, 623–5, 681; positions in, 625; scope and purpose, 624
vocational history, 19, 300–1
voice disorders, 276, 681

warming-up, 241
Washington School of Psychiatry, 79, 220
Wechsler Adult Intelligence Scale, 417, 438, 442–3, 682

Wechsler-Bellevue Intelligence Exami-
    nation, 401, 416–26, 438–43, 682
Wechsler Intelligence Scale for Chil-
    dren, 401–6, 453–4, 682
Weltanschauung, 191, 682
will, 76–7, 130, 682; ego, 130, 682;
    -to-power, 74, 682
Wisconsin Card Sorting Test, 457–9,
    682

withdrawal, 185–6
Worcester State Hospital, 250
word-association tests, 527–8, 682
working through, 90, 92, 682
World Test, 515–16, 682
World Wars I and II, 11, 639–40

A NOTE ON THE TYPE

The text of this book was set on the Linotype in a face called TIMES ROMAN, designed by STANLEY MORISON for THE TIMES (London), and first introduced by that newspaper in the middle nineteen thirties.

Among typographers and designers of the twentieth century, Stanley Morison has been a strong forming influence, as typographical adviser to the English Monotype Corporation, as a director of two distinguished English publishing houses, and as a writer of sensibility, erudition, and keen practical sense.

In 1930 Morison wrote: "Type design moves at the pace of the most conservative reader. The good type-designer therefore realises that, for a new fount to be successful, it has to be so good that only very few recognize its novelty. If readers do not notice the consummate reticence and rare discipline of a new type, it is probably a good letter." It is now generally recognized that in the creation of *Times Roman* Morison successfully met the qualifications of this theoretical doctrine.

Composed, printed, and bound by THE PLIMPTON PRESS, Norwood, Massachusetts. Paper manufactured by S. D. WARREN COMPANY, Boston. Designed by HARRY FORD.